THE
CLASH

Return of the Last Gang in Town

All lyrics quoted are for review, study or critical purposes.

Library of Congress Cataloging-in-Publication Data

Gray, Marcus.
  The Clash : return of the Last gang in town / Marcus Gray.
    p. cm.
Revised and updated edition of Last gang in Town: the story and myth of the Clash.
Originally published: London: Helter Skelter, 2001.
Includes index.
  ISBN 0-634-04673-X
  1. Clash (Musical group) 2. Rock musicians--England--Biography. I. Title.
  ML421.C57 G73 2002
  782.42166'092'2--dc21

                    2002008977

CLASH

Return of the Last Gang in Town

MARCUS GRAY

HAL•LEONARD®

ACKNOWLEDGEMENTS

First and foremost, my thanks to Caroline Kerlin for all her support, and for giving me the time and space to write this revised edition.

My family and friends have had enough to cope with over the years without being named and shamed again here, but I hope they know they also have my undying gratitude. Cheers also to the staffs of the Big W Charing Cross Road 1998-99 and Birmingham High Street 1999-2001.

To business: special thanks are due to Mark Woodley, Mark Gibson-White, John Holmes, and Mark McDonald. They provided most of the secondary source material without which this book would have been a pamphlet.

They who also served: Julian Alexander, Alan Anger, Hilary Arthur, Nick Beacock, Sean Body, Jane Carr, KH Carter (Head of Upper School, Dover Grammar School for Boys), Dougie Cameron, Jeff Dove, Peter Drum (College Secretary, Chelsea College of Art and Design), Graham Fraser, Pat Gilbert, Daniel Gooding, Julian Gray, Neil Halliday, David Haywood (Headmaster at City of London Freemen's School), RE Hough (Assistant Registrar, John Lewis PLC), Phil Jew, Alison Jinks, Sharon Kerlin, Sarah Kightley, Pattie Kleinke, Phillip McIllmurray, Iain McNay (of Cherry Red Records), Joyce Moore (of Moore Management), Tami Peterson, Nicole Pickford, Joanne Richards, Pete Rippon, Haddon Smith, Spud, Gary Sutton, John Talbot, Sarah Talbot, Sophie Talbot, Julien Temple, Gene Turbett, Kosmo Vinyl, Horst Weidermuller (of Studio K7), Adrian Whittaker, Thelma Winyard (Principal's Assistant at the Byam Shaw School of Art), Tim Young, and the staff at the National Sound Archive, the Guildhall Library, the London Metropolitan Archive, the Central Reference Library, and the Public Search Room at St Catherine's House.

Some of the people I interviewed went a good deal further out of their way to assist than others, but lest special mentions lead to accusations of favouritism, I'll be alphabetical in my appreciation: Steve Allen, Bill Barnacle, Gary Barnacle, Pete Barnacle, Steve Barnacle, Kelvin Blacklock, Brady, John Brown, Simon Cassell, Jack Castle, Terry Chimes, Sebastian Conran, Tom Critchley, Robin Crocker, Andy Czezowski, Matt Dangerfield, Alan Drake, Richard Dudanski, Vaughan Flood, Jerry Green, Johnny Green, Rob Harper, Simon Humphrey, Brian James, Jiving Al Jones, Wynn Jones, Liz Lewis, Keith Levene, Ray Lowry, Glen Matlock, Andrew Matheson, Barry Miles, Dave Mingay, Mole, Mick Morris, Patrick Nother, Chris Parry, Tony Parsons, Alvaro Peña-Rojas, Mark Perry, Honest John Plain, Esperanza Romano, Beryl Ritchie, Rat Scabies, Nick Sheppard, Pennie Smith, Clive Timperley, Geir Waade, Stephen Williams, Jules Yewdall.

This book builds upon foundations laid by other writers, reviewers and interviewers for the music, mainstream and underground press, all of whom I have acknowledged in the main body of the text.

Other sources: *Clash Songbook* (Wise Publications); *Clash Second Songbook* (Riva Music Ltd); *Armagideon Times*, 'The Story Of The Clash' by Mick Jones and Joe Strummer; *The Clash: Before & After* by Pennie Smith (Eel Pie/Plexus); *Clash On Broadway* booklet (Epic Legacy); *The Story Of The Clash, Volume 1*, sleevenotes by 'Albert Transom' (CBS); *Joe Strummer With The 101ers & The Clash 1974-1976* by Jules Yewdall (Image Direct); *A Riot Of Our Own* by Johnny Green and Garry Barker (Indigo).

1988: The New Wave Punk Rock Explosion by Caroline Coon (Orbach & Chambers); *The Boy Looked At Johnny* by Julie Burchill and Tony Parsons (Pluto Press); *Vacant: A Diary Of The Punk Years 1976-79* by Nils and Ray Stevenson (Thames And Hudson); *Like Punk Never Happened: Culture Club And The New Pop* by Dave Rimmer (Faber and Faber); *From The Velvets To The Voidoids* by Clinton Heylin (Penguin); *Please Kill Me* by Legs McNeill and Gillian McCain (Little, Brown); *The Dark Stuff* by Nick Kent (Penguin); *Punk Diary 1970-1979* by George Gimarc (Vintage); *No Sleep Till Canvey Island: The Great Pub Rock Revolution* by Will Birch (Virgin).

England's Dreaming: Sex Pistols and Punk Rock by Jon Savage (Faber & Faber); *Sex Pistols Day By Day* by Lee Wood (Omnibus Press); *Sex Pistols: The Inside Story* by Fred and Judy Vermorel (Omnibus Press); *Sex Pistols File* edited by Ray Stevenson (Omnibus Press); *I Was A Teenage Sex Pistol* by Glen Matlock and Pete Silverton (Omnibus Press); *Rotten: No Irish, No Blacks, No Dogs* by John Lydon and Keith and Kent Zimmerman (Hodder & Stoughton).

The Jam: A Beat Concerto by Paolo Hewitt (Riot Stories/Omnibus Press); *The Jam: Our Story* by Bruce Foxton, Rick Buckler and Alex Ogg (Castle Communications); *The Light At The End Of The Tunnel: The Biography Of The Damned* by Carol Clerk (Omnibus Press); *The Old Testament*, booklet entitled *The Stranglers: The Men They Love To Hate* by Chris Twomey (UA); *No Mercy: The Stranglers* by David Buckley (Hodder & Stoughton); *Too Much Too Soon: The New York Dolls* by Nina Antonia (Omnibus); *Take It Like A Man* by Boy George and Spencer Bright (Sidgwick & Jackson); *Diary Of A Rock'Roll Star* by Ian Hunter (Panther); *All The Young Dudes: The Biography Of Mott The Hoople* by Campbell Devine (Cherry Red Books); *People Funny Boy: The Genius Of Lee 'Scratch' Perry* by David Katz (Payback Press); *Bass Culture: When Reggae Was King* by Lloyd Bradley (Viking); *Psychotic Reactions and Carburetor Dung* by Lester Bangs (Minerva/Serpent's Tail); *Let It Blurt: The Life And Times Of Lester Bangs* by Jim DeRogatis (Bloomsbury); *Needs Must* by Kris Needs (Virgin); *Ginsberg: A Biography* by Barry Miles (Harper Perennial).

BAMN: Outlaw Manifestos And Ephemera 1965-70 edited by Peter Stansill and David Zane Mairowitz (Penguin); *Underground: The London Alternative Press 1966-74* by Nigel Fountain (Comedia-Routledge); *Paris '68* by Marc Rohan (Impact Books); *Revolt Into Style* by George Melly (Penguin); *Style Wars* by Peter York (Sidgwick & Jackson); *The Hit Men: Power Brokers And Fast Money Inside The Music Business* by Fredric Dannen (Muller).

Rock Dreams by Guy Peelaert and Nik Cohn (R&B); *The Penguin Encyclopedia of Popular Music*, edited by Donald Clarke; *The New Musical Express Book Of Rock No 2* edited by Nick Logan and Bob Woffinden (Star); *The Guinness Book Of British Hit Singles* and *The Guinness Book Of British Hit Albums*, edited by Jo and Tim Rice, Paul Gambaccini and Mike Read; *London's Rock Landmarks* by Marcus Gray (Omnibus Press); *Rolling Stone Rock Almanac* (Papermac); *Music Master* (John Humphries); *The Great Rock Discography* by MC Strong (Zweitausendeins); *The Time Out Film Guide* edited by Tom Milne (Penguin).

CONTENTS

FOREWORD:
ONE MORE TIME

When I began work on the first edition of this book – *Last Gang In Town: The Story And Myth Of The Clash* – I was denied direct access to the Clash. As a result, my research was necessarily an exercise in investigative journalism. It soon became clear that there were significant discrepancies between the information I was uncovering and the way the band members had portrayed their backgrounds and beliefs.

All of us are guilty of unconscious and semi-conscious revisionism, reworking our past histories and past opinions to fit our present day circumstances and outlooks. Anecdotes are elaborated. Opinions change. It could even be argued that evolution requires re-evaluation. Ralph Waldo Emerson is famed for remarking, 'A foolish consistency is the hobgoblin of little minds.' All well and good. To qualify as large brained, though, should a biographer ignore *conscious* revisionism, on a large scale over many years, the intention of which is to disguise or deny the truth? In 1977, Richard Hell observed that rock'n'roll is an arena in which you reinvent yourself. In fact, such reinvention is practically a job requirement. The Clash's story offered me an opportunity to examine how artists, managers, publicity people, media commentators and fans collude to build myths around rock'n'roll bands.

I concede that indulging in a little self-aggrandisement is hardly a crime. But the Clash went further than that. In 1976-77, punk's Year Zero mentality and its determined striving for supposed authenticity – 'street credibility' – obliged the band members (or so they evidently believed) to rewrite their pasts in order to give credence to the rhetoric they were spouting. Having set this precedent for themselves, they continued to rewrite history periodically to support whatever happened to be their position at the time. Such self-serving revisionism was a disconcerting habit to adopt for a leftist band who claimed to hold the truth in high regard.

It's hard to reply in the affirmative to Lester Bangs's sardonic query, 'I mean, does everybody always sit down with this slide-ruled plan and 10-point moral code on the wall behind 'em and then go into battle for the clear-cut Cause with all this pat as that and never deviating?' Defending his mentor Andy Warhol from the accusations of charlatanry that dogged him from soup tin to grave, Lou Reed remarked, 'You get less time for stealing a car.' With such words of wisdom in mind, I can understand why, when *Last Gang In Town* was published – 10 years after the band had broken up and nearly 20 after they had formed – some people thought I could perhaps have cut the Clash a little more slack.

It's worth restating that the Clash were not just some rock'n'roll band who happened to make a few rash statements, tell a few porkies, and flirt a little with rebel chic. Or if that's what they turned into, it certainly wasn't what they set out to be. They were originally conceived and marketed as street-level political activists who happened to have chosen rock'n'roll music as the medium for their message. Admittedly, they did back-pedal at times when this burden proved too heavy to bear, most notably during 1979 and 1982-83. Nevertheless, over half the Clash's song lyrics and almost all the media interviews they gave were devoted to expounding the band's ideology. Throughout their career, Joe Strummer in particular never stopped preaching and proselytising. Ultimately, it was the band's own recognition of the crooked mile between what they had first aspired to be and what they had become that prompted them to split.

Naturally, since that split, the initial impact of the polemic and the promises has receded. The relevance has not. When I wrote the first edition, it was my belief that the only way to come to an understanding of the Clash was to examine how and why they ultimately failed to live up to their declared aims. This remains my belief.

My investigation required some straight talking, which in turn influenced the general tone of the book. I deliberately did not wax sycophantic about particular songs, recordings or live shows because I believe there is nothing more nauseating than an extended open love letter posing as a critical biography. That said, *Last Gang In Town* did attempt a spirited defence of the previously much traduced *Sandinista!*, and I would hope that some inkling was conveyed of my enduring opinion that *The Clash* is the greatest high-energy rock'n'roll album ever made.

Two (spookily similar) reviews of the first edition compared my efforts to those of Albert Goldman, the now-deceased rock biographer who provoked the ire of millions of Elvis Presley and John Lennon fans with his detailed exposés of the – alleged – real lives behind the legends. The implication that I set out to desecrate the Clash's memory is abhorrent to me. In *Return Of The Last Gang In Town*, I have made strenuous efforts to stress the good as well as the bad and the ugly, the comic as well as the serious and tragic. (And I've spiced things up with a little more sex and drugs and violence as well, just to prove what un-Goldmanlike restraint I showed last time around…)

I've also altered the structural balance of the book. The first section has been trimmed, without sacrificing any of the vital information it contains about the band members' true backgrounds and the roots of both the Clash in particular and punk in general. The second has been expanded to cover the Clash's punk period in its entirety (1976-78). The third has been completely rewritten, and now includes a wealth of new information on the remainder of the Clash's career (1979-86), including the commercial breakthrough in America, the original band's demise, and the failure of a new line-up to sustain the achievements of the old. A new fourth and final section examines the posthumous marketing of the Clash and the band's cultural legacy.

Two last points. Firstly, I'm well aware that there's an element of irony involved in publishing a revised edition of a biography which criticises its subjects for constantly revising their pasts. The difference is, *Last Gang In Town* has become *Return Of The Last Gang In Town* in an attempt to get *closer* to the truth…

Secondly, from commencing research for the first edition, upon which I worked full time for three years, to completing the second edition, upon which I worked part time for 18 months, has taken nearly nine years. That's almost as long as the Clash's entire career lasted – considerably longer, if, as the Clash themselves would now prefer, you draw the line at Mick Jones's departure – during which time they managed to release six studio albums, one of them a double and another a triple. Two of the six are widely considered to be among the best rock albums ever made. In terms of both output and achievement, it's a humbling comparison.

Marcus Gray, 2001.

PART ONE:
ROCK DREAMS

1
ALL THE WAY FROM STREATHAM

'Mick was always Rock'n'Roll Mick.' So says Keith Levene, who knew him well only for the six months or so they were both members of the Clash. As sweeping statements go, it turns out to be a remarkably accurate one. Michael Geoffrey Jones was born on 26 June 1955. '1955!' he crowed to *Blitz*'s William Shaw 33 years later. 'The birth of rock'n'roll!' That he arrived at much the same time as the musical movement which helped establish the concepts of youth culture and the teenager is a coincidence that Mick would evidently prefer to see as an act of fate. This despite the inauspicious choice of venue for his début appearance: the South London Hospital for Women in Clapham.

Mick was an only child. Eighteen months earlier, his father, Thomas Gilmour Jones, then a 26-year old taxi driver from Clapham, had married Renee Zegansky, a 25-year old fancy jewelry saleswoman from neighbouring Streatham. By the time of Mick's birth, they had set up home together at 20 Fair Green Court, Mitcham, far enough to the south of London to qualify as part of Surrey. Mick's earliest recollection is a musical one: the Life Guards Band marching down Mitcham's main street. In 1957, the Joneses briefly moved in with Renee's mother Stella at what had been Renee's pre-marital residence, 61 Christchurch House, Christchurch Road, before taking their own flat at number 109. This late Thirties council block, located on the north west corner of the crossroads where Brixton Hill meets Streatham Hill, was to remain Mick's home for the next 10 years. Though not number 109: Stella's second husband died in May 1961; soon afterwards, her daughter's family rejoined her in number 61.

Mick's happier memories of his childhood continued to revolve around music. As was the case with many young kids at the time, his life was brightened considerably by the Beat Boom, and all the colour, style, noise and excitement that went with the burgeoning UK mid-Sixties pop scene. Renee, still relatively young – and even younger at heart – was an ardent fan of Elvis Presley. The radio was often tuned to the pirate stations, and Mick had little to overcome in the way of parental prejudice. He gave his first 'concert' miming to a Beatles song with a tennis racket on the front lawn outside Christchurch House. While most of his contemporaries lost their hearts to the winning smiles, fluffy mop-tops and memorable melodies of the Fab Four, though, Mick went on to join the fan clubs of the Animals and the Kinks, displaying a predilection for the kind of raucous showmanship that was to dominate his tastes well into the next decade.

Mick claims that his parents divorced when he was eight, but the split was not a sudden one. Mick recalls them arguing a lot, and Stella taking him down to the bomb shelter in Christchurch House's basement to await the cessation of hostilities. Renee had always been fascinated with America – indeed, had tried to stowaway on a ship bound for that destination at the age of 19 – and could no longer resign herself to life in Streatham. She emigrated, settling down in Armwood, Michigan. Here, she married again, to copper mine engineer George Tiitu, and opened a second hand clothes shop. Leaving Mick in the care of his Nan, Tommy continued to work as a taxi driver in south London.

Stella was herself no stranger to the vagaries of marital life. Born Esther Stella Class on 7 December 1899 in Whitechapel, she became a milliner. Her first marriage, to Russian émigré and furrier Morris Zegansky, took place at Holborn Register Office on 30 May 1927. Morris claimed to be 22 at the time, and – as was then considered to be a woman's prerogative – so did the 27 year-old Stella. Renee came along in late 1928, by which time her parents had moved from Holborn to Kensington. The fate of the daughter's marriage was prefigured by the mother's: Stella and Morris went their separate ways, then divorced. During World War Two, Stella and Renee took up residence in the newly built Christchurch House. On 17 December 1952, less than a year before her daughter took the plunge for the first time – and in the same place, Wandsworth Register Office – Stella married again. Hyman Markis, known as Harry Marcus, was a 49 year old divorced wireless salesman. Stella, a gown saleswoman at the time of the wedding, once again knocked five years off her real age. Harry succumbed to a fatal heart attack nine years later.

The separation from his parents came when Mick was at an impressionable age. Although both maintained regular contact – Tommy calling around to see him, and Renee sending over comics and magazines from the US – in 1976, Mick admitted to *Melody Maker's* Caroline Coon that he had felt abandoned. 'They decided I weren't happening, I suppose. Psychologically, it really did me in. Now I know it isn't that big a deal. But then at school, I'd sit there with this word "divorce, divorce" in my head all the time. But there was no social stigma attached to it because all the other kids seemed to be going through the same thing. Very few of the kids I knew were living a sheltered family life.'

No-one could say Mick was starved of affection following his parents' departure. If anything, he was a little spoiled to compensate for the upset. Despite the generation gap, a close relationship had already developed between grandson and grandmother which was to last until Stella's death in 1989. During his 'difficult' teenage years, the way Mick talked to his Nan in front of his friends could be brusque to the point of unpleasantness, but no-one who witnessed it was ever in any doubt about his true feelings for her. In his early twenties, Mick occasionally lived apart from Stella for short periods, but even in the first days of the Clash, he still considered the flat she occupied to be his main home. In the BBC2 retrospective *That Was Then, This Is Now*, filmed shortly after her death, he declared, 'I always used to come back to my Nan, because I loved her.' Big Audio Dynamite's *Megatop Phoenix*, recorded that same year, is dedicated to her memory.

In September 1966, Mick began to attend Strand School, on Elm Park, just around the corner from his home. A bright boy, he did well for the first few years, particularly in English and Religious Instruction. Before long, though, his extracurricular activities began to dominate.

In 1995, Mick told *Vox*'s Ann Scanlon that he 'nearly' had a trial for Crystal Palace. His enthusiasm for the sport was by no means partisan. He supported Queen's Park Rangers, but he used to collect the autographs of all the name players of the day. 'I knew all the hotels where they stayed and I'd wait outside and ask them to sign my *Topical Times Football Book*. Some of them were really kind, like Bobby Moore and Dennis Law, and some were particularly mean. The way I was treated then has always stuck in my mind, and it stood me in good stead for when it was my turn to give autographs.'

Even when he was at his most football crazy, music never really went out of favour. By 1967, the R&B that had both inspired and provided the original repertoire for the Rolling Stones and the Yardbirds – as well as the Animals and the Kinks – was enjoying a second coming in the guise of the British Blues Boom. At home, Mick commandeered the flat's mono radiogram to listen to the *Perfumed Garden* show on pirate station Radio London, where DJ John Peel mixed the new heavy blues with 'underground' music from both the UK and the West Coast of America. At the age of 12, Mick saved up the necessary 33s 3d and bought his first album, Cream's *Disraeli Gears*, closely followed by the Jimi Hendrix Experience compilation *Smash Hits*. It became impossible to prise him away from the radiogram. 'I used to stick my head to the oval-shaped speaker for hours,' he told William

Shaw in 1988. He began reading the music press, and before long had become the music industry's dream consumer, spending the money he earned from his paper round on whatever the critics happened to be praising that week.

When talking to Jay Cocks of US magazine *Time* in 1979, Mick described his upbringing thus: 'I stayed with me gran and a lot of wicked aunts!' The aunts came into the picture early in 1968, when Stella and her grandson moved north of the river and into the flat at 90 Park West, Edgware Road occupied by Cissie Class and Celia Green. They were actually great-aunts, Stella's sister and sister-in-law. For all the lack of wickedness on display, sharing his new home with three elderly ladies must have been a strange experience for the teenage Mick.

He and the rest of the band would later get considerable mileage from Mick's immediately pre-Clash address – a depressing Sixties tower block – but, perhaps unsurprisingly, no mention would ever be made of the place he lived for much of the remainder of his schooldays. A nine-storey, late Deco-period private mansion block with porterage and its own underground car park, Park West was and is considerably more upmarket than the average council high-rise. 'It was close to Hyde Park, very exclusive,' says Mick's latter-day schoolfriend, Kelvin Blacklock. 'I only went there about two or three times, but it was really quite ultra-posh when you got inside as well. There was a swimming pool in the basement, and we used to sneak in.'

The central location also had its perks. It enabled Mick to attend his first live show on 27 July 1968: an open air free concert in Hyde Park featuring Traffic, the Nice and the Pretty Things. This was arranged by Blackhill, a young management organisation which, 11 years later, would briefly look after the affairs of the Clash. On 5 July 1969, just nine days after his 14th birthday, Mick attended a much larger free concert in the park headlined by the Rolling Stones. It was dedicated to founder member Brian Jones, who had drowned in his swimming pool just two days earlier. The emotionally charged occasion had a considerable effect on the starstruck Mick.

In the autumn of 1969, the beginning of his fourth year, Mick turned up for one of his classes to find himself sitting next to Robin Crocker, a year his senior. Robin was loudmouthed and disruptive, a classic attention-seeker. 'He was just cocky, and trying to impress everybody,' says Kelvin Blacklock. In the booklet accompanying the 1991 boxed set CD compilation *Clash On Broadway*, Mick said of Robin, 'He was a wild one. Everybody used to get him to do the things they wished they could do themselves, so he always got into trouble.' One result of this was that he was required to resit a year, which is how he came to be sharing a desk with Mick.

'There's a marvellous story to be told about how we met,' says Robin. 'We had a fight in the Maths class on the floor in front of everybody about who was better: Bo Diddley or Chuck Berry.' Once they had settled their dispute, they found they had a lot in common. Not least was a love of the Rolling Stones and – a little later – the Faces, the sloppy, goodtime rock'n'roll band fronted by Rod Stewart who were very much in the Stones tradition. It was, however, another band that was to prove responsible for widening Mick's circle of friends even further.

Mott the Hoople came into being when producer, manager and svengali Guy Stevens teamed up a Hereford band called Silence with permanently shaded singer-songwriter Ian Hunter, with the intention of creating a cross between the Rolling Stones and Bob Dylan. Renaming them after a Willard Manus novel, he secured them a deal with Island Records, and their début album, *Mott The Hoople*, was released in November 1969. Not long afterwards, they were discovered by a bunch of the Strand School's sixth formers, among them Kelvin Blacklock, Jim Hyatt and John Brown. 'We thought Mott the Hoople were a great rock band,' says Kelvin, 'and accessible, because they were playing venues like the Roundhouse [in Camden's Chalk Farm Road] and wherever for the equivalent of 50 pence.'

Between their first and their fourth and final Island album, 1971's *Brain Capers*, Mott the Hoople continued to record mostly with the febrile, inspirational Guy Stevens. The quality and mood of the albums swung wildly, but the last of them was almost hysterically aggressive. The band were always guaranteed to deliver a souped-up live show, acknowledging their debt to the rock tradition with wild rock'n'roll medleys and extended manic cover versions of songs like the Kinks' 'You Really Got Me'. Kris Needs, who ran Mott the Hoople's fan club and went on to edit *ZigZag* magazine during its punk phase, later described them thus: 'They had the loudest amps, the longest hair, the hardest rock and the baddest attitude, although their ballads could have a whole hall in tears.'

The Mott the Hoople craze spread among the Strand's musically aware pupils. The sixth formers were two to three years older than Mick, a considerable age gap at school. Nevertheless, his friendship with Robin went some way to bridging it, and Mick's home situation also proved to be an advantage. 'He had a lot more freedom than a lot of us, actually,' says Kelvin. When Kelvin and company planned outings to live concerts, Mick was usually able to tag along. 'I think the thing that brought everyone together was a general appreciation of Mott the Hoople,' says John Brown. 'That and going down the Roundhouse on a Sunday afternoon for Implosion. You used to pay your money, go in, and spend the whole day there from midday on. Loads of bands all through into the evening.'

There were also numerous outings to see Mott the Hoople further afield. Once he began to recognise the Strand boys' faces, the band's deposed former vocalist and now road manager Stan Tippins would let them in for free. This in turn encouraged them to attend every Mott concert they could, distance no object. 'We'd bunk the fares on trains, leaping off just before we got to our destination,' Mick told *Vox*'s Ann Scanlon in 1995. John and Kelvin both recall being chased down the track by irate British Rail employees. Kris Needs recalls seeing Mick 'at many of the 80 or so gigs I caught'. Together with other committed fans, the Strand boys helped keep up Mott's spirits through some hard times, and it was to them and their ilk that later band songs like 'Ballad Of Mott' and 'Saturday Gigs' were addressed.

Even at the time, the band were appreciative of their committed followers and generous with their time and attention. Particularly in Kelvin's case. Ian Hunter took to inviting him up on stage to join in on 'Walking With A Mountain', letting him sing on the section interpolating the chorus from the Rolling Stones' 'Jumping Jack Flash'. 'That was why I became a singer, really,' says Kelvin. 'It was so great, such a buzz up there.' 'Kelvin was always pushy, you know,' says John. 'He told Ian about his aspirations, what he wanted to be… The whole Mott thing had a vast and far-reaching impact on all of us, really. It changed our lives, everyone who got involved. It was very infectious.' 'Following Mott the Hoople taught us that we could all live our lives the way we wanted to,' agreed Mick in 1995.

Inspired, Kelvin and the others decided to form their own band. The initially nameless outfit first started playing together in June 1970. Instrumental duties were assigned by Kelvin, the most forceful personality. He himself played guitar and sang lead vocals, John played second guitar and also did some singing, and Bob Goffman took up the bass. 'Jim Hyatt was very laid back, the sort of guy who wouldn't create any waves,' says John. 'So he was told he was going to play drums, and just accepted that.' Kelvin lived on a council estate in Battersea, and the band used to rehearse on Thessaly Road; sometimes in the youth club, and sometimes in the same church hall the Who would shortly take over and convert into Ramport Studios. According to Kelvin, the music was 'just straight-ahead blues, simple little riffs. That's all we could play.' Other people went along to sit in occasionally, including a guitarist from Mick's year named Paul Wayman. Mick used to go and watch. 'I don't think Mick had even been contemplating playing at that point,' says Kelvin.

Kelvin is wrong. There were two Micks in the gang: the other, being more extrovert, was known as Mad Mick, while Mick Jones, younger, and yet to shoot up to his not inconsiderable adult height, was known as Little Mick. Although not cruelly meant, the diminutive gives some idea of Mick's status among the older boys, and he was as inhibited and full of self doubt as might be expected under the circumstances. Although delivered in somewhat melodramatic terms, his true feelings spilled out during a 1976 interview with Steve Walsh of punk fanzine *Sniffin' Glue*: 'I was the last kid on my block to pick up a guitar 'cause all the others were repressing me and saying, "No, you don't want to do that, you're too ugly, too spotty, you stink!", and I believed 'em. I was probably very gullible. And then I realised that they weren't doing too well, and I said, "Ah, fuck, I can do that!"'

It would be two more years before he came to this realisation and acted upon it, but the desire to be actively involved in rock'n'roll dated from his first record purchase. In addition to his deep love of the music itself, Mick was also taken with the camaraderie of band life and the glamour of pop stardom. On *That Was Then, This Is Now* he declared, 'There's a time when you have a choice between football or music, or you just do what everybody does, and you ain't gonna get out.' Although still keen on football, his overriding ambition was to be part of a rock'n'roll band. 'That was it, really: be in a group.'

Although credited to Strummer-Jones, the 1978 Clash song 'Stay Free' was written entirely by Mick, and at the time of composition its apparently autobiographical subject matter aroused much speculation about his past. It tells of a couple of friends who meet at school, mess around, and get thrown out; it details a shared south London nightlife spent dancing, drinking, laughing, fighting and playing pool; but while one of the two devotes the rest of his time to learning the guitar, the other slips into a life of crime, as a result of which he and his cohorts end up serving a three year sentence in Brixton Prison. In 1978, Chris Salewicz of the *New Musical Express* (*NME*) asked Mick to verify that the song's other main protagonist was currently working as a 'dilettante journalist' for another music publication. Although he did not name him, he meant Robin Crocker. 'It's not just about him,' answered Mick. 'It's about all my gang in Brixton. That guy's the lucky one: he's escaped. Two of the others work in butchers' shops and are in the National Front [the UK fascist party]. Twenty-three, and they're in the Front. I don't not talk to them because of that, though. I go and see them. Show them what *I've* done. Show them the possibilities.'

Mick's explanation raises the question, among others, just what was it that had to be escaped? As he suggested on *That Was Then, This Is Now*, sporting achievement and, since the late Fifties, success in popular music are traditionally perceived to be the only two legitimate ways for working class people in inner city slum areas to throw off the shackles of poverty. For those unwilling to submit to the relentless drudgery of life as fodder for the factories or dole queues, the remaining option is crime. The story of East End boxers-turned-gangsters Ron and Reg Kray adds credence to this viewpoint. As Mick claims, some – though by no means all – of his schoolmates lived on the area's numerous council estates, and the pressures of urban life may well have resulted in a higher than average number of broken homes. Nevertheless, the pupils at Strand School had one passport to freedom that Mick has tended to gloss over in interviews, and comes close to denying altogether in 'Stay Free': a privileged education.

Strand School was not some gang-dominated, drug-infested, anarchic hell-hole, the sole purpose of which was to keep the lid on its inmates until they reached minimum leaving age. Established in 1890 as an offshoot of King's College in the Strand, central London – hence the name – it had moved out to the Elm Park site 20 years later. 'It came, as a fairly snooty school, to Brixton, which at the time was a very prosperous suburb,' says John Brown. 'Of course, the area changed over the years.' The school refused to follow suit. Even in the early Seventies, the Strand was still an old-fashioned, boys-only grammar attended by less than 500 pupils. Situated next to two much larger comprehensive schools,

Tulse Hill and Dick Sheppard; it made a mockery of the very notion of comprehensive education, the original intention of which was to provide equal opportunities for all.

Grammar schools had supposedly been rendered obsolete by the change to the comprehensive system at the end of the Sixties, but a few had held on. They accepted only the more academically oriented pupils, as determined by the 11-Plus, an examination taken in the final year of primary school. Such children were considered the most likely to go on to gain Ordinary (O) or even Advanced (A) Level General Certificates of Education, and were groomed accordingly. In the early Seventies O Levels practically guaranteed a reasonably paid white collar job, and A Levels either a well paid one or the opportunity to go on to college.

John Brown makes the perfectly valid point that children of 11 have next to no say in the matter of their education. Even when they get a little older and gain some understanding of its implications, they have relatively little power to effect any changes. 'There was never any looking down, though, although you were maybe aware that you were a bit privileged,' he says. 'Especially with 2,000 kids crammed into a skyscraper nearby, which is what Tulse Hill was.' 'Strand was a really uptight school, quite strict, actually,' recalls Kelvin. 'We could never really grow our hair long. We used to try and get away with it and all that sort of bollocks, but we used to get in trouble for it. The tough nuts ended up with the school next door, Tulse Hill. There was never really any trouble. I had a few fights at school, but I think everybody has a few fights at some point.'

Both John and Kelvin say that most problems came from external, rather than internal sources, as a direct result of inequalities that could be perceived clearly by the pupils of the neighbouring comprehensive schools. According to John's estimates, Dick Sheppard and Tulse Hill were both over 90 per cent black, while the Strand was just one or two kids away from being 100 per cent white. 'We were like a plantation, almost,' he says. 'We inherited this, "They're the white kids, let's kill them," sort of thing. Every Friday they used to gather outside the school. Really heavy. We had to run the gauntlet.'

Up until mid 1970, Mick was still a marginal figure on the school band scene. The 'gang' he spent most of his time with consisted of Robin and his friends, recognised to be the Strand's worst element. John remembers that one was a skinhead who held racist views, and Kelvin recalls some members were involved in unprovoked attacks on local Asians, or 'Paki-bashing' as it was known at the time. Although the effective apartheid practised by the local school system did little to promote racial harmony, this type of behaviour could not be attributed to ignorance or stupidity, and was by no means typical of the Strand's pupils. There was an element of perversity in the indulgence of such moronic aggression. If members of this gang did – as Mick claimed – end up working in butchers' shops and joining the National Front, then it was in spite of opportunities they had been afforded, rather than due to the lack of them.

Certainly, the intelligent and highly articulate Robin was under no particular social or economic pressure to become a bad lot. He just chose to live that way, even when mixing with the less trouble-oriented school band circle. 'There'd be a gang of us who'd go to Leicester Square for fun,' says Kelvin. 'He was one of the outrageous ones. He'd chat girls up, and when their guy came along, go "Fuck off!": just insult people. And one day, this one particular guy who was a lot older than us ran off and raised a whole gang of people, and they came down with bottles and everything, and we all ran off. Robin was a bit of a rebel. I used to go back to his place up near Crystal Palace, and he used to go into shops and thieve and do all the things you do. He was quite out there.'

As 'Stay Free' suggests, Robin was indeed expelled from the Strand. John Brown was standing next to him when he finally pushed his luck too far. He swung a keychain around his head shortly before baiting one of the school 'wimps', and was reported to the Head, who accused him of threatening the boy with a dangerous weapon. 'He was just looking for an excuse to get rid of Robin, and that was it: he got one,' says John. 'Robin was kicked out that very moment.'

Robin had already extended the scope of his operations. 'He was in the *South London Press* for running a protection racket,' Mick told *The Story So Far* fanzine in 1980. 'He was the ringleader, he was the one that did it all. A kleptomaniac if ever I met one.' The 6 March 1970 edition of the *South London Press* carried a report about a gang of teenagers pillaging local shops. The following week's edition reported a robbery at the premises of John Parry Ltd, a betting shop in Somers Road, a stone's throw away from Strand School. Robin and his cohorts were arrested soon afterwards, which led to their incarceration as described in 'Stay Free'. Some artistic license was used in the song, though: Robin was not sent to the local Brixton Prison. Although still a minor at the time of the robbery, he was by his own account made up to a Senior Prisoner and sent to Wormwood Scrubs, before being transferred to Albany on the Isle of Wight. Johnny Green, a Clash associate who became close friends with Robin in 1978, was given to believe that a sawn-off shotgun was brandished during the raid. Both the fact that Robin was tried as an adult and the severity of the sentence handed out to him – as 'Stay Free' says, three years, of which he served two – implies that the law considered the offence a little more serious than mere shoplifting. This in turn suggests menaces of some kind were employed. Still, however unpleasant an episode it might have been for those on the receiving end, the robbery was more amateur bad boy posturing than big time professional blag. Robin's gang was relatively easily identified. Just £50 was taken from John Parry's till.

For a couple of years after Robin's release, Mick and Robin's friendship became – in the latter's words – 'hands on, hands off', but in the spring of 1977, the Clash would hire Robin as Mick's guitar roadie. Although this move was partly motivated by Mick's highly developed sense of loyalty, some of the band's critics – including Julie Burchill and Tony Parsons in their 1978 book, *The Boy Looked At Johnny* – interpreted the Clash's employment of an ex-jailbird (not their first) as a bid for credibility by association. Certainly, the mawkish 'Stay Free' was not the only way in which the Clash capitalised upon Robin's past.

Mick was not above hinting that he had been directly involved in some of his friend's lawless enterprises. 'The hooligans who never got caught make the best rock'n'roll,' he boasted to *Sounds*' Garry Bushell in 1978. As the people who knew him in the early Seventies are quick to point out, the idea of Little Mick qualifying as a hooligan is simply laughable. But it seems that his desire to be taken seriously as a bad boy during the punk era was so great that he was prepared to trumpet his association with, and – worse – mythologise in song, a bunch of characters who were about as far from embodying the Clash ideal as it was possible to get.

Robin positively revelled in the attention. For several years after he was first hired by the Clash, he divided his time between acting as the band's all-purpose clown and trouble-maker and exploiting his inside contacts to write about punk for *ZigZag* magazine under the self-aggrandising but amusingly appropriate pseudonym Robin Banks.

'Stay Free' and the story of its inspiration as offered by Mick to the *NME*'s Chris Salewicz have created a misleading impression of Mick's own teenage experience. Rather than being one of the few who 'escaped', the 'dilettante journalist' was one of the very few of Mick's friends or acquaintances who ever really risked capture. Mick's own idea of escape was not from privation and poverty, but rather from what he saw as the tedium of everyday life as lived by the majority of working stiffs. It was an escape into a fantasy world informed by his obsession with rock music. This was later summed up in a couplet from another 1978 Clash composition, 'The Prisoner', its metaphor drawn – tellingly – from the sense of euphoria and belonging engendered by the Strand boys' Mott the Hoople outings: 'You're only free to dodge the cops / And bunk the train to stardom.'

In 1979, a long way from home, and a couple of years past the heyday of punk revisionism, Mick admitted to *Time*'s Jay Cocks that his school song had been 'Servants Of The State To Be'. 'It was the high hope that you would become a Civil Servant. That was the best you could do. But rock'n'roll changed the way I look at society.' For a would-be rock star, the Civil Service might have appeared to be something to be avoided at all costs, but – when one considers some of the other career opportunities available – for most people, the possibility of becoming a clerical assistant with prospects was hardly a life sentence with hard labour.

One line in 'Stay Free', 'We got thrown out and left without much fuss,' would seem to suggest that Mick's own education was also curtailed prematurely. In fact, he was still attending Strand School in June 1971, when he sat three O Levels, in Art, History and English Language. Music mania and fooling around with the gang had obviously taken its toll, though, because he failed all three. Alarmed by the thought of the future that might await him, Mick chose to return to school for a further year and make a more serious attempt at gaining some qualifications.

Summer 1971 was also when the members of the school band sat their A Levels. Thereafter, Bob Goffman went away to university, but the others decided to persevere with their musical endeavours. Kelvin and John put long term career plans on hold, taking whatever jobs they could find to generate enough money to buy the band some equipment. Kelvin moved around, but John found steady if dull employment on the production line at the Wright, Layman and Umney factory – makers of Wrights' Coal Tar Soap – near London Bridge, where he later secured a job for the released Robin Crocker. Jim Hyatt found a job with the BBC's publishing department. One of its perks was the opportunity to attend recordings of the chart-oriented BBC1 TV show *Top Of The Pops*. Over the next year or two, Jim and his friends got to see many of their idols up close.

There were some changes in the band. John switched to bass, and Kelvin decided to concentrate on vocals. By January 1972, the line up had been augmented by a guitarist named Glen and a saxophonist and guitarist called Pete. Rehearsals continued in Thessaly Road, or at John's family home at 3 Penry Street, just off the Old Kent Road. The repertoire had been extended to include some original songs, which Kelvin now dismisses as 'a bunch of crap'. 'We used to just record onto a cassette player, and a tape that we put together at that time was actually played to Ian Hunter of Mott the Hoople.'

Having rehearsed for the best part of two years, amassed enough equipment, and finally settled on the frankly hilarious name Schoolgirl – which, understandably, Kelvin now affects not to remember – the band began looking for gigs in March 1972. There was no manager or agent, and potential venues were selected for approach almost at random. 'It was just what we called hustling, really,' says John. 'It was usually through friends. Someone who lived nearby who knew someone. That's how most of the gigs came about.' Together with his Mad namesake, Little Mick volunteered his services as a roadie, with a special responsibility for the drums. 'He wanted to be involved,' says John. 'Hang out, be part of the band and all that stuff.'

Schoolgirl were as naive and inexperienced as a young band can be. Today, the catalogue of setbacks and failures that dogged their brief career causes John to lapse into fits of embarrassed laughter. Gigs mostly took place in local pub venues, and the band also entered a couple of talent shows with little success. They did manage to persuade Ian Hunter to come down and see them on two separate occasions, but he advised Kelvin to sack the others – apart from John, according to John – because they were 'shit'. It would be possibly the last time in his life that Kelvin neglected to heed advice of this nature.

An attempt to induce Mott the Hoople's by now ex-manager and producer Guy Stevens to attend another show came to nothing. Between 10 March and 20 October 1972, Schoolgirl played a total of 15 times. They split up on the evening of what was supposed to be their 16th performance, when Glen offered his resignation in the time-honoured fashion of not bothering to turn up. During the next year, Kelvin, John and Jim did get together to play four more one-off engagements, some of which also involved fellow Strand old boy Paul Wayman on guitar, but that, effectively, was that.

In January 1972, Mick retook his Art O Level, and in June of that year he resat History and English Language, and – for the first time – sat English Literature and Sociology. While awaiting his results, he took a holiday job at a warehouse where the other workers used to call him Alice because they said he looked like Alice Cooper. The erstwhile Vincent Furnier had begun to make an impact in the UK in summer 1972, finally hitting the No 1 spot in August with what was, for Mick, the highly apposite 'School's Out'.

By that time, glam rock was already well established. David Bowie had captured the hearts, minds and imaginations of teeny boppers and 'serious' rock fans alike with his concept album *The Rise And Fall Of Ziggy Stardust And The Spiders From Mars*. Bowie and his guitarist and side-kick Mick Ronson had also produced Lou Reed's album *Transformer*, thus helping to revitalise the former Velvet Underground frontman's career. Indeed, Bowie had his fingers in everybody's pie that year: after learning that the struggling Mott the Hoople were on the point of splitting, he made them a present of the definitive glam anthem, 'All The Young Dudes', and offered to produce their next album. On the strength of this act of generosity, the band decided to give it another try, saying goodbye to Island and Guy Stevens and failure, and hello in quick succession to MainMan – Bowie's management company – CBS, and success.

One result of this glam-blitz was that Mick Ronson was now vying with Keith Richards and Mott the Hoople's Mick Ralphs for the honour of being Mick Jones's ultimate guitar hero. Another was a decidedly effeminate bent to his clothing and accessories: all tight flared trousers, fitted jackets, high-heeled boots and flowing Kensington Market scarves. Having pushed the Strand rule on hair length for much of his last year at school, since May he had not been required to heed it at all. His dark, curly locks were now a long way past shoulder length. Although he did buy a few Alice Cooper records – something he has since been reluctant to admit – Mick's hairstyle was more of a tribute to his long-time role-model, the recently glammed-up, but resolutely hirsute Ian Hunter.

After several months as a roadie for the hapless Schoolgirl, Mick no longer stood quite so much in awe of their musical skills. Jim Hyatt's were especially meagre. 'There was not a lot of technical talent there,' says John. 'He just muddled through. He never really pushed himself.' Perhaps because he was aware of Jim's shortcomings and sensed an opportunity, Mick took every chance he could to get behind the kit and teach himself to play the drums. Growing in confidence, he quickly raised his musical sights: the first purchase he made with his wages from the warehouse job was a second hand Hofner guitar. 'I paid £16 for it, and I think I was ripped off,' he told Caroline Coon in 1976. 'But I tell you something: I sold it for £30 to a Sex Pistol!' While it was still in his possession, he practiced on it diligently, playing along to his favourite records in his bedroom; that is, once Robin Crocker had shown him how to tune it and shape his first chords.

In August 1972, Mick learned he had passed all his exams and took his official leave of Strand School... with more than a little fuss, turning up for the graduation ceremony in a rented top hat and tails, and flashing V for victory signs as he took the stage to be awarded his certificates. Mick now had the educational qualifications necessary to attend an art school, for which the usual entrance requirement was five O Levels. Although artistically talented, his main motivation was not to learn how to express himself on canvas, but rather to link up with like-minded rock'n'roll fans and form a band. Steeped in rock mythology, he was aware that the likes of Keith Richards, Pete Townshend and John Lennon had all gone to art school, and so presumed such institutions to be the natural place for embryonic rock stars to congregate. 'I thought if I went to art school, I'd meet people jamming in the toilets and things like that,' he told *Blitz*'s William Shaw in 1988.

Unfortunately, at 17, he was still a year short of the minimum age requirement for most colleges. With 12 months in which to work up a portfolio, he first signed on at night school to begin A Levels as a security measure, and then capitulated to Strand School conditioning by agreeing to employ his five O Levels in the service of the state. He took a job with the Department of Health and Social Security (DHSS), working as a Clerical Assistant in the Benefit Office then located at 5 Praed Street, Paddington. In such a conservative environment, his appearance attracted even more attention than it had at the warehouse. 'They used to take the mickey out of me,' he told *That Was Then, This Is Now*. 'It didn't used to bother me, because I didn't care in those days.'

Other of his experiences there did bother him; or so he claimed during the early years of the Clash, when explaining the inspiration behind part of the lyric for 'Career Opportunities'. In a 1977 *NME* interview conducted by Tony Parsons which would go a long way towards establishing the Clash Myth, Mick – fizzing on a potent mixture of amphetamine sulphate and Bernie Rhodes's team talks – went into it all in some detail: 'The Social Security made me open the letters during the letter bomb time [an IRA terror campaign that coincided with Mick's stint as most junior employee] because I looked subversive. Most of the letters the Social Security get are from the people who live next door saying their neighbours don't need the money. The whole thing works on spite. One day an Irish guy that they had treated like shit and kept waiting for three hours picked up a wooden bench and put it through the window into Praed Street... And they degrade the black youth even more. They have to wait even longer. No-one can tell me there ain't any prejudice.'

Sometime in early to mid 1973, Mick and Stella left Park West, and were rehoused by the council at 111 Wilmcote House, an early Sixties tower block on the Warwick Estate, just off Harrow Road. Yellow panels intended to provide relief from the expanses of grey window and grey concrete lend Wilmcote House's 20-storey monolith the aspect of a particularly half-hearted prefab Mondrian. It is debatable whether anyone should be made to live in such a community- and soul-destroying environment, but few would dispute that a flat on the 18th floor of a high-rise was hardly the ideal spot for a 73 year-old woman. 'It was really a kind of horrible place to live,' Mick told William Shaw. 'At the time I was living there I didn't think much about it, but I'm shocked when I go back there, because people are still living in it. It's worse than it was. It gets worse every year.'

The one consolation was the view, south east over Bayswater, Knightsbridge and – in the foreground – the main route west out of central London, the A40(M) flyover, more commonly known as the Westway. A few years later, the strings of streetlights and streams of headlights down below as seen from the 18th floor balcony would inspire a visiting Joe Strummer to write the lyric for 'London's Burning'. That one song would establish the Westway as one of the original bastions of Clash mythology, and – albeit inadvertently – prepare the ground for the unpleasantness of tower block life to become one of the foremost clichés of punk. Even to this day, Wilmcote House is frequently used to illustrate the humbleness of Mick's origins, despite the fact he was nearly an adult when he moved there and was only resident full time for another two years (though he did return on occasions between 1975 and 1980, when Stella finally moved out).

Neither his new job nor his new home appeared to cause Mick any immediate trauma. Instead, it was at this time that he really started to come into his own. As he was no longer quite so little, and was now earning his own living, people like John and Kelvin found they had to adjust their attitude towards him. 'He had the best record collection, all these obscure records,' recalls Kelvin. 'And he always had good gear on. He was always dressed better than anybody else. That's what made us look up and notice him. When we were 19 or so and he was 17, he was getting into the Speakeasy [the favoured watering hole of London-based rock stars, located at 48 Margaret Street, off Oxford Circus]. And I remember, we were all after some groovy, lovely-looking girl, and he got her. We were all like, "How's *that* possible? He's the young guy that hangs out with us!"'

One of the less endearing traits of the new Mick was a tendency to show off to his friends at Stella's expense. 'His Nan put up with so much from Mick, honestly,' says John. 'He treated her like a slave at times. He was terrible. He was always bringing millions of people home. I used to feel sorry for the old lady.' 'I was pretty averagely brought up, couldn't be rude to the parents,' says Kelvin. 'And there was Mick's old grandmother, whom he loved dearly, and we used to go in and he'd say, "Where's my fuckin' dinner?" And you'd just go, "*Whaaat?*" Shock and horror! "And make a cup of tea for everyone, as well!" He was pretty soft, really. It was just his way.'

In September 1973, Mick commenced the Art Foundation course at the Hammersmith School of Art and Building at 40 Lime Grove, Shepherds Bush. His hopes of lavatorial jamming sessions were quickly dashed. 'First day, I rushed to the toilets to see who was there,' he joked in *That Was Then, This Is Now*. 'And there was two guys having a fag.' Nor did the course itself offer much in the way of consolation. 'You had to be traditional. I spent a whole year just doing life drawing before I could do my own painting.'

Deciding it was time he found something a little less dead-end than the soap factory, John Brown had also entered the Civil Service at much the same time as Mick. He took a job with the Property Services Agency at the Department of the Environment. John and Mick had grown increasingly close in the latter stages of Schoolgirl. Their friendship was cemented shortly after Mick started art school: still barely competent on guitar, he decided he would have a better chance of finding a band to join if he switched to bass, and asked John for some lessons. 'I gave him the rudiments, and he took it from there.' John also lent him a spare Vox Precision bass, until Mick got around to buying his own Ned Callan.

In return, Mick introduced John to the delights of the Portobello Market and the Notting Hill scene. 'We used to go down the Portobello Road and hang out every Saturday, Mick and I,' says John. 'We used to go down the Duke of Clarence, and Hennekeys [now the Earl of Lonsdale, on the corner with Westbourne Grove]: that used to be the place to go. We were in each others pockets all the time. We would see things like *Clockwork Orange* together, we'd go to concerts, we'd go and watch *The Night Porter*. We would go anywhere to see weird science fiction films. When I think about it, we had a great time.'

Over the next couple of years, although they liked to get out and about and sample what London had to offer, the duo spent much of their time in Mick's room at Wilmcote House, listening to records and flicking through his by now sizeable collection of music magazines and American superhero comics. A regular pair of popular culture vultures, they also read avidly and swapped books, with science fiction again being a particular love. 'We were into JG Ballard: *Concrete Island* – the Westway novel – *Crash, High-Rise*.' These books all deal in some way with the psychological damage inflicted by too-rapid technological advancements and harsh urban environments. The actual *Concrete Island* of the 1974 novel's title was a roundabout on the Westway less than a mile to the west of Wilmcote House. *High-Rise*, published in 1975, struck another chord with Mick, addressing as it does the alienating effect of life in a 40-storey tower block, and documenting the breakdown of the social order in one such edifice. On the mid Seventies Notting Hill cityscape, the 20-storey Wilmcote House was dwarfed by the recently constructed Trellick Tower, 30 storeys high. Representations of this distinctive local monument would later appear on most of Big Audio Dynamite's album sleeves.

Inevitably, though, music was the two friends' chief interest. David Bowie continued to draw attention to his favoured artists, involving himself with the career of Iggy Pop and the Stooges. Represented by MainMan, the band had come to London in 1972 to record *Raw Power*. Upon its release in 1973, it quickly became a Mick Jones favourite, leading to an extensive investigation of the Stooges' back catalogue. Although today Iggy Pop is a household name, back in the early Seventies he was neither commercially successful nor well known, and was not to become so even during the early years of Bowie's patronage. Equally obscure at that time to the average fan of rock'n'roll in the USA, never mind the UK, were the MC5. Although they had split in 1972, their original revolutionary political stance had been as left-field and unprecedented as their raucous high-energy rock'n'roll, and their final record, 1971's *High Time*, had been a science fiction concept album, which pushed all the right buttons for Mick and John. They also got into the Flamin' Groovies, a San Franciscan band who – originally inspired by the mid Sixties British Beat Boom – had remained faithful to the spirit of the classic upbeat three minute pop song throughout the hippy era, recording their two cult garage punk albums, *Flamingo* and *Teenage Head* in 1971. Mick went even further back, investigating all kinds of mid Sixties obscurities, including the Fugs – as in: the Fucks – and perhaps the quintessential garage band, the Standells, perpetrators of some of the period's most viciously basic teen anthems.

At the time, most of these records were deleted, or available only on import, with outlets even in the capital limited to a few speciality record stalls like Rock On. Tracking them down required both research and dedication. The duo's awareness of such American underground acts was assisted by their committed reading of the music press, and not just the domestic papers. Mick's mother, Renee, was living close to Detroit, home not only of the MC5 and the Stooges but also of semi-underground magazine *Creem*, which she sent to him on a regular basis. The star writer was Lester Bangs, whose record reviews often span off into impassioned rants championing all things primitive, trashy and noisy, and who, from 1971 onwards, frequently employed the term 'punk' to describe the kind of attitude and music he favoured.

Originally a piece of American prison slang describing the passive partner in a homosexual cell-pairing, by this time it had already developed into a more widespread and general term of abuse meaning no good or worthless. For many years following 1976, 'punk' would be almost exclusively associated with the movement of aggressive back-to-basics UK rock bands kick-started by the Sex Pistols. Malcolm McLaren and his charges were insistent that they had invented something new, and a Year Zero mentality developed which denied that the genre had a lengthy history. Behind all the posturing and denial at the time, there was some recognition that the term punk had enjoyed a previous life; but what little had been written about the subject was not widely circulated, and the general understanding of its background remained vague.

In the mid Sixties, British bands inspired by American R&B and rock'n'roll began to export the music back to its place of origin. In their turn, young American musicians formed bands to attempt to emulate what they were hearing. Like all second generation copies, the result was so badly distorted that it was almost unrecognisable. There were other factors in the mutation. Many of those inspired had little or no previous musical experience, and so were more enthusiastic than skilled, making for basic chord structures and minimalist solos. Drugs reared their multiple ugly heads, producing speedy thrashes, plodding downer grinds, or hallucinogenic organ swirls and eerily phased guitars and vocals. Improved and affordable amplification encouraged the use of volume as a means to excite and to mask a multitude of technical limitations. The result was sometimes known as 'garage' rock, after the favoured rehearsal spot of America's suburban bands, and usually led to a couple of local hits rather than a long term career.

Other bands originated in industrial urban centres like Detroit, which inevitably influenced lyrical subject matter, attitude and sound. The Stooges' Iggy Pop, for example, decided that instead of trying to portray the experiences of a middle aged black man, he should try to make his own version of the blues by singing about boredom, lust and alienation over a simplistic, repetitive, loud, annoying rhythm based on the noises made by the Detroit automobile assembly plants. The MC5 tried to marry the revolutionary spirit of Sixties free jazz to the sound of the revving engines and screaming brakes and tyres of the Detroit drag racing strips.

In New York, the Velvet Underground crossed the noise of free jazz with the repetition and drones of the classical avant garde to provide suitably disconcerting background for Lou Reed's street life vignettes. The Fugs, meanwhile, revelled in their complete lack of musical training, using skiffle or jug band-type instrumentation to accompany comical agit-prop lyrics. In the late Sixties, band mouthpiece Ed Sanders was the first to describe his music as punk. Writer Nick Tosches borrowed the term for a July 1970 piece in *Fusion* magazine entitled 'The Punk Muse'. Lester Bangs borrowed it from him.

In the early Seventies, this kind of music influenced the likes of Jonathan Richman's Modern Lovers, the New York Dolls and Ziggy Stardust-era David Bowie. In 1972, rock writer and future Patti Smith Group guitarist Lenny Kaye compiled *Nuggets*, a double album of one-hit wonder classics from the original garage era, including the Standells' 'Dirty Water', the Strangeloves' 'Night Time', the Seeds' 'Pushin' Too Hard' and Count Five's 'Psychotic Reaction'. All of the above would combine to inspire a New York scene centred on the Bowery club CBGBs, which by 1974 included the Patti Smith Group, Television and the Ramones. When, in December 1975, Legs McNeill and John Holstrom launched a new magazine to cover that scene, they would give it the title *Punk*. The label stuck, but when the New York bands began to record, their record companies opted instead for the less confrontational genre term 'new wave'.

The Sex Pistols would remain condescending about such groups as the Damned and the Clash who formed in their wake and ostensibly hitched a ride to success on their bandwagon. That the Pistols as a live attraction would prove highly inspirational to the rest of the UK punk scene cannot be denied, but they themselves were hardly originators. Back in 1973, before the New York scene that gave Malcom McLaren most of his ideas existed, at a time when Malcolm was still selling drapes to teddy boys, John Lydon was a greatcoated Krautrock fan, and the prototypical Sex Pistols were still trying to work their hamfisted way through the Faces songbook, Mick Jones was already listening to a wide array of punk music and had a rare and comprehensive understanding of the genre's history.

At that time, left-field rock'n'roll bands were not well represented on UK television. The only real alternative to BBC1's chart-oriented prime time show *Top Of The Pops* was BBC2's late night rock show, *The Old Grey Whistle Test*. This attempted a magazine format, featuring interviews, the odd album track accompanied by some antediluvian cartoon footage, and a band playing a two or three song set live in the studio. Presenter Whispering Bob Harris made a trademark of his laid back delivery, and as his own tastes tended towards the West Coast and muso end of the rock spectrum, the *Whistle Test* was hardly compulsive viewing for those who liked their music with hairstyle and attitude. Even when a live act did threaten to ignite, the lack of a studio audience to supply the necessary reaction tended to throw a bucket of cold water over proceedings.

Not so on one particular show on 28 November 1973, when the New York Dolls, visiting from the US, managed to secure a performance slot. They conformed to very few of the programme's 'quality music' criteria, so they were probably booked to pander to the prurient interest raised by a feature on the immediately pre-CBGBs New York scene in the 5 October issue of *Melody Maker*. Loud, lewd and outrageous in their habitual glam drag, the Dolls looked and sounded like transvestite hookers from hell as they preened and pouted their way through 'Looking For A Kiss' and 'Jet Boy', two songs from their recently released eponymous début album. Unusually for the programme, they were miming, but they did it with such total commitment it hardly showed or mattered.

The Dolls prided themselves on living out the ultimate decadent rock star fantasy. Singer David JoHansen was an even camper Mick Jagger. Guitarists Johnny Thunders and Sylvain Sylvain were ardent Anglophiles, with images reminiscent of Keith Richards and Marc Bolan, respectively. Bassist Arthur Kane was a blond Frankenstein's monster in hot pants. Since replaced by Jerry Nolan, original drummer Billy Murcia had died from drugs-related causes during the band's first visit to London, a demise documented in the track 'Time' on Bowie's 1973 album *Aladdin Sane*... All in all, they were the perfect band for Mick Jones. Surprisingly, then, it took several months for the Dolls influence to sink in. According to John Brown, it wasn't until the band's second album, *Too Much Too Soon*, came out in June 1974 that his or Mick's interest was sufficiently aroused for them to dash down to a speciality record shop near Leicester Square and buy both albums – one each – on American import.

Liking punk rock at that time did not require the exclusive commitment it would in 1976-77. Mick and John's tastes were nothing if not eclectic. They also appreciated commercially successful mainstream artists, and some obscure cults not destined to become as retrospectively hip as the Dolls and the Stooges. John was a big fan of Free. When bass player Andy Fraser left that band in late 1972 to form the Sharks with guitarist Chris Spedding and vocalist Snips, John and Mick were intrigued enough to investigate their 1973 début album, *First Water*. 'We loved the Sharks,' says John. 'We saw them whenever we could, the second incarnation of the band, after Fraser had left [later in 1973, to be replaced by Busta Cherry Jones]. They were a big influence on Mick.' He goes on to draw attention to what is indeed a remarkable similarity between the stop-start riffs opening the Sharks' 'Sophistication', included on their late 1973 post-Fraser album *Jab It In Yore Eye*, and Mick Jones's most famous and commercially successful Clash composition, 'Should I Stay Or Should I Go'.

Something that the Year Zero mentality of the UK punk scene would also cause to be denied was the sizeable debt it owed to the exuberant mainstream glam rock scene that immediately preceded it. Although this music dominated the UK singles charts between 1972 and 1974, very few music press commentators would remark upon the debt, either. The terrace choruses of Slade and Gary Glitter, the shock theatrics of Alice Cooper, the couldn't-give-a-fuck attitude of the Faces, and the mannered, sardonic vocals of Marc Bolan, David Bowie, the post-'All The Young Dudes' Ian Hunter and Steve Harley would all have a contribution to make to the sound of Class of '76 London punk.

Some of the music produced under the genre label glam played it strictly for laughs, but other artists cast a baleful eye upon contemporary events. During 1973, the Watergate hearings undermined faith in the integrity of political leaders. Meanwhile, rising oil prices triggered a world-wide recession. In the UK, inflation ran amok, peaking the following year at 25 per cent. A miners' strike called at the end of 1973 led to the declaration of a State of Emergency, extensive power cuts and a three-day working week. David Bowie had an instinctive feel for the zeitgeist, and a profound sense of turmoil and urban alienation fuels the apocalyptic visions of his music of this period. *Mott* and *The Hoople*, the two CBS studio albums recorded in 1973 and 1974 respectively by Mott the Hoople – still Mick Jones's favourite band – offer an even more direct reflection of the State of the Nation. The subject matter of Ian Hunter's lyrics is especially noteworthy: mean streets, poor education, dead end jobs, the dole, repression of 'the kids' by the police, the government and other authority figures, and the venting of boredom, frustration and anger through vandalism and mindless violence.

Despite being disappointed by what he believed to be the limited opportunities offered by his foundation year at Hammersmith Art School, Mick applied for and was accepted onto the full-time Painting course, due to commence in September 1974. 'You get a grant, don't you?' was his cheeky explanation. To pay for those of his interests not covered by that grant, during the long summer 1974 vacation Mick took a job at the Economists' Bookshop, then located at 106 Hampstead Road. Kelvin Blacklock, between bands at the time, worked there, too. 'It's possible, actually, that Mick got me that job,' he says. 'It was a mail-order book thing, you'd pack up the books and send them off.' Before Mick returned to college Kelvin was sacked for spending too much time on the phone trying to arrange band auditions. Thereafter, he and Mick lost touch for a while.

That year Panther books published Ian Hunter's account of Mott the Hoople's late 1972 US tour under the title *Diary Of A Rock'n'Roll Star*. 'It was especially interesting to us, because we knew all the people involved intimately,' says John Brown. There was enough name dropping, rock'n'roll romanticism and vaguely decadent behaviour to fire Mick's imagination. 'It was the brochure at the time, the brochure for how I wanted to be,' he admitted laughingly on *That Was Then, This Is Now*. 'It ain't how I want to be *now*, but it was then.' The book's tales of touring America's pawn shops in search of cheap classic second hand guitars brought back memories. 'Mott would come back and they'd have 20-25 guitars, Les Paul Juniors,' says John. 'Made us drool, you know. Us with our Hofners and nameless Japanese things.'

Mick decided it was about time he rectified the situation. To make up the money, he took a stall at a science fiction convention at a hotel in Russell Square, and sold £80 worth of his rarer American comic books. In a guitar shop in the West End's Denmark Street-Charing Cross Road area, he bought a second hand black Fender Telecaster with a maple neck. 'It wasn't cheap,' says John. 'He saw it and he just loved it. He wanted to buy it no matter what it sounded like. I advised him against it. I didn't like the tone on it: it was very thin. It never suited his playing.'

By the time he commenced the Painting course that September, Mick's glam look had reached a level of excess worthy of the New York Dolls themselves. He would turn up in leather trousers – decidedly rare in pre-punk days – and women's high-heel sling-back shoes. Future Slits guitarist Viv Albertine was also attending the school. 'I thought he looked great, because he stood out a mile from the other students,' she told *Blitz*'s William Shaw in 1988. 'Half the college was like a builder's training college, and so when you went to the cafeteria, you used to walk past all these building students. It wasn't easy to walk past them if you were wearing leather trousers. Everyone knew who he was. He was always flamboyant. Always a bit of a star.' 'He got known as a bit of a poseur at that place,' says John. 'Because he used to do a bit of a Keith Richards, and just hang around. "Hanging out" was his main thing!'

The relationship between rock music and art, forged in the Sixties, had grown even stronger in the Seventies, as exemplified by the work of Belgian artist Guy Peellaert. In 1974, he designed the covers for David Bowie's *Diamond Dogs* and the Rolling Stones' *It's Only Rock'n'Roll*. That same year, he also published *Rock Dreams*, a collection of fantasy illustrations depicting popular music luminaries as the inhabitants of a decadent netherworld, wealthy and pampered, but willing slaves to drug abuse and sexual perversity.

It was an accurate reflection of the current state of play with the rock aristocracy: much of the music produced in the early Seventies betrayed the effects of a post-Sixties comedown, with ideals giving way to cynical self-interest, love and peace to fear, loathing and casual sex, and experimentation with drugs to oblivion-seeking and addiction. Many would-be Neros chose to fiddle while Rome burned. Decadence was one of the buzzwords of the era. Thus, the generation of music fans that had become teenagers in the late Sixties and early Seventies had been encouraged to believe that Peellaert's almost Burroughsian vision of a rock'n'roll parallel universe actually existed. It was a further reflection of the zeitgeist that many of those fans found it appealing.

His year of line drawing over, Mick was finally able to pursue his own artistic interests, producing paintings which – unsurprisingly – owed a great deal to the tradition of pop iconography, 'all razor blades and Marilyn Monroe and limousines and so on,' as he told the *NME*'s Paul Rambali in 1981. 'He did some great work there,' says John. 'Some great photo-collages, but his heart wasn't really in art, I don't think.' Although art could take rock'n'roll as its subject, and hold a mirror up to popular culture, it was still at one remove from the experience itself. Mick didn't want to paint that kind of picture; he wanted to be in it. He had always thought of art school as a means to an end. 'It was all a bit disappointing,' he told William Shaw. 'I didn't manage to meet *anybody* at college to form a group with.'

In January 1975, the second term of Mick's first year on the Painting course, Hammersmith School of Art and Building became part of Chelsea School of Art (today known as Chelsea College of Art and Design). The college's records show that he 'had a good year's work in 1974-75', 'a satisfactory year in 1975-76' but that 'for 1976-77 he hardly attended during the first two terms'. Mick signalled his true priority early in 1976, at the beginning of the second term of his second year, when his entire grant cheque went towards the purchase of another new guitar. It was a Fifties vintage Les Paul Junior, a model described by Ian Hunter in *Diary of a Rock'n'Roll Star* as the guitar collector's equivalent of a Penny Black. This was the 'heart-attack machine' Joe Strummer would enthuse about in the 1978 Clash song 'All The Young Punks (New Boots And Contracts)'.

By the time his third year began, in September 1976, Mick was rehearsing and playing with the Clash. Although he occasionally still went along to 'hang out', his formal attendance at college was limited to turning up on the first day of term to collect his grant cheque. His artistic output was restricted to his part in decorating the band's rehearsal room, equipment and clothing. Towards the end of the year, on one of his infrequent visits to Lime Grove, Mick was accosted by a staff member who accused him of not having produced any paintings the previous term. 'I said, "Hey, look at this!" and showed him my shirt,' Mick claimed on *That Was Then, This Is Now*. Quick thinking, maybe, but it failed to have the desired effect. 'It wasn't acceptable. I got chucked out in the end.' On 4 April 1977, the Head of Department advised the Inner London Education Authority that Mick had withdrawn from the course. 'I went back for the last day, when they have the show and you go up and get your diploma, and there was a space instead of my stuff. So I never got to have that.' He didn't get that last term's grant cheque, either.

2
DIARY OF A ROCK'N'ROLL STAR

When the UK punk movement first broke, rumours began to circulate about a by-then-defunct band named the London SS. Apparently, it had included Mick Jones in its line-up along with – at one time or another – nearly every future punk star; and it had been managed by Bernie Rhodes, later to perform that task for the Clash. When he was questioned about it, Mick remained noncommittal. In January 1977, Bernie admitted to short-lived music paper *National Rock Star* that the pre-Clash rehearsal band had existed, but insisted that the phrase 'London SS' had been nothing more than a slogan on a T-shirt worn by one of its members.

At the time, going into detail about the London SS would have compromised the Clash Myth. For the duration of the Clash's existence, only odd snippets of information emerged from the band camp. It was left to various of the other people involved in the London SS to supply their versions of events. In September 1977, *ZigZag* printed a Pete Frame Rock Family Tree entitled 'The Influence Of The New Wave Nine'. It included the most detailed account of the London SS yet committed to print, tracing the band's origins back to the summer of 1975, and drawing its information from contemporary interviews with Brian James, Rat Scabies and – principally – one of the longest-serving members of the group, Tony James. A slightly expanded version was reprinted in the Christmas 1978 issue of *Sounds* under the title 'Children Of The Revolution 1976-78'.

Once the Clash had split, Mick started to open up a little more about his previous band, particularly in the retrospective interviews he gave in 1988-89. Even in the booklet accompanying 1991's boxed set *Clash On Broadway*, though, his version failed to expand much on Tony's. Bernie, meanwhile, still avoided referring to the group by name, and endeavoured to give the impression that it had lasted a couple of weeks at most. In truth, the name London SS was first conceived in March 1975, and was actually in use from – at the latest – October of that year until January 1976. The roots of the band, and therefore of the Clash itself, can be traced all the way back via Schoolgirl to Strand School and the Thessaly Road blues band...

Mick made the transition from bedroom strummer and part-time roadie to performer as early as May 1974. By that time, he had been playing bass for several months, and was already spending a lot of time with John Brown. Schoolgirl was long defunct. Knowing that his older, slightly more experienced friend had no other irons in the fire, Mick made the tentative suggestion that the two of them should start a group of their own. 'I said, "We've got a fundamental problem here,"' says John. '"We've got two bass players!" And he said, "No, you can be bass. I'll switch to rhythm, and take it from there."' Hence the Telecaster purchase.

John recalls that the plan to form a band was hatched while he and Mick were attending a season of science fiction films at the National Film Theatre on the South Bank. The band name came along at the same time, with both possibilities considered illustrating the extent to which Mick was already in thrall to punk rock. His first suggestion was the Coca Cola Douche, the title of a Fugs song. 'I said, "I don't think we're going to get much record company interest with *that* one!"' laughs John. 'Then the Juvenile Delinquents came up. I said, "That's too much of a mouthful." So we ended up with the Delinquents.'

The history of the London SS might have remained shadowy, but mention of the forerunning Delinquents has been almost non-existent. Their first recruit, in late May 1974, was lead guitarist Paul Wayman, who had been in Mick's year at Strand School and also briefly involved with both the school blues band and Schoolgirl. Early the following month, a drummer was located via a classified advertisement in *Melody Maker*, the traditional notice board for the UK's amateur and professional rock musicians. Mike Dowling lived in Dalston, north east London, with his wife, the daughter of a Greek garment manufacturer. 'She was difficult, and she made things difficult for him,' says John. 'And he wasn't really totally the right guy.' One compensation was that Mike's father-in-law owned a garment sweat shop near Dalston Lane, where he allowed the band to rehearse two or three evenings a week. Additional weekend rehearsals were held at John's house at 3 Penry Street. 'Saturday morning, my dad would be upstairs watching the racing, and the gas fire would be bouncing along the wall with all the noise coming up from downstairs. They were very understanding, my Mum and Dad.'

The Delinquents rehearsed intensively, but allowed themselves remarkably little time to gel before they played their first gig – also Mick's first ever – on 19 June in the Students' Union bar at Queen Elizabeth College, Campden Hill Road, Kensington. 'Everyone was pretty nervous,' says John. 'We didn't have a lot of our own material. That was the only time I know for sure that we played "Ohio" by Neil Young.' A response to the 1970 demonstration at Kent State University, where the National Guard fired into the crowd, killing four students, 'Ohio' had also been a feature of Mott the Hoople's live set throughout their Island years. Other than that, John can remember little about the evening, but it is telling that the band did not play another gig proper until the end of November. Rather than repeat Schoolgirl's experience of lurching from disappointment to disaster in the hope of the occasional small victory, they decided instead to adopt as businesslike an approach as possible.

The first step was to develop a strongly identifiable band sound, and work up a few original songs. 'The music played is in a Mott-Sharks vein, loud and punky,' claimed the Delinquents' promotional leaflet, first sent out in late September 1974. It estimated that, by then, only half the band's repertoire was made up of cover versions. John recalls these were relatively – and deliberately – obscure, including 'World Park Junkies' and one other from the Sharks' début album, 'Second Cousin' by the Flamin' Groovies, and a couple of songs by the MC5. Original material was composed by all three of the band's frontmen. 'Mick was really the songwriter in the band,' says John. 'I contributed a few ideas, as did Paul Wayman, but beyond that it was a showcase for Mick's writing, really.' That said, most song ideas were developed by the band as a whole. 'I don't think we ever actually sat down and said, "This is my song, that's your song."' All three frontmen shared the vocals, but again, Mick tended to dominate.

Still a limited guitarist, Mick's ambition and creative bent had nevertheless led him to begin experimenting with songwriting as soon as he could string a few basic chords together. John cannot remember any titles, but says, 'He wrote some good stuff, even then.' In order to help with work on his compositions, Mick invested in a relatively sophisticated tape recorder. 'I think it was an Akai 4000 DS, which was the earliest reel-to-reel machine in this country that would do sound on sound,' says John. 'You could do overdubs, multi-tracking: you'd just bounce between tracks until the hiss got so loud you couldn't hear what you were doing.' Mick also used the machine to tape Delinquents rehearsals at the Dalston sweat shop. 'Mick must still have those recordings, if he's bothered to keep them,' says John. 'There'd be a lot of his early stuff on there, but he's quite close to his chest about stuff from the Delinquents days.'

According to the promotional leaflet, the next step to success was to obtain 'a good PA system courtesy of a friendly bank manager'. John also registered 'the Delinquents' as a business name. Similar attention to detail was evident in the promotional package the band prepared for prospective venue bookers and management companies. The leaflet outlined the Delinquents' history to date and listed the personnel, revealing that Mick was calling himself 'Michael J Jones', although everyone – except Stella – had always known him as Mick. He was to experiment with several other pseudonyms over the next couple of years, partly to avoid confusion with another guitarist named Mick Jones who had joined Spooky Tooth in 1973. Also, stage names were very much in vogue in the prevailing glam rock climate. 'At one point, I called myself Lance Rock, after the unfortunate guy in [Russ Meyer's cult film] *Beyond The Valley Of The Dolls*,' recalls John. 'Real kitsch stuff.'

September 1974 also saw the Delinquents arrange a photo-session to provide illustrations to accompany the leaflet. The photos were taken at Butler's Wharf on the River Thames. Although this former warehouse district has since undergone gentrification, at the time it was largely derelict – 'a bombsite, basically' – and as such was perfectly suited to the dead end kids image the band wanted to project. John still has in his possession two of the photographs the session produced, but he later gave a third – the best of them – to a girlfriend. 'Someone had written "SPUNK" on this wall, and one of us stood in front of the "S" – me, in fact – so that it spelled the word "PUNK". Mick's got really long hair, and evening gloves on.'

The most impressive part of the Delinquents' promotional package was its audio element. In the *Melody Maker* classifieds, John found an advertisement for Budget Studios, 'cheaper and better than the average studio. Professional recording from £3.50 per hour.' They booked a session to record two original songs in mid September. 'It was like a mansion block fronting onto High Holborn, by the tube station,' says John. 'The crappy bit up at the top where the attic is, that's where we were. The thing that was quite unique about it was, it was a rare 3-track, from Philips's studio. They were so proud of it, this hi-tech machine! They said, "Dusty Springfield used this to record 'I Only Want To Be With You'!"'

The quality of the demo recording might have left a lot to be desired – 'they dampened the drums so much, they sounded like marshmallows!' – but nobody could fault its presentation: the band had the tape transferred to a single, using the pressing service attached to Pye Studios on Bryanston Street, off Edgware Road. 'They'd press it for you on acetate,' says John, 'and it cost something like £16 for five copies. And £16 in 1974 was a fair amount of money for aspiring musicians.' Mick held onto the original tape, and most of the acetates were sent out with the other promotional material (along with the obligatory advice to 'play loud'), but John still has one copy. Atypically, neither song was originated by Mick: John came up with the basic idea for the A-side, 'You Know It Ain't Easy', and Mick finished it off; the B-side, 'Hurry', was primarily Paul's song.

Both illustrate the band's marked Sharks influence, being based on Keith Richards-style sloppy stop-start guitar riffs, courtesy of Mick, overlaid with fluid-but-precise melodic lead guitar lines, courtesy of Paul. The B-side's lyric is unremarkable – boy advising girl she'd better hurry up or else, then taking the sting out of the threat by telling her he'll wait anyway – and Paul and Mick sing it in unison. The A-side is a little more noteworthy. Its verses, sung clear and high by John, string together aspirational rock'n'roll clichés, charting the protagonist's progress from attending rock'n'roll shows to playing in the band. The chorus, sung by Mick, offers the observation, 'You know it ain't easy, but it ain't hard / It could be so easy if you'd drive my car.' 'That's Mick's input,' says John. 'I did the rest of the lyric, he did the hook.'

Beatles enthusiasts will recognise a subversion of the chorus from 'The Ballad Of John And Yoko', with a reference to 'Drive My Car' squeezed in for good measure. This, and Mick's sardonic, exaggeratedly yob Cockney delivery, work against the drift of the verses, and transform the song from a teen fantasy into a wry comment on the rock star lifestyle. Despite Mick's dirty rhythm guitar work, Paul's aggressive lead guitar wig-out coda to 'Hurry', and Mike's lo-fi drums, this is as 'punky' as either song gets. The Clash would later make regular use of similar marked contrast in their vocal interplay, only this time with Mick taking the high role and Joe Strummer taking the low.

Finally ready to go out into the world, the Delinquents paid for two classified ads in the issue of *Melody Maker* dated 26 October 1974 (although it would have been on sale at least two days earlier than that). The first ad, carried in the Groups section, read: 'THE DELINQUENTS, Raunch'n'roll, want gigs,' followed by a daytime number for John at the DOE, and evening numbers for Paul at home and for Mick at Wilmcote House. The same numbers appeared in the second ad, in the Management Wanted section. A model of succinctness, it read: 'THE DELINQUENTS want management/agency.'

There was some response. An agency invited the band to audition in a rehearsal studio at 101 St John's Hill, Clapham. Gigs in Sweden were promised, but nothing was delivered. Next to call was a publishing company, still in existence, but nameless here for reasons that will become all too obvious: 'It was in this really plush office above Oxford Street. We went up there, and the guy listened to the record. The thing I remember is, he was talking to us about what we were after, and all this sort of stuff, and he walked over to the fire exit, pushed the doors open, got his todger out, and started pissing out over the fire escape! "What the fuck's going on?", you know. He was a weirdo: one of those guys who's a bit of a paedophile on the quiet. There's a lot of those in the biz.' After having successfully exposed himself to the still mostly teenage band, he quickly lost interest in them.

For all their determination to take a more professional route, the Delinquents' second live performance – and indeed, all subsequent gigs – came as a result of Schoolgirl-style hustling. John got things off to a start when he approached the landlord of his local pub rock venue, the Thomas à Beckett, 320 Old Kent Road, and was offered a gig on 25 November. The Delinquents advertised their appearance on the Club Calender page of *Melody Maker*, and made sure the gig was no secret to the members of their respective social circles. 'All our friends came, colleagues from work, my Mum and Dad, my sisters,' says John. 'I think Mick's Dad might have popped in. Everybody we knew.' The partisan crowd reacted favourably, ensuring that the band was offered a return date on 9 December.

On 26 November, the Delinquents played the Woking Community Centre, courtesy of one of John's friends who lived in the Surrey town. They hired a van, which Mike Dowling drove. The 20 mile journey discouraging any travelling support. 'It was playing in front of 14 year-old girls who didn't have a clue what we were about,' says John. Three days later, the Delinquents played the Target pub in Reading, 30 miles west of London. 'It was a real squaddies' pub: there was a barracks nearby, or something. It was a bad booking for us. We were all dressed up like the Dolls, knocking out all this fast stuff, and they weren't really into that.' Following the return engagement at the Thomas à Beckett, the Delinquents played their sixth gig on 12 December at what was, for Mick, who arranged it, an even more familiar venue: Hammersmith College of Art. Although most of the audience knew him, his reputation as something of a poseur did not make for a warm reception, and John remembers him being particularly self-conscious that night.

Thereafter, the band began to make inroads on the traditional pub rock circuit. Even so, not everyone involved, however indirectly, considered this a good enough return for all the time, rehearsing, planning and expense that had gone into launching the Delinquents. Mike Dowling's wife had always believed he should be seeing more of her than of his bandmates. This conflict of loyalties led to his departure in mid January after the band had played only three more gigs and were just beginning to get into their stride.

Hardly pausing for breath, Mick and John placed a classified ad in the Musicians Wanted section of the 25 January 1975 issue of *Melody Maker*. In addition to making pointed reference to the perceived shortcomings of their former drummer, it left no doubt about their determination to continue in much the same musical vein: 'DRUMMER REQUIRED for ambitious together rock band, influenced by Rolling Stones, Free, Sharks etc. Must have view to turning professional in near future and have no commitments which might impede the band's development. No jokers.' It was accompanied by John's work number for days and Mick's home number for evenings. Shortly after it was placed, Paul Wayman found his own commitment wanting. Deciding he'd given rock'n'roll stardom a fair enough shot, he not only left the band, but also quit music altogether in order to devote himself to a career with the Post Office.

Any brief feelings of confusion or doubt Mick and John might have experienced were brushed aside in a matter of days, when they met Geir Waade.

Drummer Geir Waade and his keyboard-playing friend Casino Steel had moved to London in 1971 from Oslo, Norway, to improve their chances of becoming rock stars. Geir took a brief side trip to Amsterdam, returning to discover that Casino had found himself a band for which the drum stool was already taken: the Queen.

Andrew Matheson, the band's singer, frontman (and, in his own words, 'mouthpiece and lead sex symbol') came over to the UK from Canada in 1971 with the same ambition as Casino and Geir, only more so. Via the inevitable *Melody Maker* ads, he recruited drummer Lou Sparks and Casino for what he envisaged as the ultimate in camp, sluttish trash glam bands. Originally from Dublin, committed Keith Richards fan Eunan Brady moved to London in 1969, also in search of the rock'n'roll dream. After a brief spell with Love Affair – of 'Everlasting Love' fame – he filled in his time with pub bands while waiting for his big break. It came via Andrew's late 1972 *Melody Maker* advertisement for a guitarist 'drunk on scotch and Keith Richards'. Although impressed by the new applicant's credentials, Andrew decided that Eunan was far too un-rock'n'roll a name, and decreed that he should henceforth be known simply as Brady. Finding a suitable bass player proved to be the greatest problem. Andrew finally settled for Brady's friend Derek, whose given name was also found wanting and was promptly changed to Wayne Manor, 'after Batman's house'. Early in 1973, following the emergence of Freddie Mercury's Queen, Andrew also changed the band's name to the Hollywood Brats.

'We loved make-up, noise, aggression, outrageous clothes, and female tourists,' writes Andrew, now once again resident in his native Canada. 'We used to stop traffic on Oxford Street in the middle of the afternoon because we looked like we were from some planet you didn't want to visit.' It is tempting to describe the Hollywood Brats as London's answer to the New York Dolls, but – despite similarities in dress, attitude and name – both Andrew and Brady insist no plagiarism was involved.

The London-based group found the going even tougher than their New York counterparts. According to Andrew's admittedly highly embellished account, throughout 1973 they provoked much the same outraged reaction at their various London club gigs as would the Sex Pistols a few years later. 'We were hated everywhere we played. There was always violence at our gigs. I once had a tooth knocked out by some deranged perspiring disco Don Juan. He screamed that I'd licked his girlfriend's hand, and smashed me in my lipsticked mouth. Brady booted him in the V of his Sergio Valentes, and all hell broke loose.' Brady remembers things slightly differently:

Andrew, being fleet of foot, usually managed to avoid physical repercussions, but the others were not always so lucky. It was Lou who lost the tooth.

The band's problems were exacerbated by its members' penchant for Dolls-style hard living, and Andrew's oversized ego, which tended to rub potential allies up the wrong way. Despite this – and signing with a legendarily suspect management company – the Brats did finally land a record contract. Between December 1973 and January 1974, they recorded an album's worth of material for Arista, managing to completely alienate the production staff in their search for a suitably raw sound. Upon delivery of the master tapes, the contract was cancelled, and after a few more months of 'backbiting and nasty words', the band began to fall apart.

Casino and Andrew retrieved the masters and Casino took them over to Norway. As a result, the eponymously-titled album was released posthumously, at first only in the four Scandinavian countries. It finally won a UK release on Cherry Red in 1980, whereupon *Record Mirror*'s Peter Coyne gave it an ecstatic five-star review. (Cherry Red released the first CD version of the album in January 1994, with new sleeve notes by Andrew and Brady.) The final track, 'Sick On You', written in 1973, had anticipated one of punk's major calling cards by three years…

While his friend Casino was engaged with the Brats, Geir Waade worked for Virgin Records and – in the late spring of 1974 – auditioned several times for eccentric glam rock outfit Sparks before finally being turned down. 'Then I answered an ad in the *Melody Maker*,' he says. 'I remember talking to Mick Jones on the phone, and going up to see him in his grandmother's flat.' Conveniently, Geir was living just around the corner from Wilmcote House, at 107 Elgin Avenue. 'I met Mick, and we sort of liked each other, I reckon. I didn't think he was rock'n'roll enough, myself, because he wore white silk gloves. He looked like a right twit, I'll tell you. Tiny Tim!' With his long blond tresses and classic Nordic good looks, Geir made a far better initial impression on Mick and John. He was also no mean talent at selling himself. 'He had a bit of the gift of the gab, did old Geir,' laughs John.

Egos in the rock'n'roll world being what they are, allowances usually have to be made for jealousy and spite whenever musicians appraise one another's talents. However, John, Brady, Kelvin Blacklock and Andrew Matheson all agree that Geir was and is a personable enough human being, which gives some credence to their separately volunteered observations that he was a simply terrible drummer. 'He was an excuse on legs, really, Geir,' says John. 'He had a great image, and we were swayed by good looks as much as anything. "We can *make* him a good drummer! We can work on him." But it never really happened. He had a couple of shining moments.'

It was as a motivator that Geir really excelled. Not content to take a back seat – other than literally – with the band he had just joined, he was quick to suggest a candidate for the remaining gap in the line-up. 'He came in like a bullet,' says John. '"Oh, I got this guy, he's great. He used to be in the Hollywood Brats, you know. You must have heard of them?" "No!"' Nevertheless, when Geir talked up Brady's talent and image, he aroused Mick and John's interest. Meantime, he was doing a similar PR job with Brady, emphasising Mick and John's fondness for the Stones, Mott the Hoople and the Dolls.

Brady's diary entry for 9 February 1975 was, 'Had a blow, after much hassle, with Geir's guys. I might join.' Part of his initial hesitancy can be attributed to what he perceived to be the others' musical shortcomings. He was already familiar with Geir's playing. 'The guy had no sense of rhythm! At the end of the day, he just couldn't hack it, you know. Mick was OK. He was a good rhythm player, but I think that's as far as it went. And John was steady on the bass: he wasn't exceptional.' 'Brady could plumb the depths of sheer crap, or hit the pinnacles of sheer genius,' is how John assesses Brady's skills. 'He was that sort of guitarist.' Brady suspects that Mick paid more attention to the pinnacles, and was a little in awe of him. 'I don't want to sound pompous and arrogant, but I was very self assured, and I had this lovely Gibson Firebird. I think it was the first time Mick had met some guy where, whenever he said, "Can you play this?" I could.' Brady was concerned by Mick and John's inexperience, and – like Geir – thought Mick's look bordered on the ludicrous. 'He had long, black curly hair down to his arse! Like one of those Pre-Raphaelite paintings. And he used to wear black leather gloves.' Nevertheless, he went along for a few more rehearsals and, having felt somewhat directionless since the Brats split, he soon found himself carried along by the others' enthusiasm.

Inevitably, the addition of the experienced Brady and the forceful Geir altered the balance of power in the group and influenced its direction. Previously, Mick and John had considered themselves strong enough singers to share the lead vocals. Both newcomers favoured the idea of recruiting a frontman in the tradition of the Stones' Mick Jagger, the Dolls' David JoHansen and the Brats' Andrew Matheson: someone who could both sing and provide the band with a focal point on stage. On 22 February 1975, a display ad was placed in the *Melody Maker* classifieds: 'DECADENT VOCALIST REQUIRED for newly formed contemporary Rock'n'Roll Band. Front man/personality essential.' Again, it was accompanied by Mick's home number and – to his subsequent regret – John's number at the Department of the Environment. 'Someone tried to get through to my extension and ended up somewhere else, saying, "Yeah, I'm really decadent!" to the Sub-Permanent Under-Secretary of State, or something. And they traced where the call was supposed to be going. I got hauled on the carpet for that one…'

The ad failed to produce a suitable singer, but it did attract the attention of someone who was possibly even more welcome. 'A guy called Tony Gordon answered,' says Geir. 'He was a sort of manager who said he was interested in us.' Phoning up an unknown and incomplete band might sound an unlikely move for a management company, but Tony's company, Wedge, were keen to build up a roster of clients. Two weeks later, they even placed their own *Melody Maker* ad for 'Together bands with image and original material.' Tony – who Brady describes as 'a dead ringer for Neil Sedaka' – listened to the band rehearse, made appreciative noises, and said he would return once the line-up was complete.

Not having access to a regular practice room, the band split their rehearsal time roughly equally between Geir's flat in Elgin Avenue, Brady's squat at 28 Boundary Road in St John's Wood, and 111 Wilmcote House. Brady chuckles when he recalls trying to work on ideas in Mick's bedroom while being told to keep the noise down by Stella. 'We spent more time looking for a lead singer than we did actually rehearsing,' he says. 'We did a lot of ligging and checking people out.'

After leaving the Economists' Bookshop, Kelvin Blacklock had joined a band called Overtown, subsequently bringing in former Schoolgirl drummer Jim Hyatt. They had managed to secure a residency at the Marquee club on Wardour Street, alternate Wednesdays running from 15 January to 26 February. John and Mick took Geir and Brady along to see their old schoolmates play, and both were strongly impressed by the singer. 'We thought Kelvin looked brilliant,' says Brady. 'He was a tall, skinny guy with blond hair, and he leapt around.' 'I said I liked the guy,' says Geir. '"This is definitely a singer we should have."'

Knowing Kelvin of old, neither John nor Mick were particularly keen on the idea of poaching him, and Mick was especially vocal in his objections. 'He apparently said, "Kelvin's a breadhead,"' is Kelvin's own explanation. Brady and Geir recall it differently. 'Mick warned us that Kelvin was very unscrupulous, and only thought of number one,' says Brady. 'Mick said, "If you have him in the band, you'll get the sack,"' says Geir. '"He'll split the band up."' In Mick and Kelvin's relationship, the latter had always been the dominant party, and another likely reason for Mick's unwillingness to consider him was fear of a further diminishment of his own status within the group.

The search for a singer continued to prove unsuccessful, but the ligging helped strengthen the bonds between the band members. Both John's and Brady's diaries recorded the extent to which social activities were band-oriented: going to gigs together at the Windsor Castle on Harrow Road, the Marquee on Wardour Street and the Greyhound in Fulham, attending parties, hanging around at each others' homes, and spending Saturday afternoons drinking down the Portobello Road. Mick borrowed Brady's clothes, and Brady even gave him a pair of tight flares he had worn with the Brats. There was a certain amount of sexual braggadocio and one-upmanship, and even longer-lasting relationships had an incestuous edge: earlier in the year, Mick had been seeing a girl called Jane Crockford; in March, she started going out with John.

Andrew Matheson begs to differ, but Geir, Brady and John all insist that it was at this time that the London SS was first suggested as a band name. Certainly, the Delinquents had been dropped almost immediately following Geir's arrival. Brady confirms Geir's claim that it was the drummer who came up with the alternative, but John insists it was the result of a general brainstorming session with a dictionary and thesaurus. Obviously, the London prefix was a nod in the direction of the New York Dolls and the Hollywood Brats, but there is some disagreement about the SS part. 'I didn't mean like a Nazi thing,' says Geir. 'It was because we all went on the dole, you see: Social Security.' John and Brady's accounts indicate that Geir is guilty of some face-saving revisionism. The pun may well have occurred to him and other original and future members of the band at a later date, but the Nazi allusion was originally both deliberate and deliberately tasteless. It might seem irresponsible in today's post Anti-Nazi League world – as Geir is obviously well aware – but taken in context, it was merely another indication of the mood of the times.

Luchino Visconti's 1969 film *The Damned* focuses on decadent behaviour in its portrayal of the rise of Nazism in the Thirties. Its dark mood chimed with the similar one developing in the rock'n'roll world. There is an infamous photograph taken the same year of the Rolling Stones' Brian Jones in an SS uniform, posing with one jackboot on the neck of a doll. The 1972 hit film *Cabaret* did much to strengthen the association between decadence, the trappings of fascism, and the theatrical rock'n'roll of the early Seventies. In 1973, *The Damned*'s stars Dirk Bogarde and Charlotte Rampling were reunited for Liliana Cavani's *The Night Porter*. The film played up the S&M connotations of the uniforms, and the dominant and submissive roles of oppressor and oppressed. In the process, it established the decadent Nazi movie as a genre. All kinds of B-movies jumped on the trend, lending the Nazi theme schlock value and even a certain humorous appeal: several of Russ Meyer's trash films feature a character dressed as Martin Boorman.

Guy Peellaert was indebted to the Nazi-S&M craze and the earlier Brian Jones photograph for his 1974 *Rock Dreams* paintings of the Stones. One of them depicts the band in SS uniforms – or in Mick Jagger's case, jackboots, stockings and suspenders – lounging around a sumptuous suite in the company of several naked pre-pubescent girls. Peellaert was playing with the general public's media-fed image of the Stones as Satanic outlaws, intent on breaking every possible social and sexual taboo. The Nazi trappings were not intended to reflect the band's own political sympathies: the shock factor was everything. The same urge to provoke explains the swastika armband worn by Johnny Thunders in a late 1973 Bob Gruen photograph of the New York Dolls, and why Ron Asheton of the Stooges liked to take the stage in one of his comprehensive collection of Nazi uniforms. In thrall to such rock myth-making, the London SS were aspiring to appear just as decadent and amoral as their rock'n'roll heroes.

'I'll never forget,' says Brady, 'on his bedroom wall, Mick had this great poster of some terrible little cheap B-movie about concentration camps. "Hitler did *this!*" We both just laughed about it.' 'On Portobello Road, across the road from Hennekeys, there used to be a guy selling Nazi memorabilia,' says John. 'We used to go and buy bits there. I'm not too proud about that, but it was the decadent thing, rather than the Nazi skinhead thing. More shock value than anything else. London SS was a name to slap you in the face. That was it, really. When it was suggested, we said, "Yeah, that's a great name!" and I started going away working out logos and stuff, as you do.' The decadent pose is a justification of sorts, but it should be remembered that Mick was half-Jewish, and living with a Jewish grandparent. His flirtation with the visual symbols of Hitler's Germany might have been superficial and tongue-in-cheek, but his willingness to adopt them give some indication of just how naive and apolitical he was at this time.

Approximately a year later, the Clash would adopt the stern political stance that permeated all their early interviews, and helped set the agenda for what was and was not acceptable in punk. One issue would be the wearing of the swastika, which Malcolm McLaren promoted – and the likes of Sid Vicious and Siouxsie of the Banshees took up – for its nuisance value. One of the people annoyed was Clash manager Bernie Rhodes, also Jewish, who felt that, in the prevailing social climate, with the National Front steadily increasing its membership, flirting with fascist symbols was 'a loaded gun'. Under the circumstances, one can understand his reluctance to have revealed the extent of his, or any of his charges', prior involvement with a band called the London SS.

Back in March 1975, making the final decision about a name was not of vital importance. The London SS was not officially adopted at this time, and appears to have been just one of several possibilities under consideration. 'I remember Mick suggesting something like the Suicides,' says Brady. 'I'm sure we had loads of New York Dolls-type names, but we couldn't settle on one.' Robin Crocker recalls the Cyanide Sweeties being another option. According to Brady, Mick also toyed with the personal pseudonym Mick Stabs. But everything was left very much up in the air while the band concentrated on more urgent matters. The Vocalists Wanted section of the *Melody Maker*'s 22 March issue carried another display ad, this time accompanied by just Mick's telephone number: 'DECADENT MALE VOCALIST. Must be exciting, pretty and passionately committed to the rock'n'roll lifestyle.'

Although much of the next week was given over to auditioning the various applicants, none of them had the requisite looks and talent. Then, on 1 April, Tony Gordon sent John a letter reading, 'I have not heard from you for a few weeks and I wondered if you had yet acquired a singer? Perhaps you will let me know how things are going at your earliest opportunity?' Worried about losing Gordon's interest, the band felt compelled to take drastic measures: Mick's objections were overruled, and Kelvin was approached.

John's diary entry for 3 April noted, 'Kelvin is leaving Overtown and wants to join us. Dodgy!' On Friday 11th, Kelvin was given a proper audition, as a result of which he was offered the job. 'Could be so good with all of us in a band,' began John's diary entry for that day. If he sounded tentative, it was because – inevitably, with Kelvin – there were complications, as the diary further recorded: 'He can't join for a month: a single and two gigs.' Kelvin's Overtown commitments took up most of the rest of April, but he managed a few covert rehearsals with his new band.

At the time, he was living in the first floor flat at 22 Gladsmuir Road, Archway, and it was here that early rehearsals took place, 'with Geir on pads for drums, really quiet'. Someone moved out of one of the bedsits upstairs, and towards the end of the month, Mick moved in to live with his new girlfriend, Debbie. 'Just one room with a little grill in it,' recalls Kelvin. 'And for a while it was heaven, because we'd go and hang out at concerts and stuff.'

The band had only really been together for six or seven weeks, but it had already gone a considerable way towards establishing a musical identity. The choice of covers reflected the members' shared tastes. A feature was a version of Chuck Berry's 'Little Queenie', owing much to the Rolling Stones' reading of the song as immortalised on the 1970 live album *Get Yer Ya-Ya's Out*. 'We used to do an old Yardbirds' song called "I'm Not Talking",' says Brady. 'I think we did a couple of the original Sixties American underground things from Mick's record collection, one called "Sometimes Good Guys Don't Wear White" [originally recorded by the Standells]. It was one of those tunes that was a bit like [Them's] "Gloria", with a very simple riff.' Mick was by now a far more prolific composer than anyone else in the band. 'He'd write about 10 songs, and nine would be crap, but one would be really good,' says Brady, who had quickly come to realise that Mick made up in other areas for his limitations as a guitarist. 'He was a good songwriter, and great at ideas and arranging.'

When Kelvin signed up, he was by no means content to accept the band as it was. There were two reasons for this. Firstly, Kelvin was a little more inclined towards the rock mainstream than the others. 'I was a musical snob,' he admits. 'I'd gone out and played with a bunch of musicians who'd had their trip together, which became a disadvantage in the punk days, but then I thought was fantastic.' 'Kelvin used to sing in an American voice,' says Brady. 'Paul Rogers [of Free and Bad Company], sort of thing.' Secondly, Kelvin had a typical frontman's ego, and could not accept Mick as the band's principal songwriter. 'After Kelvin joined, every time Mick came up with a song, it was rejected by Kelvin,' laughs Geir. 'There was a big argument: "Shut up, Mick, your songs are crap!", you know...' Kelvin confirms this. 'I was trying to monopolise the songs, but I wasn't really much of a songwriter, so I was also doing other people's songs. Mick was doing originals, and he had more than anybody else, so he probably got about four in, and I got about four in. And his were much better, actually. He had a way of writing lyrics that I hadn't sussed. My lyrics were dire, looking back.' According to Brady, Kelvin's songs were not even necessarily Kelvin's songs. 'Kelvin was so bad! He'd say "I've written this great song," we'd rehearse it, and two months later he'd tell us that it was actually off some American album! Stuff like that.'

Except for Mick, no-one considered Kelvin's pushiness to be particularly threatening: at the time, would-be rock'n'roll stars were *supposed* to be prima donnas. Besides, the band had other things on their mind. On 25 April, they arranged a showcase performance for Tony Gordon at a seedy rehearsal room in King's Cross, as previously used on occasion by the Hollywood Brats. Despite the shabby surroundings and the limitations of the equipment, Gordon liked what he saw and heard. He had only one proviso for taking on the band. 'He suggested calling it Little Queenie, which I thought was *ridiculous*, because you already had Queen,' winces Brady. 'But he said, "It's a great name, and you've got a great image," so we went along with that.' Queen had recently had a hit single with 'Now I'm Here', a song that included a lyrical quotation from 'Little Queenie' over its closing bars. In retrospect, it would seem that Tony was hoping his flamboyant new discoveries would tap into the same market as the more established glam rockers. If nothing else, he showed considerable astuteness in anticipating trends: just seven months later, Queen would begin an eight week run at number one in the UK with 'Bohemian Rhapsody'.

On 7 May, a second showcase was arranged, this time at the more salubrious Tracks studio in Acton. Tony Gordon had connections at Pye records, and he brought along a representative from the record company. 'I think he liked us,' recorded Brady's diary. This was indeed the case. The following day, the newly renamed Little Queenie were invited up to the Wedge office at 13 Duke Street and offered a management contract, which they read with mixed feelings. 'We signed to Tony Gordon,' Brady wrote in his diary, 'but Kelvin says it's a crap deal.'

With a management contract secured and a recording contract in the offing, certain members of the band felt it was time to take the musical side of things a little more seriously. Two days after they signed the contract, a meeting was convened at Gladsmuir Road, and Geir was sacked. 'Geir was a great bloke,' says Brady, 'but if you have a dodgy drummer, the whole band's dodgy.' Mick – upset at what he considered to be the betrayal of a friend – offered the only real objection. He was partly mollified when it was decided that Geir's replacement should be another Strand School old boy, Jim Hyatt. The fact that Jim, himself not the world's best drummer, had always been close to Kelvin supports Geir's belief that Kelvin was responsible for instigating the switch.

On 30 May, the new line up of Little Queenie went into Pye's Bryanston Street 16-track studio to record a couple of demos with Tony Gordon producing. 'We were rehearsing in Acton, and they took us from there in cabs,' says John. 'We felt like royalty. Mick and I were together, and he was sitting back and he was *enjoying* it! It was the first taste of someone taking over, and providing for us. Treating us as though we were important.' Both John and Mick were enthralled by the whole experience, especially Mick. 'He was like a little kid in the studio,' recalls Brady. 'Saying, "Oh, what does this do, and what does that do?" I thought it was a bit embarrassing.' The songs recorded were the inevitable 'Little Queenie' and Frankie Miller's 'Fool In Love', which Kelvin used to sing with Overtown. 'It was quite a good version of "Little Queenie", if I do say so myself,' is John's opinion. Having been in a studio before, Brady was not so easily impressed, as his diary entry testified: 'Put two songs down. Ropy. Tony Gordon sucks!'

Kelvin was also feeling uneasy, and had been ever since signing the contract. He had spent the latter part of the month sounding out various of his contacts to see if he could come up with anything better. Having failed to entice Guy Stevens to come and watch Schoolgirl two and a half years previously, he now found him more approachable. This had as much to do with Guy's own reduced circumstances as Kelvin's redoubtable powers of persuasion.

Charles Shaar Murray provided perhaps the most concise summary of the Stevens career in a 1979 *NME* retrospective: 'Kingpin Mod DJ at the Scene Club in '64, Our Man in London for Sue Records, first house producer for Island Records, where he signed and produced Free and Spooky Tooth as well as inventing Mott the Hoople… the man who got Chuck Berry out of jail in 1964, the man who supplied the Who with the compilation tape that gave them most of their pre-original material repertoire, the man who introduced Keith Reid to Procol Harum and generated "Whiter Shade Of Pale"…' Quite some CV, and those are just the edited highlights. Since losing Mott the Hoople in 1972, however, Guy's legendary fondness for speed and booze had taken its toll. 'I never really recovered from Mott the Hoople,' he told CSM. 'I never really got over working with Ian Hunter.'

By 1975, despite being something of a music industry joke, Guy was still well connected, and on a retainer from Mo Ostin, head of Warner Brothers US. For his part, when he heard that Kelvin's latest band was on the point of signing a contract, Guy thought it might just provide him with the opportunity to make a come-back. The day after the Pye session, Kelvin took the others along to meet Guy in a pub. Mick, John and Jim had been fascinated by him since their schooldays, and Brady was swayed by Guy's track record, fund of anecdotes and fondness for a good time. 'Had drinks and lots of laughs,' he informed his diary. The Stevens charm was at work.

By the time Little Queenie turned up as scheduled for a meeting at the Wedge office on 2 June, Kelvin had decided to get the band out of its contract with Tony Gordon by any means necessary. 'He said, "I'll do it,"' recalls Brady. '"You guys just sit there, and don't laugh."' Kelvin's ploy was to leap onto the table in Tony's office, shout, 'I can't handle it!', and pretend to have a full-blown seizure. '*And he pulled it off!*' laughs Brady. 'That was the kind of guy Kelvin was in those days. In the end, I think Tony just said, "Oh, get out and leave me alone!" So we got out of the deal.' 'We got the contract back,' adds John, 'and we ran around the corner to the pub where Guy was, and we tore it into little bits and threw them into the air.' Perhaps unsurprisingly, Tony Gordon – who went on to manage Sham 69 and Culture Club – now claims to have no recollection of the band or any of its members.

The following day, Guy turned up at the Acton rehearsal room to watch Little Queenie run through a half-hour set. It must have been a glorious moment for Mick. Not only was he finally playing on equal terms with the older friends he'd once looked up to at school and roadied for in Schoolgirl, but he was also working with the mentor and producer of his all-time favourite group...

Then what should have been a dream come true turned decidedly nasty.

Eighteen months earlier, Mott the Hoople had finally split. Ian Hunter teamed up with Mick Ronson, and the rest of the band commenced what proved to be a fairly rapid slide into oblivion under the truncated appellation Mott. The temptation to relive his own past and fill the gap with a new, younger version of the original band proved too strong for Guy. He had a long history of meddling with line-ups – during his time as Mott the Hoople's manager, not content with replacing original vocalist Stan Tippins, he had also attempted at various times to fire both Verden Allen and Ian Hunter – and he would not accept Little Queenie as they were. 'He took Kelvin aside and said, "Well, I think you need keyboards. Brady can handle all the guitar,"' says Brady. 'He didn't think Mick was very good, and he wanted a Mott the Hoople again.'

A band meeting was arranged for 5 June 1975 at Gladsmuir Road, and Kelvin gave Mick the bad news. 'A month after I got the sack, Mick got the sack,' says Geir. 'He was right when he said, "As soon as you get that singer in, he'll split the band up." That's Kelvin!' Kelvin concedes the point. 'I made the cardinal sin of thinking, "I've got to listen to all these other people telling me what to do." I've always been a bit naughty like that. "You've got to get rid of Mick!" "But he's been my friend for years!" "Sorry, he's out." "OK, fine."' Brady's attitude was revealed the following day. 'Mick was really, like, mega-depressed,' he says. 'He phoned me up and said, "I told you this would happen! How can you do this to me, Brady?" And I said, "Look, Mick, we've got a bit of a deal with the band now, and we might go places. *That's rock'n'roll*, you know?"'

As well as being hungry enough for success to sacrifice anything or anyone, Kelvin and, to a lesser extent, Brady both had ulterior motives for acceding to Guy's demands. Although prepared to accept external control from a management figure, Kelvin wanted control within the group itself. For his part, in an era when musicians were supposed to exhibit rock'n'roll cool, Brady was unhappy about what he perceived to be Mick's naivety. They both liked Mick – Brady in particular being much taken with the younger guitarist's ready wit – but at the time their ambition allowed no room for sentiment.

Jim Hyatt was too easy-going and too new to the band to have much of a say. Only John showed any kind of loyalty at all. 'I voted against it. I said, "Fuck off! Mick and I formed this in the first place. This is *our* project." There was Guy Stevens saying, "I want to keep order in the band. Mick's excess baggage," and all this. Complete crap.' He threatened to leave, too. 'Then I got people ringing me up and coming around, saying, "You can't do this! It's all going to happen. Stevens has got Warner Brothers in his pocket." And, eventually, they talked me around to it. I stayed on to see what was happening. Mick was completely nonplussed by the whole thing. Such a kick in the teeth! I went straight to him and said, "Look, this is what's happening," and he's never, as far as I know, held it against me.'

Looking back on it, John and Brady now agree that it was a mistake to allow Kelvin to get rid of the band's main songwriter on the whim of the erratic Guy. 'Mick's was still the major writing input, and he was given the order of the boot, which was crazy,' says John. For his part, Kelvin has pulled too many similar stunts in his career to waste time regretting one error of judgement in the distant past, but he is far more sensitive to the repercussions of his actions today than he was at the time. 'It must have hurt,' he acknowledges. 'Four friends who have all been school friends, and three saying, "Sorry, goodbye." Mick was very responsible for getting it together. It was his energies.'

At Guy's suggestion, the band changed their name to Violent Luck. 'We started doing Mott the Hoople-type stuff,' says Brady. 'Which I thought was a bit dated then.' On 27 June 1975, Violent Luck auditioned for a Warner Brothers representative at PSL rehearsal studios in Battersea. Thereafter, Jim Hyatt met a similar fate to his predecessor. The remainder of Violent Luck's career was to be dogged with difficulties in establishing a permanent line-up: they never did find either a full-time drummer or a keyboard-playing replacement for Mick. On 21 August, the remaining trio went into Air studios on Oxford Circus to record some demos for Warner Brothers with Guy as producer, Bill Price as engineer, and with a couple of guest session musicians: Leo Sayer's drummer Theodore Thunder and Mott the Hoople's original keyboard player Verden Allen. Tracks recorded were the Flamin' Groovies 'Slow Death', Mott the Hoople's 'No Wheels To Ride', and Kelvin's 'That's Why My Baby (Let Me Go)'. The others later discovered it was pretty much a carbon copy of the J Geils Band song 'Nightmare'.

While still with Overtown, Kelvin had kept his options open by attending auditions for several other bands. One of the *Melody Maker* ads he answered had been placed by a bassist named Tony James. Tony was reading Mathematics at Brunel University in Uxbridge, on the western outskirts of London, and living at home with his parents in Twickenham a few miles to the south. Kelvin went down there four times before electing not to join Tony's band. 'He had all these really long songs with long lyrics.' After some initial hostility, Tony accepted Kelvin's decision, and a friendship of sorts developed. Tony became interested enough in Little Queenie to attend some of their rehearsals. In a vague effort to soften the blows of sacking Mick and rejecting Tony, Kelvin suggested the duo team up. In Pete Frame's two Family Trees, the story of the London SS starts with this meeting. 'And I didn't get any credit for it,' complains Kelvin, straight-faced.

Geir Waade, John Brown and Brady are all highly disparaging in their comments about Tony James. This is partly because he was later instrumental in writing them out of the history of the London SS, and partly because when they first met him, he was a denim and greatcoat-clad fan of Blue Öyster Cult who changed his style overnight upon befriending Mick. 'Everyone used to think, "Ah, Tony James: he's such a little wanker!"' says Brady. 'He really latched onto Mick. Mick was his idol. He was really infatuated with him, because he saw Mick had something.' 'Tony was a Mick clone,' says John. 'Mick would wear something, and the next day Tony would turn up in a replica. It was that bad.' Since he had recently become an outsider himself, it is possible that Mick felt sympathetic to Tony's position. More probably, he enjoyed having his torpedoed self-esteem buoyed by Tony's attentions. Whatever, Mick decided to form another band in much the same vein as Little Queenie/Violent Luck, only this time with himself as undisputed leader and Tony as trusty lieutenant. 'It was probably, "We'll show the bastards!"' says Brady.

The first step was for the duo to place a classified ad in the *Melody Maker* for further musicians. Appearing in the Musicians Wanted section of the 19 July 1975 issue, it read: 'LEAD GUITARIST and drums to join bass player and guitarist/singer, influenced by

Stones, NY Dolls, Mott etc. Must have great rock and roll image.' Hopefuls were asked to phone 'Michael' at Gladsmuir Road. Nothing much resulted, so a second ad was placed in the 9 August issue for the same two vacancies. The Stones and the Stooges were quoted as influences before the ad outlined its other key requirement: 'Decadent 3rd generation rock and roll image essential. New York Dolls style.'

The first caller was Brian James, a somewhat older lead guitarist with a passion for the Stooges. A meeting was arranged at Gladsmuir Road. 'A dingy little flat,' recalls Brian. 'I came up, and I played them a tape of stuff I'd been doing in Brussels with a band called Bastard. It was rock'n'roll, and they liked it. Kindred spirits, you know.' The tape of Bastard's energetic MC5 and Stooges-inspired material did indeed impress Mick and Tony, but it was just the icing on the cake as far as they were concerned. 'As soon as we saw him, we said, "This is the guy!"' Tony told Pete Frame in 1977, 'because he had just the New York Doll image we wanted.' Although keen to throw in his lot with the other two, Brian first had to return to Belgium, break the news to Bastard and sort out his affairs.

At the end of August, Kelvin returned to Gladsmuir Road with a copy of Violent Luck's demo tape for Warner Brothers. Still living under the same roof as Kelvin, Mick had tried to hide his bitterness and maintain a certain level of civility towards his old schoolfriend, but the demos proved to be the last straw. 'I remember going upstairs to play them to Mick, and he was really, really upset,' says Kelvin. 'I'll never really forget that. I thought, "Maybe I am a complete cunt," you know? He was saying, "I'm going to leave here!" He was really timid and everything else, but one thing he said was, "I'll be a better guitarist than Brady! I'll succeed!" Quite a statement...'

Mick moved back in with Stella at Wilmcote House, whereupon John took over his room at Gladsmuir Road. Shortly afterwards, Violent Luck finally began playing gigs, but the Warner Brothers deal did not materialise, and by the following spring Guy's unreliability had made a parting of the ways inevitable. According to John, Kelvin was moved to write a song in Guy's honour entitled 'It's Not So Easy (When You Fall)'... but it's worth noting that Ian Hunter's 1975 eponymous début solo album contains a track entitled 'It Ain't Easy When You Fall'.

Sometime before Mick's departure from the original line-up of Little Queenie, Kelvin had made yet another useful musical connection. 'I met this guy Barry Jones, who used to work with [fashion designer] Zandra Rhodes,' he recalls. 'I'd gone up to her office for some reason, and I bumped into Barry, who said, "I've got a studio in Warrington Crescent." And I ended up going round there and meeting Matt.'

Barry Jones and Matt Dangerfield had attended the Jacob Kramer School of Art in Leeds before moving to London in 1972. Soon afterwards, Matt had discovered a basement flat, 47A Warrington Crescent, recently vacated by a colony of hippies. He and Barry were guitarists and songwriters, and were attracted to the flat because it was large, bright, and had lots of rehearsal space. According to Matt, 'You could play really loud rock'n'roll without worrying about the neighbours.' There was also a coal storage area under the steps leading down from the street that was just large enough to house their studio. 'A 4-track, the first home studio that was available on the market, TEAC job. That was my connection with a lot of people at that time.'

Others who lived in the flat included 'Honest' John Plain, also ex-Joseph Kramer, and Barry's then girlfriend Celia Perry, a fashion design student. In addition, number 47A was invariably packed with musicians hoping to jam, form bands or record demos, and assorted friends and acquaintances who came there to hang out and play pool on the flat's own table either before or after a night's drinking at the nearby Warrington pub. One such was Steve Hershkowitz, known as Fat Steve, whose father owned the Clearlake Hotel off Kensington Gore.

Not being a man to pass up on an opportunity to network, Kelvin was soon a regular caller at the flat. One by one, he introduced all the members and former members of Little Queenie/Violent Luck to the Warrington Crescent scene, which was made up of the like-minded and similarly-attired. 'When Biba's was closing, Mick and I bought all this ocelot, leopardskin and tiger-striped velour material,' says John Brown, 'and we all had trousers and tops made out of it by Celia.' As Warrington Crescent was situated no more than a couple of hundred yards from Wilmcote House, the flat became an especially convenient hang out and meeting place for Mick and his new shadow. It had the disadvantage of being frequented by certain members of his ex-band he would have preferred not to see, but it did offer the opportunity to make new alliances.

'Mick and I got on, started talking about getting a band together, pooling ideas. We had the same sort of influences, more or less,' says Matt. Although his main love was the Velvet Underground, he was also a fan of the New York Dolls and had even heard the Hollywood Brats album. 'I must admit, I didn't think much of Mick or Tony as musicians: I wasn't a great musician, but I definitely wasn't impressed by them. I thought Mick was a good songwriter. I remember one song called "Always the Bridesmaid, Never the Bride" which I thought was pretty good until, years later, I found there was an old country or blues song with the same title. That's the only one I can remember. Most of the time it was just jamming, fucking about.'

Things were so fluid at the Warrington Crescent Trainee Decadent Rock Stars' Workshop and Social Club that, over the late summer of 1975, there was never really a set band line-up. 'People were in and out,' says Matt. 'Whoever was available. Like Honest John, for instance, was only ever in it when we needed someone who could drum, or someone who could play guitar; just fill in, because he's a good all-rounder.' Matt recorded some of the sessions, but unfortunately, the tapes have since been mislaid. Or perhaps, at least from Mick's point of view, fortunately: one song featured a Jones vocal ad-lib that walked the fine line between sexual innuendo and obscenity for some considerable time before finally falling off on the latter side. 'Embarrassing!' grins Matt. '"Get down on your knees, baby…"' 'Definitely Blackmail Corner,' agrees Honest John, who played guitar on the session. 'I mean, I'm sure Mick Jones'd pay a *lot* to get hold of that. In fact, I think some record companies would pay a lot as well…'

September and October 1975 brought a number of key encounters that would encourage the resumption of a more businesslike approach. Mick had not ceased his regular gig-going activities, and it had become his habit to introduce himself to anyone he thought looked interesting enough to be potential band material. One night at the Nashville in West Kensington he bumped into a small man with thick glasses and thinning hair who was destined to have more of an influence on his musical future than anyone he had listened to or met thus far. 'I thought he was a piano player,' Mick told the *NME*'s Paul Rambali in 1981. 'He seemed like a really bright geezer. We got on like a house on fire.'

Bernard Rhodes objects to being called Bernie – 'I'm not a bloody taxi driver!' – but perhaps for that very reason almost everyone who has ever been associated with him refers to him by the diminutive. Not a piano player, or a musician of any sort, Bernie was always more interested in popular music's associated culture than in the music itself. His background is similar to that of Mick's maternal grandparents. Born in Russia, Bernie was apparently brought to London in the Fifties by his mother, who found work as a seamstress in Soho. 'I was on the street when I was 12,' he told *Mojo*'s Pat Gilbert in 1999. 'I was living in a one-room shack in the East End. Prostitutes used to take me in, and that's where I heard [R&B pianist] Amos Milburn and all the greats, because American servicemen used their services.' Bernie – it hardly needs to be said – would later be a major influence on the Clash's tendency to self-mythologise. Nevertheless, although much of what he claims sounds improbable, even fantastical, there often turns out to be some factual basis underneath all the embellishment.

According to Bernie, then, he was one of the original early Sixties mods, and befriended Guy Stevens while hanging around on the Soho coffee bar scene. He knew Mick Jagger when Mick was attending the London School of Economics. As the Swinging Sixties progressed, Bernie went on to become an 'ideas person' for the Who, share a flat with Graham Bond, work in famed Kings Road boutique Granny Takes A Trip, become 'ideas person' for Marc Bolan's Tyrannosaurus Rex, and involve himself with Jerry Rubin and the American Yippie movement. 'There was a very optimistic feeling,' he told the *NME*'s Paul Rambali in 1980. 'The underground press was coming up, and together with that there was a lot of literature that one was consuming; knowledge, both from books and experience. Going abroad, checking it out. There was a lot of intake.'

Bernie soaked up the rhetoric of America's late Sixties underground groups like the Black Panthers, John Sinclair's White Panthers, the Motherfuckers and the Weathermen. He was even more open to the challenging work of the Situationist International, a late Fifties French radical art movement whose provocative anarchistic sloganeering had done so much to establish the tone of the 1968 Paris Riots. He was also aware of Britain's home grown Situationist splinter group, King Mob. The Situationists had been inspired by the revolutionary Surrealist movement, committed not only to changing the world but also to changing how we look at the world.

In 1972, when the politically clueless Marc Bolan – another graduate of the Soho mod scene – released a single entitled 'Children of the Revolution', Bernie grew disillusioned with music's potential for creating change. He opted out, and invested in a Renault garage in Camden Town. There proved to be an even more limited scope for innovation and ideas in the motor trade, however, and a year or so later Bernie found himself drawn back to the cutting edge of pop culture. He returned to the fray as a designer and silk screen printer of T-shirts.

Although both were ex-mods, it is most likely that Bernie and Malcolm McLaren first became acquainted through Bernie's efforts to sell his designs to the Kings Road boutiques in the early Seventies. As neither of them was in Paris at the time, they did not – as one persistent and probably self-originated tale has it – meet during the 1968 Riots. But they did share an interest in Situationism. Bernie was fascinated by the designs Malcolm and his partner Vivienne Westwood were creating and selling from Sex, at 430 Kings Road, and went on to help conceive and print some of the T-shirts that would soon make the shop notorious. Bernie's triumph was a late 1974 shirt that contrasted lists of cultural and political likes and dislikes beneath the slightly clumsy would-be Situationist International/Class of '68 slogan 'You're gonna wake up one morning and *know* what side of the bed you've been lying on!' Back in 1968, a popular challenge among American radicals had been, 'If you're not part of the solution, you're part of the problem!', a sentiment paraphrased by the MC5's 'Spiritual Advisor' Brother JC Crawford in his rabble-rousing introduction to *Kick Out The Jams*. Bernie was intent on drawing the same kind of lines.

As early as 1973, when Sex was still called Let It Rock, Malcolm had been pestered by a young regular named Steve Jones to help out with the band for which he sang and his friend Paul Cook played drums. Malcolm linked up Steve with the shop's Saturday boy Glen Matlock, attended one or two rehearsals, and (eventually) suggested the name Sex Pistols, but at the time, having no real interest in contemporary music, neglected to take matters further. Over the years, Bernie has proved himself to have a pretty fair lip – and, some would say, a penchant for improvisation – when it comes to blowing his own trumpet, but Glen Matlock supports his claim to have been the Sex Pistols' true original motivator.

At that time, the unnamed band were still bashing out their Faces covers. Bernie would take them – especially Glen, the brightest, and the most amenable to discussing ideas – down the road to the Roebuck pub (now the Dôme) and talk to them about the kind of music they should be playing, the way they should be dressing and the attitudes they should be expressing. Always a provocateur, he would put them on the spot about what it was they hoped to achieve. From November 1974 to March 1975, Malcolm was in the US attempting to manage the New York Dolls, whom he had befriended on an earlier trip to New York. During this period, Bernie continued to work with the soon-to-be Sex Pistols, encouraging them to rehearse, and trying to convince the others to ditch original guitarist Wally Nightingale.

It has become something of a rock writer's cliché to say that, in terms of drink, drugs and ego, the Dolls were by this time determined to live up to the title of their second album, *Too Much, Too Soon*. In an attempt to revive their flagging career, Malcolm dressed them in red patent leather, and made them a red hammer and sickle backdrop. In America, where Communism was considered to be not so much a political system as an infectious disease, this promotional ploy succeeded in alienating whatever small audience the Dolls had left. Shortly afterwards, the band broke up.

Richard Hell, Television's original bass player, joint lead vocalist and on-stage focus, left his band the same week. He quickly teamed up with ex-Dolls Johnny Thunders and Jerry Nolan to form the Heartbreakers, but was still unsure of his future, and had several talks with Malcolm about the possibility of moving to London to form a new band there. After giving Hell his address, Malcolm returned home in May 1975 with Sylvain Sylvain's guitar and his head buzzing with ideas. He promptly switched his attentions to the Sex Pistols, originally with the intention of developing them as a prospective backing band for Sylvain and/or Hell.

Wally Nightingale was summarily dispatched. When Sylvain opted instead for joining David JoHansen on a pseudo-Dolls tour of Japan, and Hell proved incapable of choosing between staying with the Heartbreakers and catching a plane, Steve Jones was given Sylvain's guitar to learn on, and efforts were made to discover a more conveniently-located frontman. During a trip Bernie and Malcolm made to Glasgow for some nefarious purpose or other, Bernie spotted Midge Ure leaving a music shop. He had short, slicked back hair and drainpipes, all the information Bernie required to suggest that Midge step around the corner and have a word with Malcolm. It turned out that Midge could actually sing and play guitar, but he elected to stay with his own band Slik. They made number one in the UK singles chart in January 1976 with 'Forever And Ever'.

It was also Bernie who noticed John Lydon hanging around Sex in his 'I Hate Pink Floyd' T-shirt. Again, the way he looked was deemed to be the only thing that mattered. Malcolm duly auditioned John by having him mime along to Alice Cooper's 'I'm Eighteen' on the shop jukebox. Steve Jones promptly rechristened him Johnny Rotten after the state of his teeth. 'Bernie definitely influenced the start of the Pistols,' Johnny told Chris Salewicz for the *Face* in 1980. 'He got me in the band. Malcolm hated my guts, because of the way me and Sid used to take the piss out of him.'

It was the last real contribution Bernie was allowed to make. Although he was considered by many to be a Machiavellian manipulator in his own right, his friendship with Malcolm seemed to be constructed in such a way that the latter was always guaranteed the upper hand. Hardly unaware of this imbalance, Bernie asked Malcolm for what he felt he deserved, a partnership in both Sex and the Sex Pistols. He got what Malcolm felt he deserved: nothing. Although it took Bernie some time to face up to the rejection – a strong case can be made for the theory that he never really did – its initial voicing came as no real surprise to him. He later told Fred and Judy Vermorel as much for their 1978 book *Sex Pistols: The Inside Story*: 'I thought that together we could come up with something that was truly great... But I *knew* Malcolm would never give anyone half share. He'd always want to be in control.'

Melody Maker's early Seventies move from Sixties-type pop coverage to more serious muso-oriented rock journalism had left the other UK music papers behind. With the arrival of a new serious 'inky' in the shape of *Sounds*, it had looked as though the death knell was about to sound for the *NME*. Then, suddenly, early in 1972, the paper had undergone a make-over. Editor Alan Smith had drafted in former underground press journalists Charles Shaar Murray and Nick Kent, and encouraged them to establish themselves as larger-than-life personality rock writers in the American tradition of Lester Bangs. The new *NME* had promised intelligent, thought-provoking coverage of the early Seventies rock'n'roll scene. Although the usually more R&B-oriented CSM struck up a good relationship with David Bowie, it was Nick Kent who cornered the market in decadence and sleaze, and the kind of obscure bands beloved of the Warrington Crescent crowd.

Mick Jones had read Nick's rock'n'roll fashion feature of April 1974 *NME*, 'The Politics Of Flash', and from it learned that Malcolm McLaren had supplied clothes to the New York Dolls. In July 1975, Malcolm, his shop and clothes had gained more mainstream notoriety when a regular customer was arrested and charged for wearing a provocative Sex T-shirt featuring a drawing of two extravagantly endowed cowboys naked from the waist down. The shop had been raided, and a further 18 shirts confiscated. These shenanigans had made the front page of the *Guardian*, and ensured that most of the Warrington Crescent crowd was aware of Malcolm as a face on the London scene. Mick duly visited Sex, and bought one of its less confrontational lines, a T-shirt bearing the legend that had been the shop's previous name: 'Too Fast To Live, Too Young To Die'. He was wearing this at the Nashville gig where he met Bernie. It proved to be the ice-breaker for their first conversation: Bernie claimed to be responsible for its design.

Even though the Sex Pistols had been taken away from him by Malcolm, Bernie was not yet thinking in terms of going into competition with a band of his own; but he was not averse to the idea of discovering a band that would impress his friend enough to make him reconsider a McLaren-Rhodes partnership. Bernie initially encouraged Mick to believe this relationship already existed, and as a result, the guitarist was happy to agree to another meeting. 'It was just me, Mick and Tony went along,' says Matt Dangerfield, who recalls that the encounter took place at a Rock'n'Roll Revival show. 'Bernie was Malcolm's partner, or so we thought, but in fact he'd just split with Malcolm. We didn't know about that. Bernie quite impressed me because he was weird, he had weird ideas. Bernie was very inspiring. He kind of gave you the feeling that, yeah, you could create something. McLaren doesn't listen to you, McLaren just talks at you. Bernie would somehow make you do your own thinking.'

Part of the reason Mick and Tony had not been pushing too hard to form a stable line-up from the 47A talent pool was that they were still waiting for Brian James to return from Belgium. Faced with what appeared to be a golden opportunity, however, they quickly pulled together the core of a band, with Matt on lead guitar, and Geir Waade once again behind the drums. Kelvin might have stolen one band from Mick, then, but he was indirectly responsible for providing him with the bulk of the personnel for a new one. Matt believes it was at this point that the band finally made the decision to call themselves the London SS. Apparently, Bernie's principles were not yet quite so highly developed as they would become a year later. 'He said, "If you're going to have a name like that, you've got to go all the way. Are you prepared to do it?"' says Matt. 'We said, "Yeah, sure, why not?"'

Although both Matt and Mick could sing, the idea of a five-piece band with frontman was still very much in vogue. The first step towards filling the remaining vacancy was to chip in for another *Melody Maker* classified. The display ad which appeared in the 11 October 1975 Vocalists Wanted section gave 47A's phone number, and made oblique reference to the Tony Gordon interlude: 'UP FRONT ROCK AND ROLL VOCALIST, could be IGGY POP, required by pre-launched DECADENT 3rd GENERATION Rock Band.' 'We auditioned the singers with Bernie present as well,' recalls Matt. 'Bernie asking questions not about "Have you sung before?" or anything, but really abstruse questions that had nothing to do with being in a band or anything. Which quite impressed me, because it unnerved everybody. People didn't know how to behave.' Almost inevitably, the upshot of these mind games was that the band remained singer-less.

With so many musicians hanging around the Warrington Crescent flat, perusing the *Melody Maker*'s classified ads pages was something of a weekly ritual. According to Tony, the Musicians Wanted section in the 27 September issue had made everyone sit up and take notice. In among the usual pop, cabaret and muso dross was a display ad reading: 'WHIZZ KID GUITARIST. Not older than 20. Not worse looking than Johnny Thunders. Auditioning: TIN PAN ALLEY.' Those present had believed themselves to be the only people in London apart from Nick Kent and Malcolm McLaren who even knew who the Dolls were. 'We couldn't believe it,' Tony told Pete Frame. 'So we phoned up straight away to find out which group it was. They were called the Sex Pistols.' That they were managed by Malcolm and knew Nick Kent came as less of a surprise.

According to Glen Matlock, the main purpose of the Pistols' ad was to reassure Paul Cook that everybody meant business, the drummer being unconvinced that neophyte axe-hero Steve Jones could cope on his own. But Malcolm was still obsessed by the Dolls, and it is equally likely that he was also thinking in terms of emulating that band's two-guitar line-up. He had Steve Jones learning the rudiments by playing along to the Dolls' first album on Sylvain's old guitar, and having mentally cast him in Sylvain's role, it seems he was seeking the appropriate musical complement.

Malcolm did not intend to devote himself exclusively to the Sex Pistols, who at that point must have seemed an extremely long shot indeed. Since his return to London, he had been scouting around for other promising talent, and one of the exciting acts he kept hearing about was a Dolls-type band named the Hollywood Brats. He was interested in meeting the remnants, and, once contact had been made, expressed as much to the London SS camp. Geir knew Andrew and Casino were sharing a flat at 17 London Street, Paddington, and Mick and Tony took it upon themselves to pass on Malcolm's message. Mick's motive was not entirely altruistic. Keen to impress Malcolm, he was also not averse to getting on the right side of Andrew and Casino: it had not gone unremarked at Warrington Crescent that a merger with this duo would plug the gaps in the London SS line-up, add a certain amount of prestige and experience to the band, and almost certainly secure backing from McLaren.

'My memories of the era are as clear as a dry martini and twice as tart,' writes Andrew Matheson in his inimitable style. 'Well I recall the night that Mick Jones (who made up for in bottle what he lacked in chin) and Tony James (constantly blurring the edges between charming and unctuous) arrived at our sumptuous London Street dive to propose an alliance. The eagerness and optimism of Mick and Tony contrasted sharply to the negativity and disillusionment of the two of us – more so me than Cas – and when they left after expressing a desire to work with us, and after saying extremely flattering things about the Brats album, we found our passion somewhat rekindled.'

Andrew insists that it was during Mick and Tony's visit that the name London SS first came into being, and that it was the suggestion of Casino Steel. 'That is such complete rubbish!' splutters Geir in rebuttal. 'Andrew Matheson has got nothing to do with anything at all, whatsoever!' On balance, it does seem that Andrew is mistaken as to the source of the name, but he and his songwriting partner were certainly intrigued by its possibilities. Andrew was a huge fan of *Cabaret* – 'I saw it eight times in a row over two days!' – and he and Casino were themselves flirting with Nazi chic as part of their own decadent pose. The London SS struck exactly the right note. 'We went on to design a stage set-up involving dry ice, blue lighting and barbed wire.'

Indeed, Andrew and Casino sported Nazi regalia for their visit, in the company of Mick and Tony, to the Pistols' newly acquired West End rehearsal rooms at 6 Denmark Street. 'Mick asked to borrow a Nazi armband of mine,' recalls Andrew. Sex Pistols' bassist Glen Matlock also remembers the occasion well. 'It was only a titchy little place,' he says. 'There was like a downstairs rehearsal room, and an upstairs room which me and Steve Jones lived in. It was a little outbuilding. We was rehearsing downstairs, and we all had short hair, and the door squeaked open, and these blokes walked through, and it's like, "*What on earth* are these guys all about?" We just pissed ourselves laughing. Mick had snakeskin trousers on, stack-heel shoes, this flowery kind of chemise, hair down here with his earholes sticking out. And the others all looked exactly the same! Everyone else went sheepishly upstairs, but Mick clocked us. Me and Mick just looked at each other like that, *boom*, there was a buzz right away.'

All of which tallies with Andrew's version, except for which of the parties involved were behaving sheepishly: 'We walked in at the pre-arranged time (or not long thereafter), saw three guys with short hair dressed like off-duty bank tellers, and McLaren. There was an air of nervousness in the place, as though we'd caught them masturbating or something. McLaren was sort of jittery in slow motion. Hands gesticulating, wrists limp, and minimal eye-contact. He said that both his boys and the Dolls had spoken of us, and he alternately mumbled and ranted. Thoroughly peeved, I exited the scene, followed shortly by the other three, and that was it.' In fact, Mick exited quite some way behind. Any link-up with McLaren might have been off the agenda as far as Andrew was concerned, but Mick was keeping all his options open. Having made eye contact with the three musicians in the Sex Pistols, he called in downstairs to introduce himself in the time-honoured fashion of musicians the world over: 'He came and had a jam with us,' says Glen.

Back at Warrington Crescent, a rehearsal-cum-audition for the proposed new band went ahead anyway. Bernie was not present. He didn't miss much. 'Now, this is no reflection on those guys' talents today, but I class it as an absolutely disastrous musical encounter,' Andrew told *ZigZag*'s Alan Anger in 1978. Going into more detail, he now adds, 'Mick Jones had a good sense of humour and a tenacity I quietly admired. His guitar style was non-existent, though he modelled himself closely on Brady: all the moves, just none of the chainsaw panzer sound. For obvious reasons, we kept his personal yodel well away from any of the microphones.' An attempt was made at Larry Williams's 'Bad Boy', as covered by the Beatles. 'After playing it once, we tried it again, and halfway through, I just walked out. It was terrible. That really is the sum total of my involvement with the London SS.'

Not quite. A few days later, both Matt and Geir received phone calls from the ex-Brats. 'Andrew and Casino said they wanted to get a band together with me, but not with Mick and Tony, basically,' says Matt. 'I kind of weighed up the odds, and I decided to go with the Hollywood Brats thing. At that time it was down to the fact that they had a good album and I thought Matheson was great; I didn't know what to think about

Casino, but I knew he wrote good songs, which was a plus. I thought, "Why not?"' After he had broken the bad news to Mick and Tony, Matt received a visit from Bernie asking him to reconsider. 'But I'd made up my mind, for better or worse.' 'I left the band as well,' says Geir. 'I shouldn't have, but I did. I really got on with Mick and Tony at the time, and I think that was the beginning of the Clash, really.'

Again, not quite. At Andrew's suggestion, the breakaway band called themselves the Choirboys. Predictably, Geir did not last long, a fact he attributes to Andrew's 'unique personality', and Andrew attributes to Geir's drumming. The next to leave was Andrew himself. 'He went back to Canada for the Christmas holidays or something,' says Matt, 'and just didn't come back for about six months, so we carried on without him.' Casino and Matt drafted in Honest John and some friends from Leeds, and shortened the band's name to the Boys. Their eponymous début album would feature two re-recorded Hollywood Brats songs, including 'Sick On You'.

Warrington Crescent regular Fat Steve Hershkowitz was by no means obese, but he was not whippet thin either, which seems to have ruled him out as a candidate for the London SS vocalist vacancy. Similarly, several interviewees for this book have suggested the reason guitarist Barry Jones was never considered as a potential recruit was because he was black, and that Barry – not unreasonably – developed something of a chip on his shoulder about it. If this is indeed the case, it seems both were victims of the prevailing cultural fascism which dictated that rock stars had to be long-haired, skinny, effeminate white boys. After Steve had dropped his unflattering prefix and instead adopted the surname Dior, they got their own back by forming a band with a similarly Dolls-influenced name: the London Cowboys. Unfortunately, they became too enamoured of the Johnny Thunders lifestyle to deliver.

Violent Luck played their last gig under that name on 22 June 1976, supporting Eddie and the Hot Rods at the Marquee. A favourable review appeared in the very first edition of punk fanzine *Sniffin' Glue*. Thereafter, the band was taken on by former David Bowie producer Tony Visconti, who renamed them Sister Ray after the Velvet Underground song. More demos followed, but by this time Kelvin was getting that sinking feeling. According to Campbell Devine's biography of Mott the Hoople, *All The Young Dudes*, in late 1976 he tried to use the Sister Ray demos to secure the vocalist's position with the floundering remnants of Mott. Desperate as they were, the band still decided he was too unreliable. During 1977, Kelvin recorded a couple of solo singles, finally bailing out on Sister Ray at the end of the year to join Rat Scabies's short-lived White Cats. Early in 1978, Ian Hunter suggested that Kelvin relocate to America and front new wave band Tuff Darts. He seized the opportunity, adopting the cheesy alias Tony Frenzy to sing on the band's eponymous 1978 album. Ian Hunter played piano on a couple of tracks.

After Kelvin left Sister Ray, Brady and John Brown briefly formed a band called the Hitmen with drummer John Altman, later to portray ne'er-do-well Nick Cotton in the BBC1 TV soap opera, *EastEnders*. When things fell through with Tuff Darts – almost immediately – Kelvin returned to London in time to join cash-in punk band the Tools. As the other members were Brady, John Brown and Geir Waade, it was effectively a made-over version of Little Queenie, minus Mick. Demos were recorded for Virgin records. Virgin would only offer a singles deal, so the band took the tapes to Polydor. An album was recorded, but remains unreleased.

Kelvin went on to pass in and out of bands too numerous to mention – one a post-Boys outfit including Matt Dangerfield – most of them doomed by his own suggestibility and lack of commitment. Later in 1978, Geir and John teamed up yet again with Brady to become Last Orders, the backing band for Stiff recording artist Wreckless Eric. All three played on the album, *The Wonderful World Of Wreckless Eric*, but Geir did not last long after its October release, and Brady left shortly afterwards. John played with Eric on and off until 1984. Geir returned to Norway. Brady still plays guitar in bands working the London circuit.

Andrew Matheson pursued a career in Canada as a professional soccer player, before making a solo album for Ariola in 1979 entitled *Monterey Shoes*. Subsequent sporadic attempts to restart his musical career – including abortive Hollywood Brats reunions – have been hampered by his peculiarly negative brand of perfectionism. In 1993, MCA paid for him to visit Norway and record another solo album, with Casino helping out on keyboards and production and Brady supplying occasional guitar. In 1994, ex-Boys Casino and Honest John joined Glen Matlock on sessions for Ian Hunter's album *Dirty Laundry*, which features material written by various permutations of Ian, Casino, Honest John, Matt Dangerfield and Andrew Matheson.

That none of their contemporaries on the Warrington Crescent scene was destined to enjoy the same recognition or commercial success as either Mick Jones or Tony James is a fact that only carries weight in retrospect. In mid October 1975, in addition to the inferiority complex that comes with being deemed not good enough, the duo were having to cope with the ignominy of having had their band stolen from them; and, in Mick's case, not once, but twice. Although they did continue to visit Warwick Crescent, it was neither convenient nor comfortable for them to play there on anything other than a casual basis. Which meant that, in addition to their drummer and lead guitarist, they had effectively lost their rehearsal room. Tony took his revenge when talking Pete Frame through the London SS Family Tree two years later: Matt's not inconsiderable role was reduced to the same size as Casino's walk-on bit-part, and Andrew and Geir received no mention at all.

There is one last, wince-inducing postscript to the story of the abortive London SS/Hollywood Brats/Malcolm McLaren link-up. The only halfway suitable candidate for a second guitarist thrown up by the Sex Pistols' 'Johnny Thunders' auditions was 15-year old Steve New. He attended a few rehearsals, but things didn't quite gel, and he faded out of the picture about the same time Matt and Geir were poached by Andrew and Casino. Glen Matlock had been quite taken with Mick Jones, and he and Malcolm tried to track him down. 'We didn't really have a contact,' says Glen. 'All we had was this address on London Street [that of Andrew and Casino's flat]. Some bloke wouldn't let us in, so we were shouting through the letterbox, "We just want to get in touch with Mick Jones," and this bloke – I think he was Norwegian, might have been Casino Steel – goes, "Why should I tell you? What's in it for me?"' Mick remained unaware of the missed opportunity. Shortly afterwards, the Pistols abandoned the idea of taking on a second guitarist, and on 6 November 1975, they played their first gig at the art school where Glen had taken his Foundation year, St Martin's on Charing Cross Road.

As his contribution to the fledgling Sex Pistols suggests, Bernie's unorthodox management style was already fully developed when he met Mick and Tony. 'From the word go, his whole stance was, "You know nothing, you haven't got an original idea!"' Tony told *Mojo*'s Pat Gilbert in 1999. '"If you want to be another New York Dolls, then you're wasting my time. You haven't made one statement that means anything!"' But it was following the loss of Matt Dangerfield and Geir Waade, and the consequent slump in Mick and Tony's confidence, that Bernie really began to assert his influence. He handed out reading lists to his charges, prompting them to immerse themselves in books on existentialism, modern art and Dadaism. 'It taught us something important: you have to have a bigger idea,' said Tony. 'That was Bernie's lesson.'

For all his later attempts to play it down, it was Bernie who became the main motivating force behind Mick's third post-Delinquents attempt to form a band, again under the name the London SS. Bernie found a rehearsal room: a dingy basement under a café called the Paddington Kitchen, at 113-115 Praed Street, next to the Fountains Abbey pub... and no more than a hundred yards from Andrew and Casino's flat. Fortunately, someone else proved more successful in tracking down Mick than had been Glen and Malcolm. Within days of the fateful Warrington Crescent audition – Tony claims it was the same night – Brian James phoned to say he was back in the UK and ready to go to work. That meant all that was needed was a drummer and a vocalist. Once again, the band turned to the *Melody Maker* classifieds in order to fill the vacancies, providing Bernie's home phone number for what turned out to be a series of ads running up until 6 December.

By the end of 1975, glam had long since run its course as a musical genre. David Bowie was flirting with 'plastic soul'. The MC5 were long gone, the Flamin' Groovies did not have a secure recording contract, and both the Stooges and the New York Dolls had split the previous year. Luckily, the New York punk scene (from now on referred to as New York new wave in this book, in order to avoid confusion with the UK Class of '76 punk scene) was still going strong. Television and the Ramones had been joined at CBGB's by the Heartbreakers and Blondie, with more to follow. None of the New York new wave bands sounded alike, but what they had in common was a no frills approach to raw rock'n'roll. Whether their hair was long or short, whether they wore ripped jeans, leather jackets and sneakers like the Ramones, or torn T-shirts and cheap sunglasses like Richard Hell, the style of the New York bands was similarly back-to-basics.

Although next to nothing of this musical revolution had been captured on record during 1975, Bernie was full of it – thanks largely to his connection with Malcolm, who had witnessed it first hand during his time managing the Dolls – and Mick had been following its development in his imported American magazines. CBGB's summer festival of unsigned bands was also covered in both the *NME* and *Melody Maker*, and on 8 November, Charles Shaar Murray wrote an overview of the scene for the former paper under the heading 'Are You Alive To The Jive Of The Sound Of '75?'. Mid December saw the release of the first readily available recorded fruits of the New York movement, Patti Smith's instant classic, *Horses*. Mick and Tony approved of the musical trend but – for a few months more, despite Bernie's objections – still preferred to persist with the glam look of yesteryear.

The 25 October issue of *Melody Maker* carried a display ad for a 'YOUNG STOOGE VOCALIST' accompanied by a plain Musicians Wanted ad for a 'DRUMMER – YOUNG skinny psychopath.' In the 1 November issue, the request for a disturbed drummer was repeated, but a more populist appeal was made for a frontman: 'YOUNG JAGGER VOCALIST, VISCOUS [sic] skinny rock and roller wanted.' Two weeks later, a singer was no longer required – Mick having decided to reclaim the vocals – but the need for a drummer had grown urgent enough to warrant dropping the insanity qualification and investing in a display ad: 'THIN YOUNG DRUMMER REQUIRED – INTO Loud Punk Rock, MC5/DOLLS.' The last ad gave up on insider-speak altogether, and took a more formal approach: 'Wild young drummer wanted. Must be aware of current New York scene and MC5 thru to the Stooges. New energetic kids, 18-22, rather than seasoned pros with fixed ideals, although obviously ability essential. Immediate rehearsals based in central London. Must be dedicated and look great in the above terms.'

The frequency and number of the ads might suggest a lack of response, but the London SS found themselves deluged with replies. After an initial telephone vetting by Bernie, hopefuls met the band in the Paddington Kitchen, which had a jukebox loaded with London SS-approved singles. They were then taken downstairs to the basement rehearsal room. Most of those put through their paces shared too few of the same influences and cultural reference points, and either looked upon auditioning as a recreational pastime in its own right, or just wanted to be in a group, any group. Even more disturbingly for aesthetes Mick and Tony, several candidates had facial hair, poor dress sense, receding hairlines and/or weight problems. 'I've never really been able to envisage rock musicians as anything but flash dressers,' an unrepentant Tony was still proclaiming to Nick Kent over three years later. 'It's always been an integral part of it for me... I could never imagine myself being in a group with some *fat* guy.'

A rabid Dolls and Mott the Hoople fan and would-be singer called Steven Morrissey contacted Mick and started a brief correspondence, but as he was based in Manchester, it was not possible for him to contribute in a more practical way. Pushed in front of the microphone for the first time ever, a visiting Paul Simonon was deemed to have the looks, but not the presence to be a vocalist. Terry Chimes tried out as drummer, and thought he was in with a good chance, but was not called back. Nick Headon was offered the job, took it, but left after a week... Unfortunately, the few that had the musical taste, attitude, and decadent appearance to join a Dolls-style band also had the de rigueur self-destructive bent. Even a certain Roland Hot, who stayed behind the drum kit longer than most – 'probably because he had a leather jacket,' according to Tony – was deemed unsatisfactory because he 'used to get pissed a lot'.

It was Roland who accompanied the three official members of the band on the rough live-in-the-rehearsal-room demo tapes recorded on Mick's reel-to-reel towards the end of the London SS's life, with Mick providing most of the vocals. 'And you ought to hear the music on those tapes!' Tony told Pete Frame in 1977. 'It drives like fuck. Raw rock'n'roll: it's really great!' If, as has been claimed, bootleg tapes did circulate during punk's heyday, they are no longer available, which denies the rest of the world the opportunity to judge for themselves. Tony, however, revealed that the band's repertoire included the Flamin' Groovies' hardy perennial 'Slow Death', the Strangeloves' 'Night Time' and the MC5's 'Ramblin' Rose'.

Shared influences also showed through in the sex and drugs preoccupations of the trio's own compositions. Brian's were the most Stooge and MC5-like, as is evidenced by the Damned's début album, *Damned, Damned, Damned*, where most of them found a home. That album also features 'Fish', a version of a song he originally co-wrote with Tony as 'Portobello Reds'. Tony also came up with an idea for a song called 'Rockets For Sale', about nuclear warheads being retailed in Selfridges. Bernie approved of the general concept, but pushed for something a little less fanciful.

Mick's songs, meanwhile, betrayed his affection for the entire rock'n'roll tradition. They relied upon tried and tested structures, and took the vagaries of human relationships as their subjects, but like the best work of Mick's heroes, they always included some sort of thorn beneath the rose. The titles provide some idea of the songs' content: 'Ooh, Baby, Ooh (It's Not Over)', 'I'm So Bored With You' and 'Protex Blue'. The last of these was inspired by and named after the brand of contraceptives available from the vending machine in the toilets of the Windsor Castle, the pub rock venue on the Harrow Road, just around the corner from Wilmcote House.

Night after night, week after week was devoted to jamming and trying out potential fourth members. Perhaps the quintessential London SS auditioning experience was enjoyed by Chris Miller. In December 1975, Chris was based in Caterham, 20 miles south of London. A fan of the Who and Dr Feelgood who was unhappy with his present would-be progressive outfit, he had long been attending auditions for other bands. Having monitored the London SS ads since October, Chris finally decided to respond to the one in the 6 December issue. Of his initial telephone conversation with Bernie, he says: 'That was pretty stormy. I knew they were obviously looking for somebody different, just because the ad had been running for so long. It was obvious that the run-of-the-mill approach wasn't the right one. Bernie was asking me what I knew about the

New York scene, and I just said, "I live in the sticks, how on earth am I supposed to know what's going on in New York?" And we got into this, "Well, why did you bother to answer the advert, then?" "Because I knew you were looking for somebody special." And that kind of did it, because he said, "You obviously think you're really good," and I said, "Well, yeah." It was a bit of a showdown on the phone, but as soon as I'd copped some attitude, he gave me an address to go down and meet them in Praed Street.'

As was customary, he rendezvoused with the others in the Paddington Kitchen. 'We sat around and talked about what bands we were into. I liked the MC5 and stuff, and I knew the Stooges, so it was kind of like, "You got through part one." Then there was visual image...' As Chris was less than svelte, and not only had freckles, a large nose and unkempt sandy red hair, but was also attired in scruffy flared denims, his rating was not high. Nevertheless, he was taken down to the rehearsal room. 'It was just this horrible old basement with this old drum kit in it, and these great big stacks. It was kind of, "Well, here you are: impress us." They were obviously so bored with trying people out they had a TV down there that they were watching while we were playing, which was really sensitive!'

As those present knew all too well, auditioning was always a fairly brittle process, involving much ego-bruising and one-upmanship. Having quickly assessed the situation, Chris laid into the kit with even more than his usual ferocity. 'It was just one of those things where to get their attention, you had to be really aggressive.' Like the others, Brian had been devoting most of his attention to the war movie showing on the TV, but his interest picked up immediately. He and the drummer started to play off each other and show off their repertoire of tricks. At one point, Brian impressed Chris by soundtracking one of the movie's aeroplane dog fights with a screeching noise guitar solo.

Between songs, Chris was forced to down sticks and scratch himself energetically. Asked why, he admitted to having the contagious skin disease scabies, which prompted Bernie to run around covering the seats with newspaper. Despite this, it was decided that Chris was at least worth a second audition, this time on his own kit. Later that evening, after a visit to the pub, Mick and Tony returned to the rehearsal room. A mouse ran out across the basement floor, and Tony remarked on the rodent's startling resemblance to the recently departed drummer. When he next saw the band, a couple of days later, Chris found he had a new name: Rat Scabies.

'They came and picked up my kit, from Caterham, underneath this antique shop,' says Rat. 'I remember Mick was wearing parallel jeans instead of flares. It was, "Oh, wow, what are *they*?" We bundled the stuff into Bernie's old Renault, and we drove back and played some more.' One of the songs he remembers rehearsing was the Rolling Stones' 'You Can't Always Get What You Want'. After about a week, Mick, Tony and Bernie decided that Rat didn't have the right appearance, after all, and Brian finally lost patience. He had never really approved of Bernie's involvement – 'I was quite suspicious of him, to tell you the truth' – and after two months of trying out countless hopeless cases, he was disgusted that the others had rejected what he considered to be the most exciting candidate thus far. 'It was all getting a little bit too much about looking for people who looked right, you know what I mean? I don't give a fuck what people look like as long as they can play!'

One of his other auditions had landed Rat the drum seat for a Caterham pantomime performance of *Puss In Boots*. Just before Christmas, Brian informed Mick and Tony that he was leaving, with the intention of forming a band with Rat once panto season was over. Some of his irritation – exacerbated by the punk movement's then-current trend for inter-band bitching – was still evident in the explanation he offered Pete Frame for the split some 18 months later: 'Mick and Tony are basically girls, and Rat and I wanted to play man's music.'

'In January 1976, Mick and I decided to call it a day,' Tony told Pete Frame. 'It was back to the two of us after nine months of getting nowhere.' Although the duo remained close friends, and went on to share flats together, it seems that Tony did not have quite as much say in the dissolution of the partnership as he suggested. In the 1991 *Clash On Broadway* booklet, Mick revealed that Bernie, presumably still intent on joining forces with Malcolm, brought the Pistols' manager down to Praed Street to watch the band rehearse. Malcolm's outright dismissal of what he saw there might have been dubiously motivated, but it convinced Bernie that the London SS was not going to happen.

From Bernie's point of view, then, Brian's decision to defect with Rat was a blessing in disguise. It made winding up the London SS that much more simple a task. For Mick, it was the third time he had been rejected by a band he had been instrumental in forming, and, understandably, he took it less well. Dispirited, he offered no resistance to the termination of his partnership with Tony, in which he was the dominant figure, and instead formed another with Bernie in which he relied increasingly heavily on the older man's judgement. 'Bernie seemed to know more than me about what we were going to do,' he told Kosmo Vinyl for the *Clash On Broadway* booklet. 'Sometimes in the early days I lost heart, but he always saw a way through.'

The basement rehearsal space was let go. Tony began attending auditions himself, including one for the Boys. Later in the year, he joined Gene October's band Chelsea, before decamping with guitarist Billy Idol to form Generation X. He was still keeping true to the London SS's ideals in the mid Eighties, when he launched his '5th Generation' futuristic trash glam rock'n'roll band, Sigue Sigue Sputnik. Talking to Pat Gilbert in 1999, he cheerfully recalled one of the last conversations he had with his manager while still a member of the London SS. Apparently, Bernie phoned Tony at home in Twickenham, and declared 'James, you're too fucking soft! Tell your parents you're going to spend Christmas with a hooker!'

It was during the particularly down and directionless period either immediately prior to or closely following the dissolution of the London SS that Mick made his only post-Delinquents, pre-Clash live appearance. It came about at the behest of the newly-rechristened Steve Dior, who, in an attempt to kick-start his own career, had arranged a one-off gig at Chiswick Polytechnic, Bath Road. In a manner typical of the Warrington Crescent scene, the rest of the band was made up out of whoever happened to be around the flat at the time. The songs rehearsed were all covers of compositions by the likes of the New York Dolls and Hollywood Brats, and Steve cheekily billed the concert under the latter name. As everyone who was not part of the fake Brats went along to watch, there is some confusion about exactly who took the stage, but Steve certainly sang, John Brown claims he played bass, Honest John Plain says that he played drums, and – in view of his subsequent partnership with Steve – it seems likely that Barry Jones was one of the guitarists. Everyone is agreed that Mick was the other one. 'I definitely remember Mick,' says Honest John. 'He had hair down to his waist, and black and white striped trousers: well MC5!'

It was that night at Chiswick Poly that Mick met Glen Matlock again. Unaware that Celia Perry was – nominally, at least – going out with Barry, Glen had made a tentative date to meet her there. He arrived too late to catch the band, but he, Celia, Mick and another girl decided to go on somewhere else in an ultimately fruitless search for after-hours fun. Thereafter, Celia and Glen began seeing one another (they eventually married) and Glen and Mick became good friends, both of which relationships helped bring the Warrington Crescent and Sex Pistols camps into the same orbit. Glen started accompanying Mick and various of the others on their ceaseless gig-going expeditions to places like the Royal College of Art in Kensington. 'We'd have nothing to do afterwards,' recalls Glen, 'and I'd say, "Let's go back and have a jam," because all the gear was set up. So people would come back.' The Pistols' rehearsal room in Denmark Street became another place for Mick to hang out.

The Sex Pistols had followed up their first gig with a series of largely unannounced college shows in and around the London area. By the end of 1975, the ever-ambitious Malcolm McLaren was harbouring fantasies of setting himself up as a latter-day Larry Parnes, the early Sixties manager who had run a stable of British rock'n'rollers which included Billy Fury and Marty Wilde. The end of the London SS was a godsend as far as he was concerned, releasing as it did a few more unattached musicians onto the market.

Sniffing a way to get back in cahoots with Malcolm, Bernie did not object when his former associate attempted to poach his protégé. Nor did Mick demur, having by this time had his first live exposure to the Pistols at a mutual friend's party. Reminiscing for an *NME* best-gig-ever-seen feature in 1994, he said: 'This was the most important. All kinds of things were going through my head; it was amazing. I basically felt like I'd seen the shape of things to come. Which I had.'

'There was this thing where Richard Hell was writing to Malcolm saying, "Honest, I'm not a junkie. I really want to come over to London,"' Mick told the *NME*'s Nick Kent in 1978. 'So I was in line for that. Meanwhile, Malcolm or Bernie would be planning some new group or other, and I'd be sent over to some rehearsal. There was this pool of musicians that they'd have on tap, expecting us to form bands ultimately.' Others in the pool included Rat Scabies, keeping his options open until he could begin rehearsals with Brian James, and Chrissie Hynde, former Sex shop assistant, former *NME* journalist and former girlfriend of Nick Kent.

Malcolm initially suggested that Chrissie team up with Nick and Rat to form a band. After some consideration, Chrissie decided her history with Nick would make this too painful. There followed some talk of building a group around her to be known as the Love Boys, this time with Mick on guitar, but again, nothing came of it. Malcolm then put Rat and Chrissie together in a short-lived, deliberately ludicrous outfit known as Masters of the Backside or Mike Hunt's Honourable Discharge, depending on the day. Chrissie played guitar, Rat's friend Ray Burns played bass, and vocal duties were shared between Daves Zero and White. Rat and Ray were natural extroverts, Dave Zero – a gravedigger from Hemel Hempstead – liked to model himself on Dracula, and Chrissie was supposed to dress as a boy to contrast with the effeminate mannerisms of the screamingly camp Dave White. Unfortunately, the predictable result was that nobody could take the venture remotely seriously, least of all Malcolm.

From the ashes of this quickly aborted outfit grew one of the first bona fide London punk groups to follow the Pistols: Rat got back together with Brian James, Ray Burns – later to be known as Captain Sensible – and Dave Zero, who had already rechristened himself Dave Vanian. True to the band's origin in the London SS, they stuck with the 'Nazi decadence' theme, and named themselves after Visconti's film, *The Damned*. (A name which had previously been considered by Malcolm for the fledgling Sex Pistols.) Rat and Brian finally got to play their 'man's music' with a singer seldom seen out of make up and a bassist with a penchant for taking the stage in a tutu. Rat might have left the pantomime, but the pantomime hadn't left Rat…

When the Sex Pistols began to take off in February 1976, demanding more of Malcolm's attention, Bernie took over his mix'n'match policy and suggested that Mick and Chrissie form a band called Big Girl's Underwear. The very name of this proposed outfit betrays just how much Bernie was still in thrall to Malcolm; and the fact he was willing to go along with the idea gives some indication of the blind faith Mick was by now showing in Bernie. Although Chrissie was prepared to tolerate a certain amount of high-concept self-indulgence from Malcolm, however, she was something of a rock'n'roll purist at heart and was not prepared to play the fool at the bidding of a man she – like many others at the time – considered to be McLaren's pale shadow.

While few of them are rarely mentioned in the numerous accounts of the Sex Pistols' early days – punk era revisionism having dictated that long-haired, decadent types be expunged from the records – John Brown, Brady, Kelvin, Geir, Tony, Matt and Casino were all regulars at the Pistols' early 1976 shows, along with Rat, Brian, Mick and Chrissie. They attended the band's breakthrough gig of 12 February, supporting Eddie and the Hot Rods at the Marquee. 'We helped them move the gear onstage,' says John.

As well as representing the Pistols' graduation to the club circuit, the Marquee gig was a key event for three other reasons. Firstly, Johnny Rotten damaged the Rods' monitors, which got the Pistols banned from the club and set them off on the road to notoriety. Secondly, their performance won the band their first full length live review in the *NME*. By Neil Spencer, and under the title 'Don't look over your shoulder, but the Sex Pistols are coming,' it concluded with the soon-to-be legendary band quote, 'Actually, we're not into music. We're into chaos,' making the Pistols sound like the hottest ticket in town for anyone who preferred rock'n'roll to come spiced with a little danger.

Thirdly, the spectacle of the show combined with the subsequent music press reaction to it put a rocket up the collective backside of the audience. Although it was only a couple of dozen strong – in addition to the Warrington Crescent crowd, it was made up of former and current Sex sales assistants, Johnny Rotten's friends, a few Bowie and Roxy Music-cum-*Rocky Horror Show* types from Bromley (soon to be known as the Bromley Contingent) and one or two curious passers-by – that audience quickly realised the future was there for the taking. Between them, the couple of dozen went on to form the bulk of the groups that turned punk from a one-band scene into a movement. Even those who had not seriously contemplated the possibility of becoming performers were inspired to do so. People like Mick and Chrissie, who had already been scratching around for a couple of years trying to get bands together, started to feel a renewed sense of urgency; a desire to be part of something vital and exciting, coupled with a feeling of panic about the possibility of missing the boat.

A native of Akron, Ohio, Chrissie was just under four years older than Mick. Her musical tastes had developed along similar lines, moving on from Stax soul and UK beat groups like the Kinks and the Rolling Stones to Iggy Pop and the Stooges. The Anglophile Chrissie moved to London in 1973. After a brief fling with Arthur Kane during the New York Dolls' UK visit that November, she fell in with the World's Most Elegantly Wasted Rock Journalist, Nick Kent. It wasn't long before Chrissie's opinionated views on rock'n'roll, invariably expressed at top volume, secured her a job with the *NME*. From January 1974, she wrote reviews in a casual yet scathingly witty style which owed more than a little to Lester Bangs, and in turn set something of a trend for the future Hip Young Gunslingers of UK punk journalism.

Out of step at that time, however, and increasingly bored by the kind of music she was being asked to write about, Chrissie left the paper in April 1974. Having developed a penchant for rubber mini skirts and other *outré* clothing, she went to work at Sex for a few months, during which period she became friends with Vivienne and Malcolm and got to know members of the Sex Pistols. A falling out with Nick Kent prompted her to take an extended leave of absence – sandwiching a return visit to Akron between two lengthy stays in Paris – and she arrived back in London in January 1976, just as the punk scene was beginning to get underway.

After all the talk of Love Boys and Big Girl's Underwear, it seemed fate was intent on pushing Mick and Chrissie together. Following the Pistols' 12 February Marquee gig, almost in spite of Malcolm and Bernie's scheming, they formed an uneasy sort of musical alliance that lasted, on and off, until that April. As Mick no longer had a proper rehearsal room of his own at his disposal, and Chrissie didn't even have a fixed abode, the only opportunities to play as anything like a band occurred when both parties happened to be in the vicinity of the Pistols' Denmark Street rehearsal room. Glen Matlock recalls working up a song of Chrissie's entitled 'Get On Your Hynde Legs, Baby' that was strongly reminiscent of the Kinks' 'Sittin' On Your Sofa'. 'Chrissie was singing, Mick was playing guitar, I played bass and Steve Jones played drums. It was pretty good.' More often, though, Mick and Chrissie would get together in Mick's room at Wilmcote House to play and sing as a duo. With Stella ever on hand with the tea pot, they would work through such mutual favourites as the Kinks' 'I'm Not Like Anybody Else' and the Spencer Davis Group's 'Every Little Bit Hurts', written by Ed Cobb, who had also furnished the Standells with their more memorable songs.

Despite their many shared influences, their own compositions did not have much in common. Some of Chrissie's songs were tender soul ballads, but most were feisty rockers, often in idiosyncratic timings, with lyrics largely inspired by the junky and biker subcultures she had encountered during her nomadic wanderings around London and the wider world. She remembers Mick's creations, in contrast, as 'rather dippy love songs'. The two of them continued to write separately, though Chrissie claims she changed a few lines of the lyric to 'Protex Blue', and Mick admits she helped him come up with the 'What a liar!' coda to a new song called 'Deny'.

Their different writing styles were not the only obstacles to any long term collaboration. Although mouthy, Chrissie was shy, and reluctant to perform on stage, a problem exacerbated by her worries about living up to the harsh judgements she had handed out to others while with the *NME*. Having seen a bit of the world in her 24 years, she also felt keenly the age gap between herself and the relatively innocent 20 year-old Mick, as evidenced by her affectionate, but somewhat patronising description of him as 'a really great kid'. Affecting a tough, leather clad mama style herself, she also objected to his 'long hair and skinny, faggy little jackets'.

She decided to give him an image makeover. Round at Wilmcote House one day, under the pretext of trimming some split ends, she set about his lengthy Ian Hunter-like tresses with a pair of scissors. 'He was standing up, so it was hard for him to see what I was doing. But eventually, he started to see how all over him were these pieces of hair about four or five inches long,' she told the *NME*'s Chris Salewicz. 'I can still remember how he reacted when he realised what I was doing. He clutched his stomach and was groaning, "*Oooooooh*. I've got to sit down. I've got butterflies..."' She transformed Mick from an Ian Hunter into a Keith Richards, a look that they could both appreciate.

Both Chrissie and future member of the Slits Viv Albertine – by this time his girlfriend – have testified that Mick was surprisingly sensitive and considerate for a mid Seventies rock'n'roll guitarist, but the fact remained that rock was still a man's, man's, man's world. Although his desire to emulate the debauched rock star archetype consistently lost out to his inherent sense of decency, Mick had a very traditional idea of what a band should be: namely, a gang of guys dividing their time between playing, posing, doing drugs, pulling chicks, driving fast cars and indulging in miscellaneous other male bonding rituals. It was going to take a lot more than Patti Smith's *Horses* to change that mentality.

In the end, it was the Bernie factor that hastened Mick and Chrissie's partnership to an end. Bernie might have lost the plot a little with his suggestion for Big Girl's Underwear, but the Sex Pistols' impact in the first four months of 1976 helped him regain it. He persevered with the notion of an underlying Concept, but decided it should be provocative in a rebellious manner rather than a smutty one. Initial criteria were the Look, Youth, and Attitude. Chrissie had a cool rock'n'roll image, but compared with the Pistols and Mick she was an old timer. And although she had plenty of attitude, it didn't fit in with Bernie's: as she had already proved, she simply wasn't malleable enough to capitulate to his grand design. Even while Mick was still rehearsing with her, Bernie was pushing his charge to forge new liaisons – with Paul Simonon and Keith Levene among others – which would ultimately squeeze Chrissie out of the picture.

Over the course of the next year, she had to watch as both the Damned and the Clash went on to enjoy coverage in the music press second only to the Pistols themselves. 'I wanted to be in a band so *bad*,' she told *Rolling Stone*'s Kurt Loder in 1980. 'All the people I knew in town were in bands. And there I was, the real loser.' By the time she gave that interview, however, she had bettered anything either the Damned or the Clash had so far achieved – in commercial terms, at least – by making it to number one in both the UK singles and albums charts with her own group, the Pretenders. Their eponymous début album included a Kinks cover version and several of the Hynde originals she and Mick had sung together, including an S&M biker song entitled 'Tattooed Love Boys', a nod towards the name of one of their abandoned band projects.

Having finally arrived, Chrissie could afford to look back with affection on the time she spent with Mick in Wilmcote House. 'His granny was starting to get a bit worried about him and his obsession with rock'n'roll,' she told Chris Salewicz. 'But I used to say to her, "Don't worry, he's great. He's really talented. He's going to make it…"'

3
JOHNNY TOO BAD

'I was the dark horse of the Clash,' Paul Simonon told *Melody Maker*'s Caroline Sullivan in October 1989. 'If anybody'd ever said to me, in an interview, "What do you do with your spare time?" maybe I'd have turned around and given them a big art lecture. But I think they thought I was an idiot. A thicko from South London.'

On 6 August 1955, 20 year old soldier Gustave Antoine Simonon married 19 year old Elaine Florence Braithwaite at the Catholic Church Of The English Martyrs in Streatham. Elaine was five months pregnant at the time. Although he preferred to call himself Antony, her new husband celebrated his family's Gallic lineage by passing on his other Christian name to his first son, as had his father and grandfather before him. Paul Gustave Simonon was born on 15 December 1955 in his mother's home at 1 Beulah Crescent, Thornton Heath, three miles south of the Brixton he claims as his place of birth.

Before long, the young family moved even further away: to 3 George Street in Ramsgate, a Kentish coastal town 70 miles east of London. Here, on 2 October 1959, Paul's brother Nicholas Antony was born. By the time of Paul's birth, his father had already completed his army service and taken a job as an insurance agent. By the time of Nick's, he had switched to a line of work more closely aligned to his wife's: running a bookshop. While with the Clash, Paul never admitted to having lived anywhere but London. Spending part of his childhood in Ramsgate might have made him sound too provincial. In a 1999 interview with Pat Gilbert for *Mojo*, he revealed that he had also lived in Italy for a year. Offering this information while with the Clash might have made him sound too cosmopolitan. Even in 1999, no further details were forthcoming.

Paul's parents split up when he, like Mick, was eight. Before the impasse was reached, however, the Simonons had moved back to London. When Antony and Elaine went their separate ways, Paul and Nick stayed with their mother in Shakespeare Road, Brixton. Paul attended the nearby Effra Primary School on Barnwell Road, just off what was then the notorious Front Line, Railton Road. Much later, he discovered that Robin Crocker had been one of his slightly older contemporaries there. While Robin went on to cross paths with Mick Jones in the comparatively safe haven of Strand School, the next step on the educational ladder for Paul was William Penn School: a huge comprehensive not dissimilar to Tulse Hill, situated just around the corner from Shakespeare Road, on Red Post Hill in Dulwich. In 1976, Paul told Caroline Coon that the school was 90 per cent black, also like those abutting Mick and Robin's grammar school.

In an ideal world, this figure should be meaningless, but the black population of the UK's inner cities has always been the most poorly served by the country's educational system. Overcrowding and the other environmental pressures set such schools off to a poor start. It is a statistically proven fact that – due to prejudice as much as the state of the local economy – even blacks *with* qualifications were less likely than whites to be offered an opportunity to use them in a constructive manner. This quite understandably encouraged apathy towards education itself and resentment towards authority. Teachers bore the initial brunt of both, and so were not keen to work in such a depressing, even threatening milieu. Which in turn meant that such schools could not always attract the more gifted educators. Even those teachers with a vocation, who took posts for altruistic reasons, had to be extraordinarily committed and charismatic to be able to make an impression. The result was a self-perpetuating downward spiral that, by the early

Seventies, had resulted in what Raymond Long, the head teacher at Tulse Hill, summed up as 'an urban crisis of violence, truancy and maladjustment'.

An inner city secondary school that was 90 per cent black was not going to offer much in the way of opportunity to any but the most talented and determined of its pupils, whatever their colour. 'All you done is played about and pissed on the teachers and that,' Paul told Caroline Coon in November 1976. 'There were 45 in our class, and we had a Pakistani teacher who didn't even speak English.'

As he reached his teens, Paul became caught up in the predominantly working class skinhead youth cult. The skinhead, or skin for short, emerged in the late Sixties as a more brutal and ascetic version of the early Sixties mod. There was the same obsessive attention to stylistic detail, but all hints of effete dandyism were rejected. The mod's hair had been short, but French-cut and styled; the skin's was either cropped to stubble or completely shaved. The mod had started out wearing tight Italian suits, and gradually progressed to the hipster look of outlandish Regency ruffles and flares. The skin stuck to a basic uniform of highly polished DM boots, rolled Levi's jeans or tight Sta-Press trousers held up with thin, clip-on braces, plain T-shirts or button-down Ben Shermans, worn under Harrington jackets or Crombie overcoats. Everything about the skinhead look was macho and uncompromising. While mid-period mods adopted the Union Jack as a Pop-Art symbol or celebration of Swinging London, they still prided themselves upon their cosmopolitan tastes. Skins used the flag to signal a confused, xenophobic patriotism that later made some of their number easy pickings for growing UK fascist movement the National Front.

While hippies – their despised diametric opposites – were sitting in fields lauding the arrival of the Age of Aquarius and loving their fellow man, many skins were living in inner-city council estates, absorbing the initial fallout from the collapse of the Sixties dream and looking around for ways to vent their dissatisfaction and frustration. Vandalism was one. Another was aggressive behaviour towards selected scapegoats, anyone alien to mainstream society or the skins' own subculture: hippies, supporters of rival football teams, gays, blacks and Asians. Not all skins were violent, homophobic or racist by any means, but sufficient of their number were to shape history's view of the cult. Once extreme right-wing rhetoric fed into the equation, unprovoked attacks on non-whites became commonplace, and Paki-bashing in particular was soon established as the preferred skinhead recreational activity.

Racist skinheads evidenced an almost incredible capacity for doublethink: their preferred genre of music was reggae, songs documenting life in Jamaica, written, performed and recorded by black Jamaicans; this music was only available to them in the first place because of the immigrant West Indian communities in areas like Brixton and Notting Hill; and one theory even has it that the skinhead's very look was based upon the cropped hair, big boots and rolled pants of the poor New World negro agricultural worker.

Despite the near-the-knuckle comment about his Pakistani teacher, Paul was certainly not remotely racist by the time he met Mick Jones and helped form the Clash, and he denies that he was ever involved in any racially-motivated unpleasantness. In 1978, he told the *NME*'s Chris Salewicz that he had never gone Paki-bashing, and although he did admit to stealing from shops owned or run by Pakistanis, he claimed this was due more to demographics than design. Nor did he pick fights with blacks. 'When I was at school in south London I used to always want to be mates with the hardest kids in school,' he said. 'So I could get to figure 'em out. And most of those guys tended to be black.' Not the most right-on of remarks, perhaps, but if anything, all the more convincing for that. Certainly, Paul was not so disingenuous as to pretend race was never an issue for him while growing up. Discussing the song '(White Man) In Hammersmith Palais' in 1988 for a *Melody Maker* retrospective marking the release of the compilation album, *The Story Of The Clash, Volume 1*, he said it reminded him of 'Going to blues [ie, Jamaican-style sound system] parties and being the only white boy there. When I was a kid, I wasn't so afraid of that, it's when I got to be a teenager that the feeling about race got to be a lot more powerful.'

Paul did become involved with soccer violence. 'I used to go around to football matches with me mates from the street and be a nuisance,' he told *Creem*'s Stephen Demorest in 1979. 'I remember once we'd just come from a football match and about 60 skinheads crossed over to where we was. We were skinheads as well, but we crossed over to the other side, and they crossed over again, and we ended up running down this road with them chasing us. In some ways, it's what "Last Gang In Town" is about. Stupid.'

It is not surprising that Paul's alliances at that time were motivated less by genuine friendship than by expediency. Joining a gang could offer kicks and camaraderie, but it also appealed to the survival instinct: better to be part of something than an outsider and a potential victim. In spite of such gangs' supposedly rigid codes of honour, friendships developed within their confines tend to be flimsy and seldom encourage the development of true loyalty. A casual remark made by Paul to *Melody Maker*'s Allan Jones in 1978 would seem to illustrate this point: 'Friends turn against you quicker than anyone. Like at school, it's always your best mates that turn against you. You don't think anything of it. You just have to turn the other way and get on with what you're doing.' The nature of the friendships he had in his early teens helps to explain why the Clash-era Paul Simonon appeared so self-reliant and yet – apparently paradoxically – appeared to be at his most comfortable, open and outgoing when surrounded by the band's established entourage.

Living where he did, it was impossible for Paul not to have been exposed to reggae, but his original allegiance to the music came as part of the cult experience: it was the soundtrack not only for local blues dances but also for nights spent at popular skin stomping ground, the Locarno on Streatham Hill. The attraction of the Locarno had as much to do with posing and fighting as it did with music and dancing. Inevitably, the club earned such a bad reputation for teenage violence that it closed in 1970, whereupon Mecca gave it an overhaul prior to reopening it as the more adult-oriented Cat's Whiskers.

Reggae's roots were in ska, which had developed out of Jamaica's blues dances in the early Sixties, when rival sound system operators began to cut their own discs rather than compete to be the first to play blues and soul records imported from the US. The lawn dances of downtown Kingston, Jamaica were far tougher even than the Streatham Locarno, and the argy bargy between the followers of the different sound systems did little to dispel the underlying threat of violence. Local hooligans were known as rude boys, or rudies for short.

The music did catch on to a certain extent with the mods on the early Sixties London club scene, notably at the Flamingo in Wardour Street, and Millie's 'My Boy Lollipop' was a freak number two UK chart hit in 1964. However, it was not really until 1968, by which time ska had evolved through rocksteady into reggae, that the music began to make more than a token commercial impact in the UK. In 1969, Desmond Dekker's 'Israelites' reached number one, the Harry J All-Stars' 'Liquidator' number nine, and 'Return of Django' by Lee Perry's Upsetters number five. UK reggae label Trojan's *Tighten Up* compilation album series was a huge success. Skinheads did not constitute reggae's sole market, but they were its core, as acknowledged in 1970 by Symarip's 'Skinhead Moonstomp'. By 1972, reggae had evolved yet again, into the less frenetic, more Jamaica-oriented roots style, and its UK popularity waned.

Paul's brother Nick got into Yes and other progressive rock bands of the period, but Paul could not relate to that music on any level. Instead, his affection for early reggae proved genuine and abiding, and when the Clash were interviewed by *Sniffin' Glue*'s Steve Walsh in 1976, he was still citing the Ethiopians and the Rulers as his favourite artists.

★★★

In late 1970, when Paul was 14 going on 15, he and Nick went to live with their father in Notting Hill. They shared a room in what, without ever being more specific, Paul has implied was a high-rise flat like Mick's. The explanation Paul gave Caroline Coon in 1976 suggested that it was his choice to leave his mother: 'I felt it was getting a bit soft with her. I could do whatever I liked, and I wasn't getting anywhere, so I went to stay with my dad.' In truth, the move came about because Elaine was finding it increasingly difficult to control the boys, especially her juvenile delinquent elder son. Already a regular truant, in the summer term of his third year Paul stopped going to school altogether. For him, 1970's Easter break segued into the long summer holiday, a six month absence during which he indulged his penchant for hanging around street corners, messing about on the railway line that runs parallel to Shakespeare Road, petty theft, vandalism and fighting.

To hear Paul tell it, the regime at his father's was strict enough to qualify as punishment for crimes past, or at the very least indicate the conscious deployment of a firm guiding hand. 'It was good training because I had to do all the launderette and that,' he told Caroline. 'In a way, I worked for him, getting money together.' One source of income was a Saturday job on Portobello Market. 'It used to get so cold in winter you had to stand with your feet in cardboard boxes.' The fullest account of his youthful labours appears in the *Clash Songbook*, edited by Paul and Mick Jones in 1977 and published the following year. Paul claimed he had to get up to do a paper round at six in the morning, and then make Antony his breakfast before heading off to school. During the midday break, he had to come home and make his father's lunch. After school, he would fit in another paper round before making the tea.

The school in question was Isaac Newton in Wornington Road, in the shadow of Trellick Tower. Again, the pupils at the school were mostly black, and again – or so Paul claimed in the *Clash Songbook* – the teachers were totally inept. 'It's a real sort of depressing school,' he told Janet Street-Porter on ITV's November 1976 *London Weekend Show* punk documentary. 'You go there, you don't learn nothing. All you're working for is to go into the factory that's around the corner. And, well, most of the mates I know are working in the factory.' Just over two years later, he told *Creem*'s Stephen Demorest that even school trips were geared towards introducing pupils to the army or merchant navy. According to anecdotes freely – even gleefully – offered to a string of interviewers, whenever he was away from his father's watchful eye, Paul continued to vent his frustrations by stealing from market stalls, vandalising phone booths, fighting, rolling cars down hills, throwing stones through rich peoples' windows, and dropping bricks from the landings of his high-rise block.

The picture Paul chose to paint of this period of his life in – especially, but not exclusively – the Clash's early interviews was of an unremittingly bleak, repressive home life lacking any kind of female influence; a hopeless, dead-end educational life; and a recreational life that was little more than a violent reaction to both of these. Closer examination reveals it to be an interpretation so free it borders on the abstract. Although Antony's character remains shifting and vague in Paul's possibly tongue-in-cheek accounts, he invariably comes over poorly: as a penniless loser exploiting his own flesh and blood, or a stern task-master driven solely by the work ethic. In reality, Antony was considerably more accomplished, sensitive and sophisticated than any of these options would suggest.

In 1978, while still with the band, Paul told Chris Salewicz he owed his own interest in painting to the fact that his father was always looking for some place to 'dump him' for a few days. Apparently, on one of these occasions, he was sent out to East Acton to stay with one of Antony's artist friends, who owned a coffee table book featuring the work of Henri Matisse. When his dad's friend was out of the room, Paul opened the book, and tried to copy the paintings in pencil. It was 1989, and the interview he gave to *Melody Maker*'s Caroline Sullivan, before Paul admitted that his true artistic inspiration had come not from a friend of his father, but from Antony himself. 'My dad used to paint a lot, and he'd leave them in my room to dry. I'd be like all kids, trying to copy my Dad, so I'd try and draw them.' In 1999, he told *Mojo*'s Pat Gilbert, 'My bedroom was his studio; on the walls were hundreds of postcards and pages torn out of books. Vermeers, Caravaggios, Van Goghs...'

Antony was not only an artist, but by the time Paul moved in, he was employing his talents as a junior school art teacher; one who – as Paul, in a rare lapse of consistency, admitted in his brief *Clash Songbook* autobiography – was conscientious enough to set his son extra homework because he wanted him to 'get on'. Furthermore, as Paul eventually revealed to Pat Gilbert in 1999, Antony was a committed and active communist who regularly leafleted the local area. Following the break up with Paul's mother Elaine, he had become involved in another steady relationship. Marion Clarke was 13 years Antony's junior, and just seven years older than Paul. This fact may have caused some tension in itself – though Paul has never alluded to it, or indeed to Marion – but she too was a schoolteacher, which at least suggests a certain maturity and stability.

In this educated, politically and socially conscious domestic environment, it is not beyond the realms of possibility that Paul was expected to help with various chores and work for his own pocket money. But to accept that – as he intimated during his early interviews as a member of the Clash – he was treated like a slave or that he was required to hand over all his pocket money to swell the family pot stretches credibility almost as far as *Monty Python*'s famous 'Four Yorkshiremen' sketch: 'You were *lucky*...'

As for his school experiences, even by February 1981, when he gave Chris Salewicz a rare solo interview for the *Face*, Paul was prepared to be a little less scathing. He recalled one particular teacher who was so keen for his pupils to do well that he abandoned all pretence of professional integrity. 'He was really good, this one bloke. He told us all the answers during the exam. Most still failed, though.' For all his earlier claims not to have anything to show for his formal education, Paul revealed to Chris that he had gained two O Levels, in Art and English, and further undermined the general public's view of him as barely literate by instigating a discussion about the work of Graham Greene. The author's *Brighton Rock*, it transpired, had been one of the texts on the Isaac Newton O Level syllabus, and Paul's own experience of teenage gangs had sharpened his interest in the machinations of central character Pinkie.

Pinkie might have made an impression, but most of the other heroes of Paul's mid-teenage derived from the silver screen, particularly those films – predictably enough – involving war, gangsters, guns and hard men. His curiously amoral adult interest in weaponry and violence was shaped more by movies like *Dirty Harry* than by his own skinhead activities. He grew out of the cult and its pastimes – 'Breaking things up gets a bit boring after a while. I started going out with girls. It's more fun' – but his fascination with the instant myth-making of Hollywood proved to be an enduring one. In 1978, he told *Negative Reaction* fanzine, 'I'd like to act in films like Clint Eastwood.' When he finally bought his own flat in Notting Hill, Paul decorated the walls with various rebel posters, shooting gallery targets in the shape of human silhouettes, cowboy six-guns and holsters. Chris Salewicz questioned him about a replica model of a German machine pistol propped up in the corner. 'It really seems like it's meant to be held. I just look on it as a work of art' was the not entirely successful attempt at justification.

The cinema was where the various strands of Paul's teenage interests came together: stimulating visuals, macho poses, cool styles, tough action and rebellion, yes, but also humour and creative expression. During a 1977 *Sounds* interview, Giovanni Dadomo eavesdropped on a fascinating Clash discussion about contemporary cinema, in which Paul switched without a significant change in tone from comparing the relative authenticity of the carnage depicted in two current war films, to an appreciation of the Woody Allen oeuvre, to enquiring whether anyone had yet seen *Fellini's Casanova*: 'What were the settings like? That's what I'm interested in.'

The former Isaac Newton School is now part of Kensington and Chelsea College, and no records of Paul's time there survive. If he completed his O Level courses on schedule, he should have left school at 16, in the summer of 1972. In the *Clash Songbook*, Paul stated: 'When I left school, I got a job in John Lewis carrying carpets.' Providing some background on the song 'Clampdown' for the 1988 *Melody Maker* Clash retrospective, he said, 'This was about shop-floor fascism, in so far as I worked in John Lewis carrying carpets, and not being a skilled worker, I did get the shit end of the stick.' By his own account, this dead-end job began to pall after a while, and so he decided to fall back on his one obvious talent and apply to art schools.

His dearth of qualifications held him back, but he eventually found a college, the Byam Shaw, that judged applicants solely on the quality of their portfolios. He was granted a scholarship by the local council, and so escaped from the daily grind to which he would otherwise have been condemned for life. In interviews he has always encouraged the presumption that he continued to live with Antony up to the time he started college.

The little factual evidence available suggests the truth has been bent to improve Paul's street credibility rating. Following Paul and Nick's move to Notting Hill, their mother Elaine had moved into a privately rented top floor flat at 18 Border Road, Lewisham, just two miles north-east of Paul's place of birth. The electoral roll also places Paul at this address for both 1974 and 1975, indicating that, by October 1973 at the latest, he had moved back south of the river to live with his mother once more, and that he continued to do so for much of the first year of his adulthood. This supposition is supported by the fact that, sometime in 1973, Antony and Marion – who was by now also using the surname Simonon, though the couple did not marry until November 1975 – took up residence in a flat at 63 Ridge Road, Hornsey, a move that presumably either precipitated or was made possible by Paul's departure.

He did indeed work for John Lewis, but the personnel records show that his two periods of employment at the department store's warehouse – then situated on the corner of Draycott Avenue and Ixworth Place in Chelsea – lasted from July to August 1973 and from June to August 1974. These are too brief, and too closely linked to traditional school and college summer vacations, for his carpet-carrying to have been anything other than a temporary holiday job. It appears Paul continued to attend school until the summer of 1973, presumably resitting O Levels; which in turn suggests that, however unsuccessful his efforts ultimately might have been, he was rather more serious about gaining the qualifications required by more conventional art schools than he has since chosen to admit.

In 1987, the Byam Shaw School of Art moved to 2 Elthorne Road, Archway, but in the early Seventies it was located at 2 Campden Street, Holland Park. Application is still by portfolio and interview, rather than by standard academic qualifications. Although several of the institution's staff remember Paul, once again the school's records do not go back far enough to provide any hard facts about his stay. It seems likely that his

Foundation year was bookended by his two stints at John Lewis, and that he began the Fine Art diploma course in October 1974.

'I was just hanging around a posh art college because I didn't fancy working in a factory,' Paul told *Record Mirror*'s Jan Kaluza in 1979. 'I spent a lot of time round rich girls' houses drinking wine with daddy.' Two years earlier, he told Chris Salewicz, 'It's great, because everybody there is rich. You can walk around the college, nick their paints, nick their canvases, and they don't really miss it because they can buy more. You don't get many working class kids like me and Mick going to art school. I used to draw blocks of flats and car dumps. I used to really hate Leonardo Da Vinci at first. I didn't understand him. Then I realised he'd do just a thumb and it would be the whole hand. That's what I tried to do.'

Wynn Jones, a tutor at the Byam Shaw, and Stephen Williams, an established artist who was based at the college during Paul's stay, remember things differently. The closest they come to agreeing with Paul is in allowing that his motivation was not as strong as it might have been. 'He wasn't prolific,' remembers Stephen. 'He did large paintings, and kept at them, but the commitment was 60 per cent rather than 100 per cent. There was a lot of prevarication. He wanted to finish the work, obviously, but put off doing so because he knew that meant having to start something else. My perception was that he was a "part time student": he didn't really know what he wanted to do.' Wynn picked up much the same signal. 'On reflection, I'm not sure that Paul was looking for anything as ambitious, demanding or as structured as a fine art course,' he writes. 'Perhaps, like many other young people who come to art school, he wanted a period of reflection, time to think about his life so far and to consider future options.' However, Stephen originally struck up an acquaintance with Paul because both were among the first to arrive at the college each morning, which indicates a degree of enthusiasm, and Wynn goes on to describe him as both 'clearly talented' and 'intense in his art'.

Stephen takes exception to the way Paul has portrayed the school over the years. He insists it was neither posh nor exclusive, Paul being by no means the only student on a scholarship. 'I remember reading some quote about the school being full of rich kids and him nicking their paints. There were some, sure, but there's some at every art school. The Byam Shaw had a very good cross-section of people from Newcastle, the East End, wherever, as well as the more aristocratic ones. A whole mixture of ages and social classes.' Paul had a relationship with one particular rich girl in which he might well have been cast as the Bit of Rough, but the role was hardly thrust upon him. 'I think he liked that,' comments Stephen, wryly. It was certainly not the last time Paul would play the part.

Contrary to the idea he gives of himself as a jack-the-lad working class scourge of the ineffectual posh twits, Paul was one of the more retiring pupils. 'I remember him as a quiet, modest young person,' writes Wynn. Stephen, who had more social contact with Paul, tends to concur: 'He was a very quiet, shy individual. Not at all extrovert, although he became more so. At parties, after a few jays [joints] and drinks, he'd come out with stuff in a group. He hung around with a rowdy crowd, but he was one of the quieter, more sensible ones. I find it hard to believe that the anger he expressed in the Clash was deeply felt.'

What little friction there was at college developed out of Paul's stubbornness regarding his work, which, according to both Wynn and Stephen, differed greatly in both subject matter and style from Paul's subsequent description. 'He had early on developed a fascination for the Pre-Raphaelite painters, and everything he did was strongly influenced by this, which made him quite difficult to teach in the sense of introducing him to a wide range of issues and alternative ideas,' writes Wynn. 'I do think that his preoccupation with the Pre-Raphaelites made it difficult for some tutors to engage with him, and perhaps there was eventually an element of frustration on both sides.' 'Paul was very stylised,' says Stephen. 'Large composite paintings. Very Romantic. I remember a

Bayeux Tapestry-type painting in Pre-Raphaelite colours which told a story of a battle, or fighting a dragon, or something. He didn't want to be influenced in his work. He was very defensive, to keep the tutors away.'

By the time of the Clash's first London gig on 13 August 1976, Paul had decorated the wall of the band's rehearsal studio with a mural depicting a car dump overlooked by tower blocks and the Westway. An image of urban decay, it was more in keeping with punk's new brutalism than the pastoral romanticism of the Pre-Raphaelites. *This* was the kind of subject he later claimed to have been drawing while at art school. 'That might have been in his mind,' says Stephen, 'but the manifestation of it was hard to find at the time.'

The beginning of the end of Paul's life as an art student was a chance street meeting with Mick Jones one day towards the end of 1975. Mick was still trying to complete the line-up of the final version of the London SS. 'We just sort of bumped into each other,' Paul told *Rolling Stone*'s James Henke in 1980. 'I was going out with this girl, and she was friends with this drummer, and Mick invited this bloke to rehearsal.' Paul went along to provide moral support, but following a nudge from Bernie, Mick persuaded him to audition for the vacant vocalist's job.

By his own admission, at that point Paul had never even seen a live rock'n'roll band and he knew nothing about the New York Dolls or the MC5. He was not even much of a dandy during his time at the Byam Shaw. 'It was just jeans, boots and a T-shirt, really,' says Stephen Williams. 'I remember I had some Texan [cowboy] boots which he liked, and they had got too small for me, so I sold them to him for a fiver. He wore them to death.' The invitation was therefore extended on the strength of Paul's good looks and natural poise rather than any shared sub-cultural affiliation. For his part – although he himself still preferred to wear his hair short – Paul was considerably more tolerant of long-haired types than he had been in his skinhead days. Intrigued rather than wildly enthusiastic, he took up the London SS offer.

Instead of making it easy for him, the band put him through his paces on a couple of songs that were unfamiliar to Paul and would have qualified as obscure by anyone's standards. One of them was the Standells' 1967 garage classic 'Barracuda', which includes the immortal line, 'I'm a young barracuda, don't you mess with me.' The other was Jonathan Richman's 'Roadrunner'. Although Richman's band, the Modern Lovers, had recorded the song in 1972, it was not to be released officially until 1976; 'Roadrunner' might have been destined to become a rock classic, but at the time of Paul's audition it was available only on bootleg. (According to Glen Matlock, the Sex Pistols were also covering the song in late 1975.) For both numbers, Paul – shy whenever in strange surroundings, and now completely out of his depth – just stood in front of the microphone, and chanted the few words he had managed to pick up over and over again. The result was not a great success, even forgetting the obvious limitations of the Simonon singing voice. 'He didn't get the gig,' Tony James told Pete Frame for his London SS Family Tree. 'Didn't really have enough stage presence.' Pausing long enough only to engage in the obligatory edgy verbal exchange with Bernie, Paul said what he thought was his goodbye to rock'n'roll and left.

He remained in casual contact with Mick though, and in late March of the following year – after the London SS had split – Mick suggested that Paul consider learning an instrument in order to join the new band he was intending to put together. Paul later discovered that the overture had been prompted by Bernie, who remained impressed enough by his looks and attitude to overlook his lack of any conventional musical talent. There was also the precedent set by Richard Hell, who had learned bass from scratch to join the Neon Boys, the forerunners of Television. The plans to bring Hell to London, pair him with Mick, and build a band around them had only recently been scrapped. Paul was physically not dissimilar to the American, and with a look that – more by accident than design – combined elements of both the Sex Pistols (short hair and tough demeanour) and the New York Dolls (rail-thin physique and pretty-boy features), he was close to ideal raw material for both Bernie's and Mick's dream bands.

It is perhaps not immediately obvious why Paul went along with the suggestion, especially after his London SS auditioning experience. That had been a spur of the moment thing, not particularly serious, and hardly successful enough to give him the rock'n'roll bug. He still had no real passion for the music, so why agree to put himself out in order to join a rock band? For a start, Paul was not unaware of the workings of popular culture, and he coveted the kind of attention that came with success in that field. In 1977, Joe Strummer told Caroline Coon that, 'for Paul, the Clash is a chance for him to strut his stuff', and in his contemporary *NME* feature Tony Parsons suggested Paul was in the band because 'it gets him laid a lot'. While both observations might well have contained elements of the truth, they did not represent the full extent of Paul's interest.

It was accompanying Mick to see the Sex Pistols at the Nashville on 3 April 1976 that won Paul over to the idea of punk and hardened his resolve to team up with the guitarist. Like Mick, Bernie and an increasing number of other regular attendees at Pistols shows, he saw the potential in, and felt the excitement of, a scene-in-the-making. Punk was not only about being famous and adored, but also about self-expression and self-realisation, and it was provocative to boot. Here was something that – to a physically oriented 20 year-old – was far more vital, dynamic and of-the-moment, and had far greater potential for reaching an audience than anything that could be created with paint and canvas. 'You know, you'd do a painting, and people'd love you for a week,' he told Chris Salewicz. 'But you're just in a room playing with your own ego. You're not really communicating. That's why I started playing music.' On other occasions, his rejection of his former medium of expression was total. 'Art is dead,' he told *Record Mirror*'s Jan Kaluza in 1979. 'It's not the way to reach the kids, rock'n'roll is.'

The band that became the Clash and the punk scene in general offered Paul somewhere to belong, another gang, another subculture, and one with a difference: they allowed a brooding James Dean figure to become a Rebel With A Cause. Whereas being a skinhead had been about destruction and negativity, what the Clash represented to him can best be summed up by two slogans that, in late 1976, he stencilled onto his instrument and his jacket sleeve respectively: 'POSITIVE' and 'CREATIVE VIOLENCE'. In 1979, he told *Creem*'s Stephen Demorest, 'I always wanted to be a guitarist, he's the one that looks really exciting. But when I met Mick, I couldn't sing. I couldn't do fuck all: I was useless. About all I could do was break things. But he encouraged me; I used to go round his house, and he played records to me.'

He also attempted to teach Paul some simple guitar chord shapes, but after just one painfully trying session, they came to the conclusion it would be easier for Paul to take up bass. There were two less strings to worry about, and he would be able to play individual notes rather than have to learn chords. Paul borrowed – and later bought – Tony James's spare bass, a cheap and not particularly convincing Fender copy. In order to help him find his way around it, he painted the more commonly used notes on the fretboard, under the relevant strings. In 1978, Mick laughingly told the *NME*'s Nick Kent that he gave Paul lessons 'for all of three days. Which meant that Paul got pissed off after those three days and would go away, and then return some days later to try again.' In addition to the sessions with Mick, he practised diligently on his own, playing along with reggae records and, following its release on 24 April 1976, the Ramones' eponymous début album.

It did not come naturally: Paul was still using his Play As You Learn bass when the Clash signed with CBS in late January 1977; Mick often had to cross the stage at Clash gigs to tune it for him between numbers; and Paul continued to play basslines devised and taught to him by Mick until at least 1979. Bill Barnacle – who guested on 1980's *Sandinista!* album, and whose sons Gary, Steven and Pete got to know the rest of the Clash in 1978 via their old schoolfriend Topper Headon – offers a possibly apocryphal anecdote as an illustration of Paul's limited skills. Apparently, halfway through one particular rehearsal, Mick preceded the next song on the list by yelling his customary '1,2,3,4…' while the bassist was still taking a drag on his cigarette. Paul quickly moved his hands to his instrument. Even after he started to play, though, something still sounded horribly wrong. When the band made it to the end of the song, everybody stopped on time except Paul, who hit two extra notes. 'Why did you finish two bonks after everybody else?' demanded Joe. 'Because I fuckin' *started* two fuckin' bonks after every fucker else!' came the defiant retort.

Just because he could not hope to become technically proficient overnight, Paul saw no reason to assume the traditional British bassist's role of strong silent type, standing impassively off to one side and allowing the guitarists and vocalist to hog the limelight. He decided to be a grandstanding performer from the off, wearing his bass low on his thigh Dee Dee Ramone-style, and jerking it around with a studiedly casual violence strongly reminiscent of Richard Hell. When, in 1978, Paul told Chris Salewicz, 'I want to be able to stick the bass behind my neck and play it like Jimi Hendrix played the guitar', it was the showmanship rather than the virtuosity to which he was referring. His musical ambition was the rather more modest one of fluent simplicity. His conflation of the Ramone and Hell approaches to the bass was subsequently plagiarised by both his friend Sid Vicious and Joy Division/New Order's Peter Hook. Although he has little respect for Paul's musical skills, Hooky is more then willing to give credit where it is due in other areas: 'What a strap length!'

Despite the London punk scene's Year Zero mentality and its intense rivalry with the New York scene, the Sex Pistols and the Clash were always happy to acknowledge the influence of the Ramones. This was probably because the band portrayed themselves as such two-dimensional cartoon characters they represented no artistic threat to the altogether more self-conscious and self-important London bands. Richard Hell, on the other hand, took himself equally seriously. In order to discourage the media from identifying New York as the place of origin of so many of UK punk's preoccupations, and Hell as the movement's nihilistic John the Baptist, his numerous contributions to both style and content were either played down or denied altogether.

As early as 1974, Richard was modelling the violently chopped hairstyle that was subsequently adopted by Johnny Rotten, Paul Simonon and Sid Vicious – inspired by a tousle-haired photograph of the teenage French poet Arthur Rimbaud – and was taking the stage in ripped T-shirts and wearing safety pins as jewelry. Johnny still refuses to admit an influence, and in his 1993 autobiography *Rotten: No Irish, No Blacks, No Dogs*, as elsewhere, he made a credible-enough case for having independently developed his own dyed spike-top and safety pin look. But Malcolm McLaren had brought back a flyer for the February 1975 Television residency at CBGB's to decorate the wall of Sex. In his autobiography, *I Was A Teenage Sex Pistol*, Glen Matlock admitted it was seeing the title of the Hell song 'Blank Generation' on that very same flyer that prompted him to write 'Pretty Vacant', so introducing UK punk to the lyrical theme that would go hand in hand with its characteristic pose of studied indifference. The flyer also featured a photograph of the band on stage, a spike-haired, ragged-clothed, beshaded Hell leaping into the air with his legs akimbo.

Paul teamed up with Mick in the last term of his second year of the Diploma course, but rehearsals only really began to demand all his time at the start of the summer vacation. By October 1976, when he was due to commence his third year at art school, the Clash had already played their first few gigs and received their first enthusiastic write-ups. This meant it was no great wrench for Paul to leave Byam Shaw. 'I was sorry to see Paul go as he was clearly talented, and an unusual and engaging personality,' writes Wynn Jones. 'I was delighted to hear of his great success with the Clash, and also surprised, as he had given no hint of his musical activities whilst a student!'

Although he would be closely involved in poster, clothing and record sleeve design, save for the car dump mural, one or two similar, contemporary paintings and the odd outrageous cartoon caricature of Bernie Rhodes, Paul effectively abandoned painting and drawing for much of the first six or so years he was with the Clash. This, along with his 'art is dead' pronouncement, goes a long way towards explaining why he was never offered the opportunity during that time to give that 'big art lecture' that might have convinced interviewers he was more than 'a thicko from south London'.

Back in April 1976, Paul's bass lessons by no means guaranteed him a place in Mick's new band. The day before *The Ramones* was released, the first substantial Sex Pistols interview, by *Sounds'* Jonh Ingham, hit the streets. In it, Malcolm McLaren acknowledged that unusual new bands had a difficult time getting signed by record companies. 'No-one came to sign up the Stones [in the early Sixties], no-one wanted to know. But when they saw a lot of bands sounding like that with a huge following, they had to sign them.' Malcolm wanted something similar to happen in the London of 1976; or rather, he wanted something similar to the current New York new wave scene, and the London R&B scene of a decade earlier was a convenient cover for the real source of his inspiration. Both Mick and Bernie were keen to get a band up and running, and be part of the new London scene Malcolm envisaged. Consequently – as Mick admitted in the *Clash On Broadway* booklet – they were trying out as many candidates as possible, and Paul, like Chrissie Hynde, was just one of them.

Mick's old schoolfriend, John Brown, co-founder of both the Delinquents and Little Queenie/Violent Luck, believes he might have been another, though he was still with the latter band at the time. Mick phoned him out of the blue, and invited him around to Wilmcote House to listen to his new songs. John was impressed, especially with 'Protex Blue', but less convinced by the accompanying spiel. 'He started going on about the political edge to what he was going to do, digging around to see what my reactions would be to stuff like that,' says John. 'Mick's a very proud guy. I don't think he could have asked me. I'd have to have said, "Look, I really want to get involved with this." And I think he perceived what I was giving out, really: I'm not interested in that. Not sloganeering. To me, it's "Fuck art, let's dance!"' John was subsequently approached separately by both Mick and Bernie to help out with Paul's bass lessons; although he agreed, the matter was not pursued.

Mick was also still buttonholing interesting looking strangers at gigs. 'Viv [Albertine] and I met Mick at a Roxy Music concert,' recalls Alan Drake. 'We were standing together, and we always used to dress outrageously. He just came over and started talking to us, and we thought he was pretty cool, pretty crazy. After the gig we went off to this little café he told us about. He had an expression he kept using at the time: "Oh, it's great. It's really *rock'n'roll*!"' Viv had seen Mick walking around Chelsea School of Art, but they had not talked prior to this meeting. She and Alan had once been girlfriend and boyfriend, but were now simply friends sharing a squat together at 22 Davis Road, Shepherds Bush, a few hundred yards from the art school's Lime

Grove site. 'It was a street of houses split into an upstairs flat and a downstairs flat,' says Alan. 'We had the upstairs flat. A friend lived next door, and told us about this house that had been empty for ages. I just broke into it. We lived there for nearly a year.'

Mick was soon a regular visitor. 'He just became a good friend, and used to come around all the time. Then he and Viv started an affair, so he practically lived at the place.' In spring 1976, Alan and Viv also began attending Sex Pistols gigs. Inspired by the band and by Chrissie Hynde, Viv bought her own instrument, and Mick found he had another pupil. 'Suddenly, from wanting to be an artist, she was thrown into this world of rock'n'roll and loved it, you know,' says Alan. 'She's a real perseverer. Whereas I would lose patience within five minutes, and then throw the guitar across the room because I couldn't get the sound I wanted, she'd just stick at it and stick at it.'

In spite of her commitment, it is unlikely that Viv was ever really a serious candidate for Mick's band. Alan was in with a better chance, being another pretty boy with the Bowie fan's almost obligatory love of dressing up. 'I used to get a lot of people coming up to me and asking me if I would be the singer in their band just because of the way I looked. It might sound conceited, but that's just the way it was. Mick liked the way I looked and everything, and so we thought it'd be ideal for me to be a vocalist.' They rehearsed together at Davis Road. 'But Mick was just so intense: he'd stop every two minutes to tell me, "This is very important", and I'd say, "I know Mick, I *know*! Let's just get on with it and do it." I just couldn't handle his approach to it all. As far as I'm concerned, rock'n'roll, up to a certain point – I mean, I'm not an idiot – should just happen. He was so incredibly *fanatical*, it all had to be right. I used to say, "Well, it will be…" In the end, I just kind of slipped away and stopped doing stuff with him.'

Another regular visitor to the Davis Road squat was Alan's old friend and fellow Bowie fan Keith Levene. 'We'd known each other since we were school kids,' says Alan. 'We were both from east London originally, then I moved to north London and so did he. He lived literally over the road from me. He was a few years younger, and when you're like 13, 14, just three or four years can make so much difference. I used to hang out more with his older sister, but Keith was pretty cool for his age, even when he was 11. He taught himself to play guitar. He's a genius, a really clever guy. He teaches himself things. He'll look at something, and the next minute he can work it out completely. Anyway, as he got older, we used to hang out together, and then we became inseparable.'

Keith claims to have been '17 going on 18' when he first encountered Mick, but in fact he was two years older than that. Pale, sharp-featured and edgy to the point of aggressiveness, his precocious talent as a guitarist was accompanied with an ambition almost as intense as that of his new acquaintance. 'I met Mick Jones, otherwise known as Rock'n'Roll Mick, got on really well with him,' says Keith. 'The main thing we had in common was we knew we really, really wanted to get a band together. That was it.' In the *Clash On Broadway* booklet, Mick revealed that it was again 'probably' Bernie who encouraged him to join forces with Keith, who might not have been such a glamourpuss as Paul, but certainly had attitude to spare.

Paul had been spending more and more of his time with Mick, cycling over from Campden Road to Lime Grove to hang out with him. As Davis Road increasingly became the focus of Mick's life, so too did Paul become a regular fixture there. Early in May, a decision was made: Mick introduced Paul to Keith as the third member of their band. Although he had scant respect for conventional notions of musical proficiency himself, Keith was not exactly ecstatic to hear the news. 'He couldn't play bass, but he was a good artist,' he recalls, somewhat sardonically. 'He came across thick, but apparently wasn't.'

Paul had left home the previous summer. Shortly afterwards, his mother had married for a second time, to Michael Short, who moved in with her at the Border Road flat.

Although there seems to have been no bad feeling involved on his part, Paul's family ties slackened thereafter to the point where, in November 1976, he could tell Caroline Coon, 'I get on all right with my parents, but I don't see them very much.' In May of that year, the opportunity to live rent free with his new friends proved a tempting one, and he moved into the small front bedroom of the Davis Road squat. Initially, rehearsals either took place there or in Mick's equally tiny bedroom in Wilmcote House. 'We used to show Paul where to put his fingers, and play the electric guitars acoustically, and that was a band rehearsal,' laughs Keith. 'Talk about a long shot, man!'

During waking hours, Alan's room was co-opted by Bernie for use as an office. As the whole household was now on close terms with the Sex Pistols camp, Alan maintains it was transparently obvious where most of Bernie's ideas were coming from. 'Basically, Bernie Rhodes was an arsehole, and whatever Malcolm McLaren did, Bernie would be round in a flash, and he'd say, "We've got to do this, we've got to do that," because Malcolm had done the same thing like three hours before. He'd dash back sometimes at 12 at night to my place – knowing that most of them would be there – with another idea he'd nicked off Malcolm. Give him his due: he had enough suss to realise, and jump on the bandwagon quick.'

Davis Road soon turned into a meeting place for members of the nascent punk scene. Glen Matlock found it too squalid, but Johnny Rotten's friend John Beverley, soon to be rechristened Sid Vicious, was less fastidious. He became a frequent visitor, and eventually moved in. The others got on well with him, especially Paul, but, according to Alan, 'Mick used to find Sid a bit too much.' This was at least partly because Sid became a little too friendly with Viv for Mick's liking. In addition to members of the Pistols and their followers, the household also used to hang out with Rat Scabies. As ever with Mick's circle, Saturday afternoons were spent on the Portobello Road.

One particular drinking session that May led indirectly to a moment of solidarity so memorable that it subsequently entered Clash mythology as Significant Event One in the birth of the group. Mick has told the anecdote several times, most notably on the 1989 TV programme *That Was Then, This Is Now*. Paul recounted it in the *Clash On Broadway* booklet. Here is the Rat Scabies version: 'I always remember, we went down to the top of Portobello Road, and they were doing these really gaudy leather coats for about £1 each that someone had sprayed pink and bright yellow. And everyone bought one. And there was like, me and Keith and Mick and Paul Simonon, just walking down the road, and Mick said, "Oh, look: we're in a band!" And we all wore 'em together to some dreadful party that night.'

Hanging around together in matching day-glo leather carcoats might have increased everyone's sense of unity, but there were still a couple of gaps to fill in the line-up before it was a proper band. Rat was already committed to working with Brian James, so his membership was honorary. More immediately vital than finding a drummer, though, was the acquisition of a frontman and singer. Mick was still approaching likely-looking candidates at gigs. 'There were several guys who came along to try out to be the vocalist,' recalls Alan. According to Keith, one of them was 'This awful singer that was like a Mick Jagger clone from High Wycombe. We did a few rehearsals with him, but he wasn't really working out.'

Unable to play at any volume at Davis Road – in the 1977 Clash song 'Garageland', the line 'Complaints, complaints, what an old bag!' refers to the legitimate tenant of the downstairs flat – the embryonic band would sometimes scrounge a couple of hours in the Sex Pistols' Denmark Street rehearsal room, but this was hardly satisfactory. Then Bernie remembered Wally Nightingale. Hammersmith Council had given Wally's father the contract to clear out the BBC's former Riverside Studios in Crisp Road. When Bernie had worked with the Sex Pistols, and Wally had still been in that band, they had taken advantage of this connection to use one of the Riverside's former soundtrack-dubbing rooms for rehearsals. That arrangement had terminated at the same time as Wally's involvement in the Pistols – necessitating the move to Denmark Street – but when Bernie re-established contact, Wally proved happy enough to rent out the studio on a temporary basis.

The 'Jagger wannabe', whose name was Billy Watts, appears with Mick, Keith, Paul and – to make up the numbers – Alan in some would-be promotional photographs taken outside the Davis Road squat in mid-May. One of these shots has all five posing with guitars and bass in the street. Much later, when the embarrassment it could cause was deemed to be minimal, it was used as a still in *That Was Then, This Is Now* (with Billy Watts cropped out), and as an illustration on page 22 of the *Clash On Broadway* booklet. A second snap shows the 'band', minus Keith, on the stairs leading down from the squat's back door. This photograph made its unsanctioned public début considerably earlier than the other, turning up in an August 1978 issue of the *NME* as that week's Blackmail Corner item.

As well it might, because, like the other photo, it captures its subjects in a period of transition not quite far enough advanced to justify their view of themselves as sartorial scene-setters. Alan is wearing a bomber jacket, T-shirt and baseball-boots in a vaguely Ramones-style, but his hair is straight, centre-parted and shoulder-length, recently dyed blond in a manner reminiscent of *Raw Power*-era Iggy Pop, and his baggy jeans are gathered into his ankles with bicycle clips. Billy has on a tight black suit and a white shirt worn with a skinny tie in apparent emulation of Patti Smith on the *Horses* album cover, but although his white plimsolls and centre-parted curtain of long, wavy hair could possibly be ascribed to the Ramones influence, somehow they manage to look just plain naff. Keith is also sporting viciously tapered trousers, a skinny tie and a three-button Oxfam jacket – all of which pass the Patti punk test – but he too lets himself down at the extremities, this time with unstyled, shoulder-length hair and zip-sided stack-heeled boots.

Paul is the only one with a punk coiffure – a slightly less-perfect version of his later spike-top – and is also wearing a skinny tie at half mast, plus a pair of granny-style sunglasses, as introduced to the rock'n'roll world in 1965 by the Byrds and subsequently adopted by the New York new wave and Johnny Rotten. Sadly, the remainder of his ensemble consists of a tight-fitting and tight-waisted bum-freezer jacket in a broad pinstripe, and a pair of dark Oxford bags commodious enough to obscure whatever he might be wearing on his feet. The ensemble as a whole is halfway between Richard Hell and David Bowie's then-current 'plastic soul' look. Mick is by far the most coolly attired of all. Unfortunately, he is coolly attired for 1974: Keith Richards hair and Ian Hunter shades, waistcoat over collarless shirt and necklace, and – although most people interviewed for this book remember him wearing drainpipes from late 1975 onward – tight flared trousers.

One of the London SS ads had asked for a Jagger-style singer, and Keith maintains that Mick was happy enough with Billy, someone who fitted that description. Mick still fancied himself as a Keith Richards lookalike, and the photos do suggest that it was hard for him to let go of his past musical infatuations in order to move on; the others could be accused of being copyists too, but at least they were fumbling towards plagiarising something new. Although Keith claims that the band was still nameless at the time, the photo that appeared in Blackmail Corner was captioned 'the Young Colts', which also suggests transition with its echoes of the Rolling Stones' 'Wild Horses', Patti Smith's *Horses* and the Sex Pistols.

Bernie might have already annexed the ideas department, but it was clearly Paul who was the quickest to respond to the sartorial breakthroughs of both the New York new wave and the domestic punk scene. Acknowledging that Mick 'had a lot of good ideas himself', Alan nevertheless adds, 'he did a few things that he really didn't want to do.

But he could see what was happening. Paul didn't need any telling how to look. He always knew how to look good.' Shortly after the photos were taken, Keith followed Paul's lead and had his hair cut short. Mick refused to go any further with his than Chrissie Hynde had already taken it, but it would appear that Billy opted for some kind of trim, too: by the time Terry Chimes encountered the band in late May 1976, the new look might not have taken over completely, but it was dominant enough to make an impression on both him and the general public.

It was some six months after Terry's original audition for the London SS when he finally received the follow-up call. 'Bernie said that Mick had passed his apprenticeship, whereas the other members of the London SS hadn't,' he recalls. 'And he was now in a situation where he needed a drummer to complete this new set-up. So I went down to play with them, and this time it was at Riverside Studios.' The audition was not a lengthy one, and the only song Terry can remember rehearsing is 'I Can't Control Myself' by the Troggs, one of the few UK bands who could have claimed to be punks in the Sixties. As not much polite chat was forthcoming, Terry's perception of the band he was playing with was based on visual information. The others kept their heads down, but even in rehearsal, Billy Watts was an extrovert performer. 'He made some really weird contortions of his face, which was quite… *interesting!*'

Such Jaggeresque mannerisms were too old-school for what Bernie had in mind, and Billy's time was not to be long. A suitable replacement was found shortly after Terry's audition, whereupon Billy was sacked. He went on to form his own band called the Reds, who Bernie included on one or two of the bills for gigs he promoted in 1978 under the Club Left banner. Terry knew nothing of this upheaval as he did not hear from Bernie again for two or three weeks. What stuck in his mind while he was waiting for the call was not so much the band's music, but the impact that they had on passers-by in the street. 'When we walked from where we met – which was some caff or something – to the studio, it was quite a long walk across Hammersmith, everyone was looking at us, and that struck me at the time. Everyone was staring at this group of people. It was like at your school, when you had a gang, and you could be identified as a member of that gang, sortathing.' Paul Simonon was already feeling right at home.

4
I GET AROUND

If Mick Jones's rock dreams were shaped by an early Seventies notion of rock'n'roll stardom, then Joe Strummer's had their origins in the mythology created by the lifestyles and lyrics of the blues, folk, R&B and rock'n'roll performers of between 10 and 40 years earlier. For Joe, they were a means of distancing himself from his middle class British origins. Of his real background, Robin Crocker says, 'It caused Joe a lot of problems. In terms of his personality, it's been a big dilemma for him always. He's always been very torn, felt very guilty.'

Joe's paternal grandfather, Frederick Adolph Mellor, was an official on the Indian Railway, based in Lucknow. It was there that Joe's father, Ronald Ralph Mellor, was born in December 1916. 'His father died when he was eight, so he went to an orphan school,' Joe told *Melody Maker*'s Caroline Coon in 1977. By that time, Joe's street credibility was already coming under fire from some quarters, and in the interview with Caroline, he set out to validate his position. While he gave the appearance of talking openly and frankly about his personal history, this was not strictly the case. When he spoke about his father, Joe made much of Ronald's humble origins and did his best to play down his achievements. In his version, Ronald was smart enough to win a scholarship to the 'poxy' University of Lucknow in India. He then came to London, where he worked his way up in the Civil Service from a 'junior bum' to a 'not-so-junior bum', before reaching the high point of becoming a 'diplomat going overseas'.

In fact, the Second World War insisted on a lengthy interruption to this sequence of events. Ronald served in HM Forces from 1942 to 1947, and it was not until the age of 30 that he joined the Foreign Office as a Clerical Officer. On 22 October 1949, he married Anne Girvan, known as Anna, the 34-year old daughter of David MacKenzie, a farmer from Bonar Bridge, Scotland. Following her divorce from first husband, Adam Girvan, she had been working in London as a State Registered Nurse. Ronald and Anna set up home together at 22 Sussex Gardens, Paddington. On 17 March 1951, Anna gave birth to their first son, David Nicholas Mellor. That same year, Ronald received his first posting abroad, and the family moved to Ankara in Turkey.

It was here that the future Joe Strummer was born John Graham Mellor on 21 August 1952. Ronald was transferred to Cairo in 1954, and two years later the family relocated to Mexico City. 'My earliest memory is of a huge earthquake in Mexico City,' Joe told Gavin Martin for *Uncut* in 1999. 'There was a big column in the centre, and a huge angel had fallen from the top.' In 1957 they moved yet again, this time to Bonn. Although the description 'junior bum' does not do Ronald's position justice, it is true that none of his early postings could be considered high-profile.

For his sons, the frequent moves established a pattern of removal from a familiar environment followed by introduction to an alien one. Friendships were fleeting, and a sense of security based on the notion of a stable home was difficult to maintain. In such circumstances, the tendency is for children to become increasingly self-reliant, or, conversely, introverted and insecure. It is not unreasonable to suppose that the manner in which the two Mellor brothers coped with both their early nomadic existence and the next, equally traumatic, stage of their upbringing had much to do with shaping their respective characters and fates…

In 1959, when David was eight and John six going on seven, Ronald brought the family back to Britain while he commenced another three-year stint at Foreign Office head-quarters in Whitehall. Rather than move back to the inner city with two youngsters, Ronald followed the trend of the times and elected to commute from suburbia. He bought a single-storey house at 15 Court Farm Road in Warlingham, a dormitory town 14 miles south of central London. It was to remain the Mellor family's UK base for the next 20 years. Number 15 was the property to which Joe was referring when, in 1977, he described his father's home to Caroline Coon as 'a bungalow in south Croydon'. Twenty-two years later, he was still talking it down to Gavin Martin, insisting that it only had four rooms, and a tiny kitchen with no washing machine.

The boys were sent to the primary school in nearby Whyteleafe, but this was only a temporary measure. The nature of his chosen profession dictated that Ronald would soon be posted overseas again. At the time, the belief was that, once the children of Foreign Office employees had reached a certain age, the best way to ensure they received a reasonably disruption-free education was to board them at public school. As such institutions are fee-paying, attendance has traditionally been perceived to say more about the wealth and social standing of the parents than the academic merit of the pupil. Although such an educational background might stand a person in good stead in the corridors of power and their minor tributaries, it tends to prove something of an embarrassment for would-be scourges of the establishment.

During the punk era, Joe was so worried about the threat his schooldays represented to his credibility that he constructed an elaborate five-part defence. Part one questioned that the school even qualified as 'public' in most people's perception of the meaning of that term. Joe stressed that it was co-educational, and preferred to describe it as a 'boarding school (with girls)', or, on another occasion, as 'a kind of private comprehensive'. Part two of Joe's case was that his and David's attendance was not an accurate reflection of their father's income: the fees were paid by the Foreign Office as a perk of the job.

Part three concerned itself with the school's, and young John's, lack of academic achievement. According to Joe, this was no institution offering a fast lane for the intelligent and patient coaching for the less gifted. It was – he told Caroline Coon in 1977 – a place where 'thick rich people sent their thick rich kids', and for Ronald in particular it represented something of a last resort. 'When I was eight, he made me sit all these exams for these flash public schools, but I failed the lot. Finally, I got into this other crummy school where they had this thing going, that if [one] brother [David] passed the entrance exam, his brother [John] was let in too.' Apparently, matters did not improve dramatically once he was in residence. 'I found that I was just hopeless at school,' he told *Rolling Stone*'s James Henke in 1980. 'It was just a total bore.' In 1999, Gavin Martin heard, 'I was the worst, 24th out of 24 the whole way through.'

Part four highlighted the anguish he suffered as a result of being separated from his parents between the ages of nine and 17; and not just during term time, as with other public school kids. In 1962, Ronald was posted to Tehran, and in 1966, after being promoted to Second Secretary of Information, he was sent to Blantyre, Malawi. Neither the Middle East nor southern Africa was close enough to make frequent visits a realistic proposition. For almost the entire duration of his schooldays, John only saw Anna and Ronald during the long summer holidays, when the Foreign Office would pay for his and David's return plane fares. In 1976, Joe expressed his hurt at being thus abandoned as anger towards the parties he considered responsible. 'It's easier, isn't it? I mean, it gets kids out of the way,' he told Caroline Coon. 'And I'm really glad I went, because my Dad's a bastard... I only saw him once a year. If I'd seen him all the time, I'd probably have murdered him by now. He was very strict.' By 1979, Joe's attitude had settled into a resigned melancholy at having missed out on a more family-oriented childhood. His lyric for the Clash song 'Lost In The Supermarket' refers explicitly to the lack of parental attention and consequent sense of isolation he experienced as a child in suburbia. In 1980, he told James Henke, 'It's not a lot to go back to, if you know what I mean. My Dad was working abroad, and my mother was tagging along. I don't think I really gave them a thought after a while.'

The fifth and final part of Joe's defence against having received any kind of preferential treatment was the bullying he experienced while at the school. 'On the first day I was surrounded and taken to the bathroom where I was confronted by a bath full of used toilet paper,' he told *Record Mirror* in 1977. 'I had to either get in or get beaten up. I got beaten up.' Nor was this a one-off initiation rite. 'I was a dwarf when I was younger, grew to my normal size later on,' the still fairly diminutive Joe informed *Melody Maker*'s Chris Bohn in 1979. 'But before then I had to fight my way through school.'

He mentioned regular beatings in several other interviews, and even after the Clash had split he continued to portray his schooldays as relentlessly dark and violent. On one occasion he likened them to 'eight years in the joint'. 'I went on my ninth birthday into a weird Dickensian Victorian world with sub-corridors under sub-basements, one light bulb every 100 yards, and people coming down 'em beating wooden coat hangers on our heads,' he told the *NME*'s Lucy O'Brien in 1986. While still with the Clash, he had always cast himself in the role of the downtrodden, the victim, as appropriate to the band's view of themselves as representatives of the oppressed masses. By 1986, however, he was prepared to reveal the self-perpetuating nature of ritualistic bullying. 'It brutalised me. When I got to a position of power, *I* was a bad guy. I remember slapping a guy – he was only nine or 10 – across the head – *ker-pow!* – and his National Health glasses falling off. Just 'cause he irritated me.'

For several years, it was impossible to judge the veracity of Joe's claims about his education, as he proved reluctant to volunteer the institution's name and location. In the November 1976 interview with Caroline Coon, he even tried to lay a false trail by claiming it was in Yorkshire. Not until the 1980 *Rolling Stone* interview did he admit that it was near Epsom, Surrey. It was October 1981 before he revealed its name to the *NME*'s Paul Rambali: the City of London Freemen's School (CLFS).

The CLFS was founded in central London in 1854 as a school for the orphan children of freemen of the City. In 1926, it moved out to its present location at Ashtead Park in Surrey, and the entrance requirements were modified accordingly. By September 1961, when the Mellor boys arrived, there were approximately 450 pupils, of which roughly 50 boys and 50 girls were boarders staying in two separate buildings, the boys' being known as Philp House. Joe's comments about CLFS's academic record do not hold up. The school currently boasts a success rate of over 85 per cent in GCSE and A Level examinations and Headmaster David Haywood dismisses any suggestion that standards were markedly lower in the Sixties.

Tom Critchley became a boarder at CLFS in September 1966. Although he was five years younger than John Mellor, his first four years at the school coincided with the latter's last four, and he remembers him well. In his recollection, physically at least, CLFS was not quite the Dotheboys Hall Joe has made it sound. 'In actual fact, to be growing up in 50 acres of parkland, which is basically what it was, with an old manor house and all that kind of nonsense, was fantastic.' Psychologically, however, it was somewhat less ideal, and Tom finds it easy to empathise with what he describes as the 'semi-orphaning process' experienced by David and John.

In the Sixties, the function of public schools was still very much to lay foundations for the future pillars of the establishment. Leadership qualities and team spirit were encouraged, and even some of the more disturbing ritualistic behaviour was tolerated in the name of tradition. CLFS was no different. 'It was the kind of school where you were either one of the people who played football, rugby, cricket and sang in the choir, and did the school plays, or you weren't,' says Tom. 'It was kind of participants or non-participants. And John was firmly *not* a participant in the regular kind of activities.' Such outsiders were given short shrift. Although he missed John's early years, Tom says, 'I wouldn't be surprised if he had been on the receiving end. His brother certainly had been, although by the time I got there, David was a bit too old to be bullied, if you know what I mean. But he was still regarded as being something a bit funny, a bit soft, because he was gentle. He was a loner.'

Having turned 16, David left CLFS in July 1967, at the end of Tom's first year, which meant the latter had less than 12 months to observe the Mellor brothers living under the same roof. Nevertheless, Tom got the strong impression that they were not close. 'John definitely didn't go out of his way to spend time with his brother,' he says. 'It's a difficult thing to say, but I sort of felt John was a bit embarrassed about him. But maybe what I was seeing was that he was frightened that he too could turn out like that, and therefore made himself into this more entertaining loner. Because he was a loner, too, but he was very, very funny, there's no doubt about that. Hysterically so. I remember him being in some particularly funny sketches at a DramSoc evening, which were quite *Monty Python*-esque. It's fair to say that his influences were generally more alternative than mainstream. He wouldn't perform in "regular" drama.'

Instead of using his wit as a means of buying his way into general popularity, John used it as a badge of rebellion. As with many defence mechanisms, it was at its most effective when employed as a means of attack. 'He used to hide behind his snarling lip and sharp, caustic humour,' says Tom. 'If you became the butt of it, he could be quite merciless, but never really to the point of viciousness.'

Acerbic humour might have protected John from what he considered to be the harsh realities of his existence, but he did have other avenues of escape. He read extensively, and perhaps understandably for a public schoolboy with a nomadic background, his favourite author was TE Lawrence. Although CLFS's remote location made keeping up with cinematic trends difficult, the pupils did get to watch older films on TV. In later interviews, Joe recalled both *Lawrence Of Arabia* and *Viva Zapata!* having a particular impact. He judged the former to be 'better than the book', and the latter's musical score brought back vague memories of his stay in Mexico City. Watching old Hollywood gangster and cowboy pictures certainly helped formulate his romantic vision of America and the wider world. As was also true for both Mick Jones and Paul Simonon, his ongoing interest in the cinematic arts would play no small part in the development of the Clash.

It is music, though, that Joe – again, like Mick – credits for rearranging his priorities in life. In his case, so he claimed in 1988 to the *NME*'s Sean O'Hagan, the transformation was due to one particular record: the third Rolling Stones single, released in February 1964. '"Not Fade Away" sounded like the road to freedom! *Seriously*. It said, "LIVE! ENJOY LIFE! FUCK CHARTERED ACCOUNTANCY!"' Joe might have felt obliged to reject the Stones while with the Clash, but once his own band had split, he was happy to set the record straight. 'They were definitely the first proto-punks. You can hear it all on those first few albums.'

Also in 1988, Joe made a *Desert Island Discs*-type contribution to Christine McKenna's show on KCRW, a college radio station in Santa Monica, California. At that great distance from both London and the Clash, he felt free to open up and enthuse about at least this one aspect of his time at CLFS. 'I'm going to try and spin records as they came to us in a small school 20 miles south of London in the late Sixties. This is my musical education,' he announced. 'I can even see at this moment the radio on its shelf on the wall of the Day Room. A nice big valve radio that boomed. We used to have it up loud.' First up, from 1964, was the Beach Boys' 'I Get Around'. 'You've all heard the Beatles and the Stones already,' said Joe. 'Obviously, they were cracking our heads, but also I was into the Beach Boys alone of all my friends, and I suffered a lot of ridicule for it.'

'I had "Rock'n'Roll Music" by the Beatles, and then I came across a Chuck Berry EP in Tehran, where my father was stationed,' said Joe. 'And I remember putting on Chuck Berry's "Rock'n'Roll Music" and comparing it to the Beatles and being a bit surprised that they hadn't written it.' The passionate EP sleevenotes were by none other than Guy Stevens. After learning all he could from these, young John began to pay more attention when reading band interviews in the music press. He soon discovered that the Stones and the Beatles spoke openly of their roots in R&B and the blues. This encouraged further historical research, leading him on to more records by Chuck Berry and Bo Diddley, both of whom – overlooking a brief period of denial in 1976-78 – were to remain lifelong favourites.

At this remove, it is perhaps difficult to imagine the impact the mid Sixties music scene must have had on not just John but all the pupils at CLFS. 'There was this aspect of being cut off from the outside world,' says Tom. 'Epsom was about the biggest fucking place you could go to, so it was quite strange. But people did go, and did get the records and all that.' Isolated communities are often so desperate for titbits from the outside world that their response to new cultural phenomena are quicker and more intense than those of people whose readier access encourages them to take such things for granted. CLFS was a classic hothouse environment: enthusiasm fed enthusiasm and competition fed competition. 'The release of new Beatles records, or whatever, was a really big thing,' says Tom. 'I think it was called the Hobbies Room, where the record player was, and everybody just flocked into there to hear new records.'

The 1967-68 Blues Boom, coinciding as it did with the onset of John's adolescence proper, marked the peak of his infatuation with popular music. 'That's just a coincidence, that we had a Blues Boom in '68, and I was 16, and that's when music hits you real good,' Joe told Christine McKenna and her listeners in 1988. 'It's like now, when you're 16 and you don't know nothing about hip hop, you're not hip in the schoolyard. For me, when I was young, it was blues. You had to know your blues if you wanted to be part of the in crowd at school.' As he was still largely a loner, the in crowd as far as John was concerned consisted of a few equally rabid music fans trying to outdo each other with the extent of their forays into the Mississippi Delta. 'We were sending away for Sonny Terry and Brownie McGhee records,' recalled Joe, after playing Sonny Boy Williamson's 'Bring It On Home'. 'I was always glad later that I had that grounding, that I knew Bukka White.'

By now, John was spending most of his free time with his ear pressed up against a small transistor radio and his eyes glued to the music press. 'He used to avidly consume the *Melody Maker* and seemed to have an encyclopaedic knowledge of contemporary music,' says Tom. It was something that would never desert Joe. In 1980, he told *Sounds* journalist Robbi Millar, 'You know, I listen to the radio and a record comes on and, click, I know *all* about that record. I think, "What's the use of knowing a million and one completely useless facts about rock'n'roll?" Most people forget them, but I seem to retain everything.' What John also picked up was a strong sense of rock'n'roll records and the medium of radio as his generation's principle forms of communication.

After playing their 1968 hit 'Do It Again' on KCRW, Joe explained how that song had vindicated his earlier championing of the Beach Boys. Although Joe's reminiscences might suggest otherwise, as it was a mixed school, CLFS was not as exclusively trainspotterly in its approach to popular music as an all-male school might have been. 'You used to have these weird mixed Socials on Saturday nights where the two boarding houses would get together,' recalls Tom. 'The Beach Boys were certainly very big at those.' As they did for the other boarders, the Socials gave John his introduction to the world of romance. Discussing his professed cynicism about the concept of 'love' with Caroline Coon in 1977, Joe told her that the last time he had experienced the emotion had been at the age of 16.

Along with the conventional love song, punk would do its best to rid the world of muso snobbery, and in the process succeeded in inverting the standards of the previous generation of musicians. Suddenly, it was the kiss of death to have been familiar with an instrument for more than a couple of years. In a 1980 interview for Radio Hallam, Joe went out of his way to make it clear how unmusical he had been at school. He said he had been thrown out of the choir, and that he 'couldn't even make it on a recorder' at the age of nine. In several other interviews over the years, he has claimed not to have started playing guitar until the age of 21. On more than one occasion, however, he has also contradicted himself (sometimes in the same interview) by saying he first came by a Spanish acoustic at 16. Which version is the true one depends on the rigidity of one's definition of 'playing guitar'.

John did indeed acquire a guitar in 1965, shortly after the Who enjoyed a hit with 'I Can't Explain'. It was given to him by a cousin who had been in a band named the Union at North Acton Grammar School when Pete Townshend – who the cousin claimed had been the instrument's previous owner – had been with rival outfit the Confederates. In the KCRW interview, Joe said, 'Cream had a two-note song, an old blues "Spoonful" [written by Willie Dixon] and everybody learned to go, "duh *duh* / duh *duh* / duh *duh*," and then Clapton went off into incredible improvisation for 20 minutes. So I got as far as the first phrase, and then when I heard him go "*diddlyduhdeedahdooweeoowweee*," I just threw the thing down and said, "Forget it!"' In truth, he persevered long enough to learn 'a few blues tunes', as he admitted to the *NME*'s Paul Morley in 1979. 'Although he played guitar, he didn't seem particularly brilliant,' recalls Tom Critchley. 'I remember somebody called Paul Buck, who John was friendly with, made a bass guitar in woodwork – it didn't have the normal body, it just had a block of wood [Bo Diddley cigar-box style] – and they used to jam together.'

For the duration of his A Level years, John shared a study room with Paul Buck. By this time they had their own record player. 'There was normally music being played,' says Tom. 'They were as thick as thieves.' Preferred listening for 1969, when John commenced his final year at school, was represented on Joe's KCRW special by a track from *Trout Mask Replica* by Captain Beefheart and his Magic Band. 'Out of nowhere, this dropped on our heads,' said Joe. 'That's when I became a weirdo.' Beefheart, real name Don Van Vliet, was a precocious artistic talent, having expressed himself as a sculptor and film maker before making his first recordings in 1967. One of Frank Zappa's cohorts, he started off with a psychedelic variation on R&B before really taking off into the musically avant-garde and the lyrically absurd on this, his third and most famous album. 'We sat in a dark room huddled over *Trout Mask Replica* for about eight or 10 months. We were pretty fed up of being at school at that point. Swinging London was happening only 25 miles up the road, but we were locked in behind walls and gates. Maybe it was an expression that we wanted to bust out of there.'

Beefheart's imaginative way with words and skewed, humorously shaded world-view caught the future Clash lyricist's attention at a particularly impressionable age. Certainly, the Captain's love of bizarre pseudonyms – his fellow members of the Magic Band were rechristened Antennae Jimmy Semens, Zoot Horn Rollo, Rockette Morton, Drumbo and the Mascara Snake – explains much about young John's subsequent fondness for bestowing unusual nicknames upon *his* friends and associates. It also partly explains why, when Paul Buck went out into the wider world, he did so as Pablo LaBritain, and why nobody other than representatives of officialdom would ever again know John Mellor by his given name.

In addition to Beefheart, Tom remembers John being particularly fond of the Mamas and the Papas. In retrospect, given the marked contrast between the vocal group's mellow style and the aggressive all-out assault of the Clash's early music, he finds this more than a little peculiar. Concurrent with the Blues Boom, folk rock was very much in vogue in the late Sixties. The Beach Boys had encouraged John's fondness for harmony and melody, and the blues had given him a bias towards rootsy and folksy American music in general. Just as the Rolling Stones had motivated him to backtrack and investigate the blues, so then over his last couple of years at school did the somewhat twee ditties of the Mamas and the Papas point him in the far more rewarding direction of Bob Dylan, Phil Ochs and Woody Guthrie, whose protest and social commentary songs – lyrically, at least – have far more in common with the output of the Clash.

'Yeah, you could call us a folk group,' Joe told the *NME*'s Sean O'Hagan in 1988, discussing the Clash. 'I came out of Woody Guthrie, in a way.' Indeed, upon his arrival in London, John would go one step further than Bob Dylan – who had merely borrowed Guthrie's singing voice, clothes and mannerisms – by adopting the folk singer's name. For the best part of six years from September 1970 onwards, everyone who met him would know him as Woody.

Young for his academic year, he was still 17 when he left CLFS in the summer of 1970. The school records do not go back far enough to detail his qualifications, but in 1981, Joe told the *NME*'s Paul Rambali, 'If you got three O Levels, you were top of the list. I got three: History, English and Art.' In the 1980 Radio Hallam interview, he said, 'I tried to do A Levels, but I only got Art.' He was subsequently accepted onto a Foundation course at the Central School of Art and Design, Southampton Row (now part of Central St Martin's School of Art), where the competition for places was hot: unless a would-be student's portfolio was of exceptionally high standard, the minimum academic requirement was five O Levels and/or two A Levels. It would be reasonable to assume that John was not quite the hopeless educational case he later felt punk required him to be.

Ronald and Anna Mellor returned to the UK for good in late 1969, whereupon Ronald was awarded the MBE. He continued as a Second Secretary at the Foreign Office in Whitehall until his retirement, aged 60, in 1977. In the FO, the MBE can be awarded for something as everyday as helping to arrange a royal visit; although hardly two-a-penny, it is not *that* rare a distinction for a long-serving FO official. Similarly, the rank of Second Secretary might sound rather grand to the uninitiated, but it is in fact a middling sort of grade. Nevertheless, his father's honour and title threatened considerable embarrassment to the outspokenly egalitarian punk-era Joe Strummer. He has never alluded to the MBE, and in the *Clash Songbook*, he described Ronald's position immediately pre-retirement as 'a white collar worker' in 'the Public Records Office'.

John spent the summer after he left school with Ronald and Anna in Warlingham, but this home life contact came too late to bind the family together. After eight years of regimented public school life, John was looking forward to freeing himself from his father's system of values. Although he would return a few times over the next year or two, he would gradually cut off contact with his parents thereafter, only re-establishing it during the latter days of the Clash.

As it turned out, John's identity change was by no means pure affectation. Before he could take up his place at the Central School of Art in September, something happened which quite understandably made him want to have as little as possible to do with any reminder of the youth that, while with the Clash, he would profess to having hated.

Since leaving CLFS three years earlier, John's brother David had not had an easy time. He had grown even more lonely and withdrawn, his morbid preoccupations encouraging a fascination with the National Front and the occult. At 18, David had begun to study chiropody, taking a room in a hostel at 15 Fitzroy Square, just off Euston Road in central London. Unfortunately, student life failed to bring him out of his shell, and his state of mind continued to deteriorate. In late July 1970, when he was just 19 years old, he crossed the road to Regents Park, sat down under a bush, and, according to Joe, 'took a hundred aspirins and some other tablets'. His body was found on 1 August, the official cause of death being registered as aspirin poisoning.

To his credit, the punk era Joe refused to exploit this tragedy to score credibility points. The story first came out by accident in 1977 when he was talking to Caroline Coon, and he only discussed it with one other journalist, the *NME*'s Chris Salewicz, during the band's career. He did not instigate the conversation on either occasion, and in both he gave much the same version of and unsentimental verdict on David's death. 'He was such a nervous guy that he couldn't bring himself to talk at all. Couldn't speak to anyone,' he told Chris. 'In fact, I think him committing suicide was a really brave thing to do. For him, certainly. Even though it was a total cop-out.'

Although Joe made the point that he and his brother were complete opposites, this would not have lessened the impact on him of the despair-induced death of the person who had provided his only day-to-day family contact from the age of nine to (almost) 15; especially as it occurred three weeks short of his own 18th birthday, just as he too was about to move up to London and live in a hostel. Even so, eight years later, the acknowledgement 'it happened at a pretty crucial stage in my life' was the full extent to which Joe could be drawn on the subject of his own grief.

Arriving in London in September 1970, Woody was now in a position to pursue further some of his hitherto constrained popular culture interests. He indulged his fondness for Robert Crumb comics and his taste for trash movies, the virtues of which he was still extolling when interviewed for *Creem* by Susan Whitall in 1980. He developed an allegiance to Chelsea football club, and began to attend gigs at the capital's music venues. In 2000, he told *Q* magazine that the first band he ever saw, in some club 'off Balham High Street' (probably the Castle, Tooting) was Mott the Hoople. Loath to praise Mick Jones's heroes while with the Clash, at that distance Joe was prepared to admit, 'It was magnificent. They were in their prime.'

London, however, had just about ceased swinging when Woody arrived: it was going into its post-Sixties comedown, something that did little to brighten his own mood. Listening to the radio at CLFS just two years before, songs like 'Street Fighting Man' had given him the impression that 'the whole world was exploding'. In Don Letts's 1999 documentary *Westway To The World*, he said, 'We took it all as normal, because there was no other frame of reference. By the time I reached London, the whole thing was over, which was a bit regretful.'

'Boy, that was the biggest rip-off I've ever seen,' was how he described the Central School of Art to *Rolling Stone*'s James Henke in 1980. 'It was a load of horny guys, smoking Senior Service, wearing turtle-neck sweaters, trying to get off with all these doctors' daughters and dentists' daughters who'd got on mini-skirts and stuff.' After the rigorously structured nature of life at CLFS, the 18 year-old Woody was looking for some genuine freedom, not what he considered to be the stale bohemian-by-numbers poses of his fellow pupils.

He did make friends, though. One of them, named Simon, shared a house at 18 Ash Grove, in the far-flung north London suburb of Palmers Green, with some other Central students and assorted associates. Although not a student himself, Clive Timperley secured his room there early in 1971 through a contact at the college. When he moved in, he brought along the friend who had spent the previous two months sleeping on the floor at Clive's previous flat, and who rejoiced in the unlikely-sounding name Tymon Dogg. 'Right from when I first met Woody, I was slightly in awe of him,' says Clive. 'A lot of people were. "Ooh, *Woody's* coming up for the weekend!" He turns up, and he's just a quiet guy. "*Do something*, then! What's the deal?" And then he did say something, and it was just a crack up! He always had a direct way of talking: he wouldn't say much, but what he did say was shattering.'

After Simon left, Woody took over his old room. 'He used to play little jokes,' recalls Clive. 'It was a bit like *The Young Ones*, that type of house. We were all out of our heads all the time, and he put a sign above the front door saying "VOMIT HEIGHTS", all written out nicely. It was this real suburban street, so it was quite amusing at the time.' In addition to alcohol, the more readily available drugs in those days were marijuana and LSD; a non-smoker at the time, Woody only dabbled with the former, but he relished the opportunity to experiment with acid. 'I took it about 35 times over a period of a couple of years,' he told *Melody Maker*'s Paolo Hewitt in 1980. He eventually gave it up after witnessing one bad trip too many. Although he never experienced the downside of acid himself, the drug played a part in his decision not to persevere with his studies at the Central. 'I was really shattered from this LSD pill, and I suddenly realised what a big joke it was,' he told James Henke in 1980. 'The professor was standing there telling everyone to make these little poofy marks, and they were all going, "Yeah," making the same little marks. And I just realised what a load of bollocks it was. It wasn't actually a drawing, but it looked like a drawing, and suddenly I could see the difference between those two things. After that, I began to drop right off.' In fact, he dropped right out.

Even in the period immediately following David's suicide, Woody did not discuss the subject freely, if at all. Despite knowing him well at that time, and for the next five years, Clive remained unaware of it until interviewed for this book. It is tempting to see Woody's leaving art school after just one year as not just the result of an acid insight, but also as a delayed and indirect reaction to his brother's death. Asked about David again in 1999 by Gavin Martin for *Uncut*, Joe replied, 'I still think about him a lot. He was withdrawn. It was a different world back then, no counselling or people to help you through. You just had to deal with it yourself.' Something which applied to both Mellor brothers.

Both Clive and Tymon were proficient and experienced performing musicians, but during his time at Ash Grove it seems that Woody was too inhibited to join in. Clive has no recollection of him playing an instrument while there, either with others or on his own. Three years older than Woody, and a guitarist himself, Clive had been playing live with various bands since joining Captain Rougely's Blues Band in 1965. Over the years, he had developed a style that was more technically accomplished than passionate. Although this approach to music was not to Woody's own tastes, he was not self-assured enough to dismiss it. Clive remembers one occasion when Woody came to see him at the famed Marquee club on Wardour Street, supporting Medicine Head as a member of a progressive rock band called Foxton Flight. 'He couldn't get over the fact that somebody he knew was playing at the Marquee and had got him on the guest list,' says Clive. 'He thought that was really cool. I said, "It's only a gig!" He said, "But it's the *Marquee*!" "It's only a gig, and we're supporting." "But you're *up there* and *playing*! What's it like?" Not to sound conceited, but it did affect him.'

Tymon was an altogether more idiosyncratic musician. He wrote his own strange, folk-type songs, and performed them on acoustic guitar, violin and harmonium. He could play the last two of these at the same time, holding the violin against his hip or the crook of his arm rather than his neck, and operating the harmonium with his feet. Deemed suitably eccentric, he had been signed up in the late Sixties by Apple, the Beatles' own newly-established label, and had subsequently suffered the same fate as most of the other artists involved with that disastrous enterprise. After an equally disappointing spell with the Moody Blues' label, Threshold, he had given up on the notion of mainstream success, and begun to support himself by busking on the London Underground.

The Ash Grove household broke up in mid 1971, just about the time Woody decided to leave art school. That the following couple of years are the most shadowy and vague in the Joe Strummer story has a lot to do with what happened next.

'I've been fucked up the arse by the capitalist system. Me, personally,' he told *Sounds'* Alan Lewis in 1980. 'I've had the police teaming up with landlords, beating me up, kicking me downstairs, all illegally, while I've been waving Section 22 of the Rent Act 1965 at them. I've watched 'em smash all my records up, just because there was a black man in the house. And that's your lovely capitalist way of life: "I own this, and you fuck off out of it!"' 'That was when he was living in Ridley Road in Harlesden,' confirms Clive. 'I think he moved there directly after Palmers Green. It was 1972. I wasn't living there, it was with some other people I didn't know, but they were evicted bodily. They sent the heavies round. All their goods, and all his records, were chucked out of an upstairs bedroom window into the garden. I lost touch with him for a brief period of time after that.'

Rather than transform him immediately into an angry young activist, the eviction, and loss of his beloved record collection, encouraged Woody to complete the process of dropping out from mainstream society that had begun with his leaving the Central. Like his adopted namesake, he became a drifter. 'I just went off and did absolutely nothing,' he told the *NME*'s Paul Morley in 1979. 'For at least two years, I was just bumming around. Everyone's got to bum around. I worked on a farm, but I stayed around London most of the time.'

He began to accompany Tymon on his busking expeditions, working as his 'bottler', or collector. 'It was like, I found out later, the apprenticeship of a blues musician. I got a real kick out of that,' Joe told Paul Morley. 'All the great blues players started out collecting the money for some master, to learn the licks. The guy I bottled for would play the violin, and eventually, whenever there was a guitar lying around from another busker, I would borrow it and he would teach me how to accompany. Just simple little country and western and Chuck Berry.' He also learned the tricks of the trade. 'We used to go down the tube late at night, the 11 o'clock shift, when we judged everyone in town was drunk,' he explained in a 1989 interview for Washington DC's WHFS radio. 'They'd always give more money when they were drunk.'

When it came time for Woody to buy his own instrument, he invested £2.99 in a ukulele from a music shop on Shaftesbury Avenue, believing – as would Paul Simonon later – that a four stringed instrument would be easier to play than a six stringed guitar. One day he was left on his own to work the pitch at Green Park while Tymon moved down to Oxford Circus. 'It was rush hour, and the train emptied at one end of the corridor. One second the corridor was empty, the next it was packed with people streaming through. It was like, now or never, playing to this full house. That was the first time I remember performing on my own.' Starting with 'Johnny B Goode', Woody worked up a repertoire of uncomplicated blues, country and folk tunes, all of which he would bash out with considerably more verve than finesse. 'It's no use twittering away finger-picking some delicate ballad about roses when there's like 300 elephants charging along in an echoing passage,' he explained during another radio interview, this time in 1982 for San Jose's KSJO. 'They just want to go home, they're not interested in anything else. So from the very start, when I started playing music, I realised that you had to have a rousing, thumping type of tune. Which, in a crude way, was what punk was: it had to be simple, and it had to be loud.'

The next move for Woody and Tymon was a joint European busking tour. It took in both France and Holland, and might have lasted longer and ventured even further afield had the two itinerants not been detained and deported back to England. It was just the latest episode in what was turning into a run of bad luck. Back in London, Woody continued to earn his living on the underground, until the day he underwent an unsettling Orwellian experience. He was busking at Oxford Circus, when a loudspeaker above his head crackled into life and advised him to move along quickly as the Transport Police were on their way. 'This guy walked past, and I screamed at him, "Can you hear that? This is *1984*!"' Joe told Paul Morley. 'And he gave me a funny look, and rushed off. I though, "Ah, fuck it!" and packed it in.'

Woody had maintained some of the friendships he had made through the Central School, one connection resulting in a relationship with a girl who went on to attend a course at Cardiff College of Art. Tired of roughing it in London, Woody followed her to Wales and moved in with her. Early in 1973, he paid a visit to neighbouring Newport with the intention of looking up another old Central friend called Forbes, at that time taking the Fine Art course at Newport College of Art. 'There were various bands in the college,' recalls another student there, Alan Jones. 'I suppose the most notable one was this pure rock'n'roll band called the Rip Off Park Rock'n'Roll All Stars. I can remember being in a rehearsal in the Student's Union [on Stowe Hill] in Newport, and this bedraggled sort of character – Woody – coming in with his beaten up black leather jacket, and sort of slinking to the floor with his eyes just shining. He was just electrified by what we were doing.'

It was the perfect introduction to what turned out to be Woody's spiritual home for much of the next year. 'He was so taken with this little Student's Union scene and our band,' says Alan. 'He was very affable in those days. People really took to him. He made about 10 friends a minute, because he's very sharp, very intelligent. He could switch: he could be quite fearless, but he was very charming. His wit was quite astonishing.' In addition to Alan himself, Woody connected very quickly with a girl named Gillian Calvert – 'I can remember them being just buzz, buzz, buzz. Instant rapport' – and through her with her somewhat less outgoing boyfriend, Micky Foote. Woody drifted in and out of town over the next few months, and when his relationship in Cardiff came to an end in mid 1973, it seemed only natural that he should base himself in Newport for a while.

Alan had begun to attend the college in September 1971, and had auditioned for the Rip Off Park Rock'n'Roll All Stars that same month. By his own admission, he was not then a particularly good musician; but he was informed that, despite being up to jazz standard, his predecessor had been let go because he refused to move on stage. Something of an introvert at that time, Alan had nevertheless taken the hint and essayed a sheepish version of the Shadows walk. 'I got the job on the basis of that and just about playing a bassline. I also got christened Jiving Al Jones, and it fucking stuck for years!'

Mick Jones's musical history should be enough in itself to undermine the myth that the 1976 UK punk rock movement came out of nowhere as an unprecedented reaction to the contemporary music scene's increasing pretentiousness and tendency to value musicianship over feel, but it tells only part of the tale. The 1967-68 Blues Boom had laid the ground for the Rock'n'Roll Revival, as exemplified by the 13 September 1969 Revival Concert in Toronto headlined by John Lennon's Plastic Ono Band and featuring Chuck Berry, Bo Diddley, Jerry Lee Lewis, Little Richard and Gene Vincent. Many more similar events followed over the next few years, and attracted impressive turnouts for performers and material that had until recently been considered relics of a bygone age. Fans of high energy music you could actually dance to were making a stand. There was an immediate crossover with late Sixties punk bands like the Stooges and the MC5, both of whom appeared on the bill of a similar Revival concert in Detroit. The Five went on to include tracks by Little Richard and Chuck Berry on their 1970 back-to-basics album *Back In The USA*. The following year, the Flamin' Groovies released the similarly motivated *Flamingo*, which included a version of Little Richard's 'Keep A Knockin''.

In the UK, Marc Bolan kickstarted what became known as glam rock in 1971 with a 12-bar blues-based guitar sound which borrowed heavily from his favourite late Fifties rock'n'roll records, and created the template for all future T Rex hits. With minor variations, exaggerated rock'n'roll and R&B riffs of this ilk, underpinned for the most part by similarly unsubtle stompalong drums, accounted for the trademark sounds of other glam acts like Slade, Sweet, Alice Cooper, Gary Glitter, Suzi Quatro and Mud. Pre-progressive, pre-psychedelic and pre-Beatle elements are rife in glam lyrics. Many are set not in early Seventies Britain but in a late Fifties-early Sixties American fantasyland; references to 'rock'n'roll' and 'teenage rebels' are ubiquitous. To take one particular band as an example: Wizzard allude to the jive in 'See My Baby Jive' and doo wop singer Dion in 'Angel Fingers'.

The commercial mainstream was soon saturated with glam records evoking and extolling – to borrow the title of a Mott the Hoople song – 'The Golden Age Of Rock'n' Roll', but the appreciation was not reciprocated. The common ground represented by a raw and basic approach to music was not enough to encourage Rock'n'Roll Revivalists to cross over the other way. The bulk of the UK's more purist rock'n'roll fans could be found in areas with large working class communities. More interested in a boisterous fun time out with a few beers than in mincing around in mascara and bacofoil jump-suits, they kept their distance from glam fans. Some did dress up, but preferred the period costume of the teddy boy. In London, they provided Malcolm McLaren with the market for his Let It Rock shop. Funnily enough, in 1976-77 these same teds – still suspicious of upstart rival youth cults – would do battle with punks who bought their clothes from the same premises. Rock'n'roll fans did not have to rely wholly on Golden Oldie records and Revival Shows for their musical fix, though: a new generation of bands took up the challenge of providing them with live entertainment, even if they did concentrate mostly on cover versions of the classics. Wales produced more than its fair share of such bands, including Shakin' Stevens and the Sunsets and Crazy Cavan and the Rhythm Rockers, both of whose paths would later cross with that of the Clash.

The Rip Off Park Rock'n'Roll All Stars formed when this retro trend was relatively young. They did their best to put on a good show and look the part, but they were not inclined to take themselves or the music overly seriously. Their repertoire was all first generation rock'n'roll covers, but their approach to it was both over-the-top and tongue-in-cheek, a nod towards glam's inherent sense of irony. 'It was well into leaping about performing. Not exactly Gary Glitter proportions, but very into caricaturing rock'n'roll,' says Jiving Al. Fittingly, all the other members of the band had pseudonyms too: Cool Hand Clive played guitar, Bob Jackson was the Wailing Saxman, and Knock-Out Neil played drums. Almost everyone in the band had the unstyled long hair that was de rigueur at the turn of the decade, but they added leather jackets or, in Bob's case, 'a shiny, tight blue lurex suit which his girlfriend made him'.

Although the band was popular with both students at Newport College and the regulars at the local rugby clubs, it had pretty much run its course by mid 1972. Jiving Al believes the rehearsal Woody caught was for a one-off gig played early the following year, for which a new guitarist, Rob Haymer, was added to the line-up. 'He'd just bought a guitar and taught himself to play in three to six months,' says Jiving Al. 'A really determined man.' Playing with Rip Off Park had changed Jiving Al's own approach to music. 'That band straightened me out no end, because before, I think, I was a very messy, confused bass player. I was also a very laid back character, but it completely brought me out, and I saw rock'n'roll in a much more positive, exciting way afterwards.' Following the Rip Off Park All Stars' final gig, Rob and Jiving Al decided to form a similarly basic rock band of their own. They advertised for a drummer and received a reply from a slightly older non-student named Jeff Cooper, who dressed soberly in a tie and jacket and worked in the local mortuary. 'His main job was cleaning up bodies, and he just used to talk about death all the time,' recalls Jiving Al. His age, attire and profession were not considered handicaps, a more immediate problem being the fact that he did not own a drum kit.

'When I was a teenager, I thought musicians were a world apart,' Joe told Vic Gabardini for a feature published in the *Musician* magazine book *The Year In Rock 1981- 82*. 'A secret society I could never join.' Rip Off Park's gung ho approach to basic rock classics and self-deprecating, vaguely Beefheartian pseudonyms had gone a long way to altering that opinion. The newly relocated Woody saw his main chance, and volunteered himself as vocalist and second guitarist for Jiving Al and Rob's new band. The others had mixed feelings about the offer. 'At that particular time he hadn't mastered many skills, it has to be said,' laughs Jiving Al. 'It was like, "No, you can't join the band. You can't *do* anything!" He was such a bad guitarist that we wouldn't let him go near a guitar. He actually couldn't play barre chords, and you can't really play rock'n'roll if you can't. What he seemed to have accomplished was kind of Dylan tunes, really. He'd been busking folk tunes.' Nor did his singing voice offer much in the way of compensation. 'Very nasal, very adenoidal, but deep. He's got something not naturally right about his nasal passages.'

As they were not technically minded themselves, Rob and Jiving Al could see at least some merit to the idea of Woody as a frontman. 'The fucking charisma of this guy was just phenomenal. The atmosphere that came off him.' And Woody did have one other thing going for him. He had recently swapped an unwanted camera for a secondhand drum kit, and was not beyond resorting to bribery. 'He said, "Well, as I see it, it's like you've got a drummer with no drum kit, and I've got a drum kit. So you ain't really got a lot of choice, have you?"' laughs Jiving Al. 'And everybody looked at one another and went, "He's got a point!"' The drum kit was duly loaned to Jeff Cooper, and Woody became the new band's lead vocalist and – very – occasional second guitarist.

Jiving Al was living in a flat at 12 Pentonville, above a taxi rank behind the train station. Woody moved into the spare room for the remainder of his stay in Newport. 'This flat was very seedy, very basic. I remember the rent, actually: £15 a month. Always trouble with the landlord, all the usual stuff. Not to sound boring, but we were seriously poor. I can recall coming home one night after going to see my parents, and Woody said he'd had a whole weekend with no money, and there'd been great excitement because he'd found 50 pence down the back of a chair. I suppose we weren't very clean, and we weren't hygienic, and there were an awful lot of mice. Loads.' Determined to address the problem, Woody set a trap one night with a piece of cheese on a ruler hanging over a bucket of water. When the first little victim plopped in, he was so overcome with remorse that he leaped out of bed, fished it out and attempted to give it the kiss of life.

Little has been written about the band Woody joined in Newport, but it has been reported that they were originally called Flaming Youth before Woody took over and renamed them the Vultures. Jiving Al has no recollection of the former name, and insists that Rob was responsible for the latter. There is a strong possibility that it was inspired by a popular humorous T-shirt of the time. It depicted two such carrion-eating birds of prey sitting on a heat-frazzled tree branch, one addressing the other thus: 'Patience, my ass! I'm gonna *kill* something!' This was certainly in keeping with Rob's personality. 'I would say we were co-leaders, but Rob led more than me, if that makes any sense,' says Jiving Al. 'I do think he tried to manipulate me. He tried to… Well, he didn't just try, he succeeded in manipulating Woody, too.'

Rob's control extended to the choice of material. 'Rob used to learn a song and say, "*We're fucking doing this!*" He was quite… forceful.' In the *Clash Songbook*, Joe stated that the Vultures 'played R&B when it wasn't fashionable', but their repertoire was more eclectic than this might suggest. No tapes of the Vultures in rehearsal or at any of their six or so undocumented Student Union gigs exist, but Jiving Al recalls that the band always opened with JD Loudermilk's 'Tobacco Road', a mid-Sixties hit for the UK's Nashville Teens. 'For a simple number, it's really beautifully aggressive.' US band the Blues Magoos' version of this song appears on *Nuggets*, Lenny Kaye's famed 1972 compilation album of original Sixties punk rock classics, which lends the selection a certain retrospective cachet. The same cannot be said for a vaguely-remembered song from Jethro Tull's early blues period. 'Rob wanted to play it because it had a very biting wah-wah guitar solo.' The band's sole original composition was – perhaps unsurprisingly – a Rob Haymer song, entitled 'I'm Nuthin' But A Country Boy At Heart' which, as the title hints, was in the then-popular country rock tradition.

The only bona fide first generation R&B song in the set was 'Johnny B Goode', and that was reserved for the encore. According to Jiving Al, Woody's record collection in Newport consisted of one solitary Chuck Berry EP. Sounds familiar. 'He'd say, "It's the only fuckin' record worth fuckin' having!"' Despite coming on like an R&B purist, Woody made no real attempt to change the Vultures' repertoire. 'I remember him pulling faces, and he was very unhappy about a lot of it, but he still went along with it,' recalls Jiving Al. 'I don't remember any big fights.' Although this may have been because Woody was wary of tackling the dictatorial Rob, Jiving Al believes that it was more a case of being content to keep his head down while serving out his apprenticeship as vocalist and frontman.

There may be no audio record of the Vultures in action, but Jiving Al has kept a pictorial one. It includes some of his own shots of Woody, and others of the band in action taken by various students on the college's Photography course. One of his photos depicts Woody in the Pentonville flat, his shoulder-length curly hair framing his serene, cherubic face. Wearing his habitual uniform of jeans, boots and checked shirt – an early Seventies update of the Woody Guthrie look – he is sitting with an electric guitar resting on his lap in front of a bank of amps and speakers, on unofficial loan from Newport College. The performance shots show Woody either clutching the mike and contorting his features like a young Joe Cocker, or hanging off the mike stand and gazing at his fellow band members with an expression of childlike rapture on his face. His only concession to rock star glamour is the black varnish on his finger nails; otherwise, he's in his standard attire, complete with beat-up black leather jacket. The same is true of Jiving Al; but, hilariously, not of Rob, who is wearing a grotesque rubber face mask and a flasher's mac with an empty Persil packet attached to the belt.

'I can't imagine what that band sounded like,' says Jiving Al. 'I'd love to go back and be someone in the audience. Our intent was 100 per cent. Funnily enough, a bit like 1977 [and the punk rock movement]: people who really mean it, but can't play too good, and yet something comes out. I think it was tough, very hard, very basic.' Someone who was in the audience at almost every gig was another student who, confusingly, was only one 'l' away from having exactly the same given name as Jiving Al. *Allan* Jones began to write for *Melody Maker* shortly after leaving Newport, and, in a July 1975 feature on the 101ers, he reminisced about the Vultures thus: 'an erratic but occasionally stunning formation that played a handful of gigs before sinking without trace'.

Although not himself a student, Woody was benefiting from his close relationship with people at Newport College, and was living a life that was as full, stimulating and healthy as poverty would allow. 'He didn't drink or take drugs much at all: I remember him having two pints and falling over,' recalls Jiving Al. 'He had a lot of friends. Women were quite fond of him. There were one or two I felt he knew really well, but I never really saw him having a relationship.' One of these women was involved with the Communist Party, then the dominant force in the Newport Student Union. Jiving Al suspects that Woody's brief flirtation with organised politics at this time was more to do with his interest in her than any burning desire to overthrow capitalism. 'He never talked politics to me. I wouldn't have said he was unaware, but it wasn't something he talked about.' Even if his interest in communism was genuine, it was not particularly long-lived. 'Toeing any line is obviously a dodgy situation, because I'm just not into a policy or I'd have joined the Communist Party years ago,' Joe told *Musician*'s Vic Gabardini in 1981. 'I've done my time selling the *Morning Star* at pit heads in Wales, and it's just not happening.'

He might have known a lot of people, but Woody was not a great mixer. Much of his time was spent on his own, in his room, indulging in what Jiving Al refers to as his 'activities'. 'He was very well-read. He'd go from reading to strumming his guitar, to writing, to painting.' Woody's environment was inevitably very art-oriented: everyone painted or took photos of everyone and everything else. His own work conformed to a narrower brief. 'He always painted cowboys eating baked beans! He had this obsession with cowboys.' Partly, Woody was reflecting the Vultures' country rock leanings, but he was also betraying a fascination with pop iconography not dissimilar to that evident in Mick Jones's art school output. Whereas Mick's collages were Warholesque reflections of the superficial glamour and disposability of contemporary culture, however, Woody's paintings celebrated a Hollywood version of American folk mythology. The cover art for the Clash's 1978 album *Give 'Em Enough Rope* – which depicts a couple of vultures feeding on the prone corpse of a cowboy – has more resonance for Jiving Al than for people who did not know the band's singer in 1973-74.

One result of the hours Woody spent writing and strumming was his first attempt at a song, a copy of which Jiving Al still owns. 'It's very telling. At the beginning of the tape, he says, "Really make it nasty and home-made, all right?"' It also reveals the extent to which its composer – already seeing himself as an outsider – both identified with and romanticised the outlaw figure. 'It's not "Bankrobber", but he does sing something about wanting to rob a bank at one point.'

Woody's songwriting talents might have been overlooked in the Vultures, but his artistic endeavours were held in higher regard. Despite the fact that Rob was himself on the college's Fine Art course, when the band decided to try their luck out of town towards the end of 1973, it was Woody who was commissioned to come up with a suitable promotional poster. The A3-sized result takes the form of a strip cartoon, very much in the style of Robert Crumb. In a doomed quest for some peace and quiet, Percy sets out on a bicycle ride, is plucked from the saddle by a giant vulture, and is deposited in its mountaintop nest near a precariously-positioned roadhouse, from which are emerging the strains of 'I'm Nuthin' But A Country Boy At Heart'. 'Trapped in a giant vultures' nest,' thinks Our Hero, 'slap bang next to the raunchiest R&B band you ever heard.' 'I just love this shit-kicking music,' comments Fat Freddy's cat.

Along the bottom of the strip are impressively accurate caricatures of the various band members, all of whom are given nicknames and/or brief character sketches in the tradition of the Magic Band and the Rip Off Park All Stars. The latter outfit's saxophonist had just been added to the Vultures' line-up, and he is listed as Bob 'Blow' Jackson, retaining his 'Wailing Saxman' tag; Rob becomes 'Bobby Angelo, guitars and singing, rumoured to be the illegitimate son of Bert Weedon' (Weedon being the author of the *Play In A Day* guitar book); long haired pretty boy Jiving Al is 'the so-called

Mona Lisa of the electric bass'; Jeff Cooper 'plays drums and eats concrete for breakfast'; and 'Woody Mellor' self-deprecatingly describes his own contribution as 'blues shouting and pick and shovel guitar'.

These posters were dispatched to various venues with a selection of performance photos. Almost immediately, they won the Vultures a gig at the Granary, a 500-capacity venue located at 32 Welsh Back in nearby Bristol. 'Lots of good people played there, so you were supposed to have a high recommendation or to be someone,' says Jiving Al. The advance publicity was so successful that the venue was full, but the gig itself was a disaster. 'Something went wrong. Strings broke, equipment broke down, whatever. It was one of those moments where everything went quite surreal. The next thing I remember was some army guy on stage who was threatening to take his trousers off. The music had completely collapsed. I remember Woody – I'd never seen him like this before – sort of egging on the audience to egg on this guy. He was just punching his fist in the air, like, "Off, off, off!" The whole audience was into it, thrusting its fists in the air and screaming, "*Off!*" I was having flashbacks to Nuremberg! "What *is* going on, here?" But what I was watching was him controlling the audience in a big way. It was the first time it ever happened, and I think he learned something that night.'

The Granary's promoters were not so impressed, and were reluctant to pay the band. 'We had to point out that the place was having a fucking good time, and it was packed out, whether they thought we were rubbish or not,' says Jiving Al. 'I do remember bad vibes, and thinking, "We're not going to be booked here again!" And that was the big gig for us.' It was the Vultures' first out of town gig, and their first paid gig in a proper venue. It was also their last ever. There was no immediate bust-up, but the experience left the band feeling deflated, and rehearsals gradually petered out. 'We were completely disorganised, basically. We were the typical band who didn't know their arses from their elbows.'

Tired of having to turn the furniture inside out for loose change, Woody took a job tending the graves in the town cemetery. 'I wasn't strong enough to actually dig the graves, so I just used to wheel the barrow around and collect the broken jam jars,' he told the *NME* in 1988, referring to the receptacles provided for flowers. 'I spent a whole winter doing nothing but this in Newport.' As jobs go, there can be few worse: not only boring, repetitive and lonely, but also outdoors in the cold and surrounded by constant reminders of death. 'I remember him coming home from that and being really low,' says Jiving Al. '"What the fuck am I doing?"' Without the Vultures to keep his spirits up, even the usually buoyant Woody succumbed to depression. 'I didn't get much out of him for a while. He was just hidden in his room. I was invited in, but I wasn't wanted. He didn't speak.'

In spring 1974, Woody cut his woolly hair short, and began to wear it combed back in the rocker style he would continue to favour thereafter, save for brief periods at the beginning and end of the Clash. Late one night, Jiving Al was asked to take a picture of the newly-shorn Woody posing with artefacts pertaining to his 'activities': books, a typewriter, transistor radio, valve amplifier, several guitars (including a couple of Telecaster copies 'worth about a fiver each'), and a cowboy painting. 'I think cutting the hair was quite symbolic,' says Jiving Al. As was the photograph. In the mid Sixties, Bob Dylan was fond of staging similar pictures, posing with guitars, favourite records and 'meaningful' possessions, the best known of which shots adorns the cover of the transitional 1965 folk-to-rock album *Bringing It All Back Home*. 'Woody was always very aware of that sort of thing.' Some of Woody's Newport friends had already completed their courses and moved on. Most of the remainder were due to leave in the summer of 1974. That May, Woody also came to the conclusion it was time to take it all back home. Or at least, to the closest place he had to a home at that time: London.

5
ROUTE 101

When he arrived back in the capital in May 1974, Woody headed straight for the current base of his old busking partner Tymon Dogg, a squat at 23 Chippenham Road in Maida Hill. The other side of the Westway from Notting Hill, it was also just a couple of hundred yards from Mick Jones's high-rise. The other inhabitants of Tymon's squat were Dave and Gail Goodall, the proprietors of That Tea Room on Great Western Road. Since demolished, That Tea Room was then the unofficial centre of the sizeable squatting community occupying Chippenham Road, Elgin Avenue and other smaller thoroughfares in Maida Hill. As a result, Dave and Gail were very well connected in the area, and were able to point Woody in the direction of a spare room in a neighbouring street. He moved in that same month.

101 Walterton Road had been opened up a year earlier by Patrick Nother and Simon Cassell. They had previously shared a squat near Euston station, before being informed about Walterton Road by Dave and Gail. Pat's brother Richard had moved in too, but had left again at the beginning of 1974 to complete his Zoology degree at Chelsea College in a calmer environment. In the interim period, the household had been swollen further by: Jules Yewdall, a friend from the Nothers' hometown of Leek, Staffordshire; another previous squatmate of Simon, a Chilean named Antonio Narvaez; and Antonio's friend and fellow countryman, Alvaro Peña-Rojas. Just after Woody moved into number 101, Richard Nother returned to the area. Finding the house full, he took a room in the squat that backed onto it, 86 Chippenham Road.

Back in the mid Seventies, it was relatively simple to gain access to empty property, especially in areas which, like Maida Hill, were awaiting redevelopment by the Greater London Council (GLC). If you knew the right people, making the place halfway habitable was no problem, either. 'You had to rewire the whole house, because everything's been ripped out, pipes, everything,' Joe told *Rolling Stone*'s James Henke in 1980. 'We'd get a specialist who'd go down to this big box under the stairs and stand on this big rubber mat and make a direct connection to Battersea Power Station. *Bang! Bang!* I've seen some explosions down in these dark, dingy basements that would just light things up.' They might have had electricity at 101 Walterton Road, but other home comforts were in short supply. Many of the windows were broken out, the cooker was the sole source of heat, and there were no washing facilities other than a tin tub that was kept in the bike room and had to be emptied into the back garden.

Life might have been hard, but actually staying in residence was nowhere near as difficult as it is today. If a few properties in a particular street were already squatted, the GLC would not usually bother to have inhabitants evicted until they were ready to demolish and rebuild. 'You knew that,' says Jules Yewdall, 'so you could more or less say, "OK, we'll get in here now, and we're going to be all right for another year or two."' When the GLC decided it was time to clear a street, the gloves came off altogether. For the Elgin Avenue-Chippenham Road area, the first move was made in late summer 1974. 'The GLC tried to get the LEB [London Electricity Board] to cut off our electricity,' says Richard Nother. Court proceedings to evict the squatters were instigated on 1 September. In early November, the Maida Hill Squatters and Tenants Association organised a demonstration in Notting Hill, and 200 squatters objected loudly to the prospect of being made homeless en masse. 'It got quite heavy,' recalls Richard. 'The police charged us, the Special Patrol Group.' Nevertheless, the action won the squatters a brief reprieve.

At that time, the general public perceived squatting, a communal lifestyle involving youngish people most of whom had long hair, to be the preserve of hippies and alternative-type left-wing radicals. Events such as the November demonstration only served to reinforce this view. On the whole, though, it was a misleading one. True, there were many exiles from dictatorial regimes in the Maida Hill area, including representatives from almost every South American country; but many of them had left their homelands simply to be able to pursue a less restrictive lifestyle, rather than with the intention of grouping together to plot or campaign. There were some households intent on reforming society in the UK – radical feminism, one of the major issues of the day, was not without its proponents – but there were also some that were simply anti-social: Richard's house was dominated by a motorcycle gang who used to ride their machines into the front room. 'They were *crazy*,' he says. 'They'd destroy the house during the night, then spend the next day repairing it.' The Maida Hill squats housed a cosmopolitan mix of all kinds of people with all kinds of beliefs and agendas.

Neither Joe himself nor any of his crowd was involved in radical politics at this time, but theirs was hardly a lifestyle that conformed to the values of mainstream society. 'If you hadn't got any money, it was a political act to take over an empty property and declare yourself as legally living there,' maintains Jules. Both he and Richard agree that most people involved saw it as a simple trade-off: if you were prepared to cope with relative squalor, you did not have to pay any rent, and, as a consequence, you were reasonably free to live the life you chose. As Richard notes, it might have had its roots in the values of the late Sixties counter-culture, but the squatting movement also foreshadowed the punk ideal of taking control of your own destiny and making things happen for yourself. 'We were doing it ourselves,' says Richard. 'There were a lot of people doing their own project, whether it was art, photography, music – at least, in our houses – and it meant you could do it in your own way.'

★★★

Woody's return to musical performance was inspired by seeing a trio playing Irish folk music in the Elephant and Castle pub on Elgin Avenue. 'All these people were hanging around my squat just doing nothing, and I thought, "I'll just whip up a few of these guys, and we'll play in a few Irish pubs. I can do that!"' The idea of forming a band was not without precedent among the members of the squatting community. Doing their own thing musically often coincided with the need to provide their own entertainment, and musicians got together to jam for fun or to play parties. One such band, named the Derelicts in honour of the state of their dwellings, featured the Gogan sisters Barbara and Sue and a bass player named Dan Kelleher. They formed early in 1974 and went on to play squatters and action group benefits as well as gigs at local pub venues.

Woody's intentions were not quite so community-oriented. He wanted to make a little money over the summer of 1974, or so he told the *NME*'s Paul Morley in 1979. Pat Nother remembers it differently: 'It was two or three months after I met him that he said, "I've got a great idea: I'm going to be a pop star!" And he'd decided this, which I thought was quite funny. "What, you're just going to *be* one? You can't play anything!"' Indeed, Woody's guitar playing was still so rudimentary that Jules Yewdall was under the impression he had just picked up the instrument for the first time. Although Alvaro Peña-Rojas recalls Woody staying up all night trying to work out songs, the improvement was not immediate. Luckily, Woody was not the only one living in the squat who refused to see inability as an obstacle. 'I had an alto saxophone which I'd got in Portobello market a year or so before,' recalls Simon Cassell. Between them, they managed to cajole a couple of the others into participating in a jamming session in the basement of 101. Antonio Narvaez, who had some experience as a drummer, borrowed a kit from someone in a nearby squat, and a bemused Pat did likewise with a bass, despite the fact he had never played the instrument before. Woody and Simon shared the vocals.

The results were not astounding, and it is doubtful that anyone other than Woody and possibly Simon would have wanted to persevere had not Alvaro decided to co-opt the unlikely outfit for his own purposes. An experienced tenor saxophonist, he had enjoyed three hits in Chile with his bands the Boomerangs and the Challengers before moving to the UK in 1970. In September 1973, a military coup in Chile had overthrown the world's first ever democratically elected Marxist government, and the Chile Solidarity Campaign (CSC) had formed to co-ordinate support for the victims of the struggle. Alvaro volunteered the services of the squat rehearsal group for the CSC's upcoming benefit concert, An Evening For The Chilean Resistance.

It was already nearly the end of August 1974. The gig, to be headlined by reggae band Matumbi, was scheduled to take place on 14 September at the Telegraph music pub at 228 Brixton Hill. Alvaro joined the rehearsals, and the band concentrated on working up a set of six songs. Out of necessity, these were the simplest of rock and R&B classics, something which suited Woody perfectly. They included Chuck Berry's 'No Particular Place To Go' and 'Roll Over Beethoven', Them's garage band staple 'Gloria', and Larry Williams's rock'n'roll evergreen 'Bony Moronie'. No sooner had these been knocked into some kind of recognisable shape than, just two weeks before the benefit was due to take place, Antonio suddenly left to go on holiday.

Desperate for a replacement, the band asked Pat's brother Richard to sit in on drums. 'I had a clarinet at the time, and a pair of bongos,' says Richard. 'Occasionally I used to bash about on the drums without actually playing with anyone. They asked me to sit in and see how it went.' Then the gig was brought forward a week. There followed what Richard wryly refers to as 'a couple of days of frantic practice'. On Friday 6 September – according to London listings magazine *Time Out*, not 7 September as is usually reported – just five days after Richard's first rehearsal, and only two or three weeks after Woody had told a disbelieving Pat that he intended to become a pop star, all three turned up with Simon and Alvaro at the Telegraph to play their first gig. They were billed as El Huaso and the 101 All Stars, something which presaged a future power struggle within the band: El Huaso was Alvaro, being Chilean Spanish for 'countryman'; but the latter part of the name was a nod in the direction of the Rip Off Park Rock'n'Roll All Stars, the band Woody had really wanted to join in Newport.

As they had no serviceable equipment of their own, the band rather naively hoped they would be allowed to borrow that of the headliners. Matumbi were delayed when their van broke down, and arrived two hours later then scheduled. Almost unbelievably, under the circumstances, they acceded to the 101 All Stars' request. 'There was hardly time for them to do their set, but they still lent us their drum kit and their amps,' Joe told *Melody Maker*'s Paolo Hewitt for a 1981 101ers retrospective. 'I thought that was great.' Clive Timperley, who had connections with the Maida Hill squatting community, had heard that his old housemate Woody now had a band, and went along to watch. 'They did their six songs and ran out of material, and that was it. They weren't very good, but they tried hard, and it was nice to see your mate on stage. They were very nervous about it. To get a gig at a place with a stage where everyone can see you, supporting a fairly well-known reggae band, in Brixton, out of your home territory, must have been quite daunting for them.'

For the past month or two, Richard had been sharing his room at 86 Chippenham Road with a 17 year-old Spanish girl named Esperanza Romano. Within a day or two of the Telegraph benefit, they both departed for Spain. Rehearsals continued, but the line-up remained fluid. 'We got through about two or three guitarists a week, who Woody was into attacking,' says Pat. 'It was just fucking around on crap instruments with a bunch of crap musicians, you know. But there was some ego stuff went down. Rivalries, just silly boys' stuff.' Pat's distaste for such unseemly jostling meant that at least two other bassists sat in with the band during this period.

Woody, meanwhile, had taken a job as cleaner and maintenance man at the home of the newly formed English National Opera (ENO), the London Coliseum in St Martin's Lane. His goal was to save enough money to buy himself a decent guitar amplifier. His duties were no more arduous than carrying out the rubbish, cleaning the toilets and sweeping the pigeon droppings off the roof. 'A fucking great job,' he told *Melody Maker*'s Allan Jones in 1975. 'Only had to work two hours of the day. There was this hole in the basement where I'd creep off to play my guitar.' He befriended 17-year old fellow employee Gary Hardy, who was also learning to play guitar. Interviewed in 1994 by Ralph Heibutzki for a Clash retrospective in *DISCoveries* magazine, Gary recalled that the 'hole' in the basement was in fact a space the duo created for themselves by moving a wall of lockers. On one occasion, Woody spent the whole day in this makeshift bunker trying to work out the chords to Marvin Gaye's 'I Heard It Through The Grapevine'. The Coliseum's manager must have heard it through the lockers, because he sacked Woody shortly afterwards. Woody was hardly heartbroken, as he later told Allan Jones. 'He gave me £120 to get out as soon as possible.' Before he obliged, he smuggled in Pat to watch a dress rehearsal of *Die Fledermaus*, due to begin its run on 31 September. Sitting up in the Gods, they decided it was a good time to take a rest from the pressures of squat and band alike, and set off for a holiday in Wales.

Pat's motive was entirely recreational, but in addition to looking up a few old friends, Woody was intent on checking up on various bits and pieces of musical equipment in Newport. Pat stayed away for over a month. Woody returned like Santa Claus after just a fortnight, not only full of bonhomie and enthusiasm, but also with the promise of rather more than a sackful of new gear. It was relatively easy for him to persuade Simon and his girlfriend to drive him back to Wales to pick it up. It included his collection of electric guitars, a custom-made semi-acoustic bass with violin holes, and an AC30 amplifier, which he'd bought with his pay-off from ENO. His drum kit had already made its way back to Surrey, on loan to his old school friend Pablo LaBritain.

Woody was once again able to use the possession of coveted musical equipment to improve his position within a band, but the other members of the 101 All Stars had also missed the driving force of his personality. Nominally, at least, the band continued to be run as a democracy, but it was tacitly understood by most of the people involved that, without Woody, it would not be run at all. Nevertheless, Alvaro did not immediately retreat into the shadows.

The line-up was brought back to full strength by the return of Pat and Antonio. The band managed to borrow two caseless Linear Concorde speakers, which Woody housed in a couple of knocked-together kitchen drawers; when combined with his amp, this represented the band's entire PA. 'We had a broomstick handle as a microphone stand,' recalls Pat. '"One microphone…", you know.' Indeed, the '22 singers but one microphone… five guitar players but one guitar' coda to the 1977 Clash song 'Garageland' has far more to do with the early days of Joe's second band than those of the decidedly better-equipped Clash.

Perhaps unsurprisingly, the band – their name now officially truncated to the 101 All Stars – found that securing bookings was not easy for such a ramshackle outfit with a repertoire in the process of being extended from six songs to 10. Pat recalls a lot of rehearsing and another three or four 'weird' gigs taking place in October and November. 'I can remember playing in an abandoned cinema, I think it was in Lancaster Road, and there were puddles of water everywhere. I was terrified all through the gig that my lead might be running through them. "Surely, water and electricity don't go together?"'

One of the more memorable of these early shows was another Chile-related event. Artists For Democracy arranged a two-week exhibition-cum-cabaret at the Royal College of Art under the title Arts Festival For The Chilean Resistance. It ran from 14 October to 1 November, and Alvaro volunteered the All Stars to play on one of those nights. 'It was the Chilean Refugee Exhibition, and we started playing "Bony Moronie", and they went, "Get this capitalist rock'n'roll out of here!" Really!' Joe told Paolo Hewitt in 1981. 'We got two numbers in and then we had to fucking clear out.' Pat confirms the story. 'They had a hall draped with revolutionary flags, Che Guevara, Allende, Marx and Lenin on massive banners everywhere. There was a lot of money's worth of art on display. It was a whole cultural convention thing, and then this bunch turn up and play "American imperialist juke box music"! We were slung off.'

The impetus that brought about the next stage in the 101 All Stars' development came from a source outside the band. 'We never really got off the ground until this girl pushed us into renting that room above the Chip. Because we couldn't play, how could we get any gigs?' Joe told Melody Maker's Paolo Hewitt. 'The only thing we could do to learn to play was to start our own club up.' The girl in question was Liz Lewis; the Chip was the Chippenham public house, situated on the corner of Malvern and Shirland Roads where they form a crossroads with both Chippenham and Walterton Roads; and the club was the pub's small upstairs room. Liz hired it for the first time on Wednesday 4 December 1974, and once again, having a deadline to meet helped galvanise the band. As if to pay testimony to this change of gears, the band name was truncated yet again to the 101ers.

Everything appeared to be moving a little too fast for one of the band's two latest recruits, who – due partly to his physical appearance, and partly to his nocturnal lifestyle – was known to everyone as Mole. 'I didn't think we were anywhere *near* ready to do a gig!' he says. Pat had finally left the band and given up the bass. 'I think I was chucked out,' he says. 'I *think* so...' Acquainted with Mole via Mole's girlfriend, Barbie, Simon had invited him to replace Pat on bass. 'I could play guitar, but I'd never played bass before,' says Mole. 'I said, "Yeah, why not?"' His first rehearsal, sometime in mid November, left him in no doubt about the kind of band he was joining: the bass gave him an electric shock. When he ran a mains tester over the strings, it lit up. The 101ers had been playing for over three months without any earth connections.

The other new recruit was more casual about the imminence of the gig, partly because he was conversant with both the 101ers' style and material, and partly because, from a musical viewpoint, his role was a less demanding one: Jules Yewdall had been asked to take over as lead vocalist and occasional harmonica player. Although Woody – like Simon – still intended to sing some numbers, he wanted to be able to concentrate on his guitar playing. Also, he was beginning to have doubts about his voice. Besides being limited in range, it was now distorted by both his adenoidal problem and the appalling state of his teeth. These combined to dampen some of his consonants and sibilate others to such an extent that it was almost impossible to tell what he was singing. It has been suggested that his dental decay was due to unrestrained abuse of amphetamine sulphate, but, as he later admitted to Caroline Coon, it was a simple case of neglect: perhaps another rejection of the public school regime.

The new club was christened the Charlie Pigdog club in honour of Charlie, the squat mascot, a mongrel with a Heinz 57 pedigree. Charlie had two names and at least that many personalities. 'If you knew him well, he was called Trouble,' says Jules. 'He used to get a bit schizophrenic, I think, because he didn't know who he belonged to. There were about eight or nine – 14, sometimes – people living in the house, and he was never quite sure who he was supposed to be following about.' On Wednesday 4 December, and most subsequent Wednesdays for the next five months, Charlie had no problem working it out: everyone he knew was going to the same place.

The Chip was number 101's local, and as it was less than 50 yards away the band's gear could be transported there in an old pram. Early audiences were made up almost entirely of members of the Maida Hill squatting community, ensuring that the atmosphere was both friendly and party-like. Woody took along his portable Dansette record player and people brought their favourite records. Alvaro even made sandwiches. 'The room cost a pound,' recalls Liz Lewis. 'When I'd collected enough money at the door – 10p each – to pay for the room and a drink each for the band and me, I'd stop collecting. It was informal. If there was any money left over, it'd be a string fund. It was a good laugh. We'd all go down That Tea Room after.'

The casual approach spilled over onto the stage. Friends who could find their way around an instrument were welcome to join the band for a number or two. Simon recalls that Mole's girlfriend Barbie sometimes played harmonica, and Clive Timperley – who, as well as knowing Woody, was also good friends with Liz – began to turn up with his guitar. 'I said, "Can I just sit in? Because you don't seem to have a lead guitar player."' Even Charlie was not averse to making the occasional guest appearance: according to Clive, when the sax players warmed up their horns prior to the gig, the dog would howl along with them. 'Used to crack us up. Hilarious.' In those early days at the Chip, the 101ers did not so much perform as provide the platform for an evening of audience participation.

Richard Nother and Esperanza returned from Spain just before Christmas 1974, and moved straight into 101 Walterton Road. Esperanza's sister Paloma came too, and she and her Bolivian boyfriend took over the squat's front room. Richard's reappearance was perfectly timed, as Antonio was just about to set off on his travels again. For the second time, the drumsticks were handed over like a baton in a relay.

Being fellow squatters, most of the neighbours were reasonably tolerant about band practices, which were usually held in the basement and further soundproofed by carpets and mattresses fastened to the walls. However, the cold encouraged the 101ers to move rehearsals a little closer to the cooker. It was at this point they received their first bad review. 'We came under fire… OK, it was from an air rifle, but it was quite a potent air rifle!' remembers Richard. 'Smashing windows, the lot. It was really like being pinned down: we couldn't come out because there was a guy in one of the houses in Chippenham Road just firing this gun into us!'

Someone who was rather more impressed by the 101ers, and especially his old house-mate, was Clive Timperley. Despite having relinquished some of his vocal duties, Woody's frenzied approach to stage performance made him the band's focal point. 'I thought, "Bloody hell, he's really come on!"' says Clive. 'A really enthusiastic frontman.' Eighteen months before he joined the Clash, all the elements of the Clash-era Joe Strummer stage persona were already in place: the slack jaw, the rolling eyes, what Clash roadies would later dub 'the electric leg', and the vicious, chopping, double-time rhythm guitar style that one journalist would later liken to a Veg-o-matic. 'I'm looking for the ultimate wipe-out, for the ultimate feeling of every song,' Joe told *Record*'s John Mendelssohn in 1984. 'It isn't something you can just do; you have to work yourself up to some elusive pitch.' It was not a rare event for Woody to make a withdrawal from Liz Lewis's string fund. Although he loved his guitars, especially his cherry-red semi-acoustic Hofner, he took a perverse pride in the brutal punishment he meted out to them. 'He'd say, "I'll know I'm doing my job properly when I break the three top strings on the guitar,'" says Clive. 'And he did it once too, later. All three of the fat strings: not easily done. And he used to draw blood. That's how hard he played. Whatever he lacked in musical expertise, he made up for in pure energy, and that's always the way he would go.'

A sense of commitment to the cause was slowly beginning to filter through the band. January 1975 saw the end of the 101ers' 'open stage' policy. Seriousness of purpose was also evident in Woody's recognition that a more musical guitarist might add another dimension to the group's sound. On 15 January, Clive was officially invited to join. At the time he was playing with 'a British Steely Dan-type band' which, although better suited to his own musical leanings, involved more rehearsing than performing. He was attracted to the idea of a little light relief. 'I remember thinking it was quite funny, because Woody phoned me up one Sunday evening in Knightsbridge – where I was living at the time – and he says, "We've had a chat, and we'd like you to join the band." I thought, "This is all very professional!" and I said, "Yes, all right," thinking, "It's one gig a week at the Chippenham: you won't get any money out of it, but it's a laugh."'

It would appear there was another motive behind Woody's invitation. His love of rock'n'roll extended not only to the associated culture, but also to the props, namely equipment and instruments. The collection of cheap guitars he had begun in Newport was continuing to grow, and Clive was someone with whom he could talk guitar. 'He used to phone me up, about 10 o'clock at night, and say, "What are you doing? I've just bought this guitar, and I want to see what you think about it." So he'd come down – walk through the park – and we'd be up till about one or two in the morning. It'd be like, Guitar Workshop: he'd learn a few licks while he was at it.' Thus Woody would parlay each new acquisition into a free guitar lesson. 'We – me, Tymon, whoever – would just teach him to hold down the rhythm, to hold down the chord and strum. "That's all I wanna do," he'd say. "I don't wanna do anything flash."' It was an attitude Joe was still professing in 1988, when interviewed by Bill Flanagan for *Musician* magazine: '*Fuck the fiddly bits!* That's my motto.'

That same year, he revealed the reason for his distinctive style on KCRW. 'It's because I play the guitar the wrong way round. I'm left-handed, but I play strictly right-hand style, because I learned on other people's guitars. And I thought I was being clever, because my more agile hand was on the fret, which I figured would be the more difficult thing. It was only after I learned, and it was too late to change, that I realised I lost all subtlety that these lead guitarists have with *their* right hand: you've got to pick that string, then that string, and come back. I found I could either hit all six strings, or none.'

As soon as the Charlie Pigdog club got underway, Woody began handing out nicknames to his fellow musicians, in the tradition of both Rip Off Park and the Magic Band. Jules and Alvaro escaped unscathed; and Mole was Mole before he joined; but the lanky Simon Cassell was rechristened Big John; Richard became Snakehips Dudanski, or Snakes for short, and still calls himself Richard Dudanski to this day; and new recruit Clive Timperley became Evil C Timperlee, usually known as Evil. 'Maybe I'm a bit boring, because all he did was reverse my first name,' says the decidedly mild-mannered Clive, still somewhat bemused. 'There was an element of irony about it,' explains Mole, deadpan.

Woody's own stagename posed rather more of a problem. His first choice was Johnny Caramello, a fairly obvious corruption of his given name. In order to legitimise it, he told Clive that he had previously used it with the Vultures. In his July 1975 *Melody Maker* feature on the 101ers, Allan Jones played along, referring to Woody's earlier band as 'Johnny and the Vultures'. Jiving Al denies that the band ever performed under that name, or that Woody was ever called anything but Woody while in Newport, and is supported in both claims by the Vultures poster. Woody had changed identity before, but this would appear to be the first time he attempted to rewrite history to suit the present, something that would become commonplace in the Clash.

His next choice was Joe Strummer. According to Joe himself, the surname was an acknowledgement of his limitations as a guitarist, and the forename of his understanding that he was nothing special: just an 'ordinary Joe'. 'That's more defensive paranoia,' he told *Sounds*' Pete Silverton in 1978. 'I could only play chords, and at the first two gigs I ever did [at the Charlie Pigdog club] there were like 10, 20 people in the room who could play better than me... I felt very inferior about it, playing music.' 'A kind of Trades Descriptions Act,' he told KCRW's Christine McKenna in 1988. 'So they wouldn't expect anything *but* strumming.'

Thus, the name Joe Strummer was self-deprecating, but humorously so. Hardly unintentionally – for one so well-versed in the mythology of pop culture as its would-be new owner – it was also pretty rock'n'roll cool. Woody certainly liked it enough to insist that everyone, bandmates and other friends alike, address him in that manner from now on. The change from John to Woody had been relatively painless, effected between the worlds of public school and art college. Attempting to switch from Woody to Joe Strummer while residing in the middle of a close community, several of whose members had known him by the former name for over four years, proved more problematic. 'There was this embarrassing period when you'd keep referring to him as Woody and he wouldn't respond,' says Jules. '"My name's Joe, man." "Oh, yeah. Sorry." But it stuck in the end.' Clive remembers it well. '"Call me Joe." "Do we have to?" "Well, in public." And you'd do whatever it was he asked you to, because you liked him.' Mole was less malleable. 'I always carried on calling him Woody, all the time I was in the 101ers.' Richard good-humouredly side-stepped the issue. 'I used to call him Luigi.' Although for the sake of convenience, this narrative has Woody instantly becoming Joe Strummer in February 1975, it was not until he joined the Clash and – temporarily at least – broke many of his ties with his former life that the long-drawn out transformation was completed.

Most members of the 101ers agree that, by February 1975, the band was beginning to shape up. Mole bought his own bass amp, and Clive brought along his own equipment, improving the sound and rendering the kitchen-drawer speakers obsolete. After Joe himself, Richard was probably the most enthusiastic participant in the band, so much so that he refused to surrender the drum stool to a returning Antonio. He became an official member of the 101ers on 15 February. 'I was dead keen by then, definitely,' he says. 'The bug had bitten. I liked it, and they wanted me to continue, so I continued.' Antonio had nothing to blame but his own lack of commitment. 'I've been in loads of different bands, and the old joke is, you can't go on holiday,' notes Clive. 'If you go away for a week or two, when you come back you're probably not going to be in the band anymore. *That's rock'n'roll*, I'm afraid.'

Up to this point, the 101ers were still using the drum kit Antonio had borrowed back in August 1974, but – not surprisingly – the original owner now wanted it back. In fact, Richard remembers him calling around for it, and both himself and Joe pretending to be non-English-speaking Spaniards in order to hold on to it for a little longer. Aware that this ruse had a limited life span, they persuaded Clive – working as a van driver at the time – to take them down to Pablo LaBritain's house in Surrey to retrieve Joe's old kit. But when Pablo demonstrated his talents, Joe didn't have the heart to take the drums away from him. A couple of weeks later, Richard bought his own Pearl kit on Portobello Market.

Towards the end of the month, the 101ers made a joint investment. They had secured bookings at a long-forgotten venue in Brixton for 22 February, and at Chelsea College of Art for 1 March, supporting Ian Dury's pre-Blockheads band, Kilburn and the Highroads.

Unfortunately, they lacked the transport to get them there. 'Simon came in one day and said he'd seen this great hearse,' recalls Jules. 'It was like, £50. Everyone chucked whatever they had in a hat, and he went and bought it. It was a great old thing.' It seemed intimations of mortality were destined to dog Joe throughout his musical career...

A photo session was arranged on the day of the Brixton gig to capture the band at this key moment in their history. In addition to photographing the band at the Chippenham and in the rehearsal room at 101, Ray Eagle snapped them posing on the kerb next to their new purchase. One of these appears on the back cover of the 101ers' posthumous album, *Elgin Avenue Breakdown*, and another in Jules's 1992 photo-book *Joe Strummer With The 101ers And The Clash 1974-1976*. The third surviving picture was taken in the basement of 101. The other band members are mostly long haired, idiosyncratically behatted, and generally attired in the floppy and flared manner of late hippy; but Joe is still favouring the leather jacket, straight jeans and boots, and shortish, swept back hair of his Fifties rocker-meets-Woody Guthrie look.

Alvaro was less happy than the others about the way the band was progressing. 'We all thought that we were making shit music,' is his recollection today. Pat's similar claim about the band circa autumn 1974 provokes little in the way of dissent, but Richard for one is keen to take issue with Alvaro's assessment of the 101ers' abilities by the spring of 1975. 'That's bollocks!' he states. '*He* might have thought that. We knew we were no great band, but we definitely thought it was something worth doing.' The selection and simplicity of the material and the generally limited standard of musicianship were two of the factors contributing to Alvaro's disgruntlement, but they were by no means the only ones. He was nine years Joe's senior, a seasoned and – in his native country – successful musician. As the person initially responsible for getting the 101ers up on stage – to this day, he insists he and Joe co-founded the band – it must have been galling for Alvaro to watch Joe assume leadership. Furthermore, the instrumental dominance of the horns, and Alvaro's own role as musical arranger and featured soloist, had been challenged by the arrival of the equally experienced and proficient Clive Timperley on lead guitar.

Alvaro left the band on 27 March to make his own music. Unless one counts the Mad Chilean, he was denied a nickname during his stay with the 101ers; thereafter, however, he dubbed himself the Chilean with the Singing Nose, and began to record and release his own decidedly eccentric compositions, commencing with the 1977 album *Drinkin' My Own Sperm*...

In his July 1975 *Melody Maker* 101ers feature, Allan Jones described his first visit to the Charlie Pigdog club that February thus: 'It was the kind of place which held extraordinary promises of violence. You walked in, took one look around, and wished you were the hell out of there... After 10 minutes glancing into secluded corners half-expecting to see someone having their face decorated with a razor, the paranoia count was soaring. The gig that particular night ended in a near massacre. As the 101ers screamed their way through a 20-minute interpretation of "Gloria", which sounded like the perfect soundtrack for the last apocalyptic days of the Third Reich, opposing factions of (I believe) Irish and gypsies attempted to carve each other up. Bottles were smashed over defenceless heads, blades flashed, and howling dogs tore at one another's throats, splattering the walls with blood. The band tore on, with Joe Strummer thrashing away at his guitar like there was no tomorrow, completely oblivious to the surrounding carnage. The police finally arrived, flashing blue lights, sirens, the whole works. Strummer battled on. He was finally confronted by the imposing figure of the law, stopped in mid-flight, staggered to a halt and looked up. "Evening, officer," he said.'

This is a million miles away from the cosy Dansette-and-sandwiches ambience of the club's early days, and it seems Allan approached his piece with the twin purposes of instantly mythologising his college buddy's band, and indulging himself in a little bravura

Gonzo-style journalism to shake up the staid and predictable pages of the 1975-vintage *Melody Maker*. Word of mouth had expanded the 101ers audience, and the Charlie Pigdog club was invariably packed. The band's full tilt approach to its material, highlighted by Joe's manic stage persona, did tend to excite the crowd. But there were no scenes of carnage. '*Downstairs*, it was a violent pub,' says Mole, 'but it really didn't happen much upstairs, because it wasn't normal local punters, it was more hippies, younger types.'

The police were called out on a couple of occasions, but usually for reasons other than violence: 'When it had gone way beyond closing time, and the band was still going,' says Jules. 'Also, I think people were just coming in and stealing stuff, and dropping it out of the windows to people down below.' Joe and Richard both alluded to this outbreak of petty theft in Paolo Hewitt's 1981 *Melody Maker* 101ers retrospective, and most people involved with the band now believe the resulting aggravation explains why the landlord shut down the Charlie Pigdog club following a gig on 24 April. At the time, the band members were given no reason more convincing than a vague plan to redecorate. The club is now a snooker room.

The Chippenham residency lasted two days and one gig longer than Jules's performing membership of the band. Joe wanted to reclaim the microphone for himself. Also, the 101ers wanted to pursue the possibility of playing more gigs further afield, and Clive in particular felt it would be practical to trim the band down to a more manageable size. 'I was sacked,' says Jules. 'It was OK. That's the way it was done. You were politely told, "You're out, man." It was democratically done, basically, by whoever was still in the band, and I can't think of a better way.' He bore no grudge, as he had been feeling vaguely embarrassed about the meagreness of his contribution for some time. 'A bit of singing and maracas. I couldn't really play anything.'

Jules continued to share accommodation with the band. For a while, he also acted as a kind of unofficial manager, finding gigs and keeping any hustling would-be official managers at bay. 'No-one was going to be told how to dress up or what to do,' he says. 'So it was easier to push all that away, and everyone did what they liked and organised it themselves.' Shortly afterwards, Jules began to study photography, film and television at the London College of Printing. He used the band, especially Joe, as subjects while honing his photographic talents. In turn, the band encouraged him to use his access to equipment and materials to produce promotional material. One poster from early 1976 boasted the slogan, 'BEAT MUSIC DYNAMITE!', which came uncannily close to being 10 years ahead of its time...

Back in January 1975, Joe had replaced the Bolivian boyfriend in the affections of Esperanza's sister Paloma. It is Esperanza's opinion that dating sisters strengthened the bond between Joe and Richard. That Easter, the foursome commandeered the hearse and set off for a decidedly non-luxurious holiday in Wales.

Within a month of returning to London, Joe got married; but not to Paloma. As part of his preparation for the next stage of the 101ers' development, he had decided that it was finally time to get himself a quality guitar. Initially intending to earn the price of one with the sweat of his brow, he took a job with the council as a gardener in Hyde Park. As with the ENO cleaning job, though, fate soon intervened to offer him enough easy money to give up work altogether. 'I met this South American chick who wanted to get married,' he told Allan Jones that July. 'To stay in the country, see? She paid me £100. So I quit the job and got a Telecaster to go with the AC30. I'll get the divorce through in about two years.'

The 'marriage of convenience' scam was fairly commonplace in the Maida Hill squatting community at that time, many of its members being foreigners in the country on limited visitors' visas. It was considered such an everyday event, and was over and done with so quickly, that none of the 101ers can remember anything about the wedding or Joe's bride; including Simon, who stood as one of the witnesses. Even Joe had trouble remembering the girl's name and nationality, which caused problems for him when he eventually did get around to seeking a divorce in 1986: T-zers, the *NME* gossip page, mentioned that he was trying to trace a 'South African' called 'Pam'. The marriage certificate states that John Graham Mellor, a 22 year-old musician of 101 Walterton Road – which by this time was no longer his real address – married Pamela Jill Moolman, a 25 year-old social worker of 51 Doynton Street in Archway, on 16 May 1975 at St Pancras Register Office, Euston Road. Only Esperanza is able to provide further background and explain the apparent confusion over Pam's country of origin: 'She was a friend of somebody called Rose who also lived in 101. I think she was travelling to South America after she married, or she'd just come back from South America and needed the visa to stay in England. But she was definitely South African.'

As it was just a paper relationship, the marriage did not upset Paloma in any way at the time, but it did affect her indirectly. 'This was when Spain wasn't in the Common Market, so all our Spanish friends had trouble,' explains Richard. 'I married Esperanza, even though it wasn't *marriage* marriage, in August 1975. At least I didn't charge her! Joe was our witness. But Paloma did have problems. She couldn't marry Joe, who she was living with at the time, so she married my brother Patrick. People married anyone!' Clive, for one, has no doubts about where Joe's affections really lay. 'Basically, Strummer married his Fender,' he says. 'It's true! I think that's a great image for him, because the Telecaster is definitely him, it's his prop.' Certainly, although the guitar-mad Joe had acquired and played many different styles and makes in the past, and would experiment with others in future, the Fender Telecaster – and, later, the lookalike Esquire – was to be his instrument of choice from June 1975 onward.

Early May of that year saw time finally run out for 101 Walterton Road. Anticipating forced eviction by the GLC, the household relocated of its own accord. Richard and Simon picked the locks of another empty house at 36 St Luke's Road, just a few hundred yards to the south. They moved in with Joe, Esperanza, Paloma and Joe's old Newport friend Micky Foote, who by this time was hanging around and showing an interest in the band. Number 36 became the new venue for rehearsals, but it never acquired anything like the atmosphere of 101. This was partly because St Luke's Road was not as squat-dominated as Walterton Road, and the new arrivals encountered sustained hostility. 'We stayed throughout the summer,' says Richard, 'but we had some pretty heavy scenes with some of the local kids: nicking, breaking in, stuff like that.'

As a band, the 101ers' immediate priority following the closure of the Charlie Pigdog club was to find a pub prepared to offer them a weekly residency, so that they could maintain the momentum they had already built up. That April, in the *Melody Maker*'s Hot Licks column, Allan Jones complained that New York bands like Television were receiving so much attention in the UK music press while 'a really exciting band like the 101ers, with a stack of AC30's [are] playing gigs like the Charlie Pigdog club for a packet of peanuts and half a bitter'. Allan's appreciation of the 101ers was genuine enough, but it is hard not to see his championing of an old college friend's band as an act of nepotism. Nevertheless, in Paolo Hewitt's 1981 *Melody Maker* 101ers retrospective, Joe was dismissive of this support. 'That was like the summit of a year's sweat. That was the ultimate, this little cutting. No-one was interested. *Nobody*.' His deprecatory remarks were questionably motivated, however, and history proves him wrong.

Micky and Jules took that cutting down to the Elgin pub, just south of the Westway on Ladbroke Grove, and used it to secure a one-off gig for Thursday 12 May. This in turn proved successful enough for the band to be offered a weekly Thursday night slot beginning on 26 May and – it turned out – lasting for the remainder of 1975. Like the Chippenham, the Elgin was chosen largely for convenience. 'It was just the next nearest place,' says Jules, who does not feel that the venue represented any kind of advancement for the 101ers. Richard disagrees. The band had found it necessary to set up the Charlie Pigdog club themselves in order to be able to play for their friends. By contrast, the Elgin was an established, if not particularly high-profile, music pub that booked the band on reputation and merit to play for an open audience. Furthermore, the 101ers were the only band to be offered a residency there at that time.

Simon 'Big John' Cassell lasted for just the first two gigs at the Elgin. With Alvaro no longer in the line-up, Simon was the sole horn player and his musicianship was not really strong enough for him to carry the burden alone. Again, the need to trim down the band was a factor; and again there was some tension with Clive regarding musical dominance. Clive went to work on Joe. 'I said, "You want to get this into a four-piece. Big John's a really great bloke, but, y'know..."' Although getting rid of Simon would make Joe sole vocalist and leave him in near-total control of the band, he resisted the idea; partly because Simon was a good friend, and partly because of the strong visual contrast he provided on stage. At the time, Ian Dury's Kilburn and the High Roads were making a feature of the physical discrepancies between their band members. The Charlie Pigdog version of the 101ers had boasted a similarly impressive range of shapes and sizes, an asset that Joe was clearly loath to let go. In the event, Simon's dissatisfaction with the change in musical style prompted him to leave the 101ers of his own accord following the 26 May Elgin gig. Soon afterwards, he moved to Germany, where he improved his skills playing sax in various jazz groups.

Up to this point, the 101ers had always announced and advertised themselves as an 'R&B Orchestra'. Their horn-dominated line-up harkened back to late Fifties urban R&B bands and even late Forties jump bands, but also reflected a by no means minor contemporary musical trend. In addition to Kilburn and the High Roads, crossover glam-rock'n'roll big bands like Wizzard and Showaddywaddy all boasted horn sections, as did the early-to-mid Seventies Rolling Stones, Van Morrison and the up-and-coming Bruce Springsteen. John Lennon was also revisiting several original rock'n'roll and R&B classics in full-blown big band style for the album eventually released in 1975 under the hardly misleading title *Rock'n'Roll*.

Richard maintains that the 1974 double live Van Morrison album *It's Too Late To Stop Now* had been the biggest influence on the sound aspired to – if not necessarily all the material played – by the Chippenham-era 101ers, which in turn evidences the sizeable input at that stage of the Morrison-loving Simon Cassell. Joe had listened to Them as a schoolboy, so it had not been too much of a leap for him to learn to appreciate the music of the post-Them Morrison. His own preference, though, was for the more aggressive, basic and guitar-dominated R&B style of the early Sixties Stones and the late Fifties Chuck Berry and Bo Diddley. With the horns dismissed, and Clive on hand to play the 'fiddly bits', Joe was now free to pursue this musical direction.

Back in autumn 1974, expediency had been the dominant factor in the 101 All Stars' choice of material, but as 1975 progressed, changes in line-up and improving musicianship did not effect the band's repertoire of cover versions in any way other than to expand it to fill anything up to a two-and-a-half-hour show. 'Bony Moronie' and 'Gloria' remained the usual opening and closing numbers, respectively, for the band's entire lifespan. Clive might have been partial to country and muso rock, and Richard – although having eclectic tastes – particularly fond of Sixties soul, but relatively little evidence of this made it to the live set. Similarly, Mole was a reggae enthusiast, but although he recalls playing a version of Desmond Dekker's 'Israelites' at the Charlie Pigdog club with himself on guitar and Joe on bass, and, later in 1975, working up a 'more roots' reggae song in the Big Youth vein, such experimentation with Jamaican rhythms was confined to soundchecks only.

That said, no member of the band was deeply unhappy about the songs the 101ers did perform, which were either vintage R&B or rock'n'roll, or compositions in a closely related style by second generation bands born of those traditions. Predictably, Chuck Berry was the main source, providing 'No Particular Place To Go', 'Johnny B Goode', 'Too Much Monkey Business', 'Maybellene', 'Roll Over Beethoven', 'Carol' and – though it was originally written in 1946 by Bobby Troup for the Nat Cole Trio – '(Get Your Kicks On) Route 66'. Bo Diddley provided 'Who Do You Love', 'Don't Let Go' and 'Six Gun Blues', and Johnny Otis the 1958-vintage Diddley-esque 'Willie And The Hand Jive'. In addition to 'Bony Moronie', miscellaneous other classics from the rock'n'roll era included Gene Vincent's 'Be-Bop-A-Lula', Little Richard's 'Slippin' And Slidin' – all three of which songs, incidentally, were also covered on John Lennon's *Rock'n'Roll* – Elvis Presley's 'Heartbreak Hotel' and Eddie Cochran's 'Summertime Blues'.

The Rolling Stones were represented by the song they wrote for Chris Farlowe in 1966, 'Out Of Time', and by the Slim Harpo song they covered on *Exile On Main Street*, 'Shake Your Hips'. The Beatles bequeathed 'Day Tripper', 'I'm Down' and – perfect for Joe – the Chuck Berry-meets-the-Beach Boys parody 'Back In The USSR'. Also from the mid Sixties came the Small Faces' 'Sha La La Lee' and Roy C's 'Shotgun Wedding'. Van Morrison was responsible not only for 'Gloria', but also the 101ers' most up-to-date number, the 1970 composition 'Domino'. Some of the band's choices of cover version were a little less obvious: Louis Jordan and the Tympany Five's 1946 hit 'Choo Choo Ch' Boogie'; what Clive describes as 'an old cajun-type R&B number from the Fifties' called 'Hoy, Hoy, Hoy' lifted from an old compilation album; and an equally obscure song called 'Junco Partner', attributed to one Shad, covered in 1972 by Dr John. 'I learned it off this bargain record I bought,' Joe told *Record Mirror*'s Billy Sloan in 1981, shortly after he had recorded a reggae version of the song with the Clash. 'Apparently, it's a 50 year-old New Orleans standard.'

By 1975, as far as London was concerned, the Rock'n'Roll Revival had been, if not superseded, then largely engulfed by yet another pre-punk back-to-basics movement. What came to be known as pub rock was a direct result of record companies being more interested in the latest creatively bankrupt supergroups or soundalike versions of established bands than in searching out new talent. It was not a unified movement as such: most of the bands had little in common save for the venues their lack of record company backing or commercial clout required them to play. Some of the outfits on the London pub circuit in the early to mid Seventies were just fairly ordinary country rock bands who had not yet managed to get a foot in the record companies' doors. Others were talented bands who were either too nonconformist to raise any interest, or who had already had their fingers burned by the music business.

A few had more in common with Joe's philosophy as expounded to Allan Jones in July 1975: 'I mean, if you go and see a rock group, you want to see someone tearing their soul apart at 36 bars a second, not listen to some instrumental slush. Since '67, music has been chasing itself up a blind alley with all that shit.' These bands were young, fresh and wired, and they played a stripped-down, pugnacious rock music, drawing their core repertoires from the late Fifties or mid Sixties Golden Ages before music – as they believed – chased itself up that blind alley. Dr Feelgood adopted a sleazy and menacing mod-meets-East End gangster look to deliver viciously fast Anglicised R&B. Eddie and the Hot Rods modelled themselves on a *Nuggets*-type Sixties US garage or punk band and covered Sixties rock classics like ? and the Mysterians' '96 Tears' and the Who's

'The Kids Are Alright'. The Count Bishops fell somewhere between the two, covering R&B classics and garage band songs like the Standells' 'Sometimes Good Guys Don't Wear White', as also played by Mick Jones's band Little Queenie. All three of these outfits crossed paths and repertoires with the 101ers, but only one earned their unreserved approval. 'The Feelgoods: we certainly admired them when we started playing,' says Richard. 'Late summer of '74 I think we saw them at the Windsor Castle. Wilko Johnson was great.' He was also, significantly, a manic guitarist who favoured a Telecaster.

In retrospect, it is clear that bands like Dr Feelgood and Kilburn and the High Roads did as much as the New York Dolls and the Ramones to prepare the ground for the UK's Class of '76 punk movement. It has even been asserted that the Feelgoods influenced elements of the New York new wave. In 1999 Blondie bassist Gary Valentine told *Mojo* that the band's drummer, Clem Burke, had visited London in 1975 and returned with Dr Feelgood's first album, *Down By The Jetty*. Shortly afterwards, he played it over and over again at a party attended by most of the key figures on the nascent New York new wave scene. Before long, short sharp songs and short sharp suits were adopted (almost) all round.

In the years immediately pre-punk, though, the London pub rock bands had to be judged on their own achievements. Against the trend of the times, Dr Feelgood were signed by United Artists in late 1974, made the transition to the UK's larger venues and, in 1975, released two albums. The decidedly Seventies edge the Feelgoods added to their R&B repertoire served – despite such idiosyncrasies as mono production – to make the band more than just a retro novelty act. In turn, the Feelgood Factor gave the 101ers commercial hope, a new-found credibility, and – paradoxically – an increased contemporary relevance.

Like the good Doctor, by mid 1975 the 101ers had another ace up their sleeve: the ability to compose their own genre-appropriate material. Joe had begun to write lyrics and vocal melody lines in Newport, and now, with a little help from his friends, was capable of working out rudimentary R&B chord progressions. 'Strummer would say, "I've got an idea for a song", and he'd come and play it: Guitar Workshop,' says Clive. 'I'd say, "OK, let's work it out. If I just make that chord this chord..."' Other band members would also add their ideas at rehearsals.

The first song completed was 'Keys To Your Heart'. It was later credited to Strummer, whereas most subsequent Joe-originated compositions were credited Strummer-101ers in acknowledgement of the others' sizeable musical input. By June 1975, the band's oeuvre also included 'Motor Boys Motor' and 'Steamgauge 99'. As the year progressed, it was further swollen by 'Letsagetabitarockin', 'Silent Telephone', 'Hideaway', 'Green Love', and a less typical Mole composition called 'Boo The Goose', which Clive describes as 'a funky soul number'. Musically, the 101ers proved they had a varied bag of tricks within the limitations dictated by line-up, genre and ability. Joe's lyrics were rendered almost incomprehensible by his mangled delivery – even on later studio versions of the songs – but evidence a decidedly Berry-esque style: verbose yet slick, with plenty of internal rhymes. The subject matter of his songs from this period is largely predictable. 'Motor Boys Motor' pays tribute to Chuck Berry's fascination with all things automotive; and, in its title at least, so does 'Steamgauge 99', harkening back to both 'Route 66' and Jackie Brenston's 1951 paean to a hot rod, 'Rocket 88', hailed by many as the first ever rock'n'roll record. 'Letsagetabitarockin' promotes the idea of a rock gig as endurance test: 'I'm ready to drop / But I don't wanna stop.' 'Silent Telephone' concerns itself with that old staple, the girl who doesn't ring; and who – in this case – is called Suzie, a name as generic to the rock'n'roll lyrical tradition as Johnny and Joe. If 'Silent Telephone' is a 'lost love' song, then 'Keys To Your Heart' is a song celebrating the redemptive power of love: 'I used to be a teenage drug-taker...'

Most of the band's early ventures away from their new base at the Elgin were local: squatters benefits and anniversary celebrations at Tolmer's Village in Euston and the Chippenham Factory in Maida Hill; a benefit for the Law Centre at Acklam Hall in Portobello Road; and the first of several occasional gigs at Mick Jones's local venue, the Windsor Castle pub on the Harrow Road. In late June and July 1975, however, Jules found the 101ers a couple of ostensibly prestige venues in the heart of Soho, where the likes of the Rolling Stones had originally made their mark.

The first of these was at the St Moritz club, 159 Wardour Street. As the club's name might suggest, the owner, a Mr Sweety, was Swiss. Jules's Swiss girlfriend was working as a waitress in the upstairs restaurant. The 101ers first played the club on 18 June 1975, and returned on 20 June, 2 July and 27 August. The repeat bookings are misleading: the shows were not a success. 'It was this tiny little basement, and it was full of students from the other side of the world who didn't really know what hit 'em when the 101ers cranked out this loud music,' says Jules. 'They did two sets, bashing out this R&B, and the people were all gawping at it because they couldn't respond to that kind of music. Then, as soon as the set was over, the juke box came back on, all pop stuff, and everybody started dancing again. It was bizarre.'

There were also difficulties with getting Mr Sweety to hand over the money. 'He did pay us, but he was busy running the restaurant upstairs, and he expected us to wait until he'd cleared it up.' The most positive outcome of the experience was a new song, 'Sweety of the St Moritz' in which Joe complains at length about the perceived shortcomings of venue, audience and owner. Apart from being a great driving rock song, it is notable for being the first Strummer composition to draw extensively on his own experiences, protest unfairness, and spit vitriol. Admittedly, it gets its knickers in a knot about next to nothing at all, but it can be seen as a precursor of some of the first Clash album's protest songs, and of such later State of the Clash broadcasts as '(White Man) In Hammersmith Palais' and 'Safe European Home'.

Jules's second coup was a gig Upstairs at Ronnie Scott's, the small room at Frith Street's famous London jazz club. Clive was not impressed. 'We got paid £15. Not bad for 1975,' he concedes grudgingly. 'Meanwhile, the money Ronnie Scott's took over the bar would pay for the evening and probably the whole week. It's crap. *Downstairs* at Ronnie Scott's: *that's* a big deal.' Richard acknowledges the point, but is less cynical about the 101ers' first forays into Soho. 'It was great!' he enthuses. 'It was an incredible feeling of non-stop progression.'

If the St Moritz spawned a song, then Ronnie Scott's led to the band's first – and only – radio broadcast, albeit on minor London pirate station Radio Concorde. The land-based station was forced to broadcast from a different location every night. On an earlier occasion Concorde had set up at 101 Walterton Terrace, and in return, the station arranged to broadcast a tape of the Ronnie Scott's gig. Unfortunately, as part of its efforts to avoid being traced, it also selected its frequency on a random basis. 'We didn't hear it,' laughs Clive, 'because we didn't know what to tune in to!' The 101ers' relationship with the station did not come to an end there, though: on 13 February 1976, they would play a Concorde benefit show at Hampstead Town Hall.

The summer of 1975 saw the 101ers venturing even further afield, usually thanks to the good offices of Dave McLardy, known as Dave the Van Driver – or D the VD for short – a friend of the band who owned a van, and was prepared to drive the band to gigs within a 50 mile radius of London. (Dave would ultimately marry Paloma: *marriage* marriage.) If the band went any further, they hired their own van. One of the furthest flung gigs at this time was the Stonehenge Festival in Wiltshire on 21 June. On the day of the event, Clive caught flu and refused to travel, leaving the others to muddle through without a lead instrument. Almost as if to compensate for this, upon their return to

London and Clive's return to good health, the 101ers again began to occasionally augment their line-up. Sometimes Tymon Dogg guested, but more often it was Dan Kelleher of the Derelicts. A good friend of Clive, Dan was often to be found in the audience at 101ers gigs. A musical all-rounder, he would be invited to join the full-strength band onstage for a couple of numbers on either slide or second lead guitar. As an honorary member, he too was awarded a nickname: Desperate Dan.

On 26 July, *Melody Maker* printed Allan Jones's enthusiastic full-length 101ers feature, which showcased the Strummer philosophy and made the band out to be the most exciting gritty lowlife band in town. Following on from Dr Feelgood's move into the big league, Allan's decidedly slanted rave write-up was almost guaranteed to make something happen for the 101ers; and it did. The review was instrumental in establishing them as a name attraction on the London pub circuit, making it much easier for them to get regular gigs and residencies at a steadily increasing number of that circuit's more prestigious venues, including the Hope and Anchor in Islington, the Nashville in Kensington, Dingwalls in Camden Town, the Red Cow in Hammersmith, and the Speakeasy in central London. In October and November 1975, the 101ers found themselves playing almost every other night. Although their schedule settled down thereafter to a less exhausting ratio of one gig every three nights, the band would never again be short of work. 'Allan Jones definitely helped,' is Richard's verdict.

More press was to follow. Not wanting to lose out to the *Melody Maker*, the *NME* dispatched Chas De Whalley to witness the 101ers' first Hope and Anchor gig on what, as the writer subsequently explained at length, was an extremely hot night to be watching a sweaty R&B band in a cramped pub cellar. His review, published on 16 August, was a deliberately oddball one which indicated that he understood the spirit of the band, even if he was not prepared to spare some of its members' feelings: 'Only Clive Timperlee on lead guitar boasts any kind of real musical ability and, as for the others... they start out of time, finish out of time, and play out of tune. They also churn out some very fine rock'n'roll with no pretence at all towards music, let alone art... When they're good, they're very, very good... and their own compositions "Steamgauge 99" and "Motor Boys Motor" can stand unashamedly beside some of the rock'n'roll standards that make up the rest of their set. Now that... Dr Feelgood have left the pubs, the 101ers are definite contenders for London's rock'n'roll crown.'

For their own part, the 101ers did not feel they had succeeded in gatecrashing any pub rock 'scene'. 'I think we thought we were totally doing our own thing,' says Richard. 'It wasn't as if we were aspiring to become part of a thing that was there already. Obviously, objectively, we were, because we were playing these pubs, but we didn't *aspire* to being part of that group. And I think, increasingly through 1975 and the beginning of 1976, there was the notion that, "There should be something better!" Which didn't necessarily mean better groups or bigger gigs, but something more vibrant. Which is in fact what happened with the punk uprising of 1976. In late '75, I remember *Time Out* once referring to us as a "punk" band.'

On 24 August, the 101ers returned to Wiltshire to play the Windsor Festival at Watchfield. Adventurously, they agreed to play three separate hour-long sets on each of the three stages, one of Fifties covers, one of Sixties covers, and one of originals. Three days beforehand, as a warm-up, they played a set entirely composed of originals at the Elgin. According to Mole, nobody seemed to notice. 'I still remember the audience talking at the bar,' he told *DISCoveries*' Ralph Heibutzki in 1994. '"The 101ers are OK, but they only do covers!"'

The demanding new schedule persuaded Clive to give up his van driving job. 'It was getting really hard to get up in the morning.' Like the others, he signed on as unemployed, but he maintains there was no real element of fraud involved: at the time, the 101ers' gigs were generating just about enough income to keep the band functioning. In anticipation of things improving, though, the band borrowed the money to pay for a halfway decent PA system. Micky Foote, now helping out as roadie and occasional driver, took over from Jules as unofficial manager and also began to mix the 101ers' live sound.

The October residency at the Nashville was where Dan's guest spot became a regular fixture. It was also where, according to both Richard and Clive, Eddie and the Hot Rods – with whom the 101ers were alternating as headliners – swiped the 101ers' extended version of 'Gloria'. The following year, the Rods' treatment of the song made it to number 43 in the UK singles charts as part of their *Live At The Marquee* EP. 'We were really pissed off with them,' says Clive. 'But there's no licence, is there? It wasn't even ours.'

By October, life at 36 St Luke's Road had become unbearable, so Micky and Jules went scouting for a new home and band HQ. Just over half a mile to the east they found an empty house at 42 Orsett Terrace. Micky, Jules, Joe, Paloma, Richard and Esperanza moved in and had the sizeable property to themselves. There was room for a studio for the two sisters, both of whom dabbled with ceramics, and also a band rehearsal room in the basement. Micky even managed to get a payphone installed, which made it much easier to arrange bookings and practices.

On 18 November, Joe went to see Bruce Springsteen's much-hyped appearance at the Hammersmith Odeon. With hindsight, Clive suspects he was very much impressed by Springsteen, another energetic, Fender-wielding fan of Chuck Berry and Bob Dylan, who was similarly intent on using his own songs as an outlet for his obsession with rock'n'roll mythology. 'When Strummer saw Springsteen, I think he thought, "Hello, this is the kind of image I've already got, and *look* at this guy!"' Certainly, thereafter, elements of Joe's stagecraft began to develop along similar lines to Bruce's. He bought an especially long lead so he was free to move around more and indulge himself in some grandstanding showmanship. 'At one gig, there happened to be a mattress lying in one corner – I don't know what it was doing there – and he jumped on it and lay down on it for about 10 minutes while we were doing "Gloria",' recalls Clive. 'He just kept looking at me while I was doing this solo, just blasting away, and I was thinking, "Come on, you've got to get back to the mike!" and he was just lying there. And then all of a sudden, he *rushed* back up on stage and got to the mike just in time. Brilliant!'

As he became more at ease onstage, Joe also developed an easy line in between-song patter. When the occasion demanded, he was more than prepared to abandon onstage wit in favour of offstage confrontation. 'There was some bloke at the back who was shouting and Joe just walked up to him – long lead – and whispered something in his ear,' says Clive. 'There was not a peep out of him after that.' Richard recalls another occasion when a front row heckler was doused with a pint of beer.

Such displays of energy and feistiness gave some onlookers the wrong impression. By this time, while the popularity of marijuana remained constant, other late-hippy favourites like acid and mandrax were being replaced in the drug-taking community's affections by amphetamine sulphate, or speed. It was decidedly unhealthy – Joe was later to liken it to a well-known brand of household scouring powder – but relatively cheap and easy to both find and take. The Feelgoods' Wilko Johnson has since attributed much of his own mid-Seventies energetic stage persona to the effects of the drug. In his 1 November *NME* 'Pub Rock Report '75', journalist Geoff Hill dropped a sly hint to those in the know when making reference to the 101ers, Eddie and the Hot Rods and other of the bands on the pub circuit, 'whose virtue is their raw energy and whose vice generally tends to be their unoriginality of material or presentation and an over-reliance on speed'.

It was a suggestion that had been made before, and it was one that used to annoy Joe, as he explained to Paolo Hewitt in 1981: 'At the Western Counties [in Paddington] one night we played this really blistering set, really firing on all cylinders. Then we went out into the bar to have a drink, and this bloke goes, "How many lines did you snort before *that* set, then?" And we weren't into speed. We couldn't afford speed.' Clive confirms that Joe was remarkably health-conscious for a squat-dwelling rock'n'roller. Already a vegetarian – like Mick Jones – he looked after his voice with regular doses of honey and lemon, and although he liked a drink when money allowed, he did not smoke tobaeco, even insisting on rolling his occasional joints with a herbal substitute.

The next development for the 101ers was the opportunity to record. In November 1975, the band was approached by Vic Maile, the man who had produced the first Dr Feelgood album, and also recorded the two 1975 gigs which, the following year, would provide that band with their UK number one live album, *Stupidity*. 'Vic Maile was an ex-BBC sound engineer,' says Clive. 'He used to mix the sound of audiences at football matches!' Which might explain his preference for recording bands as 'live' as possible, either at gigs or in the studio. Maile was looking to follow up his success with the Feelgoods. 'He wanted to sign up bands, do recording and production deals with them, and sell them off to the highest bidders,' recalls Clive. 'I think he just got a tip-off about us and turned up one day at a gig.' Maile was also interested in Eddie and the Hot Rods, and would later co-produce their *Live At The Marquee* EP. It may have been that he had taken a hint from Geoff Hill's 'Pub Rock Report', which had threatened that both bands would be 'descending on your hitherto-quiet local in the wake of Dr Feelgood'.

On 28 November 1975, Maile recorded six songs with the 101ers in the studio where he worked, Jackson's in Rickmansworth. As if chosen specifically to disprove Geoff Hill's charges of 'unoriginality of material', they were all band compositions: 'Letsagetabitarockin', 'Silent Telephone', 'Motor Boys Motor', 'Sweety Of The St Moritz', 'Hideaway' and 'Steamgauge 99'. 'We just went in and thrashed through a load of numbers,' says Mole. 'There were no retakes, or anything, just the vocals added later. The guy didn't want to listen to what anybody else wanted to do: not an amenable character. It was horrible, nobody enjoyed it. We were all in really foul moods because this bloke was really miserable.' Richard, as ever, is more positive about the experience: 'I don't remember that not being enjoyable. It was great! The first time we'd ever been in a studio…' Whatever, Maile's empire-building came to naught, and at the time the band was not too distraught that Jackson's studio retained the copyright on the material.

On 15 January 1976, after a two-week Christmas layoff, it was Mole's turn to be sacked from the 101ers. 'I certainly didn't leave of my own accord,' he says. 'I think I was an expedient sort of scapegoat. I think everyone was pissed off that we weren't getting anywhere, that there wasn't any success happening. This guy Dan was hanging around, and it was a case of, "We'll change something, and maybe something'll happen." And the something they changed was me. I was very upset. That band was part of a whole network in the Chippenham Road, a whole café scene at That Tea Room, a little alternative family there. And it almost excluded you from the whole thing when you were thrown out of the band.'

The other 101ers, most of whom have since patched up their friendships with Mole, are reluctant to go on record about what is obviously still a sensitive subject. However, the consensus seems to be that, whereas the other members of the band were basking in the attention they were receiving and becoming increasingly confident, Mole appeared to be growing less and less positive. Both the band's and Mole's explanations for the firing are perfectly credible, but Dan Kelleher was certainly waiting in the wings, keen to contribute more than just additional guitar embellishments to a couple of songs. As a gifted bass player, guitarist, keyboard player and arranger he was the obvious candidate for Mole's old job; perhaps even before the vacancy existed.

'I remember me and Joe going around to see Mole to tell him we thought that was it,' says Richard. 'Looking back, I think it was probably a mistake: the relationship between Dan and Joe was ultimately one of the reasons the 101ers didn't continue.' Small consolation for Mole. He went to see the band's first gig without him, on 16 January at Queen Elizabeth College, Campden Hill Road, Kensington, but thereafter had nothing more to do with the 101ers. It took him two years to get over the sacking, but then he formed his own late punk-era band Pitiful, and shortly afterwards another outfit named the Vincent Units.

The 101ers played what turned out to be their last Elgin gig on 8 January 1976. Their residency was officially terminated on the day of Mole's departure following complaints of noise pollution. The change in line-up and loss of their home-base venue helped spur the 101ers into action, but they had already decided to concentrate on playing further afield. Towards the end of 1975, the 101ers had turned to the Albion booking agency to help them establish themselves on the national circuit. 'That's when we started doing things like [the 500-capacity] JB's in Dudley,' says Clive. 'Albion also had the Stranglers, so we did a couple of gigs with them.'

From January 1976 onward, the 101ers played a punishing schedule of out of town dates. As the budget seldom ran to accommodation, the gigs were either in towns within easy access of London, or else hit-and-run sojourns in the Midlands and the North involving marathon overnight drives home. Between January and April 1976, as well as the gigs they played in and around London, the 101ers made a total of five trips up country to play the likes of Samantha's in Leek, Clarence's in Halifax, the Cocked Hat in Scunthorpe, and the Black Swan in Sheffield, the venue where the Clash would later make their début. As it was too much to expect Micky Foote to organise band, transport, and equipment under such circumstances, another member of the squatting community, John Tiberi, was taken on as roadie. Before long, he was given the obligatory nickname: Boogie.

A new spirit of professionalism was adopted. 'We used to be pissed a lot,' says Clive. 'But we cut that out. No smoking dope or getting rat-arsed before a gig.' Although the others continued to wear scruffy casual clothes, Joe decided it was time to create an image for himself, and – possibly as another nod in the direction of the Rip Off Park Rock'n'Roll All Stars – bought a stage suit. 'A kind of browny, sort of dirty colour,' recalls Clive, wrinkling his nose. Joe loved it, and was reluctant to take the stage in anything else, although he sometimes spoiled the effect by wearing it with sneakers. It became another of Micky's tasks to ensure that it was dry-cleaned between gigs. The closest Joe came to throwing a rock star-style temper-tantrum was if, for any reason, the suit could not be collected on time. The days of the Woody Guthrie look were over.

The 101ers had played occasional college gigs from their very early days. Most had been at London venues, like the South Bank Polytechnic, the London School of Economics, or the University of London Student Union. With Albion's help, farther-flung student gigs became a regular feature on the 101ers' schedule, both in London's satellite towns, like Gypsy Hill College in Kingston and Essex University in Colchester, and in the north, at such institutions as Nottingham and Liverpool Universities.

Albion also arranged the 101ers' one and only European tour, consisting of four one-night stands over a long weekend: Boddy's Music Inn, Amsterdam on 27 February, the Paradiso in the same town the following night, the Eksit club in Rotterdam on 28 February, and Gringo's in Ghent on 1 March. 'We got the usual English band deal at Boddy's Music Inn,' says Clive. 'The guy who owned it would liaise with a British agency, and get an English band to come over. He also owned a hotel, which we could stay at, and he'd arrange two or three other gigs. It's basically a rip off, but it gets you over there, and the guy who organises it gets an English band: the Dutch people love English bands.' The same is not necessarily true of the Belgian people. 'The place in Ghent was fucking horrible, awful. We tried to do [Hank Williams's cajun classic] 'Jambalaya' is all I can remember about it. We were at one end of the bar on a stage sweating, and there was people sitting there, no reaction. But we were having fun anyway. I mean, we were in another country.'

The 101ers did not necessarily have to travel abroad to experience that feeling. On 25 January, they played the Roundhouse in Camden Town for the first time as part of the traditional extended Sunday bill. Through the venue's promoter John Curd, they learned that it was possible to play Sunday lunchtime gigs at Wandsworth Prison, and duly signed up for 15 February. 'We walked into the sacristy, which was our dressing room, because we were playing on a big stage which they'd mounted on top of the altar in the chapel,' recalls Richard. 'Which was a *big* chapel.' Taking up a position inviting sacrifice in front of between 400 and 500 prisoners, many of them serious offenders, made the 101ers feel somewhat nervous; a feeling which intensified when there was no reaction at all during the first song. 'We were thinking, "This is going down like a concrete parachute,"' says Clive. 'But at the end of the number it was... instant eruption! They were on orders: they weren't allowed to talk or shout or do anything while we were playing. We did "Out Of Time", [Leiber-Stoller's] "Riot In Cell Block No 9", "Jailhouse Rock"...' It was another of the 101ers' themed sets. 'It was just incredible seeing the bliss on their faces as we moved through these songs,' says Richard. 'For me, that was the best gig we ever did.' 'They loved us,' agrees Clive. 'Talk about a captive audience!' As a result, the 101ers were asked back for two more shows, on 21 March and 11 April.

Dan Kelleher's arrival had a considerable impact. Live, in addition to playing bass, he added backing vocals to several songs and, being a confirmed Beatles fan, took over lead vocals on 'Back In The USSR'. It was behind the scenes, however, in the songwriting and arranging departments, that he made his most significant contributions. 'With a lot of Strummer's songs, he had the melody in his head, but he couldn't figure out the chords, so I sorted them out for him,' he told *Sounds*' Pete Silverton in 1979. As a result, the first three months of 1976 were the 101ers' most prolific in terms of song composition. Perhaps influenced by his live vocal feature, Dan came up with another cod-surf song, 'Surf City'. He and Joe teamed up to write '5 Star Rock'n'Roll Petrol'. Joe originated 'Sweet Revenge' ('I remember Clive having an input on that,' says Richard), 'Rabies (From The Dogs Of Love)' (credited to the 101ers when eventually released as a single B-side), and 'Jail Guitar Doors'. Richard offered 'Keep Taking The Tablets'. Only the last two failed to be recorded in the studio before the 101ers split.

The other songs are far more varied in subject and style than the band's earlier compositions, and with their new emphasis on musicianship, indicate a deliberate move away from the aggressive full-tilt approach of yore. At first, '5 Star Rock'n'Roll Petrol' would appear to be another Berry-inspired cruising anthem, but although the song itself is a straightforward rocker, the lyric is at the very least ambiguous. Either rock'n'roll itself is the superior energy-giving fuel in question, or else the protagonist requires some other kind of fuel in order to pass a 'Letsagetabitarockin'-type endurance test. Addiction is the song's central conceit: there are references to making connections and getting burned, and Joe declares 'I need some more petrol / But I don't really want it', before the song ends with alternating whispered pleas and screamed demands for more 5 Star. This is pretty blatant hard-drug imagery for a band claiming not to have the time, money or inclination for such pursuits.

'Rabies (From The Dogs Of Love)' opens with a classic folk song greeting, 'Come now, all you gentlemen / Come now, all you ladies', and ends with a whistle recalling Rufus Thomas's R&B song 'Walking The Dog'. If '5 Star Rock'n'Roll Petrol' concerns itself with drugs, then 'Rabies' is about sexual relations, rather than the 'madness of love' suggested by the title. Like the Rufus Thomas song, it sets itself up to be a novelty number, but the innuendo is altogether darker, and soon gives way to a blatant sleaziness unworthy even of the blues tradition. Initially, both sexes are addressed, but verse two tells of Crazy Daisy leaving something indecipherable in a plastic bag down on Shepherds Bush Green, and verse three of Jean, who passes on something that leads to the male victim spending the chorus down on his knees in the Praed Street Clinic. It almost goes without saying that the clinic in question is the part of St Mary's Hospital responsible for treating sexually transmitted diseases, and that 'rabies' is a metaphor for such afflictions. As 'dog' is a derogatory term for a supposedly promiscuous female, it's hard not to see the song as the kind of nasty little male chauvinist sexual revenge number beloved of the Stranglers at this time.

In comparison with the others, the country rock-tinged 'Sweet Revenge' could almost qualify as a ballad. Again, the subject belies the title, but this time in a positive way: it's a song *opposing* cycles of violence, the doctrine of an eye for an eye. One verse would appear to be directly autobiographical, referring to life 'back at school' where 'You hit him / He hits you back.' The conclusion is that blood is invariably spilled for nothing, foreshadowing the sentiments of the 1979 Clash song 'Last Gang In Town'.

Early in March 1976, the 101ers were approached by Ted Carroll and Roger Armstrong and asked if they wanted to make a single. In 1972, Ted had begun to feed the Rock'n'Roll Revival by selling imported and rare rock'n'roll and R&B records from his stall Rock On in a communal retail outlet in Golborne Road, at the north end of Portobello Road. Shortly afterwards, he had diversified into Sixties punk and garage music, and in 1974, had opened a second stall at a market then situated in Soho's Newport Court, managed by his friend Roger. A third outlet, the shop still to be found next to Camden Town tube station, had opened in 1975. Both Mick Jones and Joe Strummer became regular Rock On customers. Ted and Roger's professional interest in closely related musical genres made them particularly receptive to both the harder edged pub rock bands and to the emerging punk movement. In December 1975, they witnessed the Sex Pistols' fifth ever gig, by which time they had already set up an independent record label named Chiswick.

Small independent labels, funded with peanuts and run on a shoe string, go all the way back to the birth of rock'n'roll: Elvis Presley cut his first records with Sun, Chuck Berry made all his best with Chess. In those days, rock and R&B were still speciality – if hardly minority – interests, established record companies, or 'majors', being blinded to their appeal by snobbery and prejudice. Pressing a few hundred copies of a cheaply recorded single to be sold out of the back of a car after gigs or through one or two local record shops made perfect sense as a means of generating publicity and boosting a band's income from playing live; not unlike T-shirt sales and other associated merchandising today. If a single received radio play and took off, the label grew bigger, and the band made some more money (though not much, and not always). Most *Nuggets*-type Sixties garage rock was originally released on independents, the labels coming and going much like the bands. Conversely, Berry Gordy's highly organised independent soul label, Motown, grew so powerful that it could not only give its acts a platform for success, but could hold onto them thereafter and go on to develop them into huge international stars.

By the Seventies, though, the powerful multinational majors had muscled in on the independent sector with offers of huge advances, regular royalty payments and considerable marketing clout. Unable to compete, independent labels became something of an anachronism. There were exceptions. Richard Branson's Virgin label had money from the Virgin record retail operation behind it, and took off after the fluke success of *Tubular Bells*. Chris Blackwell's Island was well funded from the beginning. Other, smaller new independent labels went back to serving interests that were speciality and, this time, usually minority as well. Not being part of a corporate structure or at the mercy of sales and marketing strategies, the independent labels of the Fifties and Sixties had been able to follow their hearts rather than their wallets, and record original, idiosyncratic or just plain weird artists. One of the reasons the music industry had become so jaded by the mid Seventies is that it was missing the fresh injections of blood the independent sector of yore had administered at regular intervals.

Perhaps unsurprisingly, then, it was at least in part the resurgence of such forward-thinking independent labels that supplied the much needed transfusion over the next few years. Unable to attract interest from the majors, and with few existing independent labels to approach at that time, the New York new wave bands went one step further towards low key self-sufficiency by prevailing upon close friends to pay for one-off releases: in 1974, Patti Smith released the single 'Piss Factory' on Mer, funded by her friend Robert Mapplethorpe; the following year Television released 'Little Johnny Jewel' on Ork, funded by band friend Terry Ork.

In the UK, the punk movement came to be so closely associated with a flourishing new cutting-edge independent label movement that the genre title 'indie' would soon be bestowed upon post-punk rock. What is often overlooked is that Chiswick and Stiff were largely responsible for inspiring the development of this independent movement, and that both were set up before punk broke. The original idea behind Chiswick was to use it to license otherwise unavailable vintage material – the label's second release was a reissue of first generation rocker Vince Taylor's 'Brand New Cadillac', which the Clash would later cover on 1979's *London Calling* – but Roger and Ted's enthusiasm for the current London music scene soon got the better of them. In 1974, the Flamin' Groovies had been without a label for two years when Dutch independent label Skydog released an EP and a single, both of which enjoyed steady sales through Rock On. This suggested possibilities. Chiswick's first release in November 1975, was *Speedball*, an EP by the Count Bishops featuring a killer version of 'Route 66' which immediately prompted the 101ers to drop the song from their own set. It also had a picture sleeve, because the Rock On staff knew such things enhanced collectability, which again set a trend for future punk releases.

In 1980, Joe told Paolo Hewitt that he had been 'flabbergasted' by Chiswick's offer to make their third release a single by the 101ers, but it is hard to understand why. The 101ers had already recorded for the much higher-profile Vic Maile. Also, Joe knew Ted and Roger, knew they had a label, and knew that they were predisposed to like the kind of thing the 101ers were doing.

The first recording session took place on 4 March 1976 in the tiny Pathway studio at 2A Grosvenor Avenue in Canonbury, with Roger Armstrong producing. Roger remembers Joe being so nervous that he hid behind his AC30 when not actually playing. Two versions of 'Keys To Your Heart' were recorded, and also two of 'Sweet Revenge', the first of which featured Clive on acoustic guitar. A take of '5 Star Rock'n'Roll Petrol' was knocked off for a change of pace. The most problematic of the contenders for the single proved to be 'Surf City'. After an instrumental run-through, a version was attempted with Joe singing, which offers some idea why he did not attempt it again: the oft-repeated refrain 'stuck in Surf City' brought on an unfortunate attack of the Daffy Ducks. After two or three further aborted takes, a version was recorded with a seemingly overawed Dan supplying almost inaudible lead vocals.

On 10 March, the 101ers returned to Pathway with Roger to re-record 'Surf City' and 'Keys To Your Heart', now with a phased effect on the guitar, and to make a first attempt at 'Rabies (From The Dogs Of Love)'. Roger took the best take of 'Keys To Your Heart' from both the first and second sessions into Chalk Farm Studios, Camden, and mixed them on 24 and 25 March, respectively.

The fact that no B-side was finished at this time suggests that the second session had also been deemed wanting, especially as, on 28 March, the 101ers went into the BBC studios in Maida Vale, this time with house producer Simon Jeffes and house engineer Mike Robinson, to record '5 Star Rock'n'Roll Petrol' and yet another version of 'Surf City'. Richard argues with this interpretation of events. 'I think we were thinking of an EP, actually. I think we had the idea of bringing something out ourselves, and with the BBC masters, the copyright belonged to us and not to someone else.' This would make sense had the 101ers restricted themselves to previously unrecorded songs, but they returned to the BBC studios on 10 April to record backing tracks for a second version of 'Rabies' and yet another of 'Keys To Your Heart', vocals to which were added on 13 April.

Despite Richard's claims, it looks very much as though either Chiswick or the 101ers were unhappy with the bulk of the Pathway material. Alternatively, no contract having yet been signed, perhaps the band were not wholly convinced that Chiswick were going to put a record out. It was still early days for the label, and certainly, not every artist they recorded ended up with a record release. When the 101ers single finally came out, A-side 'Keys To Your Heart' was taken from the first Pathway session, and B-side '5 Star Rock'n'Roll Petrol' from the first BBC session. A convoluted history for what was supposed to be a quickly-recorded, low-budget, independent-label single.

As if to cement the alliance between the 101ers and Chiswick, Boogie helped arrange two gigs at the Nashville, Kensington on 3 and 23 April 1976, with the 101ers headlining, the Rock On disco providing incidental music, and the Sex Pistols appearing as the support band. The first of these nights looms large in the Annals of Punk: it was where Dave Goodman began mixing the Pistols' live sound, giving the band their own highly individual sonic identity; and it was where Joe Strummer claims to have undergone a conversion as dramatic as Saul's on the road to Damascus, Significant Event Two in the birth of the Clash.

Reviewing the gig for *Melody Maker*, Allan Jones was dismissive of the Pistols – 'a recently much-vaunted four-piece band of incompetents from West London' – but predictably fulsome in his praise for the headliners: 'From the moment Joe Strummer – one of the most vivid and exciting figures currently treading the boards – took a flying, perfectly judged, leap onto Snakehips Dudanski's bass drum, to their third and final encore, the 101ers were a complete and utter joy.' The *NME*'s Geoff Hutt noted that the Pistols' attitude seemed forced, before going on to dispute their alleged lack of musical ability and generally damn them with faint praise. He, too, reserved his plaudits for the 101ers, who he announced were musically much improved and had 'finally made the transition from playing the tiny Elgin pub to successfully dominating larger halls'.

Clive's recollection of the Sex Pistols tallies with that of Geoff Hutt. 'It was the first really important gig they did, and we had a ready-made audience who came to see us. People were all extremes in their reaction to them, appalled to very interested. A lot of the heckling was put up. It was very much a manipulative situation, I thought at the time. Not strictly my scene.' Richard did not think the Pistols were appreciably different to the early 101ers. 'I saw them as doing, really, what we were doing, but they were younger. They'd started more recently. As I said, we'd been called a punk band the year before. I didn't like their emphasis on image.' For Joe, steeped in pop culture, the 101er-with-a-suit, the image was a large part of the appeal. In Jon Savage's *England's Dreaming: Sex Pistols And Punk Rock*, published in 1991, Joe recalled overhearing Malcolm ask the Pistols what clothes they wanted to wear that night and being most impressed with this attention to detail. Rather than find the onstage affectations and poses off-putting, he was seduced by the intention behind them. In the 1981 *Melody Maker* 101ers retrospective, Joe explained the difference between his reaction and Richard's: 'You see, [I'm] talking about a movement of ideas, and he's talking about a riff on a stage. See the difference? I saw it not only as a "good group", but as a new attitude.'

In November 1976, just over four months after he had left the 101ers for the Clash, Joe told Caroline Coon, 'As soon as I saw [the Sex Pistols]… I just knew. It was something you just knew without bothering to think about.' The impact may have been immediate, but despite his melodramatic accounts in the *Melody Maker* and elsewhere over the years, his conversion to punk took place more gradually, lasting the best part of two months and involving a good deal of soul searching. Although Joe has never credited it, Jonh Ingham's 24 April interview with the Sex Pistols must have played some part in the band's effect upon him. In it, Malcolm dismissed the pub rock scene because it required its bands to pander to expectations and lean too heavily upon the familiar. 'Basically,' summed up Jonh, 'what Malcolm wants is a rumbling, anarchic, noisy energetic rock scene, the likes of which haven't been seen in this country since the mid 1960's.' As well as making references to his beloved Rolling Stones and echoing Joe's own musical philosophy, the feature was an open invitation to any rock'n'roll opportunist who wanted a fast lane to media attention: the Sex Pistols had only been gigging for six months, and here they were with a two-page spread in *Sounds*.

Significant Event Three in the birth of the Clash was a chance meeting in the street between Joe and a gang comprising Mick Jones, Paul Simonon and Glen Matlock. Glen, of course, had supported the 101ers at the Nashville; Mick and Paul, accompanied by Keith Levene and Bernie Rhodes, had been in the audience. The others approached Joe and told him he was great but his band was 'shit'. This, legend has it, hardened Joe in his resolve to follow his instincts to leave the 101ers and go punk. The incident would be immortalised in the opening lines of the 1978 Clash song 'All The Young Punks (New Boots And Contracts)': 'I was hanging about down the market street… When I met some passing yobbos / And we did chance to speak…' A popular anecdote, it was told and retold for years by all three of the Clash members involved. While the other details remained much the same, the location for this meeting varied from account to account: Golborne Road, Portobello Road, Westbourne Grove, Ladbroke Grove, Lisson Grove or even somewhere in Shepherd's Bush. The reason for this uncertainty and the fact that Glen, supposedly present, has no recollection at all of the incident was only revealed by Joe once the Clash had split: Significant Event Three in the birth of the Clash never in fact happened. It was a complete fabrication, a piece of instant mythologising intended to make it appear as though the idea to get together developed naturally from a casual meeting during which the future band members discovered they shared the same vision. Instead, it transpires the poaching of Joe was the result of premeditated and audacious head-hunting on the part of the management.

In a 1978 interview with the *NME*, Mick Jones told Nick Kent, 'With Joe, I could see he was a great performer saddled with a duff band.' Eleven years later, Keith Levene told the same paper's Jane Garcia that it had been he and Bernie who had recognised the potential of the 101ers' leader – 'Joe used to wear zoot suits and just go fucking mad all over the place. He was always so great to watch' – and that they had approached Joe without consulting Mick, thus presenting the guitarist with a fait accompli. In truth, the Davis Road contingent had *all* taken note of Joe's frenzied performance at the Nashville. They next encountered him, not on Portobello Road (or any of the other 'street' options), but at the Employment Exchange in Lisson Grove. As it was during the Easter vacation, Mick – accompanied by Paul and Viv – was there to claim benefit for the duration, and Joe was there to sign on as usual. The others stared covertly at the singer, and, vaguely aware of their shifty behaviour, Joe wondered if he was about to be attacked. No words were exchanged.

Some or all of the Davis Road bunch saw Joe once again on 23 April, at the second of the Nashville 101ers-Sex Pistols gigs, which achieved notoriety for a fight precipitated by Vivienne Westwood during the Pistols' set. On 12 May, the 101ers played the Red Cow in Hammersmith. Clive Timperley noted in his diary that various members of the Stranglers, Eddie and the Hot Rods, the Count Bishops and the Sex Pistols were in attendance. The Sex Pistol was Glen Matlock, and he was again accompanied by Mick and Paul. At this stage, seducing Joe away from the 101ers was little more than a fantasy option for the inchoate Davis Road band. They were unaware that Joe was intrigued by Malcolm and the Pistols, and could not have held out much hope that a name performer (albeit on the pub circuit) would be prepared to quit an established band to join forces with them. It was Bernie who took control of the situation.

On 11 May, the Sex Pistols had begun their groundbreaking – for the punk scene – weekly Tuesday night residency at the 100 Club on Oxford Street. Joe attended one or two of that month's gigs, where he was spotted by Bernie. Not one to give in to feelings of awe, Bernie said he had a venture Joe might be interested in, and asked him for his phone number.

Things had not been running smoothly in the 101ers camp. 'In early '76, not long after I had joined the band, we were striving to develop a fuller range of musical capability,' Dan Kelleher told Pete Frame for a Family Tree of the bands which developed out of the Maida Hill squatting community. 'And here were the Pistols playing with a rawness very reminiscent of the early 101ers!' Joe laid much of the blame at Dan's door for what he was increasingly coming to think of as the 101ers' recent musical wrong turn. 'This bloke was pushing his way in, this *multi-instrumentalist*,' he sneered to *Melody Maker*'s Paolo Hewitt in 1981.

Joe's first reaction upon seeing the Pistols was not to break up the 101ers, but to try to make them more of a punk-style band. 'I think there's no question that, before the 101ers split, Joe had a different, much more aggressive attitude while on stage,' says Richard. To be frenetically thrashing away on guitar flanked by two men known as Evil and Desperate who hardly ever moved no longer seemed like such a good joke. Performance intensity levels became another troublesome issue.

On 16 May, Joe went to the Roundhouse to watch the Stranglers support Patti Smith on her first visit to the UK. Joe was on friendly terms with Stranglers guitarist Hugh Cornwell. In David Buckley's 1997 biography of that band, *No Mercy*, Hugh recalls a tired and emotional Joe admitting his envy for the harder-hitting, but still hardly punk, Stranglers. At the after gig party, an even drunker Joe openly declared his love for Patti. He was flailing around, unhappy and confused.

Just two days later, the 101ers finally signed a recording contract with Chiswick. For Joe, being required to commit himself in such a manner to a band with which he was no longer fully satisfied proved painful, and it was Clive who bore the initial brunt of his dissatisfaction. Given his later savaging of Dan, Joe's initial choice of target might appear a surprising one. Richard believes that, while Dan's days were already numbered, Joe still held hopes of bringing Clive round to his point of view. By this time all pretence at democracy had been abandoned, and a one-to-one ultimatum was delivered on 21 May, after a gig at Camberwell Arts Centre. 'I felt pretty good, because I felt it had gone pretty well,' says Clive. 'Then Strummer said to me, "You'll have to buck your ideas up, mate, or you're out!"'

It seems likely that Bernie's approach to Joe was made at the Pistols' 100 Club gig on 25 May, because it was the very next day that Joe called around to see Clive for a more serious discussion. 'We spent the whole day in my flat talking,' says Clive. 'He was smitten by the Maximum Impact – carefully chosen words, *his* words – of the Pistols. He wanted to go in that direction. Dan and I didn't, because we were musos: we were into Steely Dan and Little Feat. There was a long discussion, at the end of which I agreed to leave. There was nothing wrong, or amiss, or inamicable about it at all.'

Martin Stone, formerly of pub rock leading lights Chilli Willi, and more recently of the Jive Bombers, who had supported the 101ers at Colchester University back on 17 March, was brought in at short notice for the 101ers gig on 28 May at Bromley College. 'He was another country-type lead guitar player,' says Clive. 'In other words, Joe got a straight replacement for me.' For this reason, Clive believes Martin was always intended to be a temporary stand-in, Joe planning to fulfil existing commitments prior to breaking up the band. Richard agrees with the first part of this assessment, but not the second. 'I don't think Martin Stone was considered as full time, no, but I don't think Joe was necessarily thinking of splitting it up. More a feeling that, "This has got to change." Joe wasn't getting on with Dan, so it was just us two. Myself and Joe had no problems. And for me, that was enough: to get in other people and carry on with the 101ers.'

The upset caused by Clive's departure was intensified when Bernie phoned to follow up his initial contact with Joe. Dan was at Orsett Terrace for rehearsals, and it was he who answered the phone. Deeply suspicious of the evasive Rhodes, he pretended to be Joe in an unsuccessful attempt to find out what was going on. Now aware of the turmoil in the 101ers camp, Bernie decided it was time to make his move. Taking Keith Levene with him, he went along to the 101ers' next gig, on 30 May at the Golden Lion pub in Fulham Road. After the show, a clandestine meeting took place outside, by the bus stop. This time, it was Joe's turn to be given an ultimatum. Bernie told him he was putting together a new band to rival the Pistols, and asked Joe if he wanted in. 'Joe was like, "Um, er, I don't know,"' says Keith. In the end, he was given 48 hours to make up his mind. Keith again insists that Mick knew nothing about this offer until after it had been made.

Joe spent the next 24 hours worrying over the decision. Then Bernie phoned him a day ahead of schedule, and demanded an answer there and then. Joe said he was interested. Although Bernie had prepared the ground well, it was meeting Keith that had finally convinced him. 'In those days people looked really boring, and Keith looked really different,' he told Kosmo Vinyl for the *Clash On Broadway* booklet. Bernie and Keith picked up Joe and took him to 22 Davis Road, where Mick and Paul were waiting to meet their new bandmate. Still in awe of the relatively experienced Strummer, they covered it up with the usual show of casual gruffness. 'When I met Mick and Paul at the squat we went in and sat on the bed and looked at each other,' Joe told the *NME*'s Paul Morley in 1979. 'And Bernie said, "This is the guy you gotta write songs with," and Mick sort of scowled, and I thought, "Well, I haven't got any choice. This is what I've got to do."'

They then took it in turns to play selections from their existing repertoires. The first song they rehearsed was Mick's '1-2, Crush On You'. Quickly determining that Paul could not really play and had simply learned his bass parts parrot fashion, Joe had a twinge of doubt. 'I thought, "Uh-oh, I've been through this one before: it took the 101ers 18 months to learn how to play R&B numbers!"' he said during the 1980 interview for Radio Hallam. 'But then I thought, "Oh, hell!" and we just jumped in.' He found some solace in Paul's dynamic approach to the bass, noting that, despite space restrictions, instruments were being slung around with abandon. 'He was like, "Wow, I really dig this, yeah, I'm gonna do it!"' says Keith.

'I remember Joe coming back one night when I was in bed,' says Richard. 'He came in and said, "Look, it's the end. The 101ers have finished." He'd met these blokes who

I'd seen around. They used to come to our gigs, so I knew who he was talking about. "I wanna start a new band, and go with a new manager," and all this.' He asked Richard to come with him. 'And I said, "Oh, God! Talk to you about it in the morning, Joe." And the following morning, the first bloke I bumped into in Orsett Terrace was Bernie, who spent a couple of hours trying to persuade me why I should go with the Clash, and telling me what the Clash were about. They weren't called the Clash then, but this new band, as it were. He turned me right off, really got up me nose. I didn't like the guy. I thought he was full of pseudo-political crap. "Words should be written about this kind of thing, we should wear this kind of clothing…" I certainly wasn't going to start wearing a uniform. I thought, "I'm not packing up *this* to go with that wanker!" So that was it, as far as I was concerned. I wouldn't have said no to going with younger people, but I wasn't going to go and be run by Bernie Rhodes, basically.'

Richard having stated his position, a band meeting followed at which Dan was informed of Joe's defection. It was decided to disband the 101ers after one last gig – Martin Stone's third – on 5 June at the Clare Halls in Haywards Heath. Clive turned up for the show, and joined the others on stage for the last few numbers. 'I happened to be in the area: I'd gone to an audition. I was on the way back, and I said, "Right, I'll play!"' Some subsequent bookings were cancelled. One slot, part of a Midsummer Music Festival Benefit on 17 June at Walthamstow Assembly Hall, with the Stranglers and the recently rechristened Ian Dury and the Kilburns, was taken over – fittingly – by the Sex Pistols.

Richard kept his drum kit, Clive a Gibson SG guitar and Dan his bass amp, but Joe took the rest of the band gear, including the PA, on which money was still owed. Boogie went his own way, eventually becoming a roadie for the Sex Pistols at the beginning of 1977. Micky Foote decided to follow Joe and the PA.

It was Dan who felt most aggrieved by the split, as he intimated to Pete Silverton in 1979: 'I think Joe was really cuntish when the 101ers broke up.' 'I think Dan would say that what he hated, what he felt very resentful about, was that it was all behind our backs, the Clash thing,' says Clive. 'But that was Bernie, not Strummer.' Richard is less sympathetic to any dissatisfaction Dan may have felt. 'He'd only been in the band six months, or something! I don't think the split was engineered. Dan could have carried on, if he'd wanted. *I* wasn't going to work with him.'

What Dan did do was rejoin the Derelicts for six months. In 1978, he recorded a solo single for Chiswick, 'I Couldn't Help But Cry', on which he played every instrument. That same year, he formed a band called the Martian Schoolgirls in Dorset, where he still lives. A couple of years after leaving the 101ers, Clive Timperley hooked up with former Derelict Barbara Gogan to form the Passions. 'Which was a huge step forward for me; maybe not musically, but creatively.' Their 1981 hit single, 'I'm In Love With A German Film Star', was a song about a former Clash roadie named Roadent. When the Passions came to an acrimonious end, Clive left the music business for a while, but eventually returned to the London circuit again.

Richard Dudanski decided to take a long holiday in Sicily with Esperanza, and they stayed there for three or four months. Upon returning, Richard teamed up with Tymon Dogg in a band called the Fools. Then, in 1978, he formed his own band, Bank of Dresden, before joining Public Image Ltd for a brief spell. He then followed his sister-in-law Paloma onto the drumseat for the Raincoats. He now lives in Spain, still with Esperanza, and plays for a band called Por Si Las Moscas.

In the *Clash On Broadway* booklet, Mick revealed that when Joe turned up for the Clash's second rehearsal 'he was in the gear and everything, he was already part of it, he was there'. But it transpired that making a commitment to this 'new attitude' required more than a change of clothes. Since much of the 101ers' career had taken place in the limelight, Joe was unable to pretend the band had never existed, as Mick Jones did with the Delinquents and – albeit less successfully – the London SS. The only other way he could prevent his very public defection from R&B to punk rock appearing like an act of cynical opportunism was to exhibit the fanatical zeal of the convert and denigrate his former band and musical tastes at every turn.

The first opportunity presented itself when Chiswick posthumously released the 'Keys To Your Heart' single, and Caroline Coon invited Joe to comment on the 101ers split in her *Melody Maker* singles column of 24 July 1976. 'It was very traumatic, yes,' he said. 'I formed the group with my sweat. I slogged at it. Then I met these others. Before, I used to think I was a crud. Now, I realise I'm the king, and I've decided to move into the future.' Within a couple of months, he was wearing a shirt bearing the legend, 'CHUCK BERRY IS DEAD' and performing a song, '1977', with the chorus, 'No Elvis, Beatles or the Rolling Stones / In 1977'. In November 1976, Joe told Caroline that he had realised R&B was dead the moment he saw the Sex Pistols.

That December, something occurred that made it even easier for him to shake off his recent past. He was squatting in the newly vacated premises of Robertino's Ice Cream Company at 7 Foscote Mews, just off the Harrow Road. 'I lost all my stuff at the ice cream factory, just under Mick's tower block where I lived,' Joe told *Sounds*' Pete Silverton in 1978. 'Some guy went and threw it on the skip. Everything, even my suit, still in its paper from the dry cleaners. I've got nothing left from the 101ers, not a tape, a poster, even a photograph.'

In March 1977, Joe told Caroline Coon that he had always felt inferior as a musician and singer before seeing the Pistols, but that their 'so what' attitude had inspired him to adopt the same approach. He even insinuated that the other 101ers had previously played upon his self-doubts to steer the band's musical direction away from the true path. These remarks, it has to be remembered, came from the person who had been the single most dominant figure in the 101ers from February 1975 onwards. Having knocked two years off his own age upon joining the Clash, he added insult to injury by accusing the 101ers of having been 'just too old'! He reluctantly conceded that they had been a good band – 'in fact, as far as sound and excitement went, we were much better than Eddie and the Hot Rods' – but this interview was to be the last time he said anything positive about them for years. His subsequent references to the 101ers amounted to a long-running series of deprecatory remarks about both his own abilities and the unrealistic aspirations of the band as a whole.

'I certainly don't feel it now, but at the time I felt bitter that the 101ers were denied,' says Richard, whose commitment to the band had rivalled Joe's, and ultimately outlived it. 'Not by Joe so much – although to an extent, to start with – but certainly by Bernie Rhodes. He didn't want any connections, any references from Joe to his past. I think he was a little bit embarrassed by the fact that Joe was involved with what he would consider a *hippy* band. We never considered ourselves hippies. It was all rather ironic to me, because the Clash's so-called political philosophy was for me trying to uphold a political reality that had actually existed in the 101ers. There was another ironic touch – I don't know who originated it – in saying that the 101ers' name came from the cell number of that bloke [actually, the torture room] in *1984* by George Orwell. Not relating it to squatting, but relating it to some "political" thing. Which is totally ironic when you think that one of the themes behind Orwell's book was the rewriting of history.' This popular misconception about the origin of the 101ers' name was propagated in Tony Parsons and Julie Burchill's 1978 book, *The Boy Looked At Johnny*, and subsequently by several popular music encyclopaedias. 'That's a load of bunk!' Joe admitted in 1989, when questioned about it on Washington DC's WHFS radio. Who made it up, then? 'I probably did,' he chuckled.

The cumulative effect of what Mole calls 'Clash propaganda' has been to give the impression that Joe had the foresight to jump a doomed ship just before it broke up against the rocks. This was simply not the case. Maybe overnight success did not look likely for the 101ers in May 1976, but reviews had been positive, there was a single in the offing, and both the Feelgoods and Eddie and the Hot Rods had come from the same background with a similar sound and made the charts. As things were to turn out, within a year a revamped, back-to-basics 101ers would almost have certainly benefited from a climate made receptive to almost all aggressive uptempo music by the punk explosion. The Stranglers certainly did, with not inconsiderable help from Albion, the booking agents they had shared with the 101ers.

It could be claimed that a contract with the small and determinedly eccentric Chiswick offered the 101ers little guarantee of a high profile career. But, had their alliance continued, the 101ers might well have been the band to turn Chiswick's fortunes around, enabling the label to emulate the triumphs of Stiff. Stiff was a similarly tiny, oddball organisation formed in July 1976 by Jake Riviera and Dave Robinson with a £400 loan from Dr Feelgood. Nevertheless, it provided the launching pad for the artistic and commercial successes of former pub rockers Nick Lowe (ex Brinsley Schwarz), Elvis Costello (ex Flip City) and Ian Dury (ex-Kilburns), among many others. As Roger Armstrong notes, the 101ers' disintegration, following on almost immediately from the similar fate of the Count Bishops, did little to get Chiswick off on the right footing.

When Joe made his decision, he was leaving a going concern playing a style of music he had always loved – if not quite in the style he wanted to play it at that particular moment in time – for an almost completely unknown and unproven entity. Getting in early for the Clash backlash, *The Boy Looked At Johnny* implied that to base such a major life choice on the surface impressions made by clothes and attitude was indicative of a certain shallowness of character. For a start, Tony Parsons and Julie Burchill did not present quite the full picture: at least part of the motive behind Joe's decision was Bernie's forcefully expressed determination to create something similar in spirit to the Sex Pistols. Even if clothes alone had been enough to persuade Joe to sign up, then what of it? As Tony and Julie well knew, rock'n'roll developed hand in hand with popular culture and the mass media. As early as the late Fifties, it was already almost impossible to experience contemporary music in a hermetically sealed bubble. The wider cultural context was bound to influence consumer response. Some people profess to judge music entirely on its own merits and ignore all the trappings. But however knowledgeable about music or musically gifted they may be, if they deny that – from Elvis Presley onwards – popular music has always been at least as much about image, attitude and hype as 'the riff onstage' or on disc they are not only kidding themselves, but also failing to understand a large part of its effect and appeal.

Leaving the 101ers was a gamble that involved considerable sacrifice, but the only person who had to find his defection reasonable was Joe himself. As long ago as 1970, he had shown that he was prepared to change his clothes, name and even his identity to become the person he wanted to be. In the summer of 1974, when he was barely functional as a performing musician, he had told a friend and housemate that he intended to be a pop star. For all the self-doubt experienced since that day, he had not wavered in his determination to do whatever he deemed necessary to make that ambition become a reality, providing it was on his own terms.

In 1999, the Clash documentary *Westway To The World* included some previously unseen colour film footage of the 101ers on-stage. As his younger self delivered a typically frenzied performance, Joe's voiceover finally admitted the 101ers' worth.

Back in 1976, while he was busy divorcing himself from the 101ers, Joe's new manager was organising a new rehearsal room-cum-HQ. At the end of the first week of June, Joe took his PA, his soundman, his new clothes and his new cropped hairstyle along there in search of the new attitude. 'And – *bang!* – that was it,' says Keith Levene. 'We had the band.'

PART TWO:
RIOT ACTS

6
GARAGELAND

When Malcolm McLaren made his call for a London popular music scene reminiscent of the glory days of the early to mid Sixties, it struck a chord with the generation of music fans who, like Joe Strummer and his peer group at the City of London Freemen's School, had been unable by reason of youth or distance to participate first time around. 'That generation that came of age in the Seventies, we'd grown up in the Sixties, but we'd missed the Sixties,' says punk period *NME* journalist Tony Parsons. 'It was a party we'd been too young to be invited to. A party of fucking girls who looked like Julie Christie, and stopping the war in Vietnam, and the Kings Road, and all that kind of thing. And by the time it got to the mid Seventies, and we'd turned up with our bottle of cider and our peace badges, it was over, finished. Now, it's too far away: it's history to teenagers today. But we were close enough to it to want our turn.'

At the beginning of June 1976, Bernie Rhodes took it upon himself to locate a more suitable rehearsal space for the Davis Road band. Joe had just been recruited, and the musicians needed to pool their respective talents, work on a band identity, and develop a live repertoire. Bernie found what he considered to be the ideal place right under his nose: not too far from his flat in Camden Town, and next door but one to Harry's, the Renault garage in which he still owned a share. Situated just inside the gates of the British Rail Yard, on Chalk Farm Road, halfway between Dingwalls and the Roundhouse – those two pillars of the Camden music scene – it was a damp and dilapidated two-storey end-terrace railway storage shed.

The amps and speakers were set up in the relatively large downstairs room opposite a somewhat incongruous line of old barbers' chairs. The back room was used to store pinball and fruit machines. (Bernie was a great hoarder.) Upstairs, a small front room became an all-purpose band office and recreation area. The back room was derelict, the floorboards rotted through. Most of the tiny panes in the building's high, narrow windows were broken, and stuffed with newspaper. The skylight was in a similar state, and was positioned directly over the water cistern, which had weeds growing out of it. There was a sink and a toilet, but no hot water and – a one-bar electric fire aside – no form of heating. Until it broke down for keeps a couple of months after the band arrived, entertainment was provided by another of Bernie's acquisitions: a jukebox, which they stocked with an eclectic selection of singles. As well as tracks by Jimi Hendrix and the Doors, there were some of Paul's reggae favourites – including Desmond Dekker's 'Israelites' and the Rulers' 'Wrong 'Em Boyo' – and the song with which he had failed his audition for the London SS, Jonathan Richman's 'Roadrunner', since released as a single. A payphone on the wall was fixed to accept the same coin over and over again. The source of the electricity supply was similarly dubious. Bernie dispelled any possible lingering doubts about the function of the premises when he christened them Rehearsal Rehearsals. When the novelty value of this mouthful wore off, unsurprisingly quickly, the band and their associates shortened it to just plain Rehearsals.

In Keith Levene's mind, the band might have felt complete with the addition of Joe, but there was still one vital gap in the line-up to be filled: the drummer. Richard Dudanski having refused to join, Joe called in a drum kit and a favour from his schoolfriend Pablo LaBritain, who sat in for the first couple of rehearsals while the band made up their mind about a full-time member. As a result, Pablo features in the first photographs of the band in their new habitat. Although a proficient drummer and visually more in keeping with the general band style than, say, Mick Jones (as the photos testify), Pablo did not stick around to fill the vacancy long-term. The fact that he went on to join the Clash-influenced punk band 999 suggests this decision was not entirely of his own making. Joe was in the process of shedding his past; it may have been that Pablo knew too much about it for Joe to be entirely comfortable having him around. Whatever, sometime in mid-June, Terry Chimes received another call from Bernie.

Born in 1956, in east London's Mile End, Terry had grown up in a stable, supportive and competitive environment. His two brothers were also musicians. The younger was a bass player, but, predictably, Terry took his lead from the elder. 'He plays timpani in orchestras. He's three years older than me, and when he was 18, he was going to the Royal College of Music. And so I thought, "If you're going to do that, I'm going to be a rock'n'roll star!"' An intelligent youth who had developed an early fascination for matters scientific – 'I was the kind of kid who would ask for a microscope at Christmas rather than a football' – Terry successfully juggled both interests while at school, playing drums in school bands and also passing the A Levels he required to pursue a career in medicine. It was at this point that he felt pressured to make a choice; instead of abandoning one or other of his ambitions, however, he came up with a typically level-headed compromise. 'I figured that I could just be a rock star for a year or two, and then go and do medicine after that. Now, a year goes very quickly, and I thought that I'd better make a go of this, so I auditioned with every band I could find.'

Terry was as assertive as he was pragmatic. One of his auditions, in August 1975, was for Violent Luck, and Kelvin Blacklock recalls the drummer being mouthy and pushy to the point of obnoxiousness, refusing to leave until he was told whether or not he had the job. Three months later, Terry tried out for the London SS. He was not impressed by the likes of the New York Dolls, and – despite being fond of Free and Led Zeppelin – had no unshakeable allegiance to any particular band or genre of music. As a consequence, he did not fare well in the interview part of the audition. Nevertheless, he came away with the feeling that his loud, steady, precise drumming style had made a favourable impression. Which proved to be the case when he was called back to try out first for the Billy Watts line-up at Riverside Studios, and then – following the Pablo LaBritain interlude – with the Joe Strummer line-up at Rehearsals.

Initially, Terry was bemused by the change in singers, which no-one took the trouble to explain to him. 'Billy had seemed such an integral part of what was going on at the time. And, also, Joe seemed such a weird sort of guy. He's not the archetypal rock'n'roll singer, is he? They didn't say, "This is the new singer *because…*" they just said, "This is the new singer", and I looked at him and thought, "So what's so special about you that they booted the other guy out?" I got to know him quite quickly, and then it became evident why he was there.'

At first, Mick was the only person who made an effort to communicate with Terry. Joe's initial remoteness could be partly attributed to the adjustments he himself was having to make. Terry quickly came to understand that Paul's was due to shyness. 'Paul wasn't *un*friendly. He just spoke so little that you weren't sure what was going on in his head.' Although he never became particularly close to Mick, Joe and Paul, it was not long before Terry felt able to get along with them well enough. The same was not true for the two remaining members of the team. 'Bernie irritated everyone intensely. One hundred per cent of the people he met, he irritated them intensely. That was a deliberate policy of his. He's a one-off, a strange guy. I've never met anyone like him, before or since.' Keith was equally 'quick to take people out of their comfort zone'. While Terry found Bernie annoying yet intriguing, he found Keith just plain annoying. 'I said to Joe that Keith was very hostile, and it was a pain that he was like that. Joe said that he'd agreed at first, but that he'd been at McDonalds with him, and they'd both ordered a milkshake. Joe had tasted his, and thought that it wasn't very good, but had decided just to carry on drinking it. But when Keith had taken a sip of *his*, he'd immediately started giving the staff there a hard time. And Joe thought this was the challenging sort of behaviour we should have in the band.'

Terry recalls that they began 'rehearsing frantically' straight away. 'After we'd done about three, at which time I felt I was still in the process of deciding whether they were any good, Keith announced to me that I was now a member of the band. Which offended Bernie, who jumped in, "You can't say that till I've given the go-ahead! I'm in charge here!" And then Keith and Bernie proceeded to argue about it, which was quite amusing to me. I was sitting there thinking, "Well, when you've finished, I'll tell you whether or not *I* want to join." Then we just carried on. Nothing more was said about it.'

This kind of despotic outburst was not untypical of Bernie. It begs the question, why would a group of imaginative, intelligent and mostly articulate young men put up with such behaviour?

Mick, Joe and Keith – Paul largely being content to follow their lead – still held the belief that Bernie would be able to help them hitch a ride on Malcolm's Sex Pistols wagon. The band members' encyclopaedic knowledge of rock'n'roll history included a sizeable entry under 'creative management'. It listed empire builders like Larry Parnes, seemingly avuncular hucksters like Elvis's manager Colonel Tom Parker, daredevil scammers like the Rolling Stones' Andrew Loog Oldham and the Who's Chris Stamp and Kit Lambert, intimidatory hard men like the Small Faces' Don Arden and Led Zeppelin's Peter Grant, shameless financial stroke-pullers like Allen Klein, political activists like the MC5's John Sinclair, and, of course, half-crazed vibe-merchants like Guy Stevens. These were people who – for all their various personality traits – had made names for themselves by making things happen for their respective artists. In mid 1976, there was no reason to doubt that there was room at the bottom of the encyclopaedia entry for the names of Malcolm McLaren and Bernie Rhodes.

What makes it difficult to assess the extent of Bernie's control and to establish an understanding of what he set out to achieve are the discrepancies among his role as he understood it, his role as the band perceived it, and his role as he portrayed it to people outside the band. It was important *at that time* to make it look as though the ideas were coming from the youngsters, rather than their not-so young manager. 'I have no say about what goes musically,' he told *Melody Maker* in 1977. 'My job is to co-ordinate, understand and clarify exactly what the band are trying to express; if you like, the melting pot of all their talents. It works on a basis of respect and teamwork, although of course, we argue like fuck a lot of the time, almost to the point of fights.'

Terry insists Bernie was far more manipulative than this statement suggests. He compares the numerous band discussions Bernie chaired to the kind of brainwashing one might experience in religious cults, with defences being broken down to encourage openness but also leaving the participants vulnerable to exploitation. 'Bernie was quite clever, because he drew very definite lines, and said, "Everything this side of the line is your responsibility," and challenged people. So they didn't think he was controlling everything so much as he was doing his job and expecting them to do theirs. But he actually was controlling an awful lot.' Sebastian Conran, soon to be a band associate, believes this control was established with sheer verbosity: 'Paul Simonon used to laugh about "Bernie and his parables", because Bernie always talked in metaphors the whole time, all the time. He didn't actually ever stop talking. But he had some good ideas.'

Much of the style and content of the Clash's rhetoric came from Bernie: Joe's Tale of Keith and the Milkshake was a parable very much in the Rhodes tradition, while Paul's 'Art is Dead' pronouncement was one of the many Situationist International/Class of '68 slogans with which the manager was wont to embellish his tirades. Bernie took Situationism a little too literally at times: his catchphrase was 'that's the/our/their situation', and it too found its way into general Clash-speak.

Fired up, the rest of the band quickly became as intense and serious about what they were doing as Mick had been during his abortive rehearsals with Alan Drake. 'It all seems a bit daft to have argued about, in retrospect,' says Terry. 'But however we managed it, we did get a lot of intensity going, and that was what we needed. At the time, we weren't aware that the main function of all this marvellous arguing was just to get everyone wound up and get a performance.'

They might not have been fully aware of all the manifestations of Bernie's influence in 1976, but the band have always been prepared to acknowledge it since… even at periods in their lives when they might have been forgiven for badmouthing him. 'He made us actually *think* about what we were doing,' Paul told *Melody Maker*'s Allan Jones in November 1978. 'Bernie was really responsible for a lot of the way we thought, and how we put ourselves across,' Mick told *That Was Then, This Is Now* in 1989. Joe went even further on MTV's 1991 Clash *Rockumentary*: 'Bernie imagined the Clash, and he built it to fit the specifications of his vision. The Clash wouldn't exist without Bernie's imagination.'

Other of the band members' friends and associates tend not to be quite so generous in their appraisals of the manager's talents. Alan Drake, Chrissie Hynde and Richard Dudanski are not alone in considering him a Malcolm McLaren wannabe hoping to emulate his supposed mentor's successes with his band of Sex Pistols wannabes. Even Glen Matlock – who knows better – is wont to dismiss him as a plagiarist: 'Everything Bernie did was the same thing Malcolm had done, but second hand.' While it was certainly true that Bernie monitored Malcolm to the point of obsessiveness throughout 1976, it could be argued that this was only because Malcolm was further down the track with something that Bernie himself had helped set in motion in the first place.

In Stuart Bailie's 1990 *NME* overview of the Rhodes career – by which time there was no need for him to be modest – Bernie stated, '*I'm* the guy that created punk rock… If I told you that I wrote and produced the first Clash LP, you wouldn't believe me.' This seemingly wild boast contained a kernel of truth. Bernie had been the one who encouraged Glen Matlock to think about what he was doing, and who had suggested Johnny Rotten as vocalist for the Sex Pistols: two vital factors in establishing the band which did indeed spearhead the UK punk movement. In the 1980 interview with Paul Rambali, Bernie explained his original inspiration and motivation thus: 'I was listening to the radio in '75, and there was some expert blabbing on about how if things go on as they are, there'll be 800,000 people unemployed by 1979. Another guy was saying if that happened there'd be chaos, there'd be actual… *anarchy in the streets. That's* what was the root of punk.' Bernie had sounded off about this a good deal at the time, and believes it is no coincidence that the Sex Pistols' first single and cultural calling card was entitled 'Anarchy In The UK'. 'Malcolm McLaren was a good marketing man, but he stole all my ideas,' he told *Mojo*'s Pat Gilbert in 1999. Similarly, although Bernie did not actually 'write' the Clash's first album, its lyrics give voice to many observations and beliefs that were undeniably his, even if they were mostly adapted from ideas that had been in circulation among late Sixties radical groups.

Joe's *Rockumentary* comment was typical of his post-Clash tendency to self-effacement, and he was overstating the case. Much of the time, the band were indeed responding to Bernie's stimulus, but their relationship with him was a symbiotic one, and the venture they were embarking upon was a joint one. Whatever other criticisms could be levelled at the Rehearsals set-up, everyone involved was hoping to contribute to something new and exciting within the rock'n'roll medium, and everyone who stuck with it did so because he had committed himself wholeheartedly to the project. By no means every new development in the band's character was originated by Bernie.

His proprietorship of Rehearsals encouraged the others to indulge their manager to a certain extent, but only to a certain extent. Arguing requires input and suggests dissent, and as both Terry and Bernie testify, there was a lot of arguing. In addition, Paul ran a non-stop one-man campaign of pranks and insults designed to undermine the manager's efforts to assert his authority. It would be wrong to assume, just because Bernie had taken a key role in assembling the group's personnel, that everyone willingly placed their destinies in his hands in June 1976, and was from that moment on in agreement that it was his group operating under his instructions. As with the Sex Pistols, although there were large elements of prefabrication involved, the band was not manufactured *wholly* at their manager's whim in order to embody his fantasy, test his theory or follow his game-plan. Whatever they might have heard on the radio about the potential for rioting in the streets, read in the music press about the need for a new street-level rock'n'roll movement, or believed in their gut about the time being ripe for something like punk, neither Bernie nor Malcolm possibly could have known for sure what was about to happen during the course of the coming year.

Andy Czezowski first met Malcolm and Bernie in 1974, when he began doing the accounts for Kings Road clothing emporiums Acme Attractions and Sex. During 1976, he would briefly manage both the Damned and Generation X before going on to open the Roxy punk club. 'I don't believe anyone who ever says they actually *created* a scene,' he says. 'It's all accident, it's never design. The sort of people that get involved in band management, or clubs and promotions, are able to see and exploit something coming along. People like Malcolm, who people may now revere as being The Man Who Invented Punk. He was nothing of the sort: the man was nothing more than a T-shirt salesman. People came through the shop, ideas bounced off, and he was sufficiently aware and astute to realise that there might be an angle there somewhere. You roll with it. But believe me, if it hadn't have worked, it would have been on to the next thing.' Although he did not quite go so far as to admit opportunism, in a 1980 *Melody Maker* interview with Paul Rambali, Bernie did acknowledge that the London punk explosion was not as planned as it has since sometimes been made out to be: 'We didn't know it would spread so fast. We didn't have a manifesto. We didn't have a rule book.'

★★★

Following on behind the Pistols put Bernie and his charges in a difficult position. In Jonh Ingham's April 1976 *Sounds* feature, the Sex Pistols had stated their desire for a scene with 'more bands like us'. That the Rehearsals band had been inspired by the Pistols was something which they did not try, and have never since tried, to deny; and they did very much want to be part of the Pistols' scene. On the other hand, they did not wish to be dismissed as second rate copyists. It was a dilemma also being faced by the Damned, then in rehearsal at a gay club in a deconsecrated church hall off Lisson Grove. The trick was to be similar, yet different, as Rat Scabies explains: 'I certainly don't think that any of the bands who were there right at the start of punk dreamed of sounding or looking even vaguely like one of the other bands. In a lot of ways, it was a very mod mentality at that point. It was important to have your own identity, but to be cool with it. I remember, none of us would wear Malcolm's clothes, because that was the Pistols camp, and you had to have your own thing.'

'At this stage, we looked like the cat's whiskers, all this good gear from Malcolm's shop, and they used to look like a bunch of squatters,' is how Glen Matlock sums up the gulf between the Pistols and the Rehearsals band. 'We had the style and they didn't.' They may not have had the advantage of being backed by the proprietor of Sex, but by this time Bernie's charges were not attired quite so desperately as Glen suggests. While the Damned made do with an image that, out of financial necessity, began with army surplus and then shifted quickly towards kitsch fancy dress, perfectly complementing music and presentation that was part stormtrooper assault and part theatrical high camp, the Rehearsals band were a little more literal in their response to the mod parallel.

The few photos that have since emerged of their June rehearsals show the band – excepting Mick – looking like scruffy Ivy League college boys, with hair short enough to recall early Sixties crew cuts, drainpipe jeans and trousers, sharp-looking small-collared shirts, skinny ties and narrow-lapeled jackets. Such details were rare in 1976, the era of unstyled shoulder-length hair, A-line jeans, jumbo collars, kipper ties and jacket lapels wider than the jackets themselves. Although the band's gear was mostly bought second hand, considerable thought and taste had obviously gone into its selection, and the overall effect was not so much Squatter as Oxfam Mod. It had come to them not direct from the Sixties, but via Dr Feelgood and the mostly Anglophile New York new wave bands. Mick was still a little out of step with the others, but his version of the band look – skinny black tie, leather trousers and shaggy mid-length hair – contained the most clues as to its immediate origins, being strongly reminiscent of Patti Smith on the cover of *Horses*. Whereas Patti was both paying tribute to the Sixties and subverting gender stereotypes, though, the signals given off by the remainder of the Rehearsals band were unequivocally macho. There was a hint of the skinhead in the stance, if not quite the hairstyle. 'I can remember having this conversation with Joe, and him saying, basically, that what one did was, one dressed to intimidate other people,' says Sebastian Conran. 'You would walk down the street, and people would have to get out of the way.' This was the effect Terry had noted prior to his Riverside Studios audition, and it was largely attributable to Paul Simonon.

Bernie and the other members of the band had been quick to realise they had a trump card in Paul. The way he dressed, the way he looked, and the way he carried himself were the epitome of cool. Mick was working class, from a broken home, and lived in a council high-rise, but he was grammar school-educated, vaguely effete and had an embarrassing past as a long-haired glam rocker. Joe was on the dole and lived in a squat, but he was a middle class ex-public school boy and ex-pub rocker. Paul, by contrast, *appeared* to have all the credentials of a bona fide punk: he was not only from a broken home, but he was also a former skinhead and football hooligan. He could get away with playing the Man With No Name because he brought next to no baggage with him to Rehearsals. Unlike Mick or Joe, he had no previous musical history, and none of his former school or college friends was inducted into the band's entourage.

Later, when the band began doing interviews, they were more than happy for Paul to be portrayed as a tough nut, hard man, bad lad or rude boy, because the resulting street credibility rubbed off on everyone else. The real Paul Simonon was a considerably more complex character than his media persona suggested. Most of those who knew him at 20 recognised – like Terry – that his self-contained manner was due neither to ignorance or arrogance. 'I think he's sure of himself as well, but he's not a way out front sort of chap,' confirms Rat Scabies. 'I think he is genuinely shy, and it can sometimes get misinterpreted.' This also partly explained Paul's lack of volubility. Although certainly no intellectual, and not really a match for the verbal gymnastics of either Mick or Joe, when relaxed and in the right mood, he could reveal himself to be reasonably eloquent and informed. The band member most given to laddish larking around, his humour did not begin and end with slapstick. A highly developed sense of the surreal manifested itself in off the wall monologues that could keep his companions in stitches, and he quickly usurped Joe's role as chief dispenser of nicknames. Prepared, when he thought it necessary, to put the hard face to the rhetoric of the others, he was also the most consistently polite and charming member of the group.

As well as being responsible for the band's style, Paul also provided its name. Various options were in consideration from the moment the band first arrived at Rehearsals. The Phones and the Mirrors both had a shiny, modern feel to them and, with connotations of communication and image, respectively, also brought to mind Television. The names that came closest to sticking were even more interesting in view of subsequent developments in the band's identity. The Psychotic (or Psycho) Negatives recalled the Count Five's garage classic, 'Psychotic Reaction', and revealed the strong influence at the time of Johnny Rotten's nihilistic outlook. The Weak Heart Drops was taken from the 1975 track 'Lightning Flash (Weak Heart Drop)' by reggae toaster Big Youth. But even in its shortened form of the Heartdrops, it sounded too soft, and was too close an echo of Johnny Thunders's Heartbreakers. The Outcasts suggested alienation and rebelliousness, in the tradition of Mick's original band, the Delinquents. Unfortunately, the next time they visited Rock On, Mick and Joe found an album by a Sixties American garage band with the same name. Then, flicking through London's *Evening Standard* newspaper one day, Paul noticed how often the word 'clash' recurred in titles and subtitles as shorthand not only for violent confrontation, but also disagreement and friction of any kind. The word seemed to sum up both the dynamic in the band camp and the impact they desired to make in performance. It also had a mod sharpness and directness to it, in the tradition of the Who. He suggested it to the others, and it struck an instant chord with everyone except – predictably – Keith. 'I wasn't too crazy about it, but there you go.' The guitarist was outvoted, and the band became the Clash.

Their Sixties urchin look was not inappropriate to the Clash's early material. Joe had rejected the 101ers and R&B on the grounds that both were old hat and he was loath to play songs he had written while with his former band. 'Jail Guitar Doors' and the others were quickly sidelined. Which left Mick's songs. Listening today to the stockpile Mick had amassed by the time of Joe's arrival, it comes as no surprise to learn that the guitarist had previously rehearsed with bands playing – at his instigation – songs by the likes of the Standells, the MC5, the Troggs and the Flamin' Groovies: the influence of original punk rock is all there in the riffs and the high harmonies of 'Ooh, Baby, Ooh (It's Not Over)', '1-2 Crush On You', 'Bored With You', 'Deny', 'Protex Blue', 'She's Sitting At My Party' and 'Mark Me Absent'. Lyrically, these songs evince a ready wit, a neat turn of phrase, and a suitably knowing mid-Seventies take on teenage life. This is demonstrated by 'Ooh, Baby, Ooh (It's not Over)', a song based on the riff from Booker T and the MG's 'Time Is Tight': 'Now, I don't care how many of my good friends that you kiss / I'll just have another drink, it's better when I'm pissed / 'Cos if I start a fight, I'll lose / But if I'm drunk, then I won't feel the fists.' Nevertheless, the teenage life they depict – as defined by crushes, broken romances, school canteens, drunken parties, and token rebellious gestures towards such everyday authority figures as teachers and parents – is highly stylised, and a hangover from the mid-Sixties. Mick might have been updating, adding new twists and a veneer of dirty realism, but, like his musical influence, his lyrical influence was coming second hand from the original garage bands. As their recently-released album demonstrated, the Ramones were ploughing a similar furrow, but at least their approach to teen angst was *deliberately* cartoonish.

Following the acquisition of Johnny Rotten in summer 1975, the Sex Pistols had begun rehearsing the Count Five's 'Psychotic Reaction', the Who's 'Substitute', the Monkees' '(I'm Not Your) Steppin' Stone', the Flamin' Groovies' 'Slow Death', Jonathan Richman's 'Roadrunner', the Kinks' 'I'm Not Like Everybody Else' and a couple of Small Faces songs, all of which had put them in very much the same territory. Yet as they began to play more and more of their own songs, Johnny's mannered delivery and idiosyncratic lyrical perspective made the band's growing repertoire at least seem original. Mick's were good songs of their type, but, understandably, Bernie did not think they had enough firepower to go up against the Pistols' canon. Both Keith and Joe agreed, the latter being aware of the irony of his having abandoned one band exhibiting retro-tendencies in favour of another.

The matter of song content was where Bernie's guidance was to prove most valuable. As both Mick and Joe have explained on numerous occasions, Bernie helped them to realise that songs about love were really just a convention of safe, commercial pop, and that truly cutting-edge songwriters should be reflecting their own environment and experience. 'He said, "Don't write love songs,"' Joe told the NME's Paul Du Noyer in 1981, '"write about something you care about, that's real."' The problem for Mick was that so much of his experience – so much of what he cared about, of what affected him – was second hand and unreal. 'He was a bedroom kid: one of those kids dreaming that someday he'll be as big as the guys on the posters, learning his chops in the bedroom,' Joe told Creem's Bill Holdship in 1984. At the time he made this remark Joe was intent on portraying Mick in as poor a light as possible, yet his assessment was essentially correct. Shortly after rehearsals had got underway at Rehearsals, former bandmate Matt Dangerfield met Mick wandering apparently aimlessly around the streets near Warrington Crescent. Matt asked what he was doing. 'Mick said, "Bernie says I've got to hang out." "Hang out?" "Yeah. He says I need to be streetwise,"' laughs Matt.

Before Joe joined the band, Mick had attempted to convey street wisdom in 'Deny', the lyric for which denounces a girlfriend locked into the cycle of mendacity and denial that comes with a hard drug habit. Certainly, there were people close to him who were intravenous drug users at this time – more of which later – but the song evokes the petulance engendered by personal betrayal rather than offering scathing social commentary.

The tune and chorus to Mick's first truly classic song, 'Janie Jones', came to him while he was riding the number 31 bus from Harrow Road to Chalk Farm Road for yet another rehearsal. When completed, it told the story of someone working at a dull office job and resenting having to do so when he could be listening to music, getting stoned or driving over to see his girlfriend. Janie Jones was a real-life vice queen who had enjoyed a spell of tabloid notoriety before being given a seven-year jail sentence for controlling prostitutes and attempting to pervert the course of justice by threatening witnesses. As a result, according to Joe, she 'seemed impossibly glamorous' to someone stuck in a tedious workaday routine. A few months earlier, Bernie had told Tony James to spend Christmas with a hooker. Now Mick was writing about a madam. Catchy and powerful though the song undoubtedly is, it is perhaps telling that Mick felt he had to go back to 1973, the year that Janie Jones was imprisoned and he himself last worked in an office, to find an experience that conformed even vaguely to the Rhodes brief. And again, like 'Deny', it was still a love song of sorts. 'Janie Jones' was originally written in the first person, which made Joe uncomfortable. When he took over the vocals, he opted to sing it in the third person.

In the Clash On Broadway booklet, Joe stated that most of the early songwriting consisted of 're-vamping', for which one should read 'adapting Mick's existing songs'. 'It was obvious from the start that Jonesy was great at melody and totally useless on lyrics,' Joe told Gavin Martin in 1999 for Uncut. 'It dovetailed into me: not so bad on the lyrics, not so great on the melody.' Another of the first songs to be written after he joined the band was 'Listen', which remained an instrumental. Soon thereafter Joe took over most of the lyric-writing for new compositions, but it would be some time before he felt secure enough with his position in the band to rework the words to material Mick had written before his arrival. In the meantime, he and the others had to accept them as they were, with the exception of 'Ooh Baby Ooh (It's Not Over)', which was dropped. '1-2 Crush On You' remained in the band's set, unaltered, for the rest of the year, eventually becoming the light relief encore. It is not insignificant that, when it was eventually recorded, in March 1978, it was sung by its composer.

Initially, then, most of the re-vamping consisted of arranging the music, and it is in this department that Keith Levene maintains he took a leading role. 'There's a lot of me in the Clash. I was contributing to the helter-skelter factor, to the velocity of how the songs were played, making things go much faster,' he told the *NME*'s Jane Garcia in 1989. The key word here is 'contributing'. Mick was a fan of the high-energy MC5, and few songs are faster than Mott the Hoople's version of 'You Really Got Me' or the Flamin' Groovies' 'Roadhouse'; Joe had been known as a frenetic live performer for well over a year; the whole group had been bowled over by the Ramones album; and one of the few things there had been no arguments about was that the Clash should *move*. 'The idea of the band was to try to play it *maximum*,' Joe told Harold De Muir of the *East Coast Rocker* in 1988, echoing the line he had taken with Clive Timperley 12 years earlier. 'That when we were onstage, there wouldn't be anybody standing around loafing.' Rob Harper – who would join the band as drummer for the December 1976 Anarchy Tour – recalls a conversation between Mick and Joe in which Mick said, 'Do you remember when this band started, and we said it was gonna be like an *explosion* coming off the stage?' Thus, although the band's uptempo policy was one of the ways in which they first distinguished themselves from the more mid-paced Sex Pistols, Keith was by no means its sole originator.

On the 1977 album *The Clash*, Keith receives a co-composer credit for 'What's My Name', the tune and chorus of which he and Mick wrote together at Riverside Studios shortly before Joe's arrival. 'I wrote more than I got credited for on the record,' Keith now insists. 'Basically, I got credited for "What's My Name" because I wrote the whole fucking thing, really. Let's face it, all the other tunes I had a good fucking hand in. I mean, it was me and Mick that wrote those tunes. Mick is definitely more responsible for the inception of most of them than I am, but it was me who put any bollocks there were into them.' He becomes irritable when pressed to reveal for which compositions in particular he feels he deserves credit, and memory does not serve him well: he states that all the songs written and performed during his time with the band appear on, and make up the bulk of, *The Clash*. In fact, apart from 'What's My Name', and the songs listed above that were already in Mick's songbook by the time the Clash started, only four others dating from the time Keith was still making a contribution to the band would survive to make it onto either the first album or single: 'Janie Jones', 'London's Burning', '48 Hours' and '1977'. Mick and Joe have detailed the circumstances of composition for all four, and Keith was not involved.

It is perhaps understandable that lead instrumentalists should object to the way their contributions – which define so much of their bands' musical identities – are considered mere embellishments, when even the most familiar (even blatantly stolen) three-chord skeletons of tunes they work on are termed 'compositions', and later generate royalty payments for the person claiming authorship. In a 1980 *NME* interview with Chris Bohn, Keith likened his role with the Clash to that of Brian Eno with the early Roxy Music, and when he speaks of 'putting bollocks' into the songs, he does not mean just mere speed, but also a weird spin, an attacking edge. 'I think the ideal band the Clash should have been, as far as Mick Jones was concerned, was Squeeze,' he says. 'That's what he was going after.'

Bearing in mind the type of song Mick had been writing up to that point, it is not so strange a claim as it may first appear. The question is whether Keith was any more responsible for changing that than Bernie, Joe, Paul, or the events of late summer 1976.

The only listenable surviving tape of a gig involving Keith was made at the Roundhouse on 5 September 1976, which turned out to be his farewell performance. On that tape, the band sound nothing like Squeeze, but they also sound nothing like they do on *The Clash*, recorded just five months later. It may be that they had to go through sound B to get from sound A to sound C, but it would be hard for anyone to make the case strongly enough to squeeze composer credits out of it. Nevertheless, Keith's guitar style is revealed to be inventively harsh and metallic, working off Terry's thunderous staccato drumming to create the kind of industrial noise that was to typify the experimentation of the period immediately post-punk; including that of Keith's own subsequent band, Public Image Ltd. If nothing else, it is quite clear that he did indeed play a large role in establishing an early Clash sound that was not retro, not remotely similar to that of the Pistols, and – although ultimately not something with which the other band members cared to persevere – quite possibly a couple of years ahead of its time.

Details of name, image, performance style, repertoire and sound had to be sorted out quickly to at least temporary satisfaction because the Clash's début appearance was scheduled for Sunday, 4 July 1976. They were to support the Sex Pistols at the Black Swan – known as the Mucky Duck – in Sheffield. The headline band, time and place were not without significance. It was Bernie's relationship with Malcolm that brought about the opportunity to play. From the point of view of Bernie and the Clash, supporting the Pistols was both an acknowledgement of influence and a chance to buy into the Pistols' scene. From the point of view of Malcolm and the Pistols, it established the rightful pecking order.

The Clash had been rehearsing for less than a month, and this rush to get on stage also demonstrated how fearful they were of being left behind by other bands. The venues the Stranglers usually played, the length of time they had already spent on the scene, and the band members' relatively advanced ages marked them down as a pub rock band. Nevertheless, the 101ers' old agency mates had plenty of punk attitude and were beginning to make all the right connections. Back in May, they had supported Patti Smith. On 4 July – the same day as the Sheffield gig – the Stranglers were due to appear at the Roundhouse once again, this time supporting the Ramones and the Flamin' Groovies as part of the American Independence Day Bicentennial celebrations. Of even more significance to Bernie and Mick was the fact that the Damned, the Clash's closest rivals for the position of number two bona fide punk band, were due to make their début just two days later at the 100 Club, also supporting the Sex Pistols. While the Damned were planning to walk straight into the lion's den, the Clash were choosing to take their first faltering steps in an altogether less perilous environment; but at least they were going to beat the Damned onto the public stage. Suspicion that they were hardly ready at this time is reinforced by the fact it was to be another five weeks before the Clash performed live again.

The band set off for Sheffield at 5 am, in a lorry that was so large that their equipment could be packed onto the ledge behind the cab while the band members stretched out on the floor and caught up on their sleep. Asked about the show on San Jose's Radio KSJO in 1982, Joe offered 'I *think* it was good. I'm not sure...' The Pistols were a lot less vague. 'I remember talking to John, and asking, "What do you think?"' says Glen Matlock. 'I really wanted it to work, because Mick was my mate, and I was keen for something to happen. And John went, "They're not very good, are they?"' For the documentary *Westway To The World*, some 23 years after the event, Joe did manage to dredge up one memory of the show. The Clash began with 'Listen', which opens with a bass riff. Everyone was nervous, but it proved particularly stressful for Paul to have his rudimentary skills spotlighted so early in the set: his fingers locked, repeating the first few notes over and over like a stuck record, denying the others their cue to come in. They fell about laughing, then made him start again.

Some feedback from their peers was inevitable, and – given Johnny Rotten's personality – predictably negative, but the Clash might have expected such a low-key gig to avoid the attentions of the media. True, there were no representatives of the music press there, but an unsolicited review appeared anyway, on the letters page of the 17 July edition of the *NME*. The correspondent, 'an anonymous music lover, Sheffield', passed the following verdict: 'Clash were just a cacophonous barrage of noise. The bass guitarist had no idea how to play the instrument, and even had to get another member of the band to tune it for him. They tried to play early Sixties R&B, and failed dismally. Dr Feelgood are not one of my favourite bands, but I know they could have wiped the floor with Clash.' For a band doing their best *not* to play early Sixties R&B, that must have stung. In the interests of balance, though, it is worth noting that the Sex Pistols received a similar trashing. The general drift of the letter was established in the opening paragraph: 'Both bands were crap. It's enough to turn you on to Demis Roussos.'

The night after the gig, back in London, came the first example of the rivalry-induced squabbling that was to dog the punk scene and undermine any attempts to promote a spirit of unity among the bands involved. Following the success of the Ramones-headlined Roundhouse gig – the first truly excited reaction that band had experienced outside New York – a second show involving the same line-up had been hastily arranged down the road at Dingwalls. Offered an unexpected opportunity to catch one of the best bills London had seen that year, most members of the Pistols and Clash attended. After the gig, while Mick, Glen, Steve Jones and Viv Albertine were backstage chatting to the Flamin' Groovies, Joe approached Hugh Cornwell in the bar and said, 'I think your bass player's having a scuffle with my bass player: they've both been thrown out.'

According to Stranglers follower Gary Coward-Williams, interviewed by Chris Twomey for the booklet included in UA's Stranglers 1992 boxed set *The Old Testament*, everyone piled outside to find Paul Simonon and Jean Jacques Burnel squaring up to each other in the courtyard. A full-scale brawl seemed about to break out between the Pistols and Clash on one side and the Stranglers and their followers on the other. Ultimately, though, everyone was so confused about what was happening that the situation was defused without further violence. Perhaps fortunately for Paul: JJ was an aggressive karate enthusiast. The incident deepened the mistrust between the Stranglers and the Inner Circle punk bands. JJ continued to bear a grudge against Paul for years, and former friends Joe and Hugh hardly spoke afterwards.

That week, the Clash resumed intensive rehearsals, and also began working up the first fruits of the Strummer-Jones writing partnership. Over the next year, while Joe would remain mostly responsible for words and Mick mostly responsible for music, there would be no set pattern for song construction. Sometimes Joe would write a lyric at home and bring it in for Mick to put a tune to it; sometimes Mick would write the tune first, and suggest a chorus or rough lyrical theme for Joe to expand upon; and sometimes both would work on the tune and lyric simultaneously in the upstairs office at Rehearsals, Mick with his guitar and Joe with a big pad of paper and – by his own account – a crayon. (He would later progress to a manual typewriter.) In the *Clash On*

Broadway booklet, Joe claims that if a song took more than a day to write it was abandoned. Whereas this is undoubtedly true of the unsuccessful efforts, those with which the band chose to persevere continued to be refined – especially lyrically – until such a time as they were either dropped from the set or recorded.

In *Diary Of A Rock'n'Roll Star*, recalling a song he had co-written with Kim Fowley named after 'romantic' LA crossroads Hollywood and Vine, Ian Hunter noted how much harder it was to achieve the same effect with British locations like 'the corner of Wardour and Old Compton'. Mick and Joe had started groping their way towards this goal before joining the Clash, as is evidenced by their respective songs of sexual disgust, 'Protex Blue' and 'Rabies (From The Dogs Of Love)'. The former makes reference to a West End bar and the Bakerloo tube line, and the latter to Shepherds Bush and the Praed Street Clinic. But Bernie wanted more than just a sense of place. 'The thing was to be relevant, to have some kind of root in human existence,' was how Joe summed up the Clash's original ideal to the *East Coast Rocker*'s Harold De Muir in 1988. 'We wanted it to have something to do with the times we were living in. We wanted the songs to be about the everyday, and not about a romantic fantasyland, or whatever.'

Sneaking a reference to the 100 Club into 'Deny' was a start. As the Sex Pistols' home base for the summer of 1976, the 100 Club was where the band's following had evolved into a recognisable punk scene. It was certainly the place of origin for most of UK punk's distinguishing features: the pogo dance (courtesy of Sid Vicious, too full of speed to stand still, and too hemmed in by the crowd to move in any other direction but up); gobbing (courtesy of Rat Scabies, who, during a Damned gig, spat into the crowd, which promptly spat back); the bin-liner clothing craze (courtesy of Johnny Rotten, according to Johnny Rotten); the safety pin jewelry craze (courtesy of Johnny Rotten, according to Johnny Rotten, but actually stolen from Television-era Richard Hell); the razor blade jewelry craze (courtesy of Johnny Rotten, according to Johnny Rotten, but actually stolen from Kilburns-era Ian Dury); the dog collar jewelry craze (probably courtesy of Gaye Advert, but actually stolen from Stooges era Iggy Pop); and the toilet chain jewelry craze (anonymous, but using chains stolen from the 100 Club toilets).

Following the dissolution of the 101ers and Richard Dudanski's departure to Sicily, Paul, Keith and Sid Vicious had joined Joe and Paloma in the squat at 42 Orsett Terrace. It was Paul who was responsible for giving Joe's girlfriend the name by which she would be known from this point onwards. Deliberately mishearing her given name, he dubbed her Palmolive, after the soap, and it stuck. In the booklet accompanying the 1988 double compilation album *The Story Of The Clash, Volume 1*, Joe's alter ego 'band valet Albert Transom' described life at number 42 in lurid detail. In his version, the inhabitants picked up discarded vegetables from Portobello Road market stalls for sustenance, preferring to spend their DHSS money at other stalls selling second hand goods. These included clothes, at least one television on which the sound did not work, a Dansette record player, and scratched bargain bin records by the Who, Bo Diddley, the early Rolling Stones, Woody Guthrie, Howlin' Wolf, Leadbelly and Big Youth, among others. The large communal basement room, where the food was eaten, the TV watched and the records played, was filthy, and in the relentless heat of that summer was also home to a dense cloud of flies. Reflecting his squalid environment, Joe came up with a lyric which, when married to a tune carried along by a distinctive Terry Chimes drum pattern, produced one of the more disquieting songs in the Clash's early live repertoire: 'How Can I Understand The Flies?'

Except for Terry, the entire band were now living within a hundred yards of the Westway. Mick, Paul and Joe had been based in and around the Notting Hill area for years. 'Four-square Portobello Road boys,' says Glen Matlock. 'Which was good, because it gave them a sense of identity. It gave them a base to work from, a foundation.'

'There wasn't a lot to do, so we'd just hang around,' said Joe, when interviewed for Channel 4 TV programme *Wired* in 1988. 'We had to make it better. And glamorising it was part of it. We wanted to make ourselves feel good. Because the songs I was listening to were all about Mississippi or Alabama or Lafayette – all these exotic places – and what we had here was another world, so we wanted to bring some mythology to our world.'

He wrote his first fully fledged attempt to rise to Ian Hunter's challenge at Orsett Terrace, after a visit to Mick's 18th floor flat in Wilmcote House. Although also a nod in the general direction of the MC5's 'Motor City Is Burning' – a song inspired by the Detroit inner city riots of 1967 – the title of 'London's Burning' makes more direct reference to the eponymous folk-cum-nursery rhyme celebrating the Great Fire of London of 1666. Joe adopts a sing-song voice and childish language to tell of a different kind of conflagration: the lights of the Westway and its vehicles as seen from the balcony of Wilmcote House. When both JG Ballard and the Clash wrote about it, the Westway still carried some of the shock of the new. It had been built in the late Sixties, a neo-brutalist structure forcing its way through West London on compulsory purchased land, an all-too concrete metaphor of the future for life in the inner city.

In *Search And Destroy* fanzine, Joe credited Mick with supplying the line about TV being the new religion – and, by extension, the new opiate of the masses – probably inspired by the similar sentiments expressed in John Lennon's 'Working Class Hero'. 'London's Burning' rails against boredom and the apathy of couch potatoes and ends with a bleak expression of despair, but the urgency of the chorus's repeated emergency call, the movement of the cars and the momentum generated by the band's performance serve to subvert its negativity: in the end, the song's very frustration generates a sense of excitement, anticipation of something about to happen.

It is no mean trick to simultaneously celebrate and condemn your environment without causing head-scratching bewilderment. 'London's Burning' is informed by the same ambivalence that provokes street gangs to fight for territory one day and vandalise it the next: the kind of behavioural response to habitat explored by JG Ballard in *High-Rise* and *Concrete Island*. 'Can you understand how much I hate this place?' a melodramatic Mick Jones demanded of the *NME*'s Tony Parsons at the end of March 1977. Just two weeks earlier, Joe told *ZigZag*'s Kris Needs, 'We love the place. Blocks of flats, concrete,' and Mick himself chipped in with, 'I hate the country. The minute I see cows I feel sick.' What 'London's Burning' really celebrates is the point at which adolescent confusion meets urban alienation, something that Sixties punk rock (and even mainstream pop) had always toyed with, and a subject that Seventies punk rock was setting out to make its own.

As is true of most great rock'n'roll anthems, the song also documents a lifestyle. Like '5 Star Rock'n'Roll Petrol', it contains implicit drug references, but the difference is that this is no longer merely a metaphorical device. Joe might have eschewed amphetamine while with the 101ers, but most of his new squatmates were enthusiastic users, and time hung heavy between rehearsals. By the time of the song's composition, cars weren't the only things 'speeding around underneath the yellow lights'. 'All we'd do was take blues [pills] or snort loads of cheap sulphate and get out there and live all night,' Joe told the *NME*'s Sean O'Hagan in 1988. 'We'd take amphetamines and storm around the bleak streets where there was nothing to do but watch the traffic. That's what "London's Burning" is about.' ...With the melancholy final verse representing the comedown. Joe might have had to spell it out 12 years after the event, but speed was the punk drug of choice in 1976 and the original scenesters had no trouble identifying with the song. Just as, in 1965, any mod who had ever been pilled up knew why Roger Daltrey was stuttering his way through 'My Generation'.

For such an ostensibly simple jingle, then, 'London's Burning' carries a complex series of messages. It would be difficult to overstress its importance as a cornerstone of Clash Mythology. Early interviewers would be fascinated by the song's origins on the balcony of 111 Wilmcote House, which would inspire headlines like the *NME*'s 'Eighteen Flight Rock And The Sound Of The Westway', and earn the Clash the nickname 'The Westway Wonders' and the band's music – and by extension punk music in general – the label 'Tower Block Rock'. The Westway would remain a potent symbol for the Clash throughout their career, and beyond: hence its appearance on the cover of the 1999 retrospective live compilation album *From Here To Eternity* and in the title of the accompanying biographical documentary *Westway To The World*.

In 1991's *Clash On Broadway* booklet, Mick recalled '48 Hours' being completed in a 96th of that time in the upstairs room at Rehearsals, because the band required an additional song 'for some reason'. That reason was almost certainly to provide them with a full-length set in time for their second live performance. Understandably, given the circumstances, '48 Hours' breaks little new ground. Like 'Janie Jones', it concerns a working stiff feeling oppressed by the tediousness of his job, but it harks back even further to buy into the early-to-mid-Sixties mod-culture notion of living for the weekend, as exemplified by the Easybeats' 1966 hit 'Friday On My Mind'. What it adds is a whole new level of desperation: the working week is a 'jail on wheels' hurtling ever closer. The search for kicks is so panic-driven and couched in such violent language that any possibility of fun is denied, ensuring that the quest is unsuccessful. Like 'London's Burning', it is locale-specific (the protagonist 'takes the tube'), the influence of amphetamines is blatant, and the loser message is overwhelmed by the song's sheer kinetic energy. Nevertheless, the Clash were still looking to mod to provide a blueprint for punk culture.

Between their first and second gigs, the Clash received their first real music press coverage, courtesy of the *Melody Maker*'s Caroline Coon. At 32, Caroline belonged to the previous generation. A former child ballet dancer and sociology student, she came from a wealthy background but had done more than pay lip-service to the late Sixties counter-culture. In 1967, she had co-founded Release, a legal aid support group for defendants in drugs-related cases, and had contributed to the underground magazine *It*. Along with several of her contemporaries, she had moved on to the mainstream music press in the early Seventies, and was now responsible for a weekly singles column in *Melody Maker*.

Her interest in clothes had led her to the Sex shop, and her fascination with the sociological aspects of youth culture from there to the Sex Pistols' early gigs. Unfortunately, *Melody Maker* had so far lived up to its reputation as a bastion of muso snobbery and shown a marked unwillingness to let her report on the antics of these primitive row-makers. Caroline had had to watch in frustration as the *NME*'s Neil Spencer wrote the first sensationalist music press review of the Pistols at the Marquee. Then as a representative from her own paper – none other than Joe Strummer's old Newport friend Allan Jones – had rubbished the Pistols while praising the 101ers in a review of the same Nashville gig that had ultimately caused Joe to renounce R&B: 'They do as much for music as World War Two did for the cause of peace. I hope we shall hear no more of them.' Then as her gig-going partner Jonh Ingham – his imagination fired by Neil Spencer's write-up – had stolen a march on everyone by conducting the first full-length interview with the Pistols for *Sounds*.

Worldly wise, Ingham hailed from New Zealand via Los Angeles, where he had run his own science fiction magazine. He later admitted to Jon Savage that he had deliberately mythologised the Pistols as a means of establishing himself as one of the foremost rock journalists of a new generation. Andy Czezowski for one believes this kind of attitude was instrumental in breaking punk. 'When you consider the amount of journalists in the rock business at that time – I don't know how many, but assuming there were 50-100 – you had only really two or three rooting for punk: Jonh Ingham, Caroline Coon and Giovanni Dadomo,' he says. 'That's probably it. But it created enough of a stir to ensure the papers were taken over. Because those writers were the useful energy on the music paper scene. They would not have been *allowed* to interview Mick Jagger. They were nothing journalists. The bigger guys would have got that job. So who could they deal with? The people that were their peers, the new up-and-coming scene.'

To avoid being scooped entirely, Caroline resorted to subterfuge. A review of the posthumous 101ers single 'Keys To Your Heart' gave her a transparent excuse to sneak the first brief interview with the Clash into her 24 July column. Under the memorable headline 'From a Crud to a King', Joe told of his conversion to punk, and Caroline prompted Mick to refute her colleagues' dismissal of the new movement as (courtesy of Richard Hell) 'the Blank Generation': 'We don't see ourselves that way. We're showing you music that's great. We're challenging complacency, standing up for rock'n'roll. We want to get rid of rock'n'rollers like Rod Stewart, who kiss royalty after gigs.' Like many others, Mick had found it difficult to forgive Rod for disbanding the Faces and teaming up with Britt Ekland in the international jet set.

Thereafter, editor Ray Coleman finally responded to the growing media buzz around punk rock. Competition among the three leading weekly music press 'inkies' was intense. If punk was, after all, destined to be the next big thing, *Melody Maker*'s survival might depend on its coverage of the scene. He gave the go-ahead to Caroline for a positive-overview feature, but just to hedge his bets, commissioned Allan Jones to offer the alternative opinion. Published side by side in the 7 August issue, Caroline's piece was headlined, 'Punk rock: rebels against the system?' – firmly establishing 'punk' as the title for the Class of '76 UK scene – and Allan's response, 'But does nihilism constitute revolt?'

Given that UK punk was in its infancy – she had to include Manchester yob rockers Slaughter and the Dogs, Birmingham glam rockers the Suburban Studs, and London pub rock stalwarts Eddie and the Hot Rods, the Stranglers and the Jam in order to even begin to make it sound like a scene – Caroline showed a grasp of its antecedents, aims, affectations and rhetoric that would have been truly remarkable had she not spent much of the previous six months observing its development. And if she hadn't been given considerable uncredited help by supposed rival but in fact good friend Jonh Ingham, as she later acknowledged in *1988: The New Wave Punk Rock Explosion*, the 1977 book that compiled her punk writings. Even so, this does not detract from what was an undeniably impressive feature.

Caroline made comparisons with the impact the Beatles, the Rolling Stones, the Who and the Kinks had made on the insipid British pop scene of the early Sixties. She made the point that those bands and their contemporaries were now part of the rock establishment, and that the subsequent generation of bands had abandoned the visceral and immediate in favour of the progressive and academic. She felt the State of Rock was symbolised by the stadium-type concerts given earlier that summer by the likes of the Who, the Stones and Elton John, causing her to opine, 'The time is right for an aggressive infusion of life blood.' She also claimed the new London punk scene had not been inspired by the New York new wave, but was instead developing parallel to it. This was rubbish, and was an example of Caroline toeing Malcolm's party line, as established in Jonh Ingham's earlier feature. Although she acknowledged that, like the New York scene, the London one did betray the influence of original Sixties punk, she stated that it was determined to develop its own identity: 'Nostalgia is a dirty word'. This much was true. She went on to explain that the music was performed with the minimal amount of equipment, the songs were short, basic and fast, with cynical lyrics and no solos or indulgent improvisations. Boredom was a pose, but it was a badge of punk in the same way brooding cool had been of the original Fifties rock'n'rollers and haughty detachment of the Sixties rock aristocrats. The youth of its performers was a crucial issue: punk was, after all, a youth culture.

A slick piece of propaganda, Caroline's feature was to remain the closest thing UK punk had to a manifesto for some months. In contrast, Allan Jones – despite weighing in with some perfectly valid points about its obvious debt to the likes of the New York Dolls, its violent overtones and depressing nihilism – came over like an old fogey. He shot himself in the foot by signing off with yet another World War Two analogy: if Johnny Rotten and his ilk represented the future of rock'n'roll, then Allan was 'off with the old lady to the air raid shelter until it all blows over'.

The timing of the *Melody Maker* feature was perfect for the Clash, who were now ready to make their London début. Cannily, Bernie rejected the idea of a public show, where the band would be at the mercy of all kinds of variables – nerves, sabotage from headliners, indifferent or hostile crowd reaction – in favour of a controlled environment: Rehearsals, in front of a select, invited audience of potentially useful bookers and music journalists. No effort (but plenty of expense) was spared in transforming Rehearsals into a venue appropriate and sympathetic to such an event: the band and their friends were volunteered to redecorate it. 'We all did it up,' recalls Alan Drake. 'We all put a bit of work in.' The walls of the downstairs rehearsal room were painted shocking pink and black – these having been designated the band's colours – and so were the amps and speakers. Pink drapes were hung at either side to make the performance area look even more like a stage. The finishing touch was added by Paul, who painted his mural behind the drum kit to provide the Clash with their first ever backdrop. The view from a window overlooking a car dump, tower blocks and the Westway, it was 'London's Burning' in oils.

But the band didn't stop at the walls and the amps. They also dripped, splashed and sprayed – courtesy of the nearby garage – bright colours over some of their Oxfam Mod clothes to provide eye-catching stage gear. Paul also custom-splattered his near-worthless bass; which provoked Joe into daubing black paint all over his Telecaster, making it appear near-worthless. Over the years, the band have repeatedly claimed that what came to be known as their 'Pollock look' – after action painter Jackson Pollock, famous for his splash- and drip-painted abstracts – came about purely by chance. Decorating Rehearsals without benefit of overalls, they had inevitably got paint on their clothes, and had decided to add more in order to make a feature out of a flaw... Glen Matlock takes exception to this version of events. He maintains that it was *he* who originated the look after accidentally dripping white paint on his expensive and hard-to-find black drainpipe jeans while redecorating the Pistols' rehearsal room. 'So I thought, "More paint on 'em! Jackson Pollock!" I really went to town, and everyone was like, "Wow, yeah, that's cool!"' Photographs prove that he wore the jeans onstage at the Nashville on 23 April 1976. 'Next thing, when the Clash started gigging, it was, "Do you like our stage gear, Glen? Good, eh?" And it was all paint-splattered stuff. I thought, "You bastards!"'

Whether or not it came via Glen, with three art students and three students of rock'n'roll history in the band, and a manager who claimed a previous association with the Who, it is difficult to believe that the Pollock look was not a pre-meditated punk adaptation of the Who's mid Sixties Pop Art look. Influenced by the likes of Jasper Johns and Robert Rauschenberg, the Who had covered their clothing in targets, flags, arrows and medals. The intention behind the adoption of these Pop Art trappings was as ironic as that behind Pop Art itself, but they were appropriate to the rigidity of mod culture's values, and gave the Who something to burst out of, sometimes literally. In contrast, Pollock's abstract expressionism conferred upon the Clash a visual expression of unfettered action, and amplified the supposed spontaneity and rage of their performances. Terry was not impressed – 'I quite liked the idea of outrageous clothes, but I didn't like all the paint splashing. It seemed a bit messy to me' – but the others were pleased to have their own image. At first, though, they did not take it as seriously as they would later. 'Me and Mick wrote this song in answer to Jonathan Richman's "Pablo Picasso",' remembers Glen, referring to the song on *The Modern Lovers* featuring the line, 'Pablo Picasso never got called an asshole'. 'It went, "I don't give a bollock about Jackson Pollock." We didn't get very far with it, but it was a giggle.'

In a suitably punkish gesture of defiance, the showcase took place on Friday 13 August. At first, it looked as though the fates were intent on wreaking immediate revenge, because – although a few bookers were present – only three of the numerous invited music journalists turned up. But, as Andy Czezowski has indicated, they were the right three to attract: Caroline Coon, Jonh Ingham and Giovanni Dadomo. Ultimately, by means direct and indirect, all of them would play a vital part in advancing the Clash cause. Bernie's plan was vindicated almost immediately, when Giovanni reviewed the show for *Sounds*, his piece illustrated with a photo taken by his wife, Eve.

At 9 pm, the band walked downstairs to where the small audience had been enjoying free drinks and listening to the juke box, plugged in their guitars... 'And for the next 40-odd minutes, it was like being hit by a runaway fire engine,' wrote Giovanni. 'Not once, but again and again and again.' Making allowances for one or two 'little cock-ups', he was quick to 'dispel any notion that the music is one relentless semi-cacophony, because in all that nuclear glare, there are incandescent gems of solos and references to everything from "You Really Got Me" to *you-name-it*. Also, Strummer seems to have finally found his niche, his always manic deliveries finally finding their place in a compelling tapestry of sound and colour.' He praised the band's image, 'as much the antithesis of the bearded bedenimed latterday hippy as the mods were the rockers. Clash have plenty of that old mod flash, too.' He signed off by declaring that he couldn't wait to see them again in a real venue – and, like Caroline and Jonh, he would indeed attend many of the band's gigs over the next few months – but the key sentence, part of which was blown up and used as the headline, was, 'I think they're the first band to come along who'll really frighten the Sex Pistols shitless.'

Naturally, the Sex Pistols were among those who read the review. The Clash in a subservient, supporting role was one thing, but the Pistols were not so happy that the band now seemed to be striking out for glory on their own; or with how they had set about it. 'We persecuted them mercilessly about that showcase,' says Glen. 'We thought it was well out of order. Not because we didn't know about it – although, looking back, we were a bit peeved that we weren't in on it – but the fact that it was really pandering to the press.' Giovanni's challenge to the Pistols on behalf of the Clash had followed on from Caroline Coon's earlier assertion that 'the atmosphere among the punky bands on the circuit at the moment is positively cut-throat. Not only are they vying with each other, but they all secretly aspire to take Johnny Rotten down a peg or two.'

Competition between bands on the scene was inevitable, and in his 1994 autobiography, *Rotten: No Irish, No Blacks, No Dogs*, Johnny blamed the Clash for introducing 'the competitive element that dragged everything down a little. It was never about that for us.' In an interview he gave for the same book, Paul Cook rather more astutely observed that the music press was largely to blame for stirring things up. Back in August 1976, however, the Pistols camp responded as though the gauntlet had been thrown down by the Clash themselves. Even today, Johnny and Glen display an astounding capacity for doublethink when it comes to the topic of competition: both are capable of adopting a self-righteous tone to blame others for the destruction of punk solidarity one minute, and of turning around to cackle about some wounding example of Sex Pistols one-upmanship the next. The Clash might have been in competition with the Pistols, but they remained deferential to them, and persevered longer than most with the idea of presenting a united punk front to the world. Malcolm and the Pistols gave almost all their attention to looking after their own interests; whatever was left, they devoted to sabotaging the interests of others.

Both bands had been approached to play the First European – in fact, first ever – Punk Festival on 21 August 1976, in Mont de Marsan, France. The Sex Pistols' connection with various destructive and violent incidents resulted in their being dropped from the line-up, and the Clash pulled out as a gesture of support. The Damned did go, and what a long, strange trip it was for them. Along the way, Ray Burns became Captain Sensible; they fell out with manager Andy Czezowski; and they met their future record company boss and manager Jake Riviera. Their blatant 'betrayal' of punk unity also did little to endear them to the Pistols and Clash camps, who already believed that the Damned's unremitting hedonism devalued punk's supposed seriousness of purpose.

By late August, the Clash's repertoire was going through changes in an effort to reflect this attitude. At Bernie's insistence, 'She's Sitting At My Party' was dropped for good at the end of the month. It was replaced by four new songs, none of which – as it turned out – would be officially recorded, but all of which were preserved on the tape of the 5 September Roundhouse show, eventually released as the bootleg CD *5 Go Mad In The Roundhouse*. Thematically, one would seem to be a close cousin of 'Janie Jones' and '48 Hours'. Built on a dramatic guitar riff, it lacks an official title but is listed on the CD as 'Work', quite possibly because the chorus appears to consist of that word repeated over and over again with no great fondness. The occasionally discernible line from the verses takes a pop at teachers and other everyday authority figures. 'I Don't Want Your Money' is a rejection-by-numbers of superficial materialism. 'I Know What You Do' (aka 'You Know What I Think About You') recycles the staccato riff of the Who's 'I Can't Explain'. Lyrically, it passes moral judgement on the behaviour of an acquaintance, much like 'Deny'; and the reference to a hospital room would suggest it does so for much the same reason. The song listed on the bootleg CD as 'Going To The Disco' – another close cousin of 'I Can't Explain' – is in fact 'Deadly Serious', which would seem to attack the empty hedonism associated with the rock'n'roll life.

At least one of these songs represented an attempt by the Clash to use their differences with the Damned as a departure point for the development of their own ideology. Early Clash interviews were mostly devoted to expanding or expounding on the band's lyrical themes, and the one Steve Walsh and Mark Perry conducted with the band for the October 1976 issue of *Sniffin' Glue* was telling, without making specific reference to any particular song:

Mark: What do you think of bands that just go out and enjoy themselves?

Mick: You know what I think, I think they're a bunch of ostriches, they're sticking their heads in the fucking sand! They're enjoying themselves at the audience's expense...

Mark: What if the audience say they're enjoying themselves?

Joe: Look, the situation is far too serious for enjoyment, man...

Mick: I think, if you wanna fuckin' enjoy yourselves, you sit in an armchair and watch TV, but if you wanna get actively involved, rock'n'roll's about rebellion. Look, I had this out with Brian James of the Damned and we were screaming at each other for about three hours, 'cause he stands for enjoying himself, and I stand for change and creativity.

For the next few months, the Pistols contented themselves with keeping the Damned at arm's length, but an opportunity to show the Clash who was boss offered itself within a matter of days. As a result of the Pistols' bad reputation, Malcolm was finding it hard to schedule gigs at London venues other than the 100 Club. For the same reason, it was difficult to raise any firm record company interest in his band. Through his friend Roger Austin, he arranged a concert for Sunday 29 August at the Screen On The Green Cinema, in Islington's Upper Street, and set about promoting it as an unmissable punk rock event: the Midnight Special. For all the scorn they had voiced about the Clash's showcase at Rehearsals, the Pistols' motive was the near-identical one of attracting music journalists and record company A&R men.

Following a trip to London to see the Pistols, Manchester-based Howard Devoto and Pete Shelley had set up a gig for their new heroes on 20 August at their home town's Lesser Free Trade Hall. The bill on that night had been completed by Slaughter and the Dogs, and – making their first ever appearance – Howard and Pete's own band, the Buzzcocks. So when Malcolm included the Buzzcocks and the Clash on the bill at the Screen, it looked as though he was reciprocating both bands' recent displays of loyalty. By offering them this platform to make their respective bona fide London débuts – an almost unprecedented opportunity to impress the music media and business alike at such early stages in their development – he appeared to be making an extremely magnanimous gesture of solidarity. If anything, the opposite was true.

'It didn't do us any harm to have other bands of our sort supporting us,' says Glen Matlock. 'Made it look as though there was a bit more of a movement, you know.' As Malcolm had suggested in the April 1976 *Sounds* interview, a group identified as being leaders of a movement would be a more exciting prospect for representatives of the music business. It was relatively easy to limit any danger of being upstaged by the hired help. One of the conditions of being allowed to play the cinema was that the Pistols supply a stage, a problem which they instantly passed on to the Clash. 'Malcolm said they could support us as long as they built it. And Bernie said, "Yeah, we'll provide a stage," and Malcolm said, "No, no, you've got to *build* the stage!" I thought that was really out of order, you know,' sniggers Glen, none-too convincingly. 'They had to put up the posters as well, which were basically Sex Pistols posters. That must have been very demeaning for them, having to build the stage *and* stick up posters of another band with "the Clash" in small writing at the bottom. So I went out and helped 'em stick up a few.'

For all the would-be originality of punk, the Midnight Special was an event styled on a late Sixties 'happening', and actually borrowed its title from a late night music show on American TV. The band's sets – which could not begin until after that evening's movie feature was completed, hence the event's title – were interspersed with a couple of Kenneth Anger's underground films and a Bowie and Roxy Music-dominated disco, which encouraged members of the Bromley Contingent to strut their stuff like so many extras from *The Rocky Horror Show*. The Clash had got up early on Sunday morning to build the stage, and did not get to take it until the small hours of Monday. Tired and nervous (in addition to the media presence, Mick was aware that most of Violent Luck were in the audience), the band were mean-spirited towards opening act the Buzzcocks backstage and under par in performance. Just to cap it all, both support groups were plagued by an appalling sound which – miraculously – improved as soon as the headline band plugged in. Glen admits that this was no accident. Again, here was punk rock resorting to one of the oldest dirty tricks in rock'n'roll. 'Of course. Yes, indeed,' admits Glen. 'But the band had no part of that. It's managers and roadies that do that, because they're there for one band and paid by one band.'

Whether due to the mix on the night, a primitive recorder, or multi-generational copy distortion, the tape of the Clash's performance currently in circulation among collectors preserves a muffled roar of white noise, with one song barely distinguishable from the next. At least it documents the band's core set at this early stage of their career: 'Deny', 'How Can I Understand The Flies?', 'Janie Jones', 'Protex Blue', 'Mark Me Absent', 'She's Sitting At My Party' (for the last time), '48 Hours', 'Bored With You' and 'London's Burning'.

Apart from Bromley Contingent member Susan Ballion attracting a disproportionate amount of the photographers' and journalists' attention with her peek-a-boo plastic underwear, fishnets and swastika armband, things went much as Malcolm had hoped. Giovanni Dadomo and Charles Shaar Murray, reviewing the show for *Sounds* and the *NME*, respectively, were less than complementary about the general tone of the event, dismissing the twilight decadence of films and fans alike as embarrassing and old hat. However, the Pistols themselves went down extremely well. Giovanni refuted any notion that they could not play with the repeated upper-case assertion that they were 'ONE DAMNED FINE ROCK'N'ROLL BAND.' CSM declared, 'The first 30 seconds of their set blew out all the boring, amateurish, artsy-fartsy, mock-decadence that preceded it purely by virtue of its tautness, directness and utter realism.'

In contrast, Giovanni described the Buzzcocks as 'boring and unimaginative' and 'rougher than a bear's arse'. Disappointed by the Clash's follow up to the Rehearsals showcase, he astutely laid the blame on the equipment, which did them 'a grave disservice tonight, losing Joe Strummer's hard-to-mix vocals until they became an unintelligible mumble, and generally poleaxing the band's nuclear potential'. CSM made no mention of the Buzzcocks at all, and gave the Clash what was destined to become the most famous review of their career: 'They are the kind of garage band who should be speedily returned to their garage, preferably with the motor running, which would undoubtedly be more of a loss to their friends and families than to either rock or roll.' For the Sex Pistols, the Midnight Special proved to be a giant step towards securing a recording contract; for both support bands, it was a case of taking one step forward to collect a slap in the face that sent them reeling two steps back.

7
WHITE RIOT

On Monday 30 August 1976, the day after the Midnight Special – or, to be precise, later the same day – Joe, Paul and Bernie went along to the Notting Hill Carnival for a little light relief. An annual event, taking place over the Bank Holiday weekend, the Carnival represents an opportunity for the local West Indian community to let its hair down in a manner more usually associated with the climate and culture of the Caribbean than with inner city Britain. In 1976, the weather might have been more accommodating than usual, but the attitude of the host culture had grown admonitory and harsh. The police presence had increased eightfold from the previous year to well over 1,500. The atmosphere grew more and more tense until, around teatime on Monday, there came the inevitable face-off between the police and disgruntled local black youth. An attempted arrest close to the Westway on Ladbroke Grove involving what Joe later described as a 'conga line of policemen' resulted in much jeering and the throwing of a few empty cans. Then the police charged, a few terrified middle-aged women started screaming, a member of the crowd threw a brick, and a full-scale riot ensued.

Caught up in the first charge, the Clash representatives were scattered. Having lost his glasses, Bernie withdrew. Paul threw a traffic cone at a passing police motorcycle. Then he and Joe spent the next couple of hours bombarding the police line with anything that came to hand. 'It was brilliant,' a still unrepentant Paul told the *Melody Maker* 12 years later. 'The coppers were standing there and they couldn't do a thing. We could throw bricks right at 'em. It was great.' Joe dove into his old stomping ground the Elgin for a couple of quick bracers, before – or so he claimed in 1999 – joining in with a failed attempt to torch a car.

With 60 arrests and over 450 injuries, it was the biggest – though not the only – UK riot since Notting Hill had erupted in 1958 (as documented in Colin Macinnes's *Absolute Beginners*, later filmed by Julien Temple). It provided Paul with an obviously welcome opportunity to relive his not-so-distant hooligan past, and Joe with a slightly more romanticised vision of himself as a street fighting man at society's cutting edge. However, any feeling that they were at one with the almost entirely black crowd was dispelled when they became the near-victims of a mugging attempt. 'We got searched by policemen looking for bricks, and later on we got searched by Rasta looking for pound notes in our pockets,' Joe told Janet Street-Porter that November on ITV's *London Weekend Show*. Paul came away exhilarated. Joe, equally fired up, found himself wrestling with the implications of the experience.

The Notting Hill Riot was the catalyst that brought together and to the surface a lot of disparate elements already present in the Clash. Before meeting Bernie, Mick had been largely apolitical, but he was quick to learn, well-read, and had a good grounding in anti-authoritarian and socially conscious rock'n'roll, from the MC5 to Mott the Hoople. Joe was equally adept at taking in new information, had experience of living in society's underbelly, and had a predilection for the sort of music that was intent on documenting its ills, from protest singers like Woody Guthrie and Bob Dylan to counter-cultural commentators like the Rolling Stones. Paul had been a football hooligan and part of the skinhead sub-culture, and was just waiting to have his own rebellious instincts channelled in a more positive direction. Bernie himself had come up through mod and the harder edge of the counter-culture, and was looking for a way to synthesise mod flair with late Sixties street politics. Suddenly Notting Hill happened: a flashpoint just like Watts in '65, Detroit in '67, Paris in '68, and Ohio in '70 had been, only *now*, right here on their doorstep, in their time and place.

The one snag, as the attempted mugging incident had illustrated so graphically, was that the Notting Hill Riot was not their fight. It was a spontaneous reaction to an apparently racially motivated – and certainly culturally ignorant – act of police oppression; but it was also the expression of resentment generated by years of harassment and denied opportunity, an experience specific to the inner city black population. As Bernie was aware, though, the quality of life for urban youth was deteriorating across the board, and it was not unrealistic to construe Notting Hill as a taste of what was to come for the general population. The economy was in recession, and unemployment was not only at its highest since the war, but increasing steadily, especially amongst the young. History shows that, in such situations, people look for scapegoats. Racial tension was rising, and the National Front were finding it easier to recruit youngsters hanging around aimlessly on estates and street corners, and to take advantage of the mob mentality already present on the terraces at football matches. In the excitement immediately following the Notting Hill Riot, it looked to the Clash camp at least as though the whole country could go up at any moment.

The soundtrack to – and possibly even fuel for – the riot was the menacingly heavy beat and militant lyrics of that year's crop of reggae sounds, reflecting the even more unsettled political climate of Jamaica. In the year-long run-up to the country's elections on 15 December, supporters of the rival Jamaican Labour Party (JLP) and People's National Party (PNP) had exchanged gunfire. Ostensibly to quell a situation bordering on civil war, but also as a means of exerting control, current PNP premier Michael Manley had declared a State of Emergency. Jamaica, as he put it, was 'under heavy manners', and about to experience some 'heavy duty discipline'. To the Rastafarian religious cult – usually the first to be on the receiving end when such discipline was being meted out – it seemed like a reaffirmation of the apocalyptic visions encouraged by their literalist Old Testament theology. Their fascination with prophecy and numerology found great significance in the fact that the coming year would bring two sevens together.

In his 1994 autobiography and elsewhere, Johnny Rotten claimed that reggae remained a minority interest in the UK in general and on the punk scene in particular until he played Dr Alimantado's 'Born For A Purpose' and expressed his fondness for the genre on Capital Radio's *Tommy Vance Show*. 'Then suddenly you'd get Joe Strummer and the Clash saying, "We always loved reggae." But those fucks never did.' The statement is as inaccurate as it is spiteful. The admittedly influential Capital show was not broadcast until July 1977. Although reggae's first wave had slumped in popularity around 1971 in the UK, by the mid Seventies the slower, heavier roots reggae that had superceded it was beginning to win converts outside the Jamaican immigrant community. In 1974 Eric Clapton had reached the Top 10 with a cover of Bob Marley's 'I Shot The Sheriff'. Thanks to that and 1975's breakthrough album *Bob Marley And The Wailers Live!*, by 1976 Marley was already an established name. There was regular coverage of the more hardcore releases in *Time Out*, *Sounds* and *Melody Maker*, Caroline Coon being just one of several music press enthusiasts.

Paul Simonon had remained loyal to reggae throughout the Seventies. The 'likes' list on the 'What side of the bed' T-shirt Bernie Rhodes had designed for Sex in 1974 includes Jamaican rude boys, Bob Marley, dreadlocks and King Tubby's sound system. Although Joe Strummer had shrugged off the influence of the reggae-loving Mole while with the 101ers, when, during her July 1976 singles column interview, Caroline Coon asked him if he was into the music, he had replied, 'There's not much else around to listen to, is there?' One of the early contenders for the Clash's band name had been borrowed from a Big Youth track. Certainly, by the late summer of 1976, most of the Clash had already recognised reggae to be the most vital contemporary musical genre, and the entire band's interest increased dramatically once the Riot gave a local context to its wrathful denunciations of Babylon. That autumn and winter at Rehearsals, in place of the non-functioning jukebox, a turntable was linked up to a guitar amp and speaker. Between practices this rough and ready sound system blasted out, among others: Big Youth's *Screaming Target*, Tapper Zukie's *Rockers* and *MPLA*, Prince Far I's *Under Heavy Manners*, Joe Gibbs and the Professionals' *State Of Emergency* and Culture's *Two Sevens Clash*.

The Clash camp began to see reggae culture as a blueprint for the development of both their own music and of punk in general. The punk scene, still largely an elite club for art school students and decadent poseurs, could be co-opted for the disaffected white equivalent of the rioting black youths; and could provide a more positive politicisation process than that offered by the National Front. 'We know the blacks've got their thing sewn up,' Mick told the *NME*'s Barry Miles that December. 'They got their own culture, but the young white kids don't have nothing. That's why so many of them are living in ignorance and they've just gotta wise up… They used to blame everything on the jews, now they're saying it about the blacks and the Asians. Everybody's a scapegoat, right?' 'We're hoping to educate any kid who comes to listen to us, right?' added Joe. 'Just to keep 'em from joining the National Front when things get really tough in a couple of years.'

The Rasta was too laid back and long-haired to provide a direct role model. Instead, the Clash version of the punk persona underwent a small – but significant – adjustment. The Paul Simonon-style skinhead overtones grew stronger, moving the band further towards the football terraces; and their updated take on mod culture gave ground to that of the rude boy outlaw figure mythologised in Paul's beloved early reggae records. The yob element of this new band character had already introduced itself into the Clash's music via the terrace 'harmonies' of 'What's My Name'. Now repetitive chanted choruses became as prevalent as the previously dominant high pitched 'oohs'.

The reggae influence first manifested itself in the band's live variation on the 'drop-out' production technique. Drop-out was a feature of dub, or version, reggae. As these names suggest, it was a largely instrumental version of an existing song, stripped down to basics, heavily doctored with echo and reverb, and imaginatively overdubbed with musical and lyrical snippets by such groundbreaking producers as Lee Perry. At first placed on single B-sides of the original song so that Jamaican sound system DJs could toast – that is, chatter and rhyme – over the top, dub became a popular musical form in its own right. Before long, it was taking up entire albums, and feeding back its influence into the parent genre. (It also contained the seeds of both sampling and rap.) In the context of a Clash gig, the use of drop-out meant that instead of the entire band playing all together all the time in ramalama Ramones style, at key points in certain songs one or more musicians would cease playing. This not only highlighted the efforts of those remaining, but also made a drama out of the absentees' eventual return to the fray. Although Jonh Ingham was the first to remark upon it as a 'Clash trademark' in his *Sounds* review of a 27 October gig at Barbarella's in Birmingham, the Clash were employing the technique as early as their 5 September Roundhouse appearance.

The first fully fledged articulation of the new Clash outlook was '1977', introduced into the band's set within a week of the Riot. It owes much to Culture's contemporary 'Two Sevens Clash'. The vocal trio's song evokes the prophecies of Rastafarian founder

Marcus Garvey, warning in the most apocalyptic tones and terms of violent confrontation in the year 'when the two sevens clash'. The destiny- and mythology-conscious Clash reworked this message to reflect their own environment and experience. For reasons that had more to do with subsequent band posturing and rhetoric than any shortcomings in its lyric, '1977' became one of the Clash's most misunderstood and maligned songs. Charges of portraying the band as a highly romanticised cell of urban guerrillas were levelled at Joe for the lines in which he warns of 'knives in West 11' and 'sten guns in Knightsbridge'; charges which he did his best to refute. 'I imagined having a knife pointed at *me*, right?' he explained – not for the first or last time – to *Melody Maker*'s Allan Jones in November 1978. 'I imagined sten guns in Knightsbridge pointed at *me*. But people took it to mean that WE had them and we were pointing them at other people. That was a song written about the future. I thought the future was going to do us in. I really imagined it.'

As Mick's tune is a blatant lift from the Kinks' 'All Day And All Of The Night', the song's chorus, 'No Elvis, Beatles or the Rolling Stones / In 1977', also invited criticism. In 1979, the Clash's supposed reinvention of themselves as a more traditional Rolling Stones-type rock'n'roll band encouraged further retrospective sniping about those particular lines. In fact, Joe's words have their origins in one of his genuine reasons for leaving the 101ers and joining the Clash: the feeling that playing cover versions of songs made famous by Elvis, the Beatles and the Rolling Stones was no longer enough. Instead of looking to heroes for answers, he believed, it was time for Joe and his peers to take responsibility for themselves.

Overall, the lyric takes as its starting point the dire warning of 'anarchy in the streets' Bernie had heard broadcast on the radio in 1975, factors in the Notting Hill Riot, and projects from that a deliberately sensationalist worst case scenario. The first verse addresses rising unemployment; the second predicts a potential breakdown of the social fabric, as presaged by the Notting Hill Riot; and the third offers examples of the kind of apathy and denial that might let this state of affairs come to pass. The chorus hints at racial tension or war ('you better paint your face').

Joe had flirted with apocalyptic imagery before, most notably in 'London's Burning', but '1977' lays it on especially thick. Year titles were nothing new in punk: the Stooges had bestowed the mark of the iguana on both 1969 – 'Another year of nothing to do' – and 1970, and '1977' can be seen as a continuance of this tradition. Just to cap it all, after the band had been playing '1977' for a couple of months, Joe added a countdown coda, starting with 1977 and ending suddenly with the year 1984, thus also evoking George Orwell's dystopian novel of that title.

'White Riot', destined to become the Clash's theme song, came along in mid September 1976, and represented an attempt to make a much more straightforward and direct reference to the Notting Hill Riot and the black-white cultural divide than '1977'. In 1999, when expressing admiration for the Rolling Stones was no longer verboten, Joe acknowledged the thematic influence of 'Street Fighting Man' to *Uncut*'s Gavin Martin. The title of the Clash song had other, even more militant counter-cultural antecedents. The Weathermen – the late Sixties American urban guerrillas who had taken their name from a line in Bob Dylan's 'Subterranean Homesick Blues' – had published a 'revolutionary songbook' including a number entitled 'White Riot' to be sung to the tune of 'White Christmas'. If Joe knew this, he probably heard it from Bernie.

One of the most famous Situationist International slogans, intended to underline the mind-numbingly repetitive nature of life for the average working stiff, was: 'Tube – Work – TV – Sleep – Tube – Work – TV – Sleep...' Originally, the Clash's 'White Riot' included references to 'reading papers and wearing slippers' and, somewhat more abstrusely, eating 'supermarket soul food' as similarly scornful comments on a life of passive acceptance. Joe – who was largely responsible for both lyric and tune – later replaced both lines with the more direct refrain 'And nobody wants to go to jail'. As with the Situationist slogan, the point is still that nothing will change if people are too scared to challenge the status quo.

'White Riot' suggests that disaffected white youths should learn to express their anger like their black counterparts: through direct action. The Clash had realised that the Notting Hill Riot was a black issue; but making a clear distinction between black and white in song took the band into a sensitive area. 'The only thing we're saying about blacks is that they've got their problems and they're prepared to deal with them,' Joe explained to the *NME*'s Barry Miles later in 1976. 'But white men, they just ain't prepared to deal with them. Everything's too cosy. They've got stereos, drugs, hi-fis, cars...' (And TVs, papers, slippers and supermarket soul food...) Nevertheless, the song remained open to misinterpretation. ·

In the early Seventies, rock'n'roll had flirted with the trappings of fascism as part of a decadent pose. In the summer of 1976, the National Front polled nearly a fifth of the vote in a Leicester by-election. That autumn, rock'n'roll luminaries Eric Clapton and David Bowie made highly publicised comments that seemed to be, respectively, racist and pro-fascist. Although these were later retracted and dismissed as drug-addled ravings by the guilty parties, the political situation had grown too volatile for them to be swept under the carpet as minor embarrassments: Clapton's outburst led directly to the founding of Rock Against Racism, which was announced in letters to the music press.

In the context of the times, then, a band of short-haired, aggressive youths bursting onto stage to chant 'White Riot' were asking for trouble. Were the Clash skinheads, racists, National Front members? Why a *white* riot? Was the call separatist; was it urging white-on-black violence? The confusion would reach its apogee following a gig on 29 November 1976 at Lanchester Polytechnic in Coventry. 'They said we couldn't use the stage as a platform to spread racist propaganda!' remembers Terry. 'They needed to get their ears washed out.' For all his protestations, the members of the Lanchester students entertainments committee were not the only ones with hearing difficulties.

Whatever the tangled web of its genealogy, in both its Sixties and Seventies guises, punk was an almost exclusively white musical form, so far removed from its roots in the blues that almost all the black influence had been lost: it was noisy, uptight and aggressive, the very antithesis of funky. In 1976, most mainstream British rock'n'roll bands emulated current American styles, and their vocalists affected American accents, whereas punk prided itself on its rejection of US cultural imperialism, and trumpeted a return to Britishness. 'We sing in English' was a message that Joe – still keen to distance himself from his own years playing 'American imperialist jukebox music' with the 101ers – proudly spelled out in the band's earliest interviews with *Sniffin' Glue* and *Melody Maker*. The fierceness of this parochial urge bordered on the xenophobic, running the risk of attracting and encouraging racist thugs rather than achieving the stated aim of encouraging them to rethink their position. The concerts of later yob-punk band Sham 69 would be regularly ruined by their unsolicited and unwelcome right-wing skinhead following, something which hastened the band's demise. Ultimately, it would be their enduring reggae influence that saved the Clash from a similar fate. For the Clash, cultural enslavement to America might have been out, but reflecting and celebrating the multi-cultural nature of their own country and neighbourhood was most definitely in.

Later, there would be another misinterpretation of 'White Riot', but this was a wilful one, made by the Clash themselves. In 1980, tired of being pilloried in the music press for failing to live up to their rhetoric, they attempted a retrospective shift of meaning: apparently, the song had never been intended as a literal incitement to riot or revolution; rather, it was merely supposed to encourage listeners to think and act for themselves...

While that underlying message is undeniably as present in 'White Riot' as it is in '1977', this was still a disingenuous claim. In the immediate aftermath of Notting Hill, the word 'riot' was too specific and loaded to be interpreted as a metaphor for general pro-activism, as indeed was the taunt sung over the bridge in the single version: 'Are you taking over, or are you taking orders?' In other words, are you part of the problem, or part of the solution? Which side of the bed?

During an interview for BBC Radio One's *Rock On* programme, which took place in May 1977, shortly after a Clash audience had trashed a number of seats at the Rainbow Theatre, Joe, admittedly irritated by the condescending manner of presenter John Tobler, nevertheless made it quite clear that the Clash meant it, man. Were the band trying to incite their audience to riot? 'Of course. We try it every night. I want to hear the smashing of those seats, and the crumpling of the wood, the snapping of the iron.' Suppose the rioters tried to take your money away from you? 'I don't *care*. I don't care if the ceiling falls down and kills everyone in the theatre. Me included. I don't care what happens as long as it's out of hand, you know? As long as it's *out of control.*'

On 31 August 1976, the Tuesday immediately following the Riot, the Clash were again booked to support the Sex Pistols, this time at the 100 Club. The bill was completed by Birmingham's increasingly confused glam rock band, the Suburban Studs. Once again, the Clash's set was marred by equipment problems, this time when one of Keith Levene's guitar strings broke. With no back up instruments, they were forced to wait until the string could be replaced, an unenviable position for any performers onstage in front of 200 people.

Joe improvised with the aid of a recent Portobello purchase. 'I'd been lucky, and bought a cheap transistor radio in a junk shop for ten bob [50 pence] and it worked quite well,' he told the *Sniffin' Glue* team the following month. 'When someone broke a string, I got it out, and it just happened to be something about Northern Ireland.' 'A State of Emergency,' added Mick, drawing a parallel between the Troubles in Ireland and those in Jamaica. Held up to a microphone, with heavy dub-style delay added by the Pistols' quick thinking soundman Dave Goodman, the news report echoed around the 100 Club and turned a potentially embarrassing hiatus into a Clash Statement. 'The club was filled with words like, *bombs, bombs, bombs,*' Joe reminisced to *Uncut*'s Gavin Martin in 1999. 'It sounded like a Radio Four discussion at the end of the world!' Inspired by this fortuitous occurrence, the band would continue to experiment with variants on the spoken-word address for the remainder of their career, both live and on record.

Five days after the 100 Club gig, on 5 September, the Clash made their first venture out into the wider world without the spurious patronage of the Sex Pistols. It only took them a matter of yards down Chalk Farm Road, but it also took them a long way outside the punk milieu: to the Roundhouse's traditional Sunday band-fest, as attended by Mick Jones while still at school, and played by Joe Strummer while with the 101ers. The headliners were the Kursaal Flyers – an established pub rock band – and the main support were Welsh rock'n'roll revivalists Crazy Cavan and the Rhythm Rockers. The Clash went on first, at 6 pm, before the bar had even opened, and certainly before the typical Roundhouse audience of bedenimed latter-day hippies were in the mood to give their full attention to something so demandingly different.

Up to this point, the Clash had eschewed direct verbal communication with their audiences, preferring instead to hit them with song after song, and hopefully leave them as overawed as had been Giovanni Dadomo at the Rehearsals showcase. Suspecting this tactic would have next to no chance of achieving the same results at the Roundhouse, the band instead opted for confrontation. After 'Janie Jones', Joe tried to provoke some 'audience participation'. There followed a painful four or five minutes of desultory heckling. Joe – who later explained he was unable to hear properly – found his famed 101ers era repartee had deserted him. Following a few snide remarks about denims and mind-altering drugs, he berated one person for the sin of being overweight, and dismissed another as a 'big twit'.

After 'Mark Me Absent', he abandoned attempts at dialogue, and instead offered a sermon against boredom and the evils of television, culminating with a plea for anyone who wasn't 'past it' to get involved and make something happen. Quoted by Jon Savage in *England's Dreaming*, and included on the *Lipstick Traces* album issued by Rough Trade to complement Greil Marcus's book of the same title, this Stage Rap has latterly come to be portrayed as a punk landmark, the earliest articulation of punk's DIY ethic: if you're bored, do something about it; if you don't like the way things are done, act to change them; be creative, be positive, anyone can do it. The attitude expressed would soon change the face of punk, but in the context of the gig, it's hard to believe the frankly excruciating Stage Rap converted any of those present and persuaded them to shed their denims, cut their hair, and form a punk band. Plus, it was little more than a reiteration of a remark made by Johnny Rotten to Jonh Ingham during the Sex Pistols' April 1976 *Sounds* interview: 'I'm against people who just complain about *Top Of The Pops* and don't do anything. I want people to go out and start something, to see us and start something, or else I'm just wasting my time.'

The Clash played a varied and mostly proficient 15-song set at the Roundhouse, but its pacing was ruined by these lengthy interruptions, which failed to generate any compensatory dramatic tension. The band left the stage to that most humiliating of noises, lukewarm applause. This had not been the object of the exercise, and Bernie was neither one to accept faint praise, nor to give it. 'I remember coming up to Bernard after the gig,' says Keith, 'and he was saying, "It was fucking shit! It was fucking *shit*!"' Although his language was more restrained, Chas De Whalley intimated much the same in his *Sounds* review. In addition to dismissing the bulk of the songs – authorship of which he attributed solely to Joe – as being 'little more than rewrites of this year's punk classics', he compared the Clash unfavourably to the 101ers, whose 'love and warmth' he believed had given way to 'aggression and belligerence'. Chas's review was filed quickly enough to make the 11 September edition, and was printed on the page opposite Giovanni Dadomo's fair but hardly uplifting Screen On The Green review. After this damaging combination punch, the coup de grâce was delivered by CSM's mauling of the latter performance in that week's *NME*. A few days later, Keith Levene left the Clash.

The first music press reference to Keith's departure was made during Caroline Coon's late September 1976 *Melody Maker* review of the 100 Club Punk Festival. She gave the official line that Keith had quit of his own volition to form a new band of his own. The initial assumption – propagated by Pete Frame's punk Family Tree in September 1977's *ZigZag* – was that the *Sounds* and *NME* reviews had rendered Keith too depressed to carry on. Keith's subsequent spell with squat rehearsal band the Flowers of Romance came to an end when Sid Vicious left to join the Sex Pistols. Thereafter, Keith played with Cowboys International before teaming up with the former Johnny Rotten – by then trading under his given name John Lydon – in Public Image Ltd (PiL). During PiL's May 1978 interview with the *NME*'s Neil Spencer, Keith gave his own reason for quitting the Clash: 'I wasn't into politics.'

In that same feature, Neil offered an alternative reason of his own, voicing a rumour that, by then, had been floating around the music scene for 18 months: 'A flirtation with drugs is apparently another reason why Levene didn't stay the course; certainly, "Liar" [he meant 'Deny'] on the Clash's first album is widely reputed to refer to him at this time.' Tony Parsons and Julie Burchill went even further in *The Boy Looked At Johnny*, published in October 1978: 'Keith Levene was soon too involved with heroin to devote any time to playing guitar, and quit the Clash leaving behind him only one song...'

During another *NME* interview, given to Julie Panebianco in November 1983, Keith came clean about his use of heroin. While admitting that he had indeed developed an addiction to the drug, he insisted this had happened during his time with PiL; he had not even begun to dabble while still with the Clash. In those days Keith's drug of choice had been speed. Joe confirmed as much in *England's Dreaming*, describing the former Clash guitarist to Jon Savage as something of a speed connoisseur who used it 'in a very pure form'. The confusion came about because, unlike the rest of the band, Keith was an intravenous user, and in those days most people automatically associated syringes with heroin. As for 'Deny': it is indeed addressed to someone with the tell-tale marks left by needles, but that someone is female, and most of the lyric was in place before Keith left the band. The song may well have taken on a new relevance thereafter – rumours that it was about him were never denied and were quite possibly encouraged by his erstwhile colleagues – but this was largely serendipitous.

Alan Drake is incensed by what he perceives as the hypocrisy of the Clash camp's suggestion that his friend was too drug-oriented to take an active interest in the band. 'It's absolute bollocks! It wasn't that at all. I mean, *everybody* was doing drugs at that time. If it wasn't for speed, I don't think half the punk scene would have happened anyway. At that point it was speed, speed, speed.' 'They intimated that it was drugs, but it wasn't,' agrees Keith. 'Basically, I was very down; and when I was down, I was very quiet.' Many people baulk at the idea of shooting up, even those who are generally liberal-minded about the issue of recreational drug use. Somehow, intravenous administration suggests deeper commitment to a drug: there are more attendant risks, and it offers a more intense experience of both the immediate effects and the after-effects. In a March 1988 *NME* interview with Sean O'Hagan, Joe described his own experiences with speed thus: 'I'd have these comedowns where I'd want to bash my head in with a hammer. The up wasn't worth the down in the end. Like, what we were doing was next door to Vim: cheap and nasty.' If it was like that for Joe snorting, it must have been at least as bad for Keith injecting, for all the relative purity of his supply. Despite his and Alan's protestations to the contrary, it is almost certain that Keith's drug use at least contributed to his mood swings from uptight hostility to non-communicative withdrawal, and consequently to the on-off nature of his commitment to the Clash.

As Keith suggests, though, there were other reasons for his unhappiness. He may not have been 'into politics', but as his interest was always more with the band's sound than the subject matter of the songs, and as he loved a good argument, it is hard to credit that the lyrics or Bernie's band meetings were enough in themselves to prompt him to leave. What did concern him was the extent to which the lyrical content was taking precedence, the other band members seemingly pushing for increasingly direct and simplistic musical frameworks for the words. 'White Riot' was the prime example and, in fact, the final straw. Although the song was mostly Joe's, and – as it turned out – it was Joe whose patience with Keith was the first to snap, the single greatest reason for Keith's departure was the musical power struggle between himself and Mick.

Being devoted to the songwriter's craft as well as a fan of the punk rock tradition, Mick was as uncomfortable with Keith's avant garde reworkings of his songs as Keith was with the songs themselves. 'Mick was always Rock'n'Roll Mick,' Keith told the *NME*'s Chris Bohn in 1980. 'I didn't realise then just how much I resented rock'n'roll.

Any numbers I got together, they didn't really understand.' Alan agrees: 'I think, to be honest, Keith was just too radical for Mick.' Also, replacing Billy Watts with Joe had caused an imbalance in the group: three guitarists might perhaps have been justifiable had the intention been to indulge in endless Lynyrd Skynyrd-style boogie workouts, but in the minimalist world of punk it was at least one guitarist too many. Joe was strictly rhythm, but the other two had trouble defining their roles.

The best possible scenario for Mick was that Keith should leave and that Mick should become the band's sole lead guitarist and musical director. (Joe, as he admitted to Caroline Coon the following year, was at this time no more capable of hearing full arrangements in his head than he had been in the 101ers. Paul was still learning his bass parts by heart.) It was a situation of which Keith was well aware – or at least, with the benefit of hindsight, it is a situation of which he is now well aware. 'It was quite possible for it to be Mick's *and* my band from my point of view, but it was not possible from Mick's point of view. So therefore, it had to be Mick or me, and I decided, let it be Mick.'

How much say Keith actually had in the making of that decision is open to debate. In various interviews given since the break up of the Clash, Joe has taken responsibility for instigating what he describes as Keith's sacking, and his 101ers track record certainly proves him capable of such ruthlessness. 'Keith rang up and said, "What you doin'?"' Joe told Sean O'Hagan in 1988. 'I told him we were rehearsing "White Riot", and he goes, "Uh, it ain't worth me coming in then." So, basically, I told him to fuck off. Which he did. Me and Mick and Paul and Terry Chimes did it that afternoon.'

Terry remembers the lead up to the confrontation differently. In his version, tellingly, it was Mick who first floated the idea of a showdown. 'I turned up one day, and Keith wasn't there,' says Terry. 'There were four of us sitting around waiting for him to arrive. There was this conversation where Joe said he saw Keith as the Phantom Guitar Player: although he comes and goes, he's never really there. Paul said something vaguely agreeing with it, and then Mick said, to my astonishment, "Do you think he should leave, then?" And they all thought for a second, and then Joe and Paul nodded and said, "Yeah." I was just dumbfounded. I said, "You can't just make decisions like that! You sit down and discuss the issues, and work it out. You can't just suddenly, on a whim, sack him!" Which is weird, because I'd found him harder to work with than anyone else, and now I found myself defending him. Anyway, by the time he arrived, I'd reluctantly given in and said, "OK, let's sack him", so he was sacked, and he was about as shocked as I was, I guess.'

Keith's version has the issue being put to the vote in his presence. Although he could not have known it, this was a display of 101ers-style 'democracy': the outcome was a foregone conclusion. 'The band got me upstairs and confronted me,' he says. 'Basically, they said, "Well, Keith, you're a miserable git. What's going on?" And I said, "I don't like what we're doing. It's not coming across like the thing I want it to be." What happened then was, there was this kind of vote, which I had the casting decision on. And I said to them, "Look, I'll fuck off, and if in two weeks you think it was a bad move, I'll still be open-minded. But after that, things have got to change or I'll be gone." But they never really changed their minds, and that was it.' 'I remember the first thing Mick said after Keith had left the room, slamming the door behind him,' says Terry. 'He looked around and said, "I'd better learn how to play the guitar then, hadn't I?"'

It seems not everyone in the Clash camp was confident about Mick's ability to do so. Bernie had not been party to the Keith-shedding exercise, and was initially as unhappy about the hole in the line-up as he was about it having been made without his knowledge. According to Mick's former bandmate in Little Queenie, Bernie briefly considered Brady as a replacement for Keith... until he found out he was 27 years old.

The showdown having taken place over the weekend following the Roundhouse gig, the new four-piece Clash had just over a week to knock themselves into shape for their slot at the 100 Club Punk Festival, due to take place on Monday 20 and Tuesday 21 September. Terry does not recall it being a particularly arduous task. 'After Keith left, it seemed like it had been the right decision, just because of the mix of personalities,' he says. 'Mostly we were aware of fewer arguments, less tension in the band, and everything being a bit simpler.' Having one guitar less to weave into the songs' arrangements helped, and Mick's necessarily economical lead guitar style also encouraged the Clash to experiment further with drop-out, heeding dub's lesson that musical dynamics are governed as much by what is not played as by what is.

'White Riot' was worked up in time to make its début at the gig as part of an 11-song set, four less than at the Roundhouse, and seven less than the band's full repertoire. Terry has no recollection of songs being dropped specifically because of any close association with Keith or because their lead guitar parts posed Mick any problems. It appears that the band simply took advantage of the situation to cut out a little dead wood. Joining Mick's school fantasy number 'Mark Me Absent' in the dumper were three of the more recent attempts to capture the Clash outlook, 'I Don't Want Your Money', 'Work' and 'I Know What You Do' (aka 'You Know What I Think About You'), although the following year would see the last of these tunes cannibalised to form the basis of 'Clash City Rockers'.

If Keith's departure gave Mick the room to grow musically, it gave Paul more literal room to develop as a performer on-stage: he was able to move up to join the front line, and from this point on had more space in which to fling his bass around. Visually, at least, the Clash were now perfectly balanced.

The Screen On The Green gig had given the Sex Pistols' career a considerable boost. Malcolm McLaren devised the Punk Rock Festival of 20-21 September 1976 as an even larger promotional event. It was intended to showcase his band as leaders of an ever-growing movement, and completely overshadow the French festival from which the Pistols had been banned earlier that summer. This time there would be no hippy trappings: the presentation would be as raw and basic as the music, and the venue would be the Sex Pistols' long-time favourite, the 100 Club. If there was any stylistic model at all, then it was CBGBs' unsigned bands festival of July 1975.

Less straightforward was the task of finding enough bands on the London scene qualifying as 'punk' to fill two nights and justify the description 'festival'. As the Pistols were booked to appear in Cardiff on the Tuesday, they were forced to headline the Monday night. The ever-faithful Clash agreed to be main support. The scarcity of alternative options meant the Damned had to be included whether Malcolm liked it or not, but they were placed insultingly low on the second night's bill. The Buzzcocks headlined, and main support were the Vibrators, a pub rock band with an eye for the main chance and a guest spot reserved for former Sharks member Chris Spedding. In the event, they were also joined by a French punk band called Stinky Toys, held over from the Monday.

Eking out the first night's entertainment were two outfits making their débuts. Festival openers Subway Sect were a bunch of teenage soul boys who had caught the Sex Pistols' Marquee gig back in February and been inspired to form a band of their own. They took a self-consciously anti-rock stance, but their music tended more towards the avant garde than to soul. Malcolm paid for a week's solid rehearsal in Chelsea so the band could whip their five song set into shape, and then Bernie offered them some time at Rehearsals over the weekend immediately preceding the Festival. Siouxsie (billed as Suzie) and the Banshees formed specifically to fill the remaining slot, with members drawn from a cross section of the Sex Pistol's more ardent followers: the Bromley Contingent's Susan Ballion (soon to become Siouxsie Sioux) and Steve Bailey (then calling himself Steve Havoc, soon to become Steve Severin) on vocals and bass, respectively, Marco Pirroni on guitar, and Sid Vicious on drums. Sid's friendship with the Clash enabled the Banshees to squeeze in a rehearsal at Rehearsals on the Sunday. Although neither he nor Steve had played their instruments before, Sid decided 20 minutes was more than enough: the idea of the band was to celebrate its own disposability by making a horrible noise for as long as the audience would or could tolerate it before splitting up for good.

Subway Sect habitually wore dull grey clothes resembling school uniforms, anticipating the look favoured by post-punk 'industrial' bands like Joy Division, and their demeanour was more enervated than aggressive. Nevertheless, the band's gang sensibility was similar to that of the Clash, and a kinship was recognised. Following the Festival, and the Pistols' success in finding a record contract, Malcolm's concern for Subway Sect's welfare suddenly disappeared. Planning some empire-building of his own, Bernie stepped in and effectively became their manager, although he continued to deny having an interest in anyone but the Clash for months afterwards. The Sect, accompanied by their friend, roadie and driver Barry August, began rehearsing at Rehearsals full time, alternating shifts with the Clash. In the interview the Clash gave to *Sniffin' Glue* later that month, Mick talked up his stablemates as being one of the very few worthwhile punk bands (along with the Pistols, the Clash and 'maybe' the Buzzcocks). When Bernie's Number One band began to headline their own gigs in late October, he would have a Number Two band conveniently on hand to offer regular support.

It would appear the Sect helped out the Clash in at least one other area. In the *Clash On Broadway* booklet, and numerous times thereafter, Joe claimed that 'Bored With You' became 'I'm So Bored With The USA' when he misheard Mick's title during the very first band rehearsal at Davis Road. Subway Sect singer and lyricist Vic Godard begs to differ. In September 1977, he told Steve Walsh, by then contributing to *ZigZag*, 'We had this song called "USA" that the Clash nicked and changed to "I'm So Bored With The USA".' The transformation of the Clash song's title and chorus actually occurred sometime between the Roundhouse and Punk Festival gigs, and so did coincide with the band's first exposure to Subway Sect. While it is safe to assume the inspiration to give Mick's twisted love song yet another twist came from 'USA', however, Joe did not work up a coherent lyric for another four months, and *that* was extensively rewritten prior to being recorded for *The Clash*. Accusations of extensive plagiarism are therefore somewhat overstated.

Sounds' Jonh Ingham used the Festival as an excuse for a six-page overview, launching a belated and doomed attempt to rechristen punk '? rock'. The Festival was given substantial coverage as a live event by both the *NME* and *Melody Maker*. Geoff Hill maintained the former paper's unofficial policy of amused condescension, but Caroline Coon fulfilled Malcolm's wildest dreams. She complemented her own enthusiastic response with a vox-pop assembled by eavesdropping on audience members, so conveying the excitement of a scene on the cusp of becoming a movement. Indeed, both nights of the Festival attracted full houses, and the recognisable punk faces from the Pistols' earlier gigs were swamped by inquisitive newcomers. Again, just what Malcolm wanted. Geoff Hill claimed he was impressed by the Clash's potential, but contradicted this claim by saying all he had to say about them in three short sentences, one of which, in punk terms, bordered on the damning: 'they perform as if they actually *dig* rock music'. Caroline predicted they would be 'a cornerstone of the developing punk rock scene', but her critical perspective was compromised by her determination to portray everyone and everything to do with the Punk Festival in as glowing a light as possible. She neglected to mention the inter-band squabbling that marred the first night, and, in woolly-minded liberal mode, shifted the blame for the kind of senseless violence that marred the second night onto promoters who did not do enough to anticipate and prevent it. In reality, it was the absence of the very spirit of punk unity she was trying to evoke that precipitated both incidents.

The Clash had offered to allow the Banshees the use of their equipment, but Bernie withdrew that offer when he saw that Siouxsie intended to take the stage wearing her swastika armband. Instead, the Banshees borrowed the Pistols' gear, and Sid preceded their 20-minute version of 'The Lord's Prayer', with an announcement to the effect that Bernie was 'a fucking old jew'. Bernie's rejection of the swastika was a brave stance to take, because it openly set him against Malcolm, who made frequent use of the Nazi symbol on his Sex shop clothes.

There was no antagonism between members of the Clash and the by now supposedly defunct Banshees when they returned as audience members for the second night. They even joined forces to heckle the Damned, who had not only annoyed the punk Inner Circle with their perceived betrayal in going to Mont de Marsan for the European Punk Festival, but also with their claims to be 'better than the Pistols'. Jealousy was undoubtedly a factor, too: the Damned had become the first punk band to sign to a record label, even if it was the small independent Stiff. Part way through the much-reviled funsters' set, a bottle was flung at the stage. Shattering against a pillar, it sprayed the front of the audience with broken glass. It was subsequently reported that one girl suffered permanent damage to her sight. Although this may have been a case of hysterical exaggeration – the extent of the injury was never verified – Caroline herself noted that several people were cut. Damned vocalist Dave Vanian's girlfriend was among those who required hospital treatment.

The police came to investigate, and arrested Sid Vicious. Although originally identified as the thrower of the glass, he was ultimately charged – after allegedly having been roughed up a little – with possession of an illegal weapon, namely a knife. Paul and Mick later testified that he had not thrown the glass. Caroline was taken into custody at the same time as Sid for putting on her Release hat and objecting to his arrest. She did not think he was guilty then, and was still reluctant to believe it when interviewed for both *England's Dreaming* and *Rotten*. After reading a letter written by Sid from Ashford Remand Centre expressing contrition, the author of the former book, Jon Savage, concluded that Sid had indeed thrown it. Eyewitnesses Marco Pirroni and Steve Severin confirmed as much in Johnny Rotten's autobiography. It was the Pistols' future bass player, then, who was responsible for getting the group banned, in their absence, from the 100 Club, and who deprived the punk scene of a home base venue for the remainder of 1976.

Not that this mattered to the Pistols: the Festival and its accompanying propaganda finally won them their coveted recording contract. Nick Mobbs turned up at the death to narrowly squeeze out scene regular Chris Parry, A&R representative for Polydor, and sign the band to EMI on 8 October.

By contrast, the fortnight immediately following the Festival was relatively quiet for the Clash. It was enlivened only by their first full length interview, conducted in the last week of September for October's *Sniffin' Glue*, the fourth issue of the UK punk scene's original fanzine. Editor Mark Perry – then calling himself Mark P – was a 19 year-old former William and Glyn's bank clerk. He had launched the magazine that July, taking its title from the Ramones song 'Now I Wanna Sniff Some Glue' and a Lenny Bruce comedy routine with the same general theme. 'They call *Sniffin' Glue* the first ever fanzine, which is a load of crap, basically,' says Mark. 'There was a fanzine tradition in things like blues, country, jazz: non-mainstream musics that needed to be written about because *Melody Maker* and *Sounds* weren't doing it. I didn't suddenly invent the idea of fanzines, but I was lucky to be the first to do a fanzine within the English punk scene.' As Mark suggests, fanzines had developed to serve much the same speciality collectors market as the small pre-punk Seventies independent labels. The first fanzine to specialise in punk had been New York's *Punk*, launched by John Holstrom and Legs McNeil in September 1975, which had covered the Ramones in its first issue.

The first issue of *Sniffin' Glue* also covered the Ramones, the Flamin' Groovies and even Blue Öyster Cult; by the time the second came out, Mark had seen the Sex Pistols. 'A month later, it was *forget it!* We didn't even want to know about American bands.' *Sniffin' Glue* was a long way down market of its American counterpart. Mark had access to free photocopying, and his fanzine consisted of a few A4 sheets covered in scrawled handwriting and hamfisted typing, with – by the third issue – occasional poorly reproduced photos. The results were sold for a nominal amount at punk gigs, or at record stores like Rock On and Rough Trade. The determinedly amateurish presentation set the tone for the glut of punk fanzines that followed in its wake. Although it was not out of keeping with the style of the Sex Pistols' flyers, and was totally in sync with the Clash's Oxfam Mod/Pollock look, the two foremost Inner Circle bands were not quick to recognise a kindred spirit at work. Glen Matlock recalls being introduced to Mark by Caroline Coon, and being horrified by the cheap'n'nasty production values of the fanzines he was holding in his hand.

'Some of the bands that didn't feel part of the Inner Circle welcomed us with open arms, but the Pistols and the Clash were initially a little bit hostile towards *Sniffin' Glue*,' recalls Mark. 'The Pistols and all their entourage were always very fashionable, going to clubs and all that. But the Clash became a little friendlier, particularly Mick Jones.' It took a while, but the penny finally dropped for the Clash that the fanzine offered them a platform from which they could communicate their ideas to their audience, without worrying too much about any editorial tampering: *Sniffin' Glue* interviews were reproduced verbatim, right down to the ums and ers, a tradition begun by the late Sixties underground press.

'Where I was coming from was a totally naive area,' says Mark. 'I wasn't a journalist, I wasn't interested in being cynical about it all. To hear a young band saying they were gonna do all *this*, and writing songs like "London's Burning", I loved all that. I wanted to believe in it. But then again, I wasn't a sycophant.' Steve Walsh was mainly responsible for conducting the interview with the Clash, but he was accompanied to Rehearsals by Mark, and it was the latter who took issue with some of the band's more questionable statements. The band were intent on establishing themselves as Angry Young Men, so there was a good deal of attitude-striking, and even some would-be-intimidatory fooling around with an air pistol. Even so, because the encounter was more of a peer group conversation than a formal interview, and because they were talking to a fanzine they believed to have a small circulation and to be ephemeral, the Clash gave a less studied performance than they would in subsequent interviews with the more established media. While the first sketchy attempts to outline a Clash manifesto were being made, a few stray cats were let out of the bag. Mick confessed to being a Mott the Hoople fan, to having been naive enough at one time to believe everything he read in the music press, and to having a huge collection of embarrassingly uncool records that he was in the process of unloading for a fraction of their original cost. He also admitted to having had a previous musical life – 'I've played with so many arseholes, and my whole career has been one long audition' – something he would not do again for many years.

Sniffin' Glue went on to achieve legendary status. Despite Mark's own efforts to make it disposable, this guaranteed it a longevity the Clash could not have anticipated. As a result, their more dogmatic pronouncements – the ones Mark argued with at the time – came back to haunt them over subsequent years. Their insistence that punk should be taken deadly seriously characterised them as po-faced and dour, an impression that stuck, ensuring that the humour that was so much a part of the Clash's daily lives and, more importantly, Joe's lyrics, was too often overlooked. The almost immediate payback for this ill-advised preciousness was the mockery heaped upon a pronouncement Joe made elsewhere in the same interview. At the end of a discussion about the significance of clothing within rock'n'roll – during which Steve Walsh and Mark Perry took the position that such superficial details were irrelevant, and Mick and Joe argued that they were an important part of the sub-cultural package – Joe quipped, 'Like trousers, like brain!' Taken seriously, and out of context, which, perhaps understandably, it invariably was, it is indeed a facile remark. Obviously intended to be tongue-in-cheek at the time, it followed on from Mick's perfectly valid point that the then-ubiquitous flared denims and cowboy shirts were indications of the lack of individuality and imagination in contemporary mainstream rock.

The rest of the Clash manifesto-in-progress went as follows: they were hoping to shake up the music scene; they were 'definitely political'; they were against apathy, and 'into encouraging creativity'; although they would not accept that they were part of an American rock heritage, they would accept that they were part of an English one; despite their aggressive image, they were against violence; although they wanted change, they were not anarchists and not into chaos; they were against government secrecy; they wanted more punk bands, more venues and more events, and if they had the money, they would do their best to make these things happen. Over the years, the Clash would be brought to task about their failure to live up to many of these and other, later, claims, but at the time their chief aim was to communicate their own passion and to encourage it in others.

In this, they were successful. 'I think at first, if you look, earlier on, we're all sort of floundering around to try and find something to latch onto,' says Mark Perry. 'We're desperate, in a way.' Ideas were already circulating between the bands, the involved journalists on the established music press, and *Sniffin' Glue* – soon to be joined by other fanzines – so the Clash were by no means solely responsible for making punk more than just a cocked snook at establishment values. The UK scene's DIY ethic, for example, was inherent in both the musical genre and the fanzines, and, as already mentioned, had first been voiced by Johnny Rotten. What the Clash brought to the party was a sense of purpose and righteousness. At the beginning of December 1976, via the *Today* television programme, mainstream culture was to be fed an image of punk based on Sex Pistols-style outrage and nihilism. By that time, though, as far as commentators within and around the movement were concerned, punk had already been remade in the image of the Clash. 'The Pistols: a lot of their songs were just nasty love songs, except for "Anarchy In The UK",' says Mark. (Most of the others were more like pure hate songs.) 'But the Clash: you're listening to them, and they're saying something. And they were saying things lyrically that became elements of the punk thing, [tackling] the important issues like unemployment.'

Many of these commentators, awed by the Sex Pistols, but troubled, like Allan Jones, by their relentless nihilism, found this new *positive* version of punk ideology far more appealing. They continued to cover the Sex Pistols with the appalled fascination of the audience at a freak show, but they increasingly got behind the Clash as a force for Change, Honour and Truth. The cliché describing the Clash as the new Rolling Stones to the Sex Pistols' new Beatles gets it nearly right: in fact, the roles were reversed, with the Clash playing the good guys to the Pistols' bad. Inevitably, this meant that the Clash were loaded with the expectations of others in a way that the Sex Pistols never were. It was something for which they would ultimately pay dearly.

Mick and Joe rose to the challenge of standing for change with 'Career Opportunities', introduced to the band's set during October 1976. There is some confusion as to who originated the song. 'Mick came up with the idea, because we were laughing about the careers master at school,' Joe told *Melody Maker* in 1988. In the 1999 documentary *Westway To The World*, Mick recalled Paul getting the inspiration from a newspaper article. It was certainly a topical issue. In 1975, Bernie had heard a radio broadcast threatening anarchy on the streets if the UK's unemployment figure reached 800,000 by 1979; by June 1976, it was already 1,500,000. Joe wrote a lyric to order, the chorus inverting the promise of longrunning amateur variety TV show *Opportunity Knocks*, and the verses listing various unappetising job options. Some of the latter were imagined, some of them drawn from experience, like Mick's stint with the Civil Service, when he was required to open the mail during the IRA letter bomb campaign. The first draft also contained a line about old age pensions which Paul was supposed to sing, but he rejected the idea out of hand. He could still be heard griping about it in the interview included on the following year's *Capital Radio* EP, and again over 20 years later in *Westway To The World*.

When Mick added his tune, 'Career Opportunities' emerged as one of the more powerful songs in the band's repertoire. In the wake of the 1976 unemployment figures and the opening lines of '1977' – about having been 'too long on the dole' – it moved the employment issue to the centre of the Clash's agenda. Mick had already told *Sniffin' Glue* that the band were 'all down the dole, coppin' our money off Rod Stewart's taxes'. The following March Joe would give both Tony Parsons and Caroline Coon the impression that 'Career Opportunities' and the relevant part of '1977' had been written in response to a Department of Employment threat to send him to Birmingham for rehabilitation, as he had been unemployed for so long.

The threat had possibly been made, but Joe's case was by no means as desperate as was suggested. None of the band was long-term unemployed in the true sense of the phrase. As soon-to-be Clash aide Sebastian Conran observes, 'Musicians live like that anyway. The life of a musician on the dole, and the life of someone who's genuinely looking for a job and on the dole, well, you couldn't get further apart. Most of the [punk era] people who used to talk about being on the dole would not have *dreamed* of getting a job. And times were nowhere near as hard then as they became later, in the Thatcher years, and recently.' Although the Clash never went so far in their interviews as to claim they were unemployable, they did say the only alternatives for them were late night washing-up marathons, menial warehouse stacking jobs, or the factory production line.

This was simply not the case: had they so desired, any one of them could have walked into a white collar office job the next day, and could have probably found something more stimulating, even creative, within a few weeks. Joe had chosen to live the life of a drop-out, and Terry was taking time out between A Levels and higher education. In October 1976, Paul had only just left art school and Mick was still attending, officially, at least. Paul was so unaccustomed to signing on that he was under the mistaken impression the process allowed room for self-respect: 'I wasn't on anything for a whole year,' he told Mary Turner in 1982 for San Jose's Radio KSJO. 'You go down, stand in line and get insulted. I just got fed up with it after a while. I decided I'd much rather starve than have to deal with all that.'

If the notion of punk as 'tower block rock' derived from 'London's Burning', a song inspired by a high-rise flat that was not quite the long-time Mick Jones domicile the band made it sound, then the notion of punk as 'dole queue rock' derived mostly from 'Career Opportunities', a song which came nowhere near to reflecting the realistic employment prospects of the band as a whole. The Clash were so obsessed with the concept of 'authenticity' that they put themselves in the confused position of misrepresenting the truth in order to project it.

Aware that the folk, R&B and rock'n'roll records they loved reflected the humble origins and necessarily marginal lifestyles of the songs' composers, Sixties musicians like Bob Dylan, Mick Jagger and John Lennon had played down *their* middle class origins, and assembled their public personas out of working class and bohemian characteristics. Such reinvention of self quickly became established as a rock tradition, and for all their punk era rejection of the past, the Clash were too steeped in such traditions to do anything but follow suit. As their notion of street credibility drew so heavily on the terrace yob mentality, their own public personae required even more artistic license than those of the Sixties stars, and threw up even more contradictions. 'We urge people to learn fast,' Mick told Barry Miles in November 1976. Two months earlier, during the Roundhouse show, Joe had made a sneering onstage remark about A Levels being 'a trick'. 'Your drummer's got them,' piped up a girl in the front row who knew Terry from school. 'Joe confessed to me after the show that he'd been lost for words at that point,' laughs Terry. Joe, of course, had at least one A Level himself. In 1978's *The Boy Looked At Johnny* Tony Parsons and Julie Burchill made a snide remark about Joe having taken 'de-elocution lessons'. Snide, but fair: in truth accentless and eloquent, punk era Joe contrived a mangled Cockney speaking style, punctuating his affectedly impoverished vocabulary with many an assertive 'right?' and 'see?'. So there he and the Clash were: feeling obliged to sound inarticulate and unlearned while outlining their commitment to communication and education...

Before the late Sixties brought increasing musical and lyrical sophistication, pop music had been aimed at teenagers, and had played a major role in shaping youth culture. Its resulting penchant for teenager-friendly subject matter involved much celebration of 'the kids', a generic term for the young rock'n'roll audience. Progressive rock might have fancied itself more mature, but both garage rock and glam rock remained true to this original following. So too did the insistently non-pretentious, back-to-basics Class of '76 punk bands. 'The kids' who had been regularly addressed in the lyrics of the Who, the Standells and the MC5, among (many) others, and namechecked in interviews by Marc Bolan, Slade and Mott the Hoople, were now the target audience of the Sex Pistols, the Damned and the Clash.

Generation gap-inspired ageism had been politicised in the late Sixties by the Woodstock Generation's warning not to trust anyone over 30. By the mid Seventies, many of that same generation were still around, themselves now over 30, and clogging up both the charts and the music business. As part of punk's campaign to shame the old guard into moving over, it used their advanced age and self-consciousness about it as weapons against them: they were dismissed as 'boring old farts'. It became a necessary qualification for members of punk bands to be at least approximately of the same generation as 'the kids' they were addressing, as Brady had already found to his cost.

In late 1976, the Pistols were all still safely between 20 and 21. So were all of the Clash... except Joe, who was a comparatively ancient 24. As he had spent two years prior to joining the Clash playing in a pub rock band, some people on the punk scene thought he was even older than that. 'When they got Joe, we was *really* surprised,' recalls Glen Matlock. 'Short on style there in a big way! I said that to Bernie Rhodes, and he said, "Give me a couple of weeks, and I'll have 10 years off him." I don't think he ever did, really.' But he did have two years off him: in November 1976, Joe told Caroline Coon that he was 22, again in the name of authenticity. 'When you're 22, you're still a young man, you're practically a teenager,' Joe explained to Paul Morley of the *NME*, finally coming out of the closet about his real age in October 1979. 'It's a great relief for me to be 27 in a way, 'cause I think the worst time of my life was when I was 24. I used to lie about my age, make myself younger, say I was 22 or something. I was so paranoid about it. It was the early days of the Clash, like, "Fuck, if they find out how old I am, that's it! I'm in the bunker, the dumper…"'

All this fake authenticity was bound to invite accusations of phoniness when the truth was inevitably discovered. Lester Bangs, covering the Clash's late 1977 Get Out Of Control Tour for the *NME*, dismissed such accusations as irrelevant. 'I surmise,' he wrote, 'that this is supposed to indicate that Joe isn't worth a shit, and that his songs are all fake street-graffiti.' He went on to state that the same could be said of Dylan, Jagger, Pete Townshend and Lou Reed, before asserting, 'all this blathering about authenticity is just a bunch of crap. The Clash are authentic because their music carries such brutal conviction, not because they're Noble Savages.' This was true, but the fault for not realising it lay with the Clash themselves, rather than with their critics. There was no need for the band to tell lies in order to validate their work, yet they chose to do so. And anyone who stands for office on a platform of truth yet practises to deceive is in danger of losing credibility, on the street and elsewhere.

'Career Opportunities' is a case in point: it was not necessary for the band to offer exaggerated or fabricated dole experiences and dead-end work histories in order to legitimise the song. There is a distinction to be made between the issue of unemployment, that is, not being able to find a job at all, and the issue of limited career opportunities, that is, not being able to find a job you want. Like 'Janie Jones' and '48 Hours' before it, 'Career Opportunities' is perfectly effective as a straightforward rejection of the work ethic and an exercise in social observation. It was explained much better by Mick in his November 1976 response to Caroline Coon's deliberately provocative suggestion that *someone* has to do the dirty jobs like working in a factory. '*Why* have they?' he demanded. 'Don't you think technology is advanced enough to give all those jobs over to a few people and machines? They're just keeping people occupied by making them work. There's a social stigma attached to being unemployed. Like "Social Security Scroungers" every day in the *Sun*. I don't want to hear that. I cheer them. You go up North and the kids are *ashamed* that they can't get a job.' Or as Joe would succinctly put it in the lyric of another song that he wrote four years later: 'Who gives you work, and why should you do it?' This was more in keeping with the Situationist International slogan 'Never work!'

'The only thing I'm interested in is personal freedom,' Joe told Caroline Coon in March 1977. But even by October 1976, punk in general and the Clash in particular were being infected with the kind of Orwellian revisionism and doublethink that was guaranteed to deny personal freedom. Placed in this constantly shifting, paranoid context, a jocular remark such as 'Like trousers, like brain' could be strongly reminiscent of the *Animal Farm* dictum 'Four legs good, two legs bad'. 'Punk *was* very Stalinist in that respect,' agrees Tony Parsons. 'It was very much like that: "Denounce your parents! Turn them in to the Punk Police for having flared trousers!"' As he was arguably the member of the band with the most to hide, Joe was particularly susceptible to this Year Zero tendency. 'You had to shed all your friends, everything you'd known, everything you'd played before, all in a frenzied attempt to create something new,' he admitted in *Westway To The World* in 1999. 'We were insane, basically. Completely and utterly insane.'

Like most subcultures, punk rejected the values of the parent culture, yet imposed its own set of rules upon its followers. There might have been some room for self-expression in the punk look, but a certain degree of conformity was insisted upon. Flared trousers were out, so it was conveniently forgotten that Mick had been photographed standing outside the Davis Road squat in a pair just four months before the *Sniffin' Glue* denouncement. Although prepared to laugh about the matter in 1995, Mick was still having trouble with his memory when interviewed about his punk days by Ann Scanlon for *Vox*: 'For me, the real battle was The War Of The Flares. I've never gone for the flared look, and as a war veteran, I still feel really strongly about them.'

In October 1976, much to Mick's chagrin, it was also finally decreed – by Bernie, according to Glen – that long hair was unacceptable under any circumstances. 'We had to tie Mick down to cut his hair,' laughs Alan Drake. 'He liked it long, because he thought he looked a bit like Keith Richards, which he did. But we said, "Look, Mick, you've just got to fucking shut up and sit down!" And I cut his hair, and we dyed it black.' Although his new hairstyle was still markedly longer than those of his fellow band members, it was the first time the Jones ears had seen daylight since the mid-Sixties. 'I'll never forget the day he knocked on the door and I opened it,' says Honest John Plain, then still living at 47A Warrington Crescent. 'There he was in a ragged suit and really cropped hair, and I said, "What the fuck you *done*, Mick?" and he went, "It's punk rock, innit?" And it was! It freaked me out, anyway. One extreme to the other, overnight. It was funny, but he became very serious about it.'

The new overtly political direction and seriousness of purpose greatly influenced a new Clash look, also introduced in October 1976. For all Joe's claims that '1977' was not a call to armed insurrection, the new band uniform was a flagrant attempt to cast the Clash in the role of urban guerrillas. The band had been without protection for their clothes when painting Rehearsals – or so their explanation for the Pollock look would have it – but they now miraculously managed to locate some boiler suits. Out of their intended work context, such all-in-one outfits remained functional and practical, but acquired other connotations. Used by criminals, revolutionaries and paramilitaries to protect their own identities, their very featurelessness also encouraged prisons and oppressive regimes to employ them in order to *deny* identity. For the Who's performance at Woodstock in 1969, in what amounted to a one-man rejection of flower power, Pete Townshend had taken the stage in a white boiler suit and Dr Martens work boots. In Stanley Kubrick's 1971 film version of *A Clockwork Orange*, Alex's ultra-violent gang habitually wore similar outfits.

The four members of the Clash did not wear their navy blue boiler suits all the time, but for the next couple of months there was usually at least one in evidence when photographs were being taken, and the band did their best to exploit and emphasise the residual signals of the garments with accessories and slogans. Paul added some punk studs to the seams of his. Joe mocked up a fake ID from Sebastian Conran's Student's Union pass and attached it to his breast pocket. Mick affected an armband bearing the legend 'RED GUARD' (taken from the military arm of Communist China, it was a response to Siouxsie's swastika, and, perhaps less intentionally, an indication of the distance Mick had travelled from his own flirtation with the decadent Nazi style). Boiler suits, shirts and T-shirts alike were daubed with patches of colour, some abstract, but some attempting rough approximations of recognisable shapes and images, such as the Union Jack. Jackson Pollock was giving way to Jasper Johns and Robert Rauschenberg, splatter painting slipping into Pop Art via tachism.

The slogans were initially crudely hand-painted, but before long were being applied with the aid of packing case stencils. This was partly to increase the suggestion of institutionalisation, but also because Bernie recognised some connections – above and beyond those with Pop Art and, again, the Who – that were almost pleading to be made. Firstly, with the Lettrists, a Fifties Parisian avant garde movement who had also turned themselves into walking art statements by writing on their clothing. Secondly, with the Situationist International, who had brought art and politics together in their determination to stimulate a reaction with their provocative slogans. Thirdly, with Malcolm McLaren, who had already combined both influences at Sex, decorating the shop's walls and clothing stock with similarly pithy turns of phrase.

The Boy Looked At Johnny's assertion that Bernie set about using the Clash as 'blank T-shirts on which to superimpose his own self-conscious political posturing', if taken literally, was actually not far from the truth. Certainly, the Clash's flirtation with Lettrism was Bernie's idea: Joe admitted as much to Jon Savage for *England's Dreaming*. It might seem strange that Bernie should invite yet more accusations of plagiarising Malcolm, even if he could counter it by insisting that he had been part of the Sex creative team when such influences were first being explored. The opportunity to bring all his beliefs and fascinations together in his new venture was clearly too great for him to resist. Also, the Clash approach differed from Sex's in two key respects: Malcolm sold his clothes, but the Clash's were DIY, in keeping with the new punk ethic, a point they made repeatedly; and Malcolm's slogans tended to the glib or smutty, whereas the Clash's were *politically* provocative.

Crossover with the Sex operation was limited to one slogan: 'PASSION IS A FASHION', which Joe stencilled onto his boiler suit, had already adorned the wall of Malcolm's shop. Other slogans were inspired by reggae records, 'UNDER HEAVY MANNERS' and 'HEAVY DUTY DISCIPLINE' both coming from Prince Far I's album and song of the former title. Phrases from the Clash's own songs turned up too: 'KNIVES IN W11', 'STEN GUNS IN KNIGHTSBRIDGE', 'WHITE RIOT' and 'JANIE JONES'. Social Security and other state registration and reference numbers were reproduced as comments on dehumanisation and government control. Individual band members pursued their own agendas: Mick challenged 'DON'T JUST TAKE PICTURES'; Paul advocated 'CREATIVE VIOLENCE'; Joe declared 'CHUCK BERRY IS DEAD' and inverted the hippy slogan 'Love and Peace' to rub the previous generation's face in the new reality of 'HATE AND WAR'.

8
HATE AND WAR

October 1976 saw the true beginning of the Clash's live campaign. Although there had been nothing so confrontational as a row, the disagreement over the use of the swastika had further strained the relationship between Bernie Rhodes and Malcolm McLaren. So had Malcolm's evident loss of interest, following the signing of his band to EMI, in promoting punk as a multi-band scene. The Sex Pistols devoted the next two months to recording their first single and playing numerous gigs around the national club circuit. The Clash were not invited. It was time for them to strike out on their own.

In addition to the Three Wise Journalists – Caroline Coon, Jonh Ingham and Giovanni Dadomo – who were prepared to attend most gigs, the band had a small but committed following that could be relied upon to take the chill off any strange venue accessible by tube, even if the heat they generated was not always beneficial to the band's cause. Tony James, Chrissie Hynde, Alan Drake and Viv Albertine seldom visited Rehearsals, but they were still in Mick and Paul's social circle, and Sid, when not in the remand centre, was ubiquitous. 'He was around a lot. An awful lot,' says Terry. 'I remember him turning up at Rehearsals once with a suit on and a tie made from toilet paper. It looked quite neat, actually. Not that he'd say so, but I think he was trying his ideas out on us to see what we thought.' Through Glen, with whom he had attended St Martin's, the Clash also became friendly with Mark Helfont, known as Frothler because of his tendency to dither in a manner reminiscent of Frankie Howerd. Jane Crockford, her relationship with John Brown over, had drifted onto the punk scene and back into Mick Jones's orbit via a brief relationship with Sid. Something of an unstable character, she quickly earned the not particularly kind nickname Mad Jane. The absence of the Sex Pistols from the London stage also saw the Clash's audience swollen by several other punk scene stalwarts, among them Shane MacGowan.

Two other newcomers to the scene were so taken with the band that they started to hang around on a regular basis, gradually joining Micky Foote as semi-official members of the Clash team. The first to arrive was Sebastian Conran, son of millionaire designer Terence Conran (founder of the Habitat furniture empire) and author Shirley Conran (author of the bestselling book *Superwoman*). Sebastian had developed an acquaintanceship with Glen Matlock after booking the Sex Pistols for their gig at the Central School of Art back in November 1975. 'Sebastian said to me, "Do you want to come back to my place?" after we'd been somewhere, and it was this massive big house,' recalls Glen. 'I said, "Is it a squat?" And he said, "Well, sort of." And it weren't, but it was unhip to say that.' 'I had got a lease on a house near Regent's Park, a huge squat, basically, is what it was,' says Sebastian, apparently still intent on propagating that myth despite all evidence – much of it provided by himself – to the contrary. '31 Albany Street. Well, the punks came in at 31 Albany Street, but when my brother [fashion designer] Jasper moved there, Bianca Jagger would come in at 9 St Andrew's Place, which was the other side. There was a smart side and a seedy side to the whole thing. I was renting it out to students. This was my Dad's idea. Because I didn't get a grant at the Central, he thought it would be a good idea for me to earn the money, so he found the house and got me the lease, but I had to pay it all. It was gigantic, huge, 15 bedrooms, and the lease was £400 every six months.'

One of the students living there at the time was the then-girlfriend of Micky Foote.

This guaranteed that Micky was a regular visitor, and that the entire household was aware of the Clash. Being an art student hang-out, 31 Albany Street was a hive of creativity. Jasper Conran lived and designed his clothes in the ground floor front room. There was a darkroom set up in the basement. Another tenant, Rocco Macauley, took the live photos of the Clash that were used to illustrate the *Sniffin' Glue* interview. Yet another, Sebastian's friend Henry Bowles, later did some radio commercial voiceovers for Clash record releases. According to Sebastian, Henry possessed 'a nice South London accent, and Joe thought he had a street cred voice'.

Although he was impressed by the Clash live experience, the attraction for Sebastian himself was the overall atmosphere of creative energy surrounding the band. That, and Joe Strummer's punk persona. 'Joe was my absolute big hero. I used to dog him around, follow him everywhere. He seemed so clever and so glamorous. Micky Foote was a mate who I hung around with and saw a lot of, but it was a real privilege to go out for the night with Joe.' The rough-edged loner Joe and the eager, naive Sebastian were an unlikely pairing, but it seems Joe found it easy to sympathise with another ex-public schoolboy attempting to shrug off a supposedly advantaged background. 'He's got a very high-class voice, but he means well,' he told the *Sunday Times Magazine*'s Gordon Burn in May 1977.

Paul and Terry were pleasant enough to Sebastian, being laid-back characters prepared to be open-minded about almost anyone they encountered. Also, both appreciated the fact that Sebastian was a kid with a lot of toys: the high-powered air pistol Paul wielded during the *Sniffin' Glue* interview – and which featured as a regular Clash prop over the following couple of years – was his; and Terry was so taken with Sebastian's Norton Commando motorbike that he eventually bought it from him. Mick, usually the most approachable member of the Clash, was the only one who was openly antagonistic. 'Mick Jones was just fucking rude, really.'

It was Bernie, with his keen eye for voluntary – that is, cost-free – assistance, who realised Sebastian's true potential. Like his father, he was not only a skilled and creative designer, but practically minded and industrious with it. As well as undertaking the more mundane tasks like helping the band move equipment, Sebastian increasingly found himself relied upon to realise Bernie and Paul's ideas for presentation. Initially, he was entrusted with designing and printing (for free, at the Central) the flyers advertising the Clash's headlining gigs. Their cut-and-paste Xerox'n'scrawl style was partly derived from *Sniffin' Glue* and its disciples, but – as his portfolio proves – Sebastian had already been experimenting with a similar kind of minimalism at college. Under Bernie's direction, Sebastian would go on to design the band's early tour posters and single picture sleeves, manufacture their stage backdrops, and produce and market T-shirts and other assorted items of clothing.

The Clash acquired their other helper in November 1976. Steve Connolly, who hailed from Coventry, caught the band's ICA performance at the end of October. During a conversation with Joe, he mentioned that he had just come out of prison, and had nowhere to sleep. Shortly beforehand, the squat at 42 Orsett Terrace had been cleared. Joe had found himself alternative accommodation at the disused Robertino's ice cream factory in Foscote Mews, close to Wilmcote House. There was no heating or lighting except candles, and there was no toilet until he appropriated one from a 'a gaff near Bristol Road'. ('Strangest thing I ever stole,' he reminisced to *Q*'s Andrew Collins in 1999.) Paul had instead elected to sleep at the only marginally more salubrious Rehearsals. Joe suggested that Steve also stay there for the night. Steve offered to work as the band's roadie if he could stay there long-term, and, glad of the company, Paul made no objection. Steve got the (unpaid) job, and was promptly rechristened Roadent.

Within a few short months, Roadent was attracting almost as much media attention as the Clash themselves. This was partly due to his mischievous personality and undoubted talent for self-promotion, but the version of his recent personal history that emerged also fitted in neatly with the yob-cum-rude boy image the Clash wished to promote – much more so than did, say, Sebastian's, whose very name was a dead giveaway – and Roadent's rapid promotion to centre-stage has sometimes been interpreted as another Clash bid for credibility by association. 'He went along to see the Clash soon after his release from prison,' wrote Tony Parsons in March 1977. 'At the time he was carrying a copy of *Mein Kampf* around with him. Prison can mess up your head. Strummer, in his usual manner of abusive honesty, straightened him out. Roadent's been with them ever since, and sleeps on the floor of their studio.'

In those few short sentences, Tony portrayed Roadent as a tough, simple, yet basically decent working-class lad who had been led astray, but had now seen the errors of his ways and thrown in his lot with his wise, compassionate saviours. The true picture was not so black and white. Roadent came from a working-class background, but had won a scholarship to board at a public school. Upon leaving, he had fallen out with his father and lived semi-rough in Coventry in much the same way Joe had in London, while running through a bizarre series of temporary jobs, including selling bibles. His period of incarceration immediately prior to meeting the Clash had been for a mere two weeks, and not for theft, but for lapsed maintenance payments or non-payment of a previous fine (depending on whether one believes the version he gave *Melody Maker*'s Frances Lass in 1979, or *England's Dreaming* author Jon Savage 12 years later). The restless curiosity that had led him to flirt with both religion and fascism by the autumn of 1976 was indeed quickly re-channelled by Clash-style punk rhetoric, but no-one had to do Roadent's thinking for him. 'Roadent was intelligent,' says Sebastian. 'He probably had as much to do with the political background [of the Clash] as anyone else.' In addition, he earned his favoured position with the band not by being an amusing tame thug like certain others of their hangers on, but by being prepared to accept hardship and muck in and help. 'He was a good bloke, and he worked hard,' says Sebastian. 'He and Paul Simonon lived in the most disgusting manner. They used to smell dreadful. Personal freshness was not something they went in for.'

Bernie came up with a two step plan to establish the Clash in their own right. The ultimate goal was to headline the kind of events at which they had previously supported the Pistols. Step one was the more traditional and decidedly less glamorous rock'n'roll process of hustling support slots wherever possible. Thanks to Sid and the Pistols, at this time punk was not only banned from the 100 Club, but also effectively banned from Dingwalls, the Nashville and the Marquee. In 1980's *Armagideon Times* tour programme, Mick and Joe revealed that the Clash approached and were turned down by the last of these clubs. Like the Roundhouse, some of the venues Bernie did line up had previously hosted gigs by the 101ers, which suggests a degree of trading on Joe's past reputation. Most of the places were low-key and obscure enough to qualify as anonymous, and though this was partly forced by punk's bad public image and the band's limited financial resources, it was not really a problem. The primary aim was not so much to increase the band's exposure as it was to hone their live sound and stage presentation. As Glen Matlock so pithily puts it: 'You get a set together, but it doesn't mean jack shit until you've played it in front of a few people, regardless of the reaction.' 'In the early days, we had a little Ford Transit, and we were going all over the place,' says Sebastian. 'The concerts out of town, the teeny-weeny ones, were all good fun. We'd all travel up there sitting on top of the gear in the back of the Transit.'

The first of these gigs took place on Saturday 9 October 1976, at Tiddenfoot Leisure Centre, Leighton Buzzard, about an hour's drive north west of London. Along with local band the Aylesbury Bucks, the Clash were support to a pub rock outfit named the Rockets. The gig was attended by an old acquaintance of Mick from his Mott the Hoople gig-going days, Kris Needs, who lived nearby. Kris had graduated from managing Mott's fan club to writing for *ZigZag*, the semi-underground music magazine founded in 1969 by Family Tree cultivator Pete Frame. Responding with enthusiasm to punk, Kris would take over as editor early in 1977, when *ZigZag* decided to devote the bulk of its coverage to the new movement. In April that year, he reminisced about his own first encounter with the Clash at the October gig, which was responsible for turning him into another regular Clash gig-goer, ligger and media champion: 'The hall was like a large hotel lounge, which encouraged the crowd to drape itself over the seating. The Clash taking the stage was like an injection of electricity into the smoky air. They charged headlong into "White Riot" with shattering energy, strutting and leaping like clockwork robots out of control. They never let up for half an hour. Despite sound problems, they were astounding, almost overpowering in their attack and conviction.'

The band's second trip out on their own, not long afterwards on some forgotten date in October, was to a pub-cum-disco in Guildford, Surrey, run by Marmalade's ex-bass player. In February 1980, Joe informed *Sounds'* Robbi Millar that it was the smallest venue the band had ever played. The audience had consisted of 'one lone drunk refugee from the club/disco below, where the bouncers were having the shit kicked out of them by a bunch of squaddies'. Terry remembers that the Marmalade man came upstairs while this fracas was taking place and apologised to the band for the low turnout. On Friday 15 October, according to that week's *Time Out*, the Clash were scheduled to appear bottom of the bill to a couple of bands called Spartacus and Sukuya at the Acklam Hall, off Portobello Road in the shadow of the Westway. If this spiritual homecoming actually took place, it appears to have left no lasting impression on anyone involved.

The same cannot be said of the following night's show, at the University of London Union (ULU), on Malet Street in central London. Here, the Clash were third on a bill of four, following Please Y'Self, and preceding Brett Marvin and the Thunderbolts and headliners Shakin' Stevens and the Sunsets. Although the bulk of the audience consisted of mainstream student types, the Sunsets' substantial teddy boy following was well-represented, as indeed was that of the Clash. 'To the Social guy at the Union, it must have looked OK on paper,' reflected fictitious band valet 'Albert Transom' in 1988. 'A good rock'n'roll band from Wales and to warm up, this new London group. Well, he wasn't up on his street culture.' Punks and teds were yet to reprise the mod-rocker battles of the mid Sixties, but such conflicts were inevitable; and if ever an event was liable to provide the spark, it was the ULU gig.

There was no friction between the groups themselves while setting up – 'We even lifted Shakin' Stevens's piano onto the stage,' laughs Terry – but the Clash had only played five numbers of their set when, according to 'Albert Transom', a ted approached the front of the stage, held up a five pence piece and said, 'Here's your bus fare home.' Further insults were exchanged and, upon leaving the stage, the band and their followers were forced to barricade themselves in the changing room to keep at bay a small but rabid mob. Grabbing a chair apiece, the Clash camp threw open the doors and prepared to meet their assailants. Only two rushed in, one of whom promptly tried to throttle Sebastian with his own tie. Faced with the prospect of having half a dozen chairs broken over his head, however, he quickly decided discretion was the better part of valour, put Sebastian down and retreated.

'I remember Bernie Rhodes came over to me, and he made a great statement,' says Polydor A&R man Chris Parry, who was there that night. 'There were these student girls in normal clothes, and he said, "In a very short period of time, they're going to have to decide which way to dress." And he was absolutely right.' Bernie was evidently still intent on finding a market for his 1974 'What side of the bed' T-shirt.

The Clash weren't the only punk, or would-be punk, band making waves that October, although none of the others were truly accepted by the Inner Circle. Following their support slots with the visiting New York new wave bands, and their inclusion in Caroline Coon's August *Melody Maker* punk feature, the Stranglers had cut their hair short, abandoned flares, and further speeded and toughened up their already menacing sound. Patti Smith's second visit to the UK was scheduled for October, and the Stranglers were again the support for her two London dates on the 22nd and 23rd, this time at the 3,500 capacity Hammersmith Odeon. The offer of a recording contract seemed inevitable.

The Jam had also been playing the minor pub rock venues since 1974, wearing black mod suits to perform their Who and Dr Feelgood-influenced R&B material. Caroline had been stretching a point when she included them in her who's-who-in-punk roundup. Nevertheless, on 16 October – watched by the Clash, who were grabbing a pre-ULU gig snack at a nearby café – the band set up in Soho market, plugging in at the Newport Court Rock On stall, and played an open-air gig showcasing new, punk-tinged material like 'In The City'. The outcome was namechecks for the band in both *Sounds* and *Melody Maker*, though the latter did accuse them of the ultimate punk crime of revivalism.

October was also the month that two further offshoots of the London SS chose to make their débuts. Matt Dangerfield and Casino Steel's the Boys had originally dressed like a latter-day version of the Hollywood Brats to play their melodic high energy rock'n'roll, but they cut their hair and adopted vaguely punk-style clothing in time for their first gig at the Hope and Anchor in Islington.

On 18 October, it was the turn of Tony James's new band, Chelsea, managed by Andy Czezowski, and featuring Gene October on vocals, the Bromley Contingent's Billy Idol on guitar, and John Towe on drums. In 1976, the Institute of Contemporary Arts (ICA), located at the other end of the Mall from Buckingham Palace, was making a concerted effort to live up to its name. Ted White, the events organiser, Mike Laye, who ran the theatre side, and his assistant (future comedian and actor) Keith Allen were interested in the radical and provocative end of the arts spectrum. From 19 to 26 October, a performance art group named COUM Transmissions was given free rein to hold a show-cum-exhibition entitled Prostitution, the general theme of which, according to group leader Genesis P-Orridge, was that art is prostitution. The promotional flyer made it clear that, 'For us the party on the opening night is the key to our stance, the most important performance.' On that night, the 18th, COUM set out to be as anti-art as possible, hiring strippers and blue comedians, and launching their own avant-garde rock band, Throbbing Gristle.

A friend of Acme Attractions' John Krivine, Genesis knew that Andy Czezowski was managing a new punk band, and invited Chelsea to provide musical support on one condition: that for this one-off performance they rename themselves LSD, a name deliberately chosen to jar with the punk movement's prevailing anti-hippy sentiments. COUM invited as many way-out people as possible, and Chelsea brought along representatives from the punk scene – including the Bromley Contingent and Mick Jones – to mingle with the critics and other media representatives. Entering into the spirit of the evening, Mick tried to persuade some of the female punks in the audience to get up onstage and disrupt the strippers.

That the mainstream press were more genuinely outraged by COUM's stunts was perhaps predictable, but not even Genesis expected to be physically attacked by the *Evening News* critic, who had to be forcibly subdued and ejected, and who still hadn't calmed down when he filed his vituperative review. The *Daily Mail* followed up with a photograph of various Bromley Contingent members, captioned 'This is the art connoisseur of today,' going on to describe the audience as comprising 'Hell's Angels, girls dressed as whores, and boys with dyed hair and nail varnish'. Tory MP Nicholas Fairburn, also present at the show – but presumably failing to fall into any of the above categories – supplied the comment, 'These people are the wreckers of civilisation.' The press continued to exploit the Shock Horror Outrage value of the Prostitution exhibition until the Arts Council themselves joined in and denounced COUM. It was a foretaste of the media-manipulated fear and loathing that was soon to be directed at the punk movement itself.

The Chelsea connection, and Bernie's own longstanding friendship with Mike Laye – who would go on to become a photographer and take the back cover picture for the Clash's 1985 album, *Cut The Crap* – resulted in the Clash securing their own ICA performance slot later in the week. Although Prostitution was still running, 23 October received the individual billing A Night of Pure Energy: the band's first headlining gig in the punk-event style pioneered by Malcolm and the Pistols. The Subway Sect were given the support slot, and Sebastian and Bernie designed a flyer, which the Clash took out and pasted up around London. Upon returning from this mission, Paul heated up the remaining flour-and-water paste over Rehearsals' one-bar electric fire, and ate it. Never ones to let a useful anecdote go to waste, the Clash subsequently parlayed this isolated act of bravado into an illustration of the direness of their circumstances at that time. First recounted by Caroline Coon in her spring 1977 *Melody Maker* Clash feature, it was also dusted off years later for both the *That Was Then, This Is Now* TV programme and the *Clash On Broadway* booklet.

Barry Miles attended the gig on behalf of the *NME*. At 33, Miles – as he preferred to be known – was, like Caroline Coon, another veteran of the late Sixties London counter-culture. In 1966, he had co-founded underground magazine *It*, the launch party for which had simultaneously opened up the Roundhouse as a rock venue and introduced London to the kind of hippy happenings that Malcolm's Midnight Special had copied 10 years later. In 1973, he had written a glowing review of a New York Dolls show at the Mercer Arts Centre in New York. Unlike Charles Shaar Murray, Miles was prepared to let the Clash push all his anti-establishment buttons. He had read the *Sniffin' Glue* piece, and – no doubt thanks to his former *It* colleague Caroline Coon – generally done his homework on the band. He opened his review of the Clash's show by announcing that he had enjoyed them a lot more than Patti Smith, who he had seen the previous night. 'It was as if they had crystallised the dormant energy of all the hours of crushing boredom of being an unemployed school-leaver, living with your parents in a council flat, into a series of three-minute staccato blasts delivered like a whiplash at the audience, who were galvanised into frenzied dancing.' He went on to liken their 'musical intensity' to that of the Ramones, although he believed the Clash's lyrics to be far superior.

Miles also cast a keen sociological eye over the audience, noting the Sex-style clothes, the safety pins, the pogo dancing and various other bizarre rituals of this new youth cult. His sensationalised report of one of these, illustrated by two Red Saunders photographs, ultimately overshadowed everything else about the gig and gave one of the two people involved his first 15 minutes of fame: 'A young couple, somewhat out of it, had been nibbling and fondling each other amid the broken glass when she suddenly lunged forward and *bit his ear lobe off* [while the crowd] watched with cold, calculated hipitude.' Like the COUM party, the Clash gig was a wild night fuelled by speed and alcohol. The bar staff entered into the spirit of the evening to such an extent that they gave away a further £80 worth of booze – with Sebastian's unsolicited assistance – and the twosome Miles observed, Mad Jane and Shane MacGowan, were by no means content to loiter at the back of the queue.

'Me and this girl were having a bit of a laugh which involved biting each other's arms till they were completely covered in blood and then smashing up a couple of bottles and cutting each other up a bit,' Shane informed *ZigZag*'s Granuaille in 1986, setting the record straight on the occasion of punk's 10th anniversary, and, in the process, offering another insight into the mythopoetics of punk. 'That, in those days, was the sort of thing that people used to do. I haven't got a clue now why I did it or why anyone would want to do it, but that was how teenagers got their kicks in London *if* they were hip. Anyway, in the end she went a bit over the top and bottled me in the side of the head. *Gallons* of blood came out and someone took a photograph. I never got it bitten off – although we had bitten each other to bits – it was just a heavy cut.' As Shane noted, though, the anecdote was exaggerated with each retelling. 'It's like the old story about the bloke who catches the fish. He says that it weighs *this* much and it's *that* big, and within a couple of days it's a whale.' Over the years, few have been prepared to let the fact that his earlobes are both present and correct stand in the way of a good story.

Like Miles, members of the Clash had been to see Patti Smith the previous night. She took them up on their invitation to attend the ICA gig – thus becoming the Clash's first celebrity guest – and responded to the band's set with typical Smith reserve, leaping up on the stage to dance. 'I did it because I do it all the time,' she told Caroline Coon the following January. 'To me, that's what a fan does. I was really excited about the Clash. I thought they were great and I knew I wasn't going to be back in London for a long time and I thought they wanted a reaction.' They did, and were more than a little pleased with the one they got. Joe Strummer was not the only Clash member to lose his heart to Patti. Much later in his career, by which time he had met many of his former heroes, Mick would name her as one of the few who had lived up to his expectations. Back on 23 October 1976, though, it was the brooding Simonon charm to which Patti responded. She invited Paul to accompany her to her next gig, scheduled for the following night in Birmingham. Fortunately, it was also where the Clash's next show was due to take place.

The list of provincial cities responding to punk did not begin and end with Manchester: back in early August, Birmingham's Suburban Studs had been included (albeit incorrectly named as the Suburban Bolts) in Caroline Coon's punk overview feature. At that time, the band had been glam-rockers, still looking decidedly out of place on 31 August when they supported the Sex Pistols and the Clash at the 100 Club. Birmingham Barbarella's had hosted a Sex Pistols gig on 14 August, and afterwards the Studs contacted the club and persuaded the management to designate Wednesdays Punk Night. The Studs volunteered to get proceedings underway by headlining the first gig, and bringing up a bona fide punk band from London for both moral and literal support. After catching the Clash again at the ICA, the Studs approached Bernie, and explained their desire to ignite a Birmingham scene. Their missionary zeal thus appealed to, the Clash agreed to appear second on the bill to the local heroes that coming Wednesday, 27 October.

Upon arrival, the Clash found the Studs had undergone a miraculous change of image, starting, but not ending, with haircuts all round. 'When we played with them in London, they had satin flares on,' recalls Terry. 'When we went up to support them in Birmingham, they were in straight trousers like us, and Bernie was going, "Where's your flares, then? I want to buy 'em for my band."' Unfortunately, according to Jonh Ingham, who reviewed the gig for *Sounds*, the transformation in the band's material was not extensive enough to allow the Studs to grab a seat on the punk gravy train.

By contrast, Jonh believed the Clash's 45 minute set to have been their finest yet, despite the now obligatory sound problems. This time a PA malfunction meant that only the vocals could be routed through the club system, with the band's own amplification equipment being required to project the sound of the guitars throughout the venue. At least this made for one of the clearest vocal mixes they had ever experienced. When it came to stage presentation, the word 'relaxed' was not in the Clash lexicon, but away from the largely self-imposed restrictions of the London scene, they felt able to adopt a more populist, even humorous approach. The second number, 'London's Burning', became 'Birmingham's Burning', establishing something of a local-relevance tradition for the song, and the encore '1-2 Crush On You' involved some frantic self-deprecatory mugging from Joe. The crowd loved it. 'Every song is pared to the minimum required to get it across with maximum energy and zero flab,' concluded Jonh.

The band's next gig took place back in London, on Friday 29 October at Fulham Old Town Hall on Fulham Broadway. The Clash appeared second on a three-band bill topped by Roogalator and tailed by the Vibrators. The show was again covered by *Sounds*, this time represented by Giovanni Dadomo. Giovanni was in a mood to be kind to all involved, although Roogalator were about to slide down the slippery slope of unfashionability and the Vibrators were among the most opportunistic of punk bandwagon-jumpers. He gave the Clash as much space as the headliners, blamed the venue's acoustics for their poor sound, and enthused loud and long about their passion and commitment.

While he did mention there were 'a hundred or so' in the audience, Giovanni neglected to point out that this meant the hall was only half full. That the Clash's friends in the music press were giving them an inordinately high ratio of reviews per number of gigs played was already plain, but only careful reading of their shameless propaganda revealed the supposed importance of the band to be out of all proportion to the size of the crowds they were able to draw. Nevertheless, Giovanni's hyperbole was far from being cynically motivated: he was genuinely entranced by the Clash experience, and he was by no means alone. Jon Savage, future author of *England's Dreaming*, saw his first punk concert that night, and recorded his response to the Clash in his diary: 'Within 10 seconds, I'm transfixed, within 30, changed forever.'

The next Clash-organised event was scheduled for Friday 5 November 1976, at the Royal College of Art (RCA). Called A Night Of Treason in honour of Guy Fawkes, it featured the Clash supported by the Rockets (whom the Clash had supported at Tiddenfoot Leisure Centre) and Subway Sect. Bernie had lined up press and record company interest, and Pennie Smith was sent along by the *NME* to take her first shots of the band.

As at the ULU, though, the RCA gig was marred by an ugly outbreak of violence. For years afterwards, no reason other than subcultural antipathy was given to explain why a contingent of long-haired types in the audience began hurling abuse and glasses at the stage during the Clash's set. Legend has it that Sid Vicious, determined to protect his friends, ran out from behind the stage and leaped, kamikaze style, into their midst. Whereupon, incensed by the bombardment, and inspired by Sid's fearless display, Joe and Paul downed instruments and jumped in after him. Truth to tell, though, the long-haired contingent was not particularly large, as Paul eventually revealed in a 1991 interview with the *NME*'s Mary Ann Hobbs. 'Me and Joe checked these two blokes who was, like, chucking the stuff. We put our guitars down, jumped into the audience and gave 'em a kicking. I got back on stage and said to Mick, "Why wasn't you there?" And he goes, "Well, somebody's got to stay in tune."' Whatever his motive, it would appear that Mick's refusal to get involved was the morally correct decision. Interviewed for Johnny Rotten's autobiography, Marco Pirroni insisted that the glass-throwing long-hairs were actually intent on seeking revenge for an earlier incident in which Sid Vicious – newly released from Ashford Remand Centre after the 100 Club incident, but evidently not much the wiser for the experience – had himself thrown bottles at the support band.

One of the enduring myths about the punk scene is that it only became violent when it was inundated with newcomers – labelled 'outside punks' by Caroline Coon – who received all their information about punk behaviour from sensationalist reports in the tabloid press. While such coverage would certainly exacerbate the problem during late 1976 and early 1977, it was not responsible for starting it, and nor were the 'outside punks'. Violence had always been an integral part of the scene. Vivienne Westwood had provoked the fight at the Sex Pistols' show on 23 April at the Nashville, and Mad Jane and Shane MacGowan had been responsible for the bloodshed at the Clash's ICA gig. Almost all the other more legendarily unpleasant incidents can be attributed to one person: Sid Vicious. It was he who had been first to back up Vivienne at the Nashville, he who had famously chain-whipped Nick Kent at the 100 Club, he who had thrown the glass at the Punk Festival, and now he who had started the fight at the RCA.

'That can happen and *does* happen at many "hippy" rock concerts,' was temporary editor Steve Mick's spirited defence of such incidents in the October edition of *Sniffin' Glue*. 'It's just stupid, that's what it is, to blow up the violence in punk rock and so badly distort the truth!' Maybe, as he claimed, the violence was not widespread at that time, but it has always been pervasive stuff: a little goes a long way.

Trouble was also being directed onto the scene from without well before the media really got to grips with punk. In an attempt to deflect blame from the punks for instigating violence, Steve Mick's editorial also made vague references to street attacks on scene habitués by what he termed 'discos' and 'footballs': that is, nightclub-goers and football hooligans. His admirable conclusion was, 'It's all a bit silly, ain't it?' but the sub-heading he used for this part of his editorial sounded a tellingly defiant note: 'US AND THEM'.

The Clash's own reaction was at best ambivalent. Onstage at the ICA, responding to Jane and Shane's exhibition, Joe had sneered, 'All of you who think violence is tough: why don't you go home and collect stamps? That's much tougher.' Commenting on the same incident in Miles's December *NME* interview, Mick said, 'We definitely think it ain't hip. We think it's disgusting to be violent.' In the Clash *Sniffin' Glue* interview, Steve Walsh had queried the band's image, wondering whether it was 'violent or suggestive of violence'. Mick had claimed that it reflected the band's 'no-nonsense' attitude. Although he believed violence on the punk scene was liable to escalate, both he and Joe elected to take this as an indication that at least apathy was not holding sway. He hoped people would learn to 'channel their violence into music, or something creative'. This remark was the source of Paul's boiler suit slogan. When Miles attempted to quiz the band about it, Joe responded by waving a switch-blade under his nose, and saying: 'Suppose I smash your face in and slit your nostrils with this, right? Well, if you don't learn anything from it, then it's not worth it, right? But suppose some guy comes up to me and tries to put one over on me, right? And I smash his face up and he learns something from it. Well, in a sense that's creative violence.' And in another sense, it's almost unbelievably stupid.

Bernie's contribution to the debate was a fragment of text lifted from Charles Hamblett and Jane Deverson's 1964 pop-sociological document *Generation X*, which he had Sebastian incorporate in the flyer advertising the ICA show. Therein, 18-year-old mod John Braden recalled his part in seaside skirmishes with rockers: 'I'm not ashamed of it: I wasn't the only one. I joined in a few of the fights. I haven't enjoyed myself so much in a long time. It was great: the beach was like a battlefield. It was like we were taking over the country.' Paul was wont to boast in similar terms about his part in the Notting Hill Riot, not least in November's *London Weekend Show* TV interview. During that same brief spot Mick facetiously – but irresponsibly – advocated beating up hippies:

'If there's any around, you should, like, jump into action immediately.' The following March, he defiantly informed the *NME*'s Tony Parsons, 'We ain't ashamed to fight', conveniently forgetting both his earlier rejections of violence and, indeed, his preference for staying in tune at the moment of truth.

Intimidatory clothing, bullying harangues – *right?* – and a tendency to wave guns and knives around during interviews were by no means the only confused and confusing signals the Clash were giving off. The band's songs were characterised by aggressive delivery, mob-mentality terrace harmonies and brutal lyrical imagery, some of them including direct references to 'throwing a brick' or 'fighting in the road'. In late November, the Clash were to add two more songs to their repertoire. 'Hate and War' was partly inspired by the slogan on Joe's boiler suit, once more adapting the hippy salutation to state, 'And if I get aggression / I give it to them two time back.' 'Cheat' opens with the similarly uncompromising, 'I get violent when I'm fucked up.'

The Clash may have claimed to be dealing in the currency of the day, accurately representing the experiences of 'the kids' they were representing, but they often seemed to be justifying, even encouraging, violence as an expression of frustration and alienation. A reasonably well-centred individual like Paul Simonon might have been able to cope with the contradictions implicit in a glib slogan-concept like 'creative violence', but it gave unstable, high-velocity personalities like Mad Jane and Sid Vicious carte blanche to push the outside of the behavioural envelope. Instead of disowning Sid, or even remonstrating with him, Mick and Paul had covered for him following the Punk Festival incident, and Joe and Paul had backed him up in the RCA fight.

By the end of November 1976, the paranoid siege mentality hinted at in Steve Mick's October *Sniffin' Glue* editorial was already well established on the punk scene. The Clash had missed an opportunity to take a moral lead worthy of the rest of their largely upbeat, positive rhetoric. Nobody in the band camp had bothered to draw up the kind of pros and cons lists featured on Bernie's 'What side of the bed' T-shirt, and nobody seemed to be thinking clearly enough to make the distinction between civil disobedience and mindless aggravation. As Bernie would tell Paul Rambali four years later, everything had happened too fast. A messy and unfocused battle was already underway, and it looked as though it might already be too late to establish the true identities of, and draw clear lines between, the 'Us' and the 'Them'.

In terms of personal career development, the Clash's ambivalent attitude towards violence rebounded on them almost immediately. The Damned had gone for the carrot and signed to Stiff, the first label that showed an interest. The Sex Pistols had played a waiting game, gigging for nearly a year before finally attracting the major-label deal Malcolm wanted. As the other well-known and acclaimed punk band, the Clash might reasonably have expected to be snapped up in the feeding frenzy following EMI's netting of the scene leaders, but as October turned into November the band had to sit back and watch as two outer circle bands were signed instead: the Vibrators by RAK and the Stranglers by United Artists (UA). This despite the promotional efforts of the Clash's hardly unbiased music press pals, not only in print, but also via word of mouth.

'I was friends with Jonh Ingham and Caroline Coon,' says Chris Parry. 'Neither of those two people had a car, but I had one.' Chris had chauffeured the other two to Sex Pistols gigs while himself chasing that band for Polydor. When he lost out, he had been temporarily disconsolate. 'I remember Jonh saying, "Well, don't worry. You know the Clash are a great band, and you can get them, anyway."' Chris had accompanied the journalists to the ULU gig, and been impressed enough by what he saw to bring his Director of A&R, Jim Crook, along to the RCA show. 'Somebody threw a bottle at Joe Strummer, almost took his fucking head off,' is how Chris remembers it. 'He was really angry, and quite rightly so in my opinion. He came running down right by where Jim

Crook was, and obviously thought Jim had thrown it… And it didn't do things a lot of good. Jim said, "If you think I'm signing *that* fucking band, you've got another think coming!" And he walked out.'

In spite of this not inconsiderable setback, Chris Parry refused to give up. He had the authority to commission demos without higher approval, and talked to Bernie about the possibility of making some recordings for Polydor in the hope that the results would persuade Jim Crook to reconsider. Wanting even the Clash's demos to be out of the ordinary, Bernie suggested bringing in a name producer acquaintance of his: Guy Stevens. Bernie knew Guy from his mod days and had cultivated the half-crazed producer as a potential ally in his planned assault on the fuddy-duddy record company establishment. He took him along to Rehearsals to watch the Clash play, and Guy was gripped by the high energy and passion of the performance. 'They were doing "White Riot",' he told the *NME*'s Charles Shaar Murray in 1979. 'And I just thought, "Right! RIOT! RIGHT! RIOT! Let's *goooooooh!*"'

Things had not been going well for Guy since the disintegration of his relationship with Violent Luck, and his stock had sunk even lower in music business circles. He saw the Clash as yet another chance to make a comeback. Like Brady before them, Paul and Terry were both won over by his larger than life personality. Joe remembered him as the author of the sleeve notes to his beloved Chuck Berry EP, and was quietly overawed. Mick's feelings were, understandably, mixed. As he intimated in the *Clash On Broadway* booklet, although he had never lost his admiration for Guy's talents, he still carried some resentment about his sacking from the band that had become Violent Luck, and he also harboured fears that something similar might happen again.

While discussions were going on, the Clash continued with their eclectic approach to live work. On 11 November 1976, a gig was arranged at the Lacy Lady, a soul boy haunt in Ilford, east London, with Subway Sect again providing support. Bearing in mind Steve Mick's comments about tension between punks and 'discos', the gig might well appear to have been asking for another ULU-style confrontation. Reviewing it for the first issue of his Clash-inspired fanzine, *48 Thrills*, Adrian Thrills mused on the possibility: 'the disco audience didn't know how to react. Would it be cool to dance? sit down? beat each other up?' In fact, the division between punks and soul boys was not quite so clear cut as that between punks and teds. For a start, soul boys were not exactly the same species as Steve Mick's 'discos', who were just your average nightclub-goers of the day. In effect, while punks were one type of latterday mods, soul boys were another, and the difference between them was further blurred by the fact that – in 1976, at least – they shared much the same wardrobe.

Pop sociologists have amused themselves for years debating who took the role of the chicken and who the egg in the Great Soul Boy/Punk Style-Crossover. Some commentators have maintained that the early punk look borrowed much from the soul boy styles of the 1975-76 period. Adrian Thrills made *his* position clear in his review, describing the Lacy Lady as 'one of those soul discos where kids are now starting to dress in the new trendy punk fashion'. In *Rotten: No Irish, No Blacks, No Dogs*, Johnny Rotten rubbished the idea that punks stole clothing tips from soul boys, insisting instead that he and his similarly eccentrically dressed friends had started something of a punky trend when they visited the Lacy Lady one night early in 1976 and dominated the dancefloor with their wild cavortings. His claim is both simplistic and typically self-aggrandising. There was, in truth, a two-way exchange of stylistic influence. As early as 1974, the soul boys' mod-like obsession with up-to-the minute clothing had already led some of them to investigate the wares in Sex. In return, their own short hairstyles, mohair jumpers and plastic, or 'jelly', sandals had indeed become features of the nascent punk scene.

Once that scene was established, there was also some social interaction: punks attended soul clubs like the Lacy Lady and Crackers on Wardour Street, and soul boys were intrigued enough to check out some of the early punk gigs. 'Suddenly punk was almost like a kitsch thing, in that it was totally the opposite of what the kids were listening to,' former soul boy and Crackers and Lacy Lady regular Gary Kemp told the *Face*'s Chris Salewicz in 1981. Although David Bowie's then-current 'plastic soul' period offered some common ground, the distance between the dance music and the punk rock bands of the mid Seventies was considerably greater than had been the distance between R&B and Motown singles and the music of the Who and Small Faces in the early to mid Sixties. As Gary Kemp claimed, Seventies soul boy culture was oriented more towards records and clubs than it was towards live gigs: 'I think the idea of going every night to see a band as a form of enjoyment never really appealed to a lot of those people. They *are* people who like being looked at: that's why dancing is so important, and why people try to beat each other at dancing. It's also why clothes are important. So punk soon lost that excitement, and those kids went back to the DJs, much to their delight.'

The initial musical crossover was both limited and short-lived, Subway Sect being quite possibly the only actual punk band to include former soul boys. However, the union did bear fruit a couple of years later. Late Seventies Bowie Nights in Soho and Covent Garden clubs attracted a clientele comprising both soul boys and former punks, and this cultural mix was responsible for hatching the New Romantic movement and some of the more successful UK pop groups of the early Eighties. Gary Kemp himself admits to having been inspired by punk's DIY ethic, if not the music, when he formed Spandau Ballet.

Any outbreak of violence between the two tribes at the Lacy Lady on Thursday 11 November 1976 would have been hard pushed to get out of hand: only 20 people showed up. With low audience turnouts and less than keen record company reaction, the Clash hype needed to be stepped up a notch. On 22 October, Stiff had released the Damned's single, 'New Rose', the first recording by representatives of the UK punk movement. Jonh Ingham had made it Single of the Week in *Sounds*. In the light of this development in the Damned's career, Caroline Coon was quite justified in interviewing them for *Melody Maker*. Instead of running the piece on its own, however, she twinned it with an interview she conducted with the Clash on 5 November – the day of the RCA gig – for no discernible record or tour related purpose, and rushed both into the 13 November issue under the joint headline: 'NEW FACES: Caroline Coon introduces two hot punk rock bands.'

Thus the Clash got their first full-length interview in the mainstream music press by riding piggy-back on the achievements of the Damned. It is also worth noting that the Clash piece was accompanied by a large photograph singling out Paul Simonon onstage at the 100 Club; and that by this stage Caroline and Paul's relationship was no longer purely professional. In fairness, Caroline did require the Clash to defend their position to some extent. She took issue with their dismissal of hippies; questioned whether rock'n'roll really had the power to change things; and wondered whether the band themselves would be as interested in upsetting the status quo once they themselves had achieved commercial success. All great stuff as far as it went; the problem was that it did not go far enough. Caroline neglected to pursue her arguments and to make the band justify their sometimes wild proclamations.

Asked for their comments on contemporary society, the three Clash members present volunteered answers that, for all their passion, commitment and occasional exaggeration, sounded more rehearsed than heartfelt. Mick announced, 'It's alienating the individual.' Joe bemoaned the lack of leisure options, the state of radio, and the paucity of affordable housing. Picking up the ball and running out of the stadium with it, Paul prophesised that this situation would precipitate more unrest from 'the kids', which would in turn encourage the Government to bring back National Service, whereupon 'we'll all be sent down to South Africa or Rhodesia to protect white capital's interests. And then we'll all be slaughtered...' But he did maintain that rock'n'roll had the potential to change things. He promised that, if the band made any money, they wouldn't just take it for themselves, like the Rolling Stones or Led Zeppelin, but would reinvest it in getting 'something going'. Joe agreed. 'I'm not going to spend all my money on drugs. I'm going to start a radio station.'

Sounds had already gorged itself on punk coverage with its Punk Festival issue. Furthermore, both Giovanni Dadomo and Jonh Ingham had recently filed highly partisan Clash live reviews, and any further ravings from them at this stage would be too transparently nepotistic to have the desired effect. Luckily, the Clash now had on their side another writer with access to the paper. Buckinghamshire stringer Kris Needs covered the band's next gig, on Thursday 18 November, at the Nag's Head in High Wycombe. The support was Reading band Clayson and the Argonauts. Kris blamed another poor attendance – the small pub venue was again only half-full – on that night's televised Miss World contest, but brushed aside such trifling matters, instead employing the by-now traditional combat metaphors to capture the band's impact: 'The Clash are now firing with more compressed energy than a flame-thrower at full blast. They play with almost frightening conviction and intensity, each number a rapid-fire statement delivered like a knock-out blow.'

He made no pretence at objectivity: Joe had recently dyed his hair blond, but only the truly besotted would have likened him, as Kris did, to a 'paint-spattered Greek god'. On 5 November the Vibrators had released their début single, 'We Vibrate', followed a week later by another, 'Pogo Dancing', on which they backed Chris Spedding. On the 26th of the month, the Sex Pistols were due to release their first single, 'Anarchy In The UK'. The true purpose of Kris's review was revealed in the fourth paragraph: 'The Clash... seem forced to take a back seat on the new wave recording front while groups like the Damned, the Pistols and Vibrators shove singles out. Why is it that the hottest band this country has got hasn't yet had a chance to get themselves on vinyl? Dunno, but going on last Thursday's set, it won't be long before some record company wakes up.' Wishful thinking it might have been, but Kris's attempt to push the record companies' panic buttons was timely, if not exactly subtle.

By the time his review saw print, the Clash had already recorded their demos for Polydor. Some time in mid November, the band spent two days in the record company's own studio at 17-19 Stratford Place, just off Oxford Street, and taped five songs: 'Career Opportunities', 'White Riot', 'Janie Jones', 'London's Burning' and '1977'. Discounting the static electric shocks Terry kept getting from the studio's nylon carpet, recording the basic tracks went well enough, with, so Mick told Kris Needs, Guy Stevens 'really inciting' the band. It was these same crazed urgings, however, that troubled the Polydor representatives. 'We all had a lot of respect for Guy Stevens,' says Terry. 'It was evident that the A&R man paying for the sessions and the engineer didn't have the same regard for him, for whatever reason, and they weren't working in the most positive way with him, we felt. Joe actually said to me, "They've got him numbered." So the fact that he got drunk towards the end of it, and blew it, we felt was as a direct result of the lack of co-operation he was getting from those guys.' Although himself not present for the entire duration of recording, Chris Parry admits that Guy's reputation had preceded him, and that Polydor staff engineer Vic Smith had been advised to keep an eye on the erratic producer. 'I was there for a while, and Guy was a bit all over the place.'

By no means all the tension was confined to the control room. Guy understood that feel is more important than sense in the best rock'n'roll, but Vic Smith believed that the lyrics were the most important part of the Clash's message. When it came time to record the vocals, the engineer overrode Guy, and insisted the singer make an effort to pronounce the words clearly. 'So I did it, and it sounded like Matt Monroe,' Joe told the *NME*'s Tony Parsons the following March. 'So I thought, "I'm never doing that again." To me, our music is like Jamaican stuff: if they can't hear it, they're not supposed to hear it. It's not for them if they can't understand it.'

As a result of the compound tensions and his own method of taking refuge from them, Guy was soon so tired and emotional he was unable to continue. In truth, this was nothing new: even in his Mott the Hoople days, he had been much better at starting projects than completing them. It was left to Vic Smith to finish off and mix the demos, and the band were not happy with the results. Listening to the songs today, and comparing them with the later album versions, it is not difficult to guess why: the musical fireworks Guy had supposedly ignited in the studio arrived on tape as damp squibs; and Joe's phrasing is so risibly hammy and precise it gives the strong impression he set out to express his displeasure at being given vocal instruction by deliberately sabotaging proceedings.

That the demo versions of 'Career Opportunities' and 'Janie Jones' were included on the 1991 compilation *Clash On Broadway* had more to do with paying sentimental posthumous tribute to Guy than any belated recognition of the tracks' artistic merit. In the booklet accompanying the CD boxed set, Mick put the problems at the sessions down to the differing objectives of Guy on the one hand and Chris Parry and Vic Smith on the other. Guy, as ever, wanted to make an incendiary masterpiece; Chris and Vic wanted a simple, serviceable tape to sell the band to the higher-ups at Polydor. The months immediately following the sessions found other members of the Clash camp more than willing to point the finger of blame at the disgraced Guy. 'We picked Guy Stevens because we wanted a nut case to produce the band, because that's what our music is all about,' Bernie told the *Melody Maker* in January 1977. 'But there are different kinds of nut case, and it didn't work out with him.' Two months later, talking to Tony Parsons, Joe avoided mentioning Guy by name, but was even more scathing about the 'famous producers' the band had tried who were 'all too pissed to work'. There had been only the one.

While Polydor pondered the demos, and the wider music business world digested the latest Clash propaganda, the band's campaign received yet another boost. The Sex Pistols were about to embark upon a high-profile national tour, and the Clash were invited to occupy one of the support slots. Typically, Malcolm McLaren's motive was hardly altruistic. First announced in the 13 November 1976 issue of *Sounds*, the tour was originally intended to be a package showcasing both UK punk and US new wave, co-headlined by the Sex Pistols and the Ramones, and also featuring the Vibrators (with Chris Spedding) and Talking Heads. The selection of acts was influenced by business considerations: all were signed to record companies and had records out, and the idea was that some of the costs would therefore be covered by RAK for the Vibrators, and Phonogram – the UK distributor of US label Sire – for both American bands.

The following week, the music press announced that the American bands had pulled out. Although not given at the time, the reason was record company politics: Phonogram decided they were only prepared to back a Ramones tour if it did not involve the Pistols.

Having promised name acts – that is, name to the still relatively small circle of punk and new wave cognoscenti – Malcolm was put in the unenviable position of having little over two weeks to assemble an equally prestigious package. The Damned were brought in as second on the bill support because they were the only other established punk band with a current single and with a record label willing to meet their tour costs. Malcolm fell back on his old New York Dolls contacts to find a New York band of impressive-enough status. He convinced Johnny Thunders that his still-unsigned Heartbreakers would stand a better chance of making it via an association with the UK scene. The Clash were asked along merely to shore up the bottom of the bill. When Chris Spedding and the Vibrators dropped out the following week, the poster Jamie Reid designed for what had by now been dubbed the Anarchy Tour left the Clash with no illusions about their poor-relation status among the remaining bands: there was their name, yet again in insultingly small print, crammed into the bottom left hand corner like the afterthought it was.

At least the renewal of their association with the Sex Pistols brought the Clash the immediate reward of more media interest. London Weekend Television had filmed the 15 November Sex Pistols gig at Notre Dame Hall, off Leicester Square. This, plus brief interviews conducted by Janet Street-Porter with the Pistols, various fans – including the Bromley Contingent – and the Clash, was used as the basis for the *London Weekend Show*, broadcast in the capital region only at 1.15 pm on Sunday 28 November. The Pistols had already played 'Anarchy In The UK' on Manchester-based Granada TV's *So It Goes*, and appeared as the focus of a brief run-down on the new punk movement on BBC1's national early-evening magazine show, *Nationwide*. Nevertheless, the *London Weekend Show* – despite being a local programme broadcast in a relatively low-profile slot – was the first real attempt at a documentary about punk. Its bias was still towards the Sex Pistols, but it was also the first television programme to do anything more than namecheck the Clash.

The researchers had done their job well, plainly drawing heavily on existing music press coverage of the scene, especially Caroline Coon's. Janet Street-Porter's narration touched on established rock stars being out of touch, the DIY ethic, and the difference between bands genuinely inspired by the Pistols and those jumping the bandwagon. But, like Allan Jones, she also questioned the negativity of the lyrics. Her interview with the Clash, conducted at Rehearsals, covered much the same ground. The soft target of the hippy generation received yet another broadside, with Mick making a remark that was destined to come back and haunt him: 'I suppose it ain't their fault. They've had too much dope.'

Far more impressive than the content of this somewhat stilted interview was its presentation. The band – minus Terry – were filmed in front of the pink drapes, next to the juke box, dressed in their Pop Art/Lettrist clothes, looking romantically pale and thin. Pushed up close together to fit into the frame, they appeared to be not so much sitting in a row as wrapped around each other. The few smiles and laughs were sly or knowing, and exchanged amongst the band members. Mick gave off a brooding intensity; Paul rocked backwards and forwards throughout like a traumatised child; Joe – a smoker now – sat sideways-on to the camera and, eyelids lowered disdainfully, sneered his deliberately semi-articulate replies over his shoulder. There was, as Jon Savage suggested in *England's Dreaming*, a distinct whiff of amphetamine psychosis, whether real or affected, about the proceedings. Thus, whereas the band looked comfortable together and mutually reliant – exactly like a gang – the atmosphere between the Clash and the intruding camera crew crackled with barely suppressed hostility. They didn't get to play live, like the Pistols, but their body language was a performance in itself: pure Us and Them.

Barry Miles, genuinely enthused by the ICA gig, had turned up to interview the Clash for the *NME* not long after Caroline Coon had for *Melody Maker*. Scooped by Caroline's impressive feat of conducting her interview on the Friday and completing her feature in time for the following Monday evening deadline, *NME* editor Nick Logan – rather than take a lame second place – had chosen to sit on Miles's feature until the Clash's inclusion on the Anarchy Tour, and involvement-by-association in the attendant hoo-hah, provided justification for its belated inclusion in his paper's 11 December issue.

Miles's extensive use of quotes from lyrics betrayed his familiarity with the *Sniffin' Glue* interview, and also suggested that it had by now become band policy to hand out lyric sheets to interviewers. The topics discussed confirmed the preparation undergone by both interviewer and interviewees, tackled much the same topics as the band's two previous feature-length excursions into print. On those occasions, however, the Clash had encountered people who were, if not exactly fellow members, then at least satellites of the punk scene; as an outsider, Miles had come in for much the same treatment as would the television crew, the intimidation climaxing with Joe's totally over-the-top stunt with the switch-blade.

This lame-brained piece of shock theatre undermined an otherwise sound introduction to the Clash manifesto as it stood in early November, both by making Joe look foolish, and by contradicting his opening soundbite, 'I think people ought to know that we're anti-fascist, we're anti-violence, we're anti-racist and we're pro-creative.' Surprisingly, Miles refused either to object to the knife-wielding incident at the time, or pour scorn on it later from the safety of his desk. Instead, he gave the impression that he accepted it as proof of the band's authenticity: 'When Paul Simonon named the band the Clash, he meant it.'

The *NME*'s belated attempt to get in with punk's movers and shakers was further evidenced by the sub editor's mythopoetic feature title, 'Eighteen Flight Rock And The Sound Of The Westway', and by the selection and layout of Pennie Smith's backstage RCA photos: full-on and profile head and shoulders pictures of the individual band members close-cropped to resemble police mug-shots, then arranged in a column and captioned with quotes as if to illustrate a sensationalist newspaper report of a bank robbery or gangland purge. Again, it didn't quite come off: a stray picture of Subway Sect's Vic Godard was identified as Paul Simonon, to whom was attributed a statement actually made by Joe Strummer; the picture of Paul was identified as Terry Chimes; there was no picture of Terry; and by the time the article was printed, Terry was no longer a member of the Clash, anyway.

For many years afterwards, the Clash would make out that the threat of violence – specifically the bombardment of the stage at the RCA – had been chiefly responsible for Terry Chimes's decision to leave the band in mid November 1976, on the eve of the Anarchy Tour. Mick more than hinted at this in the stream of invective he poured onto the heads of past Clash drummers during the March 1977 *NME* interview with Tony Parsons. In his contribution to the 'Story Of The Clash' in the 1980 tour booklet, the *Armagideon Times*, Joe spelled it out in no uncertain terms: 'One day during a particularly nasty gig when the bottles and cans were coming down like rain, Terry Chimes quit after watching a wine bottle come flying over and smash into a million pieces on his hi-hat.' Paul gave the same reason in 1991's *Clash On Broadway* booklet, wherein Terry was at last offered the opportunity to deny his supposed cowardice: 'Nothing to do with bottles. I never minded that.'

In that same booklet, Paul came closer to the truth when he offered the secondary explanation that Terry was not particularly enamoured of the Clash's leftist political direction. Joe went on to suggest that the drummer was more interested in personal gain. Terry does agree with these opinions, up to a point. 'I always thought it was a mistake to overemphasise the politics, because implicit in that were the things like, "We don't want to become pop stars, we don't want to make a lot of money." And I said, "Well, we *are* attempting to become famous and sell lots of records and become very important, and if we do that, then we'll come across as hypocrites," to which they never really had a proper answer. They would just say things like, "Oh, you don't understand."' Terry did understand; he just didn't agree. He lived in Hackney, ran a car (and wanted a better one), had his own social circle, and was beginning to find the Clash regime restrictive. 'Rehearsing seven nights a week, no messing about. It was part of the brainwashing thing that your priority must be the band, and therefore you never got involved with much else. I never really subscribed to that.'

After Keith Levene's departure, Terry had taken over his role as the band's token outsider. 'He didn't really fit in,' says Sebastian, 'because he wouldn't wear the gear.' 'Terry Chimes was a one,' laughs Glen Matlock. 'We'd say, "Are you gonna come out?" and he'd say, "Nah, I'm gonna go and put some shelves up." Which is where he was at, you know.' His refusal to be bullied into wholesale adoption of the gang mentality hardly marked Terry down as a weak link, but some people construed his insistent but admittedly low-key individualism that way. 'I don't remember any reason being given to us for him not being there,' says Mark Perry, recalling the *Sniffin' Glue* interview. 'But everyone seemed to know that he wasn't a proper member of the group. That he wasn't one of the people that was going to do interviews because he was "just the drummer" sortathing. That was the impression.' According to Terry, he just happened not to be around when the *Sniffin' Glue* interview took place. He was absent from all subsequent interviews simply because he had already handed in his notice.

Tony Parsons got to know the Clash when they were officially a three-piece, which goes some way to explaining why, in *The Boy Looked At Johnny*, Terry was described as an 'unsatisfactory drummer' who was 'fired and rehired constantly throughout 1976 and early 1977'. No-one involved with the Clash has ever suggested that Terry was fired. If he were truly unsatisfactory and not a valued band member, this would have been the ideal time to replace him with somebody more sympathetic to the cause, and the others would have leaped at the chance to trade in their Pete Best for a Ringo Starr. Mick's unhappiness with Terry's decision to quit was recorded in the following spring's interview with Tony. In the *Clash On Broadway* booklet, Paul recalled being aggrieved enough to threaten damage to Terry's car. 'I could have hit him with a spade,' Joe told the *NME*'s Paul Du Noyer in 1981. 'Joe *was* quite upset about it!' says Terry. 'Even when I rejoined in 1982, he kept talking about that one day when I came in and resigned. "The sun was shining, I went into Rehearsals, I felt good… and then you came in and said you wanted to leave." He never forgave me, in a way.' But the band members were too caught up in the punk image to allow themselves to appear hurt for long. 'It was anger for a day or so, and then, "OK, so we'll find someone else. That's no big deal."' Terry agreed to stay on until a replacement was found.

On the cover of *The Clash*, Terry would be credited as Tory Crimes. This has always been taken as proof of the band's enduring spite, it being an apparently backstabbing reference to his materialist outlook. In fact the nickname was a joke thought up by Roadent – the recently converted ex-fascist – while Terry was still with the group, and one which the drummer took in good part.

Terry's bombshell left the rest of the band in a quandary. It would be difficult to impress the meaning of being part of the Clash upon a newcomer, someone who had not shared the formative experiences and discussions of the past months. Also, taking on an established musician from outside the punk scene would undermine both the DIY ethic and the band's street credibility. The most ideologically sound option would be to promote someone from within the Clash's immediate circle. Paul's brother Nick, who had begun playing the drums, was briefly considered, but even in a youth culture it is possible to be too young: he had only just turned 17. 'They wanted to teach *me* the drums at one point, but I was totally uncoordinated,' laughs Sebastian, who is also mindful of the strain his background would have placed on the Clash propaganda machine. Less testing – with the odd tweak here and there – might have been that of the recently arrived Roadent, who was also considered, at least by Joe. 'Joe wanted somebody who couldn't play fuck-all,' Roadent told *Melody Maker*'s Frances Lass in 1979. 'But Mick wasn't having any. Mick wanted to be a star.'

Joe had embraced the DIY ethic wholeheartedly. Mick was pragmatic enough to realise that the Clash already had their fair share of eager amateurs, and he knew from experience that a poor drummer makes for a bad band. In the end, his argument prevailed. The Clash came up with a solution that would side-step charges of using their high-profile position to recruit an established musician: they placed an anonymous display ad in the *Melody Maker* classifieds of 20 November. It included the Rehearsals phone number and read: 'AMAZING YOUNG DRUMMER WANTED for inciting group with exciting prospects.' With just two weeks to go before the tour started, there followed a frenzy of auditions.

In September 1975, Rob Harper began to attend Sussex University in Brighton. A drummer from the age of 15, he had switched to guitar a year or so previously, and when he met fellow student, guitarist and high-energy rock'n'roll enthusiast Bill Broad, the two decided to form a band together. The Rockettes (not to be confused with occasional Clash support band the Rockets) were a Sixties-style garage outfit whose repertoire included the Kingsmen's 'Louie Louie' and several Yardbirds songs. During the Easter break, on 4 April 1976, Bill joined his hometown friends in the Bromley Contingent to catch the Pistols at the El Paradise strip club in Soho's Brewer Street, and was immediately won over.

Attending further Sex Pistols gigs at the 100 Club over the summer vacation, Bill got to know the band and their manager. He introduced Rob to the Sex Pistols live experience, and the duo subsequently took a tape of the Rockettes along to Sex. Malcolm was still interested at that time in promoting punk as a movement. Looking to fill the bill for the Punk Festival, he gave the band an audition at Rehearsals. Malcolm thought the bassist was 'quite sexy', but was more scathing about Bill's talents, and turned them down.

Rob maintains it was via an ad that he placed in *Melody Maker* that Tony James first met Bill Broad. The former London SS bassist subsequently enticed Bill away to join Chelsea, whereupon he adopted the new identity of Billy Idol. Neither former Rockette returned to University. Billy's new alliance with Mick Jones's best friend meant that he was kept up to date with new developments in the Clash camp. Possibly to make amends for having abandoned Rob, he phoned him to tip him the wink about the forthcoming drummer ad. Consequently, Rob was amongst the select crowd at Ilford's Lacy Lady on 11 November. 'I've got to say, it just totally knocked me out. I said at the time, it was like three Eddie Cochrans onstage. The drummer played in a dry, clipped way and looked like a dry, clipped person, but the three frontmen were just the business. There was just so much force coming at you: it was so *alive* and colourful. I thought they were absolutely wonderful.'

When Rob arrived at Rehearsals for his audition, Rusty Egan had just finished trying out for the band. In October 1977, Rusty would tell *ZigZag*'s Robin Banks that 'he used to play with the Clash', but like a lot of other drummers who subsequently made this claim, Rusty's audition was the full extent of his association with the band. The Clash did not always get the chance to reject unsuitable candidates. A significantly high proportion walked in, took one look at the band, then turned on their heels and walked out again.

Rob was far more empathetic. 'I didn't judge them on ability at all, because I've always been like an educated garage player. I've got the knowledge of a lot of good players, but I hate technical musicianship. I was sort of good enough to play in the Troggs. On the other hand, they were below even that! No, the musicianship was good, really. Paul's was fairly rudimentary, but that's what I like in a bassist: like an African drum thumping away, vaguely in tune. Mick was OK. Joe was a hard, scrubbing rhythm guitarist. Once he got onstage, he was just flailing around breaking strings, but he was quite good.'

In addition to having caught the band live and having been primed by Billy about their outlook, Rob had also seen some of their media coverage. 'They'd had the press from Caroline Coon, and I sussed out when I got there that she was going out with Paul Simonon, so I knew there was a little insider dealing going on. I came to them knowing that they were going to be very big. I'd seen them, and they were marvellous. I knew that this was going to be something worth being in if you wanted a "career opportunity" in the music world.' Rob had read Sociology during his time at university, and relates his grounding in that discipline to his fascination with the sub-cultural aspects of punk. Like Brady, he was 27, so his age was a problem, but he was fresh-faced enough to pass for several years younger. Digging deeper into his past would have revealed – yet again – middle class origins and a public school education, but at least he had been brought up in a council house and had a leftist political orientation.

As for musical compatibility, when his turn came to sit behind the drums, he made an instant impression. 'They definitely perked up as soon as I played, because I was very good in terms of what they were used to,' he says, matter-of-factly. 'I'd been playing drums for 12 years at that point. There's a part of me that's a complete maniac, and I can really do that on drums, which is what they liked. I had some skill, but I was really violent.' Rob might not have been 100 per cent ideal for the Clash in every department, but of the people they auditioned he came closest. After some deliberation, they offered him the job. Amazingly, he turned it down.

Rob found Bernie 'provocative and unpleasant', but clever and intriguing. He thought Mick was a bit of a poseur, but friendly and charming. He found Joe likeable, but a little manipulative. Although Paul was 'a nice polite boy', Rob took an instant dislike to him. 'You meet people like that, occasionally, that you're just incompatible with.' The main reason he passed on the offer, though, was because he was used to being a leader. With so many strong characters in the band – especially Joe, who by this time had begun to assert a quiet authority reminiscent of his 101ers days, and who Rob perceived to be the true leader – he realised it would be close to impossible for him to assert himself. 'What they wanted was a really good drummer, kicking shit at the back and minding his business the rest of the time. And there's no way I could do that.' It was his not inconsiderable ego that had prompted Rob to switch to guitar a couple of years ago, and he could not bring himself to take what he saw as a backwards step.

Panic by now having begun to set in among members of the Clash camp, Terry Chimes suddenly found he was no longer being given the cold shoulder. 'After they auditioned 50 or so, and couldn't find anyone they liked, they changed to a reconciliatory mood,' he laughs. 'Bernie in particular kept on and on and on telling me I was making a mistake. He couldn't understand how anyone could walk out on what he saw as his masterplan taking shape.' Nevertheless, Terry remained adamant that he was going to quit. So Rob Harper was persuaded back for a second audition, and Mick Jones's charm was turned full on. 'Mick said, "Look, this is going to be a classic rock'n'roll tour. Why don't you come on it and see what you think? We need you." And that was the final arrangement.' He might have let himself be talked around, but Rob was under no illusions about the situation. 'You mustn't think that Mick was mad keen that I was the drummer for them: it was more a matter of expediency, because they had to have *somebody*.'

Rehearsals began immediately. 'Very thorough. Turn up every day at 11 or 12 and run through the set a couple of times,' says Rob. He never got to play 'How Can I Understand The Flies', abandoned at this point either because it no longer fitted in with the rest of the material, or because its drum pattern was more suited to Terry's clipped style than Rob's more fluid, Keith Moon-style assault. Also dropped was 'Deadly Serious', though it would resurface the following year in the guise of 'Capital Radio'. The repertoire for the tour initially numbered 11 songs, which Rob listed – along with self-addressed tips and reminders – in the front of the diary he kept for the duration of his time with the Clash: '1977', 'Protex Blue', '48 Hours', 'What's My Name', 'Janie Jones', 'I'm So Bored With The USA', 'White Riot', 'London's Burning', 'Career Opportunities', 'Deny' and encore '1-2 Crush On You'.

In order to help him learn his parts, Rob asked if he could record one of the early rehearsals. Already concerned with maintaining as tight a grip on their public image as possible, the Clash initially refused permission, but in view of the limited number of rehearsal opportunities remaining, reluctantly gave way. The tape is fascinating, catching the Clash with their guard down at this, the most self-conscious and studied period of their career. Rob insists they were 'just slopping through the material', explaining why there is only occasional evidence of his characteristically fluid, vigorous style, 'Janie Jones' misses Terry's crisp staccato, and '1977' sounds particularly lifeless. Joe's guitar was down to two strings on this day, and funds did not appear to be available for replacements, so he concentrated on singing. Or rather, he just sang: the evidence suggests that his concentration was somewhat lacking. Most of the time, he cannot remember all the words, and in the case of 'Protex Blue', usually sung by Mick, he cannot remember any. Conversely, 'I'm So Bored With The USA' and 'What's My Name' are indecipherable because Joe had not yet written full lyrics for the songs. Although the tape catches him in loose rehearsal mode, a tendency for him to mess up the words during bona fide performances was to remain a feature of Clash gigs.

Paul's 'African drum' bass plods along, not only during the songs but also between them; in fact, so loudly and relentlessly that Mick and Joe – trying to convey the finer points of drumming Clash-style to the new recruit – are moved to express their irritation by alternately screaming at him and pleading with him to stop. Mick attempts to add some colour to this decidedly basic musical palette by breaking into frankly appalling solos at every opportunity. His contribution to '1977' is so bad it sounds like someone systematically de-tuning a guitar. Joe cracks up laughing, prompting Mick to explore new extremes of atonality, which in turn causes greater and more general hilarity. There is little evidence here of the 'deadly serious' face the Clash insisted on showing to the media. The punk code was already so rigid that it forbade anything other than the most brief and infrequent of guitar solos in more public performances. 'There's no room for instrumental excess,' Mick announced on Radio One's *Rock On* programme the following May. Interviewer John Tobler enquired whether this was because he didn't want to play like that, or because he couldn't. 'I can't at the moment,' admitted Mick, mock-sobbing while Joe chuckled.

Once Rob had mastered the established set, the band decided to work up two new Strummer-Jones compositions. These came too late to be included on the tape, but Rob duly added them to the list in his diary. 'Hate And War' betrays signs of having been written to back up some of the band's media pronouncements: it attempts to justify punk violence, the anti-hippy stance, Us and Them paranoia, and the band's love-hate relationship with their harsh urban environment. Joe's defiant, ugly lyric refuses to have any truck with right on attitudes of any kind, making reference to both 'wops' and 'kebab Greeks': even taken in context, these disparaging asides risk crossing the border into xenophobia; taken out of context, they could have caused just as many problems for the band as did the misinterpretation of 'White Riot'. Strangely, no-one picked up on them, either then or later.

Joe came up with the lyric for 'Cheat' at much the same time, and in terms of subject matter, it is clearly an offspring of 'Hate And War'. The lines which commence the latter song's second verse, 'I have the will to survive / I cheat if I can't win', provide a précis of 'Cheat' in its entirety, and also betray Joe's source material. A flyer for the UK Situationist International splinter group King Mob – as reproduced in the Penguin book *BAMN: Outlaw Manifestos And Ephemera 1965-70*, published in 1971 – features the following slogan: 'In order to survive, we steal, cheat, lie, forge, deal, hide and kill.' This was revolutionary rhetoric, and almost certainly came to Joe via Bernie. Like 'White Riot', the new brace of songs pitched the band directly against the forces of law and order, forcefully making the point that only a fool obeys rules made by an oppressor for the express purpose of keeping the oppressed in their place. All heady, confrontational stuff, and the Clash's subsequent backtracking about the 'political' content of their songs suggests that, yet again, not enough thought had gone into the possible repercussions.

In the *Clash On Broadway* booklet, Joe said he wrote the lyric for 'Hate And War' by candlelight at Foscote Mews, brought it in to Rehearsals the following day, whereupon Mick immediately knocked up a tune. The fact that it was written in this fashion at such a rushed and stressful time goes some way to explaining why Mick's musical contribution fails to live up to the anger of Joe's words. The quality control was beginning to slip. Compared to the band's other material, the backing for 'Hate And War' verges on the insipid. Surprisingly, it was chosen for inclusion in the set for the tour, while the more assertive 'Cheat' would never be performed publicly prior to being recorded for *The Clash*.

On Monday 29 November, the Clash supported the Sex Pistols at Lanchester Polytechnic in Coventry. To all intents and purposes, the bands were using it as a warm-up gig for the Anarchy Tour, due to open that Friday, 3 December. Instead of taking the opportunity to let Rob break himself in for live work, however, the Clash asked Terry to play what was supposed to be one last farewell gig. The students proved far more deadly serious than the Clash even at their most intense. Not only was 'White Riot' misinterpreted, but also the Sex Pistols' new song 'No Future' (later to be re-titled 'God Save The Queen'): an emergency committee meeting decided both were fascist. 'They didn't want to pay us,' says Terry. Thus, he left in the middle of a fraught situation that was, if nothing else, at least typical of his time with the Clash.

For the remaining members of the two bands, notice had been served that the images, meanings and signals of punk were not only ambiguous to outsiders, but also no longer wholly within the control of the scene-leaders and their supporters.

9
ANARCHY IN THE UK

The Anarchy Tour had been set up, not without considerable difficulty, by Malcom McLaren's inexperienced secretary, Sophie Richmond. By the end of November 1976, at which time she also began the diary that was subsequently used as the basis for Fred and Judy Vermorel's *Sex Pistols: The Inside Story*, she had confirmed a total of 19 gigs all over England, Scotland and Wales, running from 3 to 26 December. Although there were occasional relative tiddlers like the 550-capacity Torquay 400 Ballroom, most venues held around 2,000 and the Glasgow Apollo stretched to 3,000: the largest audiences any of the bands had faced thus far. The tour was due to end on Boxing Day with a triumphant homecoming gig at the Roxy Theatre, a former cinema in Harlesden, north-west London.

It was here that the bands – including the Heartbreakers, who had flown in that same day – were supposed to spend 1 December running through a last minute stage rehearsal, timing sets and changeovers. In the event, the Sex Pistols were unable to take their turn. Label-mates Queen had been forced to drop out of a brief interview on *Today*, Thames TV's London-region early evening magazine show, and the Pistols were suggested as a last minute substitute. Feeling the publicity potential was too great to miss, Malcolm agreed to the band being ferried back from Harlesden in an EMI limo. They were joined in the studio by several 'typical punks', represented once more by members of the Bromley Contingent. After this programme was broadcast, the punk scene would never be the same again.

The story of the band's fateful encounter with 52 year-old presenter Bill Grundy has been told and retold countless times. The cause of all the fuss, essentially, was that Bill was either annoyed at having to interview the band without adequate preparation, or drunk, or both. Consequently, instead of carefully manoeuvring the Pistols through a few token rebellious utterances suitable for the tea-time viewing slot, he openly sneered at them, made Johnny repeat a rude word, leered at Siouxsie, and when Steve Jones – justifiably – called him a 'dirty old man', Grundy goaded him into adding, 'You dirty fucker!' and 'You fucking rotter!'

Such public misbehaviour was meat and drink to the UK's tabloid press. A typical flurry of 'outraged' headlines ensued, the most memorable of which was the *Daily Mirror*'s 'THE FILTH AND THE FURY!' Bill Grundy was suspended for two weeks for his part in the fiasco, but as far as the newspapers were concerned it was open season on the Sex Pistols in particular and punk in general. Initially panicked by their response, Malcolm soon adapted and began to revel in the opportunity to play Fagin to the Pistols' street urchins. It would prove to be a role that he found difficult to relinquish.

The music inkies were wrongfooted by the timing of the incident: that week's papers had already gone to press. It was not until the issues dated 11 December that they could offer more sympathetic coverage from a pop cultural perspective, and by then the Grundy Incident was old hat. There is a certain symbolic resonance to this fact: the music papers and the fanzines would go on commenting about punk, examining its ideas and refining its rhetoric, but punk was now out in the public domain, and as it developed into a mass movement it would move further and further away from their influence.

The tabloids had taken punk national, emphasising its more negative and lurid aspects for the sake of outrage and titillation. From now on, Caroline Coon's comments about 'outside punks' bringing the movement into disrepute would hold sway. By taking a stuffy, pompous, establishment stance, the predominately right-wing UK tabloids unwittingly created the ultimate Us and Them situation. Any teenagers who did not hold with the repressive dark age values and blatant hypocrisy those newspapers represented were now going to call themselves punks. And the hints they picked up on typical punk behaviour would come from those same tabloid punk exposés: wearing bin liners, swastikas, and safety pins (sometimes through their cheeks), and trying to look as ugly as possible while spitting, swearing, jeering and generally being obnoxious.

It would be several months before these new punks would be able to buy albums and so pick up from the bands' lyrics a first-hand idea of what punk was about. Even then, it would be all too easy for them to find reaffirmations of their negative stance in the nihilistic posturing that had so troubled *Melody Maker*'s Allan Jones back in August 1976. There was a comic mania about the Damned's presentation, but their more wantonly destructive and self-destructive side was echoed in Brian James's proto-goth songs about drugs and pain. The Stranglers, marketed as punks, and the first to score big with the new following, wallowed in sleaze and violent misogyny. The Sex Pistols introduced themselves with 'Anarchy In The UK', the initial impact of which owed much to Johnny Rotten's drawled 'dee-stroyyyy'. The negativity manifested in his habit of stubbing cigarette ends out on his arm was echoed by much of the Pistols' remaining repertoire, which – as Glen Matlock pointed out in *I Was A Teenage Sex Pistol* – consisted of songs whose very titles conveyed their singer's outlook: 'No Lip', 'No Feelings', 'No Fun', 'No Future'.

Not surprisingly, the Clash's would-be pro-creative message was initially swamped by the output of their contemporaries. The new punks were encouraged to be anti-everything: anti-establishment, anti-authority, anti-parents, anti-work, anti-education, anti-morals, anti-hope, anti-life. Sid Vicious would provide them with their ultimate role model when his introduction to heroin-addicted Heartbreakers groupie Nancy Spungen set him off down his rapid slide to oblivion.

There were problems that threatened to have a more immediately damaging effect upon the Sex Pistols and the punk movement as represented by the bands on the Anarchy Tour. Concerts were being cancelled even before the tour began. At that stage, though, the scale of the eventual devastation to the schedule could not have been guessed at, and preparations for departure went ahead as planned. At manager Jake Riviera's behest, the Damned were to travel in their own van and stay separately from the others in bed and breakfast accommodation, as befitting both Stiff's limited funds and the band's outsider status. Neither the Heartbreakers nor the Clash had any record company support, but their travel and board was to be taken care of by EMI, while their share of the receipts from the gigs would supposedly cover other expenses. Along with their managers, they were to travel in a coach with the Pistols, and stay with them in upmarket hotels. Also in the retinue would be a couple of people Malcolm had enlisted to make a record of the 'classic rock'n'roll tour': photographer Ray Stevenson (brother of Pistols' road manager Nils) and student film-maker Julien Temple.

When the tour party set off on 3 December, its initial destination had already been altered. Despite the objections of the Student's Union social committee, the Vice Chancellor of Norwich University had refused permission for them to use the hall on the night in question. Instead, the coach went straight to Derby for the following night's concert at the King's Hall. By the time it arrived, a total of five concerts had been cancelled or banned. Any thoughts the bands might have had of escaping the media and allowing the uproar to die down were dashed as soon as they checked into the Derby Crest Hotel. 'Cannot go to bar,' Rob Harper wrote in his diary. 'National press there.' Included among their number was a reporter from muck-raking Sunday paper, the *News Of The World*, who offered Malcolm £500 for an interview and followed the tour for the next four days. 'We thought, "Shall we go out there with syringes stuck in our arms just to get 'em going?"' Mick Jones told Tony Parsons the following March. 'Yeah, and the furniture seemed to have labels saying, "Please smash me," or "Out the window, please."'

On the following day, the 4th, the local council tried to arrange a private 3.30 pm viewing of the Sex Pistols in performance for its Leisure Committee to assess their suitability. Most accounts have it that Malcolm refused outright. Thereafter, the Pistols were denied permission to play, but the other bands were offered the chance to go on without them; and whereas the Clash and the Heartbreakers closed ranks and refused, representatives from the Damned made statements indicating that they would be prepared to do so. This latest failure to show solidarity would be given as one of the reasons for the Damned's eventual ejection from the tour. In truth, Malcolm's own stand was not quite so firm. At first, he agreed to the councillors' demands, and the 15-strong delegation duly turned up at the venue. However, a police escort was sent to accompany the Pistols there, and it seems that it was the prospect of having the sizeable press contingent photograph and report on this far more visual symbol of the band's taming that prompted Malcolm's refusal to let his charges leave the hotel. It was only after being kept waiting for over an hour that the council representatives withheld their permission and made the alternative offer. In the light of this information, it is difficult to see why the Damned – physically isolated from the other bands, and therefore not in constant contact – should have been castigated for what amounted to the sin of failing to keep pace with the change of policy from compliance to defiance.

The following day's concert at Newcastle City Hall had already been banned by that city's councillors 'in the interests of protecting the children'. Instead, the coach made straight for Leeds, where the bands were due to play the Polytechnic the following night, and the tour party booked into the Dragonara Hotel. By 6 December the rest of the tour was already in a shambles. It being a Monday, the music press were putting the following week's issues (dated the 11th) to bed, and were finally able to provide a different perspective on the drama. All three major inkies reported in some detail both on the immediate problems facing the bands on the tour and the other repercussions and implications of the Grundy Incident. *Melody Maker* proved particularly good at ferreting out the reasons given for the numerous cancellations, now standing at 13 of the original 19 dates. The final tally would be 16.

There was no longer much point in treading softly. 'This is pure censorship and a complete denial of the principle of free speech,' Malcolm told *Melody Maker*. 'I don't see why councillors should dictate to people what kids go out and listen to any night,' added Johnny Rotten. 'It's ludicrous that people who are 102 years old should be passing judgement,' Bernie Rhodes chipped in over at *Sounds*. Malcolm took it to the masses – or, at least, the local masses – that same day when he told a Yorkshire TV news team, 'People are sick and tired of people telling them what to do.'

That night, the Leeds gig went ahead as planned. Both the national and the music press were heavily represented. Caroline Coon was, of course, there on behalf of *Melody Maker*. Tony Parsons represented the *NME*. 'I've been going around for two days thinking Big Brother is really here,' was how Joe opened proceedings when the Clash took the stage at 8 pm, but his remark failed to ignite the crowd of polytechnic students. It quickly became apparent that most of the audience had come along in a spirit of curiosity rather than enthusiasm: they stood still, hardly applauded, and occasionally indulged themselves in some supposedly punky act, like gobbing, or the throwing of slightly larger missiles. It was not a reaction peculiar to the Clash's set: Johnny Rotten was moved to comment, 'You're not wrecking the place. The *News Of The World* will be *really* disappointed.' The music press reviewers also remarked on the apathy of the crowd, which turned what could and should have been a defiant celebration into an anticlimax. The music journalists gave predictably good reviews to all four bands, but their disappointment at the lack of atmosphere inevitably came through in their less-than-scintillating reports.

The gig originally scheduled for 7 December at Bournemouth Village Bowl was cancelled by Rank Leisure Services. So the tour party made for Sheffield, where a last minute replacement gig had been arranged at the University. Whether or not it would have been allowed to go ahead is debatable, but, upon arrival, the bands discovered that the PA truck was stuck in Berkshire anyway. Thereafter, they spent a frustrating two hours in the Union bar before making for Manchester, where the next gig was scheduled to take place at the Electric Circus in two days' time.

Prior to leaving Sheffield, with nothing more constructive to do to occupy his time, Malcolm paid back a few grudges old and new by throwing the Damned off the tour. The Damned had already played around the country, and had their own following. An album was in the pipeline. Rat Scabies for one believes that, at the time, Malcolm saw the band as the only real threat to the Pistols. Glen Matlock maintains that, while Malcolm viewed Bernie Rhodes as a sort of unofficial lieutenant, he could not cope with the idea of an outsider like Jake Riviera setting himself up in direct competition. Inviting the Damned onto the tour had caused him discomfort from the very beginning, and he had only done so because he believed the package needed their added pull. 'But once Malcolm got the infamy with the Grundy show, he felt he could call all the shots,' says Brian James. 'Really, he just figured we weren't needed any more,' agrees Rat.

Bernie was also kicking up a fuss about the Clash having to open for the Damned. 'Malcolm suddenly shoved us down the bottom of the bill,' says Brian, 'and it was because Bernie was in cahoots with him.' Malcolm never did anything for Bernie unless it suited his own purposes, and his juggling with the running order was intended solely to humiliate the Damned and provoke a confrontation, which it did. The reason Malcolm gave the press for dismissing them was their supposed treachery in Derby. 'At the time, it served the political purpose of stuffing the Damned and making us look unreasonably unhip,' says Rat. 'Which wasn't that difficult.'

It was not just the tour that was being affected by the aftermath of the Grundy Incident. Workers at EMI's pressing plant refused to handle 'Anarchy In The UK'; one of the country's largest retail outlets, Boots, refused to stock it; John Peel excepted, Radio One DJs were not playing the record; and this unofficial ban also extended to Radio Luxembourg, Capital Radio in London, Piccadilly in Manchester, BRMB in Birmingham, and Radio Hallam in Sheffield.

This was the background to EMI's Annual General Meeting, held on 7 December. When it was over, Chairman Sir John Read made the following statement to the press: 'Whether EMI release any more of their records will have to be very carefully considered.' This information slowly percolated through to the tour party, then at the Midland hotel in Manchester. Rob Harper's diary entry read: 'During afternoon learned that EMI have withdrawn money for rest of tour and want Pistols back in London to "cool out". What will happen now?'

What happened then was that Malcolm refused to heed EMI's advice, deducing that the ongoing publicity of the tour would at least keep the Pistols' chance of a future career alive, even if that future ultimately might be with a slightly more daring and supportive record company than EMI. The other bands agreed to continue as well, but more as a gesture of support than with the expectation of playing anything like the number of dates originally scheduled. It certainly wasn't because they were having a good time. Rob's diary recorded a few examples of high jinks in the early days of the tour which, had they heard about them, would have given the tabloids a little more to work with. A huge communal meal at the Dragonara on the 5th only just stopped short of degenerating into a full-scale foodfight. Following the Leeds gig, Jerry Nolan was so keen to play his part in a mass attempt to drown Johnny Rotten in the bath that he kicked a hole in Mick Jones's door. Further light relief was provided in Manchester, when the Buzzcocks – added to the bill to replace the Damned for this gig in their hometown – took the other bands to a local pub named Tommy Duck's. 'It was a place where local women donate their underwear and it gets stuck to the ceiling,' Pete Shelley told *Mojo*'s Johnny Black in 1996. 'They seemed quite taken with it.' But the dominant mood was one of sheer unmitigated *boredom*, with the bands being stuck in hotel rooms and on the coach day after day, besieged by the press, with all prospects of release through performance frustrated, and with nothing to do but drink. As Johnny Rotten told *Melody Maker*: 'We feel like a bunch of prisoners.'

On the morning of the 9th, the Midland hotel management asked the tour party to leave, requiring them to look for their third base in the Manchester area in as many days. A booking was finally arranged at the 'decidedly downmarket' Arosa hotel in Withington.

In spite of the hostile locals outside the venue, some of whom gained entry and started fights with ticket holders, the gig at the Electric Circus took place as planned. It was reviewed by Pete Silverton for *Sounds*. Although he believed that the tour was 'shaping up to be an all-time rock'n'roll classic', his examination of its component parts did not quite justify this statement. The Sex Pistols were 'visibly tired and disoriented by the happenings of the past week' and 'lacked a degree of certainty and concentration'. The Buzzcocks were dismissed as 'a second-rate provincial Pistols copy'. The Heartbreakers were praised but deemed to be 'in need of match practice'. Pete also remarked on how the audience seemed to be reacting to the media representation of punk and, indeed, to the presence of the media themselves. Predictably, there was some half-hearted pogoing and – despite the bands' objections – a lot of gobbing. Glen Matlock was hit on the head by a flying bottle. There did seem to be pockets of enthusiasts, however: Pete talked to a group of young lads who were already planning to form a band called the Stiff Kittens. Two of their number, Hooky and Bernard, would follow through: the Stiff Kittens became Warsaw who became Joy Division. Future Smiths vocalist Morrissey was elsewhere in the crowd.

Rob's diary entry described the Clash's soundcheck earlier in the day as 'really shitty and depressing. Quote from EMI press rep: "You really must get in tune and balance it properly. It sounded terrible."' On the night, according to Pete's review, the Clash were 'probably the best-received band'. After requesting that the psychedelic lightshow be turned off, they stormed through their full set, a flurry of furious sound and vision. 'The gig was *amazing*!' wrote an incredulous Rob. 'Encore, second encore.' 'Shitty soundcheck, brilliant gig,' he says now. 'Sometimes, the Clash took over. Other times they were just OK.' Pete took the trouble to give Rob the only full namecheck he received all tour, noting that he 'beat hell out of his kit and had lots of fun'. His greatest compliments were reserved for Joe, whom he had met previously when covering the 101ers for *Trouser Press* (the band broke up before the feature could be used): he likened his presence at the microphone to the image of Che Guevara on the popular early Seventies bedsit poster and declared 'I still reckon he's currently *the* quintessential English rhythm guitarist.'

Sounds' news pages of the following week reported that the police forced the coach driver to park a mile away from the hotel to avoid trouble. Yet more police had been stationed at the Arosa, just in case that trouble arrived. Some tabloid journalists had also been stirring it up with the management, and so – once again – the tour party was asked to leave.

The next week of the tour calendar looked particularly bare. On 10 December, the bands had originally been scheduled to play Lancaster University. The gig had been cancelled, but at least this time not for the usual reasons. According to Lancaster student and future Clash associate Johnny Green, a group of feminists had called a special meeting of the Union because they believed punk bands to be, not racist, as had the students at Lanchester Polytechnic, but sexist. An attempt to reschedule the earlier cancellation at Norwich University also failed, as did last minute talks with the Preston Charter. The gig on the 11th at Liverpool Stadium had fallen foul of the local council, who had also put a block on what was to become the leading punk venue in that city, Eric's. The original booking on the 13th had been at Bristol Colston Hall, but council opposition had seen it switched to the city's University, where it had also been cancelled. Rank Leisure Services had pulled out of another gig originally lined up for the 14th at Cardiff Top Rank – 'we had signed no contracts' – but a substitute venue had been found in the shape of the tiny Caerphilly Castle Cinema. With no hope of playing until that date at the earliest, Malcolm decided it was pointless running up any more hotel bills. So the coach drove back to London through the night, arriving at 9 am on Friday the 10th.

The pressure did not lift even then. Sophie Richmond's diary entry for the following Monday recorded arguments about money, and Malcolm's attempts to prise more from EMI. The record company was playing it cool. Also ongoing were frantic efforts to patch up the remnants of the tour schedule. The previous week, the manager of the Roxy in Harlesden had cancelled. Sophie and Malcolm tried in vain to line up a replacement London venue for the tour's finale, with the manager of the Rainbow in Finsbury Park among those who proved reluctant to offer shelter from the storm.

Inevitably, local councillors tried to ban the Caerphilly Castle Cinema gig on 14 December, but it was still going ahead when the Anarchy Tour party set off that morning. It was a long way to go to play a one-off show in a seated venue capable of holding just 110 people – especially with losses on the tour already estimated at £9,000 – but it was now a matter of principle. 'It's a piss-off, but we're not going to give up,' Johnny Rotten told journalist Brian Case. 'We're now bankrupt. But if we give up, no new band will get a chance to play again. Ever.' Brian – a sometime *NME* contributor – was covering the gig as the basis for a four-page examination of the aftermath of the Grundy Incident in the *Observer Magazine*: the first mainstream paper to attempt a balanced overview of the punk phenomenon.

The bands arrived in Caerphilly to discover that, although their attempts to have the gig cancelled had failed, two Labour councillors had refused to give up without a fight. Joining forces with members of the town's Pentecostal Chapel, they had arranged a carol concert in the carpark outside the cinema. 'That was insane!' says Rob. 'All these idiots denouncing us in religious terms.' Indeed, there was a distinct odour of witch hunt to proceedings. 'Are children's minds to be vandalised and prostituted?' frothed Councillor Ray Davies. Again, the bastions of the local establishment were not the only ones to have been affected by what they had read. Brian Case noticed that the seated audience seemed subdued and self-conscious, before finally responding with 'an unconvincing spit fight and some desultory pogo dancing in the aisle'. Talking to some of the audience members, he found their thoughts on the 'meaning of punk' consisted of phrases regurgitated from newspaper articles. Song lyrics remained largely unknown or only vaguely understood. More worrying still were some of the style accessories: bandaged wrists were the latest thing in faked self-mutilation and the swastika was by now ubiquitous. 'I've got pictures of Hitler in my bedroom,' announced Josie Rafferty. 'It's not that I admire him. I just like the way he shows all his wickedness and that.' More clued up was Steve Harrington, already showing some of the elan that would establish him as one of the crown princes of the New Romantic movement when he moved to London and changed his surname to Strange.

Following the show, it was back to London once more. The gig originally scheduled for 15 December at Glasgow Apollo had been scuppered by the local council who had revoked the venue's license for one night only. An alternative gig at Lafayette's in Wolverhampton had also been blown out. Although it had survived on the itinerary longer than most, the original gig on the 16th at Dundee Caird Hall had been cancelled. Sheffield Council had taken the 'unprecedented' step of banning the Pistols from the City Hall on the 17th; the replacement show arranged at Carlisle's Market Hall had met a similar fate. Southend Kursaal had been cancelled for the 18th; likewise a replacement gig at Maidenhead Skindles. Guildford Civic Hall had pulled out of the show scheduled for the 19th, but at least this had been replaced by a fairly safe bet in the shape of a second night at Manchester's Electric Circus.

In the interim period, the situation on the home front did not improve. According to Sophie's diary, influential American syndicated music columnist Lisa Robinson made derogatory noises about the Pistols, as did Capital Radio DJ Roger Scott. Tension in the band's office resulted in outbursts and a (temporary) walkout by Sophie herself. The Sex Pistols might have been saving on hotel bills, but the PA and lighting crews still insisted on being paid. Billeted in Earl's Court with very little money, the Heartbreakers were making mutinous noises. Nor were things appreciably better in the Clash camp. It was at this time that Joe returned to Foscote Mews to find renovators had taken over the ice cream factory and thrown all his possessions onto a skip. So he too moved into Rehearsals to share one room, a couple of blankets, one couch and the tiny electric fire with Paul and Roadent, which did nothing to alleviate the place's overpowering smell of old socks. On the 18th, members of all three bands, plus members of the Damned, attended the *NME*'s Christmas party at Dingwalls, where the attraction was as much the free food and drink as the entertainment courtesy of the Flamin' Groovies. At least this time there were no fights in the courtyard.

The following day, the coach set off once more for Manchester. Although there were no choirs and councillors lying in wait outside the Electric Circus, the audience did have to run another type of gauntlet. The venue was surrounded by old Thirties council blocks, about a third of which were boarded up, and – turning up for a rematch – the local hooligans climbed onto the roofs and rained bottles down upon the heads of the punks below.

Paul Morley reviewed the show for the *NME*. Back in July, at least partly inspired by the punk attitude, editor Nick Logan had placed an ad in the paper for 'Hip Young Gunslingers' to cover the new music scene. Tony Parsons and Julie Burchill had secured the staff jobs, but fellow applicant Paul had been offered freelance work as a consolation prize. Ambitiously, Paul attempted to describe the three bands on the Anarchy Tour bill as representatives of three separate strands of the rock tradition. His distinction between the Clash and the Heartbreakers was unconvincing, but the one he made between the Clash and the Sex Pistols contained more than a kernel of truth. For all Joe's attempts to distance himself from 'nostalgia bores' the 101ers, Paul saw the Clash as a hard rock'n'roll band, with echoes of Eddie Cochran as well as the Ramones, and (perhaps less persuasively) 'only a few steps removed from Showaddywaddy'. At the time, this did not sit well with punk's stated desire to forge something new; but in retrospect, it reveals that the musical and stylistic change of direction the band would take in 1979 was not totally unsignalled. Paul saw the Pistols as more of a pop group. Again, it was tantamount to heresy to make this claim for such a determinedly left-field act; however, at today's distance from the initial shock of the band's image and presentation, the pop sensibility in Glen Matlock's tunes is more than evident. In *I Was A Teenage Sex Pistol*, he acknowledged musical borrowings from Abba. Paul's other comments were more down to earth: he echoed Pete Silverton's appraisal of the previous Manchester gig, contrasting the Clash's energy and total commitment with the Pistols' evident weariness and resultant sloppiness.

On 20 December, the tour had been originally due to visit Birmingham, but the local council had banned the bands from playing the Town Hall, and a subsequent arrangement with the city's Bingley Hall had also fallen through. Instead, a gig was quickly arranged, and played, at the Winter Gardens in the Humberside seaside town of Cleethorpes. The following day, after an exhausting coach journey almost the length and breadth of England, the party turned up at Plymouth Woods Centre to play only the third date of the Anarchy Tour's original schedule. According to Glen, it was a great show, with all three of the bands going over really well to a packed and enthusiastic audience.

The following night had originally been scheduled for the 400 Ballroom in Torquay. It had subsequently been replaced by Penelope's Ballroom in nearby Paignton, with a second show at Plymouth Woods Centre belatedly tacked onto the end of the tour, on the 23rd. The Paignton date fell through at the last minute, and to save unnecessary hanging around, the second Plymouth show was brought forward a day. Unfortunately, it was too late to advertise it properly, and hardly anyone turned up. In her diary, Sophie Richmond – who travelled down from London especially for the show – estimated the audience at 'about 10'; in his autobiography, Glen reckoned 'six Hell's Angels'.

Each band took it in turn to get up onto the stage and play their set while the others watched. According to Sophie, the Clash and the Heartbreakers played 'brilliant', but although the Sex Pistols did their best to compete, they were bedevilled by sound problems: ironically, for once it was their own mix that was sabotaged – inadvertently – by their soundman Dave Goodman, 'out of his head on pills'.

Thus, after only playing three times in the first two weeks of the tour, the bands had managed to string together four consecutive shows at its close, but still had been unable to end on a high note. Even the national media had got bored and gone away, missing the opportunity to capitalise on the wild goings on at the end-of-tour party back at the hotel. Among several other incidents, Roadent had to be taken to hospital for stitches after diving in to the shallow end of the hotel pool, and the road crew got their own back on Bernie – who had been typically high-handed with them throughout the tour – by using his bed as a communal lavatory. The Sex Pistols were consequently banned from the premises for life. Photos of the evening's events later appeared in Ray Stevenson's 1978 book *The Sex Pistols File*, and again in his 1999 collaboration with his brother Nils, *Vacant: A Diary Of The Punk Years 1976-79*.

While the final gig was played in a spirit of mutual support, the punk solidarity it represented had long since evaporated. The tour's hothouse atmosphere had made it all too easy for personality conflicts to come to a head. According to Glen Matlock, Malcolm McLaren and the rest of the Pistols had never been too happy about his friendship with Mick Jones; Malcolm and Johnny Rotten in particular believed that the Pistols should hold themselves aloof from the competition. Glen and Mick roomed together for much of the Anarchy Tour, which invited comment. 'As they went up the stairs one night, Johnny Rotten turned to Strummer and said, "Good boys in together, eh?"' recalls Rob. Glen himself perhaps took the significance of this a little far in *I Was*

A Teenage Sex Pistol, where he mused on the possibility that his friendship with Mick was to blame for the deterioration of his relationship with the rest of the Pistols, ultimately leading to his departure from the band. As Malcolm, Steve, and Johnny have all been more than happy to point out on numerous occasions over the years, the reasons were entirely personal.

Glen repeats another claim that he made in his autobiography, that 'the Clash's drummer' – namely Rob – was also ostracised by the other members of *his* band. Rob concedes that no-one in the Clash made much of an effort to bring him into the fold, but counters that he himself, not being particularly gregarious, didn't go out of his way to mix either. As much of an individual as his predecessor, he did not attempt to ingratiate himself by toeing the punk party line: he even listened to Bob Dylan tapes on the coach. Hyperactive, he tired easily, especially on the relatively few nights when the Clash did get to play… In *Rotten*, Johnny backed up his claim never to have liked the Clash as a band by criticising their live pacing, stating that they would go so crazy at the beginning of their set that they would run out of steam by the end. This charge was not without foundation. For the first couple of years of the Clash's career, Joe seldom made it through a show without being reduced to a hoarse, sweat-sodden wreck incapable of playing guitar and desperately hanging on to the microphone for support. Rob was not only responsible for detonating the Clash's onstage explosion, but, unlike Joe, was also required to maintain momentum to the bitter end while playing – at Mick Jones's insistence – double time on the cymbals. Even the relatively short half-hour Anarchy Tour sets proved shattering for him. 'It was really loud and fast,' he says. 'I could play loud, and I could play fast, but up to that point I'd never been required to do both at the same time.' The upshot of this was that Rob did not join in with the after gig revelry, drank little, and tended to go to bed earlier than everybody else.

Although, in retrospect, he can believe that adverse comments were made about him, he was not aware of them at the time. 'Perhaps the only way their sort of gang mentality could deal with it was to typecast me as a one-dimensional nerdy sort of character,' he concedes. 'But they never said anything to me about it. Maybe Glen's hit on a truth, but if he has, he's exaggerated it hugely, particularly about the people not talking to me.' Perhaps surprisingly, he cites supposed junkie bad-asses Jerry Nolan and Johnny Thunders as being among the most open and friendly, offering advice and retelling amusing road anecdotes. Johnny Rotten also made an effort to be sociable. After the first Plymouth gig, Rob recalls him admitting that the Pistols sometimes found it difficult to follow the Clash onstage, something which no bona fide member of the latter band – or, indeed, any member of the general public – has ever heard him say.

The tour was the first opportunity for Mick Jones to meet Johnny Thunders, one of his idols. Glen does not recall his room-mate being particularly star-struck, though. Tony Parsons, another fan of the New York Dolls, does recall Mick commandeering Johnny backstage after the Leeds gig, but on the whole a distance was maintained between the two guitarists, as indeed it was between their respective bands. Age difference, road experience and heroin all contributed to the gap. Jerry Nolan spent the tour trying to kick his habit, so he tended to be wrapped up in his own worries. Johnny, a more dedicated adherent to the junkie lifestyle, was not above playing street-wise one-upmanship. 'Johnny Thunders would wave a syringe in the face of some uninitiated, impressionable shill,' Nick Kent wrote for the *Face* in 1986. '"Are you a boy or a man?" he would tease, turning the issue into a matter of puerile machismo.' That such behaviour rankled with the Clash is more than suggested by 'City Of The Dead', a song they would add to their repertoire the following summer: on finding that the Clash cannot tell him where to cop heroin, 'New York Johnny' sneers '"You should get to know your town / The way that I know mine."' The ultimate put-down for a band of would-be streetwise punks.

Money was also a significant issue on the tour. Since most gigs were cancelled, some of the rescheduled venues had much smaller capacities than the originals, and there was such a poor turnout on the last night, the bands made next to nothing from door receipts. The Heartbreakers survived December on about £20 a week, and had to borrow £5 from Sophie Richmond while back in the Earl's Court digs for the few days immediately preceding the tour's final leg. Joe had taken the stage in Leeds wearing a green shirt stencilled with the legend, 'SOCIAL SECURITY £9.70' – his weekly income – and Bernie made a point of informing the *NME* that other Clash expenses were coming out of the manager's own pocket. EMI had initially footed travel and accommodation costs for all three bands, but when they withdrew support, that burden fell onto the Pistols' shoulders, with such bills coming straight out of the band's EMI advance. Before, as Glen noted in his autobiography, it had seemed unimportant when the Heartbreakers made lengthy transatlantic calls to their girlfriends and charged them to their rooms. It had even been amusing when they and the other bands had made room service orders for food and drink, signing the bills Donald Duck. Suddenly, as far as the headliners were concerned, such behaviour was no longer quite so funny. As the tour progressed, the atmosphere between the haves and the have-nots became increasingly sour.

By the time it ended, the financial drain on the Pistols had levelled both camps out somewhat, but no-one was prepared to be particularly gracious about it. The Heartbreakers found themselves stuck in London, practically destitute. 'I bumped into them in the Ship on Wardour Street,' says Andy Czezowski, referring to the pub nearest to the Pistols' office in Dryden Chambers, which for that reason was something of an Inner Circle punk haunt. 'They were moaning and groaning about how they'd been fucked over by Malcolm, how he hadn't paid them all the money he'd promised, how they'd got nothing and they were hanging out in people's flats, sleeping on the floor, couldn't eat, and all the rest of it.'

The Clash came out of it equally poorly, as Joe told Caroline Coon the following March: 'When I got off the coach, we had no money and it was just awful. I felt twice as hungry as I ever had before.' Despite the better reviews the Clash had received – and, in the main, from non-partisan journalists – their dominant post-Anarchy Tour feeling was one of inferiority. 'I *hated* it!' declared Joe. 'It was the Pistols' time. We were in the shadows in the background.' Five years later, reminiscing about the Pistols and the Anarchy Tour with Phil Gifford of the *New Zealand Listener*, Mick would be considerably more cheerful when acknowledging the headliners' superior status: 'They were just great. The best. Better than us. What they did to an audience never really came through on record, and the papers never wrote about it fairly, but the energy they put into an audience was amazing.'

Immediately following the Anarchy tour, however, such generosity was conspicuous by its absence. At a Christmas Day party at Jonh Ingham's Notting Hill home – according to Jon Savage's diary account – there was little festive spirit apparent among a gathering composed of members of the Pistols, the Clash, the Damned and the Heartbreakers. With what must have seemed like the entire rest of the world against them, they still preferred to keep to their own tight little groups and seethe at each other for the duration.

The Anarchy Tour bands had not been alone in their suffering during the aftermath of the Grundy Incident: other punk and would-be punk bands soon found themselves deemed guilty by association. After withdrawing from the tour, for example, the Vibrators had set up a series of dates of their own, three of which were subsequently cancelled by promoters.

In early December, trying to find gigs for the totally unknown Chelsea had proved even more difficult for band manager Andy Czezowski. While still managing the Damned, he had told *Sniffin' Glue* of his desire to set up a club for the London scene that would fulfil the role CBGBs had for the New York scene. It was now more a matter of necessity than of vague ambition. Luckily, Chelsea vocalist Gene October had a friend who owned a club in Covent Garden, and he took Andy along to meet him. His name was Rene Albert, and the club he co-owned with a sleeping partner – a barrister, apparently – located at 41-43 Neal Street, had formerly been known as Chaguaramas. 'It was all 40- to 50-year-old faggots who were into Gene, who used to hang around this place,' announces Andy, breezily. 'It was, I think, the first openly gay bar run as such in London, but it had failed, and they had changed the name to the Roxy literally that month. It was not my name at all: we didn't like it, and it was hardly original, but they'd done it and it didn't seem to make much difference anyway. They didn't know a thing about punk rock. They didn't care what was on at the Roxy as long as the money was paid, because they knew they were going to lose their licenses imminently, anyway.'

The Roxy was not really suited to live rock music, being tiny, laid out on two levels, and consisting of little more than an upstairs bar area, a downstairs dancefloor and an office. Nevertheless, Andy gave Gene the go-ahead to set it up. Andy had met Barry Jones via the Damned, members of which band were regulars at 47A Warrington Crescent. 'Barry became a partner because he had a guitar, which he managed to hock in order to get the money [£50] to get the first night going,' recalls Andy. Although Andy maintains that he himself shouldered the bulk of the actual work involved in running the Roxy, Barry employed his artistic talents to design the flyer for the first gig, due to take place on 14 December, and continued to take responsibility for publicity when the club's life as a punk venue was extended.

For more practical help, Barry's ex-girlfriend Celia Parry was brought in to run the office, and Acme Attractions shop manager Don Letts as DJ. In his turn, Don volunteered his brother Des and his good friend Leo Williams to man the bar. This Rasta contingent was initially suspicious and contemptuous of the punks, but when some of the regulars showed an interest in the reggae he was playing – there being precious little recorded punk material available at that time – Don responded in kind. Having just bought a Super 8 camera, he was eventually inspired enough by the DIY ethic to film events at the club. He and his friends also made a more immediate connection with the punks when they realised they represented a hitherto untapped market for ganja, and began selling them Jamaican cone-style joints over the bar.

In the time between Gene October arranging the first gig and Andy paying for it and commissioning the publicity, Chelsea underwent a change of personnel. Gene October was ousted, Billy Idol became the singer, and a new guitarist was hired. The band also changed their name, to Generation X, after the Sixties book that had provided the quotation for the Clash's ICA flyer back in October.

Before the band played the Roxy gig – actually their second under the new name, following their 10 December début at the Central School of Art – Andy arranged a second Roxy show. This time it was a lifeline for the Heartbreakers, penniless in London following the Anarchy Tour. Generation X and support band Siouxsie and the Banshees – reformed around the nucleus of Siouxsie and Steve Severin – drew about 120 people for their first show, who were given flyers advertising the Heartbreakers' appearance. This number was close to being the venue's full capacity by any reasonable standards, but the Heartbreakers – being better known than Generation X – pulled in 300.

An application form for membership of the club had been included in the November-December issue of *Sniffin' Glue*. Andy was hoping to open the Roxy as a regular venue with a New Year's Day show featuring the Sex Pistols and the Damned. He had suggested the idea to Malcolm following the cancellation of the Anarchy Tour's Boxing Day gig at the other, larger Roxy in Harlesden, and before he learned of the Damned's disgrace. Even so, it looked for a while as though the Pistols at least would be playing the gig. 'We were talking and talking, and then, at the last minute, he changed his mind, which was typical of Malcolm.'

One of the reasons Glen Matlock gives for the decision not to play was the size of the venue, but the audience would have been larger than it had been at the Caerphilly Castle Cinema. Anyway, the idea behind the gig was less to do with attracting a big crowd than with defying the powers that be. 'All the papers were saying how they'd been banned, that the GLC was going to stop them playing anywhere,' says Andy. Rumours of a Greater London Council blacklist had indeed begun to spread. They were given some credence when the GLC forced the plug to be pulled on the Stranglers on 30 January 1977 after Hugh Cornwell defied a contract restriction at the Rainbow forbidding him to swear onstage or wear his beloved 'Fuck' T-shirt. Questioned by the music press, although the GLC were openly hostile to both punk and the Pistols, they denied the existence of any such ban. After the evidence was weighed, the Stranglers incident was deemed to have been an isolated one, almost entirely due to the band's wilful behaviour. Although it was true that fewer and fewer London venues were willing to book the Pistols, that was attributable to the managements of those venues rather than a local government conspiracy. As both Glen and Andy soon came to realise, Malcolm had decided to play up the idea of a ban for promotional purposes. 'It was a complete hype and a complete lie,' says Andy. 'The GLC didn't have those sort of powers.'

In addition, Malcolm did not like the fact that the Roxy was a punk venture outside his control. Andy Czezowski, like Jake Riviera, was not someone he could manipulate to his own ends. 'He felt, "This is punk: *I* should be doing this nightclub,"' says Andy. 'I have heard since that he had always wanted to run his own club.'

Shortly after Generation X's arrival on the London scene it was Andy's turn to find his services no longer required by the band. Jonh Ingham had been included on the press list for the band's first Roxy show, and liked what he saw. Now that punk had established itself in the national consciousness, he had ambitions to do more than just comment on it. He seized his chance to sweet-talk Billy and Tony, and before they played their second gig at his new club, the band told Andy of their plans to defect and join forces with Jonh and his managerial partner, Stewart Joseph from the Rough Trade record shop.

Andy was beginning to think that groups in general were more trouble than they were worth. He decided to put his full energies into running the Roxy. He rented the premises for three months, at £350 a week. 'Quite a lot of money.' In order to get the club off the ground, he still needed a guaranteed crowd-pulling band, so he approached the Clash to play the New Year's Day slot abandoned by the Pistols. According to Andy, Bernie was just as hung up on the idea of a punk Inner Circle as Malcolm. 'It was, "Me and Malcolm, we set this scene up, we're into the politics, the anarchy, we were at the revolution in Paris. Where were *you*?" I got this sort of vibe off them because I wasn't into this deep philosophy that they had about punk, which they made up as they went along. I couldn't speak to them about those things, because I thought, "This is all absolute shit!" It sold papers, it got bums on seats, but I think they tried to believe it.' Nevertheless, not having Malcolm's advantages – nationwide publicity, however negative it might have been, and record company funding, however short-lived it might prove to be – Bernie could not afford to be too stand-offish. The Clash agreed to headline the official 1 January 1977 Roxy opening night, thus beginning the new year with a highly symbolic act: stepping into the Sex Pistols' shoes.

10
CAREER OPPORTUNITIES

Rob Harper had not exactly bonded with the Clash during the December 1976 Anarchy Tour. Once it finished, he headed home without anything further being said about his continuing to work with the band. After Christmas, however, he received a call asking him to play the Roxy gig, and duly turned up for rehearsals. Like the others, he found he had a new song to learn. 'Mick said, "I've been working over Christmas while you lot've been lazing around."' 'Remote Control' is, in part, a direct response to the experiences of the Anarchy Tour. The lyric opens with an attack on 'remote control from the civic hall', and the 'meeting in Mayfair' is an allusion to the EMI's shareholders' AGM in Manchester Square. But it widens its brief to cover other examples of perceived oppression, recalling both 'Janie Jones' and '48 Hours' in its references to dead end jobs, the lack of leisure facilities, and the restrictions placed on those twin staples of adolescent life, noise and drugs.

Joe had already made allusions to *1984* in the coda to '1977', and on-stage in Leeds during the Anarchy Tour. Orwell's novel is again echoed in the new song's overwhelming sense of paranoia; or what might have seemed more like paranoia had the establishment's attack on punk not been so overt. In 1978's *Clash Songbook*, the lyric is illustrated with a poster reading 'BIG BROTHER IS WATCHING YOU'. Like Winston Smith in *1984*, the song's protagonist sees no means of escape and reconciles himself to unquestioning obedience. What saves 'Remote Control' from sliding totally into negativity and despair is the angry finger it points at the oppressors and their agents: not just local government, but also national politicians, the business community, and the police. At last, it seemed, attempts were being made to define 'Us' and 'Them'.

Sadly, the rush to introduce this topical material into the band's set made for another weak tune that detracts considerably from the song's impact. 'Round about that time, Bernie said to Joe, "Some of these songs are getting a bit soft, Joe. Can't you come up with something a bit tougher?"' recalls Rob. 'And he said, "Yeah, don't worry about it. I've got some tough ones in the pipeline."' This vote of no confidence in his recent efforts may go some way to explaining why Mick ultimately got to sing both 'Hate And War' and 'Remote Control' on the album. Thereafter, even he came to recognise the relatively poor quality of the latter composition.

Joe's Telecaster was in for repairs, so when he took the stage at the Roxy shortly after 9.30 pm, it was with a large white Gretsch-style semi-acoustic hanging around his neck. Even that could not hide the huge slogan daubed across the front of his shirt which read, simply and appropriately: '1977'. In the packed, sweaty, low-ceilinged club, the Clash thrashed their way through a frantic set. 'I had to have bandages on my fingers,' recalls Rob. 'I did myself in, and at the end I thought, "That's over, thank God!"' Unfortunately, he hadn't read the small print on Sebastian's poster, and nobody had bothered to tell him what was due to happen at 12.30. 'There was a second set, and I had to do it all again!' At least the punters got their £1.25's worth. 'Mega-gig, sold out, so great: that paid the first week's rent,' says Andy Czezowski. The Roxy was under way.

Soon afterwards, Andy received a phone call from Jake Riviera sounding out the venue on behalf of the Damned. Andy reminded their new manager that the band still owed him money. An arrangement was swiftly worked out whereby the Damned would play the club for free on Monday 17 January if Andy would give them a month-long

Monday night residency. It proved to be a lucrative deal for both parties. Word of mouth about the new venue ensured audiences of close to 400. The Heartbreakers drew similar crowds for their return appearances.

The Roxy's size would have limited its life span as a venue for such established bands. Fortunately, one of the more positive aspects of the publicity following the Grundy Incident was a deluge of new groups. As the Roxy was the only bona fide punk club in town, the spring of 1977 found it playing host to punk's second wave. 'The time was right and everything was right,' says Andy. 'I filled it up with other acts that were coming through, from Penetration to Slaughter and the Dogs, X-Ray Spex, the Slits, Johnny Moped…' He could also have mentioned the Adverts, the Cortinas, Eater, the Lurkers, Squeeze and Wire, among others. Most were from out of town; Wayne County and the Electric Chairs followed the Heartbreakers over from New York.

The Roxy became not just a venue, but – just like CBGBs – the base of what now passed for the punk scene. 'It was the core, the centre of the whole scene,' says Andy. 'Even though it lasted just a short space of time, it really did open up all these doors. I really do believe without a major club – even though we were tiny, we gave out the right vibe – the whole thing could have imploded. I think the Pistols and the Clash could have remained a left-field area of the pop-rock business, whereas, by having a central point, it actually became a movement and developed the whole thing. Unconscious, once again. It was genuinely *the* band hangout. Everybody played and everybody checked out everybody else. The Clash were always there, the Pistols. The Clash were friends of Don Letts. They would come down to listen to the reggae and just hang out and drink until the club closed at one o'clock. You came because, as a punk, where else would you go?'

Exactly. Although members of the Inner Circle bands did indeed turn up at the club, that didn't necessarily mean they were wholehearted in their endorsement. Even while the Roxy was still in operation, the Clash were prepared to articulate their doubts about the bands that played there. 'All the new groups sound like drones, and I ain't seen a good new group for six months,' Mick told Tony Parsons that March. 'Their sound just ain't exciting. They need two years.' In that same interview, Joe opined that things were just too easy for new punk bands. Talking to Caroline Coon not long afterwards, he was totally dismissive of both the current punk scene and the Roxy, which he described as a 'dormitory'. The last time he had been in the club, he had been so offended by the lack of energy on display that he had squirted tomato ketchup over the mirrored walls before storming out. 'The sooner it closes the better.'

Harsh words, and ones betraying complicated and even contradictory feelings. Like the Sex Pistols before them, the Clash had pushed for new bands and a new surge of energy, but when they got what they asked for they were no longer quite so sure they wanted it. Admittedly, some of the new groups were and would remain untalented bandwagon-jumpers, but by no means all of them were as one-dimensional as the Clash's appraisals suggested. Rough-and-ready as performers and musicians these bands may have been, but the Clash – who had been together for little over nine months when they made their comments – were not that much more advanced themselves. And wasn't the whole point of the DIY ethic that such things didn't matter? The new bands might well have needed to gain some experience, but that was exactly what they were setting out to do by playing the Roxy.

Similarly, the Clash, like the Pistols, had always said they wanted the punk movement to grow, but now it was beginning to do so they were unhappy with the people it was attracting. True, they had not anticipated the influence of the tabloids' twisted version of what punk was all about; but one cannot help suspecting an element of elitism in their attitude to what Glen Matlock dismisses as 'the safety-pin and bin-liner brigade'. Following the ICA ear-lobe incident, Shane MacGowan had started to run Sid Vicious a close second as Most Famous Punk Scenester, even being identified as such on the front cover of *Sounds*. In a 1986 *ZigZag* interview, he summed up the general feeling among his contemporaries about the post Grundy Incident days: 'One thing that's got to be pointed out about the original punk scene is that it was extremely elitist, like the mod scene in the early Sixties. The whole thing was basically created by the beginning of 1977, and anyone who got into it after that was just a pile of shit, in terms of the way people thought.'

Many of the original punk followers had themselves started bands by the turn of the year. The mass-media interest saw off the remaining soul boy followers, and also the style-obsessed and unrepentantly elitist art school types like Alan Drake. Some old faces did continue to hang around. As far as hard-line Sex-clothed poseurs like Marco Pirroni were concerned, though, even the presence on the scene of a drunken slob like Shane MacGowan was symptomatic of a general decline.

Joe's passionate denunciation of the Roxy also smacks of a snobbish reluctance to accept as bona fide punk anything not conceived or controlled by the Inner Circle. The Clash might have opened the club, but they never played there again. Initially, there was a practical reason for this – the lack of a committed drummer – but it did not apply for the full duration of the Roxy's existence. Until they filled the vacancy, however, former movers and shakers the Clash were forced to be mere spectators at somebody else's show, and they evidently found it hard to take. They had yet another reason for disliking the Roxy: all a record company looking to snap up a punk band needed to do was turn up there with a contract. The publicity generated by the Grundy Incident and its aftermath meant more labels were indeed sniffing around for their own pet punks. The Clash felt a mixture of envy and irritation about the lack of dues-paying involved, just as the Pistols had with the Clash.

It was 1999 before Joe relented. In *Westway To The World* – directed, it is perhaps important to note, by former Roxy DJ Don Letts – he admitted the Roxy had been a good place to hang out, and that 'the punk-reggae interface' it encouraged had proved essential for the progression of punk.

That the Clash were still suffering for their art in the early part of 1977 was supposedly evidenced by their paleness, skinniness, grubbiness and general aspect of extreme poverty. The sub-title for Caroline Coon's November 1976 interview had been 'Clash: Down And Out And Proud.' Talking to her again in March 1977, Joe looked back and said, 'A lot of the time me and Paul did nothing else but wonder where our next meal was coming from. We were hungry all the time.' The impression given by such remarks – backed up the anecdote about Paul's flour-and-water paste snack – was that they were living one step up from rough in their decrepit rehearsal room, soldiering bravely onward despite being snubbed by an unheeding music business.

Matters were not really quite so hopeless. The band's preferred drug explains both the weight loss and pallor. Speed burns up calories, which is why amphetamines were prescribed as slimming aids in the early Sixties, and it keeps users awake, promoting a nocturnal lifestyle. Hence the lines from the summer 1977 song '(White Man) In Hammersmith Palais': 'I'm the all night drug-prowling wolf / Who looks so sick in the sun.' Joe still chose to think of his Social Security Giro cheque as a 'prescription' for drugs – as he describes it in 'Career Opportunities' – rather than money to spend on food. Admittedly, people caught in the poverty trap are, if anything, more in need of escapism than the better-off and fully occupied... But the Clash members were not really caught in such a trap. Mick was still living at home with his Nan, and at least being fed and getting his washing done. As for the others, Sebastian Conran is right when he says their lifestyle was a matter of choice. Paul had two sets of parents living within daily travelling distance of Rehearsals. He was too proud to sign on, but he was more than happy to be helped out by his girlfriend Caroline Coon. A telling scene, re-enacted a year later for the film *Rude Boy*, had Paul, the Bit of Rough, sneaking money from her purse. Caroline also had her own flat. Joe was not forced to be a lone wolf, either. Although he told Caroline he did not believe in love during a March 1977 interview, he was still (apparently not so) romantically involved with Palmolive. He could have squatted somewhere slightly more salubrious with her; or indeed, with any of his erstwhile friends from the Maida Hill squatting community.

Whether self-imposed or not, the lifestyle Paul and Joe felt they needed to live in order to be part of the Clash was a hard one. Its privations were not solely physical, either. The polygraph lie detector works on the principle that it is more taxing to fabricate a story than to tell the truth. The Clash genuinely wanted to embody the myth that was growing around them, but to do so essentially involved living a lie. Of all the band members, Joe was the one who had made the most effort to reinvent himself, not only adopting his punk persona, but also keeping his previous life at arm's length. And that was not all. 'He had to get himself into a miserable state to be able to write,' says Sebastian. 'Happy people don't create anything,' Joe himself confirmed when talking to *Musician*'s Vic Gabarini in 1981. 'I find creation hinges on being well fucked-up.' It was a tough discipline, making for a lonely, stressful existence.

By the early part of 1977, it was beginning to take its toll. In addition to using speed, Joe was drinking copious amounts of Special Brew and, as a consequence, behaving erratically. His ketchup-flinging flare-up at the Roxy was by no means an isolated incident. In a July 1978 *NME* feature, Chris Salewicz referred back to 'the days when those close to the band would tell you that "the real problem in the Clash is Joe Strummer", the days when Joe would be found lying drunk in the gutter outside Dingwalls with rain water washing into his mouth'.

Some of Joe's antics verged on the kamikaze, as his alter ego 'Albert Transom' recalled in the booklet accompanying *The Story Of The Clash, Volume 1*. Already, the ted-punk violence augured by the ULU gig had developed into full scale running battles on Saturday afternoons down the Kings Road. There were also more random assaults by representatives of one sub-culture upon the other whenever their paths should happen to cross. Against this background, Joe chose to grease his hair back, dress up in ted gear, and take a besotted and similarly attired Sebastian along with him on visits to known ted pubs and haunts. Sebastian recalls these trips all too well. 'I remember going with Joe to a teddy boy gig, dressed up and hoping we wouldn't get rumbled. And then someone said to Joe, "Oi, I recognise you! You're Woody from the 101ers. Bloody great band! What you doing now, then?" We were *shitting* ourselves!' After that narrow escape, still dressed up as teds, the duo went for a late drink at the Roxy. 'Really, we were *asking* to get beaten up,' says a retrospectively appalled Sebastian.

If that were the case, Joe got his wish in February. Although the rock stars' haunt was supposedly against everything punk stood for, some of the more recognisable punk faces had taken to going along to the Speakeasy after the Roxy shut. As he claimed in *Rotten*, Johnny Rotten had befriended a ted who was also 'a Millwall football hooligan', 'a big fat motherfuck' and 'real hard'. In Johnny's typically gloating version, the ted took against Joe for being a working class fake, got him in the toilet at the Speakeasy, and 'absolutely pummelled' him. 'Soon after Joe was going on about being beaten up by gangs of teds.' It is true that Joe mythologised the incident. The following month, he told Tony Parsons, 'I had a knife with me, and I shoulda stuck it in him, right? But when it came to it, I remember vaguely thinking that it wasn't really worth it, 'cause although he was battering me about the floor I was too drunk for it to hurt that much, and if I stuck my knife in him I'd probably have to do a few years.' His account may have been so much macho posturing, but there was no mention of 'gangs of teds', just one 'giant, psychotic teddy boy', which tallies with Johnny's own description. Among other minor injuries, Joe lost part of a front tooth, which didn't do much for his already sibilant vocal delivery.

Even accepting for a moment that Joe and the rest of the Clash had no choice about living such a desperate, hand-to-mouth existence, it was not as though there were no escape in sight. They had prospects. 'I continued to pursue them, irrespective of what Jim Crook said to me,' says Chris Parry. 'As far as Bernie Rhodes and the band were concerned, when they went on the Anarchy Tour, they were going to be signed to Polydor. We were sending telegrams to the Clash wishing 'em luck, and we had a deal in place. I just needed to get Jim Crook to sign it off, and he wouldn't.'

Since returning from the Anarchy Tour, Bernie and the band had been doing their best to speed up the decision-making process. Being in such close contact with Malcolm over the preceding month had provided Bernie with the chance to exploit the latter's contacts, one of these being Julien Temple. At Malcolm's behest, Julien had filmed on- and off-stage highlights of the Anarchy Tour. Some of this footage was ultimately incorporated in 1979's posthumously released Sex Pistols movie, *The Great Rock'n'Roll Swindle*, directed by Julien and telling Malcolm's fictionalised version of the band's story, and 20 years later, Julien would use more in his own Pistols documentary, *The Filth And The Fury*.

Julien had been brought up on a council estate in St John's Wood, a fairly salubrious part of north London. After grammar school, he had gone on to Cambridge University. After completing his degree in 1975, he had enrolled at the National Film and Television School in Beaconsfield, located 25 miles north west of London. Happening upon the punk scene at a relatively early stage, he had abandoned his other projects in favour of unofficially documenting the phenomenon using the school's equipment. Bernie learned that not only did the Film School own a film studio in Beaconsfield's Station Road, but also an 8-track sound studio. Access was easy and supervision non-existent. For Bernie – always vigilant when it came to the possibility of free and freely rendered assistance in furthering the Clash's career – it represented an irresistible opportunity.

Unfortunately, the Clash still had no drummer. For the same reasons he gave prior to being persuaded to play the Anarchy Tour, Rob Harper had left immediately following the Roxy gig. Bernie phoned Terry Chimes, and the ever amenable drummer agreed to sit in as a one-off favour. He and the rest of the Clash duly made their way to Beaconsfield. Julien filmed the recording session and stills were also taken, but – as inter-song conversational snippets captured on a bootleg tape of proceedings reveal – far more attention was paid to sound than vision. Bernie was not averse to getting some potential promotional footage of the band in the can, but filming was little more than a smokescreen for covert recording. This was another opportunity to capture the true spirit of the Clash for the benefit of Polydor, and whoever else might be interested.

After the bad experience with Guy Stevens, the band had decided they wanted something closer to their live sound. The Pistols had done the bulk of their recording to date with live soundman Dave Goodman. Taking a leaf out of their book, and also living up to the DIY ethic, the Clash installed Micky Foote in the control room. Or rather, Bernie did: the between-take chatter has Mick Jones loudly expressing both surprise and dismay at this turn of events. The rest of the dialogue could give the infamously bad-tempered and expletive-strewn Troggs Tapes a run for their money. Mick whines about everything else, too: his new, enforced short haircut (this time genuinely close-cropped), being hungry, being broke, and being told by Joe to shut his face for complaining. His one halfway constructive comment is a suggestion to lose part of a Paul Simonon bass line. Joe snarls at Mick, objects at length to being asked by Micky to do a second take, and then almost immediately does a 360 degree turn and demands better and more frequent instruction from the unfortunate soundman. After some terrible boogie-woogie piano playing, everyone takes it in turn to rubbish the in-studio sound-quality.

Partly because they were consciously trying to improve upon their Polydor demos, and partly because Terry was unfamiliar with the more recent songs, the band recorded the same selections they had with Guy Stevens: 'London's Burning', 'White Riot', 'Career Opportunities', '1977', and an incomplete (that is, instrumental only) 'Janie Jones'. The one addition was old standby 'I'm So Bored With The USA'. Joe had finally got around to writing a full lyric, albeit an inchoate version of the one that would grace the band's début album. This early effort works up a head of steam about tasteless baseball shirts and soporific West Coast music – in which context the lines, 'I'll salute the new wave / And I hope nobody escapes' – make more immediate sense than they do on the album version. The band would insist the revised version of the song was not anti-American, but instead opposed to American imperialism, both literal and cultural. The Beaconsfield version is just plain anti-American. For Joe, in truth besotted with both America and American culture, it was so much punk method acting.

Overall, despite the band's expressions of dissatisfaction during recording, the Beaconsfield demos were far more aggressive and impressive than the Guy Stevens efforts. They may well have helped sway opinion at Polydor: by mid January Chris Parry had won approval, and was in a position to formalise a deal. Now it was Bernie's turn to delay, much to Chris's frustration. 'I'd say something to him, and it was always, "I've got to think about that." And I'd say, "Bernie, you're thinking too much! It's pretty straightforward." And he'd say, "Oh, you can never think *too* much."'

Bernie had good reason to stall. On 4 January, one of the Sex Pistols had been sick at Heathrow Airport, resulting in another flurry of tabloid activity. Two days later, EMI had finally terminated the band's contract, shortly afterwards handing over £30,000, the balance of the recording and publishing advances, making the total paid to the Pistols since 8 October 1976 £50,000. Almost immediately, Malcolm opened negotiations with several other record companies, including A&M, CBS, and Warner Bros. The bands involved might not have found the Anarchy Tour conducive to ongoing friendships, but that venture had demonstrated to Malcolm that Bernie could be a useful ally, after all. As ever, when not a hundred per cent sure of himself, he began to think there might be safety in numbers. Discussions took place about the possibility of keeping the Anarchy Tour bands together under some kind of joint management and recording deal.

The two managers brought out the more Machiavellian aspects of each other's characters. They decided that their first priority should be to exert more control over their respective bands, certain members of which they believed to be getting ideas above their station. Loathed by Johnny Rotten and unpopular with the rest of the band, Glen Matlock was starting to express his resentment at being treated like a pariah. Glen had written almost all the band's tunes to date, but when it came to a stand-off between the bassist and the singer, he was the expendable one. Bernie had varying degrees of trouble with all three of his charges. Mick was increasingly dominant in the musical department, Joe's charisma was such that he appeared to have assumed leadership of the band in all other areas, and Paul's pranks and open mockery undermined the manager's supposed authority. In an attempt to assert himself, Bernie held a meeting in the Ship during which he told the Clash he wanted 'complete control'. Joe and Paul's immediate response was to burst into hysterical laughter.

Without bothering to consult their respective bands, Bernie and Malcolm came to the conclusion that a straight swap of bass players would be a mutually beneficial solution. Whether this would have actually come to pass had their alliance continued is debatable. That the possibility of Paul moving over to the Sex Pistols was at least discussed was confirmed by the Clash in a late 1978 interview with the *NME*'s Nick Kent. However, when Glen left the Pistols early in February 1977, Johnny Rotten insisted that he be replaced by Johnny's old friend Sid Vicious. Sid had been singing and playing rudimentary bass with rehearsal band the Flowers of Romance. At various times the personnel also included Joe's girlfriend Palmolive on drums, and no fewer than three guitarists: Mick's girlfriend Viv Albertine, former Clash member Keith Levene, and *Sniffin' Glue*'s Steve Walsh. Sid's method of learning his instrument was identical to his friend and former squatmate Paul's: playing along to Ramones records.

As for the other part of the exchange: Glen believes he was sounded out about it in a roundabout way by Joe and Mick shortly before he officially left the Pistols on 24 February. In the absence of a firm offer, Glen went on to form the Rich Kids with one-time Pistols guitarist candidate Steve New, and one-time Clash drummer candidate Rusty Egan. Later in the year, Mick – himself a one-time Pistols candidate, had he but known it – would help out on guitar for a couple of live shows. This was never intended as anything but a stop-gap measure until Glen could secure the services of his first choice guitarist and co-vocalist: that other one-time Pistols candidate, Midge Ure.

While personnel questions regarding the Clash and the Sex Pistols were still being mulled over, the managers did some market research about the possibility of setting up a recording equivalent of the Anarchy Tour package. Only without the complications offered by the increasingly bothersome Heartbreakers. 'At one point Malcolm and Bernie both came up to me and said, "Well, what we think might be the best thing to do is, maybe we should both go to the same record company,"' says Chris Parry. '"That way we might get understood."' The Sex Pistols had already trifled with Polydor's affections once, however, and their stock was too low to make the pitch viable there. Instead it was tried out on Maurice Oberstein, head of CBS UK. 'Bernie said to him, "What we want to do is start a label," and Oberstein said, "That's interesting,"' says Glen Matlock. 'And he went away and thought about it, and phoned Bernie up and said, "Right you are: I'm going to give you £100,000 to do it."' Like the other members of both bands, Glen was unaware of this at the time, but Bernie finally let him in on the secret when they worked together briefly in the late Eighties. Bernie and Malcolm held a final meeting about the planned joint venture on 18 January. When it came to the crunch, though, Malcolm just could not bring himself to accept anything less than sole command. 'Malcolm didn't want to be one of the pack,' says Glen. 'He wanted to be ahead of the pack. So that went down the dumper.'

Malcolm was aware that by now most record companies were interested less in the tabloids' condemnation of punk than in the publicity value that condemnation gave the movement. He knew that if he bided his time he would be able to pick and choose his own deal for the Sex Pistols. Most of the other first wave bands had already signed contracts and released singles. A&R men were already sniffing around the second wave bands at the Roxy. If the Clash were not to be left out in the cold, it was time for Bernie to make his move. And, although the band had laughed at the idea of his taking complete control in other areas, it turned out to be entirely Bernie's move. 'To be honest, I'm a total idiot in business affairs, more so then, and I'm really dumb and naive now. I'd freely admit I didn't know what the fuck was going on,' Joe, in confessional mode, told the *NME*'s Paul Morley in 1979. 'When Bernie said we were going to sign to Polydor, I just left it all to him, and I just thought, "Fucking great, we can put out a record."'

In a report accompanied by a still from the Beaconsfield recording session, the 22 January issue of *Melody Maker* reported that a Clash deal was imminent. The suggestion was that it would be with Polydor. Sophie Richmond's diary entry for 26 January revealed that there had been a last minute change of plan: 'Bernie has signed with CBS. Poor old Polydor – again.' Very few people were aware there had been previous contact between Bernie and Maurice Oberstein, and the last minute switch took almost everyone by surprise. In the *Clash On Broadway* booklet, Mick admitted that even the Clash themselves were kept in the dark until it was time for them to append their signatures. Bernie simply phoned them up and told them to be over at CBS's Soho Square offices in half an hour. 'It was January 27, 1977: that was the day we signed to CBS,' Joe told *Melody Maker*'s Ted Mico 10 years later. 'I forget my birthday, but I never forget that date.' Yes, he does: it was 25 January.

Poor old Polydor, indeed. And, especially, poor old Chris Parry. He had pursued first the Pistols and then the Clash for the best part of six months, and been left with nothing. Once again, though, he was urged to pick himself up and move on to the next most likely proposition. 'It was Shane MacGowan who came to me and said, "Don't worry about it, Chris. There's a great fuckin' band playing at the Marquee you should see." So I went to see the Jam playing, and we took it from there.' This time, Chris impressed the need for rapid action upon his colleagues at Polydor – Chiswick were in the process of negotiating a deal with the band – and the Jam were snapped up immediately for a mere £6,000. Although the contract was subsequently renegotiated, it still turned out to be one of the best bargains Polydor ever got.

The angry political edge Paul Weller's songwriting had recently taken on was very much Clash-influenced, as Paul admitted to Paolo Hewitt for his Jam biography, *A Beat Concerto*: 'I sort of meddled in politics. I really just followed the Clash and I didn't really know what the fuck I was on about.' The Jam's singles would fare much better than those of the Clash in the domestic market. As Paul Weller's writing matured, the Jam would ultimately also take over from the Clash as the darlings of the UK music press and – if polls are any indication – their readership. All this helped to fuel the rivalry between the two bands. The Jam's first few records would be produced by the Polydor in-house team of Chris Parry and Vic Smith, the engineer who had worked on the Clash demos. The latter would take over as the band's sole producer – elongating his name to Vic Coppersmith-Heaven – when Chris Parry went off in late 1978 to found his own label, Fiction. From there, Chris would launch the immensely successful career of the Cure.

There was much speculation about the details of the Clash's contract with CBS. In November 1978, the *NME*'s Steve Clarke disclosed that Polydor had offered the band an advance of £25,000, plus free recording costs. Chris Parry confirms that the January 1977 offer was indeed much the same size as the one made to the Sex Pistols four months earlier. A lot had changed since then, though, with the publicity value of the Grundy Incident having upped the ante considerably. Bernie and the Clash were initially loath to reveal the size of the successful CBS bid. Rumours of a six figure sum continued to circulate until the band finally admitted to £100,000.

It seemed, and still seems, an unbelievable leap. True, according to Glen, CBS had already tabled the sum, but that had been for a joint Pistols-Clash label. Bernie had the advantage of knowing, roughly, what Malcolm was asking for the Pistols. (When the Pistols finally signed with A&M on 9 March, the overall deal was for £150,000.) For all that, Bernie's agreement with CBS was still an astounding piece of hustling on behalf of a nine month-old band which had played less than 30 gigs, most of them as a support act. Especially as CBS were still chasing the Pistols at the time, bumping the potential payout faced by the record company for the two-band package to over twice their original offer. At 50-plus years old, having spent an adult lifetime in the music business, Maurice Oberstein was a master of unsettling and intimidatory negotiating techniques. The question has to be asked: why was he prepared to throw so much money at what had every appearance of being a short-term style-led fad?

'They signed us up for that much money because they wanna try and keep us quiet,' insisted Joe that May on Radio One's *Rock On* programme. 'You watch: they're gonna attempt to muffle us up in the next six months so they can get on with their lovely little Johnny Mathis and Vibrators and Abba records. [After failing to sign the Pistols, CBS picked up the Vibrators in April.] I reckon they paid a lot of money just to silence us.' John Tobler voiced his scepticism that such industry intrigue existed. 'What do they need us for?' demanded Joe. 'I think they see us as a threat to their fantastic rivers of money, you know? They see us as something to block it up, right? So if they own us, and we haven't got any money…' At which point John interrupted to suggest that, if the Clash had already spent £100,000, then that was surely their problem. 'Exactly!' said Joe. 'They're training us to take a helicopter to the supermarket.'

At this time, CBS (short for Columbia Broadcasting Services) and Warner Brothers were the two largest of the six multi-national record companies which controlled almost the entire music business. Maurice Oberstein did not sign the Clash because he saw punk as a threat to CBS and its established artists, but because he saw no difference between the band and any other potential money-making proposition. Like all businessmen, when market forces denied him a bargain, he was prepared to pay the going rate. But that was not the whole story. Although an American, Maurice took his job as head of the UK division seriously, and objected to its poor relation status in the eyes of the parent company across the Atlantic. His personal agenda was to sign British and European acts and rub CBS America's faces in it by turning them into huge international successes. As he told the *Guardian*'s Adam Sweeting in 1993: 'It became my great joy to attend a CBS-Columbia convention in America, and have the presidents of Epic and Columbia [CBS's US labels] asking for my acts.' Punk bands might have been a risky investment, but what could have been more quintessentially British than a street-level London rock'n'roll movement?

At the time, Clash observers were more concerned about *the band*'s motives for signing to a major record company for so much money. Having not even been party to the deal, the band members found themselves having to justify it to both the music press and to fans who picked up on the critics' muttered asides about the Clash having 'sold out' to the establishment. They had two lines of defence, both of which Mick tried out on Kris Needs in March 1977. The first was, 'You've got to make records. You can do your own label, and not many people will hear it. This way more people will hear our record.' The second was that, despite CBS's investment, the band were still guaranteed complete control over creative decisions.

Mick would quickly come to rue the latter boast, but the former – that the band needed financial backing and an efficient publicity machine in order to get their message across to as many people as possible – was to be given regular outings over the next couple of years. 'If we hadn't signed to CBS, none of you lot would have heard of us. So stuff that down your gizzard!' Joe admonished a heckling audience during the May 1977 White Riot Tour. Two years later, he gave a more reasoned version of the argument to the *NME*'s Paul Morley: both Malcolm and Bernie were concerned that, without the involvement of major record companies, the UK punk scene might become as ghettoised as had the US new wave scene before UK punk's success gave it a new lease of life. 'CBGBs on the Bowery was how it stayed for five years. It never came out of there,' said

Joe. 'Our stuff and the Pistols' stuff was great. I don't want to brag, but it didn't deserve to stay in a hole in Covent Garden [the Roxy] for five years.' Bernie confirmed this position in 1980 when discussing the only other option open to the Clash with the *NME*'s Paul Rambali: 'An independent [label]? You mean a small business. If you don't have access to gain the means of production, whatever you do is peripheral.'

By June 1977, Mark Perry had handed over the running of *Sniffin' Glue* to his friend Danny Baker. The latter's editorial in that month's issue came to the Clash's defence: 'There's no point screamin' to the converted on privately owned/distributed labels that could sell about two hundred, is there? We wanna be heard, fuck being a cult.' It should be pointed out that the fanzine had itself recently moved up in the world to share offices with Miles Copeland – manager of his brother Stuart's would-be punk band, the Police – who, in March 1977, had launched an independent punk label, Step Forward, with Mark Perry as A&R man.

It was Mark himself who would prove the most vocal in his condemnation of the Clash's move. 'I was insisting it was up to bands like the Clash – that were very popular and were courting a lot of record company interest – to say, "No! We're not going to become part of the establishment, we're gonna do it ourselves." I knew it could be done. The Buzzcocks did their first EP themselves. [In late January 1977, the Buzzcocks released their début record, *Spiral Scratch*, on the self-financed label New Hormones.] We did the *Glue* without being part of a big publisher like IPC. I think the last *Glue* sold about 20,000 copies. Even if we take the Clash's arguments about wanting a bigger audience, distribution problems, and whatever, it's still possible. The Pistols had stirred this thing up. *They'd* made this thing interesting to a big audience, *they'd* made everyone look at us to see what was going to happen next. There was a massive audience for something you could have done on your own. I mean, UB40 proved that later with their own label [DEP International]. And yet the Clash go and sign to CBS.

'If you talk about just music, it doesn't matter – I've got loads of CBS albums – but if you talk about what the Clash talked about in their songs, then they completely sold out. If the Clash didn't believe, and didn't want to stick with, the ideas they were trying to put over, then they were the biggest bullshitters around. Eric Clapton wasn't, because Eric Clapton just wanted to play music, so let him sign up to whoever he wants and make loads of money out of it. But the Clash: it disappointed me immensely, and I said so. My big quote was, "Punk died the day the Clash signed to CBS." CBS were one of the biggest weapons and communications systems manufacturers in the world! This massive conglomerate. Basically, it's why the world's dying, because of industries like that. If you look at it in those terms – and I'm no longer that serious that I want to, but if you do follow my argument – they *completely sold out.*'

Joe gave his response to Mark's 'big quote' to *Melody Maker*'s Allan Jones in November 1978: 'The dirty fucking rat! When I heard that he'd said that, I was so annoyed, you know. It was like him saying, "It's all their fault. They let us down." Why should he hang on to us? Where's his own two feet?' Mark's own two feet had by then taken him from editing the fanzine he founded to talent-scouting for a small independent record label to forming his own avant-punk band Alternative TV. All were sound DIY or near-DIY ventures. (Even bearing in mind Miles Copeland's involvement, Step Forward hardly qualified as a record company in the same way CBS did, being pitched at a level somewhere between New Hormones and Chiswick.) Mark would halt production of *Sniffin' Glue* – despite the increasing sales – in September 1977 after just 12 issues because he felt it had served its purpose and was growing stale.

As Mark says, the Grundy Incident had already brought punk enough publicity to guarantee the Clash respectable sales on a self-financed or independent label. So it was not just for him but for many other thinking punk scene observers that the band's argument about needing CBS-style backing failed to stand up. Those who believed the band were responsible for – or at least involved in – their own business decisions, could not help but suspect that the Clash were suddenly placing old fashioned rock star ambitions ahead of their much-trumpeted political agenda. Of course, in reality, it was Bernie alone who was making those decisions. For all his radical claims, Bernie was as concerned with keeping up with Malcolm and the Sex Pistols as with knocking down the pillars of the existing music business establishment. Also, having reluctantly and somewhat stingily bankrolled the Clash's efforts so far, he was not uninterested in the financial rewards of signing to a major for as high an advance as possible.

As so much up-front money was involved, the CBS contract had none of the compensatory safety and support clauses the band might have enjoyed with a smaller advance, like guaranteed help with tour costs or – as with the Polydor deal offered by Chris Parry – free recording. Music business lawyer Don Engel has described a typical record deal as 'the most onerous, impossible, unfair contract'. The advance is not a payment, but rather a loan, recoupable against future royalty earnings. In the Seventies, a standard contract like the one the Clash signed with CBS required all the costs incurred by the band – living expenses, equipment, support staff, rehearsal space, studio time, hiring a producer, promotion, touring, and almost everything else – to be met by the band. This would not only eventually dispose of the advance, however large, but would continue to be a constant drain on the band's royalty account. According to Frederic Dannen, in his 1990 book *Hit Men: Power Brokers And Fast Money Inside The Music Business*, under the terms of such a contract only artists capable of selling millions of albums would ever see any more money. A massive 95 per cent of artists would not. 'The record company can make a profit off an album while the artist's royalty account is still in the red,' wrote Dannen. 'In fact, this is a frequent occurrence.' Once their £100,000 was used up, the Clash would be dependent upon CBS 'generosity' for further loans: more debt. Joe's claim about being encouraged to take a helicopter to the supermarket was not so fantastical after all. Keeping their artists in the red was how major record companies maintained control over their investments.

Bernie made sure that his own position was as secure as that of CBS. The contract stated that he was entitled to take his 20 per cent managerial cut straight off the top of the band's gross income. In other words, unlike the band members themselves, he was guaranteed a fifth of the advance, plus all future monies earned by the Clash, *before* other costs were met.

It should be noted that, whatever their hopes for punk or their own individual futures, neither Bernie or the Clash had any reason to think of the band as a long-term career option. The Sex Pistols' experience with EMI did not exactly bode well for CBS's ongoing commitment. 'Signing that contract did bother me a lot,' Joe admitted to Caroline Coon in March 1977. 'But now I've come to terms with it. I've realised that all it boils down to is perhaps two years' security. We might have an argument with CBS and get thrown off!' In this context, with a view to cutting and running like Malcolm and the Pistols whenever it might prove necessary or advantageous, it arguably made sense for Bernie to take as much money up-front as possible. As it turned out, having the Clash sign to CBS for a £100,000 advance was the worst thing he could have done to the band.

With Polydor, the intention had been to go into the studio immediately, and the band carried this sense of urgency with them when they switched to CBS. It was born of competitive drive and a need for topical relevance, two concepts that big business could readily understand. The Damned had already recorded their first album, which was due for release in February, the Stranglers were in the process of recording theirs for UA, the Heartbreakers were recording theirs for Track, and the Sex Pistols were still working on studio material with Dave Goodman ready for when Malcolm secured them a new deal. On top of which, a song like 'White Riot', with its references to the previous summer's Notting Hill Riot, was in danger of passing its sell-by-date.

'Robin Blanchflower, the CBS A&R man at the time, was the guy that phoned me up,' says Simon Humphrey, then a staff engineer at CBS studios on Whitfield Street in central London. 'He said to me, "There's a new band we've just signed. We're sending them over because we want to stick 'em in the studio straight away." I basically got the nod as the youngest engineer: he probably thought I was more suitable to do the punk stuff. I can't remember who came over. Joe, I think, and Bernie Rhodes, and they were kind of grumpy and not very communicative, but anyway, they booked in for the next day.' That was Friday 28 January, just three days after the contract was signed. The idea was to record 'White Riot' and '1977' over a three-day weekend session for the band's first single release, with an album to follow almost immediately afterwards.

As the need to record was so pressing, the Clash had spent the latter half of January doing their best to fill the gap in their line-up. A certain weariness of tone is detectable in the display ad carried in the classifieds section of the 15 January issue of *Melody Maker*: 'DYNAMIC DRUMMER WANTED for young professional Rock Group. Must look great, play great.' Once again, the anonymous band had been deluged with applications, and had spent much of the following week auditioning all those drummers who turned up and stuck around long enough to try out. Unfortunately, nobody had proved suitable, and another ad was placed in time to be included in the 29 January issue. Decidedly more buoyant, it read: 'POWERFUL YOUNG DRUMMER WANTED FOR NAME BAND. No jazz, no funk, no laid back.' This second ad hit the streets around the time Bernie secured the deal with CBS, which meant that the band signed to the record company as a three piece.

Turning up for an audition, Jon Moss was initially put off by the dirtiness and scruffiness of his potential colleagues-to-be. Then realisation dawned, as he explained six years later to *Smash Hits'* Dave Rimmer: 'I said, "You're the Clash, aren't you?" and Joe Strummer went, "How do *you* know?" And I said, "Well, it's written on the back of your jacket..."' Aside from illustrating the difficulties faced by the would-be anonymous Lettrist, this gave the Clash fair warning of Jon's far from retiring personality. Although asked back for further rehearsals, he was by no means the only candidate, and it was anyway too late to integrate a new drummer in time to record.

Both Terry Chimes and Rob Harper were approached to help out. The plan – hinted at in the following week's *National Rock Star* – was to use Terry on those tracks with which he was familiar, namely, the single and the bulk of the album material, and Rob on those songs written since the original drummer's departure. 'Bernie phoned me up, and it was like, "Come up for a meeting, and we'll all put our cards on the table and see who is in the group and who isn't,"' says Rob, 'And I said, "No, I've fucking had enough. Bye, bye." That was it, really.'

That wasn't quite it for Rob, though. The care he takes to give as balanced an account as possible of his time with the Clash stems from his irritation at the revisionism to which it has since been subjected. When Glen Matlock left the Sex Pistols, the bassist found his decision to go portrayed as a sacking. Thereafter his former group and manager vilified him at every opportunity. At first, the circumstances of Rob's departure were similarly altered. Before long, though, instead of being mocked or scorned, he found he had been written out of the Clash's history altogether. 'I ran into the Clash once or twice at clubs and things, and Mick said, "Oh, Bernie told me he'd sacked you."' Apparently, as with Terry, Bernie could not believe that Rob would walk out on him voluntarily. Only in this case, he altered reality to fit his idea of how things ought to have been. Rob may have been involved in one of the most celebrated rock events of all time – more than just 'a classic rock'n'roll tour' – but he was not mentioned in any further interviews, family trees, encyclopaedia entries or band histories, whether official or otherwise. Even when Glen Matlock's 1990 autobiography made reference to him, it did so without using his name. Only in 1991's *Clash On Broadway* booklet was he finally credited as the drummer for the Anarchy Tour. Until then, had it not been for one or two Ray Stevenson photos taken during the tour and at the 1 January Roxy gig, as far as the Clash and their followers were concerned, he might never have existed.

'The definite offer to join them wasn't there, but the possibility was there,' says Rob. 'I actually said to myself at the time, "One day you'll regret that you threw up this opportunity, and didn't just knuckle down and do what they wanted, walk how they wanted, play how they wanted, dress how they wanted and behave how they wanted, because then you could have gone around the world. And you've got to remember, years later, when you think those things, that there was no way that it was going to work, and that's why you didn't do it." I guess I *was* a bit cavalier with my opportunities back in those days.' True: in addition to passing up the chance to join the Clash, Rob turned down Mark Knopfler's invitation to help put together the band that became Dire Straits, and played roles of varying magnitude in the formation of the UK Subs, Secret Affair, and Adam and the Ants, for the last of which bands he even suggested the name. 'I've had so much of this, it means nothing to me,' he laughs. 'It's all just like fate, you know.' Since then he has played a variety of instruments in a variety of bands, but still maintains, 'The Clash were bloody good. Best band I've ever been with.'

As a result of Rob Harper's refusal to co-operate, the Clash once more had to rely wholly on the goodwill of Terry Chimes.

'Studios were a hangover from the Sixties, even in the mid Seventies,' says Simon Humphrey. 'We all had long hair – or aspired to have long hair, in my case – and we all wore cowboy boots and stuff like that. The British studio scene was a very cosy, insulated one that was full of old-time producers and techniques. We were all in love with the Beatles, and I'd grown up with progressive rock, Yes and Led Zeppelin. In the studio, we'd only heard the rumours about what was going on in the street, as it were. We weren't prepared for punk, and we didn't particularly fancy having it thrust at us head on. I must admit, I was viewing it all with a fair amount of trepidation. I mean, the girls at head office were terrified every time the band went in. They thought there was going to be a riot every time they walked through the door. None of us knew what to expect, whether they were going to burn the place down...'

In the event, his own fears proved unfounded. 'There was no smashing up of equipment, and they were reasonably civilised. But there was a vaguely unpleasant side to them. Personal hygiene wasn't of the greatest order. By today's standards it was all fairly tame stuff: a bit of swearing, a bit of rough and tumble. Nothing outrageous, really.' It was evident that the wariness cut both ways. 'They were suspicious of studios generally. They hadn't been in too many, and you've got to understand they were trying to knock down all the doors of accepted behaviour, which is why they didn't particularly want any old-school producers sorting them out, and they didn't want to do anything that was considered to be "what had gone before".'

For this reason, Micky Foote was once more appointed producer. In view of later difficulties between CBS and the Clash over their conflicting interpretations of the phrase 'complete control', it might seem odd that the record company should allow their new £100,000 investment to go into the studio with someone who was totally unknown and inexperienced. But representatives from the record company's A&R department were familiar with the Beaconsfield demos. These had informed them of two things: firstly, that Micky was apparently capable of getting the band the raw, basic sound the Clash defined as 'punk'; and secondly, that, as the A&R men themselves could not understand this sound, it was unlikely that any 'old-school' producers would be able to, either. 'Robin Blanchflower said to me, "We don't know what the hell it's all about, but they've got this *presence*,"' says Simon. 'The record company never showed their faces at all during the recording of the single or the album. They kept well away. I was given carte blanche to let them go in and do what they wanted.'

Immediately after the recording, Micky Foote explained to Tony Parsons why he had taken on the job: 'You do it yourself because nobody else *cares* that much.' In 1990, Bernie Rhodes informed the *NME*'s Stuart Bailie that it was in fact he, Bernie, who had produced (as well as written) the band's first album. During research for this book, more than one of Simon's former colleagues intimated that it was in fact the engineer who had been the 'real' producer. Although he does not wish to make this claim for himself, Simon effectively rules out the other two contenders: 'Bernie didn't really have anything to do with the recording process, to be honest with you. He used to say things to Mick, or Joe, but he never addressed me. And they would tell him to piss off anyway. They were always screaming and shouting at him. And Micky: well, he was *there*. I mean, he was really just the bloke on the other side of the control room glass. He was credited with the production, but you can't really say he contributed to it. He had the odd idea, I suppose.'

Simon and Terry's accounts of the band's initial approach to studio work suggest it was amazing anything was produced at all: the spirit of Beaconsfield certainly lived on. The band went into Studio 3 – which, Mick was ecstatic to learn, was where Iggy and the Stooges had recorded *Raw Power* – and set up as though for a live performance. This was not particularly rare in those days, even in a 16-track facility. 'But the idea was that you separated stuff off because, although it was recorded live, you still wanted some control over different things,' explains Simon. 'Then if the bass was no good, or something, you could at least have the opportunity to redo it. They didn't grasp that. The first time they came in – the first time I'd met them all – Joe put his amp right next to the drum kit, and when he played it was like, full blast guitar. You don't do that in a studio. You have it at the other side of the room, behind a screen, so you've got some kind of separation. So he was playing, and it was no good, because the sound was going right across the drums. I explained it to Joe, and he looked at me and said, "I don't know what separation is, *and I don't like it*." That was his opening shot.'

Terry recalls another early hiccup in proceedings: 'We were going great guns with the drums, got the sound we wanted, no problem. Turned to the bass, and had an immediate difference of opinion about how it should sound. I don't think Joe or I really cared much about which way the argument went, but Paul and Mick were not going to budge, either of 'em. We spent hours, completely unproductively, arguing. I just thought, "This is an incredible waste of studio time." And the engineer suddenly said, "Why don't we do *both* sounds and decide later on, at our leisure, which one to use?" So that was unanimously voted on immediately, and we carried on.'

Not all Simon's suggestions or opinions were so keenly received. It remained an uphill struggle. 'You had to be very careful about what you said. They'd be doing something, and you'd think, "Well, that doesn't sound very good," and they'd say, "How was that?" So you'd say, "Mmm, well, I dunno. I'm not sure it's right," and they'd say, "Oh, well, we'll keep it then!" Deliberately being provocative in a silly way. They just wanted to be in and out pretty quick, and they were hostile to anything that had been employed as a technique pre-punk. So, if there was like a harmony part, or a double-tracked guitar, or even dropping-in – you know, doing a little bit again because it didn't sound good enough – they'd think you were trying to polish them up or break down the whole punk ethic.'

Mick was more amenable than the others, being the band member not only most interested in the studio's potential, but also with the most emotional investment in the actual tunes. 'They were Mick's songs. Well, Mick's music, and Mick was the musical one. Terry, the drummer, was basically told what to do. I think it's pretty well known that Paul couldn't really play. There were quite a few bass parts where, I'm not saying Mick actually played the bass, but he showed them note for note to Paul, and Paul learned them parrot fashion. Paul definitely played his own parts, and I would say that, by the time it came to doing the album, he was beginning to show his own personality, but… he just did his bit, and that was it.'

It was Joe who continued to be the most troublesome. 'He was an incredible performer,' says Simon. 'It wasn't like he was in the studio doing it, he really was giving it 110 per cent at all times.' Unfortunately, out of his depth and resentful of Mick's relative capacity to adapt, he retreated further behind the gruff Joe Strummer punk persona. 'Joe's guitar sound was just *horrible*, it really was. Even Mick would say, "That is *terrible*, that sound!"' Knowing that Joe was still without a functioning guitar of his own, CBS sent over a brand new Telecaster from the shop underneath their offices in Soho Square. 'He just took the piss out of it. He certainly never used it. Anything that smacked of the establishment.' Nor were things any easier when it came to doing his vocals. Eventually convinced they would be better recorded separately, he remained extremely jittery about singing unaccompanied. 'He actually had to play the guitar at the same time as sing. We tried to get him to do it without, and he just couldn't do it. So all his lead vocals have got this unplugged guitar bashing away underneath. He also used to sing in a corner, facing away from us, but a lot of singers are like that. His vocals would be a one-off thing, like a straight-through performance. Joe wasn't really a singer in the accepted sense of the word: he just did his vocal, and that was it. There was no camouflaging or processing. He didn't take an interest in that.'

Although not always prepared to heed their engineer, the band proved suggestible when it came to advice offered by the friends and followers who accompanied them to the single session. Among them were Sebastian, Roadent, Frothler and Mad Jane. 'The Clash seemed to have this small group of middle class fans who followed them around,' recalls Simon. 'They were almost like rich kids who were hanging on to them. They liked the anarchic side to it. They would wander into the studio, and they'd be listening to the music, and they'd say, "I think it'd be really good if we had a gun firing here." And you'd think to yourself, "Christ, here we go…" And one of them would produce this gun. And I seem to remember him shooting it into the wall, and we recorded it. Of course, it didn't sound very good. And another day, they'd bring up a whole pile of corrugated sheeting from some building site. "What about if we belt this with a hammer?" This kind of stuff. So there was a bit of indulgence there.'

This was the origin of the sound effects included on the single version of 'White Riot': the siren at the beginning, the alarm bell at the end, the breaking glass, and what Simon refers to as 'the famous stomping overdub' in the middle. Sebastian's air pistol might not have made it onto record, but his feet did. Reflecting on the earlier suggestion that he might take over as band drummer, he says, 'My sole contribution to the rhythm section was, you can hear my feet stamping on "White Riot". We were all jumping around the microphone.' The single proved acceptable to CBS, although the band themselves were not overly impressed with the Studio 3 version of 'White Riot', believing the Beaconsfield demo version to be braver.

According to Simon, the record company was running on a minimum four-to-six week turnaround at that time, so the single was scheduled for the earliest possible release date in mid March. Under Bernie's direction, Sebastian was given the job of designing a picture sleeve, something which was already de rigueur for punk singles. For the front cover, he used a Caroline Coon photograph taken the previous November. It showed Joe, Mick and Paul with their backs to the camera, assuming the hands-against-the-wall position that had given the late Sixties radical group the Motherfuckers their name: from the police command, 'Up against the wall, motherfuckers!' The pose itself was actually copied from the cover of Joe Gibbs and the Professionals' reggae album *State Of Emergency*. The connection with repression in Jamaica was reinforced by the slogans 'HEAVY MANNERS' and 'HEAVY DUTY DISCIPLINE' running along the seams of Joe's boiler suit. The back of Paul's boiler suit read 'WHITE RIOT', and the back of Mick's shirt 'STEN GUNS IN KNIGHTSBRIDGE', both of which slogans related to the two songs packaged within. Less directly relevant was the large 'HATE AND WAR' slogan adorning Joe's back, but Sebastian got around that problem by blanking it out and superimposing '1977' instead. The overall effect was as clear an illustration as possible of Joe's oft-repeated claim that, rather than identifying *with* terrorists, the Clash envisaged the sten guns in Knightsbridge to be implements of state control pointing *at* the band.

In view of the escalating violence between punks, other youth cults and even 'straights', it was less wise of Bernie to have Sebastian reproduce on the back of the sleeve the provocative *Generation X* mods and rockers quote previously used on the ICA flyer. It was balanced to some degree by another quote: 'Youth, after all, is not a permanent condition, and a clash of generations is not so fundamentally dangerous to the art of government as would be a clash between rulers and ruled.' The latter was more than just a clever way of amplifying the signals given off by the band's name. The Grundy Incident had swollen the punk movement considerably, but it lacked positive direction, as had been testified by the confused behaviour of the audiences on the Anarchy Tour. Local government interference with the tour had likewise made Bernie and the band realise there was a real enemy to face, and it was no longer enough just to stir things up for the sake of it. The Clash were campaigning to win over a new constituency, hoping to persuade the nascent nation-wide punk movement to escalate from token teen rebellion to something that offered a more genuine threat to the status quo. Or, at least, they were hoping to persuade them to buy records by a band making those kinds of noises.

The Clash booked back in at CBS Studio 3 to record the album over three consecutive Thursday-to-Sunday sessions, beginning on 10 February 1977. The material had already been rehearsed to near perfection. 'Mick did all the arranging, put a hell of a lot of work into it,' Joe told Gavin Martin in 1999 for *Uncut*. 'In some ways, that's the most difficult thing: arranging when you've only got three or four elements.' Joe spent what little spare time he had in the two weeks between the single sessions and the first album sessions refining his lyrics. Most of the songs were tweaked slightly. 'London's Burning' no longer burned with boredom 'babe', but with boredom 'now', Joe trying to exclude as many clichéd Americanisms as possible.

The previously trite griping of 'I'm So Bored With The USA' was stiffened by some judicious pruning and the addition of a new first verse. Now, the USA was guilty of military and monetary imperialism as well as cultural imperialism. It made for a much stronger song, even if it did still carry a whiff of knee-jerk punk xenophobia. Ultimately, this was how most people still chose to interpret it, something which would bring accusations of hypocrisy down upon the Clash's heads when they began to turn their attentions to the American market in 1979. All three long-serving members of the band were called upon to defend themselves time and time again over the following years. 'That song is about the Americanisation of Europe,' Mick insisted when talking to *Rip It Up*'s Duncan Campbell in 1982. 'It's about the McDonalds and Burger Kings that we've got. It's about the American deployment of nuclear missiles on our island. All these things that we don't want. It's about the way America pushes around small countries, like ours, or any Central American country. It's *not* about being bored with the USA, because America is a very exciting place to be. We weren't saying, "We're not going to go," we were talking about the American imperialist attitude.'

The other lyric to undergo a substantial make-over was that for 'What's My Name'. While one or two lines that had been just about decipherable in earlier live versions do survive in the album version, Joe earned his songwriting credit by blending them in with other scattered excerpts from the mental diary of an alienated urban teen. The protagonist fails to measure up to social standards, suffers rejection, expresses his frustration through violence, is punished by authority and abused at home. This serves to confirm his outsider status – specifically, as a criminal intent on revenge against mainstream society – and his loss of true individual identity, as expressed in the title chorus and the terrace-chant method of its delivery. All in all, the overhauled song is a concise sociology lecture from the point of view of the subject under examination. Although perhaps a little overblown, it is also chilling; it would have been even more extreme in both departments had Joe, as originally planned, placed the juvenile offender 'round the back' with a 'flick-knife' rather than a 'celluloid strip': the threat of burglary replaced the threat of something unspecified but potentially much nastier.

During rehearsals for the album, the band took to fooling around with a punked-up version of the Wailers' early reggae single 'Dancing Shoes'. This was partly for their own amusement, but it was also an attempt to go one step further than the use of drop-out in exploring the reggae influence musically. It didn't quite click, and Joe was further put off the idea by Johnny Rotten, who was wont to declare that white people playing reggae was a form of cultural exploitation. In the studio, the band set up with relatively little fuss and began playing through their repertoire while Simon adjusted the levels in the control room. Soon bored of playing familiar songs, they started to mess around with another reggae tune. Junior Murvin's 'Police And Thieves', co-written by the singer and his producer Lee Perry, had been one of 1976's more popular reggae singles and a sound system smash at the Notting Hill Carnival. Murvin's high, pure voice added a despairing quality to his depiction of gangsters and policemen apparently intent upon turning Jamaica into a war zone. 'We played it through while trying to get the right sound and really started to groove on it,' says Terry.

The more serious business of recording the remaining original compositions in the band's repertoire began shortly afterwards. Or at least, eventually. 'Sometimes they didn't really talk to me, but sometimes they didn't really talk to each other, either,' says Simon. 'Quite often, Joe would turn up and he'd go, "Is anyone else here?" And I'd go, "No, you're the first one here, Joe," and he'd go, "Oh well, bugger that then!" and he'd leave. Then Mick'd turn up and repeat the whole process.'

Mick made the most effort to break the ice. The fascination with the workings of a studio that Brady had found so embarrassing during Little Queenie's Pye demo session was not without purpose. Not long afterwards, when Mick told Tony Parsons, 'There ain't no young producers in tune with what's going on. The only way to do it is to learn how to do it yourself,' he did so not in support of Micky Foote, but to promote his own ambitions. On a couple of the occasions when none of the other band members were around, he invited Simon over to the nearby Spaghetti House for something to eat. As recording progressed, he took to staying on later at the studio. 'Mick got into the techniques of guitar solo double-tracking,' says Simon. Joe remained uninterested and made little effort to improve the sound of his rhythm playing, with a predictable result: 'There's hardly any of his guitar on the album.'

Apart from an in-studio accident which resulted in the head cracking on Mick's beloved Les Paul Junior, the recording process grew easier as time went on. 'I think, once the initial suspicion had been got out of the way and they realised I wasn't going to be a pain in the arse, they saw they could make the album without too much trouble, learn a lot in a brief period of time and stamp their own mark on it,' says Simon. 'Our brief was, if they were happy, we were happy, and even if they didn't know the difference between an E major and an E minor, and wouldn't know if something was out of tune, and didn't want to do something again when you knew damn well they could do it better, you would always respect their ideas.'

One of punk's great concerns was the principle of Value For Money. It was a reaction to the inflated ticket prices charged by the dinosaur rock acts of the day. Just as entrance to gigs should be affordable, so singles should not have throwaway B-sides, and albums should not contain tracks previously issued as singles. In keeping with this philosophy, the Clash had earmarked two of their most memorable rabble-rousers for their first single. Unfortunately, this threatened to diminish the impact of the album. They side-stepped this problem by deciding to include a different version of 'White Riot' on *The Clash*. As Simon confirms, it was not another new recording, but a remix of the earlier 8-track Beaconsfield demo version.

The band's canon was further expanded in one of the midweek gaps between recording stints. Joe presented Mick with a new lyric, and Mick – back on form – came up with the music for the anthemic 'Garageland'. The lyric is Joe's reflection on the implications of punk's move from the clubs to the record companies. Dismissing any suggestion that the Clash's own record deal represents a sell out, he rubbishes the supposed attractions of upward mobility, and declares the band's intention of remaining true to its heritage (conveniently forgetting the occasional visit to the Speakeasy). The song's point of departure is Charles Shaar Murray's opinion, as offered in his 29 August 1976 Screen on the Green review, that the Clash were a garage band who should be quickly returned to the garage, preferably with the motor running. The reference is an ambiguous one: even as it acknowledges the band's humble beginnings, it is also a defiant retort to CSM, and a proud boast about how far the Clash had progressed in the intervening months.

In March, Mick told Kris Needs that 'Garageland' was to be placed last on the album, being the band's most recent composition and indication of 'where we're moving on next'. Although in itself a stirringly powerful song, both in the light of Mick's comment and with the benefit of hindsight, 'Garageland' can be seen as a bad portent. CSM's review had been both thoughtlessly flippant and unduly harsh on a band playing its second public gig – he was later to acknowledge as much and revise his opinion – but almost all the reviews the Clash had received since then had been positive to the point of sycophancy. Being mollycoddled by their friends in the music press had led the Clash to *expect* good reviews as their due. That they were still smarting at one of their very few bad ones six months after its publication did not bode well for their ability to accept criticism in future.

Furthermore, simply by existing, 'Garageland' flirts with self-contradiction: for a band to even consider writing that kind of self-referential song suggests they have an inflated idea of their own importance, something hardly concomitant with the garage band spirit. A Clash song about the problems of being in the Clash was a move away from the Everyman perspective of their other material in favour of a viewpoint that was specific and exclusive to the four – or three – band members. Joe has since defended

Clash songs like 'Clash City Rockers' as being tongue-in-cheek celebrations of self in the tradition of Bo Diddley, a performer famous for singing songs about Bo Diddley in a proto-rap bragging style as ironically humorous as it is self-mythologising. This may be true of that particular Clash song and several others, and there was certainly room for intervals of light relief between the band's more demanding communiqués. 'Garageland', however, cleaves more to the Mott the Hoople tradition of songs about the trials and tribulations of Mott the Hoople: sentimental self-aggrandisement with next to no irony or humour in evidence. At least Mott had been together and suffered hardships for three years before Ian Hunter set off down this particular compositional path; at the time they wrote 'Garageland', the Clash had been together for less than nine months. By anybody's standards, this was far too early for Mott the Hoople Syndrome to be setting in. The song was little more than food for the Clash Myth, and, as Mick suggested to fellow Mott the Hoople fan Kris Needs, there would be plenty more to follow.

When Mick also told Kris, 'We had lots of our own material, but we wanted to do one song by someone else,' he was being somewhat disingenuous. With the inclusion of 'Garageland', the yet-to-be performed 'Cheat', and the Beaconsfield 'White Riot', the band had a total of 13 self-penned tracks for the album without having to resort to novelty numbers like '1-2 Crush On You' or any of the material discarded as substandard over the previous few months. That number of songs would usually be considered generous, but as most Clash compositions lasted closer to two minutes than three, the total running time of the album was just under 29 minutes. Brevity was a virtue for individual tracks, but not for an album, where it would undermine the Value For Money principle. Someone suggested rectifying the situation by including the band's warm-up arrangement of 'Police and Thieves'. 'I think there was some laughter at the suggestion,' recalls Terry, 'but then we realised it did sound good, and we did it.'

This agreement was not arrived at quite so quickly as Terry suggests. Joe agonised a while about the cultural exploitation issue, before eventually coming to the conclusion that the Clash's version was an honest attempt to meet an inspirational musical genre and its attendant culture halfway. In the 1999 biographical documentary *Westway To The World*, Joe described Mick as 'a genius' for coming up with the Clash's arrangement of 'Police And Thieves': 'Any other group would've played on the offbeat, trying to assimilate reggae, but we had one guitar on the on and the other on the off.' Then Mick sang Murvin-style high-pitched back-up to Joe's gruff but impassioned reading of the lead vocal. In 1988, Joe told *Melody Maker*, 'I like it a lot because we're using punk language, we're not going *ninky dinky dinky poo* like the Police were to do later. It was punk reggae, not white reggae. We were bringing some of *our* roots to it.'

For Simon Humphrey, the band's decision to record the track was something of a relief: if the law of punk decreed that next to no studio effects should be used, then the law of reggae and dub decreed that everything plus the kitchen sink should be thrown on. 'That was the one that was produced, in that it had dub effects and tape phasing at the end, which was a fairly sophisticated thing to do on the album. It's the one track where everyone got into the techniques.' The same double standard applied to the duration of the song: all six minutes of it. Punk songs were intended to be short, sharp shocks, but the Clash understood that reggae worked on the principle of slowly building up to a hypnotic groove.

Accidental though its inclusion may have been, 'Police and Thieves' proved to be more than just a filler track. The song provides an almost uncanny counterpoint to 'White Riot', its lyric echoing Paul and Joe's encounters with both police and would-be thieves at the Notting Hill Riot. Spelling out the band's empathy with Jamaican and black inner-city British youth, it makes it clear that 'White Riot' is not racist or separatist, but envious. Musically, it adds immeasurably to the dynamic and the texture of the album. It also accentuates *The Clash*'s other, less immediately obvious, reggae influences: the use of drop-out throughout; the heavily echoed 'Oi!' on 'Career Opportunities'; the staccato rhythm guitar cutting across the dominant pumping bass on 'Janie Jones'; the phased guitar on 'Cheat'; and Mick's harmonica on 'Garageland', floating in the mix like the melodica on one of Augustus Pablo's dub recordings.

Recording and mixing was completed by the end of the band's third long weekend in the studio. It all happened so quickly that they later became confused about the time it took, variously boasting to have completed both single and album in two straight weeks or even two weekends. In 1978, Mick told the *NME*'s Nick Kent, 'I was so into speed, I mean I don't even recall making the first album.' Instead of offering an explanation for the confusion, however, Mick was just indulging in some punk posturing. 'That was just one of those things I said,' he admitted to the same paper's James Brown 13 years later. 'I don't recall any sort of drug-taking, and none of us was naive: the studio was a haven for drugs and rock'n'roll behaviour,' says Simon Humphrey. 'We'd had Stephen Stills in! It wouldn't have shocked me to have seen anything, but I didn't.'

The finished album was mastered and delivered to CBS by 3 March. 'Everyone knew it was punk and a New Thing, and nothing would have been rejected by the company,' says Simon. 'They just bunged 'em in the studio, let 'em do their own thing, let 'em put the album out with minimal artwork and non-existent A&R control over recordings. Not that the band would have let them have it anyway, but they certainly didn't try. And it simply went out.'

While the artwork was indeed minimal, its effect was anything but. Bernie and Paul were responsible for most of the ideas, which were realised by CBS's in-house team, rather than Sebastian. Kate Simon – one of the regular punk scene photographers – took the front cover picture, which captures the three-piece Clash posing like street fighting men in the little alleyway opposite the front door of Rehearsals. Sebastian's housemate Rocco Macauley had also been present at the Notting Hill Riot, and his back cover photograph depicts the initial police charge in the lee of the Westway. Paying lip service to the fanzine aesthetic, the photographs have roughly torn edges and are reproduced in black and white half-tone against a background of military green. The limited sleeve information appears in Xerox-decayed typeface. The typography itself is all in lurid red. So is the razor-slashed band logo-cum-album title on the front, which Paul and Bernie adapted from the lettering on the cover of the 1973 Big Youth album *Screaming Target*. These details, and the splurges of red and pink aerosol paint across Rocco's photo, recall the band's own customised clothes, suggest the neon and graffiti of the urban environment, and evoke the fire and blood of riot. As a visual introduction to everything the punk-era Clash stood for, the sleeve is near perfect, and the charging policemen photograph quickly gained the status of a rock'n'roll icon. The nearest thing to a Clash trademark, it would be reproduced first as the band's White Riot Tour stage backdrop, and then as a semi-abstract design on T-shirts and all manner of clothing.

Having been out of the public eye since 1 January, the Clash had gradually toned down the more garish excesses of their Pollock and Pop Art/Lettrist phases. Increasingly, they were tending back towards their original basic Oxfam Mod look, with the other stylistic influences reduced to details: a paint splashed tie, an arm band, a shirt with a Union Jack panel, a relatively discreetly stencilled slogan. It was in this mode – complete with mod-style white socks – that they posed for the cover of *The Clash*. Even while the album was being readied for release, though, Bernie was taking advantage of the recent cash injection from CBS to provide the band with a new image. He hired the

Clash's first professional outside helper, a machinist named Alex Michon, who initially moved her sewing machine into the noisome upstairs room at Rehearsals.

The Sex Pistols had made a big splash with Malcolm and Vivienne's bondage suit line, based, as ever, on sexual fetishist gear. The Clash's area of provocation was entirely different, so Bernie took the idea of conflict as his basic theme. With input from Paul, and practical help from Sebastian, he and Alex came up with a style that was a logical development from previous Clash looks, but which moved away from the urban guerrilla boiler suits immortalised on the picture cover of 'White Riot' towards something more reminiscent of combat fatigues. In addition to the obligatory stencils, detail was provided by numerous pockets and zip fastenings, and instead of khaki, the colours mixed sombre black, white and grey with more garish blue and red.

When these new outfits were given their first public outing on 11 March, Vivien Goldman described them as 'couture bezippered ensembles' and Nick Kent as 'pop star army fatigues'. Ironically, in the interview he gave Kris Needs that same day for *ZigZag*, Mick was still promoting the DIY ethic: 'We encourage the kids to paint their clothes. That way they get involved, feel part of it. Now they come along and show us ideas we like.' Bernie, for one, had noted how the Pistols' post-Grundy Incident notoriety had boosted sales of Malcolm and Vivienne's various clothing lines: if the new punks were wearing their clothes, then that made them Sex Pistols punks. In direct competition, as always, Bernie came to the conclusion that in order to convert them into Clash punks, he would have to sell them *his* designs. The chief problem was that, unlike Malcolm – whose Sex shop had recently been redecorated and renamed Seditionaries – he didn't have his own outlet.

During the spring of 1977, Sebastian, Frothler, Celia Parry and Sebastian's former co-Social Secretary at the Central School of Art, Al McDowell, opened a shop at 271 Brixton Road. Although an independent venture, it owed a considerable amount to the Clash, as revealed by its name, Pollocks, and its wares: 'art clothing' decorated with Jackson Pollock paint splashes or Piet Mondrian colour squares. Although not involved, Bernie was not one to stand back and be exploited when he could be doing the exploiting. Never a particularly committed project, Pollocks ran down over the summer. Before it closed, Bernie had already harnessed Sebastian's entrepreneurial flair for his own devices, using more of the CBS advance to form a company with him named Upstarts. 'Upstarts was purely there to provide the Clash with their outfits and their backdrops,' says Sebastian. 'The work I did for the Clash, I did through Upstarts: it was a design arm for the Clash.'

It was conceived as slightly more than that: it was also intended to mass-produce and market Clash-style clothes to the general public. Bernie availed himself of a free office at Sebastian's house at 31 Albany Street. Sebastian also screen-printed the T-shirts at his home base, and helped Alex design the trousers and jackets. 'We had a little pattern-cutting shop in south London,' says Sebastian, 'and we used to take the stuff to the East End to get it made up.' In his May 1977 *NME* think-piece, 'Is This What We Ordered?', Neil Spencer scornfully enquired, 'How long before "Hate And War" shirts are on sale in the *NME* mail order ads where flower-embroidered loon pants nestled a few years back?' The answer was, not long: by that time a mail order campaign was already in the offing; Upstarts ads would indeed be placed in the music press; and there were even plans for a shop.

Bernie was less keen on spending money in other areas. Both Joe and Mick had recently found themselves in difficulties when the one halfway decent guitar each owned suffered damage, and Paul's bass was a total piece of trash. Although Mick had a decent Marshall stack, the rest of the pink PA – as inherited from the 101ers – had seen some hard use and was barely functional. It had been largely responsible for the sound problems that had plagued the Clash throughout their live career to date. Not surprisingly, the band members wanted to invest some of their advance in upgrading their gear. 'We'd had enough of crappy amps and shitty equipment,' Joe told *Melody Maker*'s Allan Jones in 1978. 'But Bernie thought that us getting decent amps was contradicting the original aims of being a punk band... When we went out in front of an audience, we wanted to sound as good as possible. They've paid to see us, right? They want to be able to *hear* us, too.'

The band won that battle, and got their new backline, which was also painted pink. Mick also bought a Plexiglas guitar, typically basing his choice more on aesthetics and association – Keith Richards, Johnny Thunders and the Flamin' Groovies' Cyril Jordan all owned one – than quality: it proved difficult to keep in tune. Paul bought a brand new Rickenbacker bass, and promptly customised it Pollock-style. The band also managed to squeeze some money out of the fund for a few minor luxuries. For his part, Mick bought a new stereo, and paid for his Nan to go and visit his mother Renee in America. That aside, though, Bernie insisted on putting his charges on a wage of £25 per week. It was a considerable boost from Joe's Social Security payment of £9.70, but – as he told Caroline Coon – it hardly meant he would be abandoning his regular order of beans on toast at George's Café on Camden High Street for more exotic fare elsewhere. By this time, Paul had moved in with Caroline, Mick was still at Wilmcote House – having moved Tony James in to keep him company while Stella was away – and Joe and Roadent had taken over a squat in Canonbury, north London. Thus, accommodation expenses were not an immediate problem. Over the next year or so, the band members would find their own homes, and succeed in persuading Bernie to hand over additional money for rent. Nevertheless, as long as he managed the Clash, the weekly wage stayed the same, and the issue consequently became a source of considerable bitterness.

If getting money from their manager to meet their own needs proved difficult, it was almost impossible to do so on behalf of the band's helpers. It seemed Bernie expected them to continue working for free. 'I remember when Mick Jones was going to leave because Bernie wouldn't buy Roadent a pair of socks,' chuckles Tony Parsons. 'Great moments in rock'n'roll history! Roadent didn't have any socks, and Mick thought this was morally reprehensible, and that Roadent should be bought some out of band funds. Bernie was equivocating. "Keep 'em hungry and sockless" being the motive, I suppose.' Tony and Barry Miles were among those astounded by Bernie's tight-fistedness, especially when he took to driving around in a car bearing the numberplate 'CLA5H' while his charges were often so broke they had to catch the bus home from their own gigs. In fairness to the manager, the car in question was a battered old Renault from his own garage, albeit one with – according to future Clash roadie Johnny Green – a Ferrari engine lurking under its bonnet, and Sebastian Conran recalls that Bernie acquired the numberplate after someone phoned up Rehearsals and offered to sell it for a mere £100. Nevertheless, it did not create the best of impressions.

By early March, the band had not played live for over two months. Not only was their perceived laziness provoking occasional sniping in *Sniffin' Glue*, but they were in danger of losing ground to the groups who had either remained active during that period, or else had appeared on the scene since the Roxy opened. The Pistols had also been in mothballs while breaking in Sid and recording. It was an ideal opportunity for Bernie and his band to make their move and usurp the position of Malcolm and his band as the Kings of Punk. The Clash now had sufficient financial clout to ignore Andy Czezowski's club, and make good on their earlier promises to finance their own events. The Colosseum in Harlesden's Manor Park Road was a cinema specialising in trashy porn and kung fu films. Kris Needs was told that the band had first considered this 'classic definition of a flea pit, all peeling paint and stained seats' as a potential venue when practising changeovers for the Anarchy Tour at the nearby Harlesden Roxy. If it were indeed a mere matter of chance, the choice was serendipitous. In organising gigs as near as possible to the intended location of the Anarchy Tour's aborted finale, it was as though the Clash were announcing their intention of delivering – both literally and symbolically – where the Sex Pistols had failed.

In fact, Bernie's plans were even more ambitious. The *NME* reported that the venue was to host 'occasional gigs by upcoming bands'. *Melody Maker* went even further, stating, 'the Clash open London's latest new wave club this week'. The cinema venue may have been redolent of the Screen on the Green, and the nature of the event as originally planned may have recalled both the Midnight Special and the 100 Club Punk Festival, but it would appear that Bernie's long term ambition was to set the venue up as a rival to the Covent Garden Roxy.

To begin with, Sebastian's poster promised Two Nights Of Action on Friday 11 and Saturday 12 March. Both were to be headlined by the Clash, with support on the first night provided by the Buzzcocks and Subway Sect, and on the second by Generation X and the Slits. Previously, the Clash had been the Number Two band in an inner circle dominated by the Sex Pistols. Bernie now wanted to build a new Inner Circle around the Clash: the kind of Larry Parnes-like stable of artistes Malcolm had first dabbled with in late 1975, and finally abandoned in January 1977 when he passed up on the chance of a joint Clash-Pistols label. Due to their own drummer problems, Subway Sect had been dormant for several months, but they were already established as Bernie's Number Two band. Although pursuing their own path to success, Generation X recognised that associating with the already signed and critically lauded Clash would do them no harm at this early stage of their career.

Rehearsal band the Flowers of Romance had disintegrated following the departure of Sid Vicious, and Keith Levene was at a loose end. At the end of February, Buzzcocks vocalist Howard Devoto announced his departure from that band. For Bernie, it was a situation ripe for exploitation: he made several calls to Buzzcocks guitarist Pete Shelley, in the hope of luring him down to London to form a new band with Keith. Having already decided to persevere with the Buzzcocks and take care of the lead vocals himself, Pete declined. However, as the Buzzcocks were practically having to relaunch themselves from scratch, they were more than happy to accept the platform offered by Bernie and the Clash. Following the demise of the Flowers of Romance, Palmolive had teamed up with Boogie's girlfriend Kate Corris, who had taken up guitar and changed her surname to Korus. Along with 14 year old singer Ari Up, and – eventually – bassist Tessa Pollitt, they had formed a band provocatively named the Slits. The Colosseum gig was to be their public début.

In a 1990 interview with the *NME*'s Stephen Dalton, Julie Burchill declared, 'What annoys me is feminist revisionists now saying punk was a wonderful time for women because we all started expressing ourselves more. That's a load of bollocks because bands like the Slits actually got their gigs supporting the Clash because they were fucking the Clash! The whole casting couch routine was still going on.' The fact that Palmolive and Kate knew the Clash and Bernie through Joe was a considerable factor in the Slits being offered the gig, but no more so than Tony James's friendship with Mick was for Generation X. Bernie was simply interested in collecting Clash associate bands, full stop. Novelty value, like stimulating ideas, might have counted for something, but keeping girlfriends happy, like musical ability, did not.

Elsewhere in her *NME* interview with Stephen Dalton, Julie Burchill apparently contradicted her casting couch accusation by claiming, 'Everybody was taking so much speed there was very little sex around.' This is untrue: there were relatively few monogamous sexual relationships, but there was a great deal of casual sex. It just wasn't supposed to be a big deal. In the late Sixties, love had been free; by the mid Seventies, thrills were cheap. Richard Hell had introduced punk's cynical attitude to romance with 'Love Comes In Spurts' – another title scrawled on the Television poster Malcolm McLaren tacked up in Sex – and Johnny Rotten had followed up with his infamous remark describing sex as 'two minutes of squelching noises'. Both Malcolm and Bernie wanted love off the agenda when it came to lyrical content. The studied lack of interest in sexuality served to liberate the movement's female participants from the subservient role they had traditionally had to endure in previous youth cults.

The resulting high profile of Patti Smith, Chrissie Hynde, Siouxsie Sioux, Poly Styrene of X Ray Spex, Gaye Advert of the Adverts, Pauline Murray of Penetration, Vivienne Westwood, Caroline Coon, and Julie Burchill herself has been largely responsible for promoting the idea that punk was essentially non-sexist and pro-feminist. The Slits were especially important because they were the first all-female non-puppet punk band and arguably the first all-female non-puppet *rock* band. Julie is merely playing devil's advocate when she claims the scene did not offer wonderful opportunities for women to succeed on their own terms.

She is closer to the mark when she implies that the true attitudes of the male scenesters were questionable: behind the blank expressions could lurk some basic lusts and screwed up values. It was quite possibly the strain of keeping hidden their true, confused feelings about sexual roles in punk that made for the sexism, chauvinism, sexual disgust and misogyny that were so prevalent on the scene. In *Rotten*, Caroline Coon accused both Bernie and Malcolm of being bad influences because they were 'basically disappointed chauvinist pigs'. Both behaviourally and lyrically, the Damned, the Sex Pistols and especially the Stranglers were guilty of committing numerous offences.

For all their supposed ideological rigour in other areas, the Clash were also a long way from coming to terms with feminism, which was after all – along with gay rights – one of the key political issues of the Seventies. When Joe was asked about his personal morality in a stilted would-be promotional interview filmed around a pool table in April 1977, he replied, 'I wouldn't steal money off a friend. But I'd steal his girlfriend.' Love might have been unfashionable at the time, but the way he discussed Palmolive with Caroline Coon that same month showed scant respect for the feelings of his partner of two years' standing. Three years later, talking to *Creem*'s Susan Whitall, Joe was still struggling to get a grip on the concept of sexism. After saying such tendencies had to be watched because they were 'inbred', he lambasted heavy metal groups for their macho cockstrutting routines, then attempted to show the Clash in a more positive light: 'We'd be standing in the warehouse in Camden Town and these kind of surveyors were coming in off the pavement, and they'd go, "Oh – blah, blah, blah – these *chicks*, man!" And I remember we'd get up and say, "You can call them *girls*, or *birds*, or *women*, but you can't call them *chicks!*" I remember sometimes they could really get my goat. And then, the other day, I found myself saying it.'

The Clash's apparently unconscious sexism was evident in everything they wore, did, said and sang. Their paramilitary clothing styles, their gang mentality and their aggressive stance were just as unreconstructedly macho, albeit in a different way, as the posturing and bragging of the heavy metal bands Joe claimed to despise. In their interviews, when the Clash spoke to or about 'the kids', those kids were always male. No hint of the female urban experience emerged in their early songs, where the protagonists were also exclusively male and invariably chauvinist with it; especially in 'Janie Jones', 'Protex Blue' and '48 Hours'. In neglecting to address the female perspective, the band not only restricted themselves to painting 50 per cent of the picture, they also drastically reduced their potential appeal and market. The result was that, for the duration of the Clash's career, most thinking women – and not a few thinking men – put down the band's combative pose as trite laddish wish-fulfilment, and dismissed their recorded output as *boys' music*.

Back in early March 1977, then, the prospect of putting the Slits onstage for the first time was not particularly high on Bernie's list of interests or worries. The Harlesden Colosseum gigs represented a bold take-over bid, and as such a considerable risk. It was important for reasons of status and reputation that nothing went wrong. Unfortunately, several things did.

Jon Moss had long hair and was not particularly impressed with the Clash philosophy. Nevertheless, as well as being a good drummer, he was handsome and just 19 years old, and so had been hired on the condition that he agreed to get a haircut. Now, after five or six weeks of hanging around waiting for the Clash to finish in the studio and get active again, Jon's disillusionment was about to peak. Like Rob Harper, he felt the Clash had no room for his input. 'I had a personality and ideas, and they didn't want that,' he told Dave Rimmer. His own politics tended to the right and, like Terry Chimes, he argued with both Mick and Bernie about what he saw as the Clash's hypocrisy. 'They were always promising things, but nothing ever happened.' Shortly before the Colosseum gigs, he phoned Bernie and said, 'Look, it's not me. I don't believe all this political shit, and I don't believe you believe it.'

The band were partly to blame, in that they had failed to learn from their experience with Rob Harper that it was important to make a new recruit feel welcome. Nevertheless, it was understandable that they were furious at being let down at the last minute. Less excusable was the manner of that fury's expression. In the anti-drummer tirade Mick Jones let loose in front of Tony Parsons later that month, Jon – although unnamed – was the individual threatened with having his legs broken: the band's anti-violence stance contradicted once again. Almost immediately upon resigning, Jon formed a punk band named London who toured with the Stranglers that summer. From October 1977 to February 1978, he would replace Rat Scabies in the Damned. After briefly supplying Burundi-type drums to the remodelled 1980 version of Adam and the Ants, he would team up with Boy George in Culture Club and finally experience success on his own terms.

The timing of Jon's departure threw the Harlesden gigs into disarray. Terry Chimes agreed to sit in on drums, but it was decided to turn Two Nights of Action into one, and the Saturday gig was cancelled. Generation X were already committed to play an Easter Ball at Leicester University on Friday, and had to be dropped from the bill. The Slits were brought forward to join the remaining bands on the Friday night, which made for an earlier start time than the advertised 10.45 pm. It was too late to circulate the change of plan, and the news pages of *Sounds* reported 'confusion... disappointing many fans'.

Kris Needs covered the gig for *ZigZag*, Vivien Goldman for *Sounds*, and Nick Kent returned to the punk fray for the *NME*, having recovered from the chain-whipping meted out to him by Sid Vicious at the 100 Club Pistols' gig the previous July. Rough Trade's Geoff Travis was the DJ, playing mostly reggae. Shane MacGowan – likened by Nick Kent to 'a vole sniffing glue' – was messing around in the audience as usual, encouraging others to pogo. Don Letts filmed in Super 8, and some of the footage later appeared in *The Punk Rock Movie*. Julien Temple made another visual record of the event for the band.

By the time the Clash hit the stage, Joe Strummer was so fired up that he was actually frothing at the mouth. The tension did not diminish. Mick was incensed when the new amps initially failed to function properly, and Joe screamed abuse when one of the longhairs manning the mixing desk accidentally pulled the plug on the band. There were also a few sporadic taunts about the CBS contract from the otherwise partisan audience. Instead of succumbing to the pressure, the band fed off it. Making reference to one of the Colosseum's more traditional attractions, Joe announced, 'I'm Bruce Lee's son.'

What are you gonna do about it?' before thrashing into another song. During 'White Riot', the strap on Mick's new Plexiglas guitar broke. Instead of grinding to a halt, he grabbed it by the neck and repeatedly slashed across the strings, before, as Kris reported, 'holding up the guitar like a machine gun to finish the number'.

It was a powerful, charged, exciting performance. Vivien admitted to being equally awe-struck by the band's new image: she was so impressed by Paul's suicide blond hair-do that she became the second journalist to liken a Clash member to a Greek god. Almost against his will, even Nick Kent 'suddenly felt involved in this music', and in praising the Clash found the perfect way to get his own back on Malcolm and the Pistols: 'it's all to do with real "punk" credentials: a Billy the Kid sense of tough tempered with an innate sense of humanity which involves possessing a morality totally absent in the childish nihilism flaunted by Johnny Rotten and his clownish co-conspirators'. Perceptively, he also stated that 'the Clash took up exactly where Ian Hunter's Mott the Hoople left off'.

The Colosseum gig may have been a triumph, but despite the music press speculation that had heralded it, it was not repeated. Things had hardly gone smoothly either pre-launch or on the day, and Kris's *ZigZag* feature suggested that the venue's Pakistani owners had been somewhat taken aback by the audience the show attracted. It seems likely that the culture shock proved too much for them, and they deemed their experiment with hosting live gigs a failure. Bernie and the Clash put plans for any similar ventures on hold while they awaited the release of their single and album, prepared themselves for promotional duties, and contemplated a satisfactory long term solution to their drummer problem.

Following the abandoning of the idea for a joint label, the relationship between Malcolm McLaren and Bernie Rhodes had cooled once again. In spite of the EMI payoff, the Anarchy Tour had left a huge hole in the Sex Pistols' pockets, and after the CBS signing, Bernie had been prevailed upon to help out with the bills. As Sophie Richmond's diary entries for 4 and 17 February testified, he had done so, but 'not very willingly'. On the latter date, he had also offered her a lecture, intended for Malcolm's ears, about how mercenary, hypocritical and bitchy the Pistols camp and, by extension, the punk scene was becoming.

Apart from demonstrating Bernie's capacity for doublethink – he despaired at the steps Malcolm was taking, but following in them anyway – what he had to say represented an astute summary of the situation. By March 1977, Malcolm was far more interested in manipulating record companies and the media than he was in looking after the career or wellbeing of his band. On 9 March, the Pistols signed to A&M; on the 10th they turned up at the record company headquarters drunk and disorderly; on the 12th they had a violent tussle in the Speakeasy with *Old Grey Whistle Test* presenter Bob Harris; and late on the 16th, A&M terminated the contract, and the Pistols walked away with a total of £75,000 severance pay. The following day's *Evening Standard* quoted a blasé Malcolm as saying, 'I keep walking in and out of offices being given cheques.' The 'White Riot' single was due for release on 18 March. By this stage Bernie was so paranoid about Malcolm's stroke-pulling that he was convinced the A&M sacking was a publicity stunt conceived with the express intention of stealing the Clash's thunder. He even phoned Sophie at the Pistols office to complain.

As it turned out, the Clash record got its own fair share of attention. In conversation with Kris Needs, both Paul and Mick had expressed disappointment with the single version of 'White Riot'. Having heard an advance copy before attending the Night of

1. The Delinquents, September 1974. *Left to right:* Mike Dowling, John Brown, Mick Jones, Paul Wayman.

2. Sister Ray, formerly Violent Luck, formerly Little Queenie, summer 1976. *Left to right:* one-time London SS member Matt Dangerfield (making up numbers), Brady, Kelvin Blacklock, John Brown.

3. The Damned, 1976, with former London SS member Brian James (*right*) and rejected candidate Rat Scabies (*second left*).

4. Former London SS member Tony James with Generation X, 1976.

5. Bernie Rhodes, 1977.

6. The Young Colts, 22 Davis Road, May 1976. *Left to right:* Alan Drake (making up numbers), Mick Jones, Paul Simonon, Billy Watts. Keith Levene not shown.

7. Mick Jones's high-rise: Wilmcote House, Harrow Road.

8. Joe Strummer's Alma Mater: the City of London Freemen's School, Ashtead Park, Surrey.

9. Woody Mellor, 12 Pentonville, Newport, 1973.

10. The Vultures, Newport, late 1973. Woody and Alan 'Jiving Al' Jones.

11. The 101ers in the murk of the Walterton Road basement, February 1975. *Left to right:* Clive 'Evil C.' Timperley, Simon 'Big John' Cassell, Alvaro Peña-Rojas, Richard 'Snakehips Dudanski' Nother, Jules Yewdall, Joe Strummer.

12. The 101ers, early 1976. Joe Strummer (with suit and Telecaster) and Richard Dudanski.

13. A Night of Treason: the Clash at the RCA, 5 November 1976. *Left to right:* Mick Jones, Joe Strummer, Terry Chimes, Paul Simonon. The Pollock look gives way to Pop-Art/Lettrism.

14. The Anarchy Tour, December 1976. With Rob Harper on drums.

15. The Roxy, 1977. Johnny Rotten and Mark Perry.

16. Pop Star Army Fatigues, spring 1977.

17. Creative violence?

18. With Nick 'Topper' Headon.

19. The White Riot Tour at the Rainbow, 9 May 1977.

20. Gates of the West, 1979. The Hollywood rock'n'roll look.

21–3. On-stage during the Bonds Casino residency, New York, June 1981.

24. The first of the mohicans and the return of both Terry Chimes and the Pop Star Army Fatigues, June 1982.

25–6. The new Clash on the May 1985 busking tour. *Left to right, top:* Vince White, Paul Simonon, Pete Howard, Nick Sheppard, Joe Strummer.

Action, Nick Kent had also confessed to being unimpressed with its lack of immediate punch, before further listens revealed that 'the chorus had been made insidiously catchy enough to become a sort of football chant'. Pete Silverton's review for *Sounds* echoed these sentiments, saying that it took 'three days and maybe 25 plays' – 24 and a half more than most new singles would have been afforded – to make its mark. But make its mark on him it did, achieving Single of the Week status. Even if the production could have been a little tougher, 'for sheer power and resolute nowness it makes everything else here look a bit sick'.

Caroline Coon chose the single to lead off her *Melody Maker* singles column. The 400 words she devoted to 'White Riot' functioned as both an open fan letter to the band and a potted biography of their career to date: all valuable publicity. Even she managed to temper her swooning adulation long enough to note 'the overall sound is a little safe and the lyrics between verses are sadly unintelligible', faults she fully expected to be rectified on the – plug ahoy! – 'forthcoming album'.

Guest singles reviewer for the *NME* was Tom Robinson, a former member of acoustic trio Café Society. Although two years older than Joe Strummer, as a committed gay activist Tom had responded keenly to the political potential of punk, and was in the process of writing new material and forming a new group to play it: the Tom Robinson Band (TRB). If anything, his 250-word appraisal was more biased than Caroline's, but his perspective was both fresh and uncannily in sync with the band's. 'It's pointless to categorise this with the other records: "White Riot" isn't a poxy single of the week, it's the first meaningful event all year,' was his opening shot. After noting the crafty and unintentionally ironic cop from 'All Day And All Of The Night' in '1977', he went on to list other criticisms the Clash had attracted, many of them as valid as his conclusion: 'Go on, say they sold out to the enemy at CBS, say it's another idle London fad irrelevant to the lives of working people, say it's all a clever hype that's conned everyone, say it's just the Sixties rehashed and you can't make out the words. Say what you like, you still can't discount it 'cause Clash aren't just a band, and this is more than a single... Whatever your standpoint, everyone basically agrees there are two sides. You know it's coming, we know it's coming, and *they* know it's coming.' The importance of defining Us and Them was something Tom knew all about. He had already written 'Up Against The Wall' by this time. Although actually taken directly from the slogan of the Motherfuckers, with its chorus demand 'Just whose side are you on?', his song could almost have been inspired by the 'White Riot' picture cover and/or Bernie's 'What side of the bed' T-shirt. This was the Clash's kind of propaganda.

More was to follow. Kris Needs's interview-cum-Harlesden review, published in the April issue of *ZigZag*, was another extended fan-letter. On 26 March, Joe met Caroline Coon in Red Lion Square for a lengthy solo interview, published in the 23 April issue of *Melody Maker*. Again, she was probing in her questioning, but ended up with a feature that appeared to be more revealing than it actually was. Joe treated it as an exercise in damage limitation. Rumours about his schooling and so-called privileged past had been spreading around the punk and music press communities, as had some jibes about his opportunistic abandonment of the 101ers. As a result he was, as Caroline claimed, prepared to be 'more forthcoming than ever before', but with slanted information and partial truths rather than the whole truth.

This personal strand was interwoven with more up to date material. Joe gave his thoughts about the current punk scene, the Clash's CBS deal, and the band's supposed manipulation by Bernie. He threw in the by now almost obligatory rant about state oppression, and was generally contemptuous of politicians. His humble appraisal of his musical talents was nothing new, but something that was totally unprecedented was his admission that rock'n'roll was 'completely useless' when it came to effecting political change. 'I'm just saying that because I want you to know that I haven't got any illusions about anything, right? Having said that I still want to *try* to change things.'

Realistic maybe, but the Clash had stood for office on the positive, pro-active hopeful ticket. Coming at such an early stage, an acknowledgement of the futility of such gestures was not a little sad. Although Joe's manner was relaxed and easy-going for the duration of the interview, to read it today is to pick up a strong sense of depression, of someone who is finding it difficult to cope. During the inevitable discussion on violence, he said, 'Being honest with yourself: that's much tougher than beating someone up.' Resolving that struggle was something that being part of the Clash denied him – and would continue to deny him for years – at no small cost to his personal wellbeing.

Hardly surprisingly, in view of its raw sound and incendiary content, 'White Riot' did not immediately establish a niche for itself on the nation's playlists. When Joe was interviewed by Caroline – a week after the single's release – the band's singer still hadn't heard it anywhere but John Peel's late night Radio One show. Joe railed against Radio One's national monopoly, the enforced death of the pirate radio stations, and the failings of London's sole official independent station, Capital Radio. Capital had been founded in October 1973 with the slogan 'In tune with London'. 'What they could have done compared to what they have done is abhorrent,' said Joe. 'They could have made the whole capital buzz. Instead Capital Radio has just turned their back on the whole youth of the city.'

Later on the night of the interview, accompanied by Roadent, Joe went out and sprayed 'WHITE RIOT' across the glass-fronted street-level reception area of Capital Radio on Euston Road, and on the entrance of the BBC Radio building on Portland Place. Neither the *Melody Maker* anti-radio diatribe nor the graffiti campaign was spontaneous: the Clash had decided to launch their attack before the single was even released. At the soundcheck for the Harlesden Colosseum gig, they had worked up a version of Jonathan Richman's 'Roadrunner'. Whereas Richman's version celebrated the medium of radio, however, the Clash's was decidedly more deprecatory, with the chorus of 'radio on' changed to 'Radio One'. There had been talk of performing it as an encore, but it didn't quite come together, and Paul had hated the song ever since his London SS audition. Instead, in the week following the gig, Mick and Joe had turned the full power of their scorn upon what they considered to be the other key offender. Based on the uptempo reworking of the Who's stop-start 'I Can't Explain' riff previously employed to power 'Deadly Serious', 'Capital Radio' is an all-out assault on the station and its programme controller, Aiden Day. Joe was reading *The Rise And Fall Of The Third Reich* at the time, which explains his opening evocation of the Nazi minister of propaganda, Josef Goebbels. Adopting a line of attack similar to the one 'London's Burning' and 'I'm So Bored With The USA' had directed towards the medium of television, 'Capital Radio' accuses radio of being a mind-numbing opiate of the masses, its purpose being 'to keep you in your place, OK'. The morning after the graffiti raid, Sebastian Conran was dispatched to Capital Radio with his camera to record the results for posterity.

With next to no radio play, 'White Riot' stayed on the charts for just three weeks and peaked at number 38. It might have been helped on its way had the Clash accepted the offer they received to appear on *Top Of The Pops*. In those days, pre-MTV and *The Chart Show*, *Top Of The Pops* was the single most powerful promotional tool for a recording act, going out on primetime BBC1 and watched by a regular audience of eight million. Back in Jonh Ingham's April 1976 *Sounds* interview, though, Johnny Rotten had dismissed the show as phoney and inauthentic because it required bands to mime along to a pre-recorded backing track. An unofficial punk boycott had been declared, and the Clash were determined to honour it.

Lacking both radio and TV access, the band were forced to exploit whatever other promotional avenues were available to them. Elly Smith, Head of Press at CBS, quickly proved herself to be one of the band's few genuine allies at their record company, and she threw her weight behind the band's music press publicity campaign.

Tony Parsons had arrived relatively late on the punk scene, but he had quickly immersed himself in it, his response being more that of participant than observer. A working class and extremely class-conscious Londoner, he had worked in a gin distillery prior to securing his job at the *NME*, and it required no great leap of imagination for him to connect with the Clash's songs and rhetoric. He became particularly close to the band during the first few months of 1977, accompanying them on nights out to the Roxy, and on their not always successful attempts to gain entry to the Speakeasy. Whereas Bernie was loath to let writers who were uncommitted to the cause get too close – 'Bernie used to say, "I don't want the boys to talk to that journalist, because that journalist's a *careerist*,"' laughs Tony – he and the band were already well aware how valuable it was to have wholehearted Clash champions in the music press. The likes of Caroline Coon, Jonh Ingham and Giovanni Dadomo had all done their bit, but Tony was of the right sex, the right age, and the right background to fit right in. It was a fortuitous relationship that Bernie, the Clash, Elly Smith, Tony, the *NME* and the paper's publisher IPC all came to recognise and exploit. The advantages for the Clash camp were obvious; for the *NME*, their writer's connection with the Clash represented a belated opportunity to grab a sizeable chunk of the growing market for punk coverage.

On 21 March, the day of the Sex Pistols' first gig with Sid Vicious at the Notre Dame Hall, Joe, Mick and Paul met Tony to record an interview. 'I had to be at a certain tube station at a certain time, and a couple of trains went past, and then it was like *Help!* or *A Hard Day's Night*: suddenly these heads popped out of the door and I jumped on, and we just went round and round on the Circle Line – as you know, you can ride the Circle Line until hell freezes over – shovelling amphetamine sulphate up our noses and just talking, talking, talking.'

The resulting feature was very different from Caroline Coon's in both approach and tone. Her championing of the band was at least balanced by some would-be probing questioning, and, perhaps without fully realising it at the time, she caught a real sense of Joe's inner turmoil. Tony's fanzine-derived gung-ho writing style whipped up the intensity and excitement levels, coming on like a literary equivalent of a Clash gig. There was no room for doubt or lack of conviction. The stance was macho-militant, the feature focusing on Paul's football hooligan past, Joe's recent fight with the giant ted, ted-punk hostility in general, Mick's threats to ex-Clash drummers, the band's boisterous sense of honour, their refusal to compromise, their gang-style reliance upon one another, and Mick's repeated declaration, 'I ain't ashamed to fight.' Tony fully accepted their version of their backgrounds: the lack of career opportunities, long periods on the dole, life in high-rises and squats.

His interview took place just five days before Caroline's, but this time the *NME* beat *Melody Maker* into print by no less than three weeks. A stark Chalkie Davis photo of the three band members' heads, with Mick and Joe facing each other in profile, appeared on the cover of the 2 April 1977 issue, captioned 'Thinking Man's Yobs'. The combination of this memorable icon, the whiz-bang Parsons-Clash rhetoric inside, and the pre-emption of the *Melody Maker* piece served to make this the key feature in establishing the Clash Myth. 'It wasn't objective journalism,' says Tony now. 'It was very much a collaborative piece. They did it with me. I felt very much a part of it all, emotionally. I know that was a big piece for a lot of people. It got a lot of people into the Clash and defined what it should be for them. It was a wonderful piece of myth-making, but myth is a very important element in any type of rock music.'

A mutually advantageous deal was arranged whereby CBS would include stickers with the first 10,000 copies of *The Clash*; if one of these stickers were affixed to a coupon included in the *NME* and sent to the address supplied, the sender would receive a free Clash EP. At the Harlesden gig, Terry Chimes had taken the stage in a T-shirt bearing the legend 'GOOD-BYE', as definitive a statement of intent as he could make. Nevertheless, he was called back to sit in with the band yet again when, accompanied by Tony, they returned to CBS Studios on Sunday 3 April to produce the material for the disc. First 'Capital Radio' was recorded, then the band's early, long-since abandoned instrumental 'Listen'. One track was to be placed on each side of the disc, along with excerpts from the cassette of the Parsons-Clash tube interview. The spoken word material was spliced into 'Listen', an unusual example of early Clash studio experimentation: both a logical progression from Joe's 100 Club IRA radio broadcast, and an exercise in dialogue-sampling that predated hip hop's (and Big Audio Dynamite's) use of soundtrack samples by several years. For all that, it only just qualified as a song, and a desirable artefact though it undoubtedly was, calling the *NME* freebie an EP flirted with contravening the Trades Description Act.

Sebastian Conran designed the sleeve, which used a photo taken during the tube train interview on the front cover. The 'picture withdrawn' space on the other side had originally been intended for Sebastian's own photograph of the grafitti'd Capital Radio offices, but that was deemed to be one taunt too many for the radio station's legal department to resist. The *NME* ran the coupons from 9 April onwards, the demand was considerable, and the 'EP' has been an expensive collector's item ever since.

At the end of March, Malcolm McLaren had got Boogie – the former 101ers roadie, by then working for the Pistols – to collect together various bits of television footage pertaining to the Anarchy Tour, and Julien Temple had intercut them with his own footage to make a 25-minute propaganda short in the style of a Pathé newsreel. Entitled *Sex Pistols Number One*, its public premiere was at the Screen on the Green, immediately prior to a Pistols performance there on 3 April. The video age had yet to dawn, and promo films were something of a rarity for any but the most established and wealthiest of bands. But if *Top Of The Pops* was a no-go area, other means of conveying the strong visual element of the punk experience were required. Malcolm's band had a promo film, so Bernie's band had to have one too. Julien's black and white footage of the Clash at Rehearsals, on the Anarchy Tour, at the Harlesden Coliseum and in the Beaconsfield studio had been shot prior to the Clash's latest image change and so was outmoded. (In 1999, Julien would contribute clips of the various bands on the Anarchy Tour, the Clash rehearsing 'What's My Name?' with Rob Harper, the band overdubbing vocals to 'I'm So Bored With The USA' at Beaconsfield, and the band posing on the balcony outside 111 Wilmcote House, to Don Letts's Clash documentary *Westway To The World*. His own Sex Pistols documentary, *The Filth And The Fury*, was finally released the following year. Julien claims to have over 50 hours of Clash footage from the 1976-77 period, most of which has never been seen.)

Back in spring 1977, it was decided to dip into the CBS advance, and have another go at capturing the Clash in all their glory. The shoot took place in mid April, in the Bedfordshire town of Dunstable, home base of the PA company that had supplied the equipment for the Anarchy tour. The idea was to film the band performing live, and also in a casual interview situation with Tony Parsons. 'By that time CBS thought that I would maybe be the Clash's representative on earth,' he says. 'Y'know, kind of like the Pope, bringing their Word to the People.' The gear was set up as though for a gig, in front of Sebastian Conran's giant blow-up of Rocco Macauley's charging policemen photo. This subsequently accompanied the Clash on the White Riot Tour and became known as the Groovy Backdrop. The Clash performed both sides of the 'White Riot' single and

'London's Burning'. 'They were fucking *blistering*,' says Tony. The film evidence proves him right. 'There was nobody there, other than me and a camera crew, so it was for an audience of one. The great thing about the Clash was, you didn't actually need a head full of sulphate and a sweaty little club and five pints of lager and a packet of pork scratchings: they were great anyway. They were an incredibly exciting live band.' The interview segment was less successful. The band were filmed 'relaxing' around a pool table. 'We didn't really understand how TV worked then,' says Tony. 'It was kind of embarrassing to play pool, and talk, and have these cameras pointing at you at the same time.' Again, the film evidence proves him right, and in *The Boy Looked At Johnny*, he (somewhat hypocritically) vilified the band for going along with this 'contrived spontaneity'.

Clips from the live performance were included in the 1989 BBC2 Mick Jones career retrospective *That Was Then, This Is Now*, the 1991 MTV Clash *Rockumentary*, and the 1999 biographical documentary *Westway To The World*. The MTV programme also included a brief clip from the interview. At the time of its making, though, the film was a promotional vehicle with no real outlet. Part of it was shown in the Virgin record shop near Marble Arch, but the few dozen record purchases this possibly inspired hardly justified the expense of its making. CBS did get some mileage out of the venture, though: lifted from the film's soundtrack, the Dunstable version of 'London's Burning' would be issued as the 'live' B-side of the band's second single, 'Remote Control'.

The Clash were not making it easy for themselves to achieve and sustain any substantial commercial success. They had signed to CBS to be heard, but there were no promotional channels open to them other than live shows and the music press. Far more people bought records than attended gigs. Although the inkies did have a relatively high circulation – the best-selling *NME* got up to 250,000 during the late Seventies, no small thanks to its 'close relationship' with the Clash – they were still specialist titles read by a narrow section of the populace.

Nor was there any logic or consistency in an attitude which took moral exception to mainstream outlets like radio and television, but made excuses for teaming up with a multi-national record company and positively relished getting into bed with the music press. The inkies might have affected an anti-establishment, underground press vibe, but they were all commercial, capitalist concerns. Those two great supposed rivals, *Melody Maker* and the *NME* were both owned by magazine publishing giant IPC, and were kept afloat by advertisements bought and paid for by the major record companies. 'I can see now that there were masses of contradictions in punk,' says Tony Parsons. 'We were all part of the music business. The Clash were on CBS, and I was writing for an IPC magazine. It was all mixed up: the idea of making the world a better place, and suddenly having a career, and having excitement, sleeping with lots of girls, taking lots of drugs, fighting fascism. All that. It was all that. So that's where all the contradictions came in.' Understandable though they were, it was those contradictions that would ultimately see the end of both punk as a viable movement for change and the Clash as a functioning creative unit.

The Clash was released on 8 April 1977 to mixed reviews that often said more about the reviewer than the album or the band. The Boring Old Fart stereotype, as personified by Michael Oldfield, was alive but mellow at *Melody Maker*. He thought punk was 'an experience to be savoured in small doses... closer examination, I find, leads to headaches, due to the tuneless repetition of chords at a breakneck pace'. He commended bands like the Clash for moving away from 'moon in June' lyrics, but objected to not being able to decipher what they had replaced them with. The album, he concluded, 'should go down a treat with the Blank Generation. Thank God I'm "too old" to have to enjoy it'.

At *ZigZag*, the album also arrived on the desk of one of the old guard, John Tobler. Opening with his most enthusiastic comment of the review, 'It's all right', he went on to echo Michael's complaints about the lack of tunes and decipherable lyrics: 'It seems more likely to alienate than inform.' Elsewhere – fortunately for the Clash – the album fell on less stony ground. At *ZigZag*, Kris Needs had already pre-empted his colleague's appraisal by previewing it in the most enthusiastic of terms: 'I can't think about it for a moment without feeling like I'm going to explode (let alone write about it!). You can hear all the words, there's the hardest guitar/drum sound ever... but most of all, it's captured the essence of the Clash. Their intense conviction is here in all its blazing glory... Even if you don't buy it, at least HEAR it. It's one of the most important records ever made.'

At the *NME*, equally safe bet Tony Parsons turned in a near full-page review in much the same tone as his interview feature. As far as Tony was concerned, the Clash were Telling It Like It Is: 'Jones and Strummer write with graphic perception about contemporary Great British urban reality as though it's suffocating them... The songs don't lie... They chronicle our lives and what it's like to be young in the Stinking Seventies better than any other band, and they do it with style, flash and excitement. The Clash have got it all. I urge you to get a copy of this album. The strength of a nation lies in its youth.'

Yet to make his famed announcement blaming the Clash for the Death of Punk, Mark Perry might also have been expected to react positively to the album in *Sniffin' Glue*, and he did not disappoint. His identification with the world portrayed therein was more total even than that of Tony Parsons. So much so that his review began with a brief autobiography, then opened out to consider the quality of life for the average urban teen, before shifting into the upper case for its impassioned conclusion: 'THE CLASH ALBUM IS LIKE A MIRROR. IT REFLECTS ALL THE SHIT. IT TELLS US THE TRUTH. TO ME, IT IS THE MOST IMPORTANT ALBUM EVER RELEASED. IT'S AS IF I'M LOOKING AT MY LIFE IN A FILM.'

For *Sounds*, *The Clash* was reviewed by Pete Silverton, someone who knew too much about Joe's past to swallow the Clash Myth whole. But that did not prompt him to dismiss it out of hand. 'In their interviews... they give the impression that they're poor white trash, straight out of the tower block onto the dole queue. In Joe Strummer's case, at least, nothing could be further from the truth but, given his lack of experience of being born (as opposed to living) at the bottom of the heap, the fact that he can so eloquently express the frustrations and obsessions of society's overlooked is nothing short of an outrageous indication of his talent.' In Pete's eyes, the Clash were setting the pace for their era in the same way that Elvis, the Beatles and the Rolling Stones had for theirs. He awarded the album a maximum five stars, and signed off with the assertion 'If you don't like *The Clash*, you don't like rock'n'roll. It really is as simple as that. Period.'

Anticipation, curiosity, word of mouth and such rave reviews helped the album make it to number 12 in the UK album charts. 'I remember everyone at the record company saying, "Well, *we* don't know why!"' says Simon Humphrey. 'It was beyond their understanding that they could release an album and people would simply go out and buy it because they knew about the band. Obviously, they'd signed the band on the basis that there was a groundswell of people interested, but there was no-one at CBS who could understand what was going on musically.' Being a record company employee, Simon was by definition a representative of the establishment. For this reason he was not credited on the album, but his contribution was not completely overlooked. 'They sent me a silver disc, a proper silver disc, which was a very nice gesture. Every now and again, you work with an act that you're proud to tell people about [Simon subsequently produced 'The Birdy Song' for the Tweets], and I'll tell anyone that I worked with the Clash. The first Clash album is a real landmark album. I mean, I can barely bear to *listen* to it, because sonically it's rough, but...'

In his *Melody Maker* review, Michael Oldfield held that punk was best experienced in small doses, and it is true that most UK punk bands came over better on their early singles than they did on their first album offerings. The Damned's *Damned Damned Damned*, released in February, lacks variety, texture and, for the most part, tunes. The Stranglers' *Rattus Norvegicus*, released in April, is confident and varied, but the tracks are a too long and musically ornate to pose convincingly as punk rock, and it is difficult to get past the hateful lyrics. The Jam's *In The City*, released in May, shows promise but is as monochromatic as the Damned album and contains too much filler. The Sex Pistols were represented by nothing but singles until October 1977, by which time Steve Jones had buried most of *Never Mind The Bollocks* under innumerable layers of guitar sludge.

The Clash is far and away the best album to emerge from the UK punk scene. As Rob Harper says, 'It has such a rich sort of texture. It sounds like a silly thing to say about a punk record, but the more you looked into it, the more there was there. They just had that knack.' As happens with all great albums, the weaker songs grow in stature next to the stronger, and the whole is better than the sum of its parts. This is also the case with the lyrics. Sections are rendered indecipherable by Joe's idiosyncratic delivery, but the gist is evident almost immediately. The finer points of detail gradually fill themselves in over repeated playings: an incremental initiation to Clash culture, where the song's overlapping themes make for a unified world-view.

Caught up in the impassioned rhetoric and paranoid mood of the times, Tony Parsons and Mark Perry saw *The Clash* as a straightforward journal of the here and now, and even the Clash themselves had fallen into the trap of discussing their work in those terms. Although this did not detract from its initial impact, it suggests built-in obsolescence and fails to explain why the Clash's début album still sounds vital, relevant and – references to Janie Jones and the odd Ford Cortina apart – contemporary today, while so many other punk records sound dated, hackneyed and contrived. Pete Silverton came closest to touching on the reason when he talked about the 'SF/Fantasy phraseology' of 'Remote Control'. *The Clash* might have more than a hint of dirty realism in its language and situations, but it is as much a work of the imagination as David Bowie's *The Rise And Fall Of Ziggy Stardust And The Spiders From Mars* and *Diamond Dogs*. The futurist branch of science fiction takes the events, moods, trends, political, technological and cultural developments of the present, and from these extrapolates the possible outcomes. Invariably, the future worlds portrayed are bleak dystopias, and the implied moral is that humankind should mend its ways before it is too late. Like Bowie before them, the Clash were walking ground already trodden by such literary luminaries as George Orwell, JG Ballard and Anthony Burgess: *The Clash* is *1984* meets *High-Rise* meets *A Clockwork Orange*, with tunes and a sense of humour. Talking to *Vox*'s Ann Scanlon nearly 20 years later, Mick Jones said, 'It's still my favourite Clash album.'

Since mid-March 1977, the music press had been carrying news reports about the possibility of the Clash supporting former Velvet Underground member John Cale on his UK tour, or at least taking part in his Roundhouse gigs on 10 and 11 April. Much confusion resulted, with more than a few disappointed fans turning up only to find Generation X in the support slot. The Clash denied they had ever agreed to play, but it would appear Bernie was guilty of not making that clear to the promoter at the time.

The band were in no position to perform live. Terry Chimes had finally managed to leave the Clash following the filming in Dunstable. He joined a band called Jem, briefly replaced Jerry Nolan in the Heartbreakers, teamed up with Keith Levene again in Cowboys International, then joined Generation X in 1981. 'I thought it was stupid to do just one musical style,' he says. 'The mistake I made was in thinking it could all happen again the next time, with the next band.'

The Clash had plans to play a few dates in France in late April, however, in preparation for their own Anarchy-style package tour of the UK in May, and finding that elusive fourth member again became the burning issue. Although no new ads had been placed, auditions for a replacement drummer had been continuing on a word of mouth basis throughout late March and early April 1977. On 24 March, the band had gone along to see the Kinks at the Rainbow in Finsbury Park. There, Mick had bumped into Nick Headon, one of the few successful applicants for the London SS drummer's vacancy, and invited him along to audition for the Clash.

Nicholas Bowen Headon was born on 30 May 1955, in Bromley. When he reached secondary school age his schoolteacher parents – both of whom went on to become head teachers – moved to the Kentish coastal town of Dover. Although not particularly academically gifted, Nick began to attend Dover Grammar School for Boys: like Strand School, it had managed to side-step the educational reforms going on elsewhere in the country. Nick ended up with three O Level passes, in Geography, History and English Literature, and dropped out of school before completing his A Levels.

The loves of his life were football and music, the latter taking over when, at 14, he broke his leg so badly playing soccer that he was confined to bed for several weeks, something which ultimately required him to re-sit a year at school. A fan of the Beatles, the Blues Boom, and its spin-off sub-genre of 12-bar boogie bands like Canned Heat, he was already able to find his way around an acoustic guitar. Nick was an active – even hyperactive – youth, and his father bought him a drum kit, partly as a form of physiotherapy for his damaged leg and partly to let him to burn off some of his excess energy. He quickly became an accomplished drummer, learning all he could from heroes like Terry Williams of Man (later to join Dire Straits), and jazz drummers Buddy Rich, Elvin Jones and Billy Cobham. 'I wanted to be the best drummer in the world. That was it. And I wanted to be in *Melody Maker*. Serious!' he told that paper's Mick Mercer in 1985. 'I thought if you got your picture in *Melody Maker*, you didn't have no problems in your life at all.'

Although he would later boast that he had begun to sit in with local jazz outfits at 14, his first band, formed with schoolfriend and novice bassist Steve Barnacle, performed extended 12-bar boogie instrumentals and went by the amusing name of Crystal Carcass. Always ambitious, Nick thereafter enjoyed overlapping spells with several other local bands: the similarly influenced Back To Sanity; established progressive band Mirkwood, featuring Wishbone Ash-style twin guitars, 7/4 rhythms, three-part harmonies, and Tolkien-influenced lyrics; a hard rock outfit named Expedition; and their spin-off fun band Dead Dogs Don't Lie. As he claimed, while he was still in his mid teens, Nick was also occasionally called upon to bash the skins at local pub the Louis Armstrong for landlord Bod Bowles's trad jazz band.

Thanks largely to his obsession with Bruce Lee, some of Nick's energy was diverted into keeping fit, and especially learning Tae Kwon Do. But not enough of it. He was always a little wilder than his secure middle class background might suggest or warrant. Steve Barnacle and his brother Gary – a session saxophonist who would later play on several Clash records – both suspect the reason was because Nick's background was a little *too* secure. 'I used to steal a lot and run with a gang,' Nick told *Time* magazine's Jay Cocks in 1979. What he failed to add was that the gang were fellow Dover Grammar schoolboys, and the stealing consisted of shoplifting sweets on the way home. Small beer it might have been, but Nick always had to push his luck that little bit further than anyone else. 'We'd ask for something on the top shelf, and sort of cover him, but he'd always start giggling,' says Steve. 'Almost wanting to get caught. I think it's significant, later on. He told me as much.'

Steve is referring to Nick's interest in drugs, which he had certainly developed before he left Dover. 'At school, I was told that if you have a puff on a joint, you're a junkie, right?' he told *Melody Maker*'s Will Smith in 1986. 'So, at 17 years old I had my first puff, and I thought, "Bullshit!" So you do a bit of speed, and you can handle that, and do a few downers, and you just think you can handle anything. It progresses and progresses, and if you're in a band you can get easy access to all these things.' There is no proof that this sort of progression is inevitable for *everyone* who dabbles with recreational drugs, but, given his character, it was almost inevitable for Nick.

Having moved up to London for the first time after leaving school in 1974, he attended and failed the same auditions for Sparks as Geir Waade. When he moved back to the capital for good, in summer 1975, he did so with his new wife Wendy: they were married on 24 May that year. Shortly afterwards, Nick passed an audition with Pat Travers, recently arrived from Canada, and suggested Steve Barnacle as a bassist for a proposed hard rock trio. Unfortunately, Steve was already committed to another venture, and Nick's second choice messed up an important audition so badly that Pat's management insisted both sidemen be replaced by name musicians. Nick returned to the auditioning circuit. One of his many outings resulted in his being offered the drum seat with the London SS. Immediately afterwards, however, he was also offered a gig that paid: a tour of American military bases in Germany with a soul band called the GI's. The band's vocalist, JD Nicholas, would go on to form Heatwave and replace Lionel Richie in the Commodores. Although unknown at the time, the GI's made good money; the wages offered Nick were £50 a week plus expenses. He accepted.

Following the completion of the tour, Pat Travers – now with a record deal – put him in touch with two Canadian friends who had also come to the UK to try their luck. Nick brought in Steve Barnacle, and the resulting Travers-influenced hard rock band, Fury, began gigging on the London pub scene. A regular venue was the same Golden Lion from where the Clash poached the 101ers' Joe Strummer. Fury came close to being signed by CBS at much the same time as the Clash, but although the band had been given the firm impression that the deal was in the bag, it fell through. One of the excuses offered to Fury was that their drummer's wristy, jazz-derived style lacked sufficient power. When he met Mick Jones at the Kinks gig, Nick was still part of Fury, and still earning £50 a week, but his long-term prospects did not look good.

He had a typical long-haired muso's contempt for punk rock, but the tenuousness of his position encouraged Nick to accept Mick's invitation. He turned up at Rehearsals in the first week of April, thinking – and telling friends like Steve Barnacle – that if his audition proved successful, he'd take the job for a year or so until his name was well enough known for him to move on to something better. The Clash were considering hiring Mark Laff, who had tried out earlier that same day, but Nick soon changed their minds. The recently voiced criticisms of his style were instrumental in securing him the job: he hit the drums as hard as he could, and the deafening barrage deeply impressed the others. Mark Laff was given the consolation prize of the drum seat with Subway Sect.

Nick – or Nicky, as he was initially restyled, possibly to avoid confusion with Mick – was introduced to the general public courtesy of Caroline Coon, via the 30 April 1977 issue of *Melody Maker*. The photograph showed him after his image-makeover, wearing Pop Star Army Fatigues and with his hair dyed ginger and spiked. His past had also been rewritten to suit: he was described as an 'ex-office clerk' and claimed never to have played live before. Although from out of town, it was important that he was not perceived to be too utterly devoid of street credibility. In the *Clash Songbook*, published a year later, Wendy was even described as his girlfriend rather than his wife. Most of the bands on Nick's resumé would never be acknowledged in interview, even after he left the Clash in 1982; and somewhere along the line his time with the GI's would be miraculously transformed into a stint with the Temptations. In 1999's *Westway To The World* – four years after his fib was exposed in the first edition of this book – he admitted that, although the GI's had supported the Temptations, he had never actually played for the Motown act.

Nick's fondness for fooling around made him good company for Paul and Robin Crocker, also hired by the Clash at this time. More importantly, Nick was content just to go along for the ride, creating none of the ideological friction of a Terry Chimes, a Rob Harper or a Jon Moss. He was quickly given a nickname, a sign of his acceptance by the band which also said much about his character. *Topper* was the title of a popular weekly comic, Nick's preferred reading matter at the time. Paul thought he resembled one of the comic's characters, Micky the Monkey. Following the tour, Topper would be asked to stay on full-time – on £25 a week – without officially being made a member of the band.

'I remember, quite a long time after I left, Bernie saying, "It's too late to come back now. We've got Topper, and we're happy with him." Almost gloatingly,' says Terry Chimes. 'He was dying for me to say this upset me, but I said, "Well, it's good that you've found a drummer you like. I'm pleased." He was a bit puzzled by that.'

11
COMPLETE CONTROL

The May 1977 White Riot Tour was closely modelled on the previous December's Anarchy In The UK Tour. Bernie Rhodes was not one to pass up a good contact, especially one made through Malcolm McLaren, so he used the same promoter, Dave Cork of Endale Associates. The support acts were predictable: the Buzzcocks, Subway Sect and the Slits, in which band Mick's girlfriend Viv Albertine had just replaced Kate Korus on guitar. Generation X were unable to take part as they had just said goodbye to drummer John Towe and were yet to poach Mark Laff from Subway Sect. The only band on the bill that were not part of Bernie and the Clash's would-be new Inner Circle were the Jam, brought along for the same reason the Damned had been included on the Anarchy Tour.

The White Riot Tour was the first high profile, big name punk tour to hit the road since the tabloid uproar surrounding the Pistols' outing. Consequently, it was guaranteed a large turnout at what were admittedly still mostly small club and college venues, and an enthusiastic reaction from many gig-goers who had not even heard of punk five months previously. The tour certainly proved to be as influential as its predecessor: the show at Eric's on 5 May show was where Julian Cope, Ian McCullough and Pete Wylie first met. Mick Jones befriended Pete and encouraged his ambition by giving him a guitar 'on permanent loan'. The Crucial Three did not last, but its spirit carried over into the bands the three former members formed thereafter: the Teardrop Explodes, Echo and the Bunnymen and Wah! Heat, respectively. A new pecking order was established, with the Clash rather than the Pistols now indisputably first in line. 'I kinda liked the Clash, and I thought they had some good songs,' says Glen Matlock. 'But I just thought they wore the crown by default, really.'

Robin Crocker joined those established members of the entourage Micky Foote, Roadent and Sebastian Conran as guitar roadie for the tour. 'Basically, he was Mick's gofer,' says Sebastian. Subway Sect roadie Barry August was also taken along to look after Topper's drums. Paul rechristened him the Baker, or Baker for short, after his alleged resemblance to Pillsbury the Doughboy. Don Letts went along to look after the Slits, and brought his Super 8 camera to film proceedings, much as Julien Temple had on the Anarchy Tour. Some of the on-the-road footage he shot would appear in *The Punk Rock Movie*. Determined to make the tour a triumphant occasion, the band also invited friends like Chrissie Hynde along to share the experience. Bernie tried to persuade the Jam to cover some of the cost of supporting such a huge retinue on the road – the contribution suggested was £1,000 – but the second-on-the-bill band thought it enough that they should be required to finance themselves. Some local councils still frowned upon punk and made it difficult for venues trying to book bands. Most of the extensive rescheduling that plagued the tour was due more to the last minute organisation of the dates. This less than slick planning did nothing to keep tour costs in check.

Some of the parallels with the Anarchy Tour were almost uncanny. Just as the Pistols had fallen out with the Damned on that outing, so did the Clash fall out with the Jam about a third of the way through the White Riot Tour. The financial disagreements were still rankling when the support band accused the headliners of denying them a proper soundcheck at the 9 May Finsbury Park Rainbow show: echoes of the August 1976 Screen On The Green gig. The Jam dropped out immediately afterwards.

This failed to sour the concert for Joe. Interviewed on the Channel 4 TV show *Wired* in 1988, he chose the Rainbow show as the moment he held most dear from his time with the Clash: 'That was the first night that punk really broke out of the clubs. The Rainbow at that time was a really big venue; it was kinda, "Supergroups go there!" We played there with the Jam, Subway Sect and the Slits, and the audience came and filled it. Trashed the place as well, but it really felt like – through a combination of luck and effort – that we were in the right place doing the right thing at the right time. And that kind of night happens once or twice in a lifetime.'

In spite of the Clash's best efforts at persuasion, the Rainbow's manager Allan Schaverian had refused to remove the venue's seats. During the course of the gig, the audience took matters into their own hands, smashing them up and depositing them in a pile at the front of the stage. In another echo of the Anarchy Tour, this garnered the Clash extensive tabloid coverage. 'PUNK WRECK' declared the *Sun* on 11 May. 'I went to bed obscure and woke up famous,' Joe told *Uncut*'s Gavin Martin in 1999. 'A three-page spread in the *Evening Standard*.' Nevertheless, much of the moral wrath that had characterised press coverage of the earlier outing was missing from these reports. Allan Schaverian knew someone else was going to have to pay for the mess. He was, if anything, pleased by the publicity. 'It was not malicious damage, just natural exuberance,' he told the *Sun*. 'We shall have more punk concerts soon.'

It was left to the music press to assume the role previously occupied by the mainstream press, and admonish the band and their followers for their behaviour. Both the 'curiously self-conscious and predictable' nature of the riot and the apparent acceptance of it by the powers-that-be made the *NME*'s Neil Spencer nervous. In a thinkpiece entitled 'Is This What We Ordered?', he quoted from *Revolt Into Style*, a book published in 1972 by jazz singer and cultural commentator George Melly: 'Each successive pop explosion has come roaring out of the clubs in which it was born like an angry young bull. Watching from the other side of the gate, the current establishment has proclaimed it dangerous, subversive, a menace to youth, and demanded something be done about it. Something is. Commercial exploitation advances towards it holding out a bucketful of recording contracts... Then, once the muzzle is safely buried in the golden mash, the cunning butcher nips deftly along the flank and castrates the animal... The establishment realises it is safe to advance into the field and gingerly pats the now docile creature which can then be relied on to grow fatter and stupider.' It was a warning Nick felt the Clash and the punk movement ought to heed.

It appeared CBS were already sharpening the shears. Having recovered from the shock of scoring a hit with a cheaply-made, practically unproduced album by a band whose musical approach and general philosophy they could not begin to understand, the record company had decided it was time to start making good on their promising new investment. Without bothering to consult either Bernie or the band, they decided 'Remote Control', backed with the Dunstable version of 'London's Burning', should be the Clash's follow-up single. It was released on 13 May in a picture sleeve, designed in-house, which merely reproduced *The Clash* album cover in miniature on the front and placed a collage of policemen and high-rise blocks on the back. As the band had insisted that signing to a major label did not mean they were abandoning artistic control, they understandably felt humiliated by this turn of events. In some quarters, the fuss they made was attributed to their supposed horror at CBS's undermining of the VFM principle in releasing a second single from the album. In fact, the Clash were simply annoyed by the choice of track: the band had wanted 'Janie Jones', and back on 30 April, *Melody Maker* had even announced that it was to be their new single. The Clash encouraged their fans to boycott 'Remote Control' and, together with its own shortcomings as a song, this ensured that it failed to make the charts.

In an effort to establish a working relationship with their record company, and without really knowing what they were letting themselves in for, the Clash had already agreed to interrupt the UK dates on 14 May in order to fly to Amsterdam and provide part of the entertainment for a CBS function at the Brakke Grande. According to the 'Communiqué From Clash City' Mick and Robin sent to *Sniffin' Glue*, they were required to take the stage after 'three funk bands' and 'one country and western singer'. Insult was added to injury when 'the reaction of the Bols Advocaat set [was] mainly one of hysterical laughter.'

Back in the UK, the Clash had more irritants to contend with. While other representatives of the establishment had decided to keep their heads down for the duration of the White Riot Tour, the same could not be said of the police. The Clash would later claim their almost continual presence – at venues, hotels and even during transit – amounted to harassment. If true, it was hardly surprising: the band had appeared on television boasting about open conflict with the police at the Notting Hill Riot; they had released records featuring pictures of police charges with lyrics openly inciting their followers to riot; and they had just presided over their own mini-riot at the Rainbow. On 21 May, the Clash coach was stopped outside St Albans, and Topper and Joe were charged with stealing 11 pillows and a room key from the Newcastle Holiday Inn the previous night. The pillows are clearly evident in one of *The Punk Rock Movie*'s coach scenes. 'We were all stripped bollock naked, fingers up the anus, the works,' Bernie informed the *NME*'s Tony Parsons, in an attempt to make the police sound more oppressive and the Clash members' thievery less petty. His claim was untrue.

The disastrous Anarchy outing had lost the Pistols over £10,000; before it had even finished, Bernie claimed the relatively unhampered White Riot Tour had lost £15,000, and in 1978 Joe told *Melody Maker*'s Simon Kinnersley that the losses had eventually totalled £28,000. 'None of us had any wages for eight weeks.'

The niggles continued back in London. On 2 June, Joe was arrested once more, this time for spraying 'THE CLASH' on a wall near Dingwalls. He was required to appear in court on the 10th, where he was fined £5. Unfortunately, this was also the day he and Topper were supposed to be appearing in court in Newcastle to face the pillow theft charges. The duo were duly arrested again on the 12th, and driven to Newcastle where they spent the weekend in jail before being fined £60 and £40, respectively. As criminal records go, the Clash's was falling well short of desperado status, and it is difficult to rebuke the music press for poking fun, which they did with great glee.

The Clash were not the only ones feeling the pressure. The Roxy had set itself up as a base from which the second wave punk bands could project a collective identity. It was an environment in which a peer group made and controlled its own entertainment without undue interference or exploitation from outside agencies. All that came to an end when Andy Czezowski's lease ran out in April 1977. A friend of club owner Rene Albert saw the money-making potential of the venue and paid to take it over, placing himself in charge. His idea was to operate the club seven nights a week and book bands through established agencies, rather than follow Andy's policy of making direct contact with the bands themselves. He also intended to skim off the profits and pay Andy and his staff token wages. Unsurprisingly, Andy refused to co-operate, and when he turned up on 23 April for a Siouxsie and the Banshees gig, he was denied entry.

The rest of the Roxy staff left with him. Don Letts and Leo Williams roadied for the Slits on the White Riot Tour and for a while thereafter. A live album had been planned and recorded at the club while it was still under Andy's guardianship. Released in June 1977 on EMI's Harvest label, *Live At The Roxy, London WC2* contained tracks by the

Buzzcocks, Slaughter and the Dogs, X Ray Spex, the Adverts, Eater, Wire and Johnny Moped, interspersed with snippets of dialogue recorded in the club toilets. Other live performances are preserved on Don Letts's *The Punk Rock Movie*. These are usually thought of as posthumous souvenirs of the club, but the new owner did keep it going for a while under the same name. 'He booked in people like the Boomtown Rats and Tubeway Army,' says Andy. 'But people realised it had nothing to do with me. The attitude had changed.'

Andy himself fully intended to bounce back with a new larger club, run on much the same lines. He leased Crackers, the former soul boy haunt at 201 Wardour Street, renamed it the Vortex, booked in two weeks' worth of acts, organised the flyers, and notified the music press. Unfortunately, Andy did not get to savour his comeback. When he turned up on 4 July 1977 for the club's first night – the Heartbreakers, supported by the Buzzcocks and the newly-formed Fall – it was to go through a depressingly familiar experience. 'The people who *said* they owned the place wouldn't let me into the club! They just used me to set it up, and then they continued to book any old bands for as little as possible.' The next time Andy opened a club, the Fridge in Brixton, he made sure no-one was in a position to take it away from him.

For a while, being new, and being in a position to book the likes of Sham 69 and Glen Matlock's Rich Kids, the Vortex became by default the centre of the punk scene. Never a comfortable place, it was staffed by intimidating bouncer-types who were openly antagonistic towards the clientele. This did nothing to dispel the undercurrents of violence and paranoia in punk, but it did reveal that the rump of the punk scene was at heart timid when confronted with displays of superior force from representatives of the establishment (albeit in a decidedly shady guise). Paul Weller was so affected by the club's oppressive atmosphere that it inspired him to write 'A-Bomb In Wardour Street'.

The post-Grundy scares had died down a little by the summer of 1977. The more traditional rock clubs and clubs, including the Nashville, the Marquee, Dingwalls and even the 100 Club, started allowing punk bands to play again. Instead of representing a triumph, this was another indication of punk's toothlessness: whatever threat it had once represented was clearly no longer perceived to exist. In Manchester, punk was still based at the Electric Circus, and in Liverpool at Eric's. In London, lacking the tight focus and separate identity provided by a single high-profile club, punk started to slip from being a scene and an outlook into being just another sub-genre of rock.

The music business establishment may have been able to overlook punk's violent image, but that image was in no hurry to go away. In mid June, Johnny Rotten was attacked by a razor-wielding gang. Luckily, he only needed two stitches in his arm. The following night, Paul Cook was assaulted by five men armed with knives and a metal bar. He required 15 stitches in the back of his head. The phlegmatic Paul managed to shrug off the experience, but the far more visible and notorious Johnny felt like a marked man and spent more and more of his time at home, behind locked doors. In a thinkpiece on punk violence entitled 'We Didn't Know It Was Loaded...' published in July, the *NME*'s Charles Shaar Murray listed attacks on several other punk figures, and offered this warning to all the nation's youth cults: 'If we lose our perspective sufficiently to start mistaking the nearest target for the biggest one, then those who hate us will have won.'

Partly in recognition of the fact that punk was now more of a national movement than a London scene, partly to put the cap on the White Riot Tour by reinforcing the notion of the Clash as the movement's top dogs, and partly because promoters Endale Associates were based in the Second City, Bernie scheduled a Clash-headlined one-day punk festival for 17 July at Digbeth Rag Market in Birmingham. With line-up also featuring the Heartbreakers, the Slits, Subway Sect and the Rich Kids, among others, it was intended to attract a crowd of 5,000. The new outbreak of punk-related violence had not passed unnoticed, however. The week before the festival was due to take place, at the urging of the local police, magistrates refused Endale a music licence. The Clash declared their intention of turning up anyway, which prompted the police to warn them that this would make them liable to charges of 'conspiracy and incitement to riot'. Finding this challenge difficult to resist, the Clash duly arrived at the site. No showdown ensued. Only Joe was prepared to leave the car to talk to the crowd of 500 die-hard hopefuls, and when the small police presence insisted the band move on, they capitulated. An alternative Clash gig was hastily arranged at Barbarellas, but, inevitably, it was something of an anticlimax. Covering the event for the *NME*, Tony Parsons and Julie Burchill found it difficult to hide their scorn, especially at Bernie's repeated exhortation, 'Abstract theatre! It's great! Everything's spontaneous!'

The festival might have failed to live up to its poster billing as 'The Last Big Event Before We All Go To Jail!', but it did have an air of finality about it. There would be no further efforts to present a major punk festival in the UK. Although Bernie would continue to investigate suitable candidates for his own stable of talent, and although he and the Clash would always endeavour to arrange stimulating support bands for Clash tours, Digbeth marked the end of their commitment to staging major events and Bernie's attempts to establish the band as the leading lights of a punk Inner Circle. From this point on, it was every band for itself, which inevitably ensured that individual success was prized more than collective achievement: George Melly's observation (as quoted by Neil Spencer) was assuming the weight of prophecy.

The Clash camp was by no means blind to this state of affairs. That much is evident from the lyrics Joe – and Mick – produced for the (mostly) new batch of songs they came up with during June and July 1977. Six months previously, Mick had written the subsequently disowned 'Remote Control' to protest the treatment afforded the bands on the Anarchy Tour. In his room at Wilmcote House, he now poured the bitterness and frustration he felt about the Clash's experiences with the police and, especially, CBS on the White Riot Tour into a song with the consciously similar title 'Complete Control'. The coda's repeated chant spells out his hard won knowledge that the promise of complete control was a total c-o-n. As the title phrase was one of Bernie's favourites, the song also carries an implied dig at him. Joe liked Mick's original lyric so much he left it untouched.

The summer arrests and the Digbeth fiasco – 'We get in, but we don't have fun' – provided the Clash with the material for 'The Prisoner', named after the Kafkaesque cult television series of that title. 'City Of The Dead' alludes to police hassle – the band sing of being 'picked up' for dressing in 'dangerous gear', namely, the Pop Star Army Fatigues – and also reports that summer's terrorisation of punks by members of the general public. Urban alienation and the boredom of everyday life in, specifically, London had provided the background to *The Clash*. Both 'The Prisoner' and 'City Of The Dead' continue the tradition. Whereas album tracks like 'Hate And War' had reacted with righteous indignation, however, the new songs merely seem resigned: faced with mindless aggression from 'the jerks', the Clash no longer threaten to 'give it two time back' but instead 'hide inside / All courage gone and paralysed'.

With police oppression on the brain, Mick now found the old 101ers' song 'Jail Guitar Doors' irresistible. Overruling Joe's objections, he revived it, indulging in a little reversal of customary roles with his partner: he kept the original chorus, but rewrote the rest of the lyric to Joe's tune. The new verses namecheck Jones guitar heroes who had (in his heavily romanticised account) also previously suffered persecution by the authorities: the MC5's Wayne Kramer, Peter Green of blues-period Fleetwood Mac, and Keith Richards.

The lyric to '(White Man) In Hammersmith Palais' was inspired by two separate but, to Joe, not unrelated incidents. It begins by describing a reggae all-nighter at the Palais, as attended by Joe and Clash roadie Roadent on 5 June 1977. As the song details, they were disappointed by the general standard of the performances, and there was a bad atmosphere in the hall. 'A lot of the black sticksmen were running around trying to snatch these white girls' handbags, and I intervened,' Joe told the *NME*'s Sean O'Hagan in 1988. That same year, he went into more detail about the song for a *Melody Maker* Clash retrospective: 'I was trying to talk about revolution, and how we weren't ever going to have one, because who had an answer to the British Army? I was really getting at the division between the black rebels and the white rebels, and the fact that we gotta have some unity or we're just going to get stomped on.'

From musing on black and white solidarity, the song moves on to consider the State of Punk, and the movement's apparent lack of commitment to change. Following the Jam's departure from the White Riot Tour, there had been some inter-band jibing in the music press. Then Paul Weller had gone public with what he subsequently admitted were his confused political views, telling the *NME*: 'All this change the world thing is becoming a bit too trendy... We'll be voting Conservative at the next election.' His intention was to rile the Clash, and he was successful. Following a couple of Tory by-election triumphs, the Jam received a telegram reading, 'Congratulations on victory on Merseyside and Manchester. Maggie will be proud of you. See you in South Africa for gun practice. The Clash.' In '(White Man) In Hammersmith Palais', the Jam are used as a symbol for everything that was wrong with the punk movement at the time: they are 'the new group(s)' refusing to learn anything, 'changing their votes', wearing 'Burton suits', and 'turning rebellion into money'.

Of the five new songs listed above, no fewer than four seem to suggest the band and punk are powerless to make any difference. The protagonists of all five – three directly and two indirectly – turn to drugs to escape the situation, while 'The Prisoner' considers 'stardom' as another escape option. The band's early interviews had been full of gung ho resolve to change the world. Much of the Clash's summer 1977 output takes its tone instead from the interview Joe had given Caroline Coon back in March, smacking of complete and utter disillusion.

'Clash City Rockers' runs against the grain of contemporaneous compositions in that it represents a determined effort to throw off that prevailing downbeat mood. Like 'Jail Guitar Doors', it is partly a makeover of an old song – elements of its tune being derived from abandoned Clash composition 'I Know What You Do' – but Joe's lyric is wholly new and upbeat, bragging with tongue-in-cheek exaggeration, Bo Diddley-style, about the Clash's invincibility. It promotes the DIY ethic – 'You don't succeed unless you try' – and demands that everyone put up or shut up: if you hate your job, leave it and do something more interesting instead.

Considered together, these six songs represent a dramatic shift away from the crude sloganeering of the first album towards a brutally – even self-laceratingly – honest and noticeably more articulate examination of the mixed emotions experienced by the Clash during the punk doldrums of mid-1977. So closely linked thematically that they almost begged to be grouped together on an album, fate decreed instead that the songs would be split into pairs and issued over the course of the following year as the A and B sides of three inter-album singles. This – and the release of the ultra-positive 'Clash City Rockers' as the second of those singles – helped to mask the extent of the band's deflation.

So did the quality of the music, the texture and dynamics of which achieved a leap in evolution every bit as dramatic as that evidenced by the lyrics. In the wake of the precedent set by the band's punk-reggae hybrid version of 'Police And Thieves', Mick seized the opportunity to throw off some of the more constraining orthodoxies of punk. Inspired to push and pull at the structures of the songs, he rejected the short, sharp shock dictate in favour of adding codas, or even breaking compositions down into rhythmically varied sections: 'Clash City Rockers' has three. Guitar solos had previously been brief to the point of terseness, but Mick now allowed himself to stretch out. In 'Complete Control', Joe's half-sarcastic, half-defiant ad lib, 'You're my guitar hero', acknowledges that a taboo has been broken. When the band booked into CBS studios in August to record 'City Of The Dead', Mick would reveal his growing interest in shading and embellishment by including piano and saxophone overdubs. This was no gratuitous self-indulgence: at least half of the new songs ranked with his best compositions to date, and 'Complete Control' would remain one of the band's most popular for the duration of their career (and beyond). By far Mick's most daring songwriting liberty, though, is taken with '(White Man) In Hammersmith Palais'. Not only is it the Clash's first attempt to slow down the tempo – another act of heresy in punk circles – but also their first to play the bona fide reggae beat: a totally appropriate setting for Joe's assessment of the prospects for unity between punk and reggae cultures at a time when even the respective followers of those cultures appeared unwilling to live up to their ideals.

Fittingly, then, reggae references abound in the lyrics to the new songs. The title 'Clash City Rockers' does not refer to the mods' old adversaries but instead describes the post-'Police And Thieves' punk-reggae crossover style of the composition. Rockers was itself a hybrid, invented in the mid Seventies by Sly Dunbar: inspired by disco, he had doubled up the drums to give roots reggae a more urgent, militant edge. 'I meant it as a rockers tune from Clash City,' Joe told *Melody Maker* in 1988. Toaster Prince Far I also gets a namecheck.

Most of the references in the other songs can be traced to the soundtrack of Perry Henzell's film *The Harder They Come*, a Jamaican take on US blaxploitation movies like *Shaft* and *Superfly*. Originally given limited UK release in 1972, it was reissued at the beginning of 1977. The central character, the gun-toting Ivan, is portrayed by veteran reggae singer Jimmy Cliff. The songs on its soundtrack are from the early reggae period 1969-71. Some, like Jimmy Cliff's title track, Desmond Dekker's '007 (Shanty Town)' and the Slickers' 'Johnny Too Bad' are still largely concerned with celebrating or admonishing the rude boy; others, such as Cliff's 'Many Rivers To Cross' and 'Sitting In Limbo' and the Melodians' 'Rivers Of Babylon', deal with the black Jamaican struggle; and the Maytals' 'Pressure Drop' makes it clear what it is like to be on the receiving end of the forces of oppression.

The reissued film made an immediate connection with Paul Simonon – who not only bought the Island soundtrack album, but also eventually the video and the book – and, via him, the rest of the Clash and their circle. The band's identification with the rude boy, dating back to autumn 1976, was reinforced by the film's story and songs, which appeared relevant to their own circumstances: Ivan, up against both the police and Jamaica's notoriously corrupt music business, is – in his own mind, at least – a latter-day version of Robin Hood or Billy the Kid. The Clash had worked up a cover of 'Pressure Drop' for the White Riot Tour; 'The Prisoner' makes reference to rude boys and to the Slickers' 'Johnny Too Bad'; and the coda to 'Jail Guitar Doors' quotes the Maytals' '54-46 That's My Number', a song which was inspired by leader Toots Hibbert's 1966-68 incarceration for marijuana possession. The influence would prove enduring, continuing throughout the following year and well into 1979: the band would namecheck the film in 'Safe European Home'; the phrase 'rudie can't fail', borrowed from '007 (Shanty Town)', would also appear in 'Safe European Home' before being recycled as the title for another Clash song; and Paul would transplant *The Harder They*

Come's protagonist and basic storyline to his south London skinhead moonstomping ground for his songwriting début, 'Guns Of Brixton'.

Most of the Clash's summer 1977 compositions received their live débuts that August, when the band played a brace of festivals on the Continent. The Second European Punk Festival was held on 5 and 6 August, again at Mont de Marsan in France. In addition to the Boys and such pub rock stalwarts as Eddie and the Hot Rods and Dr Feelgood, the bill included the Damned and the Jam. In view of the Clash's strained relationship with the last two bands, a belated showing of punk solidarity seemed unlikely. In the event, though, the banter with the Jam was good-natured, and after a brief skirmish when Captain Sensible let off a stink bomb onstage during the Clash's set, the Damned and the Clash held talks and agreed to bury the hatchet.

All to the good, as both were scheduled to appear, along with Stiff's rising star Elvis Costello, at a jazz festival in Bilzen, Belgium on the 12th. Predictably, most of the other attractions were jazz bands, and the audience was largely made up of long haired jazz fans. As if their incongruity was not enough to contend with, the punk bands discovered they would be required to perform on a stage separated from the audience by a pit full of security guards and a 10-foot tall barbed wire fence, prompting the Captain to quip, 'This isn't Bilzen, it's Belsen.' Mostly hostile to the music, and even more hostile to the security measures, the crowd spent much of the Damned's set lobbing bottles over the fence, showing little discrimination in their choice of target. By the time the Clash took the stage, the audience had progressed to bricks and stones. One hit Paul on the shoulder and another whistled past Mick's face, but the band stood their ground. Although no great fighter, Mick invariably proved as resolute as the others when facing this kind of hostility, even if – as on this occasion – he was so scared that he had to throw up after the show. Having spent much of the set trying to incite the audience to pull down the fence, towards the end Joe leaped into the pit and joined in their efforts to topple it, until forcibly restrained by the bouncers. 'I don't think about things I do too much,' he told the *NME*'s Chris Salewicz afterwards. 'I just do 'em.'

The band arrived home to find that Joe's prognosis for punk and reggae unity as outlined in '(White Man) In Hammersmith Palais' appeared to have been unduly pessimistic. Bob Marley and his old producer Lee 'Scratch' Perry had teamed up in Island Records' Basing Street studio, just off Ladbroke Grove, for a recording session. *Sounds*' resident reggae aficionado Vivien Goldman had popped along for a visit, taking with her a copy of *The Clash*. She was intrigued to see how the famously eccentric Lee reacted to the band's version of the song he had co-written with, and produced for, Junior Murvin. 'They [Lee and Bob] said, "What are these people with funny hair?"' Vivien recalled in 1981. 'And I explained what I thought they were trying to do. A week later, I went round and they said, "Listen to this!"' 'This' was 'Punky Reggae Party', a song the duo had written and recorded together as a response in kind to the Clash's gesture of solidarity. Consisting chiefly of a list of reggae and punk bands invited to attend the mythical hoe-down, it relates what they have in common: 'Rejected by society / Treated with impunity / Protected by their dignity.' Released that December as a double A-side with Bob's 'Jamming', it was inevitably overshadowed by the stronger song and failed to set the world alight. Given Marley's stature, though, it was a significant boost to Clash morale.

Hearing Lee was in town, Bernie set out to track him down. Intrigued by this very different but politically and spiritually-aligned music, Lee agreed to take the matter further. Bernie persuaded him to produce a session with the Clash at Sarm East studios in Whitechapel in August. The band chose 'Pressure Drop' and 'Complete Control', one example each from the reggae and punk genres, in the hope that the master reggae producer would help them perfect the hybrid. Unfortunately, Scratch seemed more interested in learning how to capture the punk sound in a suitably punk timespan – Joe joked that he was in and out in 15 minutes – and although the band enjoyed the experience they felt the result fell between two stools. This version of 'Pressure Drop' was shelved, and Mick went back into the studio with 'Complete Control' and remixed it with louder guitars. Back home in Jamaica, the Clash became the first white group to have their picture painted on the wall of Lee's Black Ark studio.

The Clash's insistence that 'Complete Control' should be their third single was considered by music press and fans alike to be a bold move taken by artists prepared to put their entire futures at risk on a point of principle. The song's release on 23 September 1977 was construed as a tit-for-tat public humiliation of CBS by the band, a sign that the Clash had re-established in no uncertain terms the control about which they sang. Sebastian Conran's design for the sleeve accentuates the directness of the song's message, featuring a Clash-pink speaker cabinet on the front, and a collage comprising song lyrics, a band portrait and a burning building on the back. Bernie's press release for the single took an uncharacteristically reasonable position – possibly because the second instalment of the CBS advance was now due – but still reworked George Melly's words from *Revolt Into Style* into Berniespeak: 'It tells a story of conflict between two opposing camps. One side sees change as an opportunity to channel the enthusiasm of a raw and dangerous culture in a direction where energy is made safe and predictable. The other is dealing with change as a freedom to be experienced so as to understand one's true capabilities, allowing a creative social situation to emerge.' That CBS allowed the single's release says everything that needs to be said about the size of the threat they thought it represented.

It did not perform as well as was hoped, either, staying on the charts for just two weeks and climbing no higher than number 28. The Sex Pistols' 'God Save The Queen' had made number two in June, and 'Pretty Vacant' had made number six in July. The Stranglers' last three singles had all made the Top 10, and the Jam's most recent offering had reached number 13. The two last-named bands had appeared on *Top Of The Pops*, which had undoubtedly helped. Even the Pistols – who had instigated punk's boycott of the programme – had allowed a promotional film of themselves performing 'Pretty Vacant' to be broadcast on 14 July. The Clash still refused to have anything to do with the show.

In spite of the handicap this represented, the band were determined to compete with their peers. Having already returned to CBS studios during September to record 'Jail Guitar Doors' with Micky Foote and Simon Humphrey, the Clash would book back in on at least two occasions during October and November to ensure they captured a strong version of 'Clash City Rockers', their most upbeat and therefore most commercially obvious new song, as the A-side for their follow-up single.

Another brief European tour took the band to France, Germany and Scandinavia in late September and early October 1977. A German film crew led by Wolfgang Bünd had visited London in mid September to make a documentary entitled *Punk In London '77*. Wolfgang did not get to film the Clash at that time – he had to make to with interviewing Roadent instead – but now took the opportunity to capture part of the band's set in what resembles a large school hall in Munich. A high stage and bright onstage lighting make for a poor atmosphere but a clear view as the band – Mick and Joe in bright red Pop Star Army Fatigues, Paul in a fetchingly ripped fishnet top – perform 'Complete Control', 'Hate And War', 'Police And Thieves' and 'Garageland'. The camera is fixed on Joe throughout 'Hate And War', in spite of the fact Mick is singing lead; during 'Garageland', the cameraman wanders onstage for a close up, only to be prodded off again with the base of a microphone stand by a clearly angry Joe. A backstage interview finds Mick at his most obnoxious, moaning about the lack of vegetarian food, not having been able to find a hotel for the night, and Germany in general: 'We're not coming here again! It stinks.' By contrast, Paul is charm personified as he explains the problems the band have encountered with the country's more upright citizens and police. In 1991, *Punk In London '77* was released as a Studio K7 video.

Late October saw the Clash embark upon their second headlining tour of the UK, this time under the banner Get Out Of Control, a reference to their latest single release. The band still played college venues, provided they guaranteed access to non-students, but upscaled the other venues from clubs to former cinemas with capacities ranging from 1,500 to 3,000. *NME* construed this, along with the Top Rank Organisation's decision to allow punk back through its portals, as an indication that 'the Clash have at last been accepted officially by the establishment'. If so, the establishment had a funny way of showing it. The band's reputation resulted in particularly high premiums being demanded by insurance companies, which required several of the original dates to be changed during the weeks immediately preceding the tour. Insurance problems – the promoters were informed that the band had several claims outstanding against them – were also responsible for putting paid to the very first show, in Belfast on 20 October, just two hours before the Clash were due to take the stage. Efforts to find a replacement venue at such short notice proved fruitless. A few thwarted gig-goers, not understanding the reason for the cancellation, took out their frustration by pelting the band's car with beer cans.

Belfast had been chosen to start the tour because the Troubles represented the most extreme manifestation of street-level conflict and draconian state control the UK had to offer. Prior to the show being pulled, the Clash had gone walkabout in their Pop Star Army Fatigues – set off with seasonally appropriate leather biker jackets – and had been encouraged by representatives of all three leading music papers to pose for photographs against the barricades, in front of armed soldiers, and while being frisked at security checkpoints. These urban guerrilla-style pictures were duly plastered all over the following week's issues. Mick told *Melody Maker*'s Ian Birch, 'I just felt like a dick. The best time was when all the kids were in the photos with us. That was the only time when it was human and real. I should imagine they'll lap it up in London, though.' His realisation that such posturing struck the wrong note had come too late for him to object to Sebastian Conran's new backdrop. In the tradition of the White Riot Tour's charging policemen shot, it was a blow up of a violent Belfast street scene depicting armoured cars and sheltering civilians. While the Clash could justifiably claim a connection with the Notting Hill Riot, co-opting the Troubles for their own promotional ends was downright insulting to those who had to live full-time in circumstances far more soul-destroying than anything either experienced by the Clash or described on *The Clash*. By no means everyone in London 'lapped it up', either. The *NME* headlined its feature, 'The Clash Visit Belfast For Picture Session', and, despite the complicity of the inkies' photographers in arranging that session, further sarcastic comments followed over the coming months. The Belfast connection proved to be the band's crassest and most credibility-damaging error of judgement to date. The charging policemen backdrop was reinstated for the UK mainland dates.

It was a bad start to what turned out to be a troubled tour, during which the Clash would lose the services of one of their key helpers. Roadent's position was a peculiar one. He worked closely with the band, and inevitably some of their glory reflected upon him. At live shows audience members would shout his name out while he was making last minute equipment checks, and, following his encounter with the German documentary crew, he was now cheekily putting himself forward for interview at every opportunity. Ultimately, though, he was an employee, expected to do as he was instructed. The determinedly egalitarian Joe, with whom he shared the squat in Canonbury, always treated him with respect, but that was not true of other members of the Clash camp. 'Bernie was a real cunt,' Roadent told his friend Robin Banks for *ZigZag* in 1980. 'He didn't pay me proper, and I was forking out for the gear from that! Also, I felt that some members of the band needed a personal valet instead of a roadie.' That remark, as Robin well knew, was aimed at the increasingly demanding Mick Jones. 'All the high-blown ideals disappeared years ago,' Roadent had announced to a stunned Wolfgang Bünd back in September. Just over a month later, he had finally had enough. On 26 October, en route from Glasgow to Edinburgh, he had a flaming row with the band and handed in his notice with immediate effect.

He switched allegiance to Malcolm McLaren and the Sex Pistols, for whom he worked until early the following year. Meanwhile, the punk documentary of which his mischievous interview had turned out to be the highlight proved to be a massive success in Germany. In March 1978, he would be invited to Munich to act in a TV film entitled *Brenende Langweile*. Although typecast as the roadie for a band played by the Adverts, he would impress Barbara Gogan enough to inspire the Passions' single, 'I'm In Love With A German Film Star' and his new employees enough to win a few more delinquent roles. Thereafter, he would return to the UK and use some of his earnings to set up his own PA hire company.

His replacement on the Clash tour was John Broad, who had recently graduated in Arabic and Islamic Studies from Lancaster University. His two attempts to see the Clash on the White Riot Tour had failed, so when he heard an acquaintance was driving one of the band's equipment trucks to Belfast, he had cadged a lift. Bernie had noticed John helping to unload the truck, and had asked him to help give out some badges. In Dublin, he had been pressed into service operating Joe Strummer's spotlight. Offered further work, he made his way to Dunfermline on the 24th, and, despite being totally inexperienced in such matters, found himself setting up the backline for the support band. Just two days later, in Edinburgh, he took over the departed Roadent's duties: not only setting up the Clash's amps but also lurking sidestage to provide assistance when and where needed. No accommodation was booked for him on the tour, but late one night a fellow crew member read a register upside down, and noticed that a certain Johnny Green of Dagenham Plastics had not taken up his reservation. John assumed the rep's identity in order to get a shower and a decent night's sleep. In those days, the frames of his spectacles were green, and the alias stuck.

He needed the shower because the punk audience's craze for gobbing on performers was then at its height, and being spattered with phlegm for the duration of the set was one of the least attractive perks of the job for bands and roadies alike. Early in November, in another deal worked out between CBS Head of Press Elly Smith and the *NME*, Mick's favourite rock writer, Lester Bangs, was flown in from the US to join the tour for three days (extended to six by mutual consent). The resulting three-part screed, accompanied by an album's worth of photos by Pennie Smith, was over the top even by the *NME*'s Clash-centric standards, but it did offer an outsider's perspective on some of the eccentricities of UK punk. Lester was particularly bemused by gobbing, but after affording the ritual due consideration, he developed a theory about it which he promptly tried out on Mick: it added to the general atmosphere of chaos and anarchy, right? 'No,' replied Mick. 'It's fucking disgusting.' Towards the end of the tour, the band even tried preceding their shows with pleas for no spitting. It worked. Sometimes.

As ever, Bernie and the Clash both wanted to offer 'the kids' VFM, taking along Don Letts as DJ and presenting a package of bands with a decidedly international flavour. Openers the Lous were an all-female band from Paris. Richard Hell – having finally made it to the UK – provided the main support with his new band the Voidoids. As one of the originators of punk, Hell might reasonably have expected better treatment than he got: a regular drenching in spittle and, at Newcastle Polytechnic on 28 October, a firework in the face. Attempting to kick heroin at the time, he was already at a low, and would later cite his experience on Get Out Of Control as the beginning of the end of his rock'n'roll ambitions.

The audience seemed intent on living up to the tour's name. 'The gigs were mayhem,' remembers Johnny Green. 'Never seen anything like it in my life.' At the Newcastle show, overly aggressive audience members tried to drag Mick offstage, in the process breaking his recently repaired Les Paul Junior. At Manchester's Elizabethan Ballroom, the front door to the venue gave way under pressure from queuing fans causing £600 worth of damage. Following the Bournemouth Winter Gardens show, the *London Evening News* reported that 'punk fans went beserk, leaving a trail of havoc behind them'. Elly Smith refuted these allegations in the *NME*, insisting that the paper's account was highly exaggerated. Fan Paul McLaughlin wrote in to back her up, claiming he saw just one punch thrown and 'about 12 chairs uprooted' out of a total of '1,700 or so'. Nevertheless, such news reports did nothing to reduce the Clash's insurance premiums.

Granada TV's *So It Goes* had been the first television music show to feature punk bands on a regular basis, despite being based in Manchester rather than London. Presenter Tony Wilson – soon to found Factory records – was sympathetic to the spirit of the movement, recognising the importance of presenting the music in a live setting. Some bands were invited to perform in the studio – the Pistols had made their live TV début in this manner in August 1976 – and others were filmed in concert when they came to town on tour. The programme's cameras were in the front line for the Clash's Manchester Elizabethan Ballroom gig, perfectly placed to capture the chaotic energy of the Get Out Of Control experience.

In marked contrast to the *Punk In London '77* footage, the *So It Goes* segment shows, through a camera lens blurred by deposits of gob, the sweat-drenched band toiling determinedly through a hail of gob, delivering ragged but stirring versions of 'What's My Name', 'Garageland', 'Capital Radio' and 'Janie Jones'. In the spirit of the band's more recent compositions, 'Capital Radio' now has a lengthy coda, during which Joe ad libs semi-coherently. Never wholly sure of the lyric to 'What's My Name', he mumbles his way through until inspiration strikes. 'Here we are on TV,' he sings, gesturing at the camera. 'What does it mean to me? What does it mean to you?' Then he pivots around to snarl the answer into the lens: '*Fuck all!*' At the end of the song, his feet become entangled with the microphone stand, and he pitches over backwards, smashing his head onto the drum riser at an awkward angle. Evidently a commonplace occurrence: instead of downing his instrument to rush to his band mate's aid, Paul just hoists his bass strap an inch higher on his shoulder, gobs nonchalantly at the floor, and launches straight into 'Garageland'. Sure enough – as in his 101ers days – Joe hauls himself back up in time to deliver the opening line. Intense stuff.

The spitting and unruly behaviour of certain of their number failed to poison the Clash's attitude to their audience. 'One of the things I liked about them was that they really cared about their fans,' says Johnny Green. 'One of my jobs was to open up the back door – you know, like in the lyric of "Complete Control" – to make sure that no-one without a ticket was left outside.' Mick had never forgotten the kindness shown to him by Mott the Hoople, and was committed to repaying it, even going so far as to allow stranded fans to sleep on his hotel room floor. Lester Bangs was also requested to provide floorspace, and the following day was moved to tell Mick, 'I had no idea any group could be as good to its fans as this.'

Spirits remained high, in spite of the negative publicity and Joe suffering from an abscessed tooth and glandular fever, which required him to keep a low profile and conserve his energy for the shows themselves. 'When I got to know them, I found they were a lot sillier than I expected,' says Johnny Green. 'I always think Pennie Smith's description was spot on: "Being on the road with the Clash is like a commando raid performed by the Bash Street Kids". There were a lot of serious conversations, but they could be very foolish. It was delightful.' Lester's *NME* feature also captured the band's sense of fun, even when it was at his own expense. Unfortunately, an ugly incident witnessed by the writer towards the end of his time with the tour came close to changing his opinion of them and making him doubt their sincerity.

Food fights were commonplace, usually involving the unholy trinity of Robin Crocker, Topper and Paul, although *ZigZag* liggers Kris Needs and Danny Baker were never shy to join in. During the course of one exchange of sandwiches, Micky Foote, who was doubling up as soundman and driver of the band's transit van – and was clearly unhappy with the latter task – lost his temper and physically assaulted a young fan. A drunken Robin joined in with the humiliation while Paul and Topper just sat and watched. The line between the harmless – albeit irresponsible – venting of steam and the abuse of power had just been crossed. Identifying Mick as the fans' champion, Lester sought him out to make his objections. The guitarist declared that nothing like that would be allowed to happen again. Micky Foote had already departed the tour in high dudgeon, and Johnny Green found he was now also responsible for driving the Clash from gig to gig.

Another violent incident occurred towards the end of the tour, which although not serious in itself, pointed to some of the problems with communication the band would experience in future. 'Me and Mick had a punch up in this little car going down the motorway, but Joe and Topper came off worse because they couldn't get out of the way,' Paul told *Melody Maker* in 1988. In fact, Paul was the aggressor. 'Anyway, me and Mick ended up not talking to each other for ages, so when we got to the studio to record "Clash City Rockers", Joe had to run between us telling each of us what the other one wanted him to do.'

Most of the record companies that had signed punk bands at the start of 1977 had rushed out their first albums in the spring. Six months later, the bands had been pushed into recording follow-ups to cash in before the punk craze passed. The resulting second albums by the Jam, the Stranglers and the Damned were underwhelming to say the least. Nevertheless, late autumn found CBS putting the Clash under pressure to record *their* second album.

Mick and Joe were in much the same position as their peers, having relatively few new and unused songs at their disposal. CBS had just delivered the second half of the band's advance, so once 'Clash City Rockers' had been recorded, it was suggested that the duo go away together on a working holiday. Recalling a vague invitation from Lee Perry, and still in thrall to reggae and *The Harder They Come*, Mick and Joe laughingly suggested a fortnight in Jamaica. They were stunned when Bernie agreed and handed over nearly enough money. Topper was too new a recruit to have any realistic expectations, but the reggae-loving Paul was furious about being left out. In an attempt to mollify him, Caroline Coon took him on an educational trip to Russia.

Mick and Joe hoped to make a firsthand connection with the culture they had been singing and talking about for the past year. 'Kingston, the toughest city in the world,' Joe recalled in an interview with the *NME*'s Sean O'Hagan just over 10 years later. 'We came out of the Pegasus Hotel all togged up in our punk threads. I tell you, we was like two punk tourists on a package tour. Completely naive. We knew Lee Perry, sort of, but we couldn't find him, so we were on our own.' While walking down to the docks to score some drugs they were openly addressed as 'white pigs'. 'The only reason they didn't kill us was that they thought we were merchant seamen off the ships.' Supplies secured, they promptly retired to their hotel room where they remained for much of the next two weeks. The positive outcome was that they got down to some serious work. Upon returning, they claimed to have written well over an album's worth of new material. One of the songs, 'Safe European Home', detailed their Caribbean experience. Musically, another punk-reggae hybrid song – arguably the Clash's best – lyrically it was the latest instalment in the saga begun by 'White Riot' and 'Police and Thieves' and continued by '(White Man) In Hammersmith Palais'. Joe's original, more longwinded lyric was honed until it cut straight to the heart of the duo's feelings of culture shock, rejection and fear.

The influence of both reggae and *The Harder They Come* would continue, but 'Safe European Home' was to be the last Clash composition of its type for the best part of a year. The following March, Joe told *Melody Maker*'s Simon Kinnersley, 'We got swept up in that crossover reggae, but I've got over it: it's nothing more than trash reggae.' Other bands were beginning to jump the bandwagon, most notably Elvis Costello and the Attractions. Elvis later told Greil Marcus that he had written 'Watching The Detectives' after listening to *The Clash* on headphones for 36 hours straight. It reached number 15 in the singles charts while Mick and Joe were out of the country. In the event, the Clash probably took a rest from 'trash reggae' at just the right time. Within the next couple of years, the Clash-style hybrid would become something of a cliché, with numerous 'new wave' bands toying with it, and the Police and the Ruts working up entire repertoires from variations on its basic theme.

Contributing to the decision to move away from punk-reggae crossover was Mick and Joe's restless curiosity regarding other musical forms. Mick's tastes were totally eclectic: he would listen to anything and everything, new or old, sometimes because he liked the artist and sometimes in the name of production research. In spite of his denunciation of R&B in 1976, Joe still favoured various pre-Sixties roots musics, and tended to have short-lived but passionate crazes. 'A new person every week,' confirms Johnny Green. 'The most obscure people you'd ever heard of, but always retro or genre.'

This musical curiosity is evident in the new songs brought back with them from Jamaica, which Johnny Green remembers them demoing on a TEAC 4-track at Rehearsals that January with Topper. Paul was still in Russia when the others wanted to start work. He refused to curtail his holiday for the sessions, so Mick doubled up on bass. Joe's two biggest crazes of mid-to-late 1977 had been rockabilly and cajun, and 'Last Gang In Town' makes reference to both. Mick's 'Stay Free' is a Mott the Hoople-style ballad. 'Drug Stabbing Time' is carried along by a blistering sax solo, probably courtesy of Topper's friend Gary Barnacle, who remembers jamming with the band at Rehearsals around this time. Although mostly still playing what he was told to play by Mick, Topper's flexibility allowed the Clash to attempt what Joe later described as the 'pure New Orleans' of the swaggeringly loose 'Julie's Been Working For The Drug Squad', to which Mick added some bravura slide guitar. The demo tape also includes 'Groovy Times', 'One Emotion' and Mick's pre-Clash pseudo-soul song 'Ooh, Baby, Ooh (It's Not Over)'. When Paul eventually returned, he was banished to the upstairs room with the finished tapes, a pair of headphones, a practice amp, and Johnny Green to tap out a beat for him while he learned Mick's basslines by rote 'like a special needs kid'.

Johnny had found life after the Get Out Of Control Tour to be something of an anticlimax, and had phoned up Bernie to offer his services full time. He was paid £15 a week, and given another £5 to equip the freezing and damp upstairs room at Rehearsals, his new home. He bought a second hand mattress, a three bar electric fire and a camping gas stove. Over time, he acquainted himself with the various outposts of Clash territory:

George's Café, the Canaervon Castle pub (now the Fusilier & Firkin), and Dingwalls. He and fellow roadie Baker were to divide driving duties between them. Bernie provided the van, which was yellow, tiny and – hardly surprisingly – a Renault.

Recording for 'Clash City Rockers' had been completed to Mick and Joe's satisfaction before their departure for Jamaica, and the single was scheduled for release on 17 February 1978. In their absence, Bernie had deemed the recording to be 'too flat', and Micky Foote had suggested varispeeding the master to perk it up. When Mick heard the acetate, he was furious. 'He went absolutely mental, started throwing glasses at the wall,' says Johnny. Not only was such fakery considered contrary to the punk ethic – although there is a persistent rumour that the entire first Damned album was sped up in the studio – but the Clash had very publicly butted heads with CBS over the issue of creative control, and for this stance to be undermined by their own support team was too much to take. It was too late to halt the single release, but the original mix of 'Clash City Rockers' would be reinstated for the US version of *The Clash* and used on all subsequent compilations. Although Micky Foote would continue to work for Bernie, it was made clear to him that he would take no further part in the Clash's career.

For Mick, who instigated it, Micky's removal from the scene was particularly convenient: he had designs on the producer's chair. One of the reasons the Clash spent so much time in the studio during the first months of 1978 was that he was keen to gain as much experience as possible. Some of the results would be released as singles (mostly B sides) with production credited to 'the Clash', but Mick was not ready to produce anything so high profile as an album, and CBS certainly had no intention of allowing him to try. Maurice Oberstein's main motive in signing the band had been to make his counterparts in the US sit up and take notice. *The Clash*'s sound and sentiments had been deemed too raw for American radio – at the time, that market's most powerful promotional medium – and therefore the album had been denied a US release. Maurice was determined that the band's follow-up should not meet with the same resistance from CBS's American labels.

The answer was a producer with a proven track record in getting non-mainstream rock bands onto American radio. Enter Sandy Pearlman, who had recently produced the first two albums for raucous American new wavers the Dictators, but was best known for his svengali-like role with hard rock band Blue Öyster Cult. He was not only responsible for the increasingly high-tech production of their music, but also for many of their lyrics and much of their presentation, which reflected his interests in, by his own account, 'technology, science fiction, horror literature, obscure wars' and decadent Nazi-chic. On the surface, then, he was perhaps not the most obvious choice for the Clash in 1978. Nevertheless, a trio of 'secret' dates were arranged in and around Birmingham and Dunstable for late January 1978, partly so the band could work in some of their new material, and partly so that Pearlman could see them in action.

The Clash always took their pre-gig warm-up time extremely seriously, psyching themselves for performance in much the same way as a football team. To this end, Johnny Green would seal off their dressing room for the period immediately before they took the stage. Unfortunately, at the first show he attended, Pearlman made the mistake of trying to push his way in past Robin Crocker, who had no idea who he was and had already refused him entry once. Drunk, and paying no heed to Mick's recent promise to Lester Bangs regarding unprovoked assaults, Robin lost his temper and hit Sandy on the nose. 'There was blood everywhere,' says Johnny. 'Bernie pulled out this immaculate white handkerchief, folded, a thing no-one had ever seen, leans over Pearlman and starts clearing him up. There's this man on the floor bleeding, and we're all more concerned with laughing at Bernie's handkerchief. But as Bernie never did anything for anyone, we all gradually realised, "This is serious!"'

It was. Later in 1978, on the defensive, Mick would tell the *NME*'s Chris Salewicz that Sandy just 'sort of arrived' one day and Joe would insist to *Melody Maker*'s Allan Jones that 'he was the only contender. Who else is there?' The truth was that he was foisted upon them against their will. 'There was a lot of unhappiness about it,' says Johnny. Still a long way from earning back their advance, the band were now at the mercy of the record company: the release of the Clash's second album in America, and, indeed, the funding of that album's recording, were conditional upon their acceptance of Pearlman as producer. To his credit, Sandy did not let a bloody nose put him off sticking around for the show. 'They're being accepted on the basis of stage presence, their material and their performance, not on the basis of what they sound like,' he told the *NME*'s Paul Rambali shortly afterwards. 'Their sound is not good enough to succeed in the States.' That, though, was something he thought he could remedy, and he took the job.

Recording was due to start in February 1978, but Joe fell ill. He had been feeling run down since the start of the Get Out Of Control Tour, and at the beginning of the month hepatitis was diagnosed. Joe was required to spend a fortnight in St Stephen's Hospital, Fulham Road. The album sessions had to be postponed until May, the next time both the Clash and Sandy Pearlman had gaps in their schedules. In rock'n'roll circles hepatitis is often associated with careless intravenous drug use, and the virus is indeed most commonly spread via blood (needles, transfusions) or sexual intercourse. Joe himself blamed the illness on gobbing: during one of the January gigs, he had involuntarily swallowed the spittle of an audience member. His treatment – bed rest, followed by a period of abstinence from alcohol – would suggest that he had contracted hepatitis B, a strain from which 90 per cent of people recover without incurring long term or life-threatening liver damage.

The delay meant that another interim single was required. '(White Man) In Hammersmith Palais' had already been recorded at CBS studios with Mick producing, but the band still needed a B side. A series of evening sessions were booked at short notice in the Marquee studio, situated in Richmond Mews, just behind the famous Wardour Street club. With Mick again at the controls, the band recorded what became known as the Marquee Tapes. They cleaned out their cupboards of pre-Jamaica-trip material, in the process providing B sides for the next three Clash singles. Joe's throat was still sore, so he sang lead only on 'Pressure Drop', while Mick took over for 'The Prisoner' and '1-2, Crush On You'. The band also found time for a version of Booker T and the MG's instrumental 'Time Is Tight', probably inspired by its 'similarity' to Mick's 'Ooh, Baby, Ooh (It's Not Over)'. Earlier in the year, much to his bandmates' annoyance, Mick had accepted an invitation to contribute guitar to Elvis Costello's song 'Big Tears'. T-Zers, the *NME*'s gossip page, identified the pianist heard on the second and fourth of the Clash's Marquee recordings as the Attractions' Steve Nieve, repaying the debt. The saxophone remained uncredited, but the same T-Zers entry suggested that bassist Nick Lowe also contributed to the session. Upon completion of recording, the Clash returned to rehearsing and demoing new material at Rehearsals.

It was a period of limbo for the band in more ways than one. From a chart-watcher's perspective, mid 1977 to late 1978 might seem to have been a Golden Age for bands associated with punk, but by the spring of 1978 the movement had changed beyond recognition for the Clash. As they had discovered on the Get Out Of Control Tour, instead of a smart, imaginative, dynamic London scene where everyone was a product of the same environment and at least recognised everyone else by sight, the punk audience was now more diffuse, its thousands of members – 'the kids' – inhabitants of unfamiliar provincial cities and towns. Their information about punk came largely from record covers and the music press, but was still polluted by memory of the Anarchy Tour's tabloid coverage. In 1978, Joe would sometimes alter the lyric of 'What's My Name' to demand of audiences, 'What the hell is wrong with you? / You're just doing what you're supposed to do.'

Several of the second wave punk bands from the London scene had hit records, but it was difficult to identify much of punk's original spirit in their material. The Adverts' 'Gary Gilmore's Eyes', X Ray Spex's 'Germ Free Adolescents' and even the Tom Robinson Band's biggest hit '2-4-6-8 Motorway' were essentially novelty songs. Siouxsie and the Banshees drew more from the decadent glam period immediately preceding punk, and their cold, disengaged music set something of a trend soon followed by the likes of Joy Division, the Cure and Howard Devoto's post-Buzzcocks band, Magazine. These bands pioneered an arty, borderline pretentious sub-genre usually referred to as 'post-punk', some of whose subsequent supposedly punk-inspired exponents, not least U2 and Simple Minds, would be difficult to differentiate from the pompous dinosaur acts and self-indulgent progressive rockers they were supposed to have replaced.

Many of the bands comprising the third wave of UK punk were no more genuine than those most obvious of opportunists, the Police. Mostly from provincial towns, they were inspired by punk records and media reports to either form from scratch or adapt their existing musical style to fit. Dublin's Boomtown Rats, Derry's Undertones, Dunfermline's Skids and Swindon's XTC all went on to enjoy varying degrees of chart success, but only Belfast's Stiff Little Fingers and Hersham's Sham 69 attempted to express anything other than cartoon anger, and both quickly lost the plot. Contrary to the DIY ethic though it might have been, the bands that enjoyed sustained success were usually the ones whose members had the most musical experience, including made-over UK pub rockers like Elvis Costello and New York new wavers like Blondie.

Of the first wave of UK punk bands, the Boys failed to make the charts, the Pete Shelley-fronted Buzzcocks did, but with edgy love songs, and – after their Clash-lite first single 'Your Generation' – Generation X devoted themselves to facile celebrations of pop culture. Rat Scabies walked out in disgust after the recording of the Damned's second album. The others struggled on until February 1978 with Jon Moss, before going their separate ways. They would reform, initially as the Doomed, in September 1978, with Rat but without original main songwriter Brian James. The drummer also proved to be the quality controller in the Heartbreakers: like Rat, Jerry Nolan was so offended by his band's poorly mixed late 1977 album *LAMF* that he quit immediately before the tour arranged to promote it. Terry Chimes replaced him on 21 November 1977. On the 23rd, after two gigs at the Vortex, the Heartbreakers split.

More epochal, if even more inevitable, was the demise of the original UK scene leaders. Playing up to the myth of a performance ban, Malcolm had distanced the Sex Pistols from their close supporters during 1977, and the band never regained the momentum lost during the Anarchy Tour. Their development was further retarded by the replacement of main songwriter Glen Matlock with the deeply untalented Sid Vicious. By the end of 1977, the band members were barely communicating, let alone writing new material. Following a 14 January 1978 show at San Francisco's Winterland Ballroom – the last date of their brief but hardly uneventful début US tour – the band split with considerable acrimony. Glen seemed to be having the last laugh when the Mick Ronson-produced single 'Rich Kids' made number 24 in the UK charts later that month. Unfortunately, the Rich Kids failed to follow it up, and they would also split in June the following year.

The Sex Pistols had always been the Clash's pace-setters, the band against whose achievements they measured their own. 'It made us feel a bit lonely, somehow,' Paul told *Melody Maker*'s Allan Jones later in 1978. 'There was nothing to chase.' 'We'd never have beaten them anyway,' added Joe, and both Paul and Mick agreed. Their humility overlooked the fact the Pistols had long ceased to progress creatively, but their comments did illustrate the extent to which Clash were beginning to feel isolated: as though they really were the Last Gang In Town.

Unfortunately, the Clash were not even that much of a gang anymore, something that was increasingly signalled by their dress. By 1978, the uniform of Pop Star Army Fatigues had given way to the Clash members' own individual looks, both onstage and off. Paul wore his hair cropped short and favoured a skinhead-style combination of drainpipe trousers and DMs, or his new shot-silk electric blue Johnsons mod suit. Joe combed his hair back in a quiff and wore brothel creepers and flecked Fifties-style rockabilly jackets. The haircut that had been forced upon Mick in January 1977 was the last time his locks saw the barber's scissors until the end of 1978. Throughout this period, he wore it in an increasingly unruly Keith Richards mane, and set it off with flowing white shirts and scarves, waistcoats and gaudy silk smoking jackets. In short, the three original band members had reverted to pre-Clash type. Meanwhile, Topper, who had never been a punk, continued to dress like one. That is, whenever he was not living out his Bruce Lee fantasy in a variety of martial arts costumes.

In the emotionally-charged March 1977 interview with Tony Parsons, Mick had declared, 'The people involved with the Clash *are* my family!' A year later, contact between band members was limited to rehearsals, recording and playing live, and as a consequence being part of the Clash had become more like holding down a job. Having moved into a rented flat in Tregunter Road, Chelsea, Paul continued to spend much of his free time with Caroline Coon. 'She was always a bit of a joke with the band: Paul's Bit of Rich, you know,' laughs Johnny Green. 'She mothered him, and she educated him.'

Joe had split up with Palmolive in late 1977, something which contributed greatly to his unhappiness and ill health. After moving out of the Canonbury squat he had shared with Roadent, Joe had rented a room in Sebastian's house at 31 Albany Street. Much of his free time – and a publishing royalties cheque for £1,000 – was spent socialising with the Clash crew. Towards the end of 1977, he had begun a relationship with Jeanette Lee – Don Letts's former co-worker at Acme Attractions, and shortly to become a founder member of PiL – and had briefly shared her home in Holborn until the relationship ended early the following year. When Joe left hospital after his bout with hepatitis in February 1978, it was to return to Albany Street, where he succumbed to depression and slumped into one of his loner phases.

Mick had wanted to be a rock'n'roll star long before he was a punk. Now the opportunity to live out his fantasy had arrived, he had no intention of letting anything he might have said about Rod Stewart during 1976-77 prevent him from enjoying it to the full. When the second part of the CBS advance had come through in late 1977, he had prised enough money from Bernie to enable him to move out of his Nan's flat and, together with Tony James, rent what one visiting journalist described as a 'flash Jason King-style pad' just off the south end of Portobello Road. The lease expired in spring 1978, and the two friends moved to a similarly upmarket top floor dwelling in nearby Pembridge Villas. Mick used part of his £1,000 publishing royalties to buy what was at that time still a luxury item: a video machine.

His relationship with Viv Albertine was on-off due partly to conflicting band schedules and partly to Viv's lack of commitment. 'Mick used to cry and cry about Viv,' says Johnny Green. 'She broke his heart. He was in love with her. He played the rock star normally with girls, but with Viv, no.' Mick took solace in the company of a succession of what Johnny describes as 'blonde model-types', and threw himself into a hedonistic lifestyle with Glen Matlock and other members of the new aristocracy of the new wave. For Pat Gilbert's 1999 *Mojo* respective, Mick's flatmate Tony recalled, 'He had a video of his favourite film, *Zulu*, which would be playing until 3 o'clock in the morning. People would hang out and take drugs, and the partying would be going all night, every night.'

While Joe's illness had robbed him of much of his former drive, Mick was growing ever more confident in his abilities as a guitarist, songwriter, arranger and even producer, which encouraged him to be ever more assertive within the band. Rob Harper had seen Joe as the Clash's leader, but by the time Johnny Green arrived on the scene, this was no longer the case. 'I think Clash fans, looking from the outside, saw it as Joe's band,' he says. 'But from the inside it wasn't, it was Mick's band.'

Unfortunately, Mick abused his new-found power. Band rehearsals were scheduled for 2 pm, but Mick regularly kept the others waiting, and seldom apologised when he eventually did turn up. He was high-handed when giving instructions about his songs, both at Rehearsals and in the studio, and he insisted on getting his own way with what was, after all, still mostly his music. During the coming months, several music press writers would observe that his stage moves, once a valid part of communicating the band's energy, now seemed to be so much narcissistic preening. Roadent had left because he objected to being treated like a gofer. Johnny was now required to drive over to Mick's flat, wake him up, help him choose his clothes for the day, and periodically dye his hair – 'blue-black, the shade Elvis Presley used' – before chauffeuring him to Rehearsals. Sebastian Conran is not the only person to use the expression prima donna when describing Mick. Poodle, the nickname the rest of the Clash camp conferred upon the guitarist at this time, was not solely inspired by his hairstyle.

Lester Bangs's *NME* feature had suggested that the Clash got stoned a lot, and Johnny confirms that, right from the moment he started working for them, they smoked ganja much as other people smoke tobacco. 'It was always drugs, all the time. Topper was probably the one who was least into it at that point.' Undoubtedly, as Lester suggested, marijuana was a major contributory factor to the band's highly developed collective sense of humour, but by spring 1978, not all the drugs being taken were so conducive to good cheer. Joe had once represented the band's greatest worry in terms of amphetamine and alcohol-exacerbated volatility, but he had renounced speed early in 1977, recognising that he didn't have the constitution for it. At the start of the following year, hepatitis required him to stop drinking altogether for several months. By this time, Mick had already taken over his role as the loose cannon. Although speed had always been accepted on the punk scene as a cheap, no frills street drug, cocaine was frowned upon as a champagne indulgence. Johnny believes that, at first, Mick viewed it as a symbol of his recently elevated status – much like his new flat and his new video – but he became such an enthusiastic user that he very quickly developed a serious problem.

In July that year, Joe told the *NME*'s Chris Salewicz, 'If you snort coke, you're in on your own. You don't *want* anybody, and you don't *need* anybody. Which is a *horrible* place to be.' 'He was getting at me, and he was right,' Mick admitted to *Sounds*' Garry Bushell in November. 'That sort of drug is really soul-destroying.' The following month, he told Nick Kent, 'On Janet Street-Porter's *London Weekend Programme*, me being all young and naive, I blamed drugs for the great mid-Seventies drought in rock. And a year or so later, I found myself doing just as many drugs as them! Y'know, taking drugs as a way of life, to feel good in the morning, to get through the day.' For at least the first half of the year, Mick's breakfast in bed – brought to him by Johnny in the early afternoon – consisted of a line of coke, a spliff and a glass of Ribena. After that, Mick would not touch Ribena again until he awoke the following day. As with Keith Levene before him, his drug use undoubtedly contributed to both his arrogance and his moodiness, which in turn did nothing to diminish the bad feeling within the band.

'We have rows almost every day, and we split up almost every day,' Joe told Simon Kinnersley in February 1978. 'We exist in this constant electric atmosphere. We aren't at all comfortable, mentally, together in our roles.' There had always been disagreement and bickering within the Clash camp, but previously it had been harnessed to the pursuit of a common goal. Now, despite Joe's attempt to portray the tension as a source of positive creative energy, it seemed to have even greater potential for destruction.

The band's original core group of friends and supporters might have been expected to provide emotional buffers, but Roadent and Micky Foote had both departed, and Chrissie Hynde, Sid Vicious and Mad Jane – who had just formed the Mo-dettes with former Slit Kate Korus – were all pursuing their own musical interests. The Baker, determinedly teetotal and drug free, kept his own counsel, believing his responsibilities began and ended with Topper and his drums. 'Barry was so rude to the rest of the band, it was unbelievable,' laughs Johnny. '"Baker, go and get me an egg sandwich." "*Fack off!* Go and get your own facking egg sandwich!"' A man of many interests and anecdotes, and a startling capacity for hedonistic excess, Johnny himself had become a close and valued companion to most of the band's members, and did his best to cement over the cracks. Although not officially on the payroll, Robin Crocker continued to hang around, and he too could justifiably claim to have made a substantial contribution towards holding everything together.

Bernie Rhodes, the person who perhaps should have been offering the Clash the most encouragement and guidance at this difficult point in their career, was seldom to be seen. Since the Get Out Of Control Tour had come to an end, he had relied upon Johnny Green to oversee the day to day running of the band. A large proportion of his own time was taken up with record company-related business affairs, but the Clash believed too much of the rest was devoted to what they perceived to be extra-curricular activities.

In late 1977, Bernie and Micky Foote had produced a single for Subway Sect, which was finally released in March 1978 on Braik, an independent label specially created by Bernie. Before departing, Roadent had introduced the Clash camp to a punk-ska band from his home town. They were then known as the Coventry Automatics, but were soon to become the Special (AKA the Automatics). This was first shortened to the Special AKA and then to the Specials. Later in 1978, Bernie would take them under his wing. In mid 1978, a third rate third wave punk band from Birmingham called the Killjoys fell apart. Bernie showed an interest when former members Kevin Rowland and Kevin Archer started to create a new soul-oriented sound and identity under the name of Dexys Midnight Runners. He was also working with a black jazz-punk band from Harlesden which he named the Black Arabs, as well as all-female French band the Lous and, according to Johnny, 'assorted rockabilly bands'. Under the banner Club Left, he started promoting package shows around London, featuring various members of his stable of acts.

'Bernie had his fingers in a lot of pies,' says Johnny. 'I saw a lot of it because I was running Rehearsals. The Clash were allocated afternoons and early evenings, but Bernie would expect me to be there all the time and look after this parade of bands he would bring in and try out using the Clash's gear.'

Bernie had always described himself as an ideas man, and he was far more interested in possibilities and potential, scams and confrontations than in maintenance work. His other activities could all be construed as commendable attempts to make good on promises the Clash had made a year earlier to put something back into the culture – a peripatetic club presenting VFM musical events, an independent label, free rehearsal facilities for up-and-coming bands – but Bernie did not involve the Clash directly, and consequently they felt those activities had little to do with them. 'Bernie would come in and see all these little groups, but he wouldn't come to see the Clash rehearse or listen to the new material,' says Johnny. 'He wasn't interested. That's what pissed them off. He wasn't giving them the service they felt they deserved.'

Following the demise of the Sex Pistols, when not working on what was to become *The Great Rock'n'Roll Swindle*, Malcolm McLaren found himself at something of a loose end. He amused himself in his usual way, by sitting on Bernie's shoulder wearing little horns and a pointed tail. He told his friend that certain members of the Clash were betraying him with their decadent behaviour. Bernie agreed, and on the few occasions he did check in with the band, he made no secret of his feelings. 'He didn't want us to become what we'd started out against. All credit to him,' Joe told *Melody Maker*'s Allan Jones in November. 'But his method of preventing this was to come and attack us, to come in with *scorn*.'

To add further spice to all this simmering resentment, there was the age-old problem of finance. As had Roadent before him, Johnny discovered it was almost impossible to get Bernie to cover day to day running expenses. 'We never had any money. Even for silly stuff, like petrol and guitar strings. If you brought it up, Bernie would give you a talk about the Situationists and Paris '68, and you'd say, "But Bernie, *I just need some guitar strings!*"'

As individuals, the band reacted differently. 'Mick was the most critical, Paul a bit, Topper a little bit, but not Joe: Joe was always more reticent to have a go at Bernie,' says Johnny. Joe believed he had learned a lot from Bernie, and still felt a lot of admiration for him. Although disappointed that the manager was no longer closely involved with the Clash, and personally hurt that Bernie had not bothered to visit him while he was in hospital, he made allowances and simply got on with the job. The manifestation of Paul's feelings was a scaling up of his long-running mockery campaign. 'Paul was the nastiest bastard to Bernie, but in quite an affectionate way, if that makes any sense,' says Johnny. 'Paul upset Bernie far more than anyone else. He was relentless.'

For Mick, the conflict was far more serious and bitter. As early as the previous November, Bernie had told Lester Bangs – for public consumption via the pages of the *NME* – that Mick was his 'biggest problem', and Mick was now in open revolt against Bernie's managerial style. Bernie was in charge of running the band's business, Mick was currently the dominant figure within the band, and the key issues in the Clash camp were money, responsibility, conduct and creative control. This power struggle was further complicated by the duo's personal history: after all, their relationship was the foundation upon which the Clash had been built. In late 1975, Mick had been the first to be seduced by Bernie's vision, since which time his own personality had been subjugated to a band identity shaped largely by the older man. There comes a time when any protégé leaves or rejects his mentor, and much of Mick's rock star behaviour could be construed as so much acting out: the equivalent of a teenager's rebellion against an overly strict or absentee parent.

As a collective unit, the Clash bent to Mick's will, and responded to their manager's neglect with a tit-for-tat shutdown of communication. 'The band wouldn't let me ring Bernard to ask for anything or tell him when anything was going on,' says Johnny. And, with the benefit or hindsight, the dismissal of Micky Foote, instigated by Mick, but approved by the rest of the band, can be seen as a first warning strike against Bernie. Although Micky had originally come into the Clash camp as Joe's friend, by the time of his banishment, according to Johnny, he was very much perceived to be 'Bernie's man'. 'Micky always carried an *Evening Standard*, and when it rained it was Micky's job to hold it over Bernie's head to stop his hair getting wet. I'm not kidding.'

Similar political manoeuvring during the course of 1978 was also responsible for Sebastian Conran's ousting from the Clash camp. For Robin Crocker, Sebastian's accent and slight lisp were a red rag to a bully, and since his arrival on the scene, he had done his best to make Sebastian's life a misery. When Gordon Burn made his revelations about Sebastian's privileged background in the 17 July 1977 issue of the *Sunday Times Magazine*, it was as if open season had been declared. Tony Parsons was among those who began to take cheap shots at him, in his case via the *NME*'s T-Zers page. Sebastian's house in Albany Street was home to Upstarts and Bernie's office, and was within walking distance of Rehearsals. Taking a room there had been primarily a practical move for Joe. It proved to be a mistake as far as street credibility was concerned, though, even if Joe did treat it very much like the squat Sebastian pretended it was. 'I gave him this nice room,' says Sebastian, 'and the first thing he did was aerosol all over the walls.' As Joe himself admitted to *Q*'s Andrew Collins in 1999, he also urinated in milk bottles and left them lined up on the stairs because he couldn't be bothered to walk down four flights to the toilet.

Early in 1978, jibes began to appear in the music press gossip pages to the effect that Strummer had sold out by moving into the 'White Mansion' of a millionaire's son. These were repeated by hecklers in the Clash's audiences. For someone who had roughed it for the past seven years, and who was the only member of the band still living anywhere close to the gutter, this was galling in the extreme. That spring, Joe left number 31 to share a squat in Daventry Street, Marylebone, close to the start of the Westway, with Boogie, Kate Korus and various other associates of the Mo-dettes. Making a point of inviting *Sounds*' Pete Silverton around there for an interview that June, he demanded, 'You're gonna write where I live, aren't you? I've had enough of this White Mansion rubbish.'

He also began to distance himself from Sebastian, showing no more loyalty to his friend than he had to Micky Foote. That he had spent much of the last year working so closely with Bernie certainly did little to help Sebastian's cause. 'It all got a bit acrimonious. "What's *Sebastian* doing here?" when I'd been around for ages.' Sebastian believes he became a convenient scapegoat not only for the embarrassment over Albany Street, but also over Upstarts' plans for the wider exploitation of the Clash look. 'It was a very uncomfortable political situation for them,' he acknowledges. 'But the whole thing did start off as a commercial venture, and frankly, *Bernie* started it up, and he started it up with the purpose that it should be like that.' The plans for a mail order service and a shop were abandoned. Sebastian's last design for the band was the cover of 'Clash City Rockers', released in February 1978, which features pictures of punks and policemen. Thereafter, he ran down Upstarts and, from the summer of 1978 onwards, concentrated on helping Bernie with Club Left, designing posters and helping to organise the shows.

On 5 November that year, Sebastian and his friend – and sometime narrator of Clash radio advertisements – Henry Bowles were sitting having a drink at a Subway Sect gig when a bouncer took exception to the way Henry was laughing, and attacked him. He died later in hospital. The folly of his excursions into ted territory with Joe suddenly dawned on Sebastian. The Clash would subsequently dedicate *London Calling* to Henry's memory, but by the end of 1978 a grief-stricken Sebastian had already concluded that any ideal and any individual was expendable and incidental when it came to the Clash Myth and the band's ongoing success. He split with Bernie, and thereafter pursued a successful career in industrial design. It took him a long time to develop a perspective on his association with the band that wasn't tainted by resentment and self-doubt. 'I feel much more positive now,' he laughs. 'Basically, they were being a bunch of fucking hypocrites. The whole thing was completely hypocritical.'

12

GIVE 'EM ENOUGH ROPE

Mick Jones's rejection of everything Bernie Rhodes stood for had a lot to do with the band's musical adventurousness during 1978. Although many years later he would come to view the first album as the Clash's greatest moment, by the early part of that year Mick was no longer interested in writing or playing tunes that were subservient to sloganeering. The compositional and musical flourishes he introduced were an acknowledgement that basic thrashes were all played out, and also a cocked snook at Bernie. So was his revival in the recording studio of his pre-Clash love songs '1-2 Crush On You' and 'Ooh, Baby, Ooh (It's Not Over)'. In a July 1978 interview with *Record Mirror*, for which the entire band plus Bernie were present, Joe Strummer remarked that Mick liked to write about 'that lovely girl [he] saw'. Mick quietly and calmly replied, 'Yeah, I do.' One can imagine how this declaration of commitment to romantic songwriting might have provoked Bernie's ire.

Strummer lyrics with titles like 'Drug Stabbing Time' and 'Groovy Times' – however ironic their sentiments were intended to be – were no more likely to win the Rhodes seal of approval. Both Joe and Mick had realised that 'dole queue rock', 'tower block rock' and 'the Blank Generation' had become clichés. In the wake of *The Clash*, scores of other bands both major and minor had adopted the protest stance. In one short year, rising unemployment, urban decay and alienation had all been done to death. On the defensive, Joe resorted to knee-jerk revisionism of the Clash's original intent. 'All I was ever interested in, both then and now, was a social thing,' he told *Melody Maker*'s Simon Kinnersley. 'We've got nothing to do with politics.' Just over four months later, though, Mick told the same paper's Chris Brazier, 'I have leanings to the left and I have a great concern for the human race, and immediately you accept that you really care, that's when the responsibility starts.' It was the heavy weight of that responsibility and the limitations it was in danger of imposing upon the band that was the real cause of both his and Joe's wariness with regard to the P-word. Joe admitted as much to the *NME*'s Jack Basher, 'We always go on the defensive when confronted with this political stuff. We see it as a trap, a hole to get shut up in. We wanna move in any direction we want, *including* a political direction.'

Unfortunately, other satisfactory directions proved elusive. 'I remember what a fuck up it was after the first record,' Joe admitted to the *NME*'s Paul Morley in 1979. 'We kind of turned around and said, "Now what are we going to do?" We just couldn't think of anything to follow it with, really.' At first, he turned to the news for inspiration. The lyric for 'Groovy Times' was based on a report about the dangers inherent in the aggressive policing of large crowds, and includes a reference to the fencing in of the terraces at football grounds. This policy would ultimately contribute to the Hillsborough disaster. 'Drug Stabbing Time' is a lightweight spoof on committed drug abuse and its attendant paranoia. 'Julie's Been Working For The Drug Squad' was inspired by Operation Julie, named after undercover policewoman Julie Taylor, who was instrumental in facilitating a 1977 raid on an LSD factory in Wales. Media coverage of the bust and subsequent trial fired up public opinion, which may well have influenced the excessive jail sentences handed out to the defendants. While these lyrics have a tangential connection to the Clash's preoccupations of yore, the subject matter is not exactly cutting edge. The wit and wordplay, impressive though they are, only serve to draw attention to the lack of direct emotional involvement. 'One Emotion', as its title suggests, offers even less. A piece of hackwork, it came to pass after Mick and Joe saw a James Bond film starring Roger Moore, for whom acting appeared to consist of little more than looking suave and raising the occasional eyebrow. Wisely, it was left in the can until dusted down for the 1991 *Clash On Broadway* retrospective.

Bernie's disapproval and the music press's doubts about the Clash's political commitment stung Joe into looking for something that was more hard-hitting in content. 'Last Gang In Town' has its roots in the ted-punk and black-white conflicts. It also notes that the post-punk proliferation of other sub-cultures – including skinhead revivalists and rockabilly rebels – was doing nothing to allay the violent inter-tribal skirmishes that had prompted Charles Shaar Murray's *NME* warning of July 1977. Joe's lyric purports to condemn such violence outright – 'It's all young blood running down the drains' – but his depiction of street gang action comes perilously close to romanticising the subject and achieving the opposite effect to the one intended.

In May 1977, the National Front had gained 119,000 votes in London's local council elections, and had threatened to put forward 500 candidates next time around. In direct response, a year after the formation of Rock Against Racism, a cross-section of left wing political activists – with strong representation from the Socialist Workers Party – had formed the Anti-Nazi League to protest and counter the rise of fascism. On 23 August 1977, just a month after the Clash had been denied the right to play at Digbeth Rag Market, the National Front had been given permission to march through the multi-racial south-east London borough of Lewisham, protected from 5,000 protesters by 4,000 policemen. The police at the previous year's Notting Hill Carnival had been there to intimidate the black population, so it was hard not to infer a racial and political bias. Feelings ran high, and another riot erupted. Tony Parsons, present at the time, tried to contact the Clash, and was disappointed when studio commitments were cited as a reason for their refusal to come and lend their physical support to the cause. Increasingly, the more radical left wing political groups were mobilising against the fascists, and skirmishes arising from the black-white, left-right divide were to make regular appearances in the media throughout the following year.

Joe remembered 'Johnny Comes Marching Home', a traditional song from the American Civil War he had learned at school. Realising it could be adapted to fit the current domestic political climate, he retitled the song 'English Civil War' and wrote a new lyric in which he envisions an upscaling of the conflict described in 'Last Gang In Town'. As had been the case with '1977', the images of open warfare on the streets would later be condemned by some members of the music press as a hysterical over-reaction to the situation. Again, Joe would usually counter by claiming he was projecting into an Orwellian future, depicting one possible outcome if current trends went unchecked. In July 1978, though, he suggested to the *NME*'s Chris Salewicz, 'It's already started. Sure it has. There's people attacking Bengalis with clubs and firing shotguns in Wolverhampton.' In a contemporaneous *Record Mirror* interview, Mick suggested the carpers should try to learn a lesson from history: 'In 1928, Adolf Hitler got 2.8 per cent of the votes. By 1939, there was no-one voting for anyone else.'

The Clash would have a much harder time justifying some of the other products of Joe's quest for tougher subject matter. Roadent's belief in punk's power to effect change had evaporated months before he left the Clash's employ. His fascination with all forms of extremism had encouraged him to transfer his – verbal – allegiance to the bona fide urban guerrilla outfits currently operating in Europe. In September 1977, he had told Wolfgang Bünd the only thing he found interesting about Germany was the Red Army Faction (RAF; aka the Baader-Meinhof Gang), and had also made reference to the Angry Brigade, a British terrorist organisation responsible for bombing Biba's department store in 1971.

It was not only the terminology Roadent had found seductive, and his Canonbury squatmate had evidently succumbed too. 'Joe and I were completely idealistic,' Roadent told ZigZag's Robin Banks in 1980. 'We planned to bomb Selfridges! It was gonna be at night 'cause no-one would be there, but eventually we just dismissed it as a futile gesture. We also thought about joining the National Front. We were hoping to infiltrate it and do some sabotage to fuck the whole thing up! Yeah, we used to talk and talk but nothing actually materialised.' The prospect of taking direct action was evidently so much late night drunken bravado that disappeared with the advent of the new day's hangover. Towards the end of 1977, though, Joe's guerrilla fantasies received a new boost when film director Diego Cotez asked him to do some recording for the soundtrack of his low-budget arthouse film *Grutzi Elvis*. 'It's about Elvis and the Baader-Meinhof Gang,' Joe told the *NME*'s Jack Basher the following February. In the very year in which there was supposed to be no Elvis Presley, he contributed two versions of 'Heartbreak Hotel' – a song he had previously covered with the 101ers – one cajun style, the other in what he described as 'terrorist style'.

Late Sixties activists had provided the models for much of the Clash's rhetoric and lyrical content during 1976-77. As the Sixties turned into the Seventies, some of those activists had resorted to ever-more extreme forms of direct action, heralding the era of international terrorism. Thus, there was a historical precedent for the path Joe was taking. 'Last Gang In Town' and 'English Civil War' had already demonstrated his preoccupation with the rule of fist, club and gun, and it was inevitable that his associated interest in terrorist activity should also feed into his contribution to the Clash. On the White Riot Tour, he had sometimes affected a T-shirt bearing the slogan 'FACE OF THE ASSASSIN'. In spring 1978, he would take the stage in a T-shirt promoting 'BRIGADE ROSSE' (referring to Brigate Rosse, the Italian Red Brigades) and 'RAF'. Later that year, another T-shirt would proclaim 'H BLOCK' (after the prison blocks at the Maze, where many convicted IRA members were held). Joe's song 'Tommy Gun' was inspired by terrorist assassins like Carlos the Jackal. Again, the initial impetus came from a newspaper report. It prompted Joe to contemplate how media coverage turns such men into celebrities, and to wonder whether they collected their press cuttings. Another composition from this period, 'RAF 1810', which remains unreleased, concerns the supposed – but highly dubious – group gun suicide in 1977 of Andreas Baader's terrorist cell of that number while being held in a supposedly maximum security prison.

By the late Seventies, the threat to democracy offered by the resurrection of fascism in Europe and dubious military and paramilitary activity all over the world was part of the zeitgeist, and therefore a worthy subject for consideration. Elvis Costello's *Armed Forces*, released in 1979, proves that Joe's imagination was not the only one engaged. However, whereas Elvis's feelings of fear and loathing towards extremist bully-boy antics of any kind is evident throughout his caustic collection of songs, Joe's tendency to glamorise violent conflict had again got the better of him. It is as though he saw the violent actions of far left and anarchist terrorist groups as an acceptable response to repressive governments and as a necessary balance to the transgressions of the far right. 'The bad thing is that they go around murdering bodyguards and innocent people,' he told *Melody Maker*'s Chris Brazier in July 1978. 'But you've got to hand it to them for laying their lives on the line for the rest of the human race. They're doing it for everybody, trying to smash the system that has broken everybody.' Called to account for this statement later in the year by the same paper's Allan Jones, he stated, 'I *am* ambiguous. 'Cause at once I'm impressed with what they're doing, and at the same time I'm really frightened by what they're doing. It's not an easy subject.'

While it is true that one person's terrorist is another person's freedom fighter, it is hard to give credit for idealism when it results in the murder of innocents. In 1978 the Brigate Rosse were best known for the kidnap and execution of Italian President Aldo Mora, who Joe somewhat gleefully dubbed 'the equivalent of Winston Churchill'. In 1980, however, they would be responsible for placing a bomb at Bologna railway station that killed 85 civilians. Mick made a point of distancing himself from Joe's preoccupation with terrorist chic at the time, interrupting a discussion he was having about it with *Record Mirror*'s Ronnie Gurr to announce, 'I don't support this killing stuff.' Clearly, though, Joe himself had not learned his lesson from the Belfast photo shoot. 'There wasn't any thinking, or any intellectual process to it,' Joe finally conceded to *Uncut*'s Gavin Martin in 1999. 'We just did it.'

Inspired by action movies and Boy's Own comic book adventures, Paul Simonon and Topper Headon were completely besotted with firearms of all types. Unlike Mick, they had no objections to Joe's militaristic bent, and it was Topper who suggested the machine-gun drum fills for 'Tommy Gun'. 'They were always firing off guns around the back of Rehearsals,' says Johnny Green. 'And inside, come to think of it. They were always after bigger and better ones. They used to have catalogues of them. They were well into gun culture.' Their catalogues may have pictured the real thing, but as of spring 1978, the best weapon their arsenal had to offer was Sebastian Conran's air pistol. Topper was still in touch with his old Dover friend and fellow former member of Fury, Steve Barnacle, and through him with his younger brother Pete. Pete had a high-powered air rifle he wanted to sell, and on 30 March, the two Barnacles took it over to Rehearsals so Topper could try it out. Paul and Robin Crocker were also present, and all five went up onto the roof for target practice with both pistol and rifle. The idea was to shoot at cans, but there happened to be some pigeons there. Topper, Pete and Paul downed one apiece before it dawned on them how odd it was that what they took to be 'scuzzy old London pigeons' should keep coming back for more…

They were homing pigeons. Unbeknownst to the five would-be sharpshooters, George Dole, a mechanic at the garage next door – the very same garage in which Bernie owned a share – had a loft on the other side of the sloping roof. George called for one of his co-workers, and the two of them clambered over the roof, justifiably furious. Topper and company were trapped. Steve slid the pistol under a loose roof slate and prepared himself for the worst. In the event, George contented himself with smacking Topper in the face before grabbing the rifle away from him and storming off with it.

That was by no means the end of the excitement. While the confrontation had been taking place, a helicopter had appeared and started to circle overhead. 'We're going, "Is that a *police* helicopter?"' says Pete Barnacle. They had just decided it was time to leave when a mixture of plainclothes CID and uniformed officers clambered over the slope with sniffer dogs, a loud hailer and guns. Real guns. 'It was, "Put your hands in the air. Armed police!"' says Steve Barnacle. '*What?*'

Those who were responsible for shooting the pigeons admitted it at once. This failed to satisfy the police. The dogs and their handlers searched the roof but failed to find the pistol. Acting on information relayed from the chopper, police tracked down George Dole and retrieved the rifle. It was only then that the bemused fivesome were given some indication what was going on. 'The roof was level with the railway tracks, and unbeknownst to us, opposite was one of the offices of the Transport Police,' says Steve. 'They'd looked across and seen five people on the roof with guns and thought, "Armed terrorists shooting at the trains!" That's the message the CID got.' The CID proved reluctant to accept the boys' explanation. 'Everyone knew that the Clash rehearsed there,' says Pete. 'They thought they'd arrested the whole of the Clash! They said, "We've got a train driver who says you shot at the trains, and we've got a bullet hole in the train window."' Because the air rifle was so powerful, the police also maintained it qualified as an illegal firearm.

Arrested at 7 pm, all five were taken to Kentish Town police station. Here, they were locked up in the same cell before being taken out one at a time for questioning. Unsurprisingly, the police were treated to five identical stories, which did nothing to improve their mood. They placed the rifle barrel against Topper's head and pulled the trigger, at which point he discovered it was no longer loaded. They told Steve they were going to take him upstairs and 'beat the shit' out of him. And they told Pete, all of 17 years old, 'We're charging you with attempted manslaughter, and you're going to go down for 17 years unless you co-operate.' After a night in the cells, they were taken to Clerkenwell Magistrates Court. Here, after initially being opposed, bail was finally set at the then alarmingly high figure of £1,500 per person.

Pete was taken to Ashford Remand Centre and the others to Brixton Prison pending payment of the bond. Bernie was reluctant to help – possibly thinking that a few nights in jail would improve the band's street credibility no end, or possibly just loath to part with that much money – and it was Mick Jones and Caroline Coon who turned up with the cash and legal expertise, respectively, to save the Clash members and Robin from another night behind bars. Steve and Pete were not so lucky. They tried to contact their father, Bill, in Dover, but he had gone out to play a gig with his jazz band and was unable to free them until the following day.

At first, conditions of bail required that all five had to register daily at Kentish Town police station. Although these restrictions were lifted in May, the hearing, at Clerkenwell, was postponed twice, and was not finally held until 16 June, some two and a half months after the incident. Even then, the police claimed they had not had enough time to perform a ballistics test on the rifle. It was only at this juncture that the magistrate lost his patience and dismissed outright the illegal weapon, terrorism and attempted manslaughter charges. For shooting the pigeons, the three guilty parties were required to pay George Dole £700 compensation and pay a fine of £30 each. Paul had to contribute a further £20, and Topper and Pete £10 each, towards legal fees.

In the eyes of the music press, Joe and Mick carried the burden of responsibility for the Clash's ideals, and little was usually made of Paul and Topper's unruly behaviour. However, being arrested for shooting pigeons – which was how the matter was reported – was even more ridiculous than being arrested for stealing pillow cases or spraying your own band's name on the wall. It proved hard for the likes of the *NME*'s 'Inspector Migraine' to resist having a few more cheap laughs at the band's expense.

Shortly after the incident, the Clash worked up a song from a band jam – sadly, their first ever four-way writing credit was appended to yet another variation on the 'I Can't Explain' riff – and gave it the title 'Guns On The Roof'. Joe's lyric is an indictment of global arms dealing, covert military action and terrorist activity. His most histrionic and sensationalist musing on the subject to date still asserts that assassins are an inevitable by-product of corrupt societies. Joe alludes to misrepresentations of truth in the courtroom, but direct references to pigeon slaying are conspicuous by their absence. In vain did the band protest that the song had nothing but its title in common with the Pigeon Shooting Incident. Media representatives not unreasonably assumed a connection, and were troubled by the discrepancy between Joe's chest-beating and the mental picture they had of a bunch of overgrown schoolboys taking potshots at a mechanic's treasured pets. As a result, Joe took yet more flak for what was deemed to be a particularly desperate piece of Clash Mythologising.

The Pigeon Shooting Incident did nothing to diminish Topper and Paul's interest in gun culture. Paul was responsible for designing the smoking gun and human target labels which decorate the single release of '(White Man) In Hammersmith Palais', released the very day of the court hearing. The *Clash Second Songbook*, issued in 1979, illustrates the lyric of 'Guns On The Roof' with photographs of semi-automatic weapons taken from Paul and Topper's gun catalogues. Meanwhile, the piece de resistance in Paul's anti-Bernie campaign – a response to Bernie's refusal to spring his charges from jail – was a large mural-cum-collage created in the upstairs room at Rehearsals. Captioned 'Bernie Is Odd', it depicted a naked caricature of the manager in various undignified positions, including being used as a toilet by a flock of pigeons. In June 1978, Paul wound up Bernie even further by posing for *Sounds* photographer Chalkie Davis wearing a Nazi uniform: shades of Brian Jones in 1969.

Two of the lyrics Joe came up with during spring rehearsals did attempt to address issues that were more personal to the Clash. Like 'Garageland' before it, 'Cheapskates' is a direct response to music press criticism, this time of Joe's supposed mansion-dwelling and Mick's rock star behaviour. It must have been infuriating for someone kept on a tight financial leash by his manager to be accused of lotus eating, but Joe rather overstates his case. His opening description of working dead end jobs and 'picking up dog ends in the rain' is melodramatic in the extreme: 'Career Opportunities' revisited, but far less convincingly. When he moves on to deny that members of his band hoover up copious amounts of charlie and keep company with model girls, he pushes his luck too far. By the time the song was released, Mick's predilections for both would be common knowledge. This information also served to rob 'Drug Stabbing Time' of much of its comedy value, and – in spite of the fact that 'Cheapskates' was intended to set the record straight – bring down even more accusations of hypocrisy upon the Clash's heads. 'That song ['Cheapskates'] was written during a period of heavy drug taking,' Mick, attempting a salvage operation, admitted to *Sounds*' Garry Bushell in November 1978. 'The lyrics are meant as a satire on the situation. That last bit was me and Joe writing together and coming to a conclusion instead of talking it out.' Within a year of Mick's statement, Paul would be living with a model and all four band members would have, in Joe's words, 'had our moments' with cocaine.

The intentionally anthemic quality of 'All The Young Punks (New Boots And Contracts)' is signalled by the main part of its title, which updates 'All The Young Dudes', the paean to the Class of 1972 written by David Bowie for Mott the Hoople. The Clash song commences with the Clash Myth version of the band's formation, and goes on – yet again – to bemoan the State of Punk, express concern about the Clash's own future, and complain about the threat to idealism represented by the music business. It treads exactly the same ground as 'Garageland', only in even heavier boots. Mick's 'Complete Control' had included a sly dig at Bernie; in 'All The Young Punks (New Boots And Contracts)' Joe likens the Rhodes-Clash-CBS contract to a Mafia contract, which suggests that by this time even he was at best ambivalent about the Clash manager. The song's conclusion, that being part of the Clash is at least better than working in a factory, has a decidedly hollow ring.

In the lyrics to both 'Cheapskates' and 'All The Young Punks (New Boots And Contracts)' despair slips into petulance. The summer 1977 material at least strove to use the Clash's own experience as the starting point from which to make universal points, but these latest progress reports are little more than self-indulgent whinges.

Although tiresome, the bail restrictions imposed upon Topper and Paul were not too limiting for the Clash. The band had no immediate plans to tour, instead channelling their energies into preparations for the recording of their second album. In addition to their own songs, the band relaxed by playing cover versions of the Johnny Burnette Trio's 'Train Kept A Rollin' and Carl Mann's 'Your Rockin' Mama', reflecting Joe's latest musical craze. He even talked about the band recording an album's worth of such material, a Clash equivalent to David Bowie's 1973 release *Pinups*. The past, it seems, was no longer passé.

★★★

In April 1978, the Clash also committed themselves to another creative venture. The previous year, the independent film-making partnership of Dave Mingay and Jack Hazan had begun shooting 35mm footage of the Queen's Jubilee celebrations and of National Front marches with a view to documenting the UK's contemporary political climate. Dave had felt little interest in popular music up to that point, but what he read about the anti-establishment stance of punk rock intrigued him. In the interests of research, he attended various gigs at the Marquee, the Vortex and the 100 Club, and came to the conclusion that the film should not only include punk, but make aspects of the movement its primary focus. 'The idea came more from the fans of these groups and the things going on around these groups than the groups themselves,' he says. 'Most films about music pander to the public's obsession with superstars. They want to know how much money groups make, what clothes they wear, how many drugs they take, how many girlfriends they have. I was more interested in the culture and ideas surrounding them.'

He made the acquaintance of an audience member named Ray Gange, who assured him that the Clash were 'the only group to have'. Coincidentally, Dave was friendly with John Pearse, who had designed clothes for Granny Takes A Trip in the Sixties when Bernie was also working there. He prevailed upon him to arrange an introduction with the Clash's manager. Jack and Dave's approach could not have been better timed: Malcolm McLaren was still working on the Sex Pistols movie. Impressed by the duo's credentials, Bernie gave his verbal agreement to their project, but also suggested that Jack and Dave approach each member of the Clash individually. Flattered, according to Dave, all four gave their consent.

Jack and Dave, trading as Buzzy Enterprises, decided to record events around the Clash from the perspective of a band fan-cum-roadie. Johnny Green and the Baker would both feature in the film, but Ray Gange was chosen to be this central figure, envisioned as a sort of cross between Roadent and Robin Crocker. Although some attempt would later be made to pass him off as the genuine article, this was not the case. 'He was a total phoney, brought in by Mingay,' says Johnny. 'He'd never worked for us.'

Serendipitously, in view of the Clash's current lyrical preoccupations and the kind of footage Buzzy already had in the can, the first day of filming was arranged to coincide with the Clash's appearance at the Anti-Nazi League Rally on 30 April 1978. Envisioned as a show of strength in opposition to the National Front, the rally consisted of a march from Trafalgar Square to Victoria Park in Hackney, where a free concert took place. X-Ray Spex, the Clash, reggae outfit Steel Pulse and the Tom Robinson Band performed to – although estimates varied from 50,000 to 100,000 – an undeniably massive crowd.

The Clash had been late additions to the line-up, hence their low positioning on the bill, which resulted in much backstage bickering about status. Their live sound was poor, and barely carried to the back of the crowd. Almost inevitably, they blamed this on sabotage by members of the headliners' crew. Buzzy filmed the band playing 'London's Burning' and set closer 'White Riot', for which Sham 69's Jimmy Pursey took over lead vocals. The idea was to let Jimmy demonstrate to Sham's Nazi skinhead following where his own true sympathies lay. In the event, Jimmy's shameless show-stealing did nothing to diminish Joe's anger, and – he admitted to *Uncut*'s Gavin Martin in 1999 – he was tempted to boot the special guest into the photographers' pit. The Clash's own performance came to an abrupt end when the TRB's crew pulled the plugs. There was a deadline for the event to finish, and the TRB were determined to have their fair share of time on stage. Also captured by Buzzy's camera was the altercation that ensued, with Johnny and an uncomfortable-looking Ray Gange voicing their displeasure.

Mick would join an all-star line-up for the day's closing number, specially written by Tom Robinson, but punk solidarity had once again been seen to be lacking. Talking to *Record Mirror* shortly afterwards, the Clash complained about their treatment, and although Mick insisted that 'the event transcended all that stuff' and that it was 'an admirable cause', he expressed reservations about both SWP involvement in the ANL and the Clash being closely associated with any political pressure groups: 'We've never needed to affiliate ourselves with little organisations. We've been doing it our own way.'

Buzzy also filmed the Clash performing 'Police and Thieves' at a one-off gig at Birmingham Barbarellas on 1 May. The film project then took a back seat when the band booked back into the studio to record more demos. Utopia studios was situated in Fitzroy Road, close to their Camden Town base. Most of the tracks taped here had already been roughed out on the TEAC at Rehearsals, and were scheduled to be re-recorded with Sandy Pearlman within a couple of weeks. Mick later explained this attention to detail as evidence of the band's determination to get the second album right. It is also likely that the Clash were nervous about Sandy's professed desire to redefine their sound, and were hoping that providing him with polished versions of the new songs as they envisaged them would at least encourage him to think along similar lines. The demos were completed, but the Clash's relationship with Utopia came to an abrupt end when, according to a Robin Banks report for *ZigZag*, Paul upended the tropical plants and Topper took a dirt-track tour of the studio on his motorbike.

Recording for the album proper began at the end of May. CBS A&R man Muff Winwood had previously held down the same position for Island Records, and it was probably he who suggested Island's Basing Street studios. Mick for one jumped at the chance to work where Mott the Hoople had recorded *Wildlife* and *Brain Capers*, their third and fourth Island albums. Muff himself had taken over from Guy Stevens to produce Mott the Hoople's last ever tracks for the label, again at Basing Street. After the band's departure to CBS, he had also put together their first Island compilation album *Rock'n'Roll Queen*. This did not especially endear him to the Clash members, even Mick. They recognised Muff as an out-and-out company man, and promptly rechristened him Duff Windbag.

Any illusions the Clash might have had of influencing Sandy Pearlman's working methods were soon dispelled. He brought his favourite engineer Corky Stasiak with him, and the duo – nicknamed the Glutton Twins because of their obsession with takeaway food – complained loud and long about the famously disorganised Clash crew and the primitive nature of the recording facilities. They spent the first three days, a quarter of the time it took to record and mix *The Clash* in its entirety, trying to get an acceptable drum sound. The band set up to record the backing tracks live, and warmed up for the recordings with their own versions of band favourites like Desmond Dekker's 'The Israelites'. That was as spontaneous as proceedings got: starting early afternoon and working for up to 16 hours at a stretch, they were required to run through anything up to 20 takes of each song. Any minor errors were pointed out by the production team, who – despite protests that these could be masked by Joe 'shouting' or Mick 'twanging' over the top – insisted that the relevant parts be redone.

Topper, a died-in-the-wool muso, responded well to this laborious process, and was justifiably proud when the picky Pearlman dubbed him 'the rhythm machine' because he only made one error in the first hundred takes. Both Joe and Mick turned up with guitars in prime condition, Mick's a new Gibson Les Paul Special, Joe's a rented Gibson semi-acoustic of the type used by Chuck Berry. As this indicates, Joe was prepared to show far more willing than he had on previous visits to the studio. He took what visiting *Sounds* journalist Pete Silverton described as a 'disciplined, even militaristic' approach to proceedings, deferring to Sandy and Corky as 'General' and 'Captain', respectively. At the same time, though, he re-established some of his own former authority over the band itself, egging the other members on whenever energy levels were in danger of flagging. Paul got bored very quickly indeed, and turned to the Buzzy crew for help. 'I got him some war films from the National Film Archive – Rommel, the Desert War, that kind of thing – and they projected them onto the wall,' says Dave Mingay. 'Paul thought it would make for a good atmosphere in the studio, and Joe agreed.' Unsurprisingly, it was Paul's playing which most often fell foul of the Glutton Twins' quality control. 'One of mine or the Baker's jobs was to take Paul home when he'd done his takes,' says Johnny Green. 'Then Mick would do the bass again.'

In his *Sounds* feature, Pete Silverton expressed surprise to find Mick stoned to the point of near-insensibility at the beginning of a 16 hour shift, and Johnny recalls how difficult it was to get him out of bed during this period. Despite his drug use, Mick still worked harder on the project than any other member of the Clash. 'He took a huge amount of time and care,' says Johnny. 'He sat in the control room and watched everything anyone did. Pearlman controlled everything, and Mick didn't have a say in the production unless he allowed him to. But Mick was learning his craft, and he took his guitars home every night, and cassettes of the day's recordings to listen to and work on.'

At the end of May, recording was interrupted by a trip to Paris for a one-off gig arranged by Bernie, in conjunction with the Ligue Communiste Revolutionaire, to mark the 10th anniversary of the 1968 Paris Riots. As Pete Silverton reported, the trip over was a disorganised farce, the promoter was stoned, the live sound was tinny beyond belief, there was fighting between opposing political factions at the venue, tear gas was flung around in the crowd, and bottles were lobbed at the stage during the Clash's set. The final number, the inevitable 'White Riot', was performed by just Mick and Topper, as Paul had dropped his bass, and Joe thrown down his guitar and microphone in disgust. Backstage, instead of exchanging recriminations, the band collapsed in hysterics. Informed that the crowd was threatening to riot again, the Clash told the promoter, 'If you can't get 'em to leave, tell 'em we're coming back on!' Thereafter, the new album was given the working title *Rent-A-Riot*.

Overdubs and vocals took the time spent on recording to a total of five weeks. At this stage, Buzzy shot some in-studio footage of Joe singing 'All The Young Punks (New Boots And Contracts)' and Mick singing 'Stay Free', the latter to effusive praise from Ray Gange. In addition to the 10 tracks eventually released on the album, Pearlman produced versions of 'Groovy Times' and 'One Emotion', as well as a re-working of '(White Man) In Hammersmith Palais'. At the end of the year, Mick would tell *Sounds'* Garry Bushell that the Clash had 15 unreleased songs in various stages of completion. In addition to 'RAF 1810', other never released tracks mentioned in various contemporary music press reports include 'Heart And Mind' and 'Scrawl On The Bathroom Wall'.

During the latter stages of recording, relations in the studio began to deteriorate. Representatives of Epic – the CBS label which had provisionally agreed to release the album in the US – flew in from New York to listen to rough mixes of the material. They professed themselves dissatisfied with the result. Growing increasingly anxious about the fate of the project, Sandy insisted the Clash accompany him back to the States for further work and remixing in superior and – for him – more familiar studios. Having already committed themselves to a month-long UK tour beginning on 28 June, the band dismissed this as, in Joe's words, 'pie-in-the-sky'. They were not happy with the recordings either, but for different reasons. As they had just recorded a song whose chorus repeatedly addresses their listeners as 'young cunts', no-one could have accused them of being prepared to sell out completely in order to gain access to American radio. They felt the recordings were too clean, and, believing they had already compromised enough, told Sandy to leave the tapes with them so they could rough them up a little during final mixing. Meanwhile, behind the backs of both the producer and the Clash, Muff Winwood and fellow CBS UK representative Jeremy Ensall were doing their own remixes and offering them to Epic. In order to prevent their work being tampered with further, the Clash finally agreed to more recording with Pearlman and to a new completion deadline. The album's release date was consequently put back from early autumn to pre-Christmas. Bernie did not show his face at the studio, and was not involved in these dealings.

Mick's original production of '(White Man) In Hammersmith Palais' – not the Sandy Pearlman version – backed with 'The Prisoner', was released as a single on 16 June 1978, towards the end of the band's stint in the studio and a fortnight before their summer tour was due to begin. The latter had been scheduled before the final court hearing relating to the Pigeon Shooting Incident, and presupposed its favourable outcome. It was cheekily entitled Out On Parole, from the line in Mott the Hoople's 'All The Way From Memphis': 'You look like a star, but you're really out on parole...'

The venues were much the same size and type as on the last outing, still mostly standing only. Although insurance was less of an issue this time, there were the usual complications with wary venue managers, local bans in Newcastle and Liverpool, last minute schedule alterations, and problems finding a suitable London venue. Second on the bill were pioneering New York new wave synth duo Suicide, who would attract such a rabidly negative reaction that even confrontation-seeking vocalist Alan Vega was taken aback. Opening band were the seven-piece Specials, invited on the tour at Joe's insistence. They were paid £25 per gig between them – until the Clash found out and objected, whereupon Bernie begrudgingly increased it to £50 – and in order to save on costs, fended for themselves with a Dormabile and a tent.

Back in March, when he had disavowed 'trash reggae' to *Melody Maker*'s Simon Kinnersley, Joe had pronounced himself to be 'into skanga [another name for ska] and rocksteady now. That's far stronger.' Don Letts had given him an old Trojan compilation, and the Specials further encouraged Joe's enthusiasm for reggae's formative years. In June, Joe told Pete Silverton, 'I have written a couple of Bluebeat numbers, but we haven't had time to work them up yet.' 'The Israelites' became a soundcheck regular on the tour, as it had been previously for the 101ers.

The Clash's repertoire proper for the tour comprised an even mixture of the new songs, tracks from the first album, and the inter-album singles. 'Police And Thieves' was rearranged to segue into a version of the Ramones' 'Blitzkrieg Bop'. This time out, the Clash's backdrop, designed by Paul, juxtaposed a Notting Hill townscape with a blow up of a Second World War Messerschmidt: evidence of the lingering influence of the Imperial War Museum films and the dwindling influence of Bernie Rhodes. Extremely large, awkward and heavy, the backdrop became the bane of Johnny Green and Baker's lives. The Clash stuck to their amateur hour hiring policy: Paul had been hanging around with his near-neighbour in Chelsea, Johnny Rotten, now going by his given name of John Lydon, and John's tough nut friend Steve English was taken on as the Clash's tour minder. Coincidentally, original Pistols guitarist Wally Nightingale was offered the job of guitar roadie. When it came to ligging, Robin Crocker and Kris Needs were among the usual suspects helping to relieve the tedium of life on the road.

The Clash's special relationship with certain members of the music press sometimes lulled Mick especially into being more open than was perhaps good for the band's image. The Clash still prided themselves on their treatment of their fans. In front of the *NME*'s Chris Salewicz, by now a particularly close friend, Mick asked Joe about the 'problems' with the band's official fan club. It transpired that the organiser, a fan named Mary, had been somewhat distraught when Bernie had given her the princely sum of £15 to set it up. Less amusing, and potentially more damaging, was Mick's unsolicited admission, 'All of this band are a right bunch of studs. I was the only one who slept on his own last night.' Realising that admitting to sex with groupies could be construed as taking advantage of impressionable female fans – typical rock star behaviour – he added, both lamely and somewhat pompously, 'But we *do* try and treat them with respect... And it's quite difficult: making them realise that you really *are* a human being is something of a necessary strain in the job.'

'There were a lot of girls,' says Johnny Green. 'Monogamy was not an issue. Taking your girlfriend on the road was frowned upon. Paul did have Caroline along on this tour, but it was a source of discontent to the rest of the band. Normally, Paul didn't have to think twice, because girls were always interested in him. Mick only looked at model girls, wasn't really interested in pulling for the sake of it. Joe went for less glamorous women. I once asked him why, and he said, "You don't have to play silly games. It's a straight deal: they know the score." Topper went for really young ones.'

A gig was slotted into the schedule at the last minute at Rafters club in Manchester. A couple of days after Mick made his statement, it was here that Chris witnessed what he described as 'a certain drama involving Topper Headon and a girl, a situation that puts him in a position where he is forced to decide between his emotions and his loyalties to the group'. Although Wendy, Topper's wife, was doubtless amongst those who found this description of the incident intriguing, it was a good deal milder than the Clash might have expected from a less partisan observer. Topper had drunk copious amounts of vodka back at the hotel. 'He'd had these two 14 year-old girls, one black and one white, in his room,' says Johnny. 'Then he'd gone down to the dining room and got all the silverplated cruet sets, gone back up to the seventh floor, and thrown them out of the window at cars. At the club, he was so out of it that we had to do a serious sobering up job. He had one of the girls with him, and the police were looking for her. They came backstage, and we had to hide her in a flight case.'

As Dave Mingay points out, the Buzzy crew had made a conscious decision not to concentrate on sex and drugs or other aspects of the band members' personal lives (though Joe did suggest calling the film *Don't Bring Your Pyjamas*). Far more interested in the Clash's relationship with the police, they had managed to push Ray Gange into the frame when filming the aftermath of the Pigeon Shooting Incident on the steps to Clerkenwell Magistrate's Court. The Buzzy team joined the Out On Parole Tour in Glasgow on 4 July, just in time to capture the next chapter of the Clash's battle with the law, also witnessed by Chris Salewicz and *Melody Maker*'s Chris Brazier.

Their confidence growing in the project, Buzzy scaled up their sound equipment for the Glasgow Apollo concert, hiring the first in a series of 8-track mobiles. It was to be the last rock gig hosted by the Apollo before it was closed and transformed into a bingo hall. What neither Buzzy nor the band was aware of was that the bouncers had taken umbrage at the boisterous behaviour of fans on the Get Out Of Control Tour, and viewed this farewell show as the perfect opportunity to take their revenge. From the moment the Clash took the stage, the bouncers set upon the fans and beat them indiscriminately. The band realised what was going on after a few songs, and pleaded for calm, but to no avail. Buzzy filmed them performing '(White Man) In Hammersmith Palais', 'I'm So Bored With The USA' and 'Janie Jones'. It was during this, the band's penultimate song, that

Joe – his T-shirt bearing the slogan 'GET TAE FUCK' – disappeared into the audience in an attempt to restrain a particularly vicious official, only to be promised some of the same himself later on. Back on stage, Joe urged everyone to 'simmer down', and announced the Clash's last number: 'White Riot'.

It was perhaps not the most diplomatic choice. The Clash should probably have abandoned the show a lot earlier: in refusing to relinquish the stage, they had allowed their bravado to put their followers at risk. Several fans subsequently demanded to know why the band had done nothing – that is, nothing useful – to help them. Leaving the venue to jeers, Joe was so overcome he smashed a lemonade bottle on the floor. He was immediately wrestled to the ground by the police. Appalled by the rough treatment meted out to his friend, Paul tried to pull Joe free, and was hit on the head with a truncheon for his pains.

Both were arrested and locked up for the night. Paul was punched again in the van. At the police station, Joe encountered the first friendly Clash fan he'd met all night. Despite having been arrested for the heinous crime of being on the receiving end of bouncer brutality, the fan grinned at Joe and sang the chorus of 'The Prisoner'. The following morning, Joe was charged with breach of the peace, and Paul with being drunk and disorderly and 'going to the aid of a prisoner' (an offence peculiar to Scotland). Despite mitigating circumstances, Joe insisted that they both plead guilty in order not to cause delays and jeopardise the rest of the tour. He was fined £25 and Paul £45. 'That's what we get for calling it the Clash On Parole Tour,' laughed Joe afterwards to Buzzy's camera. At least this time the music press was sympathetic to their cause, and the Clash were able to turn the bad experience into a victory of sorts: a defiant version of 'The Prisoner' became a set highlight. Buzzy made a point of filming the song at the Aberdeen gig.

The Dunfermline Kinema produced a version of 'Tommy Gun', whereupon the small Buzzy crew and Ray Gange left the tour. This meant they, like the journalists, missed the next two dramas in the Clash's lives. At Crawley on 8 July, in an incident strongly reminiscent of the one involving Micky Foote on the Get Out Of Control Tour, Steve English got carried away with policing the dressing room, and started to beat up a young fan. A furious Mick Jones dove in to break it up, much to everyone's surprise. Especially English's, whose time with the Clash was not to be long thereafter. Mick got off less lightly the following day when Johnny Green accidentally slammed the van door on one of the guitarist's fingers. Hospital treatment was required, but Mick's supply of bravery had not run out, and he was able to carry on playing.

Continuing the tour's Sex Pistols theme, when the band arrived at Birmingham Top Rank on 12 July, they found the band's former guitarist waiting for them. 'Steve Jones had driven up in his black BMW,' says Johnny. 'He arrived with his Les Paul. "All right for the encore?"' Since the demise of the Pistols, apart from his work on the Pistols' film and an aborted attempt to form a band with Paul Cook and Johnny Thunders, Steve had been at a loose end. He was known as an enthusiastic ligger on the London gig circuit, so at first Mick was not too surprised by his presence. But when Steve also turned up the following night at the King George's Hall in Blackburn, Mick started to wonder what he was doing so far away from home with his guitar at the ready. 'Mick confronted him,' says Johnny Green. 'Steve, bless him, was no diplomat. "Bernie said come along for a laugh." And then he said it: "I'm after your job!" And he broke up laughing.'

Steve stayed on after the gig, and commandeered Johnny's hotel room to entertain a girl. Then another. And another. In the middle of the night, the police mounted a drugs raid. Mysteriously, Steve had sneaked out of the hotel by this time and driven back to London. Mick was caught in possession, and spent the rest of the night in the cells. Exhausted after his rough night, and understandably upset by the double whammy of Steve's revelation and the bust, Mick was suspicious of everyone. 'The whole incident was discussed by the band in a very belligerent way the next day, with Mick putting it on the agenda in the car,' says Johnny. 'Basically, the sort of thing you'd find in a relationship: "What the fuck are you trying to do here? Do you want me out? Think *you* can write songs?" And then he went quiet for a bit, and said, "It's Bernie."' Memories of being forced out of Little Queenie by Guy Stevens cannot have been far from his mind.

A prolonged heart to heart brought the band closer than they had been all year, and despite all its problems, Out On Parole ended on a high note. It climaxed with a triumphant run of four dates on 24-27 July at the Music Machine (now the Electric Ballroom), Camden High Street. On the 26th, Mick proved he was sufficiently secure in his position to allow Steve Jones to guest on 'London's Burning', while Paul Cook played a second drum kit, and then Jimmy Pursey once again grabbed the microphone for 'White Riot'. Buzzy filmed part of one of the shows, capturing 'Complete Control', 'Safe European Home' and 'What's My Name'.

Earlier in the tour, after making allowances for the venue's notoriously poor acoustics, an *NME* review of the Leeds Queen's Hall gig had noted that the Clash's music seemed to have 'graduated/shifted towards Heavy Metal', with Mick taking 'solos impressively (frequently at will)'. Over the course of the next few months, other reviewers would remark upon a dramatic change in the Clash's live sound. The Sandy Pearlman connection would be cited as the reason for this development. Most commentators assumed that the countless studio retakes had taught the Clash how to play as a unit, while the producer's own hard rock leanings had proved infectious. In fact, the Clash had always practised and rehearsed assiduously, and any musical development was attributable to their own hard work over the past two years. Pearlman's main contribution had been to convince the band that the amateur ethic was holding them back: they could no longer get away with sounding 'like a mad seal barking over a mass of pneumatic drills', as Joe once memorably put it. For Out On Parole, the Clash had hired superior PA equipment and professional soundmen: their playing had improved, and most of the time that improvement could be heard. Plus, Mick always turned his amps up as high as they would go.

Resident Dingwalls DJ Barry Myers had hosted the Anti-Nazi league event, and the band had invited him to ply his trade at the Music Machine gigs. He submitted a review to *Sounds* that was firmly in the tradition of previous Friends of the Clash: 'It was a privilege to spend four nights with the greatest band in Britain, nay, at this moment in time, the greatest band in the world.' Charles Shaar Murray attended the third Music Machine gig on behalf of the *NME*. Save for politely suggesting to Joe that he make more effort to keep his battered Telecaster in tune, he could find no fault either: 'Their emotional power is now matched with a confident, co-ordinated strength which is well nigh overwhelming in its impact. Anyone who honestly expresses a preference for the uncoordinated, unfocussed aggression of their early days is talking out of nostalgia and I-was-at-the-Roxy-and-you-weren't-elitism: *this* is the heyday of the Clash.' Barry's review was predictable, but, coming from the author of the band's first ever serious critical mauling, CSM's was particularly sweet. 'I remember taking the *NME* round to Mick's the morning it came out,' says Johnny. 'He was ecstatic.'

Almost immediately following the tour, the pressure was back on to complete the second album. Both Mick and Joe had previously insisted they wanted to make their first visit to America as part of a performing band, but this was not to be. Only the singer and guitarist were required for overdubs, and so only they flew out to San Francisco in mid

August to resume work with Sandy Pearlman. The album was now provisionally titled *All The Peacemakers*, after a line from 'Police And Thieves'. They were booked into the Automatt on Folsom Street, where they remained for three more weeks, seven days a week, 12 hours a day. The length of the sessions suggests extensive re-recording. After his two recent scares, Mick decided it was the perfect time to cut back on his drug intake and cut out cocaine altogether. Only a few of Paul's original basslines had survived the Basing Street sessions, and at the Automatt – except on the songs most obviously originated by him, namely 'Tommy Gun' and 'Last Gang In Town' – most of Joe's guitar parts were also either replaced or buried by Mick. When album track 'English Civil War' was released as a single in 1979, its sleeve would admit as much: Mick is credited with 'guitars', Joe merely with 'vocals'.

The local music community was intrigued to have representatives of a UK punk band in its midst, but the duo avoided interviews. While in the city, they did attend several gigs, and when the Automatt sessions finished, Mick spent a week in Los Angeles while Joe drove cross-country in a 1956 Chevy pick-up truck. Stopping off in New Orleans, he picked up Graham Parker and the Rumour keyboard player Bob Andrews, who was to add yet more overdubs to the album in New York.

The two band members and Sandy Pearlman reconvened in the producer's beloved Record Plant on West 44th Street. Excited to be living out their boyhood dreams of discovering America, but a little saddened by the less-than-ideal circumstances, Mick and Joe rewrote the lyric to Mick's pre-Clash song 'Ooh, Baby, Ooh (It's Not Over)' first as 'Rusted Chrome' and then as 'Gates Of The West'. Joe's final draft, sung by Mick, namechecks the studio's location and tries to celebrate making it 'all the way' there from Rehearsals in Camden Town Rail Yard, but cannot avoid a note of doubt and regret. Engineer Dennis Ferranti supplied the high pitched vocal to this track, which was ultimately left off the album. In addition to Bob Andrews, other uncredited guests on the album proper were Stan Bronstein of Elephant's Memory – best known for backing John Lennon on *Sometime In New York City* – who added saxophone to 'Drug Stabbing Time', and 60-year old local blues musicians Gloves Glover and Al Fields, known as the Living Legends, who played piano on 'Julie's Been Working For The Drug Squad'. 'We had a lot of fun watching our record being recorded by session musicians,' laughed Mick afterwards. Then followed the mixing, 'five days on each track', which took until nearly the end of September. Topper and Paul flew out to witness the last few days of this process. Mick subsequently described working with Sandy as 'a fucking misery... it was like 98 days in hell'. 'It nearly killed us,' agreed Joe. 'We came out like zombies.'

Just 10 tracks were selected, mixed, sequenced and mastered for the album, Sandy insisting that VFM take second place to avoiding the inferior sound quality caused by 'groove cramming' on the vinyl LP format. With the album scheduled for early November release, there was little time left to devote to package design. The Clash turned their attention to the title and cover while still in New York. *Give 'Em Enough Rope*, being the first half of a proverb which concludes '...and they'll hang themselves', was clearly inspired by the similar sentiment of *The Harder They Come*, a corruption of the proverb 'The bigger they come, the harder they fall.' The title manages to acknowledge George Melly's parable about establishment interference, while also sticking up two fingers at all the doubters and begrudgers in the style of album tracks like 'Cheapskates'. The cover, attributed to New York designer Gene Grief but actually borrowed by him from a Chinese government-approved postcard, shows two vultures in the desert picking at the corpse of a dead cowboy, while Chinese cavalry bearing red flags move in from the left. Oriental typography is also used for the title, so it is hard not to construe the whole as a symbolic rendering of – as Nick Kent commented at the time of the album's release – 'the triumph of East over West', or, less literal-mindedly, the overthrow of the First World establishment by the downtrodden masses. Back in London, the Clash decided to add a poster insert. One side was to feature a Pennie Smith portrait of the band posing against a map of the world, and the other side a blow-up of the map with various international trouble spots illustrated by appropriate symbols and news photos.

The relevance of the packaging – as originally conceived – to the contents is plain. The cover is a global equivalent of the first album's charging policeman photo, and both cover and poster allude to the subject matter of 'Safe European Home', 'English Civil War', 'Tommy Gun' and 'Guns On The Roof'. However, the poster's use of a cartoon of Death captioned 'Neutron Bomb' to illustrate the US, and the cover's depiction of the overthrow of the cowboy – one of that nation's most enduring mythic heroes – by the communist hordes were also indisputably provocative. Although Epic did worry about this, their lawyer's main concern was that the Chinese government might sue for copyright infringement over use of the postcard. They were persuaded the likelihood of this was minuscule, but it could explain why the typography, at least, was altered for the US edition. It was CBS UK who raised the biggest objection to the outer cover, and then only because it failed to include a photograph of the Clash. The poster did feature a band portrait, but it was withdrawn from releases in all territories at the last minute, with the exception of a few promotional copies. Not because the record company or the band got cold feet, but because – as the slogan on the shirt Joe was wearing made all too evident – the band portrait had been printed back-to-front, and there was no time to correct this glaring error. Perhaps it was for the best: both sides of the poster would be reproduced in the 25 November issue of the *NME,* accompanied by a snide comment about the band 'expounding suspect ideologies with fancy graphics'.

Completing the album had been an enervating experience. Bernie Rhodes had not helped make life any easier when, via the 28 August 1978 issues of the UK music press, he had announced that the Clash would be playing a concert on 9 September at the Harlesden Roxy (now under new management). None of the band had been consulted about this arrangement, and when Mick and Joe learned about it they correctly construed it as a desperate attempt at emotional blackmail: putting them in the position where they would be to be letting down their fans if they did not break off recording and return to the UK to fulfil the commitment. Bernie was clearly worried at not being close enough to have any control over proceedings, and was determined to bring the band back into his sphere of influence. He was right to worry, but he picked a bad time to make his point and a worse way to do it. Unaccustomed to the McLaren/Rhodes management style, and less prepared to be accommodating than their UK counterparts, CBS New York were finding Bernie difficult to deal with. According to the *NME*'s news pages of 30 September, they had declared themselves 'anxious for a management change'. Bernie would later claim they even offered the band money to get rid of him. Mick had been grumbling about Bernie all year, but following the sneaky attempt to replace him with Steve Jones, he had been more forceful than ever in urging his dismissal. The others were wavering, with only Joe still reluctant to see Bernie go.

Mick and Joe had refused to return for the Roxy concert. The week after his original announcement, Bernie responded by issuing a statement to the inkies claiming the gig was being postponed until 23 September because the band were 'on strike' in protest over the minimal radio airplay afforded their records. This total fabrication finally pushed the Clash too far. The following week saw the first signs of open revolt, with an 'untypically humourless' Paul phoning the *NME* on behalf of the band to declare,

'Bernie Rhodes makes us look daft, and it gets our fuckin' backs up the way he assumes he can just speak away for the four of us. He can't, right?' The Roxy show was postponed yet again. By the 23rd Paul and Topper had joined Mick and Joe in New York to oversee the final days of mixing and to discuss what to do about Bernie.

Bernie flew to New York for what the *NME* billed as a 'showdown' on the 26th, but no official action was taken until lawyers and accountants representing the band had examined the paperwork. Upon returning to the UK, the Clash attempted to honour their outstanding commitment. The Harlesden Roxy show had been rescheduled for the 14 October, but after 500 seats were removed to turn the stalls area into a dancefloor, the GLC made an inspection and insisted that only 900 of the 1,600 ticket holders could be admitted. Attempts to find a compromise solution foundered, and at the very last minute the gig had to be postponed yet again. Although announcements were made on local radio, it was not possible to warn everyone in advance. The Clash hung around outside the venue until 9 pm to explain the situation in person, and free 'Tommy Gun' T-shirts were given away in consolation, but some of the 400 or so fans present had travelled a considerable distance at great expense, and were understandably aggrieved.

As far as the Clash were concerned, it was to be the last embarrassment caused by Bernie Rhodes. On 21 October 1978, after the band had returned from playing a few dates in Europe, Bernie received legal notice that his services were no longer required. His contract was to terminate officially on 1 December. Bernie refused to accept this – the press statement he released to *Melody Maker* opened with the priceless claim, 'I took them off the street and made them what they are!' – and his immediate response was to obtain a court order requiring all Clash earnings to be paid directly to him in the first instance. On the advice of their lawyers, the Clash countered by claiming that 'financial accounting by the management is disastrous'. But Bernie got his way.

For some time, the inkies had been speculating about Bernie's successor. Among those rumoured to have expressed an interest in guiding the band's future career were Rod Stewart's manager Brian Gaff and Yes's manager Brian Lane, the latter much to T-Zers' amusement: 'a riot in the Topographic Ocean?' Rather than an established professional music business manager, the Clash wanted someone with whom they already had a relationship. Among those considered were Clash-friendly *NME* journalist Chris Salewicz and Clash-friendly *NME* photographer Pennie Smith. Among those actually approached, this time to manage as a team, were Clash-friendly *NME* journalist Barry Miles and CBS Head of Publicity Elly Smith, who were offered a six-way split with the band members on all future Clash income. Miles and Elly turned them down. 'After analysing the figures they provided, it seemed that managing them would amount largely to a permanent lawsuit with Bernie who, as far as the figures showed, had ripped them off something rotten,' explains Miles. 'All we would be doing would be trying to get the money back.'

Finance was the single issue over which the considerably more complex relationship between Bernie and the band was debated in public. Talking to *Melody Maker*'s Allan Jones in November, Joe said, 'The reason we had to part company is that Bernie – although he's like some kinda genius, a great *ideas* man – he can't, you know, *do sums*.' It was not until a 1985 interview with *Sounds*' Jane Simon that Topper finally put a figure to the band's financial problems as of late 1978: 'Bernie Rhodes managed the group, and after a couple of years we found out we were £250,000 in debt to the record company. He had more money than the rest of us put together.' The strong implication was that Bernie had been lining his pockets at the band's expense. The real problem with the paperwork was not that it revealed fraud, but that it was so slapdash it revealed very little at all. Bernie was prepared to admit that accounting was not his strong suit. 'I'm an artist,' he told the *NME*'s Steve Clarke. 'I have to be a manager through circumstances.'

The Clash singles had not sold in large quantities, and although the first album had enjoyed greater commercial success, that had only been in relatively minor markets like the UK. Certainly, the revenue from record sales had come nowhere near repaying the advance, and so much of that was still outstanding. In 1977, £100,000 would have been a large sum to receive as a windfall, but Bernie had to use it to run a business for 18 months with very little additional income, a lot of outgoings, and a workforce never smaller than 10. The first £50,000, received in March 1977, had gone long before the end of the year: £28,000 of it invested in the White Riot Tour, £4,000 spent on recording the first album, a similar amount on studio time for single and EP projects, and unknown but doubtless sizeable sums swallowed up by a retrospective contribution to the cost of the Anarchy Tour, new sound equipment and instruments, the Night of Action, the aborted Digbeth festival, the Dunstable promotional film, European gigs, day-to-day running costs at Rehearsals, backdrops and other Upstarts ventures, including Alex Michon's clothes, and – however low they might have been – band wages and roadies' wages. The second half of the advance, received at the end of 1977, had to cover a loss of £10,000 on the Get Out Of Control Tour, the cost of more European dates, the Jamaican songwriting trip, more studio bills for singles and B sides, more equipment, backdrops and clothes, more running costs, more wages and now flat rents as well. The band had to ask CBS – who initially refused – if they could borrow a further £2,500 in order to hire PA for the Out On Parole Tour. That tour lost another £10,000.

Johnny Green wonders how the Clash's UK tours could have cost so much money. There were three reasons. Firstly, even on the first two tours, when the band's equipment left a lot to be desired, it was still expensive in relation to the size of the venues and the low ticket prices; when they upgraded for the third tour, the discrepancy was even greater. The determination to give VFM might have been admirable, but it was hardly economically viable. Secondly, someone had to pay for the damage caused by the audiences at the venues, and for the damage caused by the band's large and unruly entourage at the hotels. The third reason comes a little closer to home for Johnny: no-one working close to the band was a professional. The Clash's amateur ethic was again admirable, and it also allowed Bernie to get away with paying low wages. In the long run, though, disorganisation and chaos are punitively expensive, and the Clash camp – manager, band and motley crew alike – were spectacularly inefficient when it came to most practical matters.

The bulk of the Clash's debt to CBS could be attributed to recording costs for the new album: two sets of demos, five weeks in a name London studio at around £50 an hour, approximately as long again in even more costly American studios, Sandy Pearlman's considerable fee, and Mick and Joe's hotel bills and other expenses. As he had expected the second album to be completed in five weeks at Basing Street, Bernie was reluctant to take the blame. 'I didn't view my job as being here to subsidise their silly indulgences, like recording in big New York studios and staying in top New York hotels,' he said in his late October statement to *Melody Maker*. This part of the Clash's debt was so much paper, though: at the time, the album was on the point of receiving its release not only in the UK, but also in the US – the world's largest single market – as well as the rest of the world, and CBS and Epic obviously believed it would stand a good chance of recouping the outlay.

As for Topper's suggestion that Bernie had made more money than the others put together: by the terms of the CBS contract, Bernie was entitled to 20 per cent of the Clash's gross income; that is, unlike the band themselves, he had a right to a fifth of their earnings before expenses. Not the gesture of a team player, perhaps, but not illegal, and certainly not unusual for a manager. (Colonel Tom Parker helped himself to 50 per cent of Elvis Presley's income.) In his press statement, Bernie claimed he had not even taken his full cut: 'It has ended with the group owing me money.' Without access to the paperwork – and, one suspects, even with it – it is impossible to say for sure whether Bernie did fleece the band for his own profit or if he has been maligned. According to Topper, in order to regain control of the purse strings, the Clash would eventually be forced to pay their ex-manager a further £25,000.

In the end, the Clash asked Caroline Coon to look after their affairs on a trial basis. The others had reservations about offering the management position to Paul's girlfriend, but Caroline met one of the main requirements in that she had been involved with the Clash since the early days. She understood what was important to them, as well as how both the music press and the music business worked. Not insignificantly, her time with Release had made her a skilled negotiator and given her a good legal grounding. 'She was appreciated for what she did in getting Topper and Paul out of Brixton jail after the Pigeon Shooting Incident,' says Johnny Green. In the summer, she had also delayed the hearing of an incontestable drunk driving charge against Johnny himself at a time when the Clash could ill afford for him to be without a licence.

'They also liked the way Caroline looked after their image,' he says. Certainly, from October onwards, the Clash began to dress more like a gang again, but this was something that Caroline capitalised upon rather than instigated. The brief October European tour preceding Bernie's dismissal had proved to be a happy affair... if one forgets for a moment the ongoing jinx on Mick's guitars: another Les Paul fell off its stand and broke its neck. In Paris, the band had visited a club called Le Palace, and danced together to the Village People. The show at the Paradiso in Amsterdam was, according to Johnny, the best one he ever saw and heard the Clash play. 'I'd always loved the band, but suddenly they were in another league.' The following day, still high on the euphoria of the gig, the entire band visited the city's flea market. They persuaded Dave Mingay to buy them a cheap second hand leather jacket apiece from one of the stalls. It was a spontaneous celebration, but also a symbolic re-enactment of the Day of the Day-Glo Leather Carcoats, Significant Event One in the birth of the Clash.

Back in the UK, the renewed spirit of unity was captured in the publicity photographs styled by Caroline and taken by Pennie Smith at Caroline's flat, one of which was to used as the (subsequently withdrawn) poster illustration for the forthcoming album. Each band member retains something of his own individual style – Joe wearing a shirt stencilled with the unusually conciliatory slogan 'REBEL TRUCE' – but Mick has finally had his hair cut relatively short again and greased back over his ears in a rocker style, and there is a strong hint of *The Wild One* – albeit updated – in the studded leather wristbands and wide leather belts worn by all, in Topper and Paul's leather biker jackets and DM's, in Joe and Mick's biker boots, in Paul's peaked cap, in Mick's leather trousers and wrist bandanna and in Joe's sheriff's badge and aviator shades. Then there is the close physical contact, the band posing with their arms resting casually on or around each other's shoulders. The image is decidedly American, suggesting that Caroline at least had not lost sight of the need to win over the US market. In truth, it is also so buddy-buddy macho it borders on camp: after the Paris disco, was this punk's answer to the Village People?

Caroline's brief was to help the Clash put their affairs in order and make a new start. She promptly severed the band's relationship with Dave Cork and Endale Associates, turning instead to Ian Flukes of the Derek Block Agency, based in Oxford Street, to book the Clash's next UK tour. Announced in late October, it was to run from 9 November to the end of December 1978 under the self-explanatory title of the Clash Sort It Out Tour. She also hired professional publicist Tony Brainsbury. 'We haven't brought any publicity man along with us,' Joe admitted ruefully to Allan Jones. 'So we have to go outside the circle.' At the time, Tony was also responsible for Paul McCartney, Queen and Thin Lizzy, among others, but he had previously provided his services for Mott the

Hoople. One business connection did survive the split with Bernie. The court order requiring all band funds to be paid to the ex-manager in the first instance meant that all financial outlay had to be approved by Bernie's Baker Street accountant, Peter Quinnell. The Clash's unhappiness at this state of affairs explains the nickname they bestowed upon him: Quister the Twister.

The new broom did not apply to longstanding assistants Johnny Green and the Baker. They had already proved their loyalty by rejecting Bernie's offer-cum-ultimatum of staying with him in favour of throwing in their lot with the Clash. But the band would have to get used to the idea of working with a professional driver, tour manager and road crew, and professional sound and light operators. This had its advantages, but came at the cost of the sense of commitment, camaraderie and adventure of yore. Rehearsal Rehearsals and the Clash's camp's other familiar Camden Town haunts were left behind. For the first time since summer 1976, the band were forced to find new rehearsal spaces. Short-term availability and affordability were the main criteria, and Johnny remembers the band working through several over the next few months, each a little seedier than the last.

The Clash's new beginning did not get off to an auspicious start. Like Roadent and Sebastian, Tony Parsons and his fellow Hip Young Gunslinger Julie Burchill had become disillusioned with the punk movement they had been hired to cover by the *NME*. In spring 1978, they had begun work on an obituary for the movement, published that October under the title *The Boy Looked At Johnny*. An extraordinary cocktail of disappointment, vitriol and amphetamine – veering from spot-on criticism to wild accusation, from eye-witness anecdote to unproven hearsay – it offered no quarter to any of their former friends as it ripped into punk's pretensions and hypocrisies. The section on the Clash indicated that the Digbeth festival farce, Belfast photo session and 'BRIGADE ROSSE' T-shirt had irretrievably soured the Clash Myth for Tony. 'What disappointed me most was that it was boring to read,' Joe told Allan Jones shortly after publication. 'And also the fact that they'd invented so many lies. They needn't have. They could've put that kind of cynical slant on the facts.' To which Tony ripostes, 'Jon Savage's *England's Dreaming* is a brilliant book, but it's a book *about* punk. *The Boy Looked At Johnny* is a punk book. It's, "Ah, bollocks to the lot of you!"' Time has mellowed the Parsons perspective somewhat. 'I was disappointed with the Clash on a personal level, because I thought they would be more involved in trying to effect change. Essentially, they were a band, and I can now see that it's ridiculous to expect a band to behave like a political party, but I think a lot of people did, then.'

The Clash finally played the Harlesden Roxy on 25 and 26 October, so that all the ticket holders could get in to see them. Just to make sure, and in order to raise a symbolic pair of rigid digits to the GLC, on the second night Johnny Green let 60 fans in free through the back door. The *NME*, ever in search of a fresh perspective, sent along recent recruit Ian Penman to review one of the shows. This is what he saw: 'A joyless, emotionless, directionless, self-important music, something like a shambolic HM quartet converted to Mao minutes before a show, but still retaining the original ego-pushy set, swaggers and all... The Clash don't know what to do with themselves, don't know what to do with rock music, but I and you know what it's doing to them. The Clash is a dying myth.'

Give 'Em Enough Rope was released on 10 November 1978. In attempting to broaden their canvas to reflect their new national – and hopefully international – audience, it sees the Clash sever the direct connection to their material that gave *The Clash* its emotional power and unified vision. On that album, when Joe sings in the first person he is either Joe Strummer the Street Punk or Everyman; on the follow-up, he attempts to play more varied roles, but only manages to send confusing messages. In the world affairs songs like 'Tommy Gun' and 'Julie's Been Working For The Drug Squad', he is just an observer, an opinionated individual tut-tutting at the newspaper. At the other extreme, the more personal songs are just too personal. Some songs of this type can convey universal truths, but songs about the woes of the Clash do not travel far beyond the walls of the Clash's rehearsal room: at the end of side two, the sentimental Ian Hunter-esque ballad 'Stay Free' is grouped with 'Cheapskates' and the Mott the Hoople-acknowledging 'All The Young Punks (New Boots And Contracts)'. This does nothing to detract attention from the Mott the Hoople Syndrome running riot through the triptych, and also suggested by the titles of 'Guns On The Roof' and 'Last Gang In Town'. The dry wit employed in the drug songs indicates the ironic distancing of satire, while the anguished howling of a good half of the other album tracks almost demands an emotional response at gunpoint; in attempting both feats at the same time, 'Cheapskates' attempts the impossible.

Sandy Pearlman's production strips Mick's guitar playing of almost all its individuality, and reduces the entire album – guest star overdubs and all – to sterile, stodgy, Adult Oriented Rock. In turn, this serves to emphasise the bombast, sentimentality, melodrama and self-indulgence of too many of the vocals and too many of the lyrics. With hindsight, perhaps the Clash would have benefited from being hustled into the studio to record their second album at the end of 1977, after all. A quickly- and cheaply-produced set made up of the inter-album single material, 'Pressure Drop', a couple of Mick's pre-Clash songs and the best of the post-Jamaica trip demo material would have been far superior, as is testified by the second half of the first CD of 1991's boxed set retrospective *Clash On Broadway*.

With its defiant-sounding title, *Give 'Em Enough Rope* was an album begging for a lashing from the UK music press. Tony Brainsbury arranged a listening party-cum-press conference at a sleazy cinema in Dean Street. Only one of the speakers on the stereo system worked, and Topper and Robin Crocker made off with most of the promotional copies of the album to sell at a second hand record store around the corner. In *ZigZag*, Robin and Kris Needs both delivered the predictable rave reviews, and at *Sounds* heavy rock-loving Dave McCullough succumbed to the slick production and gave the album the full five stars. At the *NME*, Nick Kent was similarly impressed by the sound, but was perceptive enough to take issue with the combined effect of Joe's lyrics and vocals: 'one is never entirely sure just which side Strummer and company are supposed to be taking… What it all adds up to, I fear, is Strummer's totally facile concept of shock-politics.'

The best appraisal came from *Melody Maker*'s Jon Savage. He deemed the America-oriented production to be 'an unsatisfactory compromise'. After astutely placing the album in its historical and cultural context, that is, among the ruins of punk, he paused to note the weight of expectation the Clash had to shoulder – 'it's hard when you define a period so accurately' – before expressing his disappointment with the lack of direction and mood of defeatism: 'The Clash's view of the human condition, while imprecisely expressed, isn't very sanguine this time out. The sharp, direct attack of the first album, itself holding out hope by the accuracy of targets selected and hit, has been replaced by a confused lashing-out and a muddy attempt to come to terms with the violence of the outside world, which the Clash plainly see as hostile through and through… Flicking through the titles, you catch the words repeated – drugs, guns – and the general themes of gangs and fights, all too rarely enlivened with the humour that marked the first album. They sound as though they're writing about what they think is expected of them, rather than what they want to write about, or need to. It's as though they see their function in terms of "the modern outlaw" – obligatory "rock'n'roll" rebellion similar to the Stones – and conservationists of the punk ethos they so singularly helped to create.' He concluded, 'So do they squander their greatness.'

The single 'Tommy Gun' was released on 24 November in a sleeve mimicking Sebastian's style of old and featuring text from an Arabic newspaper and photos of car bombs, peace and anti-nuclear marches, police brutality, and a corpse. In the *NME*, former *Sniffin' Glue* editor, *ZigZag* writer and Clash champion Danny Baker grumbled about the Clash releasing an album track as a single, and pointed out that the A side had already been around for the best part of a year while the 'shabby' B side '1-2 Crush On You' went all the way back to the band's earliest days. 'With "(White Man) In Hammersmith Palais", I thought the Clash were untouchable, but this is a sad report on the state of things.'

'Clash City Rockers' had lasted just four weeks on the charts, peaking at number 35. '(White Man) In Hammersmith Palais' had stayed in for seven weeks, but made it no higher than number 32. 'Which is so sad,' sighed Mick at the time. 'I thought it would have made a great summer hit.' It did not bode well for 'Tommy Gun'. The band still attributed their relative failure in the singles market to lack of radio play. Mick and Joe understandably found it bitterly ironic that the first time they heard 'Complete Control' on the radio was on KSAN in San Francisco, nearly a year after it was released, and on the other side of the world from the country that had spawned the band and provided the song's subject matter.

The Clash were capable of being their own worst enemies. They had been invited to record a live studio session for John Peel's Radio One show, but had proved too disorganised and stoned to complete it in the allotted time. Declaring themselves unsatisfied with what they had managed to record, they insisted it be scrapped. They were informed they were the only band that had ever failed to deliver, and Peel vented his disappointment with them on air. The Clash – correctly – took this to mean they would not be asked back.

The gulf between the subject matter of the daytime music programmed for workers and housewives and the harsh realities of life on the streets explains both the title of 'Groovy Times' and its refrain 'the housewives are all singing…' In January 1979, the Clash would re-record 'Capital Radio', partly to make it more widely available for fans, and partly to reassert their condemnation of nearly two years earlier. Towards the end of 'Capital Radio Two', Joe halts proceedings and announces, 'We'll never get on the radio like this…' The band respond by launching into a cod-disco coda, over which Joe parodies John Travolta and Olivia Newton John's 'You're The One That I Want' and 'Summer Nights', both from the film *Grease*, and both number one UK hits in May and September 1978, respectively.

Since the advent of punk, some new pop music programmes had appeared on TV, several of which encouraged bands to play live. One might have expected the Clash to leap at the chance. Famed glam-era producer Mickie Most had launched *Revolver* on ITV with the expressed intention of featuring punk bands; interviewed in *Record Mirror*, he admitted he disliked the music. 'How can you have a programme like that?' demanded Mick Jones. BBC2 had started up a typically worthy-but-dull programme called *Rock Goes To College*, which broadcast hour-long sets recorded live at higher education establishments around the country. 'We don't play just to students,' said Mick. The same channel's *Something Else* was more acceptable, being a magazine programme featuring a mixture of live music and discussions about contemporary issues, and conforming to the Clash's DIY ethic in that it was devised and presented for 'the kids' by 'the kids'. In March 1978, the band had performed 'Tommy Gun' on the show – Joe wearing shades to hide his hepatitis-yellow eyes – but as this turned out to be eight months before the song's release as a single, the promotional value was negligible. These shows had relatively small ratings, anyway.

The same could not be said of Saturday morning kids' programme *Tiswas*, on which

Joe and Paul had made a late January 1978 guest appearance, but it was hardly aimed at the band's target market. While being kept in a cage and doused with gunge was a reasonable replication of the Clash's own experience of a Clash live performance, it hardly communicated that experience to the television public. The appearance might have had more impact had the whole band attended, as scheduled, but Mick refused to get out of bed. *Top Of The Pops* remained the only guaranteed televisual route to the charts, and the Clash still refused to appear on the show (though, if the truth be told, they had not been invited back after refusing the first time).

The band realised something had to be done to break the deadlock. One suggestion was to make a video clip for 'Tommy Gun', similar to that made by the Sex Pistols for 'Pretty Vacant'. Having served his apprenticeship on *The Punk Rock Movie*, sometime Clash tour DJ Don Letts was asked to film the band performing 'Tommy Gun' on-stage at one of the Roxy Harlesden soundchecks. Although the result does capture some of the Clash's energy in performance, it is not wholly convincing, largely because they are clearly miming to the studio recording of the song. This is where the holes begin to appear in the Clash camp's thinking: not wishing to mime to pre-recorded tracks was the principal reason they gave for not playing *Top Of The Pops*; that programme was the only real UK outlet for the video; and when they heard CBS were attempting to slip a copy of the video to the show's producer, the Clash objected strongly and insisted it be withdrawn.

The band's core UK following had waited a long time for the album and rushed out to buy it en masse, pushing it up to number two in the album charts by the end of the month. It would remain on the charts for 14 weeks, just two less than its predecessor. Despite its reasonable sales performance, within a few weeks of its release it became evident to (almost) all that *Give 'Em Enough Rope* had nothing like the stature of *The Clash*. Although they did their best to enthuse about it while it was still their current album, the Clash themselves subsequently came to recognise it as one of their artistic low-points. Meanwhile, 'Tommy Gun', no means a classic Clash single, nevertheless proved to be the one that broke through that previously impenetrable Top 20 barrier. It reached number 19 in December, the most competitive month of the year, and remained on the charts for 10 weeks.

At least part of the success of both album and single can be attributed to the buzz generated by the Sort It Out Tour. The Clash were still playing much the same-sized venues as on the last two outings, but this was their longest tour to date, reaching more than the usual number of fans during the peak period for record sales. As the dates were arranged at short notice, they had to be announced piecemeal and there were the usual last minute alterations and additions, but Ian Flukes did his best to respect the Clash's booking conditions and made an impressive job of pulling the schedule together. When Joe phoned him to complain that two shows at Glasgow Strathclyde University had a students-only door policy, Ian calmly remarked that he had been deceived, and cancelled the shows immediately before looking around for replacements.

Support was provided by the Slits, but it was not to be a full reunion with the Clash's former 'girlfriend' band. Deciding they wanted to pursue a more reggae-oriented direction, the others had recently asked Palmolive to leave in favour of the more versatile Budgie. (She went on to join the Raincoats.) As Don Letts and his friend Leo Williams were still looking after the Slits' affairs, the Clash asked Barry Myers to be DJ for the tour.

This outing found the band playing in front of a giant cloth patchwork comprising a selection of flags from around the world, as featured in the 'Tommy Gun' video. The idea was Paul's, but the flags were chosen by all four members of the band from a catalogue supplied by Black and Edgington, who made the finished article to Clash specifications.

Relying less on material from the first album than before – they saved it mostly for the encores – the Clash added most of the new album to their live repertoire. They also worked up a new song. Shortly before his and Mick's trip to America, Joe had decided to learn to play the piano properly in order to increase his musical contribution to the group. One of the tracks selected most often by the duo on the Automatt's relaxation room juke box had been the Bobby Fuller Four's 1966 version of the Crickets' rockabilly rebel song 'I Fought The Law'. It became Joe's preferred tune to toy with on the piano, and upon returning to the UK, he and Mick persuaded the others – including an initially reluctant Topper – to arrange an uptempo band version which proved so successful it was included in the set for the tour.

The Sort It Out Tour lived up to its title in that it kept excessive behaviour and expenditure to a minimum, but it had its moments. Topper had split up with his wife Wendy. Limited though the entourage was, he was allowed to bring along his new girlfriend, Dee, presumably in the hope that this would encourage more equable behaviour. Following the show in Bournemouth, the couple decided to go skinny-dipping in the sea – on 22 November – and Robin Crocker was unable to resist the temptation to run off with their clothes. Shortly afterwards, Topper and Dee sauntered across the hotel foyer to the lifts with just one pair of boots between them.

Gobbing was still rife in the north. Joe's already battered teeth were chipped during one show when an overeager fan grabbed hold of his microphone stand. At another, Mick was manhandled offstage by a bouncer who assumed he was a fan. On the whole, though, incidents of random violence appeared to be on the wane. For the most part, Sort It Out was conducted in a determinedly optimistic spirit that not even the poor reviews for the records could torpedo. The two events that did threaten to put a dampener on proceedings came at the beginning and end, and occurred elsewhere. In the tour's final stages, Mick learned that his Pembridge Villas flat had been burgled, and stripped of its video machine, stereo, recording equipment and – inevitably – any guitars he had failed to bring with him.

A couple of months earlier, on 12 October, a pointless, drug-related fight in the room Sid Vicious shared with Nancy Spungen at New York's Chelsea Hotel had resulted in Nancy's death from a stab wound to the stomach and Sid's arrest for her murder. When Topper had left his marital flat in Finsbury Park, he had moved into Sid and Nancy's last London abode, 17 Pindock Mews, off Warwick Avenue. (After Johnny Green and the Baker had scrubbed the bloodstains off the walls.) Back in late September, while in New York working on *Give 'Em Enough Rope*, Mick had joined former New York Dolls Johnny Thunders and Arthur Kane on-stage at Max's Kansas City as the ad hoc backing band for a Sid Vicious 'solo' show. This and all the Clash's other connections with the Sex Pistols prompted Sid's mother to ask Mick to arrange a Clash benefit show towards Sid's legal fees. The band slotted it into the Sort It Out Tour schedule at the Camden Music Machine on 19 December, prior to the tour's two other London dates at the Lyceum in the Strand on 28th and 29th.

Chris Salewicz reviewed the benefit for the *NME*. His comments were encouraging, but restrained. Although he was usually happy for approved outsiders to guest with the Clash, Joe disapproved of Mick guesting with other artists, believing that it undermined the band's status. Prior to the Clash's set, Mick joined Glen Matlock on-stage to accompany support act Philip Rambow on a handful of songs. Chris mentioned Joe's evident anger at this.

During the Out On Parole Tour, as well as the live footage, Buzzy Enterprises had filmed 'behind-the-scenes' footage of Ray Gange with the band, Johnny and the Baker both backstage and in various hotel rooms. Although there was some crossover in their roles, Jack Hazan was chiefly responsible for directing the camerawork, while Dave Mingay concentrated more on shaping the direction of the film. The camera was not always present for every key event, so as time went on, he first asked members of the Clash camp to re-enact certain scenes, and then to improvise others. 'The early filming was all for real,' says Johnny. 'Then as Dave and Jack tried to give it a theme, they would start to arrange dummy shots, set-ups. Mingay would work off a little note pad, and hold up something for you to talk about. But there weren't a lot of takes. Towards the end, though, it was totally choreographed.' It had quickly become apparent that Ray did not make a convincing roadie. 'He was just a ligger, and he was not liked,' says Johnny. Ray was more interested in drinking and mouthing off than working, so Dave made a feature of these shortcomings and the resulting tensions. Ray was filmed skiving off, getting drunk, and making a hash of setting up equipment with Johnny and the Baker (the last of these scenes actually filmed at a Subway Sect show).

While Mick and Joe were in America, Ray's character had been fleshed out further with scenes of his life at home in a Brixton high-rise, collecting the dole, moonlighting as an assistant in a pornographic bookshop, getting arrested for being drunk and disorderly, and hanging around with his diminutive skinhead friend Terry, as played by fellow Clash fan Terry McQuade. Spectacularly foul-mouthed – sample dialogue: 'Fuck them, the fucking cunts!' – Terry claimed to be Joe's cousin, both in the film and in real life.

In October, Buzzy heard about Bernie's sacking. As their initial contact with the Clash had been through the manager, they were naturally concerned that their project would not survive his departure. 'I was very pro-Bernard,' says Dave. 'I thought he was a genius, and he was an expert on youth culture. He taught me a lot.' Luckily for the film-makers, the Clash agreed to continue, although they were growing increasingly curious about the film's direction. 'The ultimate structure was not known to us until very late in the movie,' Jack told the *NME*'s Neil Norman in 1980. 'The Clash always used to ask us, "What's the film about then?" as though we had something over them.'

More scenes involving Ray and the Clash were squeezed into the band's increasingly tight schedule before, during and after the Sort It Out Tour. Some had Ray spouting his right-wing and occasionally racist-sounding views to members of the band. Dave failed in his efforts to set up an ideological debate between Ray and Joe, ostensibly the most politically committed member of the band, and also the one with whom Ray had the closest thing to a friendship. 'Ray was really like that, and Joe wouldn't address the problem,' says Johnny. In the end, it was Mick who provided the required words of censure. 'It's re-enacted, but it's roughly what he did say,' says Dave.

Three of the choreographed set-ups devised by Dave required a little more planning and expense. The first was a recreation of the Clash's early days at Rehearsals, mocked up in a seedy south London studio appropriately called the Black Hole. The Clash revived some of their old Pop Star Army Fatigues for a sprint through 'Garageland'. Another rehearsal room was hired for a scene featuring just Ray and Joe, which, in the finished film, was to follow on from Mick's admonition and precede Ray's departure from the Clash's circle. Dave had asked Joe to write a song especially for his farewell to Ray, and after some hedging, he obliged. As Ray stumbles around swigging from a can of Special Brew, Joe sits at the piano to play and sing 'I Ain't Got No Reason', which specifically addresses Ray's situation as good-for-nothing poor white trash brought up in a predominately black area of town. Joe asks Ray what he's going to do next; Ray responds by suggesting that the Clash should no longer mix music with politics. Whereupon Joe smiles and plays 'Let The Good Times Roll'.

Keen to get a good version of 'English Civil War', and much taken with the band's arrangement of 'I Fought The Law', both of which they saw as particularly appropriate to the movie – at this point, they were even considering calling it *I Fought The Law* – the Buzzy team asked to film the Lyceum show on 28 December. The sound was recorded on a 16-track mobile. 'English Civil War' was subsequently dropped from the film, but 'I Fought The Law' was to provide its live finale. In the dressing room before the show, all four members of the band happened to be dressed in black. Thinking this would make for a visually striking outlaw image, Dave asked them to go on-stage like that, but credits Caroline Coon with convincing them it was a good idea. 'She was acting like a boss figure, telling them what to do. And they obeyed her, totally.' In the film, the funereal garb acquires added significance when Joe changes the lyric of 'I Fought The Law' from 'I lost my baby…' to 'I killed my baby…', an obvious reference to Sid Vicious. It would take on even more retrospective weight just over a month after the gig when, on 2 February 1979 – out on bail but almost certainly facing a lengthy prison sentence for Nancy's killing – Sid himself died from a heroin overdose.

'I Fought The Law' would turn out to be a key track both in the film, where its positioning at the end is no accident, and for the future direction of the band's career. That this live version of the song also brings to a close the first CD of *Clash On Broadway* testifies as much. During the course of 1978, criticism from the UK music press had hit the Clash hard. Despite the domestic commercial successes of *Give 'Em Enough Rope* and 'Tommy Gun', the healthy turn out for the Sort It Out Tour, and the band's impressive showing in the fans' end of year music press polls – in the *NME*, they won best group, best single with '(White Man) In Hammersmith Palais', and second best album – they took this criticism to mean their home country had turned against them. They had been playing the same-sized venues for the last three tours, and even though this was largely of their own volition, when combined with a stalemate over radio airplay and television exposure, it reinforced the feeling that they were not getting anywhere.

'Refusing to play *Top Of The Pops* spoiled their career in Britain,' says Dave Mingay, stating the Clash's point of view at this time. Their morale was very low. In performing and recording 'I Fought The Law', a vintage American rock'n'roll song, the Clash rescinded (what at least appeared to be) the anti-traditional, anti-US imperialist declarations of '1977' and 'I'm So Bored With The USA'. They had always been keen to play in America – even more so since their trip there to record *Give 'Em Enough Rope* – and they needed to be successful in the States to pay off their debt to CBS and regain their creative freedom. What they perceived to be the hostility or indifference of the domestic scene gave them the justification they needed to give an American campaign their full attention. If the UK did not want to know, they might as well go to where – in the words of 'Gates Of The West' – Eastside Jimmy and Southside Sue both needed something new.

Only not too new: the UK music press had come down hard on Joe's 'totally facile concept of shock politics', and – as though he were heeding Ray Gange's advice – 'I Fought The Law' also signalled a move away from contentious issue-based lyrics to a vaguer and more readily palatable *Rebel Without A Cause*-type stance in keeping with the Clash's new Caroline Coon-approved image. The live version of 'I Fought The Law' stands not only as the Clash's farewell to Sid Vicious, then, but also to their UK fans and to punk.

PART THREE: STAR TRIPS

13
GATES OF THE WEST

Even before the last days of shooting for the Buzzy film project, Dave Mingay had started reviewing the concert material already in the can. 'I listened for weeks on end to the 15 or so songs,' he says. He identified numerous failings. On some tracks, there was a problem with the standard of the recording. The earliest material, from the Anti-Nazi League Rally and Birmingham Barbarellas, was in mono, and not up to the standard of the subsequent, relatively sophisticated mobile recordings. Even with those, additional problems were presented by a combination of the standard of the in-house sound, the circumstances of performance and the quality of the playing.

Dave is anxious that this should not read as criticism of the Clash. '*We* chose the songs that are in the film,' he says. 'We used to go and shoot only one or two songs a night, because we didn't have the film or the money to record whole concerts endlessly, so we didn't always coincide with the part of the concert they played brilliantly. And they would be absolutely shagged out when they played the last songs, often the most visually arresting.' Consequently, he and Jack asked the Clash to do some re-recording. In early January 1979, with theatrical impresario and sometime film producer Michael White helping Buzzy foot the bill, the Clash went into Wessex studio in Highbury with studio manager and resident engineer Bill Price and tape operator Jerry Green to do as they were bid. 'Mick led the overdubbing. He was very meticulous,' says Dave. 'He only turned up later in the day, and he did manage to take a long time doing it, but he was very hard working and brilliant at it.'

Mick had several reasons for applying himself so diligently. At the time, there was talk of issuing a soundtrack album with the film, and it was in the Clash's own best interests for it to sound as good as possible. He was also, as ever, eager for more studio experience. The Clash's rise to some measure of fame during 1977 had enabled him to renew contact with former Mott the Hoople mainman Ian Hunter. Mick had managed to display a certain amount of reserve when meeting Johnny Thunders, but he still held Ian, one of his first real heroes, in considerable awe. If Ian commented favourably upon a Clash recording, Mick considered it 'the blessing'. His enthusiasm for Mott the Hoople and the Hunter-Ronson alliance had proved infectious among Mick's social circle. In spring 1978, Glen Matlock had hired Ronno to produce the Rich Kids' eponymous album and single; in September, Tony James had asked Ian to produce Generation X's *Valley Of The Dolls*, which had led to Ian securing a contract with Generation X's label, Chrysalis. In October, Ian had booked into Wessex with various musicians, including Glen, to work on new material with Bill Price and Jerry Green.

Those sessions were abandoned, but not through any failing on the part of Bill, whom Ian rated highly. While still based at his former place of employ, George Martin's AIR studios off Oxford Circus, the engineer had provided invaluable assistance on the sessions for Mott the Hoople's two self-produced CBS studio albums, *Mott* and *The Hoople*, recorded in 1973 and 1974 respectively. In 1975, he had also helped Ian and his co-producer Mick Ronson with Ian's eponymous début solo album. In January 1979, then, Mick Jones was keen to work with Bill Price for a fan's thrill and a producer's education.

The Clash had also taken note of how Bernie Rhodes had exploited Julien Temple's filmic ambitions to secure free recording time for the Beaconsfield demos. The reason the Buzzy soundtrack re-recording sessions took so long – according to Johnny Green – was that the broke and therefore necessarily canny Clash were intent on doing some secret recording of their own at Buzzy's considerable expense. 'That was fair,' says Dave Mingay now, after a brief pause. 'Because we were taking up so much of their time.'

With Mick and Bill effectively co-producing, the Clash began by recording a studio version of 'I Fought The Law' and a disco version of 'Capital Radio'. Having promised that the original version was to be exclusive to the freebie *NME* EP, the band's commitment to VFM prevented them from re-releasing it. Copies of the EP had been changing hands for upwards of £25, though, and the Clash were keen to stamp out this exploitation of their fans. The new version was their compromise solution. The delayed release of *Give 'Em Enough Rope* meant that all the material on the album was at least nine months old, and the Clash, the UK music press and – or so the band believed – the public already considered it old hat. The band's intention was to rush-release the two 'new' tracks as the follow up single to 'Tommy Gun' in the UK. The T-Zers page in the 27 January edition of the *NME* announced this plan, and also CBS's conflicting intention to release the album track 'English Civil War'.

The sessions went well, and heralded the start of a long and fruitful relationship between the Clash and the Wessex studio team. While in the studio on Buzzy's money, the Clash also did some extra recording and mixing on 'Groovy Times', originally recorded at CBS and Utopia the previous May, and 'Gates Of The West', originally recorded at Basing Street the previous June, and already revisited at both the Automatt and the Record Plant. 'The thing with the Clash was, you could go in to record a certain amount of songs, but it never worked out that way,' says Jerry Green. 'There was always between 30 and 100 per cent more stuff recorded to be used at a later date.'

None of the four songs the band worked on was a new composition, but they still represent a statement of future intent, an indication of the Clash's proposed new lyrical and musical direction. Even the two tracks dating back to the Pearlman era evince none of the album's overwhelming heavy metal bluster. The folksy harmonica and acoustic guitar on 'Groovy Times', the soul strut of 'Gates Of The West' – which squeezes in a namecheck for Little Richard – and the funky coda of 'Capital Radio Two' provide a successful showcase for the Clash's efforts to throw off the shackles of punk, and allow them to bask in their new-found freedom and space. Topper's growing influence should not be overlooked. It was he who suggested the disco pastiche for 'Capital Radio Two', hence the line about the drummer counting all the money. In the *Melody Maker* advertisement that had netted them Jon Moss, the Clash had stated their requirement for a drummer with no funk or jazz; the fact that Topper had both these in his arsenal, and much more, was playing no small part in the Clash's musical evolution.

Their secret agenda satisfied, the band turned their attention to the Buzzy soundtrack work. 'Except for the Lyceum stuff, the Clash aren't live on the film at all,' says Johnny Green. 'Totally artificial. The backing tracks were done at Wessex.' His near namesake, Jerry Green, confirms this. 'Everything needed to be redone for the film. Wessex is quite a large studio, almost like a concert hall, and we set the band up at one end like we would for a gig. We got a TV in the control room and a large TV out in the studio. We'd made a mix from the original, tarted it up as best we could, and put it on multi-track. We gave them that to play along to, basically as a guide so they knew where they were. We had a PA in there so they could hear themselves – separation wasn't important, really – and we recorded the whole thing. Then all the ambient noise from the crowd at the actual gig was synched back into the stuff we'd recorded.' The more detailed work was done at Bill Price's former base, AIR studios. Working there was another Mott the Hoople-related thrill for Mick, but AIR was chosen because it was the only facility in London where the film could be projected onto a large screen while Joe and Mick synched their vocals to their lip movements, and Mick synched guitar solos to his finger movements.

Despite the testimony of Johnny and Jerry, and the time and money spent in Wessex and AIR, Dave Mingay disagrees about the extent to which the original soundtrack was modified. 'It is true that they did redo most of the songs,' he says. 'In order to replace part of a song, you have to record more than you need. But a lot of the original stuff was not replaced. Half the stuff you're hearing is not overdubbed. Parts of the track are already there, and it's just a skilful remix to reinforce or fill in where there were some problems.'

As Dave maintains, almost all supposedly live music soundtracks and live albums are touched up in the studio. But the Clash had always insisted that any filmed appearance should capture them true to life, warts and all. Previous documents of the Clash in concert, *The Punk Rock Movie*, *Punk In London '77* and *So It Goes*, had proved them capable of triumphing over adverse conditions, even ropier equipment than they were using in mid-to-late 1978, and their own limitations as musicians without resorting to sonic revisionism. Dave counters that, unlike these ventures, the Buzzy film was intended for mainstream cinema release, demanding higher standards. The fact remains that the Clash refused to play *Top Of The Pops* because they were not prepared to be filmed miming their performance to a pre-recorded song, and yet the film project required them to re-record songs to fit pre-filmed performances: the process was reversed, but the result is still hardly cinema verité. More so even than Don Letts's video for 'Tommy Gun', the Buzzy re-recording sessions represented a perplexing lapse in consistency on behalf of the Clash.

Epic had released *Give 'Em Enough Rope* in the US the previous November. The Clash's old sparring partner Lester Bangs gave it a positive review in New York's *Village Voice*. That other doyen of Seventies American rock journalism Greil Marcus, writing for the considerably larger-circulation *Rolling Stone*, was even keener. He noted that the production was not all it could have been, but had nothing but praise for the band and the songs. 'Imagine the Who's "I Can't Explain" as a statement about a world in flames, not a lover's daze, and you've got the idea,' he wrote, before going on to condemn 'the snivelling backlash' against the band in the UK music press. It was something in which he was going to have no part: 'The Clash are now so good they will be changing the face of rock'n'roll simply by addressing themselves to the form.'

This should have augured well for the band's prospects in the US. Should have. Of CBS's two American divisions, Columbia had more name acts and the best track record. In the music business it was known, after the colour of its record label, as Big Red. Epic, the sickly younger sibling that had picked up the US option on the Clash, was known as Mediocre Orange, and the label seemed determined to live up to its reputation from the off. Although the whole point of hiring Sandy Pearlman, at Epic's insistence, had been to get the Clash on American radio, the record company neglected to release a single from the album. Consequently, *Give 'Em Enough Rope* failed to make the Top 100. When the band first suggested going to America to promote the record, Epic said it would not be convenient: they already had two of their bands out on the road. The Clash insisted, and Caroline Coon flew over at her own expense to convince the record company otherwise. Taking the initiative, she set up eight shows in venues with capacities ranging from 1,000 to 3,500, and all but one promptly sold out.

There followed a period of haggling about how much Epic would be prepared to advance to cover the cost of bringing over the band and what the record company believed to be the excessive entourage of Caroline, tour manager Ace Penna, Johnny Green, the Baker, DJ Barry Myers, the Clash's now regular soundman Rob Collins and his partner Adrian, and lighting engineer Warren Steadman. A budget of $30,000 was finally agreed. Once Caroline had tracked him down on tour in Australia, the Clash turned around and promised a sizeable portion of this to their chosen support act, Bo Diddley. Joe had loved Bo's music since he was a boy, and Mick appreciated the idea of being able to follow in the tradition of the Rolling Stones by using support slots to re-introduce American audiences to their own neglected musical legends. Epic objected strongly to what they believed to be a perverse, genre-inappropriate choice, and pushed strongly for one of their own new wave signings. The Clash stood firm.

The band flew to Vancouver, Canada on 30 January 1979. They were searched at the airport. No drugs were found, but their studded belts and armbands were confiscated. The following night's show at the Agora Ballroom went down a storm. The manic crowd, many of them decked out in 1977-era punk regalia, demanded and received three encores... and then threw cans at the road crew when they attempted to remove the equipment. Joe's Strumguard – the towel and gaffa tape protector he habitually wore on his strumming arm – had failed to take the strain, and he had gashed himself badly. Nevertheless, in order to prevent a riot, the Clash came back on to play yet another song. 'Trouble was, they didn't stop canning the stage,' Topper told *Melody Maker*'s Allan Jones a few days later. 'It was like England.' Topper's head was split open in three places.

On 2 February, the Clash stopped at the US border so that photographer Bob Gruen could mark the momentous occasion – their first time on American soil as a performing rock'n'roll band – with group photographs of the band and crew. That night, they stayed in a Seattle motel. They woke up the following morning to be informed of Sid Vicious's death. The news only served to intensify the band's determination to do things their way. They might have decided the trappings of punk were passé, but there was plenty of punk attitude to be found in the Clash's approach. They had given the tour the hardly tactful title Pearl Harbour '79. Having lost the services of Upstarts, the band had turned to Chris Townsend of 5th Column, an established punk design collective on Kilburn High Road, to come up with appropriate T-shirts. Picking up the East-West divide motif of both the *Give 'Em Enough Rope* album cover and the tour title, his design juxtaposed an image of a kamikaze pilot with one of a burning American battleship.

The first American gig was in San Francisco, preceded by an afternoon signing session at Tower Records. Uncomfortable with such celebrity behaviour, the Clash insisted their own record be replaced on the in-store sound system by a Joe Ely album. Duties over, the band made for a place they felt more at home: Leopold's, a second hand record store run by Mo Armstrong, who was a former Vietnam veteran, an ex-member of late Sixties band Daddy Longlegs, and a genuine Clash fan.

At that night's Berkeley Community Centre show, the Clash found Epic had chosen to ignore their choice of tour title in favour of the safer, more predictable Give 'Em Enough Rope Tour. The record company's promotional posters featured a picture of the Statue of Liberty bound up in rope... The Clash opened the show that night, as they would all subsequent gigs on the tour, with 'I'm So Bored With The USA'. The Berkeley audience were polite and restrained, which the Clash blamed on promoter Billy Graham's uninspired choice of venue. Caroline made the mistake of informing them that Graham had the San Francisco area sewn up and was not a man to mess with. Mo Armstrong mentioned a collective which was hoping to break Graham's near-monopoly, and which was raising funds with a benefit concert the very next night at a new venue, the Geary Theatre. It turned out to be the former Filmore West. To Caroline's disgruntlement, the Clash volunteered to play. This time, the place went wild.

The lid finally lifted on the simmering resentment the band felt towards Epic following a gig at the Santa Monica Civic Centre on 9 February. According to Joe's estimate, 40-50 Epic area representatives were flown in from all over the country for a meet'n'greet session with the band. 'I was disgusted that they were there,' he told *Melody Maker*'s Allan Jones. 'They've done nothing for us, and they were there poncing around backstage with their slimy handshakes and big smiles.' The Clash ignored them before the gig. Afterwards, when an attempt was made to set up a group photograph, the band simply walked out of the room. Followed by the representatives, humiliated and fuming.

The next gig was scheduled five days later in Cleveland. In the meantime, the Clash set off on a meandering road trip through Arizona, Kansas and Texas in a top of the range touring bus hired from country legend Waylon Jennings. The intention was to see America. Bo Diddley had already seen America a few dozen times, but went along for the free ride. Unfortunately, although the bus was equipped with bunks, they were tiny and uncomfortable, and lack of sleep soon robbed the band of their adventurous spirit. Instead, while vast tracts of America slipped by unnoticed, most of their hours were whiled away listening to music, watching videos, smoking spliff – or in Bo's case, drinking a lethal concoction called Rock'n'Rye – and listening to Bo's seemingly endless fund of road anecdotes and worldly advice: 'Tek it from an old hand: tek that dollar and fuck the rest.' Paul was moved to bestow the Clash's ultimate accolade upon him: a nickname, Uncle Skiddly Daddly.

If real-life America failed to grab their attention, then mythical America was making itself increasingly evident in the Clash's image. Their style now borrowed elements from Fifties rockers and from movie representations of Mississippi riverboat gamblers, bikers, gangsters and cowboys. Everyone bought bandannas. Baker and Johnny Green bought Stetsons. Topper bought a pair of spurs, which he fixed to his motorcycle boots.

The bus broke down in Oklahoma, allowing the band to complete the journey by plane. By the time they arrived, the cut on Joe's arm had turned septic and one of his teeth had developed an abscess. Nevertheless, he refused to cancel the Cleveland gig, another benefit, this time for disabled Vietnam veteran Larry McIntyre. Heeding a special request, The Clash added live rarity 'City Of The Dead' to their set. Cleveland took it personally, but loved it. For this date, the full extent of Epic's promotion consisted of an album sleeve pinned to the Agora's foyer wall. When the local CBS TV channel covered the gig, it made no mention of the Clash, instead suggesting that it was a Bo Diddley concert. The plane journey and bus repairs having used up their remaining funds, the Clash had to ask Epic for money to cover their hotel bill. The record company prevaricated for several hours before wiring it through.

The Clash had to get back on the bus for the remaining dates. The sound was poor at the Ontario Theatre in Washington DC on 15 February. Although the Clash dug in and ultimately triumphed over it, Mick was so frustrated that, for once, he deliberately smashed the neck of his guitar. Bruce Springsteen, the New York Dolls' Dave JoHansen, Andy Warhol, Nico, John Cale and Robert De Niro were among the star liggers who turned up on the 17th to see the band at the New York Palladium, which did nothing to hurt the Clash's credibility. Had it become common knowledge at the time, the same might not have been said of Joe's decision to accompany the Warhol entourage to exclusive disco hotspot Studio 54... Or the entire band's decision to return the following night for another spot of jigging to the Village People.

As the tour came to a close, the prestigious *Time* magazine ran a feature on the band by Jay Cocks, which concluded: 'Out of the pieces of a shared precarious existence, the Clash has fashioned music of restless anger and hangman's wit, rediscovered and redirected the danger at the heart of all great rock.' The critics in America were evidently as mad for the Clash as the UK's had once been, but by the end of Pearl Harbour '79, the band's relationship with the American branch of their record company was even worse than their relationship with the British branch. In Santa Monica, especially, the short term pleasure of expressing their distaste for smarmy and hypocritical corporate behaviour had encouraged the Clash to score a spectacular own goal: there might not have been much record company effort put into breaking the band in the States before that incident, but following it there would be next to none.

Initially, the band attempted to give the impression – and may well have believed – that their American campaign was just part of a wider bid for global contact and recognition, as indicated by their flags-of-all-nations backdrop. Joe wrote up an account of Pearl Harbour '79 for the *NME*, using the upper case on the typewriter, as was now his wont when composing lyrics. It concluded with the declaration: 'WE ARE GOING TO GO BACK AND PLAY THE US AGAIN BUT WE MUST ALSO PLAY BRITAIN, JAPAN, EUROPE, AUSTRALIA, AND IT'S FAIR SHARES ALL ROUND. HEY! I HEAR THEY'RE REALLY ROCKING IN RUSSIA...' Whether or not it was indeed fair shares all round would become a bone of contention over the next two years.

In late February 1979 the band went back into Wessex studio to complete work on the live material for the Buzzy film soundtrack. On the 23rd, CBS released a single combining 'English Civil War' from *Give 'Em Enough Rope* with 'Pressure Drop' from the Marquee Tapes. Confirmed fan Danny Baker's *NME* review was lukewarm. The band's promotional efforts were limited to an appearance on a new ITV pop programme called *Alright Now*. In their American threads – complete with bandannas – they performed 'English Civil War' as required. But they overlooked *Give 'Em Enough Rope* entirely for their second selection, choosing instead – perhaps pointedly – to blast through the first album's 'Hate And War'. The record company might have got their own way with the choice of single released but did not get the desired result: it spent just six weeks on the chart, and peaked at number 25.

Kris Needs had booked some time in Olympic Studios, Barnes, to record a single with his band the Vice Creems. This was where the Rolling Stones had recorded at their pre-tax exile creative peak. It was also where, in 1970, Mott the Hoople had recorded their second Island album, *Mad Shadows*, with Guy Stevens producing; and, in 1972, their début CBS single 'All The Young Dudes', with David Bowie producing. Mick Jones jumped at the chance to produce the single session for his friend, roping in Topper Headon and Tony James to play on the songs.

It was some welcome light relief for the two Clash members. By now, the band believed they were in real danger of being thrown off CBS. They decided to forget such worries for the time being, and concentrate instead on writing, rehearsing, and – if allowed – recording their third album. 'I don't know why, but the problem seemed to relax us,' Joe told *Melody Maker*'s Chris Bohn that December. 'The feeling that nothing really mattered anymore, that it was make or break time.'

A problem was the lack of a regular rehearsal room. At the beginning of March 1979, the Clash sent Johnny Green and the Baker out in search of a new Rehearsals. The duo found Vanilla studios at 36 Causton Street, off Vauxhall Bridge Road in Pimlico. Situated in a little courtyard where expensive sports cars were done up and resprayed, it consisted of two dingy rehearsal rooms. The legal situation with Bernie Rhodes meant that Johnny had to approach accountant Peter Quinnell for a cheque to lease the larger upstairs room. Peter was also helping out the band with day to day living costs during this time, and the nickname Quister the Twister was quickly dropped. 'At first he was like a bank manager, but he got looser,' says Johnny. 'He held us together. Very sweet man. Very understanding.'

As Johnny was now banned from driving, the Baker bought a second hand transit van – not a Renault – and moved the Clash's equipment into Vanilla. Determined to maintain the team spirit encouraged by the US tour, the Clash approached the ensuing songwriting, arranging and rehearsal sessions as though they were in training camp preparing for a major sporting event. This impression was reinforced by the regular football matches they began to host on a nearby school playground. For these, they were joined by the crew and any other friends and associates who happened to be around at the time. Wishing to work without distraction, though, the band discouraged casual visitors to the studio itself.

The equipment was set up in the Clash's traditional manner, as though they were about to play live. As ever – once the Baker had managed to rouse Mick from his bed – the band warmed up by playing their own older numbers and a few cover versions. Paul was responsible for instigating at least two of the latter. One was his teen favourite, the Rulers' 'Wrong 'Em Boyo'. Another was a more recent discovery, evidence of his growing interest in early rock'n'roll: Vince Taylor's 'Brand New Cadillac'. Both struck chords with other members of the band, an indication of how in tune their tastes were during this period. Mick's beloved Mott the Hoople had also covered 'Brand New Cadillac'. 'Wrong 'Em Boyo' was doubly attractive to Joe, who loved ska and also recognised the song as a reworking of the traditional American folk blues legend 'Staggerlee'.

Still with an eye on the possibility of a soundtrack album release to accompany the Buzzy film project, the Clash agreed to Dave Mingay and Jack Hazan's request for some new studio material for the film's credit sequences. The two songs the Clash offered and recorded also reflected Joe's ongoing affection for ska and early reggae. One was a Clashified cover of the Edwards and Ray composition 'Revolution Rock', complete with references to smashing up seats and being 'so pilled up that I rattle'. The second was a Strummer original entitled 'Rudie Can't Fail', which, at that time, was the working title for the Buzzy film. Dave Mingay describes the song as 'Joe's rather generous adios to Ray Gange', who liked a can of Special Brew for breakfast. Along with a namecheck for Dr Alimantado's 'Born For A Purpose', Joe adds some autobiographical touches, but in essence the song remains a more sprightly take on the theme of 'Stay Free'.

When it came to composing and arranging new material for their own new album project, the Clash had more options available to them than ever before. Joe's piano playing was still rudimentary, but it provided him with a more melodic writing tool than had his scrubbing guitar style. No longer taking direction from Mick, Topper had earned his (all-too-literal) spurs as a drummer of considerable imagination. He could also play guitar and piano. Though still no virtuoso on bass, Paul could pick up basslines much more quickly than before, sometimes even devising his own. A naggingly infectious reggae riff he started to play one day was developed by the others into an instrumental that became a rehearsal room favourite.

Not all the material the band worked up over the following four months was a million miles away from the offerings of the punk period. As eventually recorded for release, four of the band's new songs were in the Clash tradition of aggressive four-square rockers. Lyrically, rather than playing down a compositional tendency that had been much in evidence on *Give 'Em Enough Rope*, it could be argued that 'London Calling', 'Clampdown', 'Four Horsemen' and 'Death Or Glory' signalled a further misguided raising of the stakes: the Clash had already moved from urban rucking on the first album to global terrorism on the second; now, it seemed, they were intent on heralding the end of the world.

To put such concerns in context, though, the recent threat of meltdown at the Three Mile Island nuclear plant near Harrisburg, Pennsylvania lent such apocalyptic musings some topical weight. Joe's 'London Calling' takes its title from the BBC World Service's traditional broadcast ID. The song began life as a moan about the mobs of tourists wandering around Soho, until Mick – briefly assuming Bernie Rhodes's role – insisted that Joe rewrite the verses about something more meaningful. Explaining the final version to *Melody Maker* in 1988, Joe said, 'I read about 10 news reports in one day calling down all variety of plagues on us.' Against this background of imminent global catastrophe, the song restates punk's DIY ethic, urging 'the kids' not to follow leaders, including the Clash: 'phoney Beatlemania has bitten the dust.'

As Joe revealed in the booklet accompanying *Clash On Broadway*, Mick originated the tune for 'Clampdown'. It had a three week life as an instrumental entitled first 'Working And Awaiting' and then 'For Fuck's Sake' before Joe came up with the lyric. Like 'All The Young Punks (New Boots And Contracts)' before it, 'Clampdown' urges 'the kids' not to waste their lives in factories propagating a system apparently hell-bent on self-destruction. It seems torn between the fatalistic belief that ageing automatically equates with becoming part of the machinery of repression, and the desire to encourage organised resistance with the assertion that 'anger can be power'. The positive message wins out. Joe's belief in the potential for change was reasserting itself.

The other two rockers display Mott the Hoople Syndrome, but in a more palatable form than on the last album. The braggadocio of 'Four Horsemen' – as in, the Four Horsemen of the Apocalypse – is so over-the-top that it qualifies as self-mockery. In the *Armagideon Times*, given away free on the early 1980 16 Tons Tour, Mick denied that the song was any way intended to be autobiographical. While it certainly *is* a celebration of the Clash – Topper's spurs may have been an influence – it is at the same time a rueful acknowledgement of earlier transgressions like 'Cheapskates'.

Conversely, 'Death Or Glory' has no room for irony. At first it masquerades as a third person account of a character from, say, 'Last Gang In Town' revisited in later life, struggling – as in 'Clampdown' – to come to terms with the frustrations of settling down and selling out. That this struggle mirrors the one faced by the Clash themselves at this point in their career is hardly coincidental. Any pretence of narrative distance is dropped during the defiant coda, where Joe states the band's determination to persevere until 'you' – CBS, the critics and carpers – lose. The lyric's compassion and resolve and an inspired bass part just about triumph over sentimentality. Joe worked out the tune on piano. Dave Mingay preferred it in this original, more reflective ballad form. He believes it was given the full band treatment to disguise the fact Joe had taken his inspiration from 'As Time Goes By', the song Sam plays again in the movie *Casablanca*: 'It's just the same old story / A tale of love and glory / A tale of do or die...'

Mick's 'I'm Not Down' is another song which refuses to be beaten, restating the 'kick my way back in' theme of 'Hate And War', albeit in more vulnerable, less violent terms. Having lost most of his treasured possessions before Christmas, during the burglary at his Pembridge Villas flat, Mick had given up the lease and moved back in at 111 Wilmcote House with Stella. The sharp contrast between his old and new standards of living had evidently done nothing to assuage his blues.

'Lost In The Supermarket' makes direct reference to the drawbacks of high-rise living, touching on the sense of urban alienation expressed throughout *The Clash*, but although it is Mick's tune – a ballad with funk bass – Joe is responsible for the lyric. It evidences a sensitivity not usually associated with Joe, which might well explain why Mick was asked to sing it. At the time, Mick believed Joe had been inspired by sympathy for his plight, but the song is actually autobiographical. It opens with Joe's childhood memories of Warlingham suburbia, and the subsequent references to tower block life reflect Joe's own domestic situation as of spring 1979.

During the early part of the year, Joe had begun a relationship with Gabrielle Salter, a young – that is, recent school leaver – friend of Topper's girlfriend, Dee. Upon returning from the States, Joe had abandoned the squatting life and moved in with Gaby at her mother's flat. It was located in a high-rise block on the World's End Estate in Chelsea, where the Kings Road runs closest to the Thames. Like 'London's Burning' before it, 'London Calling' owes its panoramic scope to the fact that its inspiration came from on high, but Joe's perspective on London has moved from the Westway to the World's End. Hence the line 'London is drowning and I live by the river' in 'London Calling'. As Joe sings over the introduction of 'Rudie Can't Fail', his new home was 'on the route of the 19 bus', which took him from the King's Road to Vanilla and, when necessary, all the way to Wessex. 'Lost In The Supermarket' was conceived in the supermarket located under the block of flats, next to the car park. In reality, it was and is too small to get lost in. 'But it was 5 am, and the song occurred to me as I stumbled around, dazed by the colours and the lights,' Joe told *Q*'s Andrew Collins in 1999.

Joe might have been happy to add the retro sounds of 'Wrong 'Em Boyo' to the Clash's repertoire, but he made evident his scorn for what he perceived to be the lack of bite in so much contemporary reggae in the sub-genre spoof 'Lovers' Rock'. The song takes a swipe at such swoonsome stylings, while also spoofing sex manuals and pondering the wisdom of artificially regulating natural cycles with the contraceptive pill.

The Clash created their own versions of Staggerlee-type mythic characters in both 'Jimmy Jazz' and 'The Card Cheat'. Jimmy is another rude boy, but the Jamaican imagery of Joe's lyric – including a reference to the Abyssinians' 'Satta Massagana' – is wedded to a jazzy blues backing. Originally entitled 'King Of Hell', 'The Card Cheat' is a melodramatic ballad in the style of Phil Spector. Joe's lyric takes the (much parodied) scene where the knight plays chess with Death in Ingmar Bergman's *The Seventh Seal* and transplants it to a Wild West saloon.

As with the *Give 'Em Enough Rope* material, the new songs were not without their references to drugs. 'Koka Kola' steals a march on Jay McInerney's *Bright Lights, Big City* by satirising American Yuppiedom's cocaine culture. 'Hateful' deals with the vicious cycle of heroin addiction, and is a non-specific requiem for Sid Vicious – 'This year I lost some friends' – set to a Bo Diddley beat. 'London Calling' also contains allusions to drug dependency with its talk of 'nodding out' and hepatitis-induced 'yellowy eyes'.

Once again, though, Joe's lyrical nay-saying was not a true reflection of the behaviour in the Clash camp. Cannabis continued to be the Clash's preferred drug, and was the principal fuel for the Vanilla rehearsals, but cocaine had been both freely available and freely used on the US tour, and Sid's fate had not deterred some experimentation with heroin. 'Paul played with it for a while, and Mick did very briefly,' says Johnny Green. 'Joe had nothing to do with it, as far as I know. Paul called it sniff, and that's how we took it. An occasional fiver's worth. Not exactly Keith Richards. Topper, well… By this stage, he always needed a bung [a loan], and Vanilla was where the drum kits started disappearing. Freebie sponsorship kits from Pearl, flogged down Henritt's, the drum store.'

All four of the songs covertly recorded during the January Wessex sessions were released on 11 May 1979 as *The Cost Of Living* EP. The Seventies had been a decade of galloping inflation, and the title was something of a buzz phrase, as well as a wry acknowledgement of the Clash's own debt to CBS. As the band had not paid for the recordings, the title was also a private Clash joke, once again at Buzzy's expense. The gatefold sleeve was designed by Rockin' Russian, a company which included Sebastian Conran's friend and former Pollocks partner Al McDowell. Featured on the back cover, a snapshot of the Clash and crew in propeller baseball caps taken backstage at the

Berkeley Community Centre is another private joke: in the photo, they are mocking the visiting perma-capped Sandy Pearlman, just out of shot, and by reproducing it here the Clash are giving the finger to Pearlman's and CBS's production values. The sleeve's overall parody of a soap powder box, and the rigid digit silhouette overlying the fake bar code, comment on the difficulty of selling the Clash. Of course, this reflects the subject matter of the songs within, particularly the reworked 'Capital Radio' and the brief reprise of 'I Fought The Law', an advertisement for the very record that contains it. All this heavy irony erected upon the related concepts of selling, selling out, debt and VFM promptly dropped onto the band's own toes. CBS refused to put out the record at the standard single price of £1, instead charging what the band considered to be an exorbitant £1.49.

In the *NME*'s 5 May Election Special, the paper's readership had surprised Joe by voting him their preferred choice as alternative Prime Minister. Any renewed warm feelings towards the UK audience that being deemed preferable to Margaret Thatcher might have encouraged were dispelled by Ian Penman's review of the new EP in the following week's edition of the paper: '[The Clash] often appear to have merely the facilities to utter ill-sorted nonsense at the top of their self-servicing voices, to barge about importantly in a prison of mere topicality.' The record stayed on the charts for eight weeks, peaking at number 22.

The band had hoped to be returning to the US in June 1979 for a second, lengthier tour. John Lydon's Public Image Ltd (PiL) were asked to support, but declined, scornfully informing the *NME*'s Danny Baker that they were not as desperate to break America as the Clash appeared to be. Caroline Coon got as far as booking dates for a Clash tour before the inevitable financial restrictions and record company intransigence got in the way. It was Caroline's turn to be the scapegoat. On 16 May, while she was in New York attempting to explain to the band's New York booking agent why the Clash were going to have to pull out of two gigs at the city's Palladium for which the tickets had already sold out, Caroline was informed by the band that her services were no longer required. Paul was not happy with the decision, or how it was enforced, but – perhaps inevitably – his relationship with Caroline ended at much the same time. She flew directly from New York to LA, where she signed up as adviser on *DOA*, a documentary on punk that took as its point of departure the Sex Pistols' first and final American tour. The band decided to manage themselves, and for a while the DIY ethic applied to all areas of the Clash operation.

British reggae band Misty in Roots had recently been subjected to an attack by fascist sympathisers in Southall. A protest demonstration led to anti-fascist sympathisers being arrested, and Rock Against Racism promptly set up a Southall Defence Fund to help with costs. The Clash accepted when approached to headline the second of two benefit concerts to be held on 13 and 14 July at the Rainbow, with the Who headlining the first and providing much of the equipment and technical expertise. The band took advantage of the situation to ask Who soundman Bobby Pridden for advice on 8-track recording. After another visit to Peter Quinnell for funding, a TEAC portastudio was installed at Vanilla, and the Baker took it upon himself to man the controls while the Clash recorded demo versions of their new songs. At the end of June, Joe told the *NME*'s Charles Shaar Murray that the band were considering cutting out expensive studio costs by recording the album on two TEACs twinned to provide a 16-track facility.

In order to warm up for the Rainbow show and try out some of their new material live, the Clash arranged a couple of low key dates of their own on 5 and 6 July at the Notre Dame Hall, off Leicester Square. Joe made a collage design for the fliers, Bobby Pridden agreed to do the sound, and Joe's ex-squatmates the Mo-dettes and Terry McQuade's band the Low Numbers were enlisted to provide the support. Although the music press were not informed or invited, *Sounds* writers Garry Bushell and Dave McCullough attended the first of these shows. Having arrived eager but late for the punk scene, they were deeply unhappy to see any indications of its demise. Consequently, they parlayed a brief chat with the band into a three page feature griping about the Clash's new direction. 'Punk was *about* change!' Joe told them, but his words fell on deaf ears. On the second night, Jimmy Pursey inadvertently reinforced Mick's determination to see that change through when he yet again hijacked the microphone for 'White Riot'.

In order to discourage another in-venue riot, the seats were removed for the Clash's benefit show at the Rainbow. Reviewing the gig for the *NME*, Paul Morley described the new songs as masterpieces, and the Clash themselves as 'a sort of blank screen upon which the entire history of rock'n'roll achieves a comprehensive focus: corny, splendid and, er, *rebellious.*' At one point, though, Joe lost his temper, and sent his recently purchased Fender Esquire guitar looping high over the drum kit. Pennie Smith's dramatic shot of the incident was given the top half of the T-Zers page. As pictures go, it was worth a thousand of even Paul Morley's kind words. The Clash understood image instinctively, but the picture reminded them of the value of spectacle, something Bernie Rhodes had never tired of stressing.

Around this time, there was another addition to the Clash camp. The self-styled Kosmo Vinyl had first encountered the Clash in the late spring of 1977. Mick Jones had approached him at his Portobello Market record stall and somewhat peremptorily requested him not to sell the sole copy of the 'Remote Control' single he had in stock. A young man with a neat line in Johnson's suits and considerable reserves of front and patter, Kosmo had gone on to involve himself with Stiff records, becoming the independent label's PR and package tour MC. In June 1979, he began turning up at Vanilla, seemingly on a casual basis. 'He wasn't given a lot of time at first,' says Johnny. 'He was regarded as someone who didn't really understand where the band was coming from. But Mick started to get very friendly with him.'

In July, some representatives from CBS came down to Pimlico to hear the Clash's new songs. Despite being subjected to a vicious mauling in the guise of a Clash camp-versus-record company football match, they liked what they heard enough to approve the funding of the band's third album. The conditions were that the band forget notions of self-produced TEAC recordings and agree to book a proper studio and hire a name producer. The Clash had recently returned to Wessex to record versions of 'Revolution Rock' and 'Rudie Can't Fail' with Bill Price for the Buzzy film. It seemed logical to carry on working there. Joe, however, proved so loath to abandon the TEAC idea that, in a 1982 interview with Roz Reines for the *NME*, he was still maintaining that the album was recorded 'in a garage in Pimlico'. This misconception has persisted ever since.

Joe suggested Guy Stevens as producer. The Clash knew from both reputation and experience that Guy was great at creating a vibrant atmosphere. He offered a direct connection to the musical roots the Clash desired to investigate: he was not only steeped in US blues, soul and rock'n'roll, but on first name terms with many of the great artists of those genres. Although an aficionado of American music, Guy was quintessentially British, with roughly the same background and reference points as the band. He believed in inspiration, and valued feel over painstaking multi-tracked perfectionism, a welcome prospect after the Sandy Pearlman experience. 'We've done it the American way, and it don't work,' Mick diplomatically informed *Creem* magazine's Dave DiMartino that autumn. 'It's a load of shit!' Another not-insignificant factor was that Bill Price had worked with Guy before, most recently on the Violent Luck demos, and was therefore – in theory – more likely to humour him, and less likely to depress or offend him than had been the rest of the production team for the Polydor demos. There was also – it hardly needs to be said – the Mott the Hoople connection.

A major part of the motivation for suggesting Guy, though, was a massive fuck you to CBS, mavericks siding with maverick. Muff Winwood certainly knew all about Guy from the time they had spent at Island together. He was prepared to acknowledge his achievements, but only through gritted teeth. As Muff well knew, Guy's potential for inspiring bands to ascend to the highest peaks of creativity was at least equalled, and arguably overshadowed, by his capacity for orchestrating total and utter chaos. He was capable of single-handedly trashing a studio almost beyond repair. During the September 1971 sessions for Mott the Hoople's *Brain Capers*, Guy had gone so far as to set fire to Basing Street studios.

Joe volunteered to go out in search of Guy, and tracked him down to an Oxford Street pub. Here, they played out the prodigal father scene Joe felt the reunion required. Guy wanted to hear the demos, but no longer owned a cassette player. Johnny Green was required to visit Peter Quinnell not just once, but twice more. The first time was for the money to buy Guy a tape machine. The second time was for the money to buy Guy a second tape machine after Johnny had got drunk and left the first tape machine, plus demo cassette, on a tube train. Guy could relate to this way of doing business. He was in.

The Wessex sessions commenced at the beginning of August 1979. Shortly beforehand, the Clash had been approached by Ian Flukes – who had recently left the Derek Block Agency to set up his own Wasted Talent – to appear at the Rusrock Festival in Turka on the 4th of the month. It made little sense to interrupt recording at such an early stage and fly all the way to Finland just to support Graham Parker and the Rumour. The Clash did it because they needed the money. They travelled light: Johnny arranged to borrow Abba's equipment for the show, so the Clash were able to leave their own set up in the studio. Jerry Green – now officially Wessex's second engineer – went along as Mick's guitar roadie. Once there, at Mick's suggestion, the Clash took a leaf out of Chuck Berry and Bo Diddley's books, and insisted on being paid in cash before taking the stage. It was £7,500 that neither Peter Quinnell nor the taxman would ever see: the band and crew split it seven ways on the plane coming back.

The recording of the album took four weeks, but if Guy had been given his head it would have taken considerably less. The *NME*'s Roy Carr spoke to him while the Clash were in Finland and was informed that, after just three days in the studio – the time it took Sandy Pearlman to get an acceptable drum sound – the Clash had already recorded 12 tracks. The first song attempted was 'Brand New Cadillac', which Guy declared perfect after just one live take. 'But it speeds up!' objected Topper, the rhythm machine. 'All good rock'n'roll speeds up,' retorted the producer.

Guy's antics during the album sessions have become the stuff of legend. While the band were recording 'Death Or Glory', he stormed into the studio and began to throw chairs around. On another occasion, Guy swung a ladder at Mick for fussing too much over a guitar part. On another, Guy and Bill Price started scrapping over the mixing desk when Guy tried to push every fader into the red. On another, Guy blew up the studio TV by pouring beer into it. When CBS UK head Maurice Oberstein visited the studio, Guy lay down in front of his Rolls Royce and refused to get up until Maurice admitted the music being made inside was 'magnificent'. He regularly phoned Ian Hunter in the States for lengthy pep talks, and insisted upon being driven to the studio via Arsenal's football ground, so that he could stand on the centre circle and pay homage to Liam Brady. On one occasion, he turned up at Wessex with someone he introduced as his minder, who duly sat around the studio for 18 hours. It subsequently transpired that the man was a taxi driver whose cab was outside with the meter still running.

The mayhem appeared to pay dividends. Upon the album's release, reviewers singled out Guy's production for praise, and Charles Shaar Murray conducted a lengthy interview with him for an *NME* career retrospective. Drunk and raving for his first meeting with the journalist, Guy was nevertheless portrayed as an amusing raconteur. He turned up for the second meeting sober and buoyed by the critical reaction to the album. The Clash contributed kind words and recommendations to the feature, and it seemed as though Guy's rehabilitation was well under way. Not long afterwards, he began taking a drug prescribed by his doctor to help him reduce his alcohol dependency. Ironically, on 29 August 1981, he would overdose on it, and die.

The album he recorded with the Clash has consequently come to be seen as a testimonial to Guy's talents, the last brilliant flourish of a career otherwise on the skids. It is a view the Clash have been happy to propagate. When it came time to compile the *Clash On Broadway* retrospective in 1991, the Guy Stevens association was highlighted with the inclusion of two of the original Polydor demos, the previously unreleased tribute song 'Midnight To Stevens', and a number of Guy-related anecdotes in the accompanying booklet. Although their motives were undoubtedly pure, the result was that the Clash effectively annexed the Guy Stevens Myth to feed the Clash Myth.

Their affection and respect for Guy has prompted most of the parties who have gone on record about the Wessex recording sessions to make light of his transgressions and play up the extent of his contribution to proceedings. Although they too feel much retrospective affection for Guy, between them, Johnny Green and Jerry Green paint a somewhat different picture. In their versions, Guy's addiction to alcohol was so far advanced that he resembled a psychotic tramp. He only turned up for the first two weeks of recording, and his attendance at the studio was irregular even during that time. When present he invariably got so out of it that he had to be driven home or encouraged to sleep it off in the tape cupboard.

His wild cavortings were not always quite so amusing at the time as they would be made to sound later. Truth to tell, his routines were both tired and tiresome: he had pulled almost all the same stunts with Mott the Hoople nearly a decade before. Jerry Green remembers the Night Of The Taxi Driver-Minder all too well: he was the last one in the studio when Guy demanded £55 to pay the bill. Jerry didn't have any money, but Guy refused to believe him and poured a two litre bottle of red wine into the studio's newly acquired and extremely expensive grand piano. Jerry, responsible for the upkeep of studio equipment, was furious. So was Bill Price, who had bought the piano. So were the Clash, who had to pay for it to be professionally cleaned. This proved to be the last straw. Mick had already started playing around with the controls when Guy was absent or comatose. Now Guy was discouraged from turning up altogether, and Mick and Bill took over the production completely. 'As soon as Guy was out of the way, we got on with the serious work,' says Jerry. 'Before that, it was pretty much playtime and trying it Guy's way.'

Paul was happy that his mistakes on bass had been allowed to pass unchallenged, but Guy's insistence on no-nonsense first-take recording had been too punk purist even for Joe. Most of the dozen tracks Guy boasted about recording in the first three days were oldie cover versions, including Bob Dylan's 'Billy The Kid' and the Bo Diddley songs 'Mona' and 'You Can't Judge A Book (By Looking At The Cover)', the latter amusingly retitled 'You Can't Judge A Woman (By Making Love To Her Mother)'. Of these only 'Brand New Cadillac' made it to the record. Otherwise, Guy was nominally in control for the recording of some of the backing tracks. His main contributions to the sessions were the creation of a charged atmosphere and what Mick described to CSM as an almost supernatural ability to act as a purgative: 'All the mess goes into him, like Dorian Gray's portrait, or whatever. All the messy sound goes and it *becomes* him, and what's left on the tape is clarity.'

It was a particularly generous thing to say, given both Mick's history with Guy and the fact that Guy would receive all the credit for what were largely Mick's labours. 'Mick suddenly knew what he was doing,' says Johnny Green. 'It was a solid team, he had a lot of help from Bill and Jerry, but I could see a difference in him in the control room from how he'd been previously. He was very much on top of the whole thing.' For the last two weeks at Wessex, with Guy's luddite restrictions removed, Mick was able to experiment and overdub to his heart's content. He achieved the Phil Spectoresque Wall of Sound he required for 'The Card Cheat' by recording every instrument twice. For other tracks, he followed Kosmo Vinyl's recommendation and drafted in Blockheads keyboard player Mickey Gallagher to add organ. The Irish horns added brass. Mick himself played some piano, while Joe self-deprecatingly credited himself with 'pianner'. There were also the inevitable Jones guitar additions. Once Paul had gone home for the night Mick may also have replaced some of the less skilful Simonon basslines: Jerry Green says not, but both Johnny Green and Chiswick staff producer Roger Armstrong – working in the next door studio with the Damned at the time – claim to have witnessed Mick's meddlings.

Paul's moment of triumph came when – having realised songwriters earned more money than mere musicians – he presented Joe with a lyric for the reggae instrumental the Clash had built around his bassline at Vanilla. 'The Guns Of Brixton', inspired by *The Harder They Come*, is yet another gesture of defiance, and therefore of a piece with both Joe's 'Death Or Glory' and Mick's 'I'm Not Down'. If the rest of the band were wary of inviting more music press censure for romanticising gunplay, then they hid it well. But they did persuade Paul to 'sing' it himself.

Joe was on a compositional winning streak, and he came up with two more songs during the recording sessions. The idea for 'Spanish Bombs' came while he was travelling home from Wessex at 4 am in the morning, listening to a radio news report of Basque terrorist bombings of tourist hotels on the Costa Brava. This in turn brought to mind the recent IRA bombing campaign in the UK. Again, this kind of subject matter had proved problematic for the Clash in the past, but 'Spanish Bombs' opens up its lyrical scope to compare and contrast the modern day tourist experience of Spain with the noble cause of the Spanish Civil War. There is also an autobiographical element: Joe's ex-girlfriend, Palmolive, hailed from Andalucia. The historical perspective, romantic sub-text and acoustic pop context combine to make it a sort of latter day folk song; the overall effect is far more uplifting than a 'BRIGADE ROSSE' T-shirt.

During his tenure at the control board, Guy had lent first Johnny Green then Joe a copy of a biography of troubled method actor Montgomery Clift. After the left side of his face was paralysed in a car crash, Monty's close-ups had to be shot from the right, hence the title of the song Joe was inspired to write. Monty subsequently lapsed into the pill and alcohol addiction that ultimately claimed his life. Guy certainly recognised the parallels with his own situation, and Johnny for one believes 'The Right Profile' is in fact the first of the Clash's tributes to the producer, albeit veiled.

By early September, the band had recorded 18 tracks, including reworkings of the two songs they had supposedly recorded exclusively for the Buzzy film project, 'Rudie Can't Fail' and 'Revolution Rock'. Mixing for the album had yet to be completed, but as the Clash's second tour of the US had finally been rescheduled to start on the 8th, they were forced to leave that part of the job in the capable hands of Bill Price. Once again, America was calling.

★★★

When the return visit to the States was finally given the go-ahead from Epic, it was authorised not so much in anticipation of the Clash's third album as in belated recognition of the commercial potential of their first. By June 1979, the US release of *Give 'Em Enough Rope* had chalked up 200,000 sales, a healthy total given the lack of promotion. More impressive, though, was the fact that imports of the UK version of *The Clash* had sold 100,000 copies in the US in the two years since its release. At the time, this was the highest sales figure ever achieved by an import. On 26 July 1979, Epic finally bowed to the pressure of the US market and released a modified US version of the album: minus 'Deny', 'Cheat', '48 Hours' and 'Protex Blue'; plus all the pre-*Give 'Em Enough Rope* UK single A-sides. To make it even more desirable – and echo CBS UK's gesture of giving the *Capital Radio* EP away with the original UK album – a free 7-inch disc combining 'Groovy Times' and 'Gates Of The West' was included in the packaging.

'I Fought The Law' had been released simultaneously as the band's first US single. With no promotion from Epic, the single failed to chart, but did receive a lot of valuable radio airplay. Thanks partly to the original import's groundbreaking efforts, the album fared considerably better, going on to sell a further 370,000 copies. 'Like Francis Coppola's camera journeying upriver in *Apocalypse Now*, this LP roves over scenes of a struggle that seems as endless as it is brutal,' wrote *Rolling Stone*'s Tom Carson. (It was a review ahead of its time: 1982's *Combat Rock* would take his analogy a little more literally.) He went on to acknowledge that the chopping and changing of material had altered the original album's meaning, even destroyed its unified vision, but he maintained that the result still made for compelling listening: 'Despite the trimming and the compromises, their music remains a crackling live wire that can't be silenced. What it has to say is part of our currency, too. And anyone in America who still cares about rock'n'roll must listen.' In the *Village Voice*, Robert Christgau opined that it might just be the most important album ever released in America.

Although the Finland jaunt had been a success, albeit an unconventional one, two of the Clash's other three attempts to arrange overseas dates in late summer 1979 had come to nothing. Approached by the Undertones to headline a festival in the band's home town of Derry in Northern Ireland, the Clash had agreed. When the show was announced, loyalist paramilitary group the Red Hand Commando sent a letter to the *NME* threatening to kill Joe if the Clash appeared. Joe wanted to go ahead, but the others talked him out of it, and the band withdrew. This was terrorism coming a little too close to home. The other trip had been suggested by the band's San Francisco contact Mo Armstrong: a visit to communist Cuba. Tentative plans were made to spend a week as the guests of Fidel Castro's government, and play two shows while there. According to Johnny Green, these plans were ultimately abandoned for two reasons: fears that the US trade embargo on Cuba might subsequently be applied to the Clash; and Mick's reluctance to demonstrate his support for the revolution and belief in the dignity of labour by spending the required token day toiling in the sugar cane fields. (It was 2001 before the Clash-influenced Manic Street Preachers became the first UK rock band to play Cuba; no toiling was required.) The only date the band did manage to set up at this time, again via Mo Armstrong, was the Tribal Stomp Festival in Monterey, California.

By late August, Mick for one had come to the realisation that the band could not hope to manage themselves as well as performing all the other tasks demanded of them for the duration of a lengthy American tour. Epic and CBS certainly wanted somebody more experienced and level-headed to liaise with. Reluctantly, Joe agreed. Recently, the band had received approaches from the unlikeliest of prospective managers, including entrepreneurs Kerry Packer and Freddie Laker. More realistic a prospect was the seasoned Blackhill management team of Peter Jenner and Andrew King, as recommended by Kosmo Vinyl. At the time closely associated with Stiff, and responsible for managing Ian Dury and the Blockheads, Blackhill had previously promoted the very first concerts Mick had attended in Hyde Park, and had managed the

Syd Barrett-era Pink Floyd. Peter Jenner had even branched out into production, one of his credits being the 1973 Sharks album *Jab It In Yore Eye* so beloved of Mick in his Delinquents days.

In retrospect, Johnny Green believes that Kosmo's visits to Vanilla had never been purely social after all, but instead a canny scouting operation on behalf of Blackhill. Johnny also wonders whether the idea to make the younger, streetwise Kosmo an ambassador for the former hippy entrepreneurs came from Blackhill, Kosmo himself, or somewhere a little closer to home. A review of the beneficiaries explains his thinking: Jenner and King ended up with the Clash's management contract on a trial basis for the duration of the American tour; Kosmo duly became the Clash's PR man; and Mick Jones, who had argued most strongly in favour of abandoning self-management and who had been the first to befriend Kosmo, ended up with professional representation capable of getting his band's career back on track and his music back into the public arena.

The new management team did not get to exert complete control, and the Clash were still determined to break America on their own terms. This much was signalled by their choice of title for the enterprise: the Clash Take The Fifth Tour. By invoking the Fifth Amendment to the American Constitution – that is, by refusing to testify in case they incriminated themselves – the band were striking yet another self-mythologising, anti-authoritarian outlaw pose. Last time, Epic had objected to the size of the Clash's entourage. This time it was even bigger. In addition to DJ Barry Myers, Johnny Green, Baker and the lighting and sound crew, there was the new management team of Andrew, Peter and Kosmo. Blackhill had set the dates up through the William Morris Agency, and they supplied American tour manager Mark Wissing. Three of the band decided to forego one of touring's traditional fringe benefits, and take along their girlfriends: Topper was accompanied by Dee, Joe by Gaby, and Paul by his new New York model girlfriend, Debbie. Mick's relationship with Viv Albertine had finally ground to a painful halt. Single, he confused everyone – not least Mark Wissing – by appointing an old art school contemporary called Rory as his own personal tour manager and road companion.

Kosmo demonstrated his professional talents before the band even left the country by ensuring that the UK music press dispatched only Clash-friendly representatives to cover the tour. *Melody Maker* sent Joe's old pal Allan Jones, and *Sounds* sent long-time Clash supporter Pete Silverton for a couple of days apiece, but the real coup was with the *NME*. Feeling that the paper's epic Clash-On-The-Road sagas were getting a little predictable, recalling her startling Rainbow shot, and already thinking ahead to cover illustrations for the new album, Kosmo arranged for Pennie Smith and her camera to accompany the band for the entire jaunt. Just to be on the safe side, though, writer Paul Morley, responsible for the positive Rainbow review, was also taken along for the first nine days of the ride. Kosmo kept him supplied with his favourite tipple, and Paul duly turned in the traditional glowing two-part, 10-page account to go with Pennie's pictures. Not to be outdone, Johnny Green suggested that the *NME*'s rock'n'roll and Clash-loving cartoonist Ray Lowry come too. Epic drew the line as the Clash entourage touched 30, but Ray paid for himself and went anyway, sending back five weekly half-page illustrated reports.

Upon arrival in San Francisco, the Clash had a few days' grace to rehearse their new set. Initially, at least, 'I'm So Bored With The USA' would remain the set opener, but the other punk thrashes would mostly be reserved for closing numbers and encores. 'White Riot' would usually be the final song, as it had remained throughout 1978. Other older songs were reworked to fit in with the Clash's new material: Mick played acoustic guitar on 'English Civil War' to emphasise its folk roots. 'Guns Of Brixton' was introduced to the set, soon to become a staple, with Paul and Joe making much play out of switching their instruments and stage positions. During rehearsals, the band started playing along to Willie Williams's current reggae hit 'Armagideon Time', and quickly worked up a powerful version that was also quick to establish itself as a show regular.

The opening show was the band's sole remaining pre-Blackhill commitment, an afternoon slot on 8 September at the Tribal Stomp festival in Monterey. The Clash turned up at a fairground that was supposed to hold 12,000 to find just 500 people milling around in front of the stage. Worse, most of them seemed intent on reliving the original 1967 festival, and were attired in hippy fancy dress. The culture clash with the Clash's now even more finely tuned Fifties rocker look – hair grease now obligatory – could not have been more pronounced. Joe opened proceedings by flinging himself backwards into the drum kit, an attention-seeking device that worked only in retrospect: the LA Times photographer captured it in a dramatic motordrive sequence that made the following day's edition. Otherwise, the Clash's gung ho set made limited impression. For the band, the highlight was bringing on Joe Ely for encore versions of his 1978 single 'Fingernails' and their own 'White Riot'.

Regular opening act for the first leg of the tour proper were the Undertones, with the second on the bill slot – depending on the city – going to Bo Diddley, ex-New York Doll Dave JoHansen, or soul duo Sam and Dave. The Undertones and the American artists made their own arrangements, so the Clash entourage travelled alone; or rather, as alone as 30 people can be. Baker went with the American crew and the equipment van. The others went by a bus named Arpeggio. As on the previous tour, it was luxurious, but only in comparison with British models: the Clash and company were still to be subjected to six weeks of continuous motion and limited sleep.

Mick's choice of Rory as travelling companion rebounded on him almost immediately, as his old friend entertained the others for hours with humorous tales from Mick's Delinquent past. Kosmo proved even better value, keeping the band amused as well as focused on the task of converting America to Clash-style rock'n'roll, which he dubbed The Quest. 'You need someone, when you're flagging, to keep your spirit up so you can get back up there,' Joe told Creem's Susan Whitall in 1980. 'Kosmo's one of those sorts of human beings who's all razzle-dazzle and no downs.' 'They fell in love with Kosmo very quickly,' says Johnny, who wasn't quite as impressed with the new boy. Nor was Baker. Nor was Ray Lowry. 'Kosmo's real name was A Fucking Balloon,' he says. 'He turns up in California, a loudmouthed Cockney retard wearing a bomber jacket emblazoned with a map of Vietnam and the legend, "When I die I'll go to heaven 'cause I've served my time in hell." Notting Hell, presumably.'

Paul's own ongoing fascination with warfare was evidenced by the new backdrop, which he had conceived and the Clash had commissioned from an Islington-based designer at a cost of £1,500. It featured B52 aeroplanes with bays open and bombs raining down in the direction of Topper's drum kit, and was flown to the US at considerable expense. Despite having raised no objection to the Pearl Harbour tour paraphernalia earlier in the year, or, indeed, Kosmo's jacket this time around, Mick took one look at the backdrop and rejected it out of hand for 'promoting violence'. When the tour reached New York, Ray Lowry was commissioned to paint a replacement, but was unable to rent a studio space large enough on the budget the Clash gave him. Consequently, the flag backdrop had to be pressed into service again.

On 12 September, Mick's mother, Renee – who, according to Johnny, looked just like Elizabeth Taylor – and stepfather, George, came to see the Clash at the St Paul Civic Arena, where Renee had once seen her beloved Elvis Presley. Joe had always been the consummate showman, but his recent photo spreads had inspired him to work up a few new routines. During soundcheck at the Arena, he arranged for Warren Steadman to dim the stage lights for 'Armagideon Time', so that Johnny Green could shine a torch up under his face to chilling effect. Later, Joe found – of all things – a candelabra on the buffet table backstage. Come showtime, when the lights went down and the band kicked into the song, he appeared from behind the drum riser, flaming candelabra held aloft, before moving forward into Johnny's spooky spotlight. Unfortunately, the rest of the Clash show was a disaster, with amps breaking down and the new material failing to gel. Joe was so frustrated, he bit Paul. The following day's *Minneapolis Star* ran a review under the headline 'Hardly Transcendental'. As the candelabra routine had been just about the only thing that had worked all night, the Clash decided to keep the prop for future shows. An attempt to steal it was frustrated, so Andy King and Peter Jenner handed over $250 the band could ill afford to buy it from the venue management.

Epic had yet to come through with the $20,000 Blackhill had asked them to contribute to the tour. When the Clash checked in to Chicago's Downtown Holiday Inn, the hotel demanded payment upfront, so the credit card of *Sounds* journalist Pete Silverton had to be pressed into service to put up 30 people for three nights. Taking advantage of the stand-off with the American label, CBS UK suggested they be allowed to release the US version of *The Clash* in Britain, in return for forwarding the band some of the money they could expect to realise from sales at home. The Clash saw this as an attempted exploitation of their British fans, and refused. 'Typical of them to try and trick us while we're away,' Mick muttered to Paul Morley. 'They always do that.' Epic finally delivered some money as the band were about to abandon taking the Fifth in favour of taking the next plane home. By this time, the highly stressed Mark Wissing had had enough, and he left the tour anyway.

The financial wrangles and the poor reception for the opening shows combined to put the Clash in a pugnacious mood, and they were wound up further by their self-appointed cheerleader, Kosmo Vinyl. The media bore the brunt. In Chicago, an influential local DJ preferred to go on a coke binge rather than turn up to interview the band; he tried to make amends at the gig by presenting the band with a couple of hookers. Mick explained to him, none too gently, that the Clash did not operate that way. Meanwhile, a female journalist asked Joe if he had a message for America. 'Eat less,' was the reply. In Detroit, Joe took exception to *Creem*'s Dave DiMartino smoking throughout a pre-gig interview, but instead of explaining the reason for his agitation, blew up and stormed out. After the Boston show on the 19th, the entire band plus Kosmo took part in an unbelievably obnoxious phone-in interview at the local WBCN radio station. A couple of years earlier, Patti Smith had written an article called 'You Can't Say Fuck On Radio Free America'. Nobody, it seems, had bothered to inform the Clash. The band were not that much more co-operative with the team from ABC TV's documentary series *20/20*, who attempted an interview backstage at the New York Palladium. After clowning around for the first few minutes, first Paul and then Topper walked out smirking, leaving the presenter to cope with Mick's twinkle-eyed sarcasm and Joe's naked hostility.

The band might have believed they were giving a wake up call to the lazy, ignorant and incompetent representatives of the US mass media, but their scorn was carried via such conduits to the fans and potential fans of the band. The Clash were so determined not to compromise that they were in danger of alienating not just those in control of the American channels of communication but also the people with whom they wished to communicate. Some of their taunting was even more direct. From Chicago onwards, the band took to opening their shows with the least Clash-like of their new songs, 'Jimmy Jazz'… and *then* hitting the confused audience right between the eyes with 'I'm So Bored With The USA'. Chicago was 'a Clash city', and went where the band wanted to take them – the show on the 14th gave rise to the popular bootleg LP *All Or Nothing*, featuring label illustrations by Paul Simonon – but quiet or baffled audience responses continued to dog the tour. This was hardly surprising, given that so much of the set was unfamiliar and atypical, but – as ever 100 per cent committed to the live experience – Joe continued to take such reactions personally.

In Detroit, a notoriously hard to please city, two former MC5-ers attended the gig at the Masonic Temple. Wayne Kramer chatted amiably with Mick backstage, but 'fat Rob Tyner' infuriated Joe by sitting in the front row with his arms crossed, and a 'whaddya got to show me?' expression on his face that seemed to typify the attitude of the entire crowd. 'The British audiences that we've been brought up on have always been great, and that's our high standard. If an audience doesn't reach that, or if we can't get an audience up to that pitch, then we'll feel angry. We'll take some of the blame, but we'll also blame it on them,' Joe told Paul Morley afterwards. 'That's when I start hating it, and that's when it starts coming over really twisted.' The gig on 26 September at the O'Keefe Centre in Montreal could not have presented a more marked contrast: the crowd went berserk, pogoing, gobbing and smashing up the front row of seats. Apparently, it was still 1977 in some parts of Canada, and – needless to say – Joe didn't like that either.

Paul ricked his back and hurt his hip during the Chicago gig, and having to hoist his heavy Fender bass around every night for the rest of the tour gave him little chance to heal. Most of the time, despite the pain, he remained as stoical and easy-going as ever, but something seemed to snap on 21 September during the second New York Palladium gig: he began smashing his bass repeatedly against the stage. 'Sometimes I feel a bit funny,' was his only comment afterwards. When it came to spectacle, Joe had been upping the ante ever since Monterey. During one show he climbed up on the drum riser, and jumped clear over the kit and Topper's head. His Rainbow stunt of hurling his guitar into the wings was now repeated every night, with Johnny being trusted to perform whatever acrobatics were necessary to catch it. It's worth noting that Paul's Pete Townshend act occurred during a show that was being recorded by WNEW radio – it was subsequently heavily bootlegged under a number of titles – and at a time when Pennie Smith was standing in the wings at his side of the stage, perfectly placed to take advantage of the perfect photo-opportunity. As Paul advanced towards her with his bass aloft, she managed to squeeze off two shots before diving out of the way.

When Topper's turn to grab all the attention came, it was totally inadvertent and certainly not something the Clash wished to exploit for publicity purposes. Ray Lowry had intended to file a report per week for the entire duration of the tour, but his penultimate communiqué, covering the band's Texas shows, failed to appear in the *NME*. In his final dispatch, he intriguingly claimed it had been 'suppressed by the authorities'. For the Texas dates, Joe Ely had replaced the Undertones as support band. He invited the Clash to fit in an extra show on 7 October at Rock's Club in his, and Buddy Holly's, home town of Lubbock. The Clash visited Holly's grave, and lay plectrums there in tribute. After the show, in 'a real dodgy bar', Topper took too much heroin, and OD'd. 'I walked him up and down the road for about an hour, trying to keep him conscious and breathing,' says Johnny. 'We didn't dare risk taking him to hospital.' It was something the Clash evidently also preferred the *NME*'s readership not to know about.

With his trotting cross-stage runs, scissor kicks and star jumps, Mick continued to give good value as a live performer, but he was noticeably more of a background figure on this tour. Joe took care of most of the interviews. As the only member of the band with recording know-how, Mick had enjoyed a brief period of dominance at Wessex, but Joe had been the driving force at Vanilla, and for much of 1979 had been more productive than previously as a tunesmith as well as a lyricist. 'I watched the dynamics change,' says Johnny. 'When I joined up with them, Joe had been at a really low ebb, with hepatitis and all that, and when they came out of being a straight punk group and

with Bernie going, Mick had taken control of the group and Joe had taken a bit of a dive.
But with the new album, Joe was starting to reassert himself.'

Having lost his possessions, flat and girlfriend in quick succession, Mick was
genuinely struggling with the depression he had alluded to on 'I'm Down'. 'The Clash
is everything to me,' he told Paul Morley during the Take The Fifth Tour. 'I'm under the
impression that I have given everything else up for it. I'm under the impression that I
have lost everything: home, personal life, everything. So my dilemma is, in a way, that
I resent the Clash.' More than the others, he found the manner in which the band were
touring America to be a near-unbearable ordeal. Topper's use of heroin, though
occasionally worrying, was still part of his enthusiastic social – if not always sociable –
life. By this stage, Mick was sticking largely to smoking spliff, but he smoked it
constantly, often alone. Rory was a road manager whose role seemed to consist of
managing to find dope for Mick while he was on the road.

Blackhill's management style was more traditional, in that they endeavoured to
relieve the band of all responsibilities, save playing the gigs and doing the press. It took
much of the grit out of the Clash's lives, but during the Vanilla sessions and on earlier
tours, it had been the grit that had inspired them to overcome their differences and pull
together. Joe remained fascinated by the people he encountered, talking to anyone and
everyone, not only at the shows and hotels but also over Arpeggio's CB radio. Mick
chatted and signed autographs, but his floor was no longer available for fans to sleep on.
During the Take The Fifth Tour, a gulf became apparent between the band and even the
closest members of the entourage. Johnny for one noticed he was being treated more and
more like a valet, and not solely by Mick. Taking their girlfriends along provided the other
three with some much needed respite from the grind of touring life, but it too detracted
from the camaraderie within the band, and further emphasised Mick's outsiderdom.

Everything came to a head in Toronto, Canada, the morning after the show at the
O'Keefe Centre on 26 September. Mick had been forced to throw away his stash when
Johnny had refused to smuggle it through customs for him. Now, Mick refused to get
back on the hated bus without the makings of a joint. Seemingly impervious to their
anger, he kept the entire entourage waiting outside the hotel for hours until a supply of
ganja could be located. To kill time, Pennie Smith took pictures, one of which appeared
in her 1980 book *The Clash: Before And After*. Joe's caption makes a joke out of the
situation – 'this bus ain't going anywhere until the Man arrives' – but at the time it
wasn't funny, and grudges were held against Mick. It was beginning to seem as though
the only way he could assert himself was with such displays of petulance. Rory
disappeared from the tour around this time…

There were more enjoyable moments, most of them to do with music. The Clash
enjoyed their support groups, especially Joe Ely. The Lubbock visit precipitated a Buddy
Holly craze, and at the Kezar Pavilion in San Francisco, the rock retro vibe inspired a
final encore of Gene Vincent's 'Be-Bop-A-Lula', as previously covered by the 101ers.
On 19 September, Mickey Gallagher flew out to augment the Clash for the rest of the
tour. He rehearsed during the soundcheck at the Orpheum Theatre in Boston. That night,
he found himself onstage with a band he had never even seen live before, being required
not only to play the numbers he knew from the Wessex recording sessions, but also to
add *Blonde On Blonde*-style 'wild mercury' organ to the more punky set closers. In New
York, Bill Price arrived with first mixes of the new Clash album material, providing the
bus with its soundtrack music for the next few days.

In honour of both their musical change of direction and of the Quest, the Clash briefly
toyed with the idea of calling the new album *The New Testament*, but settled instead for
London Calling. Ray Lowry was commissioned to design the sleeve. 'The Elvis tone of
things was set by the band's own mutation into greasers and a copy of the first Elvis

Presley album that I picked up for $6 in Wax Trax in Chicago,' says Ray. He copied the 1956 Presley album's green and pink lettering, and as the Clash's 1979 look was both retro and largely monochrome, he had no trouble finding suitable illustrations among Pennie Smith's contact sheets. The band were unanimous in their insistence that one of the photos of Paul smashing his bass should be used for the front cover, despite Pennie's protestations that it was out of focus. Their instincts proved sound: over the coming years, it was to become one of rock music's most instantly recognisable icons.

The Blackhill team could iron out most minor niggles, but found themselves up against it when the money ran out again in Austin, on 4 October 1979. Approached for more, Epic initially refused, again objecting to the ever-expanding entourage – Mickey Gallagher was accompanied by his wife and young sons Luke and Ben – and the unpaid American road crew staged a drunken mutiny. When Epic finally delivered, the band, girlfriends and management used some of the money to fly to LA. Paul still managed to turn up over an hour late for the Palladium gig in that city, causing the Clash to be fined by the promoter. Mick was prepared to inconvenience his colleagues, but not 'the kids', and he joined in the chorus of disapproval.

By this late stage, everyone was becoming frayed around the edges. Always a hard drinker – in which activity he was kept company by Ray Lowry – Johnny Green was also hoovering up cocaine and anything else he could lay his hands on. As he documents in *A Riot Of Our Own*, the memoir he wrote in 1997 with the assistance of Garry Barker, his behaviour grew more and more erratic as the tour progressed. His account of the last couple of weeks read like a rerun of *Fear And Loathing In Las Vegas*. In San Francisco on the first tour, the Clash had indirectly insulted Bill Graham by playing for a rival promoter. When they returned to play the Kezar Pavilion on 13 October, Bill Graham insulted the Clash backstage, and Johnny tried to attack him. Bouncers had to pull him away. Yet to receive any payment for his work on the tour, Johnny went to Andrew and Peter's San Francisco hotel room to determine why. He learned that Blackhill had decided he was too cocky, headstrong and unreliable to remain in the Clash's employ. He had to resort to threats of violence to get his money.

On the 15th, in Seattle, Johnny's excesses required him to be hospitalised, and he missed the show. The following night's date, in Vancouver, Canada, was the last of the tour. The American crew pulled the fuses from the PA as part of another showdown over lack of pay. This time, both Johnny and the Baker resorted to threats of violence to retrieve the fuses. The gig went ahead, but like the previous few shows, it was something of a downer. Ray Lowry reported that Joe once again railed 'against passive audiences stealing his soul'. Next day, everyone involved with the tour gathered at the hotel, demanding to be paid. The Clash threatened to break up. Johnny walked out and flew home alone.

A few days rest put a different complexion on things. In spite of the mixed audience responses, the hardships endured, the tensions experienced and the enemies made, those who survived the epic trek were left with a feeling of significant achievement. 'It really started to feel as though it was starting to take off,' muses Johnny Green. Ray Lowry closed his last *NME* report thus: 'If the Clash packed it in tomorrow, we'd lose the sole living evidence that rock'n'roll aspires to be anything more than blind escapism… I'd like to be back on the bus with the last rock'n'roll band.'

A great adventure it might have been, but it is debatable to what extent the Take The Fifth Tour saw the band's American career start to take off. The entire record industry was hit by recession in 1979 – the first decline in growth since the end of World War

Two – and CBS, the biggest player, took it particularly hard. The industry's total sales slumped by 11 per cent on the previous year; over the same period, CBS saw a drop in earnings of 46 per cent. On 29 June 1979, CBS's American operation made 53 people redundant. On 10 August – which became known as Black Friday – a further 120 employees were let go. According to *Hit Men*, Fredric Dannen's 1990 exposé of the American record industry, the recession was partly due to 'Koka Kola'-style excesses in the corridors of power, and partly due to a serious misjudgement of the size, longevity and profitability of the disco craze in the wake of the huge-selling *Saturday Night Fever* soundtrack. What was really cutting in to the profits, though, was the cost of hiring 'independent promoters'.

In the States, pre-MTV, there was no single national TV show with the same power as *Top Of The Pops*, and no single national radio station with the same power as Radio One. Instead, each area had one or two leading Top 40-type radio stations with the ability to generate a local hit; if several such stations responded well, then a single could go on to become a national hit. Major record companies helped the process along by hiring independent promoters to plug their singles in the most influential areas. Or, in other words, they hired people to bribe station owners and DJs to play their records. In 1978, the leading independent promoters had formed themselves into an unofficial alliance known as the Network. This organisation couldn't guarantee a hit if you paid them; but they could guarantee there would be no hit if you didn't. Buying favours with dollars, coke and hookers was nothing new in an industry which had invented the concept of payola, but between 1972 and 1979, the price demanded per single added to an important playlist had gone up from around $100 to as much as $100,000. By 1980, CBS's total outlay on such promotion would be $8-$10 million a year: close to a third of the company's pre-tax profits.

In comparison, what the Clash had asked for in tour support was peanuts, but in a world where even the most megalomaniac record company executive was forced to take part in an eternal round of kiss-ass and bribe-ass, the Clash's refusal to play the game was interpreted as unforgivable arrogance. Some maverick DJs might play Clash songs because they liked them, the band might get the odd interview, and the odd gig might be recorded for live transmission – as the bass smashing show at the New York Palladium had been – but this would not be enough to make a significant dent on the American charts. In a nutshell, until the Clash started kissing ass, Epic were unlikely to find the money to bribe ass on their behalf; no pay, no airplay; no airplay, no hit singles; no hit singles, no hit albums; no hit albums, no American career opportunities for the Clash. No American career opportunities, no point Epic wasting money on tour support…

Back in the UK, the Clash booked back into Wessex in early November to polish the final album mix. While there, they also set up to record 'Armagideon Time' as a high profile B-side for proposed lead single 'London Calling'. The Clash realised this brace of songs offered contrasting cultural perspectives on the same basic theme, in much the same way as had 'Police And Thieves' and 'White Riot'. Even forgetting this new recording – and its dub mixes, 'Justice Tonight/Kick It Over', planned as Jamaican-style versions for the 12-inch edition of the single – the band still had 18 tracks in the can, too many to fit comfortably onto a single album.

Annoyed with CBS for charging £1.49 for *The Cost Of Living*, the Clash had been taking a stand over VFM ever since. In January, Generation X had insisted that Chrysalis knock 40 pence off the cost of their second album, *Valley Of The Dolls*. By contrast, CBS had initially wanted to charge the industry maximum of £5.99 for the Clash's new album. In the July *Sounds* interview with Garry Bushell and Dave McCullough, Joe had bellowed, 'THERE WILL BE NO SIX QUID CLASH LP EVER. It's a fact.' Reluctantly, CBS had backed down.

From August onwards, the Clash had been pushing for the album to be a double, but had insisted on keeping the low single album price tag. At first, CBS had refused. Via Kosmo, the Clash now offered to make the album a single disc if they could include a free single, as they had with the US version of *The Clash* earlier in the year. Accepting that it was a tried and tested marketing ruse, CBS agreed. Next, the Clash asked if it could be a 12-inch single. CBS agreed. The Clash then insisted that the 12-inch single play at 33 rpm and contain eight tracks…

The *NME*'s reputation as the Paper That Supports Our Boys had already been bolstered by Paul Morley's words, Pennie Smith's photos and Ray Lowry's cartoons, but Kosmo was not done yet. He reminded the inky's editorial team what a pop-cultural landmark the *Capital Radio* EP had been, and suggested arranging something similar: this time a flexi-disc to be attached to the paper itself. Back in 1972, the Rolling Stones had promoted *Exile On Main Street* in this manner. At Wessex, Kosmo asked the Clash if they had anything appropriate. That night, Mick wrote 'Train In Vain', and it was rehearsed, recorded and mixed the following day. Named after the insistent Echoplex-treated guitar riff that drives it along, the song suggests Motown in its beat, and recalls Tammy Wynette's 'Stand By Your Man' in what at first appears to be a banal off-the-peg lyric about lost love. On closer inspection, its references to homelessness, a job that doesn't pay, and a fickle ex-girlfriend reveal that it in fact draws directly upon the recent traumas in Mick's own personal life.

Had the proposed *NME* flexi-disc come off, it would have brought the paper's 1979 Clash coverage close to multi-media overkill, but IPC refused permission at the last minute. As the band's most hardcore VFM true-believer, Mick insisted 'Train In Vain' be added to the end of the second disc. It was too late for its lyric to be included on the inner sleeve, or its title to be added anywhere on the packaging. Instead, the title was carved into the plastic of the fourth side's run-off groove. As a result, a certain mystique was conveyed upon a song that would perhaps not otherwise have earned it. So began another freebie marketing trend, this time for 'secret' extra tracks, that would be more fully exploited during the CD age.

The 'free 33 rpm 12-inch single' now contained nine tracks. For once, CBS had been outmanoeuvred, tricked into agreeing to what was all intents and purposes a double album retailing for the single album cost of £5, exactly what the Clash had wanted in the first place. 'I'd say it was our first real victory over CBS,' gloated Joe to *Sounds*' Chris Bohn that December. At the time, the victory seemed a pyrrhic one: CBS felt justified in counting *London Calling* as a single album contractually, meaning that of the five albums they believed they owed the record company, the Clash were deemed to have delivered a total of three rather than four. This explains the 'three down, two to go' tally marks on the record's inner sleeve. Today, the point is largely moot: as the entire record comes in at 65 minutes, it fits comfortably onto a single CD.

Don Letts shot a video for 'London Calling' on the Festival Pier, on the south side of the river near Battersea Park. Dressed in their monochrome Hollywood rock'n'roll gear, the band played through umpteen takes of the song in the cold, dark and rain. It made for an atmospheric clip, but it ruined the hired musical equipment. At the end of the shoot, Johnny Green added a few hundred pounds to the band's debt by throwing it into the Thames. The single was released on 7 December 1979 in a sleeve that – true to the retro design of the parent album – was based upon HMV's old sleeves for 78 rpm singles, featuring illustrations of dancing couples. Andy Gill's *NME* review offered only faint praise, which did not bode well for the fate of the forthcoming album.

Initial critical response to *London Calling*, released in the UK on 14 December 1979, turned out to be mixed. Reviewing it for the *NME*, and sharing the same tastes in roots rock musics as the Clash, Charles Shaar Murray was predisposed to be sympathetic. He had a couple of reservations, notably with the macho militant stance of 'Guns Of Brixton' and the hamfisted sexual politics of 'Lover's Rock' – Joe was still finding it hard to win his PC certificate on this issue, even with his tongue in his cheek – but, those aside, his endorsement was wholehearted. 'The Clash have been criticised for becoming a "straight-ahead rock band", which is specious in the extreme,' he declared. 'The Clash love rock'n'roll, which is why they play it, but they want it to live up to its promises, which is why they play it the way they do. With groups like the Clash on the case, rock ain't in the cultural dumper: *London Calling* makes up for all the bad rock'n'roll played in the last decade.' James Truman expressed much the same feelings on behalf of *Melody Maker*, albeit in a more understated sort of way: 'the Clash have discovered America, and by the same process, themselves.' Both writers believed the band had come back from the disaster of *Give 'Em Enough Rope* with their finest album to date.

Sounds' Garry Bushell took the opposite view. After looking back fondly on the turgid *Give 'Em Enough Rope* as 'a magnificent fiery rock album, brimming with metal attack and renewed purpose', he made his feelings about the Clash's new material clear in a sneering, condemnatory two (out of five) star review headed 'Give 'Em Enough Dope'. Questionable though his taste might have been, he voiced opinions shared by other inky writers who were less punk-obsessed than Garry or roots-oriented than CSM. Garry's first point was that there was little genuinely new about the Clash's supposed new direction: 'Unable to go forward, they've clutched at straws, ending up retrogressing via Strummer's R&B past and Jones's Keith Richards fixation to the outlaw imagery of the Stones and tired old rock clichés.' In November, John Lydon's PiL – with ex-101er Richard Dudanski briefly occupying the drum seat – had released *Metal Box*, a collection of avant-garde dub-disco anti-rock tracks spread over three 45 rpm 12-inch discs presented in a circular tin. As its playing length was much the same as *London Calling* – the PiL album's second pressing would be packaged as a standard double LP – comparisons were inevitable, and the Clash's more traditional work was found wanting in terms of cutting edge experimentalism.

Garry also agreed with CSM that there was something disquieting about the band's '"guns and gangs" outlaw vision-lumpen lyrical fantasy world'. Finally – going for the jugular now – he maintained that the band had failed to live up to many of the promises they had made three years earlier: 'one of the Clash's biggest failings has been their inability to link their righteous sentiments with the power struggle in the real world. Like, shouting "Long live the revolution" don't make it come, y'know.'

In interviews he gave over the next few years, Joe affected surprise at the accusations of American influence. He cited the album's reggae rhythms and numerous London-specific lyrical references in refutation. 'I never thought about beefburgers once, or Micky Mouse, or the Statue of Liberty,' he told the *NME*'s Roz Reines in 1982. He was being not a little disingenuous. Lyrically, parts of the album do indeed follow 'Brand New Cadillac' and the Clash's own wardrobe into a mythological American fantasy land, the details and parameters of which are informed by the mythologies associated with folk, jazz, blues, rock'n'roll and Hollywood. While it could be argued that the AOR HM of Sandy Pearlman's *Give 'Em Enough Rope* was closer to the sound of then-contemporary America, many of the non-reggae songs on the new album have their origins in retro US musical genres. The overall impression is reinforced by Ray Lowry's cover, and Pennie Smith's photos from the Take The Fifth Tour of the band in their

American outlaw togs. Full page music press ads for *London Calling* depicted a 1956-era Elvis Presley holding a copy of the album.

The denunciations for having sold out the punk ideal hit even harder. The Clash could point out that it was their very insistence upon giving their British audience VFM that had put them in debt with CBS in the first place, which debt had effectively prevented them from touring the UK during 1979. But it seemed all the carpers could see was that, while the UK had seen a mere handful of shows all year, the US had enjoyed two full tours, seeming proof that the Clash had deserted their original following for the sake of breaking the lucrative American market. Even the most straightforward cause-and-effect economic arguments failed to convince some sections of the music press otherwise. Although the votes for the inkies' end-of-year readers' polls had been cast before the release of *London Calling*, they too seemed to reflect this dissatisfaction. In the *NME*, the revitalised Jam took over the Clash's crown as the erstwhile UK punk constituency's favourite band.

To retain their hardcore UK fan base, the Clash believed they would have to tour first thing in the new year. When it came to arrangements, the band proved themselves every bit as blind to economic realities as the people who rubbished them for selling out. They refused to upgrade from the size of venue they had played in late 1978. In 1989, 10 years after the event, co-manager Peter Jenner explained what Blackhill had to contend with to *Q* magazine's Paul Du Noyer: 'The refusal to face dilemmas was the essence of the Clash. I'd cost out a tour for them, and say, "With the ticket price you want, and the scale of equipment you want, even if we sell out every show, you'll still lose money. It won't add up." But they'd go, "We can't rip off the kids!" "All right, keep the ticket price down, but scale down the stage show." "But we're a big rock'n'roll band, we've got to have all the stuff!" So they'd go to CBS for extra money, and end up further in hock. CBS always had them by the short'n'curlies.'

While this demeaning process was acted out yet again – meaning that the victory over CBS represented by the cut-price cost of *London Calling* was extremely short-lived – the Clash tried to set up a brace of Christmas shows in London as a more immediate thank you for patient fans. They also bent to pressure from Blackhill to play the benefit Concert For The People Of Kampuchea on 27 December at the Hammersmith Odeon as support to Ian Dury and the Blockheads. Rehearsals for these shows and the forthcoming tour took place in an unlovely and unloved rehearsal room under a railway arch in south London. Here, Joe taught the band another new Strummer composition. Perversely, in view of recent criticisms, what was then known as 'The Bank Robber's Song', a title subsequently shortened to 'Bankrobber', presents itself as an outrageous slice of Staggerlee-goes-to-Hollywood myth-making. Behind the outlaw romanticism, though, it reveals itself to be another song with a message in the tradition of 'Clash City Rockers', 'All The Young Punks (New Boots And Contracts)' and 'Clampdown': dead-end jobs are a living death, so live your life to the full while you can. In its original form, it was a jaunty ska number, so it was presumably the lyric rather than the music which inspired Mick to play caterwauling bottleneck guitar throughout.

The band's own concerts were scheduled at the very last minute to take place on the 25th and 26th of the month at the 250-capacity Acklam Hall, off Ladbroke Grove, literally under the Westway. Money was so tight that Johnny Green remembers the Clash taking the unheard of step of skimping on the PA, while Kosmo paid for the flyers out of his own pocket. Pennie Smith's contribution was to take photos of the band round at 111 Wilmcote House for a give-away Christmas card. Even so, as they charged just 50 pence for admission, the Clash's gesture put them further in debt.

The first show was sparsely attended, partly because the flyers went up after the pubs shut on Christmas Eve – Kosmo was caught in the act by police, but let off with a caution

– partly because no-one could believe the Clash would be playing such a tiny venue at 5 pm on Christmas Day, and partly because there was no public transport available. Mickey Gallagher played organ, and Kosmo was MC. As well as Joe's newest song, the band played his oldest, the 101ers' 'Keys To Your Heart'. Mick's Nan, Stella, was one of the select few who saw the show, her first ever Clash gig. She thought Mick was 'very good', but that it was 'a bit loud'. Afterwards, Paul and Debbie went back to Johnny and Lindy's place in Hampstead for Christmas dinner and some sniff. A year later, *Creem*'s Iman Lababedi would ask Paul how he stayed so thin. 'I have no sense of smell, so I don't get that hungry. At Christmas, when everyone's starving, I can't smell the turkey.' Did he take drugs? 'Yes. Drugs are OK if you use them properly.'

Word of mouth guaranteed that the second Acklam Hall show was packed out and far more boisterous. A dozen skinheads invading the stage during the closing 'White Riot', prompting Joe to mutter that Jimmy Pursey wasn't expected. The mood was less celebratory at the following night's Hammersmith Odeon benefit show, though the band were musically and visually impressive. Alex Michon had worked up a bowling shirt-type design that was to become the Clash's regular stage wear for much of 1980: black back, shoulders, collar and sleeves – worn rolled up high on the bicep, rocker style – but with front panels in one of several contrasting bright colours. The band turned in a powerful set, and their live take of 'Armagideon Time' duly turned up on the *Concert For Kampuchea* live album and TV film, both of which came out the following year.

The real drama happened offstage. Joe had been brooding for days about being asked to support the Blockheads, believing it indicated where Blackhill's true priorities lay. When the Clash arrived at the venue, promoter Harvey Goldsmith took delight in rubbing in their lowly status. The fact the Odeon was a seated venue did nothing to improve Joe's mood. When he learned that Mick intended to join Dury onstage for 'Sweet Gene Vincent' – illustrating the song's lyric by wearing black'n'white clothes and playing a Strat-lookalike Telecaster – there was a furious row. Both Joe and Johnny informed Mick he was 'a shit' for putting star guest spots above band solidarity, but despite being so upset he cried, Mick still took the stage and played.

On the surface, it was a petty disagreement – and it appeared even pettier when Joe swallowed his anger and went on afterwards to join the others for Eddie Cochran's 'Twenty Flight Rock' – but it hinted at deep-seated resentments that would be expressed far more forcefully in the coming year. Paul Rambali's *NME* review of the show described *London Calling* as 'a naked record made by a group with a lead guitarist of tireless vanity who writes drippy, sentimental words, and a strong idealistic leader who likes reggae, rhythm and blues and George Orwell, and makes valuable propaganda against the clampdown.' More than one person within the Clash camp agreed with those sentiments.

14
VERSION CITY

The UK tour, scheduled to take up most of January and February 1980, was set up through Straight Music, run by former Roundhouse promoter John Curd. Its title, The 16 Tons Tour, was a wry acknowledgement of the band's situation. In 1956, Tennessee Ernie Ford had enjoyed a UK number one single with a song inspired by a saying of composer Merle Haggard's Kentucky coal miner father: '16 tons, and what do I get? / Another day older and deeper in debt.' DJ Barry Myers would play the single as the band took the stage. Pennie Smith went along to take more pictures, now with a book in mind. Johnny Green and Baker retained their roles, but whatever quibbles Blackhill might have had about the amount of equipment hired in relation to size of venue, they were not reluctant to invest in professional assistance. They hired experienced tour manager Hugh Price to drive the band's top of the range mini-bus, and a catering company called Bubble and Squeak to provide cooked meals for the entire crew. Straight Music supplied Ray Jordan, fake dreadlocks sprouting from under his knit cap, as the band's personal security man. The self-styled Terry Razor was loaned from Stiff Records to handle official merchandising, an increasingly important source of revenue in the music industry.

The Clash were initially wary about this last step. It smacked of conventional rock business practices, the kind of commercial exploitation of their fans that had so troubled them during the Upstarts days. They put whatever doubts they had to the back of their minds while they involved themselves in the production of an offbeat tour programme-cum-newsletter entitled the *Armagideon Times*. The first edition included photos by Pennie Smith, a band history by Joe and Mick, and a guide to the *London Calling* songs featuring hand-written notes by Joe, Mick and Topper, and illustrations by Paul. Further artwork was farmed out to a design team calling themselves Jules and Eddie, but Robin Crocker was invited to help Terry Razor with the layout. All of which made it easier for the band to overlook the fact that the *Armagideon Times* also featured advertisements for other Blackhill acts, as well various punk paraphernalia dealerships, including 5th Column. Terry further sweetened the pill by agreeing to let band cohort Terry McQuade help man the merchandising stall. Robin Crocker and Kris Needs also went along on part of the tour for the lig, but both found the hospitality to be less lavish than on previous outings.

Terry Razor tried to win over the crew by supplying them with red Harrington jackets bearing a Clash star motif. The band had their own uniform: their American retro rock'n'roll threads were sharper and shinier than ever before, and Crombie coats and trilby hats quickly established themselves as popular and practical wintertime additions to the collective Clash wardrobe. If bandannas had been optional accessories in 1979, they became compulsory in 1980; mostly red, they added a welcome flash of colour to the band's still predominately monochrome outfits.

The professional attitude was also evident on stage. The sound quality was high, and the well-rehearsed band – again augmented by Mickey Gallagher – were at their tightest ever, despite concentrating largely on the newer material from *London Calling*. Mick was still playing loud, but was more interested in treating his guitar sound with effects pedals than in straight-ahead HM bludgeon riffola. For the first time since signing to CBS, the Clash went out without a backdrop, but they more than made up for it with an impressive lighting rig. The semi-choreographed routines they had started to develop in

America had evolved into something which could genuinely be termed a 'show'. At key points, the three frontmen would run to the back or the front of the stage as one. Mick still worked through his full repertoire of Pete Townshend leaps and kicks, and Paul had even started attempting James Brown knee drops. Joe still sang 'Armagideon Time' in Johnny Green's torchlight, emoting Bob Marley-style with his forefinger to his brow. His guitar still flew into the wings on cue. It was all very dramatic, and highly effective, but whereas once Clash performances had been near spontaneous explosions of energy, now they bordered on the slick.

Toots and the Maytals, the originators of 'Pressure Drop', were pencilled in for main support on the tour. It was announced that the Clash would be encouraging local groups to come forward and open the show at each of the cities and towns they visited. At the last minute, however, the Maytals dropped out. There followed some frantic scrambling around for substitutes for the first batch of dates – Prince Hammer and Lew Lewis were among those who stepped in – before Joe Ely was confirmed for the last 10 shows, and Mikey Dread for the bulk of the tour. Christened Michael Campbell, Mikey was a DJ and producer who, from 1977 to 1979, had hosted his own massively popular and influential late night radio show in Jamaica, *Dread At The Controls*. On this, he not only played discs but also accompanied his own toasts with backing tracks built up from layers of humming and rhythmic sound effects created by an oddball selection of found objects. He oversaw the compilation of a series of dub-dominated albums, and recorded his own tunes with the assistance of renowned reggae producer and fellow technology buff King Tubby. Bravely, Mikey would go out to face the Clash's audience night after night armed with nothing but a miked-up ghetto blaster, a matchbox and a few squeaky toys.

The first gig, on 5 January at Aylesbury Friars, not only sold out, but was the venue's fastest selling show of all time. Kris Needs's Vice Creams were the evening's local heroes. Main support was provided by Ian Dury and the Blockheads, returning a favour from the Kampuchea benefit... and Mick repeated his guest spot on 'Sweet Gene Vincent', fancy dress and all. Promising an objective response in his *NME* review of the headline act, Mark Ellen noted the 'massive chasm between their overblown romanticism... and their intended feet-on-the-street directness of sentiment', questioned the show's pacing and Mick's shape-throwing, but came to the overall conclusion that 'they won'. A television documentary entitled *Rock: Ready For The Eighties?* captures Mick's cameo with Dury, and the Clash performing 'London Calling', 'Police And Thieves' and 'Complete Control': not exactly biased towards the most forward looking material in the band's repertoire.

Another of the Clash's benefit buddies, an extremely drunk Pete Townshend, turned up on the 8th, at the first of two Brighton shows, to guest on the encores. All of a sudden, it looked as though everyone wanted a piece of the Clash. The 'London Calling' single might not have been getting the amount of radio exposure the Clash wanted, but it was still creeping high enough in the charts for Joe to be invited onto Radio One's *Round Table* discussion show, alongside Blondie's Debbie Harry and DJ Kid Jensen. Another DJ, Annie Nightingale, bet Joe a Cadillac that the Clash single would make the Top 10. It spent 10 weeks on the charts, but peaked at number 11, still the Clash's highest position yet. A regular listener offered an old Caddy for Annie to give to Joe, who, being unable to drive, duly donated it to a raffle to benefit the people of the recession-hit steel town of Corby. It turned out that the car didn't actually work, which seemed vaguely appropriate, if disappointing for the winner.

More significantly, the high profile early evening BBC news magazine programme *Nationwide* considered the tour enough of an event to send a crew along to the Dundee show to film a report. The narration opens, 'They say they owe no allegiance to either the right or the left, and despite an almost contemptuous attitude to exposure on radio or TV, they're one of the most successful bands in Britain.' Far from being contemptuous, the Clash recognised this to be the best exposure they'd been offered to date, and offered *Nationwide* full access and co-operation. Footage of the band playing 'Clampdown' and 'Revolution Rock' is accompanied by shots of the trilbied and Crombied Clash walking from tour van to hotel with their ghetto blasters – Joe's blaring the inspirational speeches of Martin Luther King – and preparing for the show backstage with the crew and Mikey Dread, with Joe drinking honey and lemon for his voice. A skinhead fan named Donald is shown being bailed from police custody by the Clash, prompting Joe and Mick to hold forth about the Clash's own experience of police harassment. For the most part, though, the report goes to great pains to accentuate the positive: despite being broke, the Clash had released a double album for the price of a single, were putting on an expensive show in small venues – cue more sighing from Peter Jenner – and, as always, were going out of their way to accommodate their fans. The last of these points is illustrated by footage of Joe and Terry McQuade letting fans in free through the dressing room window. As a PR exercise designed to repair the damage caused by UK music press criticism over the past year or so, it could hardly have been bettered.

Once released by the police, Donald attached himself to the Clash touring party. In Glasgow, on 22 January, he went out on-stage in his Crombie to skank along during Mikey Dread's set. A couple of nights later, he was joined by Johnny Green, wearing a trilby, Crombie and a bandanna over his face, bankrobber style, to hide his blushes. The following night Joe went on too. Within a week up to seven members of the touring party were dancing, all in the same disguise: Donald, Johnny, Joe, Kosmo, Robin, Kris and even Mick. A hugely enjoyable in-joke, it turned sour at Tiffany's in Coventry on 7 February, when Donald grabbed the microphone and began spouting offensive racist claptrap to the audience. Ray Jordan marched him off-stage and out of the Clash's life. There were no attempts to re-educate him, as there had been with Roadent, or tolerate him, as there had been with Ray Gange. As soon as he proved himself to be an embarrassment and a liability, he was gone.

Mick's occasional inclusion in the skanking posse did not mean that the resentments festering within the Clash at the turn of the year had reached any sort of resolution. A particularly ugly scene occurred on 27 January at Sheffield Top Rank. Back in the dressing room following the rapturously received main set, Joe suggested the band finish the encores with the habitual 'White Riot'. Mick, who had been tired of the song for some time, refused point blank. Later that year, he would describe the more basic early songs in the band's repertoire to *Rolling Stone*'s James Henke as 'just *bang, bang, bang,* like a nagging wife'. What happened next was only ever alluded to in the vaguest of terms for many years thereafter. Joe finally came clean when talking to Gavin Martin for *Uncut* in 1999: '[Mick] went, "You've got no respect for the stage!" I said, "Don't fucking tell *me* about the stage!" And he threw his vodka and orange in my face. So I hit him... so hard in the middle of the head that he had my knuckle print stamped there.' 'Joe whacked Mick one,' expands Johnny Green. 'The manager of the venue was there, and I just said, "Turn your back. Close that door *now!*" and pulled the band into the room. Joe really piled into Mick, gave him a severe pasting. There was a real savagery in the attack. Mick was crying his eyes out.'

When Mick went back out on stage, the bandanna he was wearing over his nose and mouth was not a bankrobber affectation, but a necessary disguise for his cuts and bruises. He made his point by putting down his guitar and walking off-stage halfway through 'White Riot'. It's hard to say who won the battle overall: 'White Riot' would be played less and less regularly over the next couple of years, but ultimately, its tenure with the Clash would outlast that of Mick Jones. The incident was never really talked over, and Joe did not apologise. 'You're like a team going on-stage, and no-one lets anyone down,' he told Gavin Martin. 'When that happens, you have to resort to violence between each other, punch people. It's beyond discussion.'

Even before the media coverage afforded the tour and the relatively high chart placing achieved by 'London Calling', Kosmo and the Clash had come up with an imaginative solution to their between-record slumps in visibility and – or so they supposed – popularity in the UK. To counter the impression they were devoting a disproportionate amount of time and effort to breaking America, they had decided to launch a non-stop UK singles campaign, releasing a new record each time the one before dropped out of the charts. 'A Clash Singles Bonanza,' was how Joe described it to the *NME*'s Paul Du Noyer at the end of 1980. 'Fire them off like rockets all through the year.' The novelty aspect, word of mouth and the cumulative impact of the songs themselves would surely overcome all obstacles.

It was arranged for the band to record the follow up to 'London Calling' during a brief break in the tour schedule. On 1 February, the Clash booked into Pluto studios, Granby Row, Manchester for two days. Mikey Dread had taken to joining the Clash on-stage to toast along with 'Armagideon Time', a collaboration that would prove to have considerable influence on the band's development during 1980. The band found Mikey so simpatico that they asked him to produce the Pluto studio session. Bill Price and Jerry Green came up from London to assist.

During 1979 and early 1980, former Clash support group the Specials had helped establish the Ska Revival, encouraging other bands like the Beat to marry the music of mid-Sixties Jamaica to the skinhead style of 1969-70 and the social commentary of the Clash. It was by now a well-worked seam, as Mikey pointed out. Although Joe had originally written 'Bankrobber' in the ska style, Mikey persuaded the Clash to push the song in the direction of slow, heavy dub reggae. The backing track for the A-side begat two potential B-side versions: one instrumental was entitled 'Robber Dub', and a second with Mikey toasting his impressions of the 16 Tons experience over the top was entitled 'Rockers Galore… UK Tour'. The band also worked with him on a reggae-for-squeaky-toy-and-matchbox 'instrumental' called 'Shepherds Delight'. Pennie Smith took photographs during the marathon session, some of which appeared alongside resumés of the band and crew in the *Armagideon Times No 2*, distributed at the remaining gigs. Don Letts shot a video, intercutting footage of the recording process with footage of Johnny and Baker running around town with bags of swag in their fists and bandannas over their faces.

Such forced Keystone Kops-style fun failed to recapture the pre-Sheffield spirit. Following the Poole show on 10 February, the band held a party to celebrate Kosmo's 23rd birthday at the Queen's Hotel in Southsea. A number of fans were invited to join in. Once the more respectable visitors like Maurice Oberstein left, the desk clerk grew concerned that several fans were intending to bunk down for the night without paying. He phoned the police, who checked the rooms to verify his claims. Predictably, given the inflammatory remarks the band had made on *Nationwide*, the representatives of the law chose not to ignore the tell-tale aroma of ganja. Joe – who, according to the *NME* news report, was found lying in bed reading the bible – Topper and four members of the crew had various substances taken away for analysis.

The 15 February gig at the ill-ventilated Electric Ballroom in Camden was attended by the *NME*'s Gavin Martin. He caught the Clash on another bad night. According to his review, Joe was an over-emotional wreck, while Mick was once again displaying 'the complacent detachment of a guitar hero'. 'They need a rest,' concluded Gavin. 'The tour has fatigued them and sapped them of willpower and cohesion.'

There was precious little evidence of this just three days later, when the band played the Lewisham Odeon. Don Letts supervised the filming of the show, his chief aim being to capture the band performing 'Train In Vain'. This *London Calling* track had been selected by Epic to be the first single released from the album in the US, despite not being listed on the cover. Attired primarily in black, much like at the Lyceum gig of a year earlier, the Clash rose to the occasion with a performance so impressive that excerpts from Don's Lewisham Odeon film would be used to illustrate European Clash TV features for the next two years. In addition to 'Train In Vain', the highlight is a driving 'Clampdown'. Prefaced by Mick's military salute, it benefits mightily from Mickey Gallagher's feisty organ work and the heavy echo added to Joe's vocals. It also provides Topper with his moment in the spotlight: 'Let me take you into the engine room,' announces Joe – as he had done on every night that tour – before shoving his microphone in among Topper's flailing sticks. Also worthy of note is the Mikey Dread-spiced 'Armagideon Time', which was subsequently dusted down for inclusion on the 1999 live compilation CD *From Here To Eternity*.

Immediately afterwards, though, the band were forced to heed Gavin Martin's advice and take a rest whether they wanted one or not. Earlier in February, the *NME* T-Zers page had reported that Topper had cracked 'several vertebrae in his pelvis… falling off Kosmo' while messing around, something which had limited his mobility and affected his drumming. Following the Lewisham gig, the paper's news pages reported that Topper had now torn a ligament in his hand. The remaining six dates of the tour had to be postponed until June.

Upon joining the band, not anticipating a lengthy stay, Topper had not worried overmuch about the nature of his role. Having always been something of an extrovert, he had contented himself with fooling around and having a good time, living up to the classic Crazy Drummer stereotype. In his own words, he acted like 'a poor man's Keith Moon'. 'Joe was the Spokesman, Paul was the Good-Looking Moody One, and Mick was the Sensitive Songwriter,' Topper told *Record Mirror*'s Lesley O'Toole in 1985. 'The only role left over was the Wild One, and I found myself creating an image I had to live up to. I always had to be first at the party and last to leave.'

By the 16 Tons Tour, he was out of control. The incidents reported in the music press were not the only ones that occurred on the tour. Johnny Green says the reason Donald was bailed in Dundee and taken along for the ride was because he had 'taken the rap' for Topper over some now-forgotten transgression the previous night. In Pluto Studios, according to Jeremy Green, Topper threw a bottle through the control room window, substantially increasing the impoverished band's bill from that establishment. That the Southsea bust only found him to be in possession of pills prescribed to ease the pain in his lower back was more a question of luck than self-denial. At the end of 1979, Topper and his new girlfriend – who, against all reasonable odds, was, like the previous one, named Dee – had moved into a rented flat on Fulham Road, close to the junction with Fulham Palace Road. It was here, following the Lewisham Odeon show, that the incident which finally scuppered the closing shows of the 16 Tons Tour took place. Support act Joe Ely was told that the drummer sustained his hand injury while challenging an intruder. The confusion over the exact nature of the damage sustained – subsequent music press reports would describe it as a broken finger or a broken thumb – suggested that the true story was being withheld. Topper's flat was Party Central, an open house, and he was hanging around with drug users, drug dealers and petty criminals. In May 1982, Joe finally admitted to the *NME*'s Charles Shaar Murray that Topper had in fact been stabbed in the hand with a pair of scissors during the course of an altercation.

The Clash's much-trumpeted show-must-go-on pride had required all four of them to take the stage with illnesses and injuries ranging from split lips to hepatitis. Paul had been bawled out for turning up an hour late for one show in America; that Topper's behaviour necessitated the rescheduling of six entire gigs did not inspire the others to take it easy on him. Clash buddy Joe Ely had been let down badly, though on 24 February Mick and Joe did make amends by joining his band on-stage for the encores at their Hope and Anchor show. More importantly, and – in the wake of the *Nationwide* report – more embarrassingly, Topper had undermined the Clash's credibility with their UK fans.

The intention had been to get the Clash Singles Bonanza underway in late February or early March, but this too hit a snag: CBS head Maurice Oberstein took upon himself to intervene. He disliked both 'Bankrobber' and Mikey Dread's bass-heavy production, and refused to allow the single's release. Once again, the Clash's efforts to seduce Britain had resulted in frustration.

Editing of the Buzzy film project had taken the best part of 1979, with relatively little involvement from the band. At the end of the year, Dave Mingay and Jack Hazan arranged a special showing of what they had now officially titled *Rude Boy* for the Clash and the Blackhill team. It was not a success. Before the screening, Joe had still been talking up the forthcoming film to the music press. Following the screening, the Clash camp announced that the movie would never be shown in its current form. Buzzy carried on regardless, giving the film its premiere at the Zoo Palast on 27 February 1980 as an official British entry at that year's Berlin Film Festival. The Clash refused to attend, but – despite having been refused permission by Mick – Johnny and Baker did go.

Reviews were mixed, with the mainstream press being predictably less susceptible to the film's charms than the music press. The *Daily Mail*'s film critic, Margaret Hinxman, asked 'MUST WE SHOW OFF THIS FOUL VIEW OF BRITAIN?' The *Observer*'s gossip columnist, Tom Davies, was so incensed that he punched Dave Mingay in the eye. The *NME*'s Neil Norman described the film as 'an innovative piece of cinematic art... a genuine cri de coeur for a generation already on the retreat.' Although not prepared to go that far, *Sounds*' Phil Sutcliffe believed 'there's obviously a clear plan behind it.' *Melody Maker*'s Paolo Hewitt was less convinced this was the case. Like Phil, though, he found it highly ironic that the Clash, of all bands, should be distancing themselves from a film with such a strong political message.

The musical content failed to make much of an impression on the majority of older reviewers from the national press. An exception was the *Guardian*'s Derek Malcolm who, despite referring to the band as the Slash – presumably unintentionally – declared that 'musically, at least, the film is extraordinary... there could not be a better advertisement for them or their records'. Almost everyone in the music press agreed with him that the film was a fine document of the Clash as a performing band. The first UK showing of *Rude Boy* – falsely described as the world premiere – was scheduled for 13 March at the Prince Charles cinema, off Leicester Square. The Clash responded by taking out an injunction in an attempt to prevent the film being seen. Bearing in mind their own history of conflict with CBS over artistic control – and especially the then-current impasse regarding 'Bankrobber' – their actions seemed both surprising and hard to justify.

Over the years since, three reasons have been given for the Clash's sudden antipathy to *Rude Boy*. The first, offered at the time of the injunction, was business-related. In February 1980, a spokesman for the band told the *NME* that the film was 'virtually a pirate'. If the Clash had truly believed this to be the case, they would not have continued to co-operate with the project throughout 1979. Back in October 1978, just before he was sacked by the band, Bernie Rhodes had put the previously verbal contract with Dave and Jack in writing. Buzzy had been given full copyright and artistic control. That the Clash themselves had not signed this document goes some way to supporting their insistence that they did not know of its existence. However, by the start of 1980, the band had already received £2,550 of the £4,000 the document guaranteed them – along with the promise of 10 per cent of net profits over £25,000 – which suggests a degree of acceptance of terms.

It was Blackhill who were unhappy with the legacy Bernie had left the band vis-à-vis the Buzzy project. Peter Jenner and Andrew King were appalled by how little was in it, financially speaking, for their charges. Blackhill might not have had much direct influence over the Clash, but the band were even more wary of being exploited by outside agencies than they were of being railroaded by their management team. Under the circumstances, it was easy for Kosmo to work on the band's paranoia and feed them the Blackhill line. Kosmo himself had no great enthusiasm for the film. It predated his involvement with the band, and the only role it offered him was that of saboteur after the event.

The second explanation concerned some of the non-Clash-related footage. The band claimed to be offended by the scenes depicting black pickpockets being arrested and intimidated by police. 'They were shown dipping into pockets, and then they were shown being done for something, and that was their only role in the film. And that's a one-way view,' Joe told *Melody Maker*'s Paolo Hewitt in December 1980. 'That's what the right wing use: all blacks are muggers, which is a load of rubbish.' The pick-pocketing footage was among the first shot for the film, predating the Clash's own involvement, so it is hard to see how its existence could have come as such a last minute surprise to the band. It is even more difficult to credit Joe's reading of the intent behind its inclusion: Dave and Jack were hardly racist or even right wing in outlook. Plus, by his own admission, Joe's lyrics for both 'White Riot' and '(White Man) In Hammersmith Palais' were themselves at least partly inspired by black would-be muggers, and he was appalled whenever *they* were misconstrued to be propagating racial stereotypes.

Joe's bluster could not hide the Clash of 1980's evident discomfort with the Clash of two years previously. 'They got alarmed by what they were doing, and that applies to everything from the political stance to the death of Sid Vicious,' says Dave. 'If you confront the "ideas of today", then you find you're in a very hot seat.' He sees the band's need to overcome their financial problems and break America as the principal reasons for their efforts to play down the political element in their own output and for their disowning of the film.

The third reason, posited by Dave Mingay to Johnny Green and recorded in the latter's *A Riot Of Our Own*, was that certain members of the band, particularly Mick, were unhappy with the way they came across in the film. The general standard of 'acting' is indeed embarrassingly poor, but Dave suggested that Mick was required to face the greatest discrepancy between self-image and screen image. Johnny wonders whether this gulf might have been deliberately created by the Buzzy team. 'Dave and Jack got sick of Mick playing the rock star early on. It was not what they had been led to expect. I think what you see in the film is the result of their low opinion of Mick. There was some really nice stuff of him in the rushes, but that all ended up on the cutting room floor.' Dave allows that he had 'endless problems' with the 'really difficult' Mick, but cites all the incriminating material he and Jack chose to leave out as proof that no personal attack or stitch-up was intended.

Rude Boy proved to be a big hit on the Continent, particularly in France. 'It's very good with subtitles,' says Dave. 'The lyrics of the songs running along the bottom explain and illustrate the content of the film. You can see how appropriate, or ironic, or even hilarious, the whole thing is. The Clash's opposition to the film spoiled things in Britain. Their support was crucial.' Even more crucial to the film's financial success would have been the simultaneous release of the largely live soundtrack album. Predictably, that was also vetoed, though Dave believes CBS may well have been as much to blame as the band for its non-appearance.

Although there were few UK screenings of the film during 1980 and the years immediately following, *Rude Boy* has gone on to enjoy a long and healthy life on video. As a visual record of the Clash live on-stage in 1977-78 it is unparalleled, capturing all the moves and the passion, if not quite the original sound. A soundtrack album of sorts might have seen the light of day in 1990, when Dave Mingay was approached by Kosmo – of all people – and asked if the Clash could use material from *Rude Boy* for a forthcoming live album. In the event, that project mutated into the band retrospective *Clash On Broadway*, released in 1991. By this time it featured just one track from the film, 'I Fought The Law', as recorded on 28 December 1978 at the Lyceum, plus 'English Civil War', filmed and recorded by Buzzy at the same venue but not included in the movie. When the inevitable Clash live album, *From Here To Eternity*, did finally emerge in 1999, just three tracks were used from the *Rude Boy* soundtrack: 'I Fought the Law' again, 'London's Burning' from the 30 April 1978 Anti-Nazi Rally in Victoria Park, plus 'What's My Name' from the 27 July 1978 gig at the Music Machine. Another track, 'City Of The Dead' had been filmed and recorded by Buzzy at the 28 December 1978 Lyceum gig, but had not been included in the movie. A terse sleeve note acknowledges that 'some instrumental overdubs' have been added to the three *Rude Boy* tracks 'to repair technical deficiencies on the original live recordings'.

For all its limitations and rough edges, there is more to *Rude Boy* than a series of bravura Clash performances. In retrospect, the film's greatest achievement is in portraying the end of an era and anticipating the mood of a new one. The left/right, black/white tensions highlighted throughout the movie, and in the Clash's lyrics of 1977-78, evoke the spectre of extremist and/or terrorist groups taking over the political arena. In the event, the threat would not come from the likes of the National Front or some as yet unidentified paramilitary agents of the extreme right, but from within the ranks of the existing political system: namely the radical right wing of the Conservative Party.

The film closes with footage of Margaret Thatcher arriving in Downing Street on 4 May 1979 to assume power. Early in the movie, Ray argues with Joe that the right is preferable to the left, because at least they are honest about their intentions. He says he cares little if they divide the population into haves and have-nots because he – a man with no obviously marketable skills, acting included – aspires to be one of the haves, a fat cat driving around in a Rolls Royce. Thatcher and her cohorts would play upon this self-delusional facet of working class materialism as they set about dismantling the unions, the welfare state and other bastions of solidarity and community, in the process effectively dividing and conquering the opposition. In Thatcher's Britain there would be no readily accessible platform for a new equivalent of the punk movement: little cheap housing, fewer squats, less subsidised public transport, no dole-as-grant for bands or artists of any kind, fewer rights for everyone except employers, landlords and businessmen. By the end of the Eighties, the ultimate irony of punk would be self-evident: the underclass who in the late Seventies had complained about urban decay, lack of career opportunities, boredom, and oppression by the police and the government, had in fact had it pretty good. The underclass of the following generation would have it much, much worse.

★★★

Topper recovered from his injuries in time to play a gig in Paris on 27 February 1980, filmed for French TV, and then to fly out to the States for the band's third American tour. This visit, running from 2-10 March, was no longer than the band's first, concentrating on the key urban markets. It was so short that it was not deemed worthy of its own title, carrying on under the same label as the British dates. Barry Myers was DJ. Mickey Gallagher played organ. Mikey Dread stayed on as support, joined by female new wave band the B-Girls and soul veteran Lee Dorsey. The same basic crew were retained, including Ray Jordan, but the entourage was kept small, and most of the equipment was hired locally to keep haulage costs to a minimum. Sick of the bus, the band flew between shows. Pennie Smith went along, supplying a double page photo-journal to the *NME* as that paper's alternative document of the tour. *Rolling Stone* was also on the case, dispatching James Henke to interview the band at the Warfield Theatre in San Francisco, scene of the tour's opening show on 2 March.

A month earlier, speaking to *Sounds'* Robbi Millar about Francis Ford Coppola's 1979 film *Apocalypse Now*, Joe had said, 'You know, it doesn't leave you, it's like a dream.' Spookily, when the Clash arrived at the Warfield, the cinema next door was showing *Apocalypse Now*. It established something of a military theme for the band's stay. Their radically inclined San Franciscan buddy, Mo Armstrong, gave them a consignment of bandannas and posters he had bought from the Nicaraguan Solidarity Campaign. Each of them featured a picture of a cowboy and the logo of the left wing Sandinista freedom fighters, the FSLN (Fronte Sandinista Liberacion Nacional). The Clash loved them: style-conscious guerrilla cowboys were right up their street. Mo also supplied Joe with *The People's War* and other literature about the 19 July 1979 victory of the FSLN over Nicaragua's military dictator General Somoza, and the dictator-friendly US government's subsequent attempts to destabilise the new regime.

Before the Warfield show, Mick chatted to a fan named Freddie who was about to join the marines for 'a roof over my head and $500 a month'. Mick dedicated 'Stay Free' to him that night, and then – refusing to be discouraged by the band's experience with Donald – persuaded the Clash to employ Freddie as a roadie for the duration of the tour. It was a typically big-hearted gesture, but also a typically short-sighted one: the Clash could not afford to keep Freddie on, even at $500 a month, for the rest of his working life.

After a second night at the Warfield, the tour took in LA and Philadelphia before arriving at the New York Palladium on the 7th. Here the audience contained some of the usual celebrity suspects: Wayne Kramer, Debbie Harry, Bianca Jagger, Robert De Niro and Martin Scorsese. Following shows in Passaic, New Jersey and at the Orpheum Theatre in Boston, the 16 Tons Tour wound up on the 10th in difficult Detroit. Epic recording artist and wild man of rock Ted Nugent turned up and asked to jam. Johnny was dispatched to meet him with a pair of scissors and an offer to join the band on-stage if he was prepared to chop off his trademark mane. Ted demurred. Blackhill were pressured into writing a letter of apology the following day. 'What if someone said they wouldn't talk to Joe Strummer unless he fixed his teeth?' complained an Epic spokesperson. 'How *rude*!'

At least Joe took time to make his peace with *Creem* magazine, granting Susan Whitall a long and friendly interview to compensate for the roasting he had given Dave DiMartino in 1979. And when it came to artists they liked, the Clash proved they could show respect. Lee Dorsey was afforded a lot of time and encouragement, despite a serious drink problem and one or two unkind reviews. In the previous year's *Creem* interview, Joe had complained about the plight of one of the great soul men, Jackie Wilson, who had been in a coma in hospital since suffering a heart attack on-stage in 1975. This time around, the profits from the Clash's Detroit show were donated to help pay for Jackie's care. While in the city, Joe and Mick also made a pilgrimage to the original Motown recording studio, Hitsville USA.

In the US, *London Calling* had been released in early January 1980. The *Creem* review had been lukewarm. Billy Altman had found the apocalyptic language of the title track so explosive and challenging 'that the rest of the album's lyrics just seem to be a weak addendum to a case already stated as well as it can be… the absence of relief is wearisome'. *Rolling Stone*'s Tom Carson had been far more enthusiastic in his appraisal of the album, apparently able to recognise the use of light and shade and the flashes of humour that passed Billy Altman by. Tom positively revelled in the album's romanticism and variety, his review straying into the realms of hyperbole in its first two sentences: 'By now, our expectations of the Clash might seem to have become inflated beyond any possibility of fulfilment. It's not simply that they're the greatest rock & roll band in the world…'

On 12 February 1980 – without significant objection from the Clash – Epic had released the atypical, almost throwaway 'Train In Vain' as the US single. It became the band's first American hit, making number 23 in late April. This was certainly not due to any increase in effort on behalf of the record label, though Epic had agreed to the low album price rate of $9.98. As Fredric Dannen revealed in *Hit Men*, Dick Asher, overall Deputy Head of CBS, had his suspicions that Frank Dileo, Epic's Head of Promotion was putting more effort into pushing bands who showed their appreciation in material terms than into pushing bands who showed nothing but potential. REO Speedwagon had bought Frank an $8,000 Rolex for his work on their August 1979 album *Nine Lives*. Six months later, Frank was still more interested in squeezing a 10th life out of that record than he was in promoting the Clash album. (He would later leave Epic's employ to manage the career of Epic's highest earning artist, Michael Jackson.) Dick Asher challenged the Epic staff, 'Anybody want to bet me that the Clash album sells more ultimately than REO's album does?' There were no takers, but the Clash album certainly won on the proving ground of the American charts: *Nine Lives* peaked at number 33, *London Calling* at number 27, selling 200,000 in the first six weeks of its release (going on to sell 625,000 copies by the end of the Eighties). Which illustrates the importance of breaking America: in the smaller UK market, the Clash album reached number nine, stayed on the charts for the band's best stretch to date of 20 weeks – beating the début's number 16 and the follow-up's number 14 – and yet sold just 180,000 copies in the first year of its release.

The Clash were now considered popular enough in the US to be asked to do a commercial for the very American soft drink Dr Pepper. They could have used the money, but refused to advertise on principal. Of more interest to them was an approach that followed on from Martin Scorsese's attendance at their Palladium gig. One of the director's projects in development was a film based upon *Gangs Of New York*, Herbert Asbury's history, first published in 1928, of the Italian and Irish gangs who had regularly rioted and sacked New York during the period of the Civil War. Marty asked the band if they would be interested in contributing, both to the soundtrack and, possibly, as actors. Given their numerous shared interests, the Clash were keen to collaborate, but the project was still in its early stages, and everything was left hanging for the time being.

Part of the reason the American tour had been so short, and the postponed UK dates had been put back so far, was that Paul had already been offered a film role. *Ladies And Gentlemen, The Fabulous Stains* (aka *All Washed Up*), directed by Lou Adler, with a script by Nancy Dowd – previously responsible for the acclaimed 1978 Vietnam veteran movie *Coming Home* – is the story of an all-female American band called the Fabulous Stains. Paul's part was not too demanding – he was to play John, a member of a male English rock'n'roll band, alongside British actor Ray Winstone and ex-Sex Pistols Steve

Jones and Paul Cook – but his presence was required on set in Vancouver for six weeks from 11 March. Although Paul later described making the film as a 'good experience', Nancy Dowd walked off set three days before the shoot was completed, and the movie failed to make an impact. It was never given a full release in the UK.

The 16 Tons Tour proved to be DJ Barry Myers's last with the Clash, for reasons at least partly due to his preferred means of relaxation. Johnny Green's appetite for drink, drugs and adventure had also long been at odds with Blackhill's professionalism. Furthermore, Kosmo had usurped the more creative aspects of Johnny's role, and the band were now too cosseted for his liking. Dissatisfied with his lot, he accepted an offer to work with Joe Ely in Texas. He informed first the management and then the individual Clash members of his decision on the plane to Detroit. He was disappointed when Joe, who he considered to be a close friend, took the news in his stride. 'He just went, "Yeah, all right." I thought, "Cheers, mate! Talk me into staying, why don't you?!" But that was very Joe. He was always the loner.' If anything, Johnny was even more surprised by the reaction of Mick, with whom he had never enjoyed a particularly warm relationship. 'It was Mick who was the caring one, who had a long hard talk with me about it.' Mott the Hoople, Mick's model for the rock'n'roll life, had kept the same crew throughout their existence. Mick was also big on personal loyalty: after losing two parents and several bands, he did not take abandonment lightly.

Joe and Mick had been thinking about helping out with the recording of the new Joe Ely album, but that fell through. Instead, the Clash, minus Paul, booked into New York's Iroquois Hotel – having heard that James Dean used to stay there – and took advantage of their recent rise in status to prise some money out of their record company to record some material of their own. The previous year, Ian Hunter had recorded his fourth solo album *You're Never Alone With A Schizophrenic* at the Power Station, on 53rd Street, and it was possibly on his recommendation that Mick and the Clash booked a couple of days there.

The idea was to record some cover versions for fun, and maybe sketch out a couple of songs from scratch with Bill Price and Mikey Dread for release as future instalments in the Singles Bonanza. After recording a version of the Equals' 'Police On My Back', though, they felt they were beginning to get into a groove. The Power Station was fully booked for the next few days, so the Clash phoned Jimi Hendrix's old studio, Electric Lady, on 8th Street. In January 1976, this was where Ian Hunter had recorded his second solo album, *All American Alien Boy*. A three week block of sessions was available. The Clash took it, and moved their base camp to the Gramercy Park Hotel for the duration.

Mickey Gallagher was asked to fly back over from the UK and bring Blockheads bassist Norman Watt-Roy with him. Norman stayed for five days, after which the three remaining Clash members shared the bass playing duties on new material among themselves. 'We'd always make up lines in Paul's style,' Joe told the *New York Rocker*'s Richard Grabel at the end of recording, none too convincingly. Mick bumped into Joe's old busking partner Tymon Dogg on a Manhattan street corner, and invited him along to the first session, where the Clash-Blockheads aggregate backed him on his eccentric composition, 'Lose This Skin'. Tymon released it as a single that June on the Ghost Dance label. Following Tymon's departure, the others warmed up on the Spencer Davis Group's 'Every Little Bit Hurts'. Mick used to play the song with Chrissie Hynde at Wilmcote House four years previously, and was reminded of it when Chrissie called around to visit him at the Gramercy Park Hotel.

After the cover versions, things began to get a little more experimental. Almost certainly as a direct response to criticisms of the retrogressive tendencies of their 1979 recordings, the Clash and friends now started to go in every direction imaginable. They hardly left the studio, working through into the early morning day after day. Much of the material recorded over the next three weeks was written on the spot, and developed from jams. This is perhaps at its most evident in the loose skiffle sound of 'Junkie Slip' and the mellow jazzy reggae of 'Broadway'. In keeping with the spirit of proceedings, Joe improvised lyrics for both tunes as they were being recorded. The former indicates how much Topper's drug problem was playing on his mind, while the latter free-associates about the past life of a Manhattan down-and-out.

Excited by this spontaneous approach, Joe had the engineers wipe the squeaky toy background to Mikey's Pluto-recorded 'Shepherds Delight' and replaced it with a double-tracked rambling stream-of-consciousness about New York and Electric Lady which he gave the new title 'If Music Could Talk'. In Johnny Green's absence, tour lighting man Warren Steadman had stepped in as all-purpose gofer and spliff-maker, quickly earning himself the nickname Stoner for his pains. Rather than sit with the others in the sometimes overcrowded control room between takes, Joe built his own private bunker out of flight cases in the main studio. It was not unlike the hidey-hole he and Gary Hardy had fashioned out of lockers at ENO back in 1974. Here, Joe would work on lyrical ideas and – as he freely admits in 'If Music Could Talk' – smoke ganja in what consequently came to be known as the Spliffbunker. The Clash's in-studio intake of the drug had always been considerable, but Mikey Dread's arrival on the scene had nudged it up to a level that could only be described as prodigious.

While in New York, the band picked up on the still relatively new hip hop scene, tuning in to the cutting edge WBLS station. Ears as ever open to new sounds, Mick was particularly keen, and went out scouting for the records. Hip hop was then still at its nascent treated-funk-with-rap stage, which Joe recognised owed a debt to dub's treated-reggae-with-toast. Nor was rapping a million miles away from the extemporised vocals with which he was already experimenting. He was as keen to give it a go as Mick. Norman Watt-Roy had been recruited with this direction in mind: his work with the Blockheads demonstrated what an impressively fluid and funky bassist he was.

Built on a tape loop of a Watt-Roy bass riff, 'The Magnificent Seven' – originally entitled 'Magnificent Seven Rappo-Clappers' – is the Clash's tribute to the Sugarhill Gang. Joe borrows the title from the famous Western movie, but probably had in mind the full-strength skanking posse on the UK leg of the 16 Tons Tour. His mischievous rap juxtaposes the fates of the world's great free-thinkers with his own experiences of the capitalist system's daily grind: yet another angle from which he could approach his crusade against wage slavery. Japanese corporations like Honda and Sony – both namechecked – made their staff sing the company worksong each morning; 'The Magnificent Seven' is an anti-worksong, 'Career Opportunities' and 'Clampdown' played for laughs.

Everyone enjoyed the exercise so much that they did much the same again with 'Lightning Strikes (Not Once But Twice)'. Only this time the music is a kind of dub-funk hybrid, and Joe's rap is another 'If Music Could Talk'-type self-indulgent ad lib, rhapsodising at length about multi-cultural New York before almost guiltily squeezing in a mention of the Westway at the end. Joe would later claim that the New York influence was inevitable: there was a transit strike while the band were in the city, which meant they had to walk the many blocks between the hotel and studio each day, forcing them to soak up the atmosphere whether they liked it or not.

Mikey Dread was not as impressed with the Sugarhill Gang as either Mick or Joe. Responding to the rap outfit's 'Rapper's Delight', he wrote 'Rockers Delight', which puts them down in no uncertain terms – 'strictly chatting and tripe' – and extols the primacy of reggae. Mikey's distaste for the UK Ska Revival surfaces in another Clash-Dread collaboration. The general gist of 'Living In Fame' is that bands should make more of an effort to live up to their names. According to the lyric, the Specials are not that special, the Selecter do not put enough thought into selecting their material, and Madness are not crazy enough. Running out of ska groups, Mikey goes on to remark that Shane MacGowan's Nipple Erectors fail to do much for him either, before (diplomatically) proclaiming that at least the Clash get it right.

Mikey's musical influence is also evident on the Clash's own reggae track 'One More Time', the lyric for which depicts the cycle of poverty and violence to which the mostly black inhabitants of America's inner city ghettos are condemned. Relatively Mikey-free, 'The Call Up' features guest guitar from a former member of Richard Hell's Voidoids, Ivan Julian, and bookends a reggae tune with the Marines' marching song. The lyric finds Joe in 'Spanish Bombs' mode, using the slightly archaic, romantic imagery of folk songs to add historical weight to a contemporary concern. In this case, his subject is the senselessness of young people wasting their lives at war – and, indeed, work – at the behest of uncaring and manipulative political leaders. Joe's initial inspiration was Freddie, the wannabe-Marine turned Clash roadie. As Mick recalled in the *Clash On Broadway* booklet, though, registration for the draft was generally 'a big deal' in the States at the time, that year's Presidential Election Campaign having turned it into a live issue.

Some of the material recorded at Electric Lady conforms to more recognisable song structures, even if it is by no means four-square rock'n'roll. Joe's love affair with American folk culture finds perhaps its ultimate voice on 'Version City', a funky R&B paean to US roots music and the mythical train that provided so much inspiration for that music's lyrics and rhythms. The subjects of sin and temptation drive the pseudo-gospel number 'The Sounds Of The Sinners', which affectionately lampoons its religious subject matter and yet puts some real conviction into its evocation of forthcoming Armageddon. Some reviewers and interviewers were prompted to wonder whether Joe had got religion for real. 'I was just thinking that a spiritual solution is just as important as a social solution,' Joe told *Melody Maker*'s Paolo Hewitt later that year. 'Just solely talking about economics like, say, Marx did, I don't think it's enough.'

Almost inevitably, *Apocalypse Now* found its way into one of the new songs. The title, chorus and general tone of the lyric for 'Charlie Don't Surf' are drawn from a remark made by Robert Duvall's battle-crazed officer during the film. Charlie was US military slang for the Viet Cong (from the radio call sign Victor Charlie). A synthesizer drone recreates the sound of whirring chopper blades. Like 'The Call Up', the song is anti-war, and takes a global perspective. But the ironic approach gives more punch to its attack on those who impose their religious and political beliefs on other people; especially the super powers whose machinations run the risk of bringing about apocalypse soon.

The interview James Henke had conducted with the Clash at the start of the American tour ran as the cover feature for the 17 April 1980 edition of *Rolling Stone* under the title 'Rebels With A Cause And A Hit Album'. James's story rehashed the Clash myth for the mainstream American rock market, acknowledging that the band had finally broken through in that country. The lead quote, from Paul Simonon, again tried to avoid pigeon-holing with regard to politics. 'When people say that we're a political band, what they usually mean, I gather, is that we're political in the way of, like, left and right. Politics with a capital P, right? But really, it's politics with a small p, like personal politics. When somebody says, "You can't do that!" we think you should stand up and ask why, and not go, "Well, all right."' Although not published for another two months, Susan Whitall's *Creem* interview more than compensated for her magazine's poor review of *London Calling*: 'What other band has so successfully absorbed the music of so many cultures, digested it, and emerged with a startling, evocative language of their own?'

On 24 April, following Paul's return from his filming commitments, the Clash made their début US TV appearance on the ABC show *Fridays*. With Joe and Paul showing off their new cropped hair – somewhere between suedehead and army crew cut – and Mick's guitar set to effects overkill, they perform live versions of 'London Calling', 'Train In Vain' and 'Guns Of Brixton', with first Joe, then Mick, then Paul taking centre stage at the microphone. Then Joe and Mick team up for a mighty 'Clampdown'. Take that, America.

The Clash star might have been in the ascendancy in the US, but things looked much less positive on the home front. The argument over 'Bankrobber' had dragged on all through March and April. Partly as a way of hitting back at CBS, the Clash started talking about using the Electric Lady material to form the basis of another cut-price double album. In no mood to go back to Britain, they resolved to record even more material. Sticking by their choice of producer for the shelved single, the Clash flew with Mikey Dread to Kingston, Jamaica, for further sessions at Channel One studios.

Paul was delighted to make it to Jamaica at last, but his pleasure was short-lived. The sessions were quickly and forcibly abandoned following demands for money with menaces from representatives of the local music business scene, who believed a big name rock'n'roll band should be able to afford a little baksheesh. It was a long way from the truth: by this time the band were living on the credit card of Paul's girlfriend, Debbie. Much to their annoyance, CBS had to wire them enough money to make good their escape. All the band had to show for the visit was one incomplete track: the reggae-fied version of the old 101ers R&B standard 'Junco Partner', perhaps intended as another wake up call for Topper. The namecheck Joe squeezes in for his 'sweet Gabriella' could be seen as a sign that Joe was beginning to soften up on the issue of romantic lyrics… if it were not for the fact that, in the guise of the titular junky, he is envisaging pawning her for enough money to score.

In mid May 1980, the Clash returned to the Continent for more live dates. Punk had finally caught on in Europe in a big way, but again, Joe believed, too much attention was being paid to the superficial trappings at the expense of the true spirit. 'It's nothing but a complete 1976 Revival… just another fashion,' he told the *NME*'s Roy Carr later that year. 'It's become everything it wasn't supposed to be. And what we were confronted with was junior punks in their expensive designer uniforms with concrete heads and no ears.'

Having to deal with yet another wave of criticism for selling out their original punk style and principles finally proved too much for Joe on 20 May, at the Markthalle gig in Hamburg, Germany. He became so incensed by the antics of one particularly aggressive audience member – who was 'using the guy in front of him as a punch bag' – that he leaned out and swiped him across the head with his Telecaster. After the gig, Joe was arrested, and was freed only when a breathalyser test proved negative. He had not felt particularly guilty following his altercation with Mick backstage in Sheffield, but on this occasion he did express remorse. 'I nearly murdered somebody, and it made me realise that you can't face violence with violence. It doesn't work.'

Clash fan Adrian Whittaker, based in Hamburg at the time, attended the gig. 'Hamburg then had a strong, politicised anarcho-punk scene with some very heavy squats in continual conflict with the police,' he recalls. It was these squat-dwellers who came to the Markthalle en masse to crash the gig and berate the band for abandoning punk's values. 'They tried to get in free, couldn't, sat down in the main road outside and brought traffic to a standstill. They got cleared away by riot police and, tempers fraying, besieged the doors again.' Although the show had already sold out, someone decided to let them in.

'The dance floor was a seething pit of pogoing and fighting bodies. There were sorties onto the stage during early numbers to grab the mikes and make speeches along the lines of "The Clash aren't playing for revolution, they're playing for CBS!"' Despite the fact the interlopers hadn't paid to get in, Mick offered them their money back. Joe challenged them to form their own bands if they were so unhappy with the Clash.

'Mikes and stands started disappearing from the stage – possibly to start those new bands – eventually leaving the three frontmen clustered around one mike,' says Adrian. 'One particular guy was screaming at the crowd to have a go at Joe – according to the paper the next day, he was shouting "Bringt ihn um!" (" Kill him!") – as well as hitting all and sundry around him. It was this guy who Joe walloped, and fairly understandably, I reckon. It calmed down slightly then, but the Clash never really recovered their composure.' The show produced one of the more widely circulated and infamous bootlegs to emerge during the band's lifetime, *Clash In Hamburg* – the Clash's equivalent to Iggy and the Stooges' *Metallic KO* – which came wrapped in German newspaper reports of the event and carrying a declaration that the 'CBS schweine' would not see a pfennig of the profits.

Adrian feels that, in personalising the conflict – making it an incident between himself and one unruly audience member – Joe was misplacing his regret, and, whether intentionally or not, drawing attention away from the real issue. Three to four years behind the times they might have been, but the Hamburg punks of 1980 were by no means 'expensive designer' fakes. They were not only displaying the attitudes but also living for real the lifestyle the Clash had promoted on their first two albums and in *Rude Boy*; a lifestyle with which, despite Joe's insistence on continuing to encore with 'White Riot', the band apparently no longer wanted to be associated.

The contretemps evidently took its toll. Part of the 1 June show at the Piazza Maggiore in Bologna was broadcast on Italian TV, but one has to question the progammers' judgement. Mick fights a losing battle with his effects pedals throughout 'Tommy Gun', 'I'm So Bored With The USA' and 'Complete Control', producing a squalling, nerve-shredding row.

The European tour finished shortly afterwards, but was immediately followed by the UK dates which had been postponed when Topper damaged his hand. Mikey Dread had been pencilled in as a support act, but now he wanted the Clash to pay for him to bring a full backing band over from Jamaica, something which they simply could not afford. A falling-out ensued, and Mikey was replaced by rockabilly band Whirlwind. The situation was a sticky one, and not just because of Mikey's production contribution to so much of the Clash's recent work. With organisational help from Blackhill and Stiff, Kosmo Vinyl had just set up his own label, its name borrowed from Mikey's former radio show, Dread At The Controls. Kosmo had scored a personal coup by using the Clash's Martin Scorsese connection to secure the UK rights for the director's *Mean Streets* soundtrack album. The label's main function, however, was to release material either recorded by Mikey – like the June single release of 'Rockers Delight' – or leased with Mikey's aid from Jamaican record labels.

Chris Bohn's *NME* review of the rescheduled 17 June Hammersmith Palais gig did nothing to take the bad taste of the European tour away: 'At times the Clash appear so immersed in their own myth it's difficult for them and us to see each other straight. Ever conscious of their future position in the history books, they've fashioned their collective rock'n'roll persona to fit it even more perfectly since their American tour, where their less threatening traditional approach has now won them lots of new friends… While their music has been enriched by the assimilation of their roots, it does make them more conservative.'

The UK dates kept the band occupied until the end of June. By then, 'Bankrobber' had still not received an official UK release. The Clash had managed to sneak it out earlier that month as the B-side of the Dutch release of 'Train In Vain', though, and import copies were making their way into Britain. The band derived considerable pleasure from this scam, but CBS could and did go one better. For at least the past year, the Clash had kept their spirits up by telling themselves they had only two more albums to deliver before they were free of CBS for good. However, lurking previously undetected in the small print of the Clash's contract as approved by Bernie Rhodes was a sub-clause allowing the record company an option on a further five albums, which option they now elected to take up.

Exhausted after months of non-stop touring and studio work, the band had intended to take July off anyway – as long ago as the March American dates, Joe had sprayed the legend 'I MAY TAKE A HOLIDAY' onto his white Esquire – but they made sure the music press got the impression they were downing tools in protest at the 'Bankrobber' situation. Within a matter of weeks, Joe was brushing off rumours that the band had seriously considered splitting, but it was certainly a particularly low point in what had always been a fraught career.

Mick went to New York to be with his new girlfriend Ellen Foley. Meatloaf's vocal foil on the bestselling 1977 album *Bat Out Of Hell*, Ellen shared a management company, Cleveland International, with both Meat and Ian Hunter. Consequently, her début solo album *Nightout* had been co-produced in spring 1979 by Ian and Mick Ronson. Ellen had been introduced to Mick during the Clash's Electric Lady sessions, and she had expressed interest in singing on the new Clash album. As she was also signed to CBS-Epic, it was decided that her new boyfriend should produce her follow-up album. Ellen returned to London with Mick in early August. In the meantime, Joe produced some material for London R&B band the Little Roosters.

CBS finally gave 'Bankrobber', backed with 'Rockers Galore... UK Tour', a UK release on 8 August 1980. Reviewing it for the *NME*, the previously pro-Clash Paul Morley objected to the record's sentiments, and concluded, 'I just wish the Clash would go wild, and smash out of those strenuous traditionalist restrictions.' In *Sounds*, the single was dismissed as deathly slow, dreary stuff, the lyric's sub-text ignored, and Joe's claim that his daddy was a bankrobber held up for ridicule: 'Actually, John Mellor's daddy was a Second Secretary Of Information at the Foreign Office. One of my mates' daddies was a bankrobber, and he ended up in little pieces after a gangland feud.' As ever, the band refused to play *Top Of The Pops*. So Pan's People danced to the song behind bars, attired in gangster hats and slightly less conceptually relevant one-piece striped bathing costumes, black tights and high heels... Despite this, the single made it to number 12. The Clash chose to see it as a victory, but the six month delay in its release had killed the concept of the Singles Bonanza stone dead. That it was a great idea gone to waste was proved over a decade later when the considerably less commercially obvious band the Wedding Present resurrected it and made the *Guinness Book Of Records* with 12 hits in as many months.

The reason for CBS's capitulation over 'Bankrobber' soon became evident. Following the success of the band's albums in the US, Epic had taken note of the demand for Clash import material, and were keen to exploit it. The project they mooted was a 10-inch compilation album of odds and sods previously unavailable on that side of the Atlantic, to go by the apposite title *Black Market Clash*. On this album, the UK début album version of 'Cheat' was to be joined by the original 'Capital Radio' from the *NME* EP, and early single B-sides 'City Of The Dead', 'The Prisoner' and 'Pressure Drop'. 'Armagideon Time' and its twin dubs, 'Justice Tonight/Kick It Over' were also to be included, along with 'Bankrobber' – still unreleased in the US – and 'Robber Dub', originally intended for the never-released UK 12-inch single. 'Rockers Galore... UK Tour' was left off, probably because it was by now out of date. To add extra spice, and make up the numbers, that August found Bill Price remixing the band's previously unreleased March 1978 version of Booker T and the MGs' 'Time Is Tight'.

That project sorted out, the band reconvened at Wessex to work on the material for their fourth album release proper. Establishing exactly what was recorded during these sessions, and when, is close to impossible. Recording segued straight in from *Black Market Clash* and straight out into the Ellen Foley album, which would use much the same personnel. Although Mikey Dread was present in the studio at this time, engineer Jerry Green only recalls working with him on material for the Dread At The Controls label. He believes that, although he would be given a 'version mix' credit on the new Clash album, Mikey only performed this function on tracks recorded *before* the band moved to Wessex, and did not contribute further following the row over the postponed UK tour dates. Jerry is probably mistaken. Mikey had made up with the band, having joined them onstage for the encore at the 17 June Hammersmith Palais gig. Paul Simonon certainly played bass on a Dread single around this time, as well as on several tracks that would see release on Mikey's 1981 album *World War III*. Matters are confused by the fact that, during the album sessions at Wessex, the Clash continued to work on the 30 or so tracks – some nearly complete, some the most basic of backing track sketches – recorded at Pluto, the Record Plant, Channel One and especially Electric Lady, several of which had already involved Mikey's participation. Although not present on all the finished album's reggae and dub tracks, Mikey nevertheless maintains enough of a presence overall to suggest that he continued to contribute right up until the project's completion.

Even the wholly new songs were not recorded systematically. The Clash were still working experimentally, recording as they wrote. Jerry recalls that a fresh batch of backing tracks would be taped, then the band's attention would turn to older material, before returning to the overdubbing of the recent backing tracks, or even moving on again to the recording of yet another fresh batch. Bill Price tended to oversee the recording of new backing tracks, and Jerry the recording of overdubs. Blurring the picture further was the non-stop intensity Mick and Joe in particular brought to the sessions. Initially, these began at 2 pm and ended around 4 or 5 am, but they began to lose shape as August turned into September. 'It got to the stage where we'd managed to click our way around the clock several times,' says Jerry, who woke up in his flat around the corner from the studio at four one morning to find Joe, anxious to get to work, standing next to his bed. 'I'll tell you, I thought I was having a fucking nightmare!'

The recording process involved Mick at every stage: he co-wrote the songs, arranged them, played on the backing tracks, sang vocals and backing vocals, taped numerous guitar and piano overdubs, and directed the other production work with Bill and Jerry. 'Mick was the one with the overall masterplan,' says Jerry. 'Every track was written down with every overdub that would be needed to be done on it. If it was done and acceptable, it was noted in a certain colour, and if it wasn't quite right, it was noted in another colour.' Joe was involved at slightly fewer stages, but could always occupy himself writing lyrics for the growing stockpile of new material.

Paul and Topper, though, found their services were mostly only required at a relatively early point in the development of each song, and the lack of a coherent overall work schedule made for lengthy periods spent just hanging around. For Paul, it was always easy to relax – in fact, his ability to sleep anywhere at any time would be a visual joke running throughout Pennie Smith's late 1980 Clash photobook *Before And After* – but for the hyperactive Topper it was impossible. Bored, he proved easy prey to the dealers who hung around his Fulham Road flat. His new girlfriend was an intravenous heroin user, and Topper soon followed suit. Johnny Green, back in the country, visited him around this time and nearly spiked himself on a syringe left lying on an armchair. At Wessex, Topper copied Joe's flight case bunker idea, but while Joe spent most of his time in his with pen and paper, Topper, according to Jerry Green, 'would be out the back with tubes and pipes and goodness knows what, doing what he was doing'. What he was doing was getting himself in such a state that he could barely sit upright behind his drums. 'Before, he'd had that natural ability to make his drums talk, almost,' says Jerry. 'Come certain things during those sessions, it was down to the bass drum, snare and hi-hat. Y'know, nice and safe. He could keep time in that, didn't have to get out of pattern, get out of tempo, wouldn't have to think.'

The drummer's decline was an open secret in the music business. The *NME*'s gossip pages had started making digs about Topper's drug problem in the 12 July issue, reporting that he was 'sickly, his continued bad health being the cause of some band friction'. The following week's paper 'retracted' the statement by saying 'it was apparently news to both Topper and his mum, who rang up concerned after reading T-Zers, as is her habit'. Emphasis on the final word. In September, the paper recounted the story of a prank staged by the Blockheads: after appearing on *Top Of The Pops* to perform 'I Want To Be Straight' dressed as policemen, they had driven directly up to Wessex, stormed in the back door and besieged the control booth. Topper, it was reported, panicked and ran, and 'was last seen wearing a hopelessly false beard and reading a paper upside down in the Gatwick departure lounge, sweating profusely'.

'I tried to get the band to do something about Topper,' Peter Jenner told the *NME*'s Len Brown in 1989, 'and I was told to fuck off and mind my own business.' Despite this response to what they perceived to be yet more managerial interference, the other members of the Clash were just as concerned. They also recognised that it would be hypocritical to deliver ultimatums: it was not as though they themselves were practising abstinence. According to Jerry Green, when the Blockheads staged their 'police raid', it was Mick – enveloped in his habitual ganja cloud – who came closest to having a heart attack. Towards the end of September, Joe was busted yet again near Kings Cross station. Members of the SPG detained him under the sus law, and made him take them back to his flat. Here, according to the *NME* news report, they discovered three ounces of home-grown marijuana. He was duly fined £100. 'We were always a drug band,' Joe admitted to the *NME*'s Sean O'Hagen in 1988. '*Always.*'

The messiness of the album's making is masked to some extent by the abandonment of the traditional Strummer-Jones composer credit in favour of attributing all original material to the entire band. 'They said, "What we'll do is make the credit 'the Clash', and we'll split all the money four ways," so I thought, "OK, fair enough,"' Topper told *Melody Maker*'s Mick Mercer in 1985. But the democratic gesture only extended as far as the album's liner notes and label. 'When it came to the next business meeting it was decided the money should be shared out among the people who wrote the songs, so it meant people never realised that I wrote songs for the Clash.' Specifically, he claimed that he and Joe co-wrote 'The Magnificent Seven', and that he and Mick co-wrote most of the other music recorded at Electric Lady, with Topper, in addition to drums, contributing piano, guitar and bass to some tracks. Conversely, the communal credit also hid the extent to which his input tailed off at Wessex.

That said, he is the sole musical composer of the disco-funk 'Ivan Meets GI Joe', which he also sings. Talking about the prospect of the draft to *Rolling Stone*'s James Henke, Mick had stated, 'This is an important fact: people prefer to dance than to fight wars.' Joe's lyric works off both the disco rhythm and the electronic Space Invader bleeps that power the song. It namechecks former Clash disco haunts Le Palace in Paris and Studio 54 in New York, casting the personified super powers Russia and America as contestants in a dance competition. Complementing 'Charlie Don't Surf', it adds up to a droll metaphorical exploration of mutually assured destruction.

Not being present at the time, Paul had not assisted with the composition of any of the Electric Lady tracks. Although Norman Watt-Roy's bass was retained on the tracks he helped with, Paul did subsequently overdub some – but by no means all – of the basslines laid down in his absence by Topper, Mick and Joe. He contributed bass to the new Wessex material, and, like Topper, both originated and sang one song. 'The Crooked Beat' is his follow up to 'Guns Of Brixton' in more ways than one, revisiting its location, macho stance and musical genre. This was not entirely of his own volition, or so he claimed to *Melody Maker* in 1988: 'I was heavily into reggae, and whenever I had an idea for a song and played it to the others, they'd immediately start playing it reggae, which wasn't always what I intended. But me not being the musician, I felt a bit helpless.'

Contact with Mikey Dread had set Joe off on another of his periodical musical crazes, this time for cutting edge dub reggae. His exposure to Jamaican radio during the aborted Kingston jaunt had done nothing to dampen his enthusiasm. 'I heard some incredible rhythms,' he enthused to *Trouser Press* in 1981. 'Stunningly inventive. A couple of years ago, I started to think that reggae had had it, but I've since found I was a bit hasty: that music is growing all the time. I like listening to dub a lot; not a lot of people do. I'd like to hear it on the radio all night long, instead of the soothing dribble of the big band sounds.' As 'The Magnificent Seven' indicates, he had also had his enthusiasm rekindled for the writings of Karl Marx, and both interests find expression on the heavy dub sound of 'The Equaliser'.

Upon hearing some rough mixes of the Electric Lady sessions, the *New York Rocker*'s Richard Grabel had asked what had already been the band's least favourite question for the best part of a year: whether the American influence evident in their new material represented a betrayal of their original vision. To which Joe replied, 'Who gives a shit whether a donkey fucked a rabbit and produced a kangaroo? At least it hops and you can dance to it.' Which might not have made much sense in itself, but certainly sets the scene for 'Rebel Waltz', possibly the strangest of the band's musical hybrids. Joe had a dream one night which inspired another of his romantic folk lyrics about battles of long ago. His idea for a musical setting for it was to marry the whitest musical form he could think of, the waltz, to the blackest, reggae.

Joe might not have been directly influenced by Richard Grabel's question, but, it seems, the general criticism the Clash had received from fans and critics alike for abandoning both Britain and politics did provoke a reaction. Some, if not all, of Joe's Wessex lyrics deal with subject matter closer to home. Another folk ballad, 'Something About England' allows an English counterpart of the tramp in 'Broadway' to testify, and throws in a few First World War singalongs and a 'brass band' for good measure. Gary Barnacle – Topper's schoolfriend – had been invited along to play saxophone on a few tracks. Asked to recommend an appropriate brass section, he contacted his trumpet-playing father Bill, who taught at a military college in Dover. Bill duly turned up with military bandsman David Yates to record the track. Mick's vocal leads off the song, and everything about it suggests it will be one of the Clash's more sentimental indulgences until Joe, in the role of the tramp, kicks in with a venomous, heartfelt – and historically accurate – diatribe about the failure of two world wars and the technological revolution to break down the British class system.

While on home turf, the Clash also addressed some familiar subjects. His return to Wilmcote House inspired Mick to pick up the baton from the previous album's Strummer composition 'Lost In The Supermarket'. With 'Up In Heaven (Not Only Here)', he launches his own attack on 'the towers of London, these crumbling blocks'. Joe, meanwhile, was not finding the towers of Chelsea any more salubrious. 'Somebody Got Murdered' had been commissioned as 'a heavy rock number' by Jack Nitzsche for the 1980 Al Pacino movie *Cruising*. 'We wrote the song, but we never heard from Jack again,' Joe told *Melody Maker* in 1988. Although the film is set on New York's gay S&M scene, Joe drew more direct inspiration from an incident that occurred in an another underworld entirely: 'It's about the car park attendant in the Worlds End Flats that was stabbed to death for £5 while I was living there.' Topper's dog, Battersea, overdubbed the barking.

By late August, Joe and Gaby had moved into a rented flat off Ladbroke Grove. Around the same time, Paul became the first property-owning member of the Clash when he secured a mortgage on a tiny two-room basement flat at nearby 53 Oxford Gardens. That Bank Holiday saw Joe, and by extension the Clash, returning both literally and inspirationally to the Notting Hill Carnival. A 1976-vintage Rocco Macauley photo depicting a lone Rasta walking towards a line of policemen had been chosen to adorn the front sleeve of the *Black Market Clash* compilation, partly to identify it as a companion volume to the US version of *The Clash*, and partly to invite comparisons and suggest connections between the Clash music of 1976-77 and that of 1980. Although there was no riot at the Carnival in 1980, there were tensions, not least for Joe, who found it difficult to forget former associations when listening to some of the more militant sounds. Drawn there principally by the reggae sound systems, he also responded strongly to the other strains of Caribbean music on offer: calypso and its soul-crossover offshoot, soca, as performed by the Trinidadian steel bands.

Steel drum players became the latest in a long line of guest artists to grace the album sessions. Three of the tracks to which they contribute find Joe turning his lyrical focus to the Carnival. On both 'Corner Soul' and 'Let's Go Crazy' he adopts the perspective of the local black community coming to the Carnival carrying the baggage of one year of oppression and the folk memory of 400 more. The brooding reggae of the former track asks, 'Is the music calling for a river of blood?' The boisterous calypso of the latter seems to be losing itself in celebration, but in fact answers that question in the affirmative. The haunting 'Street Parade' is less genre-specific, with touches of steel drum and dub-effect guitar, and a more personal lyric which contemplates disappearing into the crowd. 'Let's Go Crazy' also affords Joe the opportunity to attack the sus law – the 'power of indiscriminate arrest' – which permitted his own Kings Cross bust.

Thoughts of oppression and the Caribbean encouraged the making of other connections. 'Kingston Advice' is a heavy rock-funk-dub crossover documenting the further escalation of poverty and violence in the Jamaican capital since the visit that had inspired 'Safe European Home'. Trinidadian steel drums become similar-sounding Central American marimbas for 'Washington Bullets', a folk-style lament about US attempts to undermine leftist governments in the lands south of its borders. As with 'Somebody Got Murdered', the song's lyric takes its cue from a real life experience – so Joe informed *Trouser Press* the following year – this time in the run up to the 1980 elections in Kingston, Jamaica while the Clash were in (Jamdown) town: 'A youth of 14 was shot dead on Hope Road just 10 minutes after we'd gone past.'

Joe goes on to consider some – relatively – local background, recalling 1973's US-backed overthrow of democratically-elected Marxist president Salvador Allende in Chile, and 1961's US-backed attempted invasion of communist Cuba, before celebrating the Sandinistas' victory in Nicaragua as a triumph over US imperialism. In the interests of balance, he also points the finger at the USSR's invasion of Afghanistan, China's invasion of Tibet, and the activities of British mercenaries and arms dealers the world over. His spontaneous closing shout of 'Sandinista!' was to give the album both its title and its catalogue number, FSLN. Once again, style might have preceded content in the

Clash's political education, but the content did come through. From humble bandannas do mighty albums grow...

Disarmament on a larger scale is the subject of 'Stop The World', a post-nuclear holocaust nightmare lyric added at Wessex to a Strummer-Headon jam held over from the Electric Lady sessions: Joe had tried to play Booker T and the MGs' 'Green Onions' on the organ, and although he kept getting it wrong, had asked Topper to play along anyway.

A more recognisable attempt at recreating a Sixties soul groove is Mick's duet with Ellen Foley, 'Hitsville UK'. The backing track is strongly reminiscent of the Supremes' 'You Can't Hurry Love'. When visiting the original Motown studios in Detroit, the band had been amazed by the primitive facilities with which Berry Gordy's independent label had made all those classic singles. The Clash had already adapted one of the label's slogans – The Sound Of The Westway derives from The Sound Of Young America – and the title and chorus of Joe's lyric to this song borrow another, Hitsville USA. Part a celebration of the British independent label scene for having picked up Motown's torch, it is also intended as a slightly less direct attack on CBS than 'Complete Control', a belated acknowledgement – in the wake of the 'Bankrobber' fiasco – that taking the big advance from a major record company had indeed been a bad idea after all.

Joe provided another break from the dominant reggae focus of the album when he brought in a cassette of Mose Allison's 'Look Here', and the band made their own attempt at capturing its jazzy R&B feel. His long-time interest in rockabilly – now also shared by Paul – led to the Clash compositions 'Midnight Log' and 'The Leader'. The former is a wry yet spooky meditation on the spiritual cost of crime and corruption. The latter is an exposé of government vice, as inspired by the Sunday papers and *The Denning Report* on the Profumo scandal. 'The hypocrisy of it all is what I'm trying to get at,' Joe told *Melody Maker*'s Paolo Hewitt that December. 'The way that people are jailed for this and that, and yet up on the Top Floor they're setting no example at all. So how can they dish it out to us?'

By the end of September 1980, the Clash already had far too many tracks for a double album. Mick's response to this information was to suggest releasing a triple set. Such epics had previously been the preserve of self-indulgent pseudo-classical progressive rock bands, the direct antithesis of everything the Clash and punk had stood for, and Joe was understandably taken aback. But he responded to both the challenge and the perversity of the gesture, and the others agreed to go along. There was also, of course, the joy of presenting CBS with such an unwieldy monster after they had expressed so much unhappiness at being given a double last time.

Back in July 1979, when accused of being a punk traitor by Garry Bushell, Joe had informed him that there would never be a 'six quid' Clash album. Resolute about maintaining their VFM policy, the band demanded that CBS put out *Sandinista!* in the UK for the price of a single album, £5. The record company refused, but after negotiation, agreed to a cover price of £5.99. There were two conditions. The first was that, once again, it would only count as one album as far as the Clash's obligation to CBS was concerned. The second was that the band would forego all claim to performance royalties – not composer royalties, which are calculated separately – on the first 200,000 copies sold. To put this in perspective: at that time, *London Calling* had sold 20,000 less than that in the UK. Amazingly, the Clash agreed to these terms.

'The thing I like about making a stand on prices is that it's *here and now*, and not just a promise,' Joe told *Musician*'s Vic Garbarini the following year. 'It's dealing with reality: how many bucks you're going to have to part with at the counter to get it. It's one of the few opportunities we have to manifest our ideals, to make them exist in a real plane. To do it in Thatcher's Britain during a recession was kind of a flamboyant gesture.' Asked how CBS had responded by Duncan Campbell of New Zealand's *Rip It Up* magazine, Mick replied, 'Let's put it this way: if it had happened in Japan, all the record company executives would have killed themselves.'

The gesture certainly proved to be, in Peter Jenner's words, 'the terminal issue' for the Clash's management. The clashes over Johnny Green and Topper had not been the only ones, and the strain had been showing for some time. More recently, bored by what he considered to be Blackhill's too frequent and interminable business meetings, Paul had insisted he would only attend if they supplied him with a rabbit costume. They called his bluff. Paul called theirs straight back by putting it on and spending the duration of the mercifully truncated proceedings hopping around the room. Such high jinks they could endure, but the *Sandinista!* royalty issue struck Blackhill as a genuine act of lunacy, and they objected strongly. Their services were promptly dispensed with. 'What offended Joe most was that I seemed schoolmasterly, and the very type of authority figure he was kicking against,' Peter later told the *NME*'s Len Brown. 'He seemed to think it was uncool to be efficient. The relationship was never easy.' Peter and Andrew would be 'thanked' on *Sandinista!*'s inner sleeve under the guise of 'the two ogres'. Kosmo was kept on as PR, and noises were made to the effect that the band would be looking after their own affairs in future, as they had done briefly following the departure of Caroline Coon.

The problem now was that the Clash didn't have quite *enough* material for a triple album. Jerry Green recalls them scrabbling around for extra tracks. 'Stop The World' had already been earmarked for the non-album B-side of the first single, 'The Call Up'. 'Every Little Bit Hurts' was dropped as one oldie cover version too many. (It would eventually be included on *Clash On Broadway*.) Although it had already been released as a single under his own name and on another label, the Clash decided to include Tymon Dogg's 'Lose This Skin' to give him wider exposure. Recordings of Mickey Gallagher's young children singing karaoke versions of 'Career Opportunities' and 'Guns Of Brixton' made the cut. So did Mikey Dread's 'Living In Fame'. 'If Music Could Talk' was included, despite having exactly the same backing track as 'Shepherds Delight', the Mikey-dominated instrumental from the Pluto sessions chosen to end the album because of its suitably apocalyptic closing explosion. Hence its title, from the proverb 'red sky at night...'

The band had already worked with Mikey on dub versions of 'Out Of Time' and 'The Crooked Beat', both of which were sequenced on the album so they ran straight on from their parent songs. They now began mixing versions of other tracks: 'Version Partner' was spawned by 'Junco Partner', and Joe's talkover track 'Sapphire and Steel' comes directly from 'Washington Bullets'. Both are included on the final side, making them seem like the afterthoughts they indeed were. Even more desperate is 'Mensforth Hill', a noise collage strongly reminiscent of the Beatles' similarly unlistenable *White Album* track, 'Revolution Number 9', and whimsically described in the liner notes as the 'title theme from a forthcoming serial'. In fact, it is 'Something About England' played backwards. As well as wanting to sequence the tracks so that they linked together – sometimes with the aid of 'found' snippets of dialogue, or Mikey Dread's exhortations – the band developed an obsession with having six tracks a side. Among other oddities, this explains why 'One More Dub' is credited as a separate track, while 'The Crooked Dub' is not. Mick oversaw the final mix.

Joe's massive sheaf of lyrics was handed over to political cartoonist Steve Bell to transcribe and illustrate for the album insert, titled *Armagideon Times No 3*. Don Letts filmed a video for 'The Call Up' at the somewhat worrying militaria collection-cum-warehouse of former Sixties pop star, Chris Farlowe, with the band performing the song attired in a selection of military uniforms. A hasty cover photo session was arranged with Pennie Smith behind Kings Cross station, the band lining up against a wall in a pugnacious pose strongly reminiscent of Kate Simon's front cover for *The Clash*, Mick still wearing a GI helmet from the video shoot. Some pro-West Ham United graffiti on the wall was later airbrushed out, presumably because the Clash members supported other London teams. The various packaging elements were then handed over to Jules, the designer who had worked on the first two issues of the *Armagideon Times*. The feeling that the band consciously wanted the cover of *Sandinista!* to refer back to *The Clash* – for the same reason as had the cover of *Black Market Clash* – is further encouraged by the use of similarly distressed red typography.

Then it was straight back to Wessex to begin work on Ellen Foley's album. As well as producing what became *Spirit Of St Louis*, Mick prevailed upon Joe to help him write six songs for the project. Having met Tymon Dogg at Electric Lady, Ellen raided his repertoire for a further three songs. Tymon also played on the sessions, along with all four members of the Clash, plus Norman Watt-Roy, Mickey Gallagher and Davey Payne from the Blockheads. The album was recorded and mixed by Bill Price and Jerry Green. Perhaps surprisingly then, it sounds nothing like *Sandinista!* Ellen wanted her approach to be that of an Edith Piaf-style chanteuse, and for their part, Mick and Joe welcomed the challenge to venture into one of the very few areas they had not already been with their own record. 'It gave us a chance to do stuff we don't regularly do for the Clash,' Mick told *Musician*'s Clint Roswell in 1981. 'It worked out well all around, letting us expand our range a little.'

October 1980's two Clash-related releases did not improve the band's relationship with the music press. The cut-price US-only *Black Market Clash* did nothing to dispel the notion that the band were favouring America. The band's position on an official UK release for the record was the same as it had been for the revised version of *The Clash*: no way. Nevertheless, the album's inclusion of the hard-to-find original 'Capital Radio' and the otherwise unavailable 'Time Is Tight' made it a desirable object for UK fans and collectors, and its ready availability as an expensive import gave some the feeling they were being exploited, after all.

At much the same time, Pete Townshend's Eel Pie imprint published Pennie Smith's book of Clash photos, *Before And After*. Although featuring photos taken from 1977 to 1980, and in the UK as well as the US, the book seemed to be dominated by the American pictures. Pennie acknowledges that the band's latter-day monochrome outlaw style lent itself to being shot in black and white against classic American backdrops, and that as a result those photographs were bound to have more impact. Although some of the shots captured the Clash members in a less than flattering light, and Mick and Joe's captions were mostly wittily self-deprecating, the book was seen by some as an attempt by the Clash to further inflate their mythic status. In his year-end *Melody Maker* interview, Paolo Hewitt gave it the unofficial subtitle, *A Book Of Clash Poses*, and asked Joe to defend it. Joe made the point that it was Pennie's project – 'she's an artist herself, and that's one of her testaments' – but did address the myth-making issue: 'That's part of the lure of hoisting yourself out of a duff environment. You can't take the glamour out of this scene, no matter how hard you try.'

It had not passed unnoticed that the Clash's promises to put something back into the culture that spawned them had gone largely unfulfilled. In the far off days of 1976 and early 1977, the Clash had promised to start up a club and an alternative radio station. In June 1979, Joe had told the *NME*'s Charles Shaar Murray that he was also trying to persuade a London TV company to create a live midweek early evening rock'n'roll show to rival the dread *Top Of The Pops*. In December of that year, Joe told the same paper's Adrian Thrills that the Clash were considering 'a disused West London theatre' – actually located on Ladbroke Grove – as a site for the club, to be called the Lucky Seven. Joe also thought it would make a good venue for the proposed TV show, the idea for which had sadly been rejected by Thames TV. 'What I need is a maverick, left field, renegade, rebel TV producer. The aim, hopefully, is to get past the blinkered, half-dead nitwits who control the media.'

Grilled in December 1980 about the band's failure to deliver, Joe explained that the attempt to take over the Lucky Seven – actually located on Ladbroke Grove – had fallen through when the landlord decided to turn it into a snooker hall. And a maverick, left field producer had failed to materialise. The main problem, though, was finance, as he told Paolo Hewitt: 'We came flooding out with these ideas, and everybody wrote them down and said, "Well, this is all really good stuff. Right on!" Then we realised we weren't getting any money... It took a couple of years for that to sink in, whilst in the meantime all these people were saying, "Where's all these radio stations? Where's all these wonderful things?"... But I haven't dropped any project at all.'

In addition to being brought to brook for perceived failings, the Clash were also beginning to find themselves out of step with prevailing musical and pop-cultural trends. The New Romantic movement shared the same Bowie and Roxy-inspired foundations as punk's art school followers, and indeed provided a new home for many of them. Culture Club's Jon Moss, Visage's Steve Strange, Rusty Egan and Midge Ure, and the Ants' Marco Pirroni had all been associated with punk in some way. Adam himself had formed the original Ants as a dark punk band in the Siouxsie and the Banshees mould, before turning his attention first to Burundi drumming and then pantomime kitsch.

Despite having many of the same origins, the New Romantic movement's flamboyant, decadent image was the diametric opposite of punk. Its practitioners were self-absorbed, clothes-obsessed, hedonistic, and (in song, at least) apolitical. 'The new dandyism is in,' Joe announced to Kosmo on the promotional interview album *If Music Could Talk*. 'Dressing up like Robin Hood and Friar Tuck, Napoleon and Billy Bunter.' Which was amusing, but would have packed more punch had not the Clash spent most of the past four years at a slightly more butch fancy dress party of their own. The bands at which Joe scoffed opened the floodgates for what became known as the New Pop of the early Eighties: music without a care in the world, its practitioners running the gamut from sophisticated ennui to screaming camp to arch naivety. Not for nothing did Dave Rimmer entitle his 1985 Culture Club biography-cum-New Romantic history *Like Punk Never Happened*.

Some of 'the kids' this music appealed to were very young indeed, and their interests were catered for by *Smash Hits*, a spectacularly successful A4 colour magazine which combined the innocence of Sixties pop journalism – songwords and questionnaires – with a cheekier, Eighties irreverence. Unlike the inkies, it did not expect its interviewees to be committed, responsible or opinionated, but nor did it pander to their egos. Early in 1980, former *NME* editor Neil Logan founded another publishing success story, glossy pop culture and lifestyle magazine the *Face*, which although eclectic in approach, tended to cover the more adult end of the New Pop spectrum.

Meanwhile, the more serious world of the post-punk bands was mutating into what would henceforth be known as indie, after the independent labels on which – confusingly – by no means all of its exponents released their recordings. New influences and technologies were being adopted to forge new directions and sub-genres. There was a stripped-down funk element to the Gang Of Four and the Au Pairs; a psychedelic edge to Echo and the Bunnymen and the Teardrop Explodes; a futuristic slant to the synthesizer music of the Human League, Ultravox! and Depeche Mode.

Concerned about diminishing sales, and mindful of the new trends indicated by the success of arriviste publications *Smash Hits* and the *Face*, the inky old *NME* tried to adapt, a move that was as expedient as any change of policy ever adopted by the Clash. Its two most willing boys about town were Paul Morley and Ian Penman. They patented an affected decadent intellectual style which initially succeeded in covering all the bases and in making some telling points about the inherent conservatism of the rock'n'roll scene. Before long, the duo would start to wear out the readership's patience with some of the most impenetrably pretentious copy ever published in the *NME*. In the short term, however, they had sufficient clout to ensure that any kind of rock music that was deemed too traditional or earnest was sneered at, with the expression 'rockist' – originally coined by Mick Jones's pal Pete Wylie – becoming a commonplace term of abuse. On the whole, this was no time for the Clash to be releasing a triple album full of brooding dub, political harangues and intimations of imminent apocalypse.

A chance for the *NME* to sharpen its teeth was offered by 'The Call Up'. T-Zers anticipated the single's 28 November release thus: 'It was inspired by the group's current bid for US citizenship.' The song was specifically targeted at American fans like Freddie – which did make it a strange choice for first single in the UK – and the front cover featured the address for the US pressure group Immobilise Against The Draft, but Joe pointed out that the lyric also referred obliquely to Soviet conscripts, and that the young soldiers pictured on the cover were actually Russian. The B-side 'Stop The World' examines the end result of military escalation, and the back cover features a picture of a 'Dead Man's Shadow' from Hiroshima, and the address of the Campaign for Nuclear Disarmament. Paul Morley used the single review proper as an opportunity to hand in his resignation from the Clash fan club. After a year of being attacked for abandoning political concerns, it must have been particularly galling for the band to read it. 'With the general shifts in moods and desires that are going on, the Clash are already old fashioned,' pontificated Paul. 'Too sternly stuck inside a political phase, too wrapped up in those used-up myths. A set of passions I can't get to grips with... "The Call Up" sounds like a lost album track, proud and bravely cheerless, but lost in the murk... It doesn't seem right for the times. They care so much but seem so lost.'

In the UK, *Sandinista!* was released on 12 December 1980. The task of reviewing it for the *NME* fell to Nick Kent, hardly one of the paper's new dilettantes, but – as someone who had responded favourably to *Give 'Em Enough Rope*'s pedestrian HM sound, if not subject matter – no more likely than Morley or Penman to appreciate the band's new direction. He dismissed the three-album set as 'ridiculously self-indulgent', and ran through the list of the band's genre-experimentations – for which he blamed Mick alone – with scorn. The Clash had made a mistake in trying to be musically *professional*, believed Nick, who went on to attack both Joe and Mick's limited vocal ranges, poor pitching and – in Mick's case – lack of projection for not being professional *enough*. Ditto the production, 'too grandly embellished by (particularly) Mickey Gallagher's keyboard work' and 'riddled side after side with a wafer-thin, soft-focus mixing down of instruments that divides everything off instead of building up textures. This mix problem is such a crippling flaw that song after song fails because its clout is dismembered... a producer would be advisable as the band have no real perspective on their work in the studio.'

Nor did Joe's lyrics get off lightly. He was criticised for failing to address the current British malaise, instead resorting to cliché, turning to freedom fighters abroad, or hiding in fantasy-land. To Nick, the songs were either 'another set of neatly-glib black and white snapshots of "the good fight" be it in Nicaragua or in a pub down Shepherds Bush Junction (after all, when you've seen one ghetto, you've seen 'em all, eh lads?)', or just plain 'blinkered romanticism'. He seemed particularly offended by the band's critical reception in America: *Rolling Stone*'s Greil Marcus had accused Nick of starting a 'snivelling backlash' against the Clash with his *Give 'Em Enough Rope* review; Nick now responded with a jibe at the 'absurdly sycophantic' reviews the band had been receiving 'across the Atlantic'. Eventually finding it in his heart to praise a select handful of tracks, he concluded: 'The Clash will survive. Why they bother to is the really painful question that *Sandinista!* forces me to ask.'

Melody Maker's Patrick Humphries continued the paper's tradition of taking the balanced approach. Three albums for the price of one was generous, he conceded, but quantity did not always compensate for quality: '*Sandinista!* is a floundering mutant of an album. The odd highlights are lost in a welter of reggae/dub overkill.' He believed it managed to suffer from both aimlessness of direction and similarity of sound. Although he found the album to be lyrically 'interesting', he agreed with Nick Kent about 'the black and white way' the band equated rebellion with just causes. He even objected to the choice of title, which 'reeks of the political "awareness" which many find so glibly unattractive'. Unlike Nick, however, he believed, 'the Clash really do still care, and remain a radical committed band'. After 'the consistent excellence of last year's offering', he found *Sandinista!* disappointing. 'That aside, I can't wait for the next Clash album.'

Surprisingly, given that a representative of the paper had been so scathing about the Clash's retreat from punk with *London Calling*, the most positive of the inky reviews came from *Sounds'* Robbi Millar. Like the other two reviewers, she worried that the band's 'busy body interference is too eager to glorify war, in Nicaragua or Brixton', though she did cite 'Corner Stone' as proof that they could 'stick the dagger in just where it's needed... the selfishness of violence is once again exposed'. Robbi was more open to Joe's romantic streak than were her counterparts at the rival inkies – 'the romantic aspects of the album are some of its strongest points whether they're social or personal' – but she too found the American references on the album to be 'a bore', and maintained that its best music 'involves Britain, whether it be a black, white or two-tone Britain'.

Her principle differences of opinion with the other two writers concerned what she perceived to be 'the fine production', 'the band's increase in technical competence' and the impressive variety of musical genres attempted. She also noted that 'rhythm is the key throughout *Sandinista!*'. Robbi concluded by asserting that too much of the band's punk spirit was still in evidence for them to be dismissed as would-be Rolling Stones, but she had already summed up her overall opinion earlier in the review: 'The fourth Clash album is an adventure of diversity and wit, of struggle and freedom, of excellence and dross. When it is good, it is very good. When it is bad... maybe aiming to provide us with three album's worth of value was aiming too high.' She gave it four out of a possible five stars.

To greater and lesser extents, prejudice lurked behind all three reviews. The accusations of an American bias on *Sandinista!* are unfounded. Aside from the fact that the bulk of the album's music is reggae-derived – reggae being a Jamaican genre with no commercial track record in the US whatsoever – only eight of the lyrics refer directly to the States, and only a couple of these indulge in the cosy American mythologising to be found on *London Calling*. Most of those tracks which do allude to the US openly criticise that country's government. The Clash were only able to make the gesture of selling the album for £5.99 in the UK because they were charging a relatively hefty

$14.98 in the US: in effect, US fans were being required to subsidise British fans, which, if anything, was an indication of bias the other way.

The reviewers' suggestion that the band should stick to British subject matter in their lyrics was evidence of a blinkered and parochial mentality – which, ironically, had quite possibly been inspired by the pro-English, anti-American rhetoric of the punk-era Clash – and just as limiting as it would have been to insist the band arrest their musical development at the sound of barking seals and pneumatic drills. The Clash had not only improved as musicians since the first album, they had also been out into the wider world. To pretend otherwise would have been a lie. 'Really to see where you've come from, you have to go someplace else,' as Mick explained to *Rip It Up*'s Duncan Campbell early in 1982. 'Otherwise you wouldn't understand that the world didn't finish at the end of your street.' Eight of the lyrics do refer to specifically British locations and experiences, but most – including those eight – have a universal relevance.

The reviewers were all lazy in assuming that 'Washington Bullets' is solely 'about' Nicaragua, when in fact it is 'about' covert armed interference world-wide. A song clearly denouncing such activity is, surely, far preferable to the bombast of 'Guns On The Roof' or the only semi-ironic celebration of terrorism that was 'Tommy Gun'. Furthermore, having spent several years in the early to mid Seventies sharing squats with refugees from various South American regimes, having formed the 101ers with two Chileans, and having played his first gig with that band on behalf of the Chile Solidarity Campaign, Joe could lay claim to feeling more genuine empathy with the Nicaraguan rebels' cause than most white middle class Britons.

As for adopting *Sandinista!* as the album title, the motive was not to bestow radical chic upon the Clash, but to draw attention to an event most people in their right minds would choose to celebrate – the overthrowing of a despot by his own people – had they only been aware of it. 'There was a media blanket covering the whole bloody thing, and people didn't even know there was a revolution there,' Mick told Duncan Campbell. 'We really wanted to have a title that was useful for once. It was something that would draw people's attention to something that was going on at the time.'

Less easy to defend was and is the band's continuing *stylistic* fascination with rebel chic. Patrick Humphries remarked upon the GI helmet Mick sports on the cover of the album, and the other two reviewers also evidently allowed it – and the band's military outfits in 'The Call Up' video – to colour their response to the lyrics within. When tackled about Mick's headgear by *Sounds*' Pete Silverton, Joe rather lamely replied, 'He's wearing that helmet for the reason that we're all going to be wearing them soon. We spent a lot of time making this album wearing helmets… Admittedly, there's nobody strafing us and napalming the neighbourhood, but it seems like war to me out there.' Those songs on the album that touch on the subject are for once unambiguously *anti*-war and *anti*-violence, as Mick had professed to be when rejecting Paul's warmongering backdrop the previous year. But once again, the Clash's love of dressing up and posing had undermined both the message of their music and their own credibility.

Sandinista! is deeply flawed. Firstly, there is, as the reviewers all agreed, far too much of it. 'It's pretty much designed to last for six months to a year of listening,' Mick explained to Kosmo for the *If Music Could Talk* promotional interview disc. 'People don't have to listen to it all at once. They can listen to it a bit at a time. However much they can take.' The band, and especially Mick, showed considerably naivety in believing that the Clash could rewrite the rules of popular music consumption overnight. Most of 'the kids' who bought a new album did so with a sense of urgent anticipation. Even the most ardent fans were going to have problems familiarising themselves with a triple album of often demanding new material. Newcomers and browsers were going to be put off by the level of commitment required. Furthermore – and not unimportantly – being forced to assimilate the record quickly in order to make deadlines, reviewers were going to feel overwhelmed, disoriented and, frankly, resentful.

Patrick Humphries was right when he said that the band's experiments with other genres were overshadowed by the number of reggae and dub numbers. Some, like 'One More Time' and its dub are both powerful and moving. Others, like 'The Crooked Beat', 'The Equaliser' and the last minute padding dubs on side six are just plain boring. The charge of self-indulgence also applies to some of the Electric Lady jams, 'Junkie Slip' in particular being a complete waste of space. 'Mensforth Hill' is unforgivable. Nick Kent's comments about the mix do apply in some – if not all – instances, simply because there was too much material for every song to be given due attention, as Joe would admit to *Creem*'s Bill Holdship in 1984. One of the victims is 'The Call Up' which, as a single, does – as Paul Morley suggested – sound like an album track. An instrumental remix made in March 1981, and released on the US 12-inch of 'The Magnificent Seven' under the title 'The Cool Out', gives some indication of just how powerful the parent song could have been.

Nick Kent saw the album's diversity of musical genres as a 'blight'. In drawing together influences and styles old and new from all over Britain, Europe, Jamaica, Trinidad, New York, New Orleans, Memphis, Detroit, Central America and – indirectly, via several of the above – Africa, the Clash were making a point about the connections that exist among them all. Nor were they content to leave it there. Their attempts at often complex fusions and crossovers made them more than just tourists or archivists. At the end of the previous year, they had been found wanting for exhibiting retrogressive tendencies, and compared unfavourably to the supposedly avant garde PiL. Even in June 1980, Chris Bohn had described them as 'conservative'. Now, they were being criticised for experimenting with form. It was more than a little unjust. Arguably, the Rolling Stones and the Beatles had both attempted similar projects in the past, but *Sandinista!* was in fact a bold exploration of world music long before such a category existed in the record racks or Paul Simon went in search of *Graceland*.

At the time, the received wisdom about the triple set was that it was the product of too much dope, Mick's November 1976 *London Weekend Show* remark about the problem with hippies come back to haunt him. In a way, this is true: it is a stoner album, just like the slow dub reggae of the mid to late Seventies is stoner music, and punk is speed freak music. Perhaps more tellingly, though, much of *Sandinista!* is groove-oriented, and rock fans and a few of the more traditional rock critics of the period were notoriously uptight about post-Motown dance music. 'Disco sucks' was still very much the prevailing mentality.

Only Robbi Millar found anything praiseworthy to say about the band's foray into funk, and only she correctly identified the Sugarhill Gang as the chief source of inspiration. Patrick Humphries avoided mention of the new departure altogether, and Nick Kent gave it one of his typically florid muggings: 'The "disco" pulsebeat – usually a surly repetitious bass figure punctuated by an ethnic piano chord – is featured twice on side one alone.' The musical branch of hip hop culture of which he was being so dismissive – aka rap – would go on to be the most innovative, influential and commercially successful force in the popular music of the Eighties and early Nineties, its crossover with rock injecting essential new lifeblood into the form. The Clash were the first non-New York rock band to get on the case.

Reggae and its various sub-genres and offshoots have gone in and out of fashion with the rock audience over the years, but heavy dub has always been a minority taste. Thus, the UK music critics' unanimous thumbs down for its dominance on the album is understandable. However, by choosing to carp on about *Sandinista!* being 'too grandly embellished' by keyboard work and 'psychedelic' sound effects, rather than acknowledging these features as conventions and techniques of dub production, Nick

Kent did rather seem to be flaunting his own lack of knowledge about – or at least, interest in – the genre.

Lyrically, the album succeeds in bringing together all the Clash's previous concerns. The Ladbroke Grove area, tower blocks, oppression and urban alienation all feature. Political machinations in the wider world are addressed without resorting to the histrionics of *Give 'Em Enough Rope*. Myths and romantic legends have a place, but are rooted in historical fact, or balanced by more realistic or satirical neighbouring songs. The sense of coming Armageddon is not mere empty stadium-rock bombast, but a genuine expression of empathy with the fears and woes of Third World peoples condemned to eke out a living against a background of disease, famine and war, and of supposedly First World peoples living in poverty in ghettos riddled with drugs and guns.

The overall impression is of a document of 1980, made up not only of first-hand experience and news, but also historical and political texts, memories, stories and dreams, and captured in a variety of folk-ballad and oral tale-telling forms. 'Up In Heaven (Not Only Here)' quotes a song by Phil Ochs, a Greenwich Village contemporary of Bob Dylan who, like Joe Strummer, was from the school of Woody Guthrie. The title of Phil's 1965 début album was an adaptation of the *New York Times'* tagline: *All The News That's Fit To Sing*. In presenting the liner notes and lyric sheets to *Sandinista!* as an edition of the *Armagideon Times*, the Clash were making much the same statement.

The much-maligned *Sandinista!*'s groove-oriented stoner music would prove to have a significant impact on the UK music scene. Along with the drum pattern from James Brown's 'Funky Drummer', it would help shape the sound of the late Eighties: the Farm and Happy Mondays have both acknowledged an influence, and the Stone Roses would be hard put to deny one. Mick Jones himself would pursue the line of enquiry instigated by 'The Magnificent Seven' with his post-Clash band Big Audio Dynamite, who in turn would inspire a posse of imitators.

In the years immediately following the album's release it became something of a standing joke that it would be a challenge to compile a worthwhile single album from the triple set's material. In fact, hindsight and a couple of judicious remixes could have produced a double that might have been praised as a worthy follow-up to *London Calling*… in almost any year other than 1980.

But 1980 it was, and the Clash had to come out and face a pugnacious music press. Or rather, Joe did. Following completion of Ellen Foley's album, Mick had returned with her to New York. Topper did a few overseas phone interviews, and Paul invited Chris Salewicz to his Oxford Gardens flat for the *Face*, but it was Joe who was left to handle the bulk of the promotion. Which meant that he spent much of December on the defensive, justifying both the album and the Clash against accusations of self-indulgence, toadying to Uncle Sam, and other hypocrisies and failings many and various. He started off in reasonable form, affable, witty and informative, but the cumulative effect of his interviewers' negativity and the poor reviews afforded *Sandinista!* – coming as they did on top of the latest in a succession of difficult, demanding years – finally proved too much.

Still susceptible to inky opinion, he privately began to blame Mick, as had Nick Kent, for forcing the band down an unpopular musical path. By 1984, Joe was openly volunteering the information that *Sandinista!* had been a wrong turning. In 1988, during the interview he gave Chris Salewicz for a promotional film accompanying the release of the compilation album *The Story Of The Clash, Vol 1*, Joe laughed, 'The sixth side: only bold men go there!' True, Mick had been responsible for suggesting a triple album, and, largely, for the production; but Joe conveniently forgot that *he* had been the one who had wanted to rap, that *he* had been the one who had fallen in love with dub, and that *he* had been the one who had wanted to improvise lyrics over band jams. In the interviews he gave in 1999 to promote the retrospective live album *From Here To*

Eternity and the re-release of remixed versions of the Clash's entire back catalogue, Joe revealed he had changed his mind once again. Now bullish in his defence of the album, he insisted that he stood by every one of its 36 tracks.

The *Sandinista!* sessions had seen Mick once again wrest dominance of the Clash back from Joe, to no immediate critical or financial reward. By the end of 1980, the Clash were close to half a million pounds in debt to CBS, a situation that sales of *Sandinista!* seemed hardly likely to rectify. In 1988, talking to Chris Salewicz, Joe ironically echoed the sentiments of Peter Jenner when he blamed Mick's idealism in insisting upon VFM for the fans – particularly with regard to *Sandinista!* – for preventing the Clash from being able to function in the real world.

At the time of the album's release, Joe's feeling that everything was turning to ashes was exacerbated by developments on the domestic front. At the age of 28, and in a stable relationship with Gaby Salter, he was growing tired of squats and borrowed flats. He had recently applied for a mortgage to buy his own home and been refused. After nearly five years of going without material comforts in an attempt to live up to the Clash's ideals, all Joe had received in return was scorn for supposedly failing to do so. A brief period of despondency was followed by a renewed determination to get back on the right track. That Joe already had his first move in mind can be inferred – with the benefit of hindsight – from the promotional interviews he gave during December 1980. He refused to blame Bernie Rhodes for signing CBS's draconian contract, or for having imposed financial hardship on the band with his legal manoeuvres over the two years since his dismissal. Joe told Paolo Hewitt: 'I'm not knocking Bernie, because I think he's the best.'

15
COMBAT ROCK

In December 1980, with Mick Ronson in the producer's chair, Ian Hunter began recording a new album at New York's Power Station. One of Ian's songs, 'Theatre Of The Absurd', had been inspired by a conversation with Mick Jones about the reggae-rock crossover the Clash had helped instigate. Wanting a reggae feel for the track, and aware that Mick was in town with Ellen Foley, Ian invited him down to the studio to offer advice. It was a fantasy fulfilled for Mick. By this time any awe he felt for Ian was more than equalled by confidence in his own powers. Initially asked to overdub guitar on just the one song, the workaholic Mick quickly asserted himself, taking over from Mick Ronson to commence his third back-to-back production job. 'He had all kinds of ideas, and used the mixing board like a musician,' a bemused Ian told Campbell Devine for his 1998 book *All The Young Dudes*. 'Couldn't argue with him. Very strong personality in the studio, very, very strong. Stronger than me. Most upsetting.'

The sessions moved first to Electric Lady, then, in January 1981, to Wessex in London, where they were completed with Bill Price engineering. Mick instigated two more songs when he persuaded Ian to set his poems 'Central Park'n'West' and 'Noises' to music. Although he remained uncredited, some of the chords and ideas for embellishments on these two songs also came from Mick, as Ian later admitted. As well as playing guitar, and joining Ellen on backing vocals, Mick brought in Topper Headon to play drums and Tymon Dogg to play violin. The album's working title was *Theatre Of The Absurd*, but Mick renamed it *Haircut* when Ian had his trademark locks lopped off, and Ian eventually decided to go with *Short Back'n'Sides*. Although production was officially co-credited to Mick Ronson, Ian admitted to Campbell Devine that both he and Ronno had lacked focus at the time, and the project had become more Mick Jones's than anyone's. Retrospectively, this was plainly not something with which Ian was 100 per cent comfortable.

During the Wessex sessions, Mick contacted his fellow Delinquents co-founder John Brown, whom he had not seen for several years. Mick informed John he was hoping to build a touring band for Ellen Foley, and asked if he would be interested in playing bass. Telling John that Robin Crocker would also be present at Wessex, he invited him along to the studio, and offered to pick him up. 'My wife had just had a baby girl, who was about three months old, and I was full of it, you know,' says John. 'Mick came in, and I said, "Look, here's my daughter!" He walked straight past, walked around the room once, and said, "Come on, let's go!" I thought, "Fuck me! You've never even *met* my wife before!" He was *not* interested, really distant. We went to Wessex. Mick had a huge lump of dope, which he would roll a jay from, and smoke it all to himself. And then he'd walk away, roll another one, and smoke *that* all to himself. He was very withdrawn. He'd come into the control room, say a few things, then disappear again. I didn't understand what I'd walked into. I couldn't feel at home, even though I'd known Ian Hunter for years. This was when I suddenly thought, "I don't know Mick at the moment." I don't think I've ever known him since.' Nothing more was said about John joining Ellen's band, though this might have been due to the damning-with-faint-praise *Spirit Of St Louis* suffered upon its release in late March 1981: according to the *NME*'s Adrian Thrills, it was just 'an intermittently worthwhile indulgence'. The album failed to chart.

Given his offhand manner towards them, it is not easy to determine Mick's motive for inviting John and Robin along to Wessex. An uncharitable interpretation is that he wished to impress upon his fellow former Mott the Hoople fans – and, in John's case, fellow wannabe rock'n'roll star – the extent to which he, and only he, had fulfilled the rock dreams they had shared as Strand schoolboys. If so, universal acclaim was still some way off. When *Short Back'n'Sides* was released on Chrysalis in August 1981, *Sounds* described it as 'irresistibly big and loud' and 'the best old rock album of the year so far', giving it five stars. But other reviewers were less impressed and the album spent just two weeks on the UK charts, peaking at number 79. Although it managed 11 weeks on the US charts, it climbed no higher than number 62.

Alternatively, rather than rubbing John's and Robin's noses in his fame and influence, it is possible that Mick simply wanted to gather people he knew, liked and trusted around him for support and reaffirmation. By late January 1981, he certainly had a lot of things on his mind. But if he did want to reach out and renew old friendships, he had clearly forgotten how. Both Ian Hunter's and John Brown's responses to Mick at this time go some way to explaining why he might have needed to go outside the Clash to search for that support and reaffirmation in the first place: professionally, he felt the need to dominate; and socially, he held himself aloof.

Joe hated Mick's moonlighting, but faced with a fait accompli, he took an opportunity to revisit his own musical roots. He saw in the New Year appearing at the Tabernacle Community Centre in Powis Square with Richard Dudanski, Mole and other former members of the 101ers in a Sixties-style soul revue outfit named the Soul Vendors. It was a reunion long in the making. The February 1978 release of the Clash's version of the late-period 101ers' song 'Jail Guitar Doors', credited to Strummer-Jones, had rubbed salt into Richard's wounds. Determined to prove the 101ers' worth, he had begun assembling various studio and live recordings by the band with a view to releasing them as an album. Bernie Rhodes objected, and made the mistake of trying to argue the toss with Richard, hardly his number one fan. 'He came down to my place and had the cheek to give me all these completely absurd reasons why I shouldn't be bringing out this album,' Richard told the *NME*'s Chris Salewicz in 1981. 'I ended up having to literally get hold of him and throw him out of the door.' If anything, his resolve was hardened.

Once Bernie had been ousted, the Clash began to move away from punk into more traditionally based music, some of which was not a million miles away from the spirit of the 101ers. In mid 1980, the band even recorded their version of the old 101ers' set staple 'Junco Partner' for *Sandinista!*. Keeping his former band's output a secret was no longer such a priority for Joe, and he gave in to pressure from Richard. Along with Clive Timperley, Dan Kelleher, Mole and Micky Foote, they became co-directors of a specially-established label, named Andalucia! in honour of Esperanza and Palmolive (and, it would appear, as a pun on the Clash's then-current album venture). A distribution deal was arranged with Virgin.

Richard set up a deal which gave them access to the Jackson's studio material recorded with Vic Maile. Understandably, when Chiswick learned that the 101ers were about to be revived as a marketable commodity, they elected to exploit their copyright material themselves. This took the form of a second 101ers single, coupling 'Sweet Revenge' with 'Rabies (From The Dogs Of Love)'. However, Chiswick did see the wisdom in synchronised releases with some crossover of material: thus, Andalucia! were allowed to use the Pathway version of 'Sweet Revenge', but were not granted permission to use 'Rabies', or for that matter, '5 Star Rock'n'Roll Petrol' and the original single version of 'Keys To Your Heart'. Luckily, the 101ers had the BBC studios material as back up, the copyright in which had remained with the band. 'Mike Robinson actually remastered them for us,' says Clive. 'He was always a big help with the 101ers.'

In order to make up an album's worth of material, Micky Foote supplied a cassette recording he had made of the 101ers supporting Van Der Graaf Generator on 18 April 1976 at the Roundhouse in Camden. 'I'd been working the audience as hard as I could and I couldn't get nothing out of them,' Joe told Pete Silverton in 1980. 'And then Trouble, the dog, wandered onstage and they all went bananas. And I gave up. The tape's really good: fast number banging into another fast number. No messing about. No sloppiness. And we couldn't impress them. Mind you, I don't know what sort of music Van Der Graaf is. It's like Shakespeare crossed with Uriah Heep.' This makes the gig sound like an unlikely choice for a permanent record of the live 101ers, but much of its appeal for Joe especially must have been that it came from that brief period between his first exposure to the Sex Pistols and the sacking of Clive Timperley.

Chiswick released the 'Sweet Revenge' single in late January 1981. The album emerged towards the end of March under the title *Elgin Avenue Breakdown*. It was named after a jazz record Joe had seen in New York, *Lenox Avenue Breakdown*, but there were multiple puns at work: the first part of the title makes direct reference to one of the main routes through the old Maida Hill squatting community, but also suggests the 101ers' longtime home base pub on Ladbroke Grove; the second part serves as both an offer to provide all the necessary facts and as an acknowledgement of the band's untidy demise. The specific sense of locale and resolutely downbeat feel are further reflected in the packaging, which makes a virtue of amateurish, sub-bootleg lettering and layout. The front cover features a picture of the Metal Man, a local hobo-type character who, during the 101ers' heyday, could be found sitting on kerbs around the Ladbroke Grove area, festooned with metal objects.

Unshakeable Clash aficionado Chris Salewicz wrote a half page *NME* feature for the 14 February 1981 issue based on an interview with Richard. A two-page retrospective by Paolo Hewitt in the 28 February issue of the *Melody Maker* – where the 101er's old champion Allan Jones was now editor – brought together Joe, Richard and Mole to reminisce about the old days. Although Joe was clearly not wholly comfortable, and showed no inclination to revise his customarily dismissive appraisal of the 101ers, he and Richard talked about their shared escapades with genuine affection. Perhaps because fewer of his memories were good ones, Mole was largely silent throughout.

Upon the album's release, Allan Jones himself waxed lyrical about the 101ers in *Melody Maker*'s review. Having never really warmed to the punk rock movement, he made the claim that 'Strummer songs like "Motor Boys Motor" anticipated the frustrations of punk, but betray none of its empty rhetoric.' In his opinion, the 101ers' 'Junco Partner' 'makes the Clash version sound stilted', and while he acknowledged the overall poor sound quality of the live material, he maintained that 'the ferocity cuts through' on certain tracks. In the *NME*, Adrian Thrills took a different perspective. As far as he was concerned, the album had arrived too long after the event, and could be of interest only to Clash fans and collectors. 'This mixture of studio and abysmally recorded live stuff is incredibly run-of-the-mill, and would be almost completely forgettable were it not for the unmistakable, unexpurgated dementia in Strummer's coarse vocalising.' On this latter point, at least, he was in complete accord with Allan Jones, who wrote: 'Strummer's coarse vocal still carries an enthralling potency, screaming through the crowded lyric [of 'Letsagetabitarockin'] in an urgent blurred torrent.'

Elgin Avenue Breakdown is a perfectly fine rough-and-ready souvenir, but it does not showcase the 101ers in a particularly favourable light. Not being able to use the majority of the Pathway material was too great a blow for the album to ride. Although the limited use of studio material is annoying, it is understandable. More mystifying is the reason why the Roundhouse tape, the sound quality of which is indeed very poor, was used as the sole source of live material. During the lengthy period he worked as soundman, Micky Foote recorded almost every 101ers gig direct from the mixing desk. Even though he did have what Richard describes as 'the horrible habit, if he didn't have a new cassette, of re-using one from two months before', that nevertheless still left a wide selection. Clive and Richard both have stashes of tapes, the latter having recently unearthed a recording of one of his favourite Wandsworth Prison gigs. Mole also has tapes of early 101ers rehearsals. 'I heard them a few months ago, and some of the songs blew my head off, because I'd forgotten all about them,' says Clive. '"Boo The Goose", "Hideaway" and "Green Love" are on there.'

By 1993, *Elgin Avenue Breakdown* was long deleted. Former 101ers roadie Boogie attempted to capitalise on this by compiling an unauthorised CD of almost all the 101ers' studio recordings for a Paris-based label named Made In Heaven under the title *Five Star Rock'n'Roll*. 'It sounds fine, and it's got good packaging, but it went out without our permission,' says Clive. 'He was just after a few bucks out of us. We went apeshit, and the French record company were really, really apologetic. It's been withdrawn.' So far, a replacement has failed to materialise, although during a 2000 *Q* interview, Joe did promise to remedy this. On a personal level, re-establishing contact during 1980-81 with his pre-Clash friends Tymon Dogg and Richard Dudanski helped take some of the pressure of band life off Joe's shoulders. He would remain especially close with Richard therafter, visiting him often even when he and Esperanza moved to Spain.

Meanwhile, back in early 1981, the *NME* reported that Topper Headon had been involved in helping the New Symphony Orchestra recover some stolen drums – in view of his own propensity for making kits disappear, there was surely more to this story than ever made the music press – and as a reward he was invited to sit in with them for their 1 February Royal Albert Hall performance of the '1812 Overture'.

Even Kosmo found a side project to occupy himself. For much of the last year, he had been going out with the – for a Clash associate – irresistibly named American vocalist Pearl Harbour, formerly lead singer with the Explosions. In January, he used his Clash contacts to put a new backing band together for a UK tour in support of her solo single 'Fujiyama Mama': ex-Rich Kid Steve New, Nigel Dixon of recent Clash support band Whirlwind, Topper's friend and *Sandinista!* session saxophonist Gary Barnacle, and Paul's brother Nick Simonon on drums. Paul himself still knew how to relax, but everyone else in the Clash camp was keeping busy. Perhaps a little too busy…

On 16 January 1981, 'Hitsville UK' became the second single to be released from *Sandinista!* in Britain. The B-side was Mikey Dread's 'Radio One', yet another of his critiques of the contemporary music scene, and also in the tradition of the Clash's own harangues about the state of radio in the UK. When released on 17 February as the first single in the US, the A-side was combined with 'Police On My Back'. As far as the American market was concerned, the subject matter of 'Hitsville UK' might not have been wholly relevant, but it was the track closest in sound to the band's only US hit to date, 'Train In Vain'. For the domestic market, the song was selected to balance the supposedly American bias of 'The Call Up'. The *NME*'s Ian Penman dismissed it as the band's creative nadir. After damning the lyrics for their romanticism, patronising tone and hypocrisy, he set about the tune in similar vein, before sticking the boot into the Clash themselves: 'What do they see when they look in the mirror? Third world guerrillas with *quiffs*?'

The slide in popularity with the British public the band had feared before devising the aborted Clash Singles Bonanza seemed to be underway: 'The Call Up' had climbed no higher than number 40; 'Hitsville UK' peaked at number 56. Although the Clash did feature in the *NME* end-of-year readers' poll, and still commanded enough loyalty to hold on to third best group, most other categories for which they qualified found them lurking mid table. The Jam once again lifted every trophy. 'If you're a musician, and you listen to the Jam, all you hear is lock, stock and barrel lifts,' Joe grumbled to *Trouser Press*.

At the end of November 1980, the music press had reported that plans were being laid for an 'extensive' Clash UK tour early in the new year. On 24 January 1981, this was amended to 'selected' dates. Apparently, no tour support was forthcoming from CBS, and the band could not afford to pay for the jaunt themselves. Following the announcement, an untypically petulant Joe volunteered another explanation during an interview with Wolverhampton's Beacon Radio: 'I'm not going to pretend that we're going to do a great big tour. There's a lot of things putting us off. Like, a group tends to believe what it reads in the press as reflecting the true mood of the country. And this past year, reading the English press has been pretty depressing for me, because every time they mention the Clash it's been a dig, or to say we're irrelevant. After a while, you start to accept that, and you think, "Obviously everybody's got a big downer on us." So we aren't too keen to come rushing out every-bloody-place and play and get gobbed on in the face by 30 people while 3,000 stand by passively watching. They can just stuff it.' Once upon a time, Us and Them had meant punk bands, the music media and the punk audience against all agents of oppression; now it appeared to be the Clash against their one-time supporters.

The 7 February edition of the *NME* announced that the tour had been called off altogether. Kosmo's reason was, 'We cannot find enough alternative venues to play.' Rumours of a split began to circulate once more, and again, they were not without foundation. Joe might have been tired of criticism, but neither that, nor Kosmo's lame excuse, was the real reason for the tour's cancellation. Joe had been pushing for Bernie Rhodes's reinstatement since the beginning of the year, even going so far as to invite him along to a band meeting. In the 1999 Clash biographical documentary *Westway To The World*, Paul professed to be 'pleased' by Joe's suggestion, and that same year Joe told *Uncut*'s Gavin Martin that 'even Mick' wanted Bernie back. At the time, though, only Joe was truly in favour of reinstating their original manager, and Topper and Mick resisted strongly. Just as the tour dates were about to go to press, Joe played his trump card: unless Bernie was brought back, he was leaving the Clash.

Faced with such an ultimatum, the others had no option but to capitulate. It was particularly tough on Mick, who had pressed hardest for Bernie's dismissal just over two years earlier. Especially as he was now put in the humiliating position of being deputised to approach Bernie and ask him to return. This may well explain why Mick appeared so preoccupied when meeting John Brown. As he had with the 101ers, when it came to the crunch, Joe had proved he was prepared to abandon his, and the Clash's, supposedly democratic principles in order to get his own way. In so doing, he had forcibly retaken control; something that was bound to have long term repercussions on his relationship with the others, and with Mick most of all. 'I could quite easily have walked out then,' Mick told Paolo Hewitt in 1986, by which time the former was with Big Audio Dynamite and the latter was writing for the *NME*. 'But it's like a marriage, or the people you love: you cling on hoping it's going to work out.'

Since late 1978, Bernie's fortunes had been mixed. The Black Arabs contributed to Malcolm McLaren's *Great Rock'n'Roll Swindle* soundtrack, but split not long afterwards. After a couple of failed attempts to record an album, Subway Sect had also broken up. Bernie had delivered where the Clash had failed in establishing a club of his own in London: the once occasional and peripatetic Club Left had become a regular faux-Bohemian joint based in the former Whisky-A-Go-Go club (later the Wag) in Wardour Street. Former Subways frontman Vic Godard became the club's resident house crooner. Still managed by Bernie, his erstwhile backing band would be teamed with American vocalist Dig Wayne and renamed the Jo Boxers. Once Bernie had secured them a 'very poor' deal with RCA, they would go on to experience chart success in 1983 with the number three single 'Boxer Beat' and an image based on that of a pre-War New York Street gang.

Bands had to be strong if they didn't want to come apart in Bernie's hands. Recalling both the habitual meddling of Guy Stevens and Malcolm McLaren's mix'n'match policy, he even tried to persuade Specials' singer Terry Hall to defect to the Black Arabs. This came after Bernie had refused to allow the Specials to play live for six months while they honed their visual and sonic identity to his satisfaction at Rehearsals. It proved to be the last straw for the band. They left Bernie, but they took a leaf out of his book when they established their own independent label, 2 Tone. The band reached number six in the charts with their July 1979 début single, 'Gangsters', which tells the story of their relationship with their ex-manager. It includes allusions to intimidation and paranoia, and opens with the quintessentially Rhodesian command, 'Bernie Rhodes knows, don't argue!' 2 Tone would prove to be hugely successful – more of a movement than a label – and the Specials would go on to reach number one in June 1981 with the single 'Ghost Town'.

Bernie followed up his own short-lived Braik label with another, Oddball, created for the release of Dexys Midnight Runners' début single, 'Dance Stance'. Production was attributed to Foote and Mouth: Micky and Bernie. It reached number 40 in January 1980, whereupon Kevin Rowland and company fled for Phonogram and a number one summer hit with their follow up, 'Geno'. The Specials' gang image and lyrical examinations of urban decay and the privations of Thatcher's Britain bore the Rhodes stamp, as did Dexys' *Mean Streets* image and their confrontational relationship with the music press (as would the Jo Boxers' gang image and Depression chic). By 1981, the Specials and Dexys had become two of the most critically acclaimed and commercially successful bands in the UK. Bernie's manner might have discouraged these and other bands from sticking with him, but he had proved he could still pick talent and point it in the right direction.

So far as he was concerned, then, he had no reason to show any humility upon accepting his old job back with the Clash. Nobody was doing *him* any favours. 'I certainly don't see it as a permanent position,' he airily informed Chris Salewicz for the August 1981 issue of the *Face*. 'Malcolm McLaren and I have plans for something quite big that we'll probably get underway in about a year or so.' Bernie was not prepared to admit that he had been at fault in any way when his relationship with the Clash fell apart back in 1978. Situationism was to blame: 'Every situation needs a scapegoat, and I became it.'

Joe's demand for Bernie's recall cannot be dismissed as mere nostalgia for the good old days, nor as an example of a rebellious son finding himself in a jam and running for help to a previously spurned father-figure. Joe did not want the Clash to become just another rock'n'roll band, a process which he believed had started to happen with Blackhill. It was Bernie's convention-bucking off-the-wall ideas that he missed. But even Joe had his doubts about allowing Bernie to regain total control of the Clash purse-strings. At no small sacrifice to their own everyday comforts, and instead of diminishing their debt to CBS, the band had only just succeeded in paying off the £25,000 Bernie claimed they owed him from his first spell with the band. This time around, Bernie was required to take his managerial percentage out of the band's net profits, rather than their gross income.

So keen were they to boost sales of *Sandinista!* that the Clash agreed to the, for them, unprecedented release of a third single – in the UK – from what was admittedly a unusually large album. CBS and Epic were unhappy with the band's choice of 'The

Magnificent Seven'. At the end of the original six-minute track, Joe mutters, 'Fucking long, innit?' with which appraisal both record companies agreed. The swearing didn't exactly endear it to them, either. The Clash came up with a compromise solution. One of the spin-offs from the rap and dance scene in New York was the tradition of employing an outside DJ to produce a 12-inch extended dance remix for the clubs: a sort of funk equivalent of a dub version. The band agreed to supply a straightforward, edited mix of 'The Magnificent Seven' along with a longer, more experimental, instrumental remix called 'The Magnificent Dance'. At the same time, they also worked on a new instrumental mix of 'The Call Up' called 'The Cool Out'.

Credit for the remixes was given to 'Puerto Rican producer Pepe Unidos'. This was a pseudonym, according to the sleevenotes accompanying the 1999 re-issue of *Super Black Market Clash*, for a collective comprising Joe, Paul and the newly returned Bernie. They worked on the tracks at Wessex in February 1981. Whether or not Mick was available at the time, it's hard to believe that the Clash's in-house producer accepted this usurpation of his usual role with good grace.

Mick found an outlet for his talents elsewhere. Former Clash merchandiser Terry Razor was now managing a new band called Theatre of Hate, and Mick produced their single 'Rebel Without A Brain'. Meanwhile, Joe's determination to take control of his life manifested itself as body-consciousness. During the Clash's time out of the public eye, he finally visited a dentist and had his teeth fixed and capped. At the end of March, he ran the London Marathon in a Clash Take The Fifth T-shirt. It was an indication of his willpower that he completed the course despite having done no training whatsoever.

In the UK, 'The Magnificent Seven' backed with 'The Magnificent Dance' was released as a 7-inch single on 10 April and a 12-inch single on the 24th. The staggered release of different formats was another typical music industry marketing ploy of the day: it encouraged repeat buying. In the US, both tracks were combined with 'The Call Up' and 'The Cool Out' and released as a 12-inch-only EP released on 27 March. At home, the *NME* swatted the single aside. Reviewing it for *Melody Maker*, however, dance music aficionado Paolo Hewitt described it as 'a great record... it features a superb bassline, an intelligent lyric, and succeeds beautifully because Joe Strummer understands that the rhythm of his words are just as important as Mick Jones's careful funk guitar'. The single failed to climb higher than number 36 in the charts.

That March, the Clash rented Vanilla studios in Pimlico once again to rehearse some of the *Sandinista!* material for live performance and to work up further new material. Efforts were also made to rebuild the Clash team. Johnny Green, now back in the country, was offered his old job back. He stuck it for two days, then asked Joe to go for a drink. 'I said, "This is crap, Joe. The music's shit, and you don't look like a band anymore. What's going on?" He had tears in his eyes, and he said, "I don't know, Johnny." And I said, "I don't want any further part of it."' Johnny went on to have his own troubles with heroin – which claimed the life of his wife, Lindy – but eventually cleaned up, left the music business and settled down in his native Kent. After a spell as Kent County Education Adviser on drugs and sex – a job which greatly amused old friends like Robin Crocker – Johnny retired. In 1997, he published *A Riot Of Our Own*, a vivid memoir of his days with the Clash co-written by Garry Barker and illustrated by fellow Take The Fifth veteran Ray Lowry.

Even the daily football matches failed to rekindle the magic at Vanilla. Mickey Gallagher fell over during one kickabout and broke his arm. It marked the end of another association: although he was involved in one short-lived side project in late 1982,

Mickey never again played with the Clash, on record, on stage or on the pitch. Gary Barnacle was chosen to be his replacement when it came to adding musical colour to the new material. He was invited down to Vanilla with his saxes. 'And I had a couple of games of football with them, yeah.'

In mid April, the Clash went back into the studio to record three of their new songs with Gary. This time the band chose Marcus Music in Kensington Gardens. Shortly after Bernie's return to the fold, he and Kosmo had cemented their new partnership by hatching the concept of Radio Clash. 'Information comes to youth through the mass organisations like record companies and TV,' Bernie told the *NME*'s Paul Rambali that October. 'In order to create an ethnic scene that these kids feel part of, they have to have their own sources of information.'

Throughout the Sixties and early Seventies – as both the young Mick Jones and John Mellor could testify – radio had provided the means for the dissemination of youth culture's ideals. A radio discussion about unemployment had provided the motivation for Bernie's involvement in punk. The failure of the UK's national and local radio stations to get behind punk had frustrated the Clash greatly, as had the lack of funds they needed to rectify the situation by setting up their own station. Now they could see stations like WBLS becoming a vital part of hip hop culture, which, like punk before it, was a creative melting pot for music, dance, graffiti, clothes, rhetoric and attitude. In the continuing absence of a real Clash-operated alternative radio station – a WBLS for the UK – Radio Clash was conceived as a radio station of the imagination, a symbolic rallying point for a new scene or culture where ideas and music of all genres would be encouraged to cross over.

The musical vehicle for the song-of-the-concept, 'This Is Radio Clash', is another funk riff, only this time one that came via an unusual source. 'That's ripped straight off Queen's "Another One Bites The Dust",' Joe admitted to *Melody Maker* in 1988. Fair enough: Queen, in turn, had ripped it off Chic's 'Good Times'. Joe's lyric carries an echo of the Days of '76, in that it equates the lack of leisure time opportunities – specifically, the non-existence in reality of the kind of radio station Bernie, Kosmo and the band envisaged – with more blatant means of oppression.

The influence on Joe of *Apocalypse Now* had not ended with 'Charlie Don't Surf'. The film takes Joseph Conrad's *Heart Of Darkness* – a book which employs a journey into the interior of Africa as an allegory for facing the darkness in one's own soul – and transplants it to the Vietnam War. Enthused, Joe was receptive to the wave of Vietnam-related films of which it was just part. Michael Cimino's *The Deer Hunter*, Hal Ashby's *Coming Home*, and Martin Scorsese's slightly earlier *Taxi Driver* are all concerned with traumatised veterans' struggles to come to terms with their experiences and readapt to life at home. The last of these films, in particular, makes its point by relocating Travis Bickle from the jungles of Vietnam to the nocturnal urban jungle of New York's Times Square region. There were multiple connections for film buffs and 'Third World guerrillas with quiffs' like the Clash to make: this was a world where rap met their fascination with New York met their acquaintances Robert De Niro and Martin Scorsese met *Apocalypse Now* met the Sandinistas.

The screenplay for *Apocalypse Now* drew in part upon the recollections of Vietnam war correspondent Michael Herr. Jerry Green recalls that Herr's own memoir of the war, *Dispatches*, was passed around the Clash camp at this time. Along with the above-mentioned films, the book is the direct inspiration for such lines in 'This Is Radio Clash' as, 'Them that see ghettology as an urban Vietnam'. It also provided the subject matter for the lyric of 'Sean Flynn', another song written at Vanilla and recorded by the Clash at Marcus. Son of Errol – namechecked in the previous album's 'If Music Could Talk' – and a friend of Michael Herr, Sean covered the Vietnam war as a member of the press corps.

In 1970, he went missing in neighbouring Cambodia, and was presumed killed. Joe imagines Sean approaching his personal heart of darkness: 'Each man knows what he's looking for.' According to Gary Barnacle, it was Topper who was largely responsible for instigating the film soundtrack-like music for 'Sean Flynn', which Gary and Mick then developed into an extended moodpiece. The eerie melancholy of the original seven-minute version of the track owes much to Gary's multi-tracked and treated saxophone contributions. Jerry Green cites Mick's guitar playing on the song as proof of his inventiveness and steadily improving musicianship: 'The way he uses the echo box against what he's playing, chromatically: he was quite adept to be able to do that. It's like an Irish reel.'

The third song, 'Car Jamming', is built on Topper's funky Motown drum pattern. Here Joe's 'urban Vietnam' emerges from a half-sung, half-rapped lyric juxtaposing images of New York gridlock with references to disabled Vietnam veterans, creating the impression of someone about to go into Travis Bickle-style meltdown. Clash buddy Mo Armstrong was himself a Vietnam veteran, and one who had been exposed to the debilitating effects of Agent Orange, which lends Joe's references to 'Agent Orange colour blindness' a personal touch. The reference to a 'funky multi-national anthem' emerging from 'a thousand King Kong cassette decks' restates the concept behind 'This Is Radio Clash'.

Although Gary would be credited for his work on 'Sean Flynn', 'Car Jamming' would be re-recorded at a later date, and he believes his efforts are poorly represented on the released version of 'This Is Radio Clash'. 'My contribution ended up virtually inaudible, just this funny little sound in the background. It sounded great, really raw, but then Mick Jones came along and smoothed it out. The final mix has got the vocals really loud, and the backing just doesn't have the necessary power. I got the impression that Mick wasn't mixing or producing completely unselfishly. I think he had two things in mind: firstly that *his* performance should be the overriding thing; secondly, that he didn't like the fact that they'd recorded some stuff when he wasn't there.' Mick was evidently intent on reclaiming ground lost to 'Pepe Unidos'. 'It was really petty by then,' says Gary. 'Mick and Joe were hardly talking.'

Topper was clearly still capable of flashes of musical brilliance, but his appalling state could no longer be ignored. As he himself admitted the following year, the cost of his heroin habit was now running at approximately £100 a day 'just to feel normal'. 'There were times when he couldn't sit on a drum stool, or even stand up properly,' says Gary. Topper had been busted earlier in the year, something that the band were able to keep secret from the music press until he appeared at Horseferry Road court in early April charged with possession. He was conditionally discharged with the threat of a one year prison sentence hanging over his head. Aware that Gary had known Topper since they were both young boys, the rest of the Clash asked if he could do anything to help sort him out. Tied up with work commitments, Gary passed on the request to his brother Steve, the member of the Barnacle family who had always been closest to Topper. Steve was willing to try, but was unable to take any immediate action because the Clash were due back out on the road.

★★★

Instead of immediately reorganising the UK tour cancelled when Joe had delivered his ultimatum, the Clash elected to launch a mammoth 60-date US tour as a bid to exploit their breakthrough into the mainstream in that market. The reasoning was simple: neither its three singles nor *Sandinista!* itself had made any real impression in Britain, and, as Joe had intimated on Beacon Radio, the band were no longer prepared to throw away money they didn't have wooing an apparently uninterested public.

In the States, the album's January release had not exactly met with unanimous approval. *Creem*'s Jeff Nesin had shown accord with his UK counterparts by venturing the opinion, 'Generally, the further the Clash stray from their great theme, The Dying of England, the more specious and patronising their songs become.' However, in the wider circulation *Rolling Stone*, John Piccarella had given it a five star review: '*Sandinista!* is an everywhere-you-turn guerrilla raid of vision and virtuosity.' The album made number 35 in the US charts. It went on to sell around 800,000 copies world-wide, well over half of them in America. Later in the year, in separate interviews, both Mick and Joe would talk about being prophets without honour in their own land, and both would say they now felt more comfortable in New York than London.

Which made it all the more surprising that the American tour was cancelled at the last minute. That August, the band told the *Face*'s Chris Salewicz that Epic had refused to help with finance, thus forcing their hand. 'The Epic decision was an odd one,' commented Chris. 'A series of 60 gigs would have cemented the already colossal Stateside Clash popularity once and for all.' He wondered whether Epic's objection to Bernie's return might have had something to do with it.

Other factors may well have influenced the cancellation of the Clash's proposed 60-date tour. Mick's interest in studio recording and dance music had eclipsed his interest in touring as part of a rock band. 'Mick doesn't like being on the road at all,' Joe had told *Trouser Press* at the beginning of the year, even before Bernie's comeback had become a factor in the guitarist's intransigence. 'So there was a conflict there in that the rest of us really enjoy touring, and Mick thinks it's a trial and tribulation. So something or somebody has to suffer.' If Mick was reluctant, then Topper was unreliable. Aside from doubts about his ability to function for the duration of such a marathon excursion, there was also the logistical problem of keeping him supplied with the massive amounts of heroin he needed while travelling across the US by coach and plane, crossing state lines on a near-daily basis. His recent bust meant that his habit was now a matter of record. The authorities would be monitoring him closely, and any future arrest might well lead to his incarceration for real.

Ultimately, though, the manner in which the Clash chose to fill the time originally allotted to the aborted American tour gave the lie to any suggestion that they had cancelled it of their own volition. On 11 April, in response to the rumours about their imminent demise, the band released details of their schedule for the rest of the year to the music press. First on the list was a European tour; and not the Clash's usual hit and run Continental jaunt, but this time starting on 27 April and lasting for a full month. After years of dividing their attention chiefly between the US and UK, the Clash, at Bernie's instigation, had decided to live up to the more globally conscious bent of their recent music. It was not so much an extension of The Quest, as a recognition that there were other markets out there besides America that could help put the Clash's finances back in order. The European tour was to begin in Spain – the economy of which country was enjoying a post-Franco boom – and take in France, Holland, Denmark, Sweden, Germany and Italy. The band would play to crowds of between 8,000 and 15,000: a significant escalation from the size of venue they habitually played in either the UK or the US. For the first time, they were intending to make a profit from touring.

Roadent briefly returned to the fold when his company supplied the PA for the outing. The Clash were experimenting with visuals: their backdrop was now a sheet of urban wasteland-type corrugated iron, upon which were affixed posters promoting selected causes, and onto which were projected slides of Right To Work marchers in Detroit, dole queues in Britain, devastation in Cambodia, and numerous other flashpoint images. Last year, the Clash had worn predominately black clothes and the two-tone bowling shirts with rolled sleeves. Although the band still favoured this kind of clothing offstage – and Joe's rocker fixation had reached its most extreme expression in the form of an elaborate Bill Haley kiss curl – Alex Michon's stage outfits for this year were markedly different. Clearly intended to reflect the 'urban Vietnam' influence, they acknowledged the Pop Star Army Fatigues of 1977 in their use of white and bold primary colours, but also incorporated stylistic details from military wear as seen in Vietnam movies. Jackets and shirts were sleeveless, designed to show off muscle; something which Paul, Joe and Topper could carry off with some elan, but which did few favours to someone of Mick's physique.

The set drew heavily on the last two albums. There were extended jams on the more funk and dub influenced tracks, while Mick's ever-growing affection for effects pedals was evident in the lengthy guitar introductions and codas tacked onto songs old and new, particularly 'Complete Control' and 'This Is Radio Clash'. The latter also found him grabbing a pair of drumsticks and adding extra percussion. The Clash had recently become prophets *with* honour in their own land: the previously slightly ludicrous lyric of 'Guns Of Brixton' had become both topical and realistic when the always touchy relationship between police and locals in that south London borough erupted into riots early in April 1981. Although no longer focusing on the UK as a market, the band were not indifferent to events at home, and Paul's vocal feature was also given the big production treatment.

Record Mirror's Mike Nicholls was in attendance at the opening show in Barcelona, and filed a revealing report. Clash camp humour was holding together, but not without underlying barbs. Everyone had been put in charge of a fictitious Department: Bernie of Ideas, Kosmo of Information, Paul of Insults, and Mick, tellingly, of Complaints. An exhausted Topper collapsed immediately following what was now typically a two hour set, which did not augur well for the rest of the tour. Although Mike believed the band's manic behaviour to be celebratory, with the benefit of hindsight his account of the two-day drinking session and compulsive wise-cracking is more suggestive of desperation. *Melody Maker*'s Paolo Hewitt caught up with the tour nearly a month later in Milan, and got the following impression: 'Now the Clash have never seemed more buoyant. Both on and off stage.' Either the drum marathon he was having to endure every night had forced Topper to channel his attention away from drugs, or the Clash and their management team were doing a better job than usual of manipulating the music press.

An indication that the latter was the case is provided by a startling Austrian TV appearance filmed towards the end of the tour. Highlights of the band's show in Vienna – 'Clash City Rockers', 'Somebody Got Murdered', 'London Calling' and 'Safe European Home' – are intercut with some of the most revealing offstage footage of the band ever broadcast. Here, in a nutshell, is the schizophrenic nature of contemporary Clashlife laid bare… Backstage, a laughing band encourage the cameraman to film their seldom-photographed manager, supine across a row of chairs, fast asleep with his mouth wide open. 'That's Bernie Rhodes. He invented punk rock,' deadpans Joe. 'It was obviously too much for him.' But earlier, during an airport press conference, a clearly below par Topper confesses to feeling sick, and a journalist passes comment on what he evidently presumes to be passé punk posturing. 'Shut up, will you, you stupid cunt!' snarls Joe, hardly helping to revise the stereotype. 'Do you think this is 1976, and you're talking to the Sex Pistols? Piss off, or I'll piss all over you.' Paul leans menacingly into frame, jaw jutting, eyes bulging. 'If he feels like throwing up, it's because his stomach hurts,' continues Joe. 'If you want to talk about puking, go home and read your teenybop magazines. We are not a teenybop puking group!' The fact that he is moved to be so aggressive in Topper's defence – and that his rant goes off on such a bizarre tangent – gives an indication of just how much strain the drummer's condition was putting him under.

Such dramas failed to make the British music press. Even the notoriously bitchy *NME* T-Zers page took the trouble to report that the European tour had been an overwhelming success, referring to crowds in Lyon and Paris going 'apeshit, monkeypoo and orangutangdung'.

Determined to make at least some kind of impression upon the American market, the Clash camp had come up with a promotional wheeze that was thematically appropriate to the Clash's current record release: a residency of a magnificent seven dates to be played in late May and the first week of June 1981 at Bonds Casino, situated on Broadway as it enters Times Square, New York: Travis Bickle country. Although events would conspire to make this seem like a stroke of promotional near-genius, in truth it was not even an original idea. Mott the Hoople had attracted heavy publicity for being the first ever rock band to play a residency on Broadway, appearing at the 2,000-capacity Uris Theatre from 7-11 May 1974, as preserved for posterity on that year's *Mott The Hoople Live*.

The tickets for all seven of the Clash's shows sold out on the day they became available. On Thursday 27 May 1981, the first show went ahead as planned, but the band came offstage to find firemen storming through the club. The next day, the Fire Department announced that Bonds' supposed 4,000 capacity represented a fire risk, and insisted that no more than 1,750 should be allowed into any future gig. Unbeknownst to the Clash, they had arrived in New York just as it was entering one of its periodic Club Wars: there were simply too many live attractions in the city to keep every venue in business, and the band and Bonds were victims of the resultant dirty tricks campaign.

Following a meeting with the club management, it was agreed that Bonds would cancel its forthcoming bookings – Gary Glitter and the Stranglers – and the band would extend their residency to a total of 16 days, including some extra matinee shows. The Clash agreed to absorb the cost of extra accommodation, equipment and crew wages in order to allow everyone who had bought a ticket to see them, if not quite on the date they had originally planned. Friday night saw a bit of bad feeling in the Square from those who were turned away, but Bonds had time to warn future audiences in advance, thus avoiding further last minute disappointments. Or so they thought: on Saturday morning, the city's Building Department declared Bonds a potential fire trap, and used a court order to close the club indefinitely. The fans who turned up for that afternoon's show blocked the Square and caused a mini-riot, requiring the area to be cleared by mounted police.

The situation was a PR man's dream come true, and Kosmo immediately started wheeling and dealing with the media. Promising each of them an exclusive, he managed to get all seven of New York's major TV news channels to carry an item on the riot. A special edition of the *New York Post* ran the front cover headline '"CLASH" IN TIMES SQUARE'; the band had the cover reproduced on T-shirts. The media were not only fascinated by the riots but also by the fact that the Clash had chosen to play Bonds in the first place, rather than the 16,000-capacity Madison Square Garden. On Sunday, having been badgered ceaselessly by his Clash-loving daughters, the New York Building Commissioner stepped in. He decreed that, providing Bonds reworked their fire escape system, improved security, and stuck rigidly to the restrictions imposed by the Fire Department, they could continue with the shows. It felt like a triumph, and it was publicised as such back home: Mick Farren filed a report for the *NME*, and Alan Lewis for *Sounds*.

This was an exciting period for the band. Don Letts was with them, with the dual intention of shooting a video for 'This Is Radio Clash' and a longer documentary feature entitled *Clash On Broadway*, capturing both the band's performances and all elements –

the rap, the graffiti, the breakdancing – of New York's emergent hip hop culture. The scenes outside Bonds provided him with ideal footage, excerpts from which were projected onto the backdrop during the shows. Don introduced the band to graffiti artist Futura 2000. The band persuaded him to spray over the backdrop while they played, and also to take the microphone while they backed him on his own rap, 'The Escapades Of Futura 2000'. Rap groups the Treacherous Three and Grandmaster Flash and the Furious Five – soon to push the idiom to a whole new level with 'The Message' – were hired as two of the many and varied support acts.

The Clash were ecstatic to tune into WBLS and find that the DJs were not only playing 'The Magnificent Dance' up to five times a day, but also doing their own remixes of it, dubbing on samples from the soundtrack of *Dirty Harry*. 'That bit where Harry goes, "To tell the truth, in all this excitement I kinda forgot myself..."' burbled Joe to Alan Lewis. 'Why isn't radio that good in Britain?' Picking up on the cue, the Clash started using Ennio Morricone's theme '60 Seconds To Watch' from another Clint Eastwood movie, *For A Few Dollars More*, as their play-on music. On 5 June, the publicity engendered by the Bonds residency won the Clash their second American TV appearance. NBC's *Tomorrow Show* catches them cracking wise in response to presenter Tom Snyder's dull questions and performing their most WBLS-friendly tracks 'The Magnificent Seven' and 'This Is Radio Clash' in front of a giant graffiti'd Clash logo.

Martin Scorsese came along to the second night's show. Although his proposed movie *Gangs Of New York* was no nearer production, he invited the band to appear, fleetingly, as street hoodlum extras in *King Of Comedy*, the movie he was currently shooting with favourite leading man Robert De Niro. It was an offer they could not refuse. Joe and Kosmo lived out a movie of their own, spending most nights after the gig drinking and playing pool in sleazy dive bars until the early hours of the morning, sometimes in the company of De Niro.

The Clash's much publicised interest in Nicaragua encouraged representatives of the Democratic Revolutionary Front of neighbouring El Salvador to approach them. Flattered, and happy to help the cause, the band agreed to allow them to man a stall at the venue, but balked at the request that they be allowed to take the stage to make speeches. Instead, Joe said he would shout 'El Salvador!' towards the end of 'Washington Bullets', and they could take it in turns to declaim over the music while information leaflets were dropped from the ceiling. Alan Lewis challenged Joe about trendy cause-hopping, suggesting that the political situation was less clear-cut in El Salvador than it had been in Nicaragua. 'They haven't been given the chance to self-determine,' Joe replied. 'You ask me how deeply I've gone into the situation, and I'd have to say not deeply at all. Where can I get my information? There's an absolute restriction on accurate information... But I've talked to a few people from El Salvador, and I know the number of people dead or missing is running at about 60 a day at this moment.' Then, tellingly, he began to relate US intervention in that country to the situation in Vietnam in the early Sixties. 'Now today, the US is limbering up for *another* Vietnam. It's only films like *Apocalypse Now* that are gonna save El Salvador.' Alan Lewis was uncomfortable that the Clash were in New York, 'getting the kudos while other people are shedding blood'. 'I have no confusion about this,' said Joe. 'I know what I'm here to do, and I'm doing it.'

Yet another stage guest-to-be presented himself at the 12 June show. Poet Allen Ginsberg was one of the leading lights of the American Beat literary movement, and therefore a figure held in some regard by Mick and, particularly, Joe, who greeted him by asking when he was going to run for President. Allen was invited to read a couple of poems preceding the band's encores, but instead suggested the band accompany him on a 'poem with chord changes' called 'Capital Air'. Everyone enjoyed the collaboration, with the exception of Paul who later admitted to Chris Salewicz that Allen, a hippy before hippies existed, was 'not exactly my cup of tea'. Allen subsequently told Barry Miles, author of the 1989 biography *Ginsberg* – the same Barry Miles who, while interviewing the Clash back in 1976, had had a flick-knife stuck up his nose by Joe – 'They're all good musicians, Mick Jones especially, and they're very sensitive and very literate underneath all the album cover roughneck appearance. I don't know of any other band that would, in the middle of a big heavy concert, be willing to go onstage with a middle-aged goose like me.' The live recording was later included on the 1994 Ginsberg anthology *Holy Soul Jelly Roll: Poems And Songs 1949-1983*.

The following night's show was recorded for the *Clash On Broadway* film and the extended 'This Is Radio Clash' promotional film. The latter is really two videos joined together. It opens with the dramatic organ pipe play-on music of '60 Seconds To Watch', while pictures of the band getting ready backstage are intercut with excerpts from the TV coverage of the Time Square riot and a huge graffiti'd Clash banner being unfurled over the Bond Casino facade. The band take the stage and kick into 'London Calling', which is in turn intercut with flashpoint images culled from TV news reports. The 'This Is Radio Clash' segment follows on, and intercuts the Bonds performance of the song with footage of the Clash dancing around on Bonds' rooftop, hefting ghetto blasters, and taking part in a graffiti raid with Futura, and with more general glimpses of New York hip hop culture, like graffiti'd trains and breakdancing challenges.

The publicity generated by the residency played no small part in taking the Clash on to the next level in the States. As former White Panther Mick Farren remarked at the time, 'America seems to need a big, bold bad-ass rock'n'roll band. For some reason they're unable to produce one for themselves. [This was many years pre-Guns'N'Roses.] Basically, the Rolling Stones' old slot is going begging... and, if not the whole of America, at least New York seems anxious to shoehorn the Clash into it.' Back in town with BAD II almost exactly 10 years later, Mick told the *NME*'s James Brown, 'We ran this town. We took Broadway. De Niro was bringing his kids to see us, and the city stopped. The Clash were in town.' The residency was certainly a key event in Clash history – and would have even greater significance thrust upon it in 1991 when the band's boxed set retrospective was given the title *Clash On Broadway* – but it was not without its attendant disappointments, failures and moments of unpleasantness.

Immediately after her January UK tour, Pearl Harbour had lost her recording contract and band and split up with Kosmo. Since then, though, she had fallen into a relationship with Paul, and been invited along to DJ at the Bonds shows. One night someone spiked her drink with acid and she began to trip so badly she had to be taken to hospital.

The marathon stint at the club, coming directly on top of the European tour, also proved too much for Topper. Perhaps Mick Farren caught him on a good, early night when he described him as 'rock steady... he lays down the foundation rhythm for the Clash with a dependability that can't be beat', or perhaps he was just trying to offer his encouragement. In March 1982, Topper himself would admit to Roz Reines that his drumming had been below par for the past two years. Louise Bolloton had won a trip to see the band at Bonds in an *NME* competition which had required readers to come up with a magnificent seven insults for the Clash. She begged to differ about the state of the drummer's health: 'Topper spoke to us a couple of times, but he seemed to be out of his brain most of the time.' She also described Bernie as thoroughly obnoxious, astutely noting that, 'It seems the only people who like him are Strummer and his girlfriend, Gaby.' Alan Lewis certainly found Bernie objectionable, and also noted Kosmo's bullying tactics in his report.

The predominately white American audience proved resistant to anything that challenged their preconceptions of a rock'n'roll gig. Most of the support bands were given a rough time, particularly Grandmaster Flash and the Furious Five, who had trash thrown at them. Mick made it a furious six. 'It's disgusting,' he fumed to Mick Farren. 'I mean, it's an insult to us when you look at it. We picked the bands that opened for us. We wanted to turn the crowd onto something. They're too narrow-minded to open up to something new.' The reality of the multi-cultural Radio Clash appeared to be a long way off.

The band's performance in *King Of Comedy* was so wooden that the bulk of it ended up on the cutting room floor. 'Nil points for us that day,' Joe conceded to *Uncut*'s Gavin Martin in 1999. 'We just kind of stood there, bumbling around.' There would be no chance for the band to redeem themselves with Martin Scorsese: *Gangs Of New York* would remain in development limbo for another 20 years.

Reports in the music press over the next 10 months made Don Letts's *Clash On Broadway* film sound an exciting (and expensive) project, a kaleidoscopic celebration of hip hop New York. In May 1982, Chris Salewicz announced via the pages of the *Face* that 'Letts and Bernie Rhodes are currently negotiating with major distributors for an autumn release'. Subsequent upheavals in the Clash camp led to the project being shelved, however. 'As far as I know, the reels were stored in a rental place in New York,' Joe told Chris in 1994 for *Mojo*. 'Bernie forgot to pay the rent, and the footage was destroyed. The only surviving bit was 10 minutes that Don found at the bottom of his wardrobe. Part of a cutting copy, but only 10 minutes of it.' That and the footage used in the promotional film for 'This Is Radio Clash' are all that remain of yet another ill-fated Clash movie attempt. It seems that the soundtrack did survive in some form. Three other tracks from the Bonds show recording appeared on the 1999 live compilation CD *From Here To Eternity*: guitar effects-drenched versions of 'Complete Control', 'Train In Vain' and 'Guns Of Brixton'.

June and early July 1981 saw further insurrectionary activity in the UK. Several areas of London, Toxteth in Liverpool, Birmingham, Wolverhampton, Reading, Luton, Chester, Hull and Preston were among the cities and towns that wanted and had a riot of their own. Some of the band's critics started to get tetchy – much as Tony Parsons had done four years earlier – about the irony of the former White Rioters playing 'Guns Of Brixton' on Broadway while genuine expressions of frustration and dissent were taking place in their home country. That October, it was Mick's turn to put the case for the defence to the *NME*'s Paul Rambali, though he also took the opportunity to send what – in the wake of the 'disagreement' over the continuing relevance of 'White Riot' – was clearly a loaded message to Joe. 'I don't think I'd make such a good rioter. I don't think I even agree with them. Destroying your own places, especially when the government ain't gonna give you another one, it seems really *double* dumb. I do my thing and it's a creative thing, that's how I feel I contribute. And if my absence is conspicuous on these occasions, then I say, "Don't look to me in the first place." I'm not a street fighting man. I still got a belief in the power of reason. I think I'd be really *stupid* to go out and think I could lead the people.'

Even Bernie took a measured approach. 'I don't know whether the riots were that major in terms of people being clear about what was going on,' he pontificated. 'It was just a fracas. The Clash are interested in politics rather than revolution. Revolution sets a country back a hundred years. Revolution is very, very dangerous. I don't think we were ever revolutionary, I think we were always interested in the politics of the situation. And I think we still are. But I think that England's less interested.' A year earlier, he had told the same writer, 'I think you could have a cultural revolution, but not an actual revolution. The culture side of it is the interesting thing. That's possible. The other one isn't.'

Bernie's argument was specific to the UK, and therefore did not necessarily contradict the band's stance on Central America. That said, both he and Mick were adopting positions that were a long way from 1976-vintage Clash rhetoric, without making any attempt to acknowledge or explain the change. And Mick and Joe's insistence that they were just artists and observers was also somewhat removed from the first person 'authenticity' of yesteryear, when Mick wasn't ashamed to fight and Joe didn't mind throwing a brick.

Having surrendered the lease to his Notting Hill flat shortly before going on tour, Joe returned to the UK to find himself in the all-too-familiar state of homelessness. There had been an element of conscious martyrdom in allowing things to get to this state: the other three members of the Clash had managed to house themselves adequately over the course of the last year. Topper was still renting in Fulham, and Paul had his tiny Oxford Gardens flat. Upon moving out of 111 Wilmcote House for good in 1980, Mick had found a flat just off Powis Square, still within a couple of hundred yards of Ladbroke Grove. Professing himself to be 'baffled' by his own situation, Joe moved into the Bloomsbury squat occupied by Tymon Dogg.

It had been arranged for Steve Barnacle to move in with Topper in order to mind him and help him get back in shape. Like his brother Gary, though, Steve was a working musician – then between tours as bassist with Rick Wakeman – and could not provide a 24-hour service. Temptation was never far away. 'Topper was telling me he didn't want to do drugs anymore, he wanted to get fit and healthy,' says Steve. 'I'd come back in of a night, and there'd be this big party going on, and it was just drugs-a-go-go. It was almost like a schoolmaster finding the pupil doing wrong. He'd be all embarrassed, but I'd say, "If you're going to do it, you're going to do it." His old girlfriend had been well into drugs herself and not a good influence on him, but the new one was an out-and-out junkie. I walked into the bathroom to use the loo once and he was in there helping her shoot up. I lived there for a couple of months, but I had to leave because I had a couple of run-ins with these dealers.' The dealers were running Topper's parties on a tab: letting him and his hangers-on have whatever they wanted, then periodically insisting on 'settling up' with the host. 'They'd turn around and say, "Right, you owe us three grand this month,"' says Steve. And he'd go, "*What?!*" Of course he's been out of his head all month, and he's got no way of knowing what he owes, and he can't say, "No way! Fuck off!" because it'll end up with his hands being broken. That's the sort of people he was in with.'

Mick was so into hip hop that he would have WBLS broadcasts taped and sent over to him. By now, he was listening to the music constantly on a ghetto blaster, and even affecting a back-to-front baseball cap. In 1986, he told *Rolling Stone*'s David Fricke that the others used to call him Whack Attack. It was not meant affectionately. 'They accused me of bringing my New York environment everywhere I went with them.' In August 1981, he brought it to AIR studios to work on alternative DJ mixes for 'This Is Radio Clash'. 'Pepe Unidos' was not invited. With Jerry Green engineering, Mick made a fair stab at squeezing a radio programme's worth of material out of the one song. The 'version' entitled 'Radio Clash' is in reality just part two of the original track, featuring alternative semi-improvised lyrics from Joe. The first remix proper, entitled 'Outside Broadcast' is an interminable wig-out, with female backing vocals, the main riff played on sampled car horns, 'typewriters going like machine guns', and Joe's nonsense lead vocal varispeeded as low as it can go. The second, 'Radio 5' features dub effects like backwards taping and heavy echo, but is really a showcase for Mick's adventures on the wheels of steel: his attempt to get to grips with scratching, another of New York DJ culture's innovations.

After the expense and time devoted to recording *Sandinista!* and the accusations of self-indulgence it had brought down upon the band's heads, Bernie and Joe wanted the follow-up album to be recorded quickly and cheaply in the UK. Joe was doubly determined to record in the Guy Stevens style when he heard about the producer's death at the end of August. Rehearsals for the Clash's next string of dates commenced at the beginning of September, in Ear studios rehearsal room, located in the Peoples' Hall, Freston Road, in the shadow of the Westway. The Clash decided to combine these rehearsals with songwriting and recording sessions, again in an attempt to recapture the spirit of *London Calling*. Joe was even harking back to his 1979-vintage idea of making an album on a TEAC portable studio. His interest in production values had never been particularly great, as he told the *NME*'s Richard Cook in 1984: 'The greatest records on my shelf are the ones made with a couple of microphones.' Paul was in accord, his passion for obscure rockabilly having grown during the course of the last two years.

Mick's interests had, of course, taken him in almost completely the opposite direction both musically and with regard to technology. To him, Joe's suggestion seemed to be – and perhaps was – another attempt to undermine his position in the band. A compromise of sorts was agreed. The Clash hired the Rolling Stones' mobile studio – several steps up from a portastudio – and linked it up to the rehearsal room, once again bringing in Jerry Green to act as engineer. Joe was still standing up for rap and dub in the interviews he gave at the end of 1981, telling Keri Phillips of Australian magazine *RAM*: 'When I put on a rap 12-inch or a Jamaican reggae record, I know that the singers are gonna hit me with something I'm not gonna expect in a million years.' By then, though, it was so much lip-service. The critics had upset Joe, and his commitment to the Clash's recent musical direction was already shaky: several of the songs recorded on the mobile evidence a bias away from the funky groove music that was Mick's preference at the time towards the retro musics favoured by Joe and Paul. The uneasy middle ground the band found persevered to some extent with the fusion trend of *Sandinista!*, but instead of frenetic globe-hopping and the throwing together of exotic hybrids, attempted to incorporate the diverse influences in a sound that was identifiably the Clash's own. 'We're just trying to boil it down to one music,' Joe told Roz Reines early in 1982. 'Not trying to ignore anything that we've heard before, but we want to make it our own, and all at once in every track.'

'Midnight To Stevens' is the Clash's tribute to Guy. Attributed to Strummer-Jones, it is a sentimental ballad, part Ian Hunter, part Sixties girl group, with a lyric listing both the producer's achievements and failings. After recording it, the band promptly forgot about it until it was disinterred for inclusion on 1991's *Clash On Broadway*. Given his recent leanings, Mick's solo composition 'Should I Stay Or Should I Go' is surprisingly old-fashioned. As John Brown suggests, it owes something to the Sharks' 'Sophistication', but it is even more strongly reminiscent of Mitch Ryder and the Detroit Wheels' 1966 US hit 'Little Latin Lupe Lu', a long-time favourite of Chrissie Hynde. Its lyric was made to seem prophetic by future events. Speaking to the *NME*'s Stuart Bailie in 1991, Mick would acknowledge that 'maybe it was pre-empting my leaving the Clash', but maintained that 'it was about a personal situation', namely, his relationship with Ellen Foley.

Paul, Mick and Joe co-wrote 'Long Time Jerk', harmonica-driven cajun skiffle with a lyric on a vaguely romantic theme, and 'First Night Back In London', a sort of club-footed rockabilly funk soundtracking the noirish account of a drug bust. Although Topper's lifestyle would seem to be the source of inspiration for this song, that lifestyle had reduced him to the status of 'just the drummer' on the sessions: he did not contribute as composer to any of the above material. Whether or not he had any say in other songs written and recorded at this time was subsequently obscured by the band's decision to persevere with the collective Clash songwriting credit for their fifth studio album.

Another hard rocking funk number – much more so in its original form than in the subsequently released version – is 'Overpowered By Funk'. In the tradition of 'Capital Radio Two' and 'Lovers' Rock', Joe's lyric mocks the song's very genre – 'asinine, stupefying' – before using it as a soapbox from which to rubbish Western capitalist greed. Political subject matter had so far been off the agenda, but Joe further redressed the balance with his sardonic 'Know Your Rights'. A souped-up rockabilly number with a rolling 'Ghost Riders In The Sky'-type guitar riff, it can only think of three basic human rights to list – all of them subject to provisos which ultimately render them worthless – before concluding that the only rights most people are likely to experience are the ones the police read them while making an arrest. 'Inoculated City' adapts a military march for another anti-war song, this time attacking the unquestioning chain of command from president to private. 'Ghetto Defendant', a laid back reggae lope, concerns New York's inner city drug crisis, blaming heroin-induced despondency for lack of positive communal action.

'Know Your Rights', 'Should I Stay Or Should I Go', 'Inoculated City' and 'Ghetto Defendant' were all worked up for the tour, the imminence of which meant further recording had to be suspended until late November.

At the end of September 1981, the Clash revived the magnificent seven residency concept at the Mogador in Paris. Robin Crocker attended. The account he filed for *ZigZag* under his traditional nom-de-plume Robin Banks was predictably upbeat, but it did include one revealing vignette: a dressing room discussion instigated by Bernie that developed into a row about Topper's condition. Robin dismissed this as 'completely unnecessary paranoia', citing Topper's ability to count off 50 press-ups before taking the stage as proof that he was in the best of health. Always a fit man, Topper's physique was just about holding together; the problems were with his timing, co-ordination and behaviour. Robin had always been a heavy drinker and gung ho hedonist, prone to violent and destructive outbursts, which goes some way to explaining his refusal or inability to recognise the damage Topper was doing to himself. Tellingly, the changing atmosphere around the Clash prompted Robin and other long-time liggers like Kris Needs to move out of their orbit around this time. Both would leave *ZigZag*. Kris would succumb to drug addiction, as recounted in his autobiography *Needs Must*. Robin would succumb to alcoholism and do another stretch in prison.

The *NME*'s Paul Rambali also caught up with the Clash in Paris, but his access was limited to Joe and Mick. He asked the usual spiky questions, and was met with defiance. Mick objected to being called a remote rock star. Joe objected to what he perceived to be the paper's relentless negativity and obsession with the band's credibility. 'If they're teaching their readers to hate us, then I'd like to ask the *NME* who they're teaching their readers to trust? Which groups? Which ideas? I'm looking hard, and I can't see anybody.'

The Clash's long-delayed UK tour commenced in October 1981: a mere six provincial dates followed by another magnificent seven residency at the Lyceum in London. As ever, the Clash had allowed themselves to be conditioned by the music press to expect hostility from the audiences on the UK leg of the tour. They were consequently taken aback by the positive reception they received, and the accompanying belated revelation that most fans were unlikely to have their opinions swayed by the odd bad review. 'They were so keen to see us, and I can't say there was any resentment, or anything like that,' Mick told Duncan Campbell in 1982. 'It touched us all.' 'That's another bum steer that the *NME* gave me,' grumbled Joe to the paper's Roz Reines in March 1982. 'I believed them when they said we weren't liked there [in the UK]. In fact, the guy on the street was digging us.'

The response of their UK fans confirmed the band in a belief that both Mick and Joe had been voicing since early that summer, when Jerry, one of the roadies, had told them that British rock fans were becoming dispirited by the Clash's failure to make it big. 'If I don't make it, then all the kids who are watching can say to themselves, "Well, shit, they didn't make it, they didn't get out, what hope is there for us to make it?"' Joe had told Mick Farren in New York. 'If we make it, then those kids know that *they* got a chance, too.' This was Mick's romanticised vision of his own adolescence writ large. Now enshrined as Clash policy, it was taken by the band as a mandate to relax more and more of their punk-era principles as they went in search of success: not to line their own pockets, heaven forfend, but as a symbolic gesture on behalf of the downtrodden masses. It was conveniently forgotten that the Clash had not previously thought of 'making it' in commercial terms as a goal in itself: before, they had aspired to make it creatively without compromising their ideals. Nor was it acknowledged that – phoney Beatlemania having bitten the dust – the idea of 'the kids' looking up to their rock'n'roll heroes was the very antithesis of punk's DIY spirit. The truth was simply that the band wanted to make a lot of money because they were sick of the restrictions their debt placed upon them. Being the Clash, though, they couldn't just admit that to journalists. Or, it would appear, even to themselves.

The Clash took the stage to the sound of an air raid siren. The stage set was still 'urban Vietnam', with tiger-striped checkpoint barriers and graffiti artist Futura 2000 working his aerosols as the band played. Barney Hoskyns attended the first of the Lyceum gigs and gave the band the now-traditional good kicking on behalf of the *NME*. According to Barney, their material consisted of 'wavering, sanctimonious pseudo-songs' and 'decisively *unloose* funk-rock'; Joe kept 'emitting that absurd screech about five times during the course of every song'; Mick played 'some of the worst guitar the Lyceum has probably ever witnessed'; and 'the Clash aren't terribly exciting on stage – had you ever noticed?'

Melody Maker's Adam Sweeting was more reserved, though he did agree with Barney about Mick's guitar playing that particular night. He began his review, 'Who'd be the Clash? Not me, squire. They can't win,' and ended it, 'They've had the sense to move on and diversify, and in many cases they've done it well… Whose fault is it that, however well the Clash play, their fiercest finest hour has passed?' After attending two more shows during the course of the residency, however, he wrote a second, longer piece acknowledging that he had warmed to the band more on each occasion, and wondering why it was they were now so out of favour with the music press. Under the heading 'The Clash And Cocktail Culture', he likened the New Pop zeitgeist to the era of the Flappers in the Twenties. 'This new attitude seems to me like an abject admission of defeat… Instead of determination we have submission. Instead of heart, we prefer plastic soul… Maybe everything's too serious and depressing for music to be serious anymore… After the challenges of punk and the earthy dynamics of its aftermath, I think we're back to worse than square one. I think we're working for the clampdown.' Over the next year, Joe too would be increasingly drawn to this line of thinking.

'This Is Radio Clash' was released as a 7-inch single on 11 November 1981 and a 12-inch single on 4 December. The debate on the Clash's relevance was continued by Gavin Martin in his *NME* review. 'Another rag bag of musical clichés and political simplifications… a sprawling, splintered fantasy which presents the zombified vision of would-be media guerrillas with rampant hysteria. "This Is Radio Clash" is a four part epic: scrubbed up, dubbed down and sellotaped together… More than any group I can think of – and that's not to say their intentions aren't sincere – the Clash highlight the age-old inadequacy of the white musician as culture vulture.' The single stalled at number 47 in the UK charts, and, when it was released there on 25 November, failed to make the US charts at all.

Satisfied with the way recording had progressed using the mobile at Ear studios, once the UK tour was over Joe suggested continuing in similar vein. Mick, however, thought the tracks were below par, and decided the shift away from what he wished to do had gone far enough. He wanted to record in New York, partly because that's where music was at its most exciting, partly because the studios were better equipped, and partly so he could spend some time tending to his relationship with Ellen Foley. Instead of taking the trouble to explain his motives, though, he elected to play Joe at his own game and deliver an ultimatum. 'He said, "Good luck to you then, because I'm not coming to the sessions,"' Joe told the *NME*'s Richard Cook in 1984. '"If you do it in New York, I'll turn up." So we got a studio there, so the Emperor could attend.'

The studio was Electric Lady: familiar, but ruinously expensive. Not only did the band have to pay for the recording facilities and hotel bills, but also for the hire of all the musical equipment. Last time, they had just completed a US tour, and therefore had their own gear to hand. Jerry Green, their engineer of choice, had recently become a father. While he would have been available for recording in London, he made it clear that he had no intention of leaving his family in order to come to New York. Which meant the Clash also had to work with unfamiliar personnel, namely engineer Joe Blaney and tape operator Eddie Garcia.

Joe, Paul and the management team shared similar feelings about the Clash's future development. Mick was out of favour because of his refusal to acknowledge budget restrictions and because of his increasingly petulant behaviour. Topper's addiction had stretched everyone's patience to breaking point. Although not necessarily of like mind, the two outcasts teamed up for mutual support, and the band thus split into two factions. Mick and Topper were still by far the most musically gifted members of the Clash, and as songwriters, Joe and Paul had previously relied heavily upon the creative input and arranging skills of the other two. With Topper's capabilities limited, and Mick's co-operation withdrawn, the singer and bassist now found themselves musically marginalised. Joe was still in charge of the lyrical content, but much of the new music recorded at the Electric Lady sessions evidences a shift back towards Mick's preferences. Mick's insistence on taking charge of production – even more assertively than on previous occasions – also gave him control over the sound of both the new material and that recorded earlier at Ear studios, most of which he insisted on re-recording from scratch. To put it mildly, this did not go down well with Joe and Paul.

The unsteady boat was rocked even further when, upon returning to the UK for Christmas, Topper was arrested – on what was indeed his first night back in London – for smuggling heroin into Heathrow airport. Prison was a real possibility, but when Topper appeared at Uxbridge Magistrates Court on 17 December, his defence counsel pleaded that he was a valuable member of the band – 'recently voted one of the world's top five drummers' – and was needed at the recording sessions. He admitted to being an addict, but claimed he was now determined to mend his ways. Topper was fined £500 and told, 'Unless you accept treatment, you will be the best drummer in the graveyard.' Realising he had pushed his luck about as far as it would go, Topper pledged to kick his habit.

Joe announced the new album was going to be a single disc. At the time, he explained this by claiming Epic had deliberately failed to promote *Sandinista!* as it was in danger of setting a precedent for economically unsound multi-disc releases. Labelmate Bruce Springsteen had responded to *London Calling* with the similarly-packaged double set

The River, and Epic – according to Joe – were determined to stop the rot. (Another possible explanation for their cancellation of the 60-date US tour earlier in the year.) 'Even here in New York,' Joe told *RAM*'s Keri Phillips during the album sessions, 'if my tape-operator wants to buy a copy of *Sandinista!*, which is supposedly my current LP – and remember we're not in Peru or Baghdad or Bombay or even Alice Springs, we're here in New York, supposedly the centre of the Western World – he can't even buy it. *That's* why it's gonna be one record.' Whether or not his conspiracy theory was grounded in fact, this was a rationalisation of an expedient move: the Clash wanted to make money from their fifth album, and would not be able to do so if they continued the trend established by their last two VFM releases.

Recording produced several new tracks. 'Cool Confusion' is sort of semi-electro dub-funk. As ever, the song Paul originated, 'Red Angel Dragnet', has a strong reggae flavour. He sang it, as usual, in what Mick kindly described at the time as his 'Jamaican Marlene Dietrich' style. 'Atom Tan' has a soul strut riding behind its call-and-response vocals. 'Kill Time' and 'The Beautiful People' are variants on calypso-funk. Topper gave some indication of working methods in the *Clash On Broadway* booklet when he revealed that 'Straight To Hell' began as a Mick Jones guitar doodle that would not work with a rock'n'roll beat; so Topper grafted on a bossa nova drum pattern, itself drawn from a Brazilian hybrid of samba, baiao and jazz.

It would be a mistake to take the fact that Topper also single-handedly wrote the music for 'Rock The Casbah' as an indication of his creative resurgence: the piano riff was one that he had been toying with for years. However, finding himself the only member of the band in the studio one morning, Topper was sufficiently industrious to record the piano, the drums and the bass for what was supposed to be a rough demo. In the event, the band just looped the tape to double its length and used it as a backing track. Joe was impressed both by the song and the speed of recording. Mick needed a little more persuasion before he added a few guitar chords. 'When you're concentrating on the latest masterpiece you've carefully put together and someone comes up with something so fast, it can be a little disorienting,' Joe waspishly remarked to Gavin Martin for *Uncut* in 1999. Joe's lyric was inspired by hearing about floggings meted out to anyone owning a disco album in Iran, a country he had visited as a schoolboy, and where – ironically – he had bought his first Chuck Berry EP, the one with sleeve notes by Guy Stevens.

The inspiration for Joe's other lyrics was varied, yet touched on several familiar themes. The New Year's Day shooting of Frankie Melvin, member of subway vigilante group the Red Angels, gave him 'Red Angel Dragnet'. As it does for 'Ghetto Defendant', the inner-city drug crisis informs part of 'Straight To Hell', a song also listing the dominant culture's rejection of unemployed English Northerners, mixed race children of Vietnamese women and American GI's, and immigrants in general. 'The Beautiful People' and 'Cool Confusion' are both vicious critiques of those who live on the other side of the social divide. 'The beautiful people are ugly, too' insists the former, while the latter takes its inspiration from a first hand observation made in Studio 54 and other bastions of New York's clubland: the In-Crowd's tendency to sweep into a place, make a show of looking around with disdain, then sweep out again. Both 'Ghetto Defendant' and 'Atom Tan' allude to the bigger picture, ending on decidedly Strummeresque apocalyptic notes.

Taking the 1981 material overall, the drug bust in 'First Night Back In London', the steel mills in 'Straight To Hell' and Jack the Ripper in 'Red Angel Dragnet' are the sum total of references to London, the UK and the culture that bore the Clash. When eventually released, the new album would carry the catalogue number FMLN 2, a gesture of support for El Salvador's rebel forces (Farabundo Marti Liberacion Nacional). Unlike *Sandinista!*, though, the lyrics for the Clash's funky multi-national anthems do not take the listener out into the wider world. Joe's central conceit requires him to adopt a specifically American perspective. A New York-like inner city ghetto awash with drugs and guns is the scene for 'Ghetto Defendant', 'Overpowered By Funk', 'Car Jamming', 'Red Angel Dragnet', and part of 'Straight To Hell'. Although their portrayal of social collapse is both vivid and realistic, the songs are not set in real New York, but reel New York. A certain South-East Asian war hovers in the background like a recurring nightmare, just a slow dissolve or jump cut away.

Joe's 'urban Vietnam' imagery owes much to the movies, and other filmic references abound. 'What is the dream? I'll tell it / To live like they do in the movies,' states 'Red Angel Dragnet'. Like 'Sean Flynn', 'Death Is A Star' could almost be an atmospheric soundtrack piece. 'It's about the way we all queue up at the cinema to see someone get killed,' Joe told Roz Reines early the following year. 'These days, the public execution is the celluloid execution. I was examining why I want to go and see these movies, because deep in my heart I want to see a man pull out a machine gun and go *blam, blam, blam* into somebody's body.' Similarly, the protagonist of 'Atom Tan' whiles away the four minute nuclear warning watching the skies for the Lone Ranger or some other comforting celluloid or comic superhero. By the end of the Electric Lady sessions the album even had a movie title: *Rat Patrol From Fort Bragg*.

The Clash were due to resume their new-market-breaking tour at the end of January 1982, with gigs in Japan, New Zealand, Australia and South East Asia. Work on the album was supposed to be wrapped up by the end of December 1981, but by that time the band were still not only overdubbing but also recording backing tracks for new numbers. The progress of the project was beginning to resemble that of the last one. Not only did the Clash end up with far too many songs – 17 – but the tracks themselves were lengthy, more in the tradition of extended 12-inch rap and funk mixes than the short sharp shocks of punk era singles and album tracks. Bernie Rhodes was heard to grumble, 'Does everything have to be as long as a raga?' It gave Joe the opening line for 'Rock The Casbah', but was intended as a real criticism of the Clash's – and particularly Mick's – self indulgence: experiments with Indian ragas in the mid-to-late Sixties had precipitated the progressive rock so loathed by Class of '76 punks. More importantly, as the tussle over 'The Magnificent Seven' had proved, the record company and most mainstream radio stations were still antagonistic to lengthy singles.

As recording went over schedule – and way over budget – tempers became even more frayed. During one memorable argument, Joe accused Mick of starting all the rot by insisting the album should be recorded in New York. 'He turned around and said, "I was only joking,"' Joe told the N*ME*'s Richard Cook in 1984, still aghast over two years after the event. In early January, Mick and Joe, again barely talking, began working separate shifts, the former recording guitar overdubs by day and the latter vocals by night. Unhappy with how things were going under Mick's direction and finding it difficult to communicate with Joe Blaney, Joe made a desperate phone call to Jerry Green, begging him to come out and help for just a little while. Against his better judgement, Jerry heeded the call on 5 January 1982, and ended up being away from his partner and newborn child for a total of three weeks. 'At the end, we had two studios going simultaneously,' he says.

Mick was playing his guitars through a battery of effects pedals to make them sound, in Paul's words, like everything from a harpsichord to an orchestra. He was no longer prepared to even pretend that Paul's musicianship was sophisticated enough to keep pace. 'I didn't really notice Paul not playing the bass until we got to New York,' says Jerry Green. As well as whatever songs Mick chose to overdub the instrument on, Topper was responsible for the bass on 'Rock The Casbah', and Jerry recalls Electric Lady tape operator Eddie Garcia playing on another song.

Futura 2000 was on hand, and the band helped him record 'The Escapades Of Futura 2000', eventually released on Celluloid records in May 1983. They roped him in to rap on their own 'Overpowered By Funk', which also features Poly Mandell on keyboards. Kosmo half-rapped his De Niro-does-Travis Bickle impression on 'Red Angel Dragnet'. Ellen Foley provided backing vocals for 'Car Jamming'. Perhaps intending a sly dig at the Little Latin antecedents of Mick's song, Joe decided that he and a visiting Joe Ely should record the backing vocals for 'Should I Stay Or Should I Go' in Spanish. He got Eddie Garcia to phone his mother for a translation. 'I've had some Spanish people tell me it's rubbish,' Joe told *Melody Maker* in 1988. 'But I've explained that it's Ecuadorian Spanish and got off the hook.'

During another of Joe's vocal overdub sessions, Allen Ginsberg turned up to visit the band. Working on 'Ghetto Defendant' at the time, Joe invited him to supply 'the Voice of God' for the track. Allen asked for the name of some typical punk dances – the Worm being a favourite in San Francisco – and improvised a poem around Joe's lyric, to which he also contributed. 'He said, "You're the greatest poet in America; what can *you* do with this?"' Allen told *Rolling Stone*, modestly. 'So I made some suggestions, and he was real smart and open, not resentful or begrudging.' Worried that Allen's contribution had been blown up out of proportion – robbing him of due credit for developing his own lyric writing skills – Joe did get a little resentful and begrudging in the *Clash On Broadway* booklet: 'I asked Ginsberg for a word once, but it was just one word.' In fact, it was slightly more than that. Barry Miles's *Ginsberg* revealed that the poet turned up to a total of seven night-long sessions, and worked on 'three or four' lyrics in total. Not all the tracks Allen contributed to made it to the finished album, however, and the verse he helped with most on 'Ghetto Defendant' was subsequently·excised from the song.

Another last minute addition was the toilet cleaner commercial '2,000 Flushes' on the fade of 'Inoculated City', evidence of Mick's continued enthusiasm for unusual samples. It was a joke that was to rebound on the Clash. Following the record's release, they had to sneak around the US like wanted men in order to avoid being served with papers pertaining to a multi-million dollar lawsuit launched by Flushco Inc, the manufacturers of the product in question. Perseverance from the company's lawyers led to a temporary injunction against further production of the album, prefiguring the sampling copyright debate of the mid-to-late Eighties. The commercial was withdrawn for the second pressing of the Epic edition.

Mick finally presented the rest of the Clash with what he considered to be a final mix for a 15-track 65-minute double album including everything the band had worked on at Electric Lady except 'Overpowered By Funk' and 'Long Time Jerk'. They rejected it out of hand. Joe later referred to it as a 'home movie mix'. There was also too much of it. 'I don't believe anyone is that great that they don't write crap sometimes,' Joe told *Creem*'s Bill Holdship in 1984. 'Mick wouldn't have that. In his mind, he was a great artist, and great artists don't write crap. It was dangerous. I think Mick's got a tendency to bring yes-men close to him, and shut out people who will tell him the damn truth. Remember, I'm supposed to be his buddy and partner, and I said to him, "Mick, I don't think you can produce." What I meant was that you can't just sit in the chair, move some faders, and claim to be the producer. And it was, "You bastard! I thought you were my friend!"'

Work finally had to be abandoned when the Clash made a last minute dash for the plane to take them to Japan. As the album was now long overdue, and CBS-Epic were piling on the pressure, it was decided that the entire band would attempt a compromise remix in Australia, the only place they could book studio space and still hope to complete the project in time for an April 1982 release.

16
SHOULD I STAY OR SHOULD I GO

It had been decided that the Australasian live shows would feature a career-summarising 'best of' set in acknowledgement of the fact that the Clash were visiting what were, for them, virgin territories. The Japanese dates opened on 24 January 1982 at Tokyo's Shibuya Kohkaida. The band demonstrated a sensitivity to the finer feelings of their hosts that was firmly in the tradition of 1979's début American tour: they included a nightly guest spot for Pearl Harbour, backing her on her 'Fujiyama Mama'. If anything, the audiences' enthusiasm was a little *too* extreme, with the band somewhat disconcerted to be treated like 'part-time Western Gods'.

Joe grumbled that the Japanese should look to themselves and their own culture. As the band had gone to Japan in the first place because the youth of the country's passion for Western popular music made it the second largest – after the US – single nation record market in the world, this was a little rich. 'If we'd wanted to make money in Japan, we would've played Budokan like Bob Dylan,' Joe insisted at a Sydney press conference that February. '30,000 Nips jumping in the air, throw yer money on the plane and – bingo! – *that's rock'n'roll*. We played nine times in as many days, and never to more than 3,000 people. And that's nine days' worth of expenses, and all.' This visit was all about exposure, though, and the Clash got plenty when Japanese TV's *Young Music Show* broadcast 60 minutes of their 1 February Tokyo Sun Plaza performance. The recording spawned another popular bootleg, *White Riot*.

The Sydney press conference was set up at short notice in the mammals section of the Museum of Applied Arts and Sciences to boost flagging ticket sales of the magnificent seven dates scheduled at that city's Capitol Theatre as part of the Australian leg of the tour. It required the band to make a stop-over on their flight from Japan to New Zealand. In full-on ranter mode, Joe didn't allow any other member of the Clash – or, indeed, the assembled press – to get a word in edgeways for the 30 minutes of the conference's duration. Standing, while the rest of the band sat by his side and nodded, he held forth on any subject that entered his head, but did not forget that the point of the venture was to hard sell the Clash as a live attraction: 'We're here because we're exciting. We jump about, wiggle our bums, and there's nothing wrong with that!'

Under the headline, 'MAMMALS BABBLE: the Flying Sydney Press Conference', Bruce Elder and Ed St John, there on behalf of the New Zealand version of *Rolling Stone*, described it thus: 'Joe Strummer's performance is an immensely amusing one. This wasn't the usual deadly serious affair as uninformed journalists ask the subjects inane questions, but a holy rollin' one-man stand up, political flag-waving harangue by a man who – if he delivers one 10th as good live on stage – must be a performer to leave others flatfooted. The Clash's Sydney press conference was a real occasion.'

Adding further to the band's jetlag was the fact that Topper's reputation had preceded him, and the band were subjected to a four hour customs examination before being allowed into Auckland, New Zealand. Having declared 1982 the Year Of The Body, Joe was physically and verbally active at all times to the point of mania. In the New Zealand edition of *Rolling Stone*, Malcolm McSporran(!) recounted how Joe had been up at 7 am the morning after his arrival, asking questions about local culture and politics and busking in the town's main street with a ukulele bought specially for the purpose: shades of 1972. During a local TV interview for a programme called *Shazam*, Mick borrowed the ukulele to lead the Clash through an ad hoc version of 'Shanendoah'.

Won over – despite Joe's initial reluctance to grant him an interview – Malcolm went on to describe him as both enigmatic and charismatic and backed up his own impressions with those of New Zealand tour manager Graeme Nesbitt: 'Joe calls all the shots. After a show, everyone goes out and rages. Sometimes he goes too, but invariably he's up at six o'clock or even five the next morning wandering the streets writing notes. He's always writing notes. Everybody wakes up to find notes from Joe under their doors bearing legends like, "The order of the songs tonight is…" or "I don't like that lighting bit…" or "Raymond, you're fucking up the backstage passes. Don't do it again!" His overview is complete, right down to the last detail.' Having had limited contact with even the Clash Myth, let alone the band itself, Malcolm and Graeme had no idea that this autocratic behaviour was a departure from the Clash's formerly – nominally, at least – democratic set-up. Nor could they imagine how difficult it was for Mick to take. Feeling isolated within the Clash camp, and therefore unable to compete, when not actually playing he stayed in his room and brooded.

Mid-February's return to Sydney for the magnificent seven residency allowed local journalist Roz Reines to catch up with the band for an *NME* interview. Aside from a few words from Mick and a message from Topper regarding the evils of heroin, Joe once again dominated the resulting feature. Still manic – lifting the hotel room television in the absence of weights – he advised, at some considerable length, mass emigration from England to New Zealand. After attacking the *NME*, he gave yet another indication that the Clash was no longer overly concerned with the UK: 'I'd rather they hated us in Britain as long as they hear what we have to say in America. I don't think that the English need the Clash too much because they're too smart.' Again, this was a convenient view to hold, and not a little glib. He side-stepped questions about any contradictions inherent in the new Clash approach by hiding behind the word 'paradox': 'don't be afraid of the word paradox'.

The band enjoyed the heat and the sunshine of New Zealand, but even when advising emigration from dull grey England Joe acknowledged that he was talking of Australia and New Zealand purely as *scenic* paradises. An acknowledgement that not all was rosy beneath the surface came during the Sydney Capitol residency, when Aboriginal Land Rights Campaigner Gary Foley was invited onstage to orate over the coda to 'Armagideon Time'. Nor did the band find their reception in the two former British colonies any less unnerving than it had been in Japan. 'Every time we come to a town, they go, "Oh, we've been waiting for five years for you,"' Joe told Roz. 'I'd rather come as an extra, a bonus to the local scene, not like the staple diet was in town for 20 minutes and then left.'

In New Zealand, Joe placed the audience at 'around 1978'. One of them even spat at him… because he thought that was what punks were supposed to do. It was like Canada in 1979 and Europe in 1980. 'The message of punk was Do It Yourself,' Joe told Roz. 'The bands were home-made, the fanzines were home-made, and sometimes the guitars and instruments. Somehow it's been distorted along the line. Now you just get carbon copies of skinheads and punks in far-flung corners of the globe. They're not dealing with their own town, they're just wishing they could be somewhere else.' Another 'paradox': didn't this contradict the notion of resorting to emigration as an escape route?

The lengthy shows were rendered even more arduous by the intense heat and humidity. The Clash really started to push themselves during the Sydney residency, when they would head for a local recording studio straight after the gig and work through the night on mixes. Before going in, Joe admitted to Roz that he had been trying not to think about the album since leaving New York, and that he was 'semi-scared'. Roz met Mick a couple of days later, and he told her that band relations had been further strained by a 4 am disagreement which had forced the most recent session to be abandoned. In an echo of the Clash's very first CBS recording session, there had been a two hour stand up row between Paul and Mick about the bass level on 'Know Your Rights', Paul wanting it louder and deeper. This time, there was no-one like Simon Humphrey on hand to mediate. 'We weren't solving anything. There was just no compromise,' Paul told the *NME*'s Richard Cook in 1984. 'With Mick, it was do it his way or sulk.' The arguments continued, with all the rest of the band trying to wrest control of the final mix away from Mick. As Topper recalled for the *Clash On Broadway* booklet, it was not easy for any of them to make the fine sonic judgements required when they had just been half-deafened by a lengthy rock'n'roll gig. The album remained unfinished, and an indication that Joe, in particular, was driving himself too hard came when he collapsed from heat exhaustion and dehydration during the Perth show.

At the end of the month, the band played Hong Kong, then went on to Bangkok. In his liner notes for 1988's *The Story Of The Clash, Volume 1*, all 'band valet Albert Transom' could recall about the gig at Thamasat University was an audience full of people in orange turbans, which unravelled as they attempted to pogo. Unlike the other legs of the tour, the motive for the Thailand jaunt was not to exploit a new market. 'We were number one there, but I think everybody who visits there is automatically number one for the time they're there,' Mick told the *NME*'s James Brown in 1991. 'I think it's quite corrupt, like the police chief and the guy in charge of the music industry are the same man. They don't have real records, just bootleg tapes.'

Not that this meant that the band were playing there for altruistic reasons: they were in search of something as close as possible to the Vietnam vibe; partly to live out their own fantasies, and partly to enable Pennie Smith to take some suitable photographs for the album cover and forthcoming *NME* feature. 'We went mad in Thailand,' Mick told James Brown. 'It was like *Apocalypse Now*. When you go that far away, it takes a long time to get back... One great thing that happened was we were out in the bars, dressed like *The Deer Hunter*, and they have these girls in the really heavy places dancing on the bar. Joe and Kosmo got up and did the frug on the bar with these girls. When you come back from that, it's hard to get back into normal life. It was a fantastic adventure.' The Vietnam veteran fantasy was given an unwelcome shot of realism when first the band's money was stolen – marooning them in their hotel until more could be wired over, a by-now familiar occurrence – and then Paul took sick.

'He'd jumped into what looked like a black puddle, and thousands of flies flew up at him,' Mick told James Brown. 'Then a couple of days after, he had some dodgy food and he got seriously ill.' The rest of the band elected to stay on and keep him company, and the supposedly brief visit was extended to three weeks. According to Pennie Smith, the local hospital diagnosed a twisted colon, and at one point were proposing removing a section of his bowel. Unconvinced, Paul postponed a decision until he was able to make it home, where doctors revealed he was suffering from a bug that, although severe, neither required nor justified such drastic surgery.

The band unity that this scare seemed to foster was illusory, though. On *Westway To The World*, Pennie claimed to have seen the Clash fall apart before her very eyes during the album photo session, their instinctive feel for group poses deserting them. The photograph ultimately chosen for the front cover is more like a snapshot of four people who would really rather not be on holiday together.

In mid March 1982, back in London, the Clash turned their attention once more to the vexatious topic of mixing the new album. Having failed to reach any kind of compromise with Mick, the others made the decision to override him completely and bring in an experienced producer-engineer to oversee a substantial editing and remix job. Drawing up a short list, Bernie astounded everyone by pushing for Gus Dudgeon, Elton John's producer. It was quickly established that he actually meant Glyn Johns.

Glyn was an inspired suggestion. Not only had he worked with the Rolling Stones, the Beatles and the Faces, but he had developed something of a speciality in salvage operations. Commissioned to put together a warts'n'all Beatles album from songs recorded in 1969 during the making of the *Let It Be* film, his *Get Back* was ultimately deemed to have a few warts too many. The source material was subsequently reworked by Phil Spector to form the frankly syrupy *Let It Be* album, released in 1970; most people who have heard it prefer Glyn's version. The following year, Glyn got another chance to prove his mettle when Pete Townshend – on the point of a nervous breakdown – brought him in to put together a single album from the over-ambitious, aborted double *Lifehouse* project. The resulting *Who's Next* was arguably the Who's finest ever album.

Rat Patrol From Fort Bragg had originally been pencilled in for release at the end of April 1982, to coincide with the beginning of a UK tour. With no time to spare, Glyn and Joe booked straight into Wessex and got to work. During the Sydney press conference, Joe had set out his agenda thus: 'We're going to deliver an album that those suckers down at CBS [including Epic] won't even suss, so they'll just serve it up with their Boston and Foreigner. Then we're going to get out there and fight for it, because it's no use being priests. It's all very well getting heard by cult freaks, but I want to get through to the creep who's filling his head with "Stuff 'er on the bed and shove it to her, yeah, yeah, yeah!" That's the person I want to reach. All eight million of him.' This had not been merely a statement to the effect that The Quest was ongoing, but a first-time acknowledgement – at least as far as Joe was concerned – that, musically speaking, artistic integrity now came second to market forces.

The album Joe had described in Sydney bore little relation to the album the Clash had recorded in New York and attempted to mix in Sydney. Glyn's job, as Joe saw it, was to do as much as possible to eradicate that discrepancy. Much of the more left-field material was dropped altogether. 'The Beautiful People' and 'Kill Time' remain unreleased to this day; 'Cool Confusion' and 'First Night Back In London' joined 'Long Term Jerk' on the future single B-sides list; 'Overpowered By Funk' was reinstated, bringing the total number of tracks to be included on the album to a manageable dozen.

These then underwent a substantial overhaul. The drums and guitars were pushed up in the mix to give the album the big sound beloved of American AOR radio. The tracks were then edited, often severely, to fit the space available. 'Straight To Hell' lost a verse from the middle, 'Red Angel Dragnet' and 'Ghetto Defendant' their final verses, 'Car Jamming' and 'Inoculated City' their codas, and the longest raga of all, 'Sean Flynn', was cut from its original seven minutes to four and a half. Two of the three more conventional sounding rock songs were also chosen to be single material, and were consequently afforded even more attention. Joe improved the lyric for his own 'Know Your Rights', and re-recorded the vocal. The Spanish backing vocals were dropped from the first verse of 'Should I Stay Or Should I Go'. Then Mick was prevailed upon to re-record the lead vocal, substituting 'If you want me off your back' for the smuttier and decidedly less mainstream radio-friendly original 'On your front or round the back?'

Futura 2000 had already designed the album's lyric sheet, and although the myriad changes rendered it obsolete, it was too late and too expensive to have him redo it from scratch. Consequently, some lyrics appear on the inner sleeve in their original form, and some have been sloppily altered. The credit to Guy Stevens for 'inspiration' has also been partially erased: a half-hearted effort to admit the fact that the Stevens spirit had left the project as soon as the Clash left Ear studios.

Everything about the salvaged album was ostensibly Joe's show: Paul and Topper were not consulted over the remodelling, and Mick was so devastated that, aside from re-recording his vocal, he effectively boycotted the Wessex sessions. 'Mick's attitude was that I ruined his music,' Joe told *Creem*'s Bill Holdship in 1984, before going on to make it clear that, had there been enough alternative material to hand, he himself would have gone even further with the changes: '50 per cent was great rock, but the other 50 per cent was what Phil Spector would call *wiggy*.' When reading that appraisal, one has to bear in mind that, by then, Joe had finally openly disowned the belief he so frequently expressed between 1980 and 1982: that rap and dub reggae were *the* cutting edge musics of the day. Joe and Glyn's final version of the album is by no means a desecration, but it goes far enough – perhaps too far – in its pursuit of the mainstream. Although it could indeed have used some editing, Mick's original double was hardly a disaster. More than anything, the salvage operation proved that effective compromise *within the band* was now totally beyond the Clash.

Joe also decided to streamline the album title to the less quirky *Combat Rock*: a comment upon its making as much as its content, but hardly an inspired choice. Along with the band's name, the title is reproduced on the record's front cover in red packing case stencil lettering similar to that with which the Clash had decorated their clothing in 1976. Although it finds the band a long way from Camden Town Rail Yard and Kings Cross, the cover photograph continues the railway association theme begun by the cover of *The Clash* and picked up again by *Sandinista!*. More than either of those albums, though, the image recalls the cover of the Animals' 1965 album *Animal Tracks*, where the band squat on a train track, dressed in combat gear and toting various weapons of destruction. The Animals fell apart shortly afterwards, too.

Upon taking delivery of the tapes at the beginning of April 1982, CBS set about a rush-release schedule that would put the album into the shops by 14 May. It was to be preceded on 23 April by a single coupling 'Know Your Rights' with 'First Night Back In London'.

Meanwhile, the band attempted to make Radio Clash at least a part time reality, taking advantage of the facilities offered by Open Access Radio, broadcasting on 103.8 megahertz from 19 Calthorpe Street near Kings Cross. Between excerpts from 'This Is Radio Clash' and the occasional link from Kosmo, Pearl Harbour, and – in outrageous cod Spanish – Joe, the Clash show finds Paul Simonon presenting a pre-recorded hour's worth of music. Unsurprisingly, the session has a heavy bias towards retro genres, drawing substantially upon early Seventies reggae, Sixties soul and Fifties rock'n'roll. Featured are tracks by former Clash support acts like Lee Dorsey, Bo Diddley and Mikey Dread, and the original versions of Vince Taylor's 'Brand New Cadillac' and Bobby Fuller's 'I Fought The Law'. The show is more like a prolonged *Desert Island Discs* than the cutting edge mix'n'match of WBLS, and Paul is hardly a natural DJ, but the Clash were happy to endorse the DIY ethic behind the station. Plus, at least two members of the band could say they had made a token gesture towards reclaiming the airwaves from the likes of Radio One and Capital Radio.

April also found the Clash going into rehearsals for the 19-date tour of the UK. Arranged via Ian Flukes's Wasted Talent agency, it went under the banner of the Know Your Rights Tour, and opened on Monday 26 April in Aberdeen. Or at least, that was the plan. The 1 May issue of the *NME*, the news pages of which went to press on Tuesday 27 April, reported that Joe had gone missing. He had disappeared on Wednesday 21st, and as a result, the first two dates of the tour had been postponed.

'Joe's personal conflict is: where does the socially concerned rock artist stand in the bubblegum environment of today?' announced Bernie, grandly. 'I feel he's probably gone away for a serious rethink.' The manager went on to make digs at both the general public – following the previous year's poor singles and album performance, the Clash had slumped to a new low in the 1981 end-of-year NME readers' poll, while the Jam still held sway at the top – and the UK music press itself: 'I think he feels some resentment about the fact that he was about to go slogging his guts out just for people to slag him off, saying he's wearing the wrong trousers. A lot of people want to destroy the group, but we won't let that happen because we're an international group. But they could still destroy the Clash in this country.' He closed by appealing to the readers for help in finding Joe, and could not resist pointing out that the situation was costing the band a small fortune. The possible seriousness of the situation discouraged the paper from chortling at Bernie's exhibition of rampant paranoia, even the part where he envisaged Joe's trouserist comment in Sniffin' Glue coming back to haunt him.

A stop press addendum in the same issue reported that Steve Taylor, a journalist for the Face, claimed to have shared a compartment with Joe and Gaby on a Thursday 22 April boat train to Paris. The following week's NME announced there was still no sign of the Clash singer, and that the first half of the tour had now been rescheduled for July. The Paris lead seemed to have been a false trail. As Charles Shaar Murray later reported, among the rumours in circulation were that Joe was living in Amsterdam, working as a navvy in Marseilles, or had been fished out of the river in Glasgow. The third week's NME – issue dated 15 May – reported he was still missing, and that another five dates had been postponed. Next week's paper announced that all the remaining dates had been blown out, but that at least Joe had been located: on Monday 17 May, Kosmo had set off to some unspecified location in Europe to fetch him back.

The news pages of the 29 May issue dropped another bombshell. Joe had rejoined the band in time to play the Lochem Festival in Holland on Thursday 20th, but, upon the Clash's return to London the following day, Topper Headon had quit the band. Topper's reason, according to Kosmo, was 'a difference of opinion over the political direction the band will be taking'. That Saturday, CSM arranged a summit in a cafe on the Portobello Road with the remainder of the band to find out just what was going on. The Clash camp made a show of displaying a united front: both Paul and Mick stuck to the party line on Topper's departure and were vocal in their support for Joe.

Joe explained his own disappearance thus: 'It was something I wanted to prove to myself: that I was alive. It's very much like being a robot, being in a group. You keep coming along and keep delivering and keep being an entertainer and keep showing up and keep the whole thing going. Rather than go barmy and go mad, I think it's better to do what I did, even for a month. I just got up and went to Paris without even thinking about it. I might have gone a bit barmy, you know? I knew a lot of people were going to be disappointed, but I had to go. I only intended to stay a few days, but the more days I stayed, the harder it was to come back because of the more aggro I was causing that I'd have to face.'

One of the other rumours that had circulated during Joe's absence was that it was all a publicity stunt. This possibility was called into question to some extent by the symptoms of stress that had been evident in Joe's behaviour before he went, and by Topper's departure upon his return, which combined to suggest that something altogether more serious had been taking place. It was to be years before anything approximating the full story began to emerge, and then it would do so in sometimes contradictory dribs and drabs.

In an apparently frank interview he gave to Channel 4's Wired programme in 1988, Joe maintained that his disappearance had indeed begun as a publicity stunt dreamed up by the band's management. On the eve of the tour, a couple of the early Scottish dates had failed to sell out. Not taking into account the sizeable 'walk-up' the Clash could count upon – people who come along on spec, and pay at the door – Bernie had started to panic that the band had finally exhausted the loyalty and patience of their UK fans. 'So Bernie Rhodes – who, like Malcolm McLaren, used to like the odd scam – came to me one night and said, "Look, you've got to disappear." I said, "Well, Bernie, if you really think I should, I will. Where do you want me to disappear to?" And he said, "Well, I don't know… Go to Austin, Texas. You know Joe Ely, go and stay with him. But ring me every morning at 10 am." I said, "OK, Bernie. I'll be seeing you." But I took the boat train to Paris instead. Then I thought it'd be a good joke if I never phoned Bernie at all. So he was going to be *thinking* he was acting, "Oh, where's Joe gone?" and after a few weeks he would be going, "Where *has* Joe gone?" I stayed with a bloke I knew in Paris, and I ran the Paris marathon, too.

'Eventually, they hired a private detective to find me, because they didn't know what continent I was on or anything. But he never found me. It was Kosmo Vinyl who eventually tracked me down.' Joe had contacted his mother to reassure her that he was well, and Kosmo managed to prise the information from her. 'One day, there was a knock on the door, and I opened it, and there was Kosmo dressed head to foot like Rambo, for some reason.' The *Combat Rock*-appropriate fancy dress had been inspired by the recently released original Rambo movie, *First Blood*, starring Sylvester Stallone as yet another traumatised Vietnam veteran.

Thus, Bernie's remarks accompanying the *NME*'s original report that Joe had gone missing had been insincere and manipulative. The first couple of dates of the tour had been deliberately sacrificed to boost ticket sales for the remainder. But neither this nor Joe's explanation fully justified his own reasons for staying away so long. Back in early 1978, he had told *Melody Maker*'s Simon Kinnersley: 'I haven't got any sense of responsibility… I'm capable of disappearing right off the face of the earth.' This simply wasn't true. Joe had always had a highly developed sense of commitment to both the band and 'the kids', as he impressed upon CSM following his return from Paris. For him to stay away for a month either meant that his joke had spun wildly out of control and he had indeed gone a bit 'barmy', or that he had some other ulterior motive: one that he was unhappy to dredge up for TV consumption even in 1988.

The 1982 year-plan Joe had outlined at the Sydney press conference had two parts. Firstly, to deliver an AOR radio-friendly album, which had been duly accomplished at the expense of Mick's finer feelings. Secondly, to go out on the road and tour hard behind the album – in Joe's words, 'fight for it' – in order to break the band into the big time internationally. Immediately before his disappearance, that part of the plan had come under threat from two quarters: from Mick, because he was still reluctant to tour; and from Topper, because his promises to kick heroin had crumbled at the first sign of temptation.

That the 'political differences' given as the reason for his departure were just an excuse to cover for Topper's heroin problem was an open secret, but was only officially acknowledged later in the year. Topper didn't leave of his own volition. He was sacked. On *Westway To The World*, Joe maintained that while heroin might suit jazz horn playing, which floats over the music, it didn't suit the more precise and rigorous demands of drumming. 'We couldn't play anymore.' In the same film, Paul pointed out that Topper's addiction was also undermining the stance on heroin that Joe had taken with the likes of 'Hateful', 'Junkie Slip' and 'Ghetto Defendant'. Talking to *Sounds*' Dave McCullough in summer 1982, Joe took full responsibility for instigating Topper's dismissal.

Three years later, Topper told *Sounds*' Jane Simon that he believed Joe's Parisian holiday had been deliberately conceived as a reprise of the underhand tactics he had employed to get Bernie reinstated early in 1981: a control-asserting gesture preceding a pre-planned ultimatum. 'They knew that if they'd said, "Get rid of Topper," Paul and Mick would have said no. But Joe proved that we couldn't go on tour without him, so I had to go.' Topper recalled that, although Paul had just gone along with whatever was easiest, Mick had spoken up in his defence – as he had done for Geir Waade in a similar situation seven years previously – but to no avail. Isolated by the loss of his one remaining ally in the Clash camp, Mick was cowed into agreeing with Joe's gameplan. 'Well, I felt that anything he [Joe] does is all right,' Mick told CSM, who, perhaps sensing that all was not as it seemed, made a point of describing the fixed stare on Mick's face while he was delivering his lines.

Meanwhile, the UK single 'Know Your Rights' had been greeted with surprising enthusiasm by the music press. For the *NME*, Paul Du Noyer wrote, 'Orator Joe storms back with a bitter-edged pep-talk for the troops, and the Clash make their best single in a long time... Hard and economic, instead of laid-back-flat and sprawling, tough and direct and properly thought-out instead of indulgent, sloppy and confused.' It's hard to see this as anything more than an expression of relief and encouragement for the move away from *Sandinista!*-era looseness: the song is tunelessly one-dimensional. It failed to climb any higher than number 43 in the UK charts.

Released during Joe's absence on 14 May, *Combat Rock* also fared well at the hands of the critics. As it was the Clash's most American-oriented and non-British album to date – both in terms of subject matter and slick sound – and further distanced itself from life's realities with its use of cinematic imagery, a savaging might have been more predictable. As it was, scorn was reserved for the album title, while the contents were judged to represent a creative renaissance. Instead of complaining about the lack of punk ramalama, *Sounds'* Dave McCullough praised the album's wordiness, AOR production, and strange musical landscapes, and awarded it the maximum five stars. 'The Clash... aren't static anymore, but sailing down into their own Heart of Darkness, trying to settle those wild contradictions they seemed doomed by.'

Melody Maker's Adam Sweeting refused to allow his aversion to the title to colour his reaction to the album. True, he also disliked opening track 'Know Your Rights'- 'the worst first' – and was unhappy with the overall 'hard, dry mix', but found 'the music increasingly effective the more you listen to it.' The Vietnam imagery was impossible to miss, but unlike Dave McCullough, Adam also picked up on the general cinematic feel. 'There's a darkness here, yes, but it's distanced, a zoom shot from a low-flying helicopter,' he wrote. 'Like editors of old documentary film, the Clash re-process imagery through the shifting lenses of their music. "Red Angel Dragnet"... isn't *really* about the people's fight against street violence, it's about a Martin Scorsese movie. With "Sean Flynn", same again... doubtless the Clash have nicked the idea from Michael Herr's *Dispatches* or *Apocalypse Now.'* His appreciation was a little more qualified than Dave's: 'I have doubts about the more exploitative aspects of the Clash, and the way they milk death and repression until they become meaningless, but I'll be listening to *Combat Rock* for a while yet.'

Over at the *NME*, their toughest taskmasters of late, the Clash benefited from another publicity stunt that was not of their own making. Early in April, the leader of Argentina's ruling junta, General Galtieri, had ordered the invasion of what Argentina called the Islas Malvinas and Britain – which claimed sovereignty despite being half a world away – called the Falkland Islands. Her popularity slumping in the polls, Margaret Thatcher seized the chance to be seen to act decisively, and dispatched a Navy Task Force to deal with the problem. Early May 1982 saw a series of sea and land skirmishes take place, the UK tabloid newspapers responding with some of their most memorably rabid headlines since the heyday of punk. Hundreds of young men, most of them teenage Argentinian conscripts, lost their lives for the sake of a few sheep and a Tory election victory.

Such goings on were more to do with the reportage of *Sandinista!* than the stylised dramatics of *Combat Rock* – Adam Sweeting noted as much in the opening paragraph of his review – but the *NME*'s recently recruited skinhead politico, X Moore (aka Chris Dean of Clash-influenced band the Redskins) believed the album 'has inadvertently become the best counterblast on the Falklands'. Whereas its predecessor had been released into a hostile environment, *Combat Rock*'s timing could not have been better. 'Listen, I'll tell you where the "socially concerned rock artist" stands in the bubblegum environment of today: s/he stands HERE!' wrote Chris, before Joe's return and Topper's sacking. '*Combat Rock* is too important to be snidely lumped with all the other dross, and this band are too important to tear themselves apart.'

Combat Rock took only a week to make number two in the UK album charts. Although this position equalled the feat of *Give 'Em Enough Rope* back in 1978, the new album eventually stayed on the charts nine weeks longer – 23 in all – making it the band's most successful in the UK to date.

Even before *Combat Rock*'s release, though, the Clash found themselves out of the red for the first time since signing to CBS in January 1977. The money they had made on the road over the past year had paid for their keep, while between them, *London Calling* and *Sandinista!* had chalked up enough sales to repay their debt to the record company and even to cover the exorbitant costs of recording their latest album. A four and a half week US tour was due to start on 29 May, and for the first time, the Clash were facing the prospect of going on the road not just to make money, but to make money for themselves.

There was only one problem: they had sacked Topper on the 21st, and therefore didn't have a drummer. So they did what they had always done in the same situation, and phoned Terry Chimes. Having worked as a session musician since the dissolution of Generation X the previous year, Terry pronounced himself available. The arrangement was temporary – to see the Clash through the gigs they had booked up until the end of the year – but it was also canny; firing one of their members had undermined the band's gang image, but bringing back a former member in his stead immediately repaired much of the damage.

Terry had just five days to work up the set before opening night. 'What made it really difficult was their policy of having a pool of 40 or so songs, and selecting a different permutation every night,' says Terry. 'But I'm used to that: I learn fast.' Nevertheless, although he had to familiarise himself with the key *Combat Rock* songs in a hurry – that being the album the band was promoting – for a long time the set was biased towards the early Clash material with which Terry was most familiar. The dictates of repertoire selection were not the only influence on the Clash's decision to rein in the extended work outs of the 1981 shows in favour of a tighter, more focused rock and roll sound. Terry was a more stylised drummer than Topper had been at his best, with – in Rob Harper's words – a distinctive, clipped sound. What started as an expedient move, catering for the introduction of a new band member, would have a significant influence on the band's future.

The US release of the album was delayed slightly when the Clash insisted Epic remove the 'Home Taping Is Killing Music' logo they were including on all album packaging at that time. The band had heard that it was common for US college bulletin boards to carry notices offering to tape an hour's worth of the customer's choice of *Sandinista!* tracks for $3, something that was at least in keeping with the original 'consume it any way you want to' thinking behind the album. 'We don't care *how* many people tape our records,' Kosmo announced to CSM. Paradoxically, they did care when no-one bought them...

Either as a consolation prize or as an attempt to mollify him following Joe's hijacking of the album production, Mick was given the opportunity to remix 'Rock the Casbah' for later US single release, and also to record a DJ-style remix entitled 'Mustapha Dance' for inclusion on the B-side of the 12-inch single. Work took place at the Power Station in New York, immediately prior to the US tour. In 1979, Ian Hunter had used America's engineer-of-the-moment Bob Clearmountain for his album *You're Never Alone With A Schizophrenic*, and had come away with nothing but praise for him. Mick hired him too, and this time produced under his own name rather than the traditional collective Clash credit.

Coupled with 'Long Time Jerk', the original album version of 'Rock The Casbah' was released in the UK that June as the second single from the album. Don Letts hastily arranged a mid-tour video shoot, capturing the band performing in front of an oil well in the Texas desert. To play up the supposed Middle Eastern theme two extras skank about 16 Tons Tour posse-style, only this time dressed up as an Arab and an orthodox Jew. These roles were subsequently reprised by Bernie Rhodes (the Arab) and long-time band buddy Mark 'Frothler' Helfont for the single's picture sleeve.

Another long term band associate had departed the Clash camp at the same time as Topper. Baker moved to New York, where he worked as a truck driver until a bad road accident forced him to quit. By now, Ray Jordan was one of the few remaining familiar faces among the Clash support staff, and the influx of new employees were wont to take the band's Pop Star Army Fatigues look at face value. An atmosphere of macho determination prevailed. New roadie Digby recalled the ambience with some glee when talking to the *NME*'s Steven Wells in 1991: 'We were all dressed in black combat gear and everybody got out of the way when we came through; *everybody*.'

At the tour's opening-night party, Kosmo had turned up with a mohican-style hair cut. This was partly in tribute to his enduring hero, Travis Bickle, but also a response to the punk-coiffured Hell's Angels in the more recent 1981 movie *Mad Max 2*. The years 1979-80 had seen the emergence of a fourth wave of UK punk bands. Incensed, like Garry Bushell, by the progressive and arty tendencies of so much post-punk/indie music, the likes of the Exploited, the UK Subs, the Cockney Rejects and Discharge proudly declared 'punk's not dead' and attempted to prove it with music that was even more basic and angry than that of the first wave, despite being highly derivative. Impressed by the *Mad Max 2* outlaws' daring juxtaposition of leathers and crazy-coloured mohican cuts, many of these bands had already picked up a few fashion tips from the film, lending the punk look of the early Eighties a decidedly cartoonish aspect.

Strangely, Joe was impressed with Kosmo's new hairstyle. In the video for 'Rock The Casbah', he too sports a red-dyed mohican. Mick refuses to be left out in the weirdness stakes: he wears a bandanna over his face until near the end of the clip. It was a look he continued to affect for the subsequent live dates. Whether intentionally or not, the band were giving off worrying signals. The militaristic Rat Patrol image suggested camaraderie and teamwork, but Robert De Niro had decided to adopt the mohican cut in *Taxi Driver* after reading that stressed-out US soldiers in Vietnam sometimes cut their hair that way when convinced they were about to die. Certainly, the gang members in *Mad Max 2* were hardly wholesome role-models. In view of Joe's somewhat desperate recent behaviour, his adoption of such an extreme image did not bode well for his state of mind, and he later admitted that his intention had been to make himself look as ugly as possible. Meanwhile, Mick's bandanna mask was not so much a reference to 'Bankrobber' as to the occasion at Sheffield Top Rank when he'd had to wear one to cover his bruises. It was an indication of just how withdrawn from proceedings *he* had become.

It was a tour of ups and downs. Support act were the Beat, and Ranking Roger took to joining the Clash on-stage to toast on 'Armagideon Time'. In Hollywood, the Clash sold out five consecutive nights at the Palladium, a feat made all the sweeter by the fact the Jam had recently struggled to sell out just one. Joe was even more pleased to learn that Bob Dylan had come to see them. 'He's said to have been recording rock'n'roll again the very next morning,' he crowed. In Atlanta, a local communist group attempted to distribute some literature outside the Fox Theatre, and a mini riot ensued. 'They pulled the police guns out on us in Atlanta,' Joe told *Sounds*' Dave McCullough. Fourteen people were arrested and charged with battery or disorderly conduct.

The first single culled from the album in the US was 'Should I Stay Or Should I Go', which, between 10 June and 20 July 1982, was released with no fewer than three different B-sides ('Inoculated City', 'Cool Confusion' and 'First Night Back In London') and in three different picture sleeves, one of which features a picture of Ronald Reagan. Despite this blatant hard sell, it stalled at number 45.

'Rock The Casbah' had peaked in the UK before the Clash returned home to commence the tour that had been postponed when Joe disappeared, but the lack of live promotion and another bad review from the *NME* had not prevented it from reaching a respectable number 30 in the charts. The tour itself, beginning at the Fair Deal in Brixton on 10 July, was rechristened the Casbah Club. The idea was that, in the absence of the permanent club they had been promising for years, the Clash would offer a peripatetic one in the tradition of Bernie's original Club Left. A statement read, 'The club will take over halls for the night as a celebration of low life and Clash fans. As well as the Clash playing, there will be guest appearances by celebrities, public figures and other attractions.'

Richard Cook paid those other attractions no mind in his *NME* review of the opening Fair Deal show, but the Clash could hardly have complained: 'Every one of perhaps 20 songs was dealt out with a surly, scorched-earth bravado, spilling accents of suspicion and untempered wrath: purpose in every turn. The Clash have learned to channel sound as never before. What the bungling theatre of sores that now calls itself British punk cannot grasp is this definition... the sound of punk shouldn't be the spluttery sprawl of mud-clogged feedback over Chad Valley drums, it should be this steeled rush, this fluorescent razor's edge!... The Clash have rediscovered something that rock is supposed to have forgotten: its grip on exhilaration... I say we need this anger, no matter how romantic it may be. I say this antidote to romantic *despair* is necessary. The Greatest Rock'n'Roll Band In The World. I guess that doesn't sit so badly, after all.'

Following the UK tour's completion early in August 1982, the Clash hardly had time to pause for breath before commencing the second month-long leg of the US tour on the 11th of that month. The venues were larger and the receptions more enthusiastic than ever, but inevitably, pressures were building. 'Terrible tensions,' recalls Terry Chimes. 'The tensions when I'd been in the band before had been flying around in all directions, but it had been mostly me versus everybody else. When I rejoined the band, they never argued with me about the politics or anything anymore. This time, it was very much Mick versus Joe and Paul, and I felt that Kosmo was very anti-Mick as well. I'm not saying whether he deserved it, I'm just saying that's how it lined up. The record kept selling like crazy [15,000 copies a week for the duration of the tour] and it seemed like we could do no wrong that year. And yet the tension was mounting and mounting.' Mick signalled his apartness by ignoring the Pop Star Army Fatigues uniform in favour of a series of increasingly loud and tasteless baggy double breasted suits with huge shoulder pads.

On 7 September, a brief respite from larger halls was provided by one of the Clash's favourite venues, the Orpheum Theatre in Boston. Here the Clash turned in what tape traders subsequently declared to be the best of their 1982 performances, something which was taken into account 17 years later when the former band members came to compile material for the retrospective live album *From Here To Eternity*. No fewer than seven of the show's songs would make it to the 17-track collection: 'Clash City Rockers', '(White Man) In Hammersmith Palais', 'London Calling', 'The Magnificent Seven', 'Know Your Rights', 'Should I Stay Or Should I Go' and 'Straight To Hell'.

The tour's second leg was originally supposed to run down in early September, but then the band were offered a support slot on eight 50-80,000-capacity stadium gigs on the Who's October 'retirement' tour. These included two consecutive nights at Shea Stadium in Queens, New York, as famously played by the Beatles in 1965. Seeing it as an opportunity to reach a new, even larger audience, the Clash accepted. In the *NME* a disgruntled T-Zers entry wondered, 'Still steering that steady course straight to hell?' It was a question worth asking. Since signing to CBS, aside from a couple of charity shows and festivals, the Clash had always refused to support anyone, let alone dinosaur acts like the Who. What had happened to 'No Beatles, Elvis or the Rolling Stones'? And *stadiums*: one of the central pillars of the Clash's ethos was that rock'n'roll should be played in venues where audiences could see the whites of a band's eyes. Just a year earlier, they had lined up seven nights at Bonds – extended to 16 – rather than play one night at the 16,000 capacity Madison Square Garden...

It was all justified in the name of breaking through, the only alternative – or so the Clash claimed – to remaining forever a cult attraction, just scraping by, perpetually at loggerheads with their record company. Rather than apologise for this change of policy, the band opted to flaunt it. Glyn Johns was hired to record and Don Letts to film their performance on 13 October, the second night at Shea, with the initial intention of making a live-style video for the UK release of 'Should I Stay Or Should I Go'. Footage was also shot of the Clash riding to the show in an open-topped car, playing at rock stars. Their stage gear plumbs ridiculous depths of self-parody: Mick is dressed all in red and wearing a beret, and Joe sports a Davy Crockett-style coonskin cap over his mohican. Irony was doubtless intended, but the band were by now relying on such none-too-convincing double-bluffs to shore up their integrity. The Clash debt had been settled long before, so there was no other reason for accepting the Who supports other than lining their own pockets. The recording of that night's concert was initially supposed to provide the bulk of the material for what became *From Here To Eternity*, only for the plan to be abandoned when the more intimate-sounding Boston Orpheum show was discovered. In the event, only the Shea version of 'Career Opportunities' made the cut. As Joe acknowledged on *Westway To The World*, it was a knowing song selection if ever there was one.

Another opportunity for exposure was offered by a 9 October live performance slot on popular NBC TV show *Saturday Night Live*. The Clash wear the same clothes in which they would take the stage at Shea and perform 'Should I Stay Or Should I Go' and 'Straight To Hell'. Joe clowns around good naturedly during Mick's song; Mick insists on dancing and prancing around embarrassingly throughout Joe's. In the UK, these two tracks had been released on 17 September as a double A-sided single with a cover illustration reminiscent of the insignia with which 'Nam grunts were wont to customise their jackets. On behalf of the *NME*, Adrian Thrills approved heartily of the latter song, while acknowledging that the less adventurous former song would probably receive most attention. This proved to be the case, with the single climbing to number 17, the band's best domestic showing since 'Bankrobber'.

In late October, the second single release in the US was Mick's remixed version of 'Rock The Casbah'. Thanks partly to the exposure generated by their own tour, partly by the Who gigs, and partly to the video's heavy rotation on the recently established cultural phenomenon of MTV, 'Rock The Casbah' climbed to an impressively high number 8 in the US charts. This in turn helped the album climb to number 7 on its way to selling over a million and a half copies. To paraphrase Joe, one should not be frightened of the word irony: the Clash enjoyed their biggest ever selling US single with a song written and almost exclusively played by their recently sacked drummer; and at least part of this success was due to a video in which they mimed to the song, shown on a TV channel which, at that time, had considerably less personal touch and live feel than even *Top Of The Pops*.

Given that CBS's financial troubles had contributed to the Epic's lack of support for the Clash back in 1979, it was also ironic that the Clash's greatest commercial success should happen to coincide with another music industry slump and an even larger purge of CBS personnel. On 13 August 1982 – another Black Friday – the record company fired a further 300 employees. That the Clash's triumph occurred without much in the way of help from Epic, and very much against the grain of the record company's overall sales performance, made it all the sweeter.

On 27 November, the Clash closed their working year by playing the Jamaica World Music Festival in Montego Bay. 'We did that because it was like a little holiday at the end of all this, because we'd worked very hard in America,' says Terry. Favouring the by-then sizeable reggae element in their repertoire, they won over the local crowd and finally gained some acceptance in the country that had inspired them but also spurned them for so long. As Richard Grabel's *NME* review summed up, 'The Clash took their chance and made it mean something.'

The upswing in the band's fortunes was reflected in the end-of-year polls. *Creem*'s review of *Combat Rock* might have been less than complimentary – Richard Meltzer had dismissed it as a 'RELATIVE PIECE OF SHIT' – but the magazine's readership refused to be directed, awarding the band third best album, best single and sixth best single, third best tour, third best band, and third best live band. Most of the first and second places went to the departing Who and poodle-haired stadium rockers Van Halen. The *NME*'s readers still placed the Jam – who had also retired that year – at the top of most categories, but the Clash claimed third best band, second best album, third best songwriters, and third best live act: their best showing for years. Most surprising of all, music columnist John Blake took half a page of trashy mainstream tabloid the *Sun* to prophesise that the Clash would be the 'Top Band of '83'...

The decision had already been made to take a few months holiday following a year of such heavy live activity. Terry Chimes had enjoyed playing with the band again, and would not have objected to staying on full time, but found it hard to envisage a long term future while the relations between the others remained so strained. 'I had other plans. I didn't want to spend six months sitting there while they argued about whether there was a band or not, so I got involved in other things.' He worked with Billy Idol for a while, joined Hanoi Rocks, and made a drumming video. 'And then I decided the time had finally come to do medicine, or else I'd never get around to it.' In 1987, he began five years of training as a chiropractor. He now also practices acupuncture, and continues to drum in his spare time.

Over the few months following Terry's departure, band-related recording activity was limited to one recording session, a debt of gratitude to the no-longer-incarcerated Janie Jones. Joe had written 'House Of The Ju-Ju Queen' for her, and on 28 December 1982 produced a session at Wessex during which both that song and a version of James Brown's 'Sex Machine' were recorded for a proposed single. Mick played guitar, Paul bass, Mickey Gallagher keyboards and fellow Blockhead Charley Charles played drums.

The single would be released in December 1983 on Big Beat under the name Janie Jones and the Lash.

By February 1993, rumours about a Clash split had begun to circulate once more. Little happened to convince people that they were unfounded. Mick insisted on extending the band's time off to six months. To anyone else, this might have seemed a reasonable enough demand following 1982's hectic schedule, and bearing in mind that the only breaks of any duration Mick had been allowed in the two years prior to that had been those enforced by Joe's walk-outs. Joe would later come to acknowledge that the Clash were burned out by this time, and would have benefited immeasurably from taking an even longer sabbatical. At the time, though, he was a man with a mission: he believed the Clash should be following up on their American breakthrough by getting out on the road and 'out-working' their heavy metal and AOR competitors. The tension continued to build.

Joe financed and helped out on the mixing of what was supposed to be a Tymon Dogg album with Richard Dudanski on drums, but it remained unreleased. On 17 March, he appeared in the *Sun*, posing in a T-shirt bearing the tabloid's logo alongside Kenny Lynch, Lennie Bennett and two other members of a team intending to run the London Marathon in aid of Leukaemia Research. The general consensus was: nice cause, shame about the sponsor. Sporting another mohican cut, Joe completed his third marathon in as many years. He and Gaby also finally bought somewhere to live. 37 Lancaster Road was situated a matter of yards away from Ladbroke Grove and the Westway, and was exactly the type of house Joe used to squat in his 101ers days. May also found the *Sun* reporting that Paul had married Pearl Harbour – whose UK visa had recently expired – in a New York register office. Meanwhile, Mick's relationship with Ellen Foley came to an end.

The Clash were not entirely inactive during this period. Early in 1983, British director Stephen Frears offered Joe the role of a hitman in *The Hit*, alongside John Hurt and Terence Stamp. Having just seen Tim Roth in the play *Made In Britain*, Joe felt honour bound to turn it down and point Stephen in the direction of the compelling young actor. Tim duly got the part. Inspired, Joe decided to make the best of his free time and make his own movie: a black and white 16 mm silent short entitled *Hell West End*. It was destined to meet the same fate as Don Letts's *Clash On Broadway* film. 'It was a disaster,' Joe laughingly informed *Film Comment*'s Graham Fuller in 1987. 'Luckily, the laboratory that held the negative went bankrupt and destroyed all the stock, so the world can breathe again. That was like a dry run for me. I managed to shoot it without a script. God knows what it was about. I'm the only other one who knows, and I'm not telling.' Pennie Smith was involved in the project as an actress, and she does have some stills from the movie which reveal it to have a – perhaps predictable – cops and robbers theme. Paul plays a street hoodlum in a po'boy cap, Mick a slick hustler in a James Bond-style white tuxedo, and Joe a uniformed – but armed – British policeman with a moustache. 'When I get the bug back, I might try another one,' mused Joe in 1987. 'I think film directing's something you have to build up to: make a few bum films like they do in college… learning as you go.'

The Clash also attempted to get some more conventional work done. To this end, they moved back into the Camden Town warehouse building that had formerly housed Rehearsal Rehearsals, now refurbished and transformed into a somewhat more salubrious rehearsal studio with a 16-track recording facility. The Lucky Seven club had not materialised, but the rehearsal room was named Lucky Eight. Here, the efforts made to write and demo new material proved about as successful as *Hell West End*.

In late spring, the Clash received an invitation to play live that they – Mick included – found impossible to turn down. The second annual Us Festival was scheduled to begin on 28 May in Glen Helen Regional Park, Los Angeles. A three-day event, it was the brainchild of Apple computers magnate Steve Wozniak. Its title derived from the banner under which it was organised, Unuson, an acronym for Unite Us In Song. The Clash were offered a staggering $500,000 to headline the opening New Music Day.

The one obstacle to the Clash performing was their drummerless state. Efforts were quickly made to remedy this situation. The classifieds section of the 23 April 1983 issue of *Melody Maker* carried the following large but anonymous display ad: 'YOUNG DRUMMER WANTED. Internationally successful group. Recording and concert appearances immediately.' After auditioning, or so they claimed, in excess of 300 applicants, the Clash finally decided upon 23 year-old Pete Howard of Bath band Cold Fish. Who happened to be signed to CBS. Appropriately enough, Pete's Clash career threw him straight in at the deep end. Within a month, the band were in America's South West, playing five dates as a warm up for the big event.

Shortly before they were due to go on at the festival itself, the Clash called a press conference denouncing what they now deemed to be a complete charade. They claimed they had been informed that ticket prices would be pegged at $17, instead of the $20-$25-plus-parking actually charged. As a consequence, they were refusing to take the stage until the promoters agreed to donate $100,000 to a Southern Californian summer camp for disadvantaged children. This act of blackmail resulted in Unuson agreeing to hand over $32-$38,000 (different sources reported different figures). Not content with this, the Clash then cornered several other acts on the bill and insisted that they too donate a portion of their inflated fees to worthy causes. The band finally went on two hours late to play an 80 minute set, throughout which Joe harangued the audience. Banners behind the band read 'SEX STYLE SUBVERSION' and 'THE CLASH NOT FOR SALE'. After the gig, the Clash brawled with event security and crew members: Kosmo punched the DJ in the nose, a bouncer hit Mick, and Paul hit the bouncer, spraining his thumb in the process.

Their behaviour raised a number of questions in music press reports of the festival. If the Clash found the idea of the event so abhorrent and were indeed 'not for sale', why had they accepted so much money to play, and even hired a drummer especially for the occasion? Some cynics noted that the band had only begun complaining when they discovered Van Halen were getting a million dollars for *their* headlining spot on Heavy Metal Day (which drew 350,000 people as opposed to New Music Day's 140,000). How could a band who prided themselves upon treating their audiences fairly justify keeping them waiting for so long, and then insult them from the stage? Last but not least, instead of resorting to blackmailing the organisers, why hadn't the Clash simply donated part of their own fee to the summer camp?

The Clash offered no explanation until the following year. 'We have to deal with the music industry, and that weekend, the whole industry was looking at the festival as *the* state of rock'n'roll,' Joe told *Creem*'s Bill Holdship. 'So we had to go in there and show them that we wouldn't be pushed under the carpet. Our second purpose was to spoil the bloody party, because I'm not going to have some millionaire restaging Woodstock for his ego gratification and tax loss in his backyard and get away with it... Don't tell me you can recreate Woodstock in the Me Generation of cocaine California in 1983... On the Van Halen day, somebody got clubbed to death over a drug deal.' He did concede that the press conference had perhaps not been the best of ideas.

Joe's justification for the band's rudeness at the Us Festival was unconvincing. It was far more likely that the Clash had been attempting to incite a riot of their own, not for any serious political reasons, but simply for promotional purposes. The media coverage of the Times Square furore following the Bonds Casino cancellations had been a godsend for the band's career... That they had clearly prepared their stage banners well in advance certainly suggests an element of premeditation. If that was indeed their intention, the Clash failed. The stunt rebounded on them, and made them appear foolish, grasping and boorish.

Regarding the band's own fee, Joe told *Record*'s John Mendelssohn that they had originally ear-marked it for the long-promised Clash-owned club: 'We needed it for London. If Wozniak wants to be a sucker and give us half a million dollars, we'll take it.' Unfortunately, for tax reasons, not all the money could be taken out of the US. Some of that which could undoubtedly went towards paying for the refurbishment of Lucky Eight, but arguments about what to do with the rest added to the bad feeling in the Clash camp. Wary of having Bernie and his appointees in control of all matters fiscal and legal, Mick employed New York attorney Elliot Hoffman to look after his interests.

Nothing more was heard from the Clash camp for the remainder of the summer. On 11 October 1983, *Us Festival*, a Showtime film of the Clash's live set and chaotic press conference was screened in the US. By this time, it no longer mattered that the Clash had embarrassed themselves on the day by trying yet failing to hijack the festival for their own ends. Subsequent events had served to make the film a more important Clash testament than the band could have realised at the time it was made. It was to stand as a record of Mick Jones's last ever gig with the Clash.

On 10 September 1983, the *NME* news pages had carried the following statement, its uncomfortable syntax revealing the hand of Kosmo Vinyl: 'Joe Strummer and Paul Simonon have decided that Mick Jones should leave the group. It is felt that Jones had drifted away from the original idea of the Clash. In future, it will allow Joe and Paul to get on with the job the Clash set out to do from the beginning.' Carried in the same issue, Mick's response was: 'I would like to state that the official press statement is untrue. I would like to make it clear that there was no discussion with Strummer and Simonon prior to my being sacked. I certainly do not feel that I have drifted apart from the original idea of the Clash, and in future I'll be carrying on in the same direction as in the beginning.' Although news of the split was not without impact, it hardly came as a surprise.

Although playing the older material with Terry Chimes had been a move born of necessity, it had reminded both Joe and Paul – as well as critics like Richard Cook – how direct and hard-hitting the Clash had once been. They had wanted their new material to pursue a back-to-basics angry punk direction. Mick, on the other hand, was bored with both his and the band's traditional role and wanted to persevere with hip hop and groove music. His demos for new songs used drum machines, synthesizers and samples. 'I was going, "Come on, let's dance,"' was how he summed the situation up to the *NME*'s Paolo Hewitt in 1986. 'And they were saying, "No, let's riot!"' The previous year, he told *Rolling Stone*'s Bill Flanagan, 'I kept movin' and they wanted to go backward.'

'I had to beg him to play guitar, and he's supposed to be the Clash guitarist!' an exasperated Joe claimed in 1984. 'It was like dragging a dead dog around on a piece of string. Insane! Better to take a dive and never be heard of again than to carry on with that ridiculous performance. I'd rather go back to busking and be a nobody than carry on like that.' Mick's refusal to take what he considered to be a retrogressive step, and the others' refusal to bend to his will, meant that the summer of 1983 had been one prolonged Mexican stand-off.

Joe's version of the final straw received several airings. 'Mick eventually said, "I don't mind what the Clash does, as long as you check it with my lawyer first,"' he told the *NME*'s Richard Cook in February 1984. 'I sat back and thought... hang on! And I said, "Go and write songs with your lawyer. *Piss off!*"' The animosity Joe and Paul had bottled up for the best part of two years continued to spill out over the next year in almost every interview they – and especially Joe – gave. Mick, to his credit, refused to enter into any tit-for-tat bickering, or even to tell his side of the story in any detail, as long as the Clash existed in any form. In early 1985, however, he did tell Bill Flanagan that – despite all ongoing rhetoric to the contrary – the Clash's original ideals had been shattered by the time of his sacking, thus making a split inevitable. 'We all knew that we were just doing it for the money. We couldn't face each other. In rehearsals we'd all look at the floor. It was the worst.' Joe had come to the same conclusion. 'I couldn't believe we'd turned into the people we'd tried to destroy,' he said in spring 1984. 'We'd turned into… *Pop Stars*!'

Back in 1974, Joe had told Pat Nother that it was his ambition to be a pop star. He had disavowed that aim upon joining the Clash two years later, but his – and the rest of the band's – attitudes to the Rock Dream had remained ambivalent ever since. The Clash's outlook had gone through many changes, but the Who stadium support shows had found them at perhaps their furthest remove from the Spirit of '76. In late 1983, Joe apparently still had no fear of the word paradox. He wanted to be famous and successful and to attract a mass audience, but he was also hankering after the provocative iconoclasm of punk's Year Zero. The next stage of the Clash's career would determine whether it was possible to reconcile these two apparently conflicting aims.

17
DEATH OR GLORY

According to the retrospective compilation *The Story Of The Clash, Volume 1*, released in 1988, the video compilation *This Is Video Clash* and the singles compilation *The Singles*, both released in 1991, the boxed set career summary *Clash On Broadway*, released in the US in 1991 and in the UK in 1994, the odds'n'ends compilation *Super Black Market Clash*, released in 1992, and the live compilation *From Here To Eternity* and its companion biographical documentary *Westway to The World*, both released in 1999, the Clash story ended with Mick Jones's departure in 1983.

In fact, with Mick out of the way, the Clash were determined to heed the warm public and press response to 1982's gigs with Terry Chimes, and forge a music which – to paraphrase Richard Cook's Brixton Fair Deal review from July that year – put the fourth wave Punk's Not Dead groups in their place with its sharpness, anger and bravado. Although the last plot to replace Mick had involved Steve Jones, the former Sex Pistols guitarist was not considered this time around. He had since joined Topper on the heroin casualty list, and it may be that this played a part in disqualifying him. But it had also been decided that the new Clash should not be some kind of punk supergroup. 'Who needs the old pals act?' demanded Joe in spring 1984, before – somewhat cheekily, bearing in mind the money the Clash had pocketed from their stadium support gigs with that band – doing his best to distance the Clash from the likes of the Who: '"Keith Moon's dead, so bring in Kenny Jones." That's not the way to do it; it doesn't work. Get some lunatic in off the street!'

The classifieds pages of the 1 October issue of *Melody Maker* carried a large display ad reading: 'WANTED. YOUNG HARD GUITARIST who can hold his own. Immediate studio and live work.' Efforts were obviously being made to put more emphasis on the 'sex' in the 'SEX, STYLE, SUBVERSION' promised by the band's Us Festival stage banner. Unfortunately, the innuendo was more worthy of a Carry On film than a cutting edge rock'n'roll band. Two weeks later, a second ad was run requesting a 'YOUNG ROCKIN' GUITARIST UNDER 25, OVER 5'9". For international live work and recording.' By 5 November, what was required was simply a 'Wild, young GUITARIST. Must look good, play good, under 25...' etc. The following week's ad took a different tack entirely, seeking a 'YOUNG UNSIGNED GROUP FOR FILM PART...'

To preserve anonymity, the initial auditions were held at the Electric Ballroom in Camden. Neither Joe nor Paul attended, and curious applicants were required to play along to tape recordings of three new instrumentals. Response was good, but, as ever, very few of those who turned up fitted the basic requirements: apparently, a total of '300 heavy metal guitarists' – 300 having by now replaced 204 as Clash-ese for 'a lot' – had to be put through their paces. Nick Sheppard was one of the earliest applicants. 'A couple of friends of mine said, "Look, here's an advert, here's a number,"' he reminisced early the following year in a rare interview with home town radio station, Radio West. 'I figured out pretty quickly who I was auditioning for. There was about 60 other guitar players there. We played along to a backing tape in front of the other 60.' In the interview, Nick was toeing the party line. The friend who tipped him off worked for Bernie, and Nick figured out who he was auditioning for 'pretty quickly' because – like Rob Harper before him – he already knew before he got there. When he was asked back for a second audition on his own at Lucky Eight, he quickly tired of the charade of anonymity, and deflated a smug Kosmo by telling him he knew why he was there. He got the job anyway.

He started rehearsing immediately with Joe, Paul and Pete Howard. A couple of weeks later, unaware that the ads had continued to run, he was surprised to be told that he was to be joined by a second guitarist. 'Joe said, "I'm going to stop playing guitar." I said that was stupid, but they brought Vince in.' By this time the Clash's secret had sprung several more leaks – Nick believes the final ad, offering a film part to a young, unsigned group, was intended to throw rumour-mongers off the scent – but Vince White was still genuinely surprised to find out he was joining the Clash. Up until five minutes before entering Lucky Eight and meeting the rest of the band, he thought he was going to be playing with Ten Pole Tudor.

There was a real sense of urgency about rehearsals. American shows had been booked for January and UK shows for February the following year. In addition to Joe and Paul's genuine desire to make up for lost time, there were two other pressing reasons to get the show on the road as soon as possible. After shedding a few tears, the first thing Mick had done upon being sacked was phone his lawyer, Elliot Hoffman. On Mick's behalf, he had immediately instigated proceedings to freeze all Clash earnings up to the point of Mick's departure, pending arbitration. 'My understanding was that our version of the Clash couldn't be bankrolled by money made by the Clash that Mick had been in,' says Nick. 'That was all tied up. We basically had to play to make money to pay ourselves.' It was a familiar situation for Joe and Paul, but if anything all the more galling for that. For Bernie, it was a taste of his own medicine. Even more disturbing, though, was the possibility that Mick might challenge Joe and Paul's right to the use of the name the Clash.

Mick Jones watchers had a few false trails to follow in the latter months of 1983. He played guitar on the début album by General Public – a new band formed by ex-Beat members Dave Wakelin and Rankin' Roger – and helped out behind the mixing desk at live shows by old friend Tony James's new band Sigue Sigue Sputnik and former Theatre of Hate frontman Kirk Brandon's new band Spear of Destiny. According to Mick, though, his competitive urge and need to prove himself – the same motivating forces that had spurred him to get up and try again when each of his pre-Clash bands fell apart – had him making plans for a new band of his own a matter of days after his sacking. His determination to stay true to the original Spirit of the Clash was clear: everything about the assembly of the personnel echoed the formation of the original Clash.

Mick started by approaching friends with like minds and similar tastes. First recruit was former Roxy barman, Slits roadie and Basement 5 bassist Leo Williams, with whom Mick had retained contact via Clash video director Don Letts. Don himself was a non-musician, and had never really thought about performing. Nevertheless, Mick found he was increasingly using him as a sounding board for his new ideas. Image-conscious as ever, he liked the idea of a skinny white guy standing on-stage between two big, beefy dreads, and appreciated the advantage of having an in-house film-maker in what he was already thinking of as a multi-media band. For his part, Don was growing bored with being a pop-promo man for hire, and responded to the same sort of opportunity that had inspired him to pick up a camera in the first place. In addition to operating as a toasting second vocalist, it was decided that Don should take charge of live sound effects. To this end, Mick taught him rudimentary keyboard skills, Don placing stickers on the appropriate keys just as Paul had once painted the notes on his bass.

Then Mick really stirred things up by inviting Topper Headon to join. Being sacked from the Clash in May 1982 had left the drummer feeling depressed, and even more susceptible to taking refuge in his painkiller of choice. Towards the end of that year, though, he found himself involved in a sort of punk supergroup with, among others, Pete

Farndon. Pete had been sacked from the Pretenders that June because of his own drug problem. On 14 April 1983, he was found dead in his bath, having overdosed on a heroin and cocaine speedball. Instead of shocking Topper into cleaning up, this merely propelled him further into his addiction. The Who's Pete Townshend – who had agreed to produce some demos for the band – had recently recovered from heroin addiction himself. Recognising the signs, he paid for Topper to undergo the Black Box treatment in LA. Within a matter of weeks, the drummer had started using again, and the supergroup fell apart.

Mick made his offer on the condition that Topper undertake an electro-acupuncture cure at his expense. Mick recognised Topper's invaluable contribution to the music and sound of the latter-day Clash, and hoped to recreate the productive working relationship they had enjoyed during 1980-81. There was probably also an element of guilt for not having been more assertive in standing up for Topper at the time of his dismissal: loyalty with hindsight. And it should not be overlooked that an alliance with his fellow Clash sackee not only gave added credibility to Mick's bid to represent the True Spirit of the Clash, but also gave that new alliance as much right as Joe and Paul to actually *call* themselves the Clash. 'One of the reasons we got out and played as quickly as possible was to establish that Joe and Paul were the Clash,' says Nick Sheppard.

Mick certainly started dropping hints that he intended to challenge for use of the name, and, according to Michael Goldberg's report in the 1 March 1984 issue of *Rolling Stone*, once Bernie had set up the American dates for Joe and Paul's new band, even went so far as to phone Bill Graham in San Francisco to tell him, 'The band you're promoting isn't the Clash. I'm going to bring the real Clash over.'

Prior to the American gigs, like Terry Chimes and Pete Howard before them, Nick Sheppard and Vince White were faced with the task of learning a pool of 40-50 songs from the Clash's back catalogue. In the interviews he gave during the course of 1984, still seething with animosity towards Mick, Joe would describe *Sandinista!* as an act of brazen stupidity and suggest that it was unplayable live. *Combat Rock* would be dismissed as half good, half bad. The selection of material rehearsed in late 1983 thus betrayed a distinct bias towards the Clash's 1976-78 material and the more basic rock and reggae numbers from the later years: anything hard, fast and direct. Surprisingly, perhaps, 'The Magnificent Seven' and 'This Is Radio Clash' were among the tracks selected for occasional performance, but like everything else, they were stripped back to basics.

Although still prepared to taunt US audiences with 'I'm So Bored With The USA', the Clash camp were savvy enough to know that they would have to perform their hits in America if, commercially speaking, they wanted the new Clash to pick up where the old Clash left off. *Combat Rock* was the band's current and best-selling album. Having at least written the lyric, Joe still had no qualms about singing Topper's 'Rock The Casbah', but Mick's 'Should I Stay Or Should I Go' presented more of a problem. Not only had its sentiment become even more loaded since Mick's departure, but Joe had always detested the song. In the end, he managed to simultaneously acknowledge and avoid the issue by getting Nick, Mick's replacement, to sing it. Nick also took lead vocals on another former Jones live feature, 'Police On My Back'.

He describes the mood in the Clash camp at this time as upbeat and positive. 'Joe and Paul were really relieved to be getting on and doing something, and we were fresh faced little juniors who were really excited, which rubbed off on them, too. We all got on OK.' Bernie wasn't around much at first, but after about a month, he came down to Lucky Eight and took everyone out to a restaurant. 'He just talked absolute nonsense for a couple of hours, and then left,' laughs Nick. 'Pete probably knew what to expect, but Vince and I were left with our jaws on the table. *Just what the fuck is this guy on about?!*" It was the first of what Nick would come to term Bernie's 'dehumanising sessions'.

The new recruits' identities were not made known to the music papers until January 1984. According to the Clash camp's press release, Nick, 23, had formerly been in Bristol punk band the Cortinas, while Vince, also 23, and a native of Finsbury Park, was previously untested. Not revealed at the time was that Nick had more recently played in a Latin American-flavoured covers band going under the somewhat dubious name of the Spics. The T-Zers page of the *NME*'s 28 January issue told the world a little more about Vince: 'Actually, "Vince" White is in fact Greg White, a one time native of fashionable Southampton, not Finsbury Park. Greg arrived in London in 1979 to study Physics and Astronomy at University College London.' It seemed that street credibility was as highly prized an asset in the new Clash as it had been in the old... and just as difficult to sustain.

The Clash image for 1984 was an updated punk style consisting of a retro jumble of 1982-era Clash Pop Star Army Fatigues, Fifties leather motorcycle jackets, and 1977-vintage punk T-shirts and accessories. For one photo-shoot, Nick even resurrected Bernie's 1974-vintage 'What side of the bed' T-shirt. The pictures strove to suggest a gang spirit, but the reality was somewhat different. In February 1984, Joe would tell Richard Cook, 'We don't want a slave syndrome!' Slaves they may not have been, but the new boys were certainly not equals, either. For a start, they were put on wages rather than a percentage of proceeds. 'The Clash wasn't really a band by this time, it was a limited company, and we were paid by that limited company,' says Nick. 'Bernie asked me, "How much do you want? So much, and your tax paid, or this much more and you pay your own tax?" And I said, "I'll take the larger amount, and you can pay the tax as well." He laughed and said OK. It was about £250 a week. I don't think the tax ever did get paid. I had a few letters from the Internal Revenue afterwards.'

Kosmo made it clear to the newcomers that they would not be taking part in interviews. 'He was probably quite wise in not having these dunderheads wandering around saying what they hadn't been properly prepared to say,' admits Nick. 'It didn't worry me at the time. It was, "Look, they want to interview Joe. They don't know who the fuck you are, so don't worry about it." To get the party line across, it always helps if you interview one person instead of five.' And that party line – the Clash's musical and political direction – had been determined long before the new boys' recruitment.

From this point onward, the Voice of the Clash was the voice of Joe Strummer, with occasional support from Paul or Kosmo, and it was invariably raised to deliver a confrontational, angry, meandering rant that made some interviewers fear for his sanity. However, he did have points to make. The 'White Riot'-era attitude to television was back with a vengeance. 'Get up off your chair, turn off the TV, go outside and deal with real life,' Joe lectured *Creem*'s readership via an interview with Bill Holdship. After a four year spell of having – at worst – ambivalent status, America was out of favour once more. 'I don't like it,' he told *Jamming!*'s Ross Fortune. 'I don't like the food there, I don't like the way everything looks the same. I don't like the signs all over the place. I don't like the plastic buildings. I don't like the imitation muzak dribbling out of the speakers, and I don't like the way they let the government get on with things.'

The new band were to be fit, hard-working and clean living, a reaction to both the old band's creative self-indulgence and the setbacks it had encountered as a result of substance abuse. 'If you take drugs, wear a kaftan,' Joe informed the *NME*'s readers via Richard Cook. 'Be honest. Wear a bell round your neck. I've smoked so much pot I'm surprised I haven't turned into a bush.' DIY was back on the agenda. 'Anybody can do it,' he told Bill Holdship. 'The fact is, we play three or four chords. On a good day, we might hit five. But dammit to hell, I challenge anybody not to be able to learn five chords in three weeks. God, I could get a penguin to do that!' The distilled essence of all this proselytising, in Joe's own words, was, 'You've got to feel like you can get involved,' and, 'Vote. Take some responsibility for being alive.'

Even more so than in 1976-77, when the punk era at least provided an appropriate context, the largely valid observations he made were undermined by the hectoring manner of their delivery. 1984 was a world away from '1977', whatever the countdown at the end of that song might have attempted to suggest to the contrary. The music scene had developed and splintered beyond recognition. True, there were fourth wave punk bands in the UK, and a similarly no-nonsense hardcore scene in the US, but at the time these were little more than cults. More commercially successful were the likes of the Alarm and U2, who had taken the Spirit of the Clash and added leather trousers, big hair, half-baked mysticism and inflated passion. Elsewhere, the New Pop bands offered vacuous entertainment-lite, while wan indie bands jangled their guitars and peddled bedsit angst. Joe not only refused to align with any of these, but also loudly trumpeted his disgust. This was hardly likely to encourage fans of such artists to make room in their hearts and record collections for the Clash. Richard Cook pointed out that, in rejecting nearly all of his new peers, Joe was in danger of talking the Clash out of any kind of an audience at all.

In fairness to the band, and despite their stated ambition to present a sexy image, they were taking their impression of the mood of the times not from *Smash Hits* and the *Face*, but from the news media. The effects of economic recession and the government's response to it had boosted the number of unemployed to a figure three times greater than that of 10 years earlier, when Bernie had first anticipated anarchy in the streets. The North, traditionally home to the bulk of the UK's heavy industry, was especially hard hit. Comparisons with the still relatively untroubled, affluent South led to talk of a North-South Divide. Britain had broken into two economically disparate factions which – bearing in mind the decidedly similar origins of the American Civil War – made the 'English Civil War' Joe had sung about in 1978 seem distinctly possible. Someone had to address these issues. To Joe, the New Pop dandies and indie naval-gazers were avoiding them, and he didn't think the fourth wave punk bands or the likes of the Alarm and U2 were up to the job, either.

As well as learning the sizeable back catalogue, the new Clash's rehearsal time was also spent working up at least nine new Joe Strummer songs. Most of these were ultra-basic rockers which found Joe treading familiar ground. 'Dictator' points the finger at a US-funded Central American despot, but the character sketch is so hackneyed that it is impossible to take the intended political point seriously: it has more in common with 'Rock The Casbah' than with 'Washington Bullets'. Knee-jerk rhymes and empty sloganeering drive 'Are You Ready For War?', another examination of escalating world conflict and the resulting threat of mutually assured destruction. 'Ammunition', also known as 'Thank You, Chief', continues to do the anti-warmongering theme to death. Its title aside, 'Sex Mad War' rings the changes to some extent: it is an anti-pornography rant. In 1976, 'London's Burning' and '48 Hours' had found Joe identifying with the underclass's reliance on cheap street drugs; by contrast, new song 'Glue Zombie'- the latest of his pronouncements on the State of Punk – reveals the now drug-free Strummer's more puritan tendencies.

The punk-reggae 'Three Card Trick' finds Joe returning to what, in his *Creem* review of *Sandinista!*, Jeff Nesin had described as the Clash's 'great theme': the Dying of England. With its references to the mill on top of the hill, steel being manufactured abroad rather than domestically, fading 'fog drowned towns' and people finding themselves on the wrong side of the scissor blade, it is clearly informed by the North-South divide and the Tories' willingness to sacrifice the hopes of the have-nots in order to preserve the security of the haves. It sets itself up as a more uptempo 'Straight to Hell' for the UK, but its overblown, almost Gothic imagery – crucifixions, wastelands, torchings, death's head legions – fails to make anything like the same direct emotional connection.

'We Are The Clash' sets out to thumb its nose at Mick Jones. It aspires to continue in the self-celebratory tradition of 'Clash City Rockers' and 'This Is Radio Clash', and makes a feature of 1976-77 era Clash terrace harmonies, but both the guitar and Joe's vocal inflections – right down to the Rottenesque rolled r's – recall no band so much as the Sex Pistols. Debating whether its self-aggrandisement qualifies as school of Bo Diddley or school of Mott the Hoople is a redundant exercise: neither would want to claim parentage of this charmless and defiantly yobbish football chant.

Nick was more impressed with the two least typical songs, 'In The Pouring, Pouring Rain' and 'Gallini'. He describes the latter, of which not even a live recording appears to have survived, as a musical and lyrical cross between 'Death Is A Star' and 'Straight to Hell'. 'It was really moody, and it didn't fit the bill as far as the back-to-basics "we are punk rockers" thing went,' he says. These were also the two songs he made the biggest contribution to, and they encouraged him to think that he might later be able to collaborate with Joe on the songwriting.

The new line up was broken in, as planned, with a few gigs in Southern California at the end of January 1984. It was a deliberate return to the scene of the Us Festival, to pick up where the previous line-up of the Clash had left off. The opening performance took place on the 19th at the 2,000 capacity Arlington Centre in Santa Barbara. The decision to play venues of this size, most of them in towns usually considered by international name rock bands to be off the beaten track, was trumpeted by Kosmo as being indicative of the new Clash's desire to take their music to the people and play it how it should be played, up close and personal. The statement didn't quite ring true, but Nick Sheppard objects to any suggestion that the band were in fact deliberately avoiding the glare of publicity. 'It might have been out of the media eye in England, but not in America. We were on TV: *Entertainment Tonight* and shit like that. I would have liked to have warmed up in a couple of clubs, but the shows in Santa Barbara and Santa Monica were on big stages in front of 2-5,000 people. San Francisco was at least 10,000. These were big gigs. As far as I was concerned, they were fucking huge!'

Not all of the larger shows sold out, though: the 15,000-capacity Long Beach Arena remained half-empty. Curiosity, it seemed, was only going to sell so many tickets. LA journalist Ethlie Ann Vare noted that the band showed 'more energy than finesse' at that show, and agreed with Mick Jones that the new Clash's new direction 'seems to be backwards'. *Rolling Stone*'s Michael Goldberg reported that fans were demanding to know what had happened to Mick. Significantly, after the first few gigs, Nick's version of 'Should I Stay Or Should I Go' was dropped. At much the same time, remarking that he felt like 'a frog in a microwave' without his guitar, Joe decided he could no longer brook spending the entire set prowling the stage with nothing but a mike stand for company. *Record*'s John Mendelssohn suggested that Joe opted to play guitar again 'primarily so that he can make a big production of angrily yanking his black Telecaster off and flinging it to a roadie in the wings every couple of numbers'.

America was where Bernie's dehumanising sessions became regular features of the new members' schedules. 'Bernie's style of management was one I'd never come into contact with before, and haven't since,' says Nick, echoing Terry Chimes's observations about his initial exposure to Bernie in 1976. 'Very controlling, lots of head games, challenges, even abuse: personal stuff about the way you looked. We'd have all these meetings. I never really got an angle on what it was all supposed to achieve, and I don't think it did achieve anything.' Although the no drugs decree was real enough, Nick is quick to point out that not everything about being part of the new Clash was grim. 'I think Joe and Paul were a bit sick of all the drugs. But we had a great time. We went and got pissed. A hell of a lot of brandy was drunk.'

For the first time since 1977, the Clash had made no show in the 1983 *NME* end-of-year readers' poll, but tickets did sell out quickly for the eight early-to-mid-February 1984 dates played in the UK and Eire under the banner Out Of Control. Recycled from the 1977 tour, this title was another attempt to stake the new band's claim to the old Clash's heritage. Ironically, what the band was now offering was closer to a traditional rock'n'roll show than anything they had ever flirted with before: banks of lights, smoke bombs and video screens. Ray Jordan and one or two of the soundmen who had worked on earlier tours were in evidence, but by now there were remarkably few other direct links to the band's past. It is not insignificant that Pennie Smith had by this stage withdrawn her services as the Clash's official photographer.

Mick Jones's legal representatives served injunctions at every venue. 'I don't know if he's trying to make his lawyer a millionaire or something, but he's going the right way about it,' grumbled Joe to *Jamming!*'s Ross Fortune later that year. 'The writs started arriving thick and fast. I haven't got time to bother with that. He obviously has.' 'The injunctions were all ignored,' says Nick. 'No gigs were ever cancelled.' Audience calls for Mick were given particularly short shrift.

It was during the UK leg of the tour that Joe came up with what he would later describe as the last great Clash song: 'This Is England'. The original tune was worked up on one string of his ukulele, and – in truth – was not really so great, bearing little relation to the subsequently recorded version. The lyric is another British take on 'Straight to Hell', a compassionate identification with life on the employment scrap heap, on decaying council estates and on the receiving end of increasingly brutal police repression.

The UK tour sandwiched a European sojourn, with the Clash playing Sweden, Germany, Switzerland, Italy and France. The show on the 17th, at Stockholm's Issatdion, subsequently spawned a host of bootlegs, and is considered by collectors to be one of the new Clash's better performances. After Kosmo had introduced the band by quoting the chorus of 'We Are The Clash', the band proceeded to reduce almost every tune they tackled to a primitive staccato stomp. Only the earlier punk tunes responded well to such treatment: everything else had its original melody, subtlety, texture, and – sadly – meaning hammered into the ground.

The second leg of the UK tour began in March, and culminated in a string of five dates at the Brixton Academy (formerly the Fair Deal) supported by former punk face Shane MacGowan's band the Pogues. Intrigued by Richard Cook's February 1984 *NME* interview with the new Clash – or, rather, with Joe and Paul – that paper's Gavin Martin went along to see them with an open mind, but was disappointed. 'This new Clash are no big departure, they are still entangled with all the old faults. The new young bloods in the pack haven't brought fresh drive and commitment, they've merely grown into and expanded the idea of the Clash as posed-perfect rebels.' Gavin failed to see any evidence of a 'return to the primal elements of real rock shock', describing instead 'the heaviest and most orthodox rock show I've ever seen the Clash play. The callisthenics, the heroic posturing, the riot scenes and war footage are all still there. For a group so against the machinations of violence, they still get an awful lot of mileage from its imagery.'

The Brixton shows earned a heavily photo-illustrated cover feature in what had once been the band's unofficial fanzine, *ZigZag*. Kris Needs and Robin Banks might have departed, but the tradition of nepotism was – it seemed – to be maintained when reporter

Paul O'Reilly admitted he also manned the Clash's merchandising stall. Surprisingly, though, his piece turned out to be both frank and critical. Joe was portrayed as something of a dictator at soundchecks, making the new boys run through numerous takes of 'Safe European Home', a song they had been playing regularly since January. Although he refused to admit that the Clash were 'a dead band', Paul O'Reilly conceded that it was now up to them to prove otherwise. Bernie's contribution also came in for some scrutiny: 'He has occasional flashes of pure brilliance, but against that you have to set an infuriatingly dogmatic side of his nature that can often reduce a situation to stalemate.' 'We had huge fucking fights backstage at the Academy,' says Nick. 'Bernie was all, "You're shit! You've never achieved anything! Have you ever thought what would you do with a million pounds?" Bullshit. Just bullshit.'

For all Joe's anti-American remarks and renewed lyrical interest in the political situation in Britain, the Clash were still determined to follow up their late 1982 success in the States. A second US tour began at the end of March 1984, and ran through until the end of May. With two full years having passed since they last had a new record to promote, though, the band were slipping even further as a live draw. 'I know some of the gigs weren't selling out,' says Nick. 'We did a lot of college shows on that tour. They weren't huge, but they paid a lot of money.' Kosmo had previously insisted on a guarantee of a front cover before he would allow music press access, but now had to suffer the humiliation of back-pedalling for a feature in *Creem*.

Everyone in the Clash camp recognised the need to release new material. 'I don't want to actually record until we've got the group as a unit,' Joe had told *Jamming!*'s Ross Fortune following the Brixton gigs. 'In my mind, I liken us to a new platoon,' he told *Creem*'s Bill Holdship, employing now tired Clash combat metaphors. 'We're going to go out and crawl right in front of the enemy lines, get fired upon, and then look at each other to see how we're bearing up. Can I rely on this guy when my gun jams? We're under fire, and we're sharing that experience. And that's what's going to make our record great.'

Not insignificant factors in the recording delay had been the freeze on Clash finances and the tussle over the right to the band's name instigated by Mick Jones. The pressure began to lift in late spring 1984, when Mick and Topper decided to go their separate ways. Topper later claimed that he was unhappy with the emphasis on sampling and technology – and, specifically, electronic percussion – in Mick's new music. In truth, the split occurred because Topper was using heroin again, and objected to the way Mick was trying to limit his access to the drug by controlling the manner in which he was paid.

Topper's replacement in Mick's band was recruited via a music press ad. Greg Roberts was hired partly because he seemed more enthusiastic than anyone else, and partly because Mick thought he looked like Richard Gere. Mick was now as keen as his former bandmates to free up the money from his time with the Clash, so that his new band could purchase more cutting edge equipment and also begin recording. He would later insist that his threat to continue performing under the name the Clash had merely been intended as a wind-up. Whether or not this was true, it is probably not coincidental that the legal matter was resolved at roughly the same time Mick finally made it known he had dropped any claim to the name. Nevertheless, all the names Mick did consider for his new outfit demonstrated his determination to be seen to be living up to the Spirit of the Clash. The first choice was Top Risk Action Company (TRAC), very *Rat Patrol From Fort Bragg*. The next, Real Westway, was a pun on football team Real Madrid and 'the real Sound of the Westway'. The one that stuck, Big Audio Dynamite, not only presented a convenient acronym – BAD as in bad-ass; BAD meaning good – but also captured the confrontational, in-your-face overtones of the early Clash: it sounded like a band that would explode off the stage.

Topper's substantial back royalties for *Sandinista!*, *Combat Rock* and, especially, 'Rock The Casbah' were also released at this time. The initial payment was enough for him to buy a flat in Abbey Road, St John's Wood. It was also enough to finance another prolonged cocaine and heroin binge. He took up with Donna, the wife of former Heavy Metal Kids vocalist and future *Auf Wiedersehen Pet* actor – and future OD casualty – Gary Holton, and tried to avoid the threatened repercussions by holing up in the Portobello Hotel, Stanley Gardens with a suitcase full of money. That summer, Topper took the inevitable fall. He awoke one morning lying prostrate in a motorcycle garage showroom with concussion and a badly broken leg, having evidently plunged through a skylight. He claimed amnesia, and pointed out to the police that it was not customary for burglars to go to work in stack heeled boots and a bright red suit. In view of Topper's complicated love life, preferred recreational habits and associated business contacts, hypnosis was not required to solve the mystery. Topper was let off with a caution. Soon afterwards, Steve Barnacle received an urgent phone call from the patient, begging to be sprung from hospital. Not only was he going into withdrawal, but he had just been visited at his sick bed and threatened by 'a person known to him'.

The new Clash were now able to make a record, theoretically at least. Joe had told Ross Fortune that the band intended to go into the studio sometime over the summer. 'We came off tour in May and we had a break,' says Nick. 'Then we began to drift into some sort of work in Lucky Eight. Joe wasn't around very much. We were told, "Oh, he's writing."' In 1994, Vince White talked to Ralph Heibutzki for a *DISCoveries* Clash retrospective, and recalled how he and the other two newcomers would be given tapes of Joe's basic chord sketches to work on. 'It was only the three of us,' said Vince. 'Sometimes, Paul would go down. Most of the time we were arranging these chords.' Nick was not too concerned. 'The summer just drifted by,' he says. 'It was a nice hot one, and I was just enjoying myself.'

With what seemed like typical bad timing, the hiatus in Clash live activity in the UK coincided with the biggest manifestation of grass roots political activism in Britain since the inner-city riots of three years earlier. The Falklands War had to some extent succeeded in externalising the nation's aggression, but now it was erupting at home once again. Margaret Thatcher's government made it clear that it was prepared to use the most draconian measures available in order to retain control, even if that meant undermining civil rights and the country's industrial infrastructure, resorting to violence in the short-term and forcing whole communities into a long-term poverty trap. The strike by miners threatened with widespread pit closures and redundancies came to embody the North-South Divide. The miners were making their stand not only for their own rights, jobs and communities, but also in order to provide a rallying point for the rest of the country's disaffected workers and unemployed. Their action entered its critical phase in late spring 1984, and the most memorable image of the conflict comes from that May's pitched battle between pickets and mounted riot police at Orgreave: a photograph of a galloping policeman, leaning out to take a full baton swing at an unarmed female spectator. Both 'Three Card Trick' and 'This Is England' reflect the brutal face of contemporary policing – batons are wielded willy-nilly in both – but the Clash missed a real opportunity to attach themselves to the miner's cause at this crucial time. The Clash of '76 had managed to generate a righteous anger and capture the imagination of the nation's youth on far less fuel than this. The Clash of '84 remained on holiday until September.

When they did reconvene, it was to play a series of gigs organised by the Communist Party. In Italy. Again, the motive was chiefly financial. Joe remained distant, travelling separately from the others, but Nick remembers the shows themselves with some fondness. 'The Communist Party held these huge festivals every year, featuring all kinds of music, partly to generate income for the party on a local level, but also to enhance the cultural life of the country. We played about five of them. They were really good and we played really well. And we all got some really cool communist flags and T-shirts out of it.'

It was upon returning to London that, from Nick's point of view, things truly began to 'get weird' in the Clash camp. The rehearsal sessions continued, again without Joe. 'At one point I was given a tape of songs numbered one to five,' says Nick. 'They had no lyrics on them, just Joe playing mad riffs over a drum machine. They made no sense to me whatsoever.' This peculiarly remote sort of collaboration depressed him. 'I realised, "Yes, I am just a hired gun. I just do what I'm told. I'm not actually going to write any songs here, or have any real interaction with anybody in that respect."'

While the Clash were dormant, BAD came out to play. They made their first low key foray onto the UK live circuit in October 1984, as unannounced support to – of all bands – the Alarm. That Mick's band were still feeling their way was evidenced by the high proportion of songs that were destined never to make it to record: in addition to 'BAD', the set included 'Keep Off The Grass', 'Interaction', 'The Nation Has A Nervous Breakdown' and 'Strike', several of these titles suggesting that Mick was paying heed to current events. The audience was taken aback by the experimental nature of the set: Mick sang and played a state of the art synthesizer guitar, Don liberally dosed the extended dance grooves with movie dialogue samples, and Tony James took time off from Sigue Sigue Sputnik to add dub effects at the mixing desk. 'Tony's role is to take the group and rip it apart and make something different every night,' Mick told *Rolling Stone*'s Bill Flanagan early the following year. 'It's like producing a new 12-inch single every time.'

Meanwhile, in the Clash camp, Bernie's head games were getting ever more twisted. 'The rest of the autumn and winter was spent with various combinations of people being told they wouldn't be on the record, which wasn't very nice, and then that they would be, which by that stage wasn't very nice, either,' says Nick Sheppard. These latest demoralisation sessions were the prelude to two shows played at the Brixton Academy on 6 and 7 December. Under the banner Scargill's Christmas Party, they were belated benefit gigs on behalf of the striking miners and their families.

Three of Joe's new songs were débuted at the Brixton gigs. 'North And South' was the most appropriate to the occasion, again examining life on the wrong side of the national divide. At times genuinely affecting, it is marred by Joe's apparent inability to tell a tale without resorting to hyperbole: he raises the stakes just a little too high for credibility to stay the course. 'Dirty Punk' and 'Fingerpoppin', meanwhile, strike self-consciously adolescent rebellious poses. Like 'Cheat' and 'Hate And War' before it, the former takes great delight in shoving punk's bad reputation back in its detractors' faces. The latter takes the mating game as its subject – even stooping to rhyming 'dance' and 'romance' – the sort of thing Mick Jones had been criticised for doing all the way from '1-2 Crush On You' to 'Should I Stay Or Should I Go'.

Joe would later voice his disappointment that he was not invited to contribute to another worthy cause that December. In response to television news reports of famine in Ethiopia, third wave punk Bob Geldof and former Rich Kid Midge Ure had written 'Feed The World' and arranged for it to be recorded by an all star cast under the name Band Aid. Recording took place at Sarm West, formerly Basing Street studio, where the Clash had recorded *Give 'Em Enough Rope*, and just a few doors away from Joe's Lancaster Road home. As he told the *NME*'s Sean O'Hagan in 1988, being overlooked made Joe feel like an outsider, and it hurt. Given that most of the artists involved were the same New Pop stars he had spent most of the last year lambasting in the music press, though, it was hardly surprising.

Recording for the new Clash album finally began in December 1984. Not in London or New York, but in Munich, Germany. Bernie chose the studio – the name of which has never been revealed – so at least one of the reasons was immediately self-evident. 'It was cheap,' says Nick. 'It was also out of the way, and it was a very early digital studio. It was owned by a millionaire who made his money in construction after the war. He built it for his girlfriend, who was a singer.'

Nick did not get to see it for some time. The backing tracks were recorded in his absence, and indeed, in the absence of every other member of the Clash camp except Bernie and Joe. With Ulli Rudolf engineering, drum tracks were programmed by session musician Michael Faye, and keyboard and synthesizer tracks were added by a German session musician subsequently credited as Herman (Young Wagner). Strangely, for someone who had expressed an interest in getting back to the fundamentals of punk-style rock'n'roll, Joe was allowing his songs to be constructed piecemeal, using the very programmed percussion and synthesizers to which he had so strongly objected when employed on Mick Jones's last demos for the Clash.

Trying to reconcile this approach to all the pep talks about the Spirit of the Clash was something that Nick Sheppard for one had given up attempting. After being told he would be playing on the album, after all, he was called down to Lucky Eight on Christmas Eve for a single day's pre-production work. This consisted of being given a tape of the backing tracks and being asked to come up with ideas for guitar parts. Some of the songs dated from the period of intensive live work early in 1984, but that did not necessarily mean they were familiar to him. He describes the recorded version of 'We Are The Clash' as 'fairly similar' to its live incarnation, but 'Dictator', 'Are You Ready For War?' – which would be listed on the album as 'Are You Red...y?' – 'Three Card Trick' and 'This Is England' were all 'very different'. 'North And South', 'Dirty Punk' and 'Fingerpoppin' had been débuted at the miners benefit shows, so he did recognise them. The remaining four tracks were completely new.

'Movers And Shakers', one of the songs Nick heard for the first time on Christmas Eve, is an attempt to promote DIY among Britain's swelling numbers of disadvantaged and downtrodden. Musically, the song carries a pungent whiff of Sham 69's 'Hurry Up, Harry'. Like 'Three Card Trick' and 'North And South', it suffers from ridiculous imagery: 'The boy stood in the burning slum.' Such failings pale in comparison to its overall message, however: it would appear to be suggesting washing car windscreens at traffic lights as a viable career opportunity. Prior to 1981, when the Clash had talked about DIY, they had meant *creative* self-expression. Songs like '48 Hours', 'Career Opportunities', 'Clash City Rockers', 'Clampdown', 'Bankrobber' and 'The Magnificent Seven' had all rubbished the notion that people should be grateful to take soul-destroying jobs for the sake of a weekly pay packet. In the wake of such broadsides to establishment values, it is not a little disappointing to hear Joe Strummer – art school drop-out, squat-dweller and dole-scrounger – promoting self-reliance as represented by such menial and demeaning tasks. He is effectively telling his followers to get on their bikes, to borrow a phrase from an infamous contemporary speech by Tory hard-liner Norman Tebbit.

'Play To Win' has a game of Space Invaders for a musical backing track, and its chorus boasts of taking the pioneer and bandit spirit to the space age. The rest of the lyric is a spoken dialogue between Joe and an unidentified second party – possibly Paul – affecting Jamaican patois. At least one verse appears to have been inspired by the tradition of English and German rivalry, which had once found its expression in war and now did so at football matches: 'If it's hooligan you want / We British will tear up on the street.' The new Clash seemed to be using terrace harmonies to carry a message of terrace chauvinism, something the Clash of '76 had tried much harder to avoid.

This latest batch of songs clearly found Joe striving for a more positive, upbeat message to balance the doom and gloom of the earlier new Clash material, but further evidence that writing to a brief was no longer his forte is provided by 'Cool Under Heat' and 'Life Is Wild': two more celebrations of punk posturing with even less to recommend them than the equally lame-brained but at least enthusiastically spiteful 'Dirty Punk'.

Nick flew to Munich early in January 1985, learning new material even as he recorded his guitar parts for the album. Joe played some guitar, and a while later Vince was brought over too. 'I'm on all the songs,' says Nick. 'I would say Vince is as well, to my recollection.' Norman Watt-Roy, veteran of the New York sessions for *Sandinista!*, played most of the bass. 'Paul wasn't really involved much, but then again, what's new?' says Nick. 'He did play on a couple of tracks.' Everyone joined in on the terrace chant choruses. Pete Howard's contribution as drummer was limited to a couple of songs the official five-piece Clash recorded live in the studio one afternoon: a recently composed paean to pro-activism, 'Do It Now' and the more venerable 'Sex Mad War', now retitled 'Sex Mad Roar'.

This last session was little more than a gesture towards the notion of the new Clash as it had been sold to the new members back in October 1983. After Joe, Nick was the musician who spent longest working on the record, and he did at least get some belated sense of being appreciated as a collaborator. 'Me and Joe would talk about the record a lot, work on guitar parts and get quite excited,' he says. One result was the overhauling of 'This Is England', its lyric now strapped to a juggernaut of a riff. 'I remember playing bass on that and Joe being ecstatic about it. He said, "That's the only bit of the record with any bollocks to it!"' That remark, plus the guilty sop of the live-in-the-studio session, gave Nick the feeling that Joe was not wholly happy with the way the album was going, either. 'When you're making a record, you try to get into it, but it was just a fucking joke, really.'

Nothing was heard of the Clash in the UK media until May 1985, when local radio and BBC2's *Whistle Test* (the show's name having been shortened to slough off the old grey image) reported the unlikely news that the Clash had been seen busking in several Northern towns over the weekend of the 11th.

It transpired that this was, indeed, true: the band were hitching from town to town armed only with acoustic guitars and, in Pete Howard's case, drumsticks, and setting up in a variety of gathering places to play for loose change. They were even sleeping on fans' floors. *NME* stringer Paul Syrysko overheard Joe say, 'If anyone from the *NME* talks to you, just tell 'em we've gone stark, raving mad.' It might have been the last thing one would have expected the average big name rock'n'roll band to do, but it made perfect sense in the context of Joe's previous remarks about getting back to basics: he was not only revisiting his own pre-Clash roots, but also the early days of rock'n'roll, blues and folk, when music was made with the most primitive of equipment. Although the press and public did not realise it at the time, it was also a deliberate and pointed reaction to the manner in which the album had been recorded.

The venture was conceived in Munich. Joe and Nick were feeling down, and Kosmo suggested they go off and do something mad. During the course of a walk around the town, they came up with the busking tour, and suggested it to the others before flying back the following day. Strict rules applied, but there was no real organisation. 'We all left London with £10. We weren't allowed to take any more than that, our instruments and a change of underpants,' says Nick. 'We had to hitch separately or in pairs. "We'll meet you by the town clock." "*Is* there a town clock?" "Dunno."'

The tour took the Clash, clad in durable leathers, from Gateshead station to Sunderland Carlton Bar Drum club to Nottingham – where they played outside the Garage club and in the Old Market Square – to Leeds, where they played outside Le Phonographique night club. They stayed on for an extra day in that city in order to entertain customers queuing to see the Alarm. Following the dismissive remarks Joe had made about the band the previous year, it was hardly surprising that the venue's bouncers were instructed to disrupt the performance. Less fathomable was the action of an irate audience member who threw a balloon full of red paint at Joe to protest CBS's involvement in South Africa. Following a half hour show in the Faversham pub, the Clash moved on to York. There, the following day, they played outside York Minster to 600 people gathered to celebrate VE Day. On Tuesday the 14th, they turned in a set at Edinburgh's Coasters disco, playing to 1,300 people without a PA, and also visited reformed hard man Jimmy Boyle's Gateway centre for young people with drug-related problems.

'We'd play anywhere, morning or night,' Joe reminisced fondly to *Musician*'s Bill Flanagan in 1988. 'We played under canal bridges, in precincts, bus stops, nightclubs, discos.' Apart from the paint-throwing incident, reactions to the decidedly rough'n'ready performances ranged from the bemused to the ecstatic. Certainly, enough fans turned up with tape recorders to provide bootleggers with the raw material for several 'commemorative' albums. New compositions 'Movers And Shakers' and 'Cool Under Heat' were given an outing, but the set chiefly comprised older Clash songs, standards like the Monkees' 'Stepping Stone', and such former 101ers' set regulars as the Beatles' 'Twist And Shout' and Gene Vincent's 'Be-Bop-A-Lula'.

Had it been intended solely as a publicity stunt, the busking tour would have been an unqualified success: it caught the public imagination in a way that the new Clash's bona fide gigs had failed to do. Kosmo's January 1984 claim that, in choosing to play smaller venues off the beaten track, the band were taking their music to the people had rung decidedly hollow. But the busking tour really was just one step removed from having the Clash come and play in your front room, and the fact that it was exclusively a Northern jaunt was strong indication of where the band's sympathies lay. 'That was probably the best thing we ever did,' says Nick. 'I think it was the only real thing we ever did. It made people sit up and think, which could be argued was what the band was supposed to be about.' Even today, it is still the abiding memory most people have of the band's final incarnation.

The *NME* report of the busking tour announced that the Clash were 'still recording' their new album, but nothing further was heard over the coming months. With Mick Jones's BAD also in the act of honing new material, it was – perhaps against the odds – Topper who proved to be the first of those who had participated in the *Combat Rock* sessions to release a follow-up record. Breaking his leg had reminded him of the childhood accident that had led to his becoming a drummer in the first place. As soon as his injury healed, he began practising again. In the summer of 1984, he took on a new manager, Andrew MacPherson, from his home town of Dover. He also exploited his Dover connections to recruit much of the personnel – including Gary, Steve and Bill Barnacle – for the jazz big band he assembled to record a cover of Gene Krupa's 'Drummin' Man'. Sessions took place at Wessex with former Clash engineer Jerry Green producing.

The track was initially intended as a calling card from the drug free Topper, an announcement that he was back and looking for work. Jerry had other ideas. He knew Topper could write his own material, and persuaded him to put together his own band.

Mickey Gallagher had played on 'Drummin' Man', and his services were retained, but Steve Barnacle never got the phone call he was promised. James Eller and ex-Roxy Music man Neil Hubbard were brought in to record 'Du Cane Road' and 'Hope For Donna', two Headon-composed movie score-type instrumentals in a jazzy R&B style. CBS agreed to let Topper go, and the tracks so far recorded helped secure him a new deal with Phonogram offshoot label Mercury.

Everyone was keen for Topper to record an album which pursued the R&B direction suggested by the instrumentals, only with lyrics and rather more adept vocals than the drummer could provide. Jerry brought in a recent acquaintance, Jimmy Helms, best known in the UK for his 1973 Top 10 solo hit, 'Gonna Make You An Offer You Can't Refuse'. By the end of the summer 1985 sessions, James Eller and Neil Hubbard had been replaced by former Jeff Beck and Van Morrison guitarist Bobby Tench and former Marvin Gaye, Detroit Emeralds and Van Morrison bassist Jerome Rimson. Some guest guitar was added by Robert Johnson, the man who had put the wah-wah into Isaac Hayes's 'Shaft'. In the meantime, in June 1985, 'Drummin' Man' and the two instrumentals were released as a taster single. The NME's Cath Carroll described the cover as 'commendable' and the other tracks as 'groovy', but it failed to make the charts.

Throughout 1984, Mick Jones had continued to send Jerry Green tapes of his works in progress. He was looking for feedback, but also keeping the engineer abreast of developments so that they would be on the same wavelength when it came time to record for real. When Mick learned Jerry was working on solo material with Topper, he saw this as yet another betrayal. 'What Mick said was, "Do you want to work with Harold Robbins, or do you want to work with Tolstoy?"' says Jerry. At the time Jerry thought he was onto a winner with Topper and his pedigree R&B band, and preferred the idea of occupying to producer's chair to the engineer's, so he chose the drummer and laughed at Mick's arrogance. In time he would come to acknowledge that the joke was on him.

Early in 1985, BAD further polished their live sound as anonymous support on a European tour by – of all bands – U2. In spring, Tony James returned to Sigue Sigue Sputnik, and Mick hired former Theatre of Hate roadie Flea as soundman. BAD continued to work on new songs, which saw an increasing contribution from Don Letts. He was now not only supplying toasting and effects, but also acting as what he termed 'Mick's lyrical apprentice'. Any hopes Mick might have had of following in Topper's footsteps and escaping from his CBS contract were dashed. In the US, though, he did manage to switch from Epic to the company's other label, Columbia.

In the summer, he hired experienced dub engineer/producer Paul 'Groucho' Smykle as Jerry Green's replacement. It was an association that would last for three albums. Accused of being a wannabe New Yorker during his last couple of years with the Clash, Mick was keen to re-establish his roots in London, and specifically the Notting Hill area. At least partly for this reason, the recording sessions took place in Sarm West, the former Basing Street studio.

Mick later insisted that the music was not intended to be hip hop, but something he had wanted the Clash to strive for on *Combat Rock* and the wasted year thereafter. 'BAD don't really rap,' he told *Good Times*'s Kevin Zimmerman in 1987. 'We like the beat. That's the thing we most go for. But we try to put it together with other things like the reggae bass and the rock'n'roll guitar, and make it something which is our own.' Lyrically, although he and Don address some serious issues, all eight tracks recorded – each as long as a raga – evince a wry, even satirical take on the world.

'A Party' takes on South African apartheid; 'The Bottom Line' is 'a dance to the tune of economic decline'; 'BAD' is a list of things 'that drive me crazy'; 'Stone Thames' considers the impact the AIDS epidemic was beginning to have on sexual behaviour; 'Sony' muses cheerfully on Japan's attempt at world domination by microchip (and would prove itself to be prophetic when, three years later, Sony bought out CBS); 'Sudden Impact' pokes fun at that particular corner of the trash culture market that responds to Satanic heavy metal and gruesome horror B-movies; 'E=MC2' celebrates the cinematic oeuvre of director Nic Roeg; and 'Medicine Show' takes its own brand of Medicinal Compound to the Wild West, an excuse for the gratuitous deployment of the spaghetti western samples and Clint Eastwood movie dialogue Mick had first heard on the WBLS Dirty Harry Mix of 'The Magnificent Seven'.

Mick believed BAD were maintaining the Clash's policy of providing social commentary, while avoiding the dogma and melodrama to which – he chose to imply rather than state – the new Clash had succumbed. 'It's important not to be too preachy, to be bumming people out,' Mick told *Rolling Stone*'s David Fricke in 1986. 'Everybody knows how shitty it is out there. It's important to say those things, but the tactical problem is how to say them.' It was also clearly important to him to repudiate the notion that it had been his fascination with hip hop that had been responsible for the Clash turning their back on London. If the Clashworld of *Combat Rock* brought Vietnam movies to the streets of New York, then BADworld takes arthouse, cult and mainstream movies from all over the world and brings them back home to Notting Hill.

When it came time to take photographs for the album sleeve, BAD brought in Dan Donovan, son of famous Sixties photographer Terence, and former assistant to the equally feted David Bailey. Dan let slip that he played keyboards; by the end of the session, he had been recruited for BAD. Mick's multi-media band now had an in-house stills photographer as well as an in-house video director. The pictures Dan took for the front cover are black and white and feature the band grouped closely around Mick. Their leader stands legs akimbo in a pose strongly reminiscent of the covers for both *The Clash* and *Sandinista!*. Rather than a military helmet, though, Mick wears a cowboy hat and holds a stick of dynamite in humorous acknowledgement of Clint Eastwood's involuntary contribution to his music. The inner sleeve shots were posed just off Portobello Road, with Trellick Tower clearly recognisable in the background, celebrating Mick's association with the area he had taken to calling the Wild West End. Mick had taken on Gary Kurfirst as the band's manager, and the office address was given as 95 Ladbroke Grove. A further declaration to the effect that it is BAD, rather than the new Clash, who embody the True Spirit of the Clash is to be found in the album's title: *This Is Big Audio Dynamite* makes sly reference to both 'This Is Radio Clash' and 'We Are The Clash'.

For Mick and Topper's former band, all thoughts of working harder than a heavy metal outfit seemed to have been forgotten. The Clash made just three conventional live appearances over summer 1985, all at large European festivals: the Roskilde in Denmark on 29 June; the Rockscene at Quehenne in Finland on 13 July; and on the second night of a two-day event at the Antic Panathinaikon, Athens, Greece on 27 August. These shows were more obviously played just for the money than any previous ones, with the Clash appearing as a support act on bills headlined by the kind of bands they had recently professed to despise.

By mid-to-late 1984, up to 40 per cent of a typical two hour Clash set had been made up of post-Mick Jones material; now just one new song, 'Three Card Trick', was included. The only other development was that Paul had dropped 'Guns Of Brixton' in favour of singing 'What's My Name'. The band's discomfort was palpable. They were unable to prevent part of the Rockscene show being transmitted on FM radio, but their truculence turned Roskilde into a mini-reprise of the Us Festival. Only this time with no-one paying any attention. Joe went on verbal attack during the press conference. Kosmo – who had long been so in thrall to his own hucksterdom that he firmly believed himself to be not only a member of the Clash but one of the more important members – joined in, interrupting and arguing with journalists and band members alike. Later, 14 songs into the set, he marched on-stage during 'Spanish Bombs' in order to object to the presence of TV cameras.

The ultimate indignity was reserved for the Athens show, headlined by the Cure and also including Culture Club on the bill. In his 1995 autobiography, *Take It Like A Man*, Boy George recalled that 200 anarchists created a disturbance because they were denied free entrance. Those who made it inside inflamed other sectors of the 60,000-strong crowd, who chose to express their frustration by throwing bottles, stones and coins. Their target was not the Clash, those veterans of missile dodging, but Culture Club, perhaps the ultimate symbol of the New Pop. Drummer Jon Moss had left the Clash because he did not share their political convictions. He happened to be the lover of Culture Club frontman George, the extent of whose political acuity is summed up by the chorus of 'The War Song': 'war is stupid'. Nevertheless, George bravely carried on performing until one of his backing musicians was felled by a brick. At what would turn out to be their last ever gig, the Clash's riot act was stolen by a man in a dress.

The UK music press had lost its fascination with the Clash a year earlier, so the next development came as something of a surprise: the late September 1985 single release of 'This Is England', backed with 'Do It Now' and, on the 12-inch version, 'Sex Mad Roar'. At the *NME*, the band were unlucky enough to encounter Gavin Martin once again: 'Still determined to slay the totems, bare the social ills, attend the wake of our crumbling banana republic, Strummer's rant bears all the signs of agit rocker well into advanced senility: voice rambling and cracking over syn-drums flutter, football chants and ugly guitar grunge.' In other singles and albums reviews, 'This Is England' was afforded considerably more respect, and with hindsight it does live up to Joe's claim for it: the last great Clash song. It failed to make any impression in the US, but reached a respectable enough number 24 in the UK charts.

Perhaps not entirely coincidentally, BAD's first single, 'The Bottom Line' was also released in September. At the NME, Charles Shaar Murray saluted Mick's musical ambition, but deemed it a 'sprawling mess' unsuited to his 'reedy voice'. He did opine that, had Joe sung it – and been flexible enough to follow this musical direction – it would have made a good Clash record. The single failed to trouble any charts at all.

The news pages of the 19 October issue of the *NME* carried the following statement from an unnamed Clash spokesperson: 'As legal difficulties over the name the Clash have forced the band off the road, the group known as the Clash hope to play some shows in the UK and Europe before the end of 1985. The long-awaited album will be released in early November, and the Clash will start touring under a temporary name until this dispute is resolved.' What it didn't explain was how, if they were suddenly unable to play live as the Clash, the band would be able to release further records under that name. The statement made no sense. The paper also reported that rumours were circulating about a possible reunion of Joe and Paul with Mick and Topper.

The Clash album, entitled *Cut The Crap*, turned up as promised. It was reviewed for the *NME* by Mat Snow, who provided some not-unsympathetic historical context to the Clash's attempt at a punk revival, before ripping the album apart. He described the sleeve as 'a marketing director's idea of Ye Style Punke', and poured scorn upon the inner sleeve 'communiqué', which reads: 'Wise MEN and street kids together make a GREAT TEAM... but can the old system be BEAT??. no... not without YOUR participation... RADICAL social change begins on the STREET!!. so if your [*sic*] looking for some ACTION... CUT THE CRAP and Get OUT There.'

On to the contents. As far as Mat was concerned, the band had succeeded in shaking off their global dabblings only to come up with a sound strongly reminiscent of Sham 69 and the Sex Pistols: 'snub nosed guitars bullying the troops and railing at the bastions of privilege whilst full-throated terraces (that's us, remember?) roar their approval'. He noted that Joe's lyrics were hard to make out, and the few examples on the sleeve indicated that this was probably for the best. 'Where's his knack for a pungently well-turned phrase?' At *Melody Maker*, the album was reviewed by Adam Sweeting. If Mat Snow was moved to sarcasm, then Adam was personally offended: 'Guess what? IT'S CRAP! And it doesn't cut it. Football chants, noises of heavy meals being regurgitated over pavements and carpets and a mix that Moulinex would be ashamed of. Who the hell does Joe Strummer think he is?... Ugly? It's painful.' Over at *Sounds*, bizarrely enough, Jack Barron liked it enough to give it four and a half out of five stars. 'Subtlety dies, but it was worth the wait for me, anyway,' he wrote. 'The Clash don't miss Mick Jones, and the band have finally managed to lucidly stitch together their love of ethnic musics with gut-level rock. The collisions of R&B, electro, funk, Tijuana horns and whatever are often splendid on a *sonic* level.' He did concede that the lyrics were not all they could be, but ventured the following justification: 'Joe Strummer has never been a poet: he deals in propaganda with broad slashes of filmic imagery.'

Back in 1984, Joe's stated aim had been to make an album that would have the same impact and longevity as the Clash's début. *Cut The Crap* is not that record. It would appear that the hip hop inflections are intended to serve the same function as the reggae ones did on *The Clash*, but in this case they fail to broaden the cultural base or to raise the quality of the music above the level of bog-standard punk. The album is a non-stop aural barrage, with too much going on, and everything louder than everything else. Except, that is, for Joe's vocals. Trying to decipher them is like straining to hear something shouted from an active construction site across a main road in the middle of rush hour. The stripped down sound of *The Clash* might have been so raw that engineer Simon Humphrey found it difficult to listen to, but this is real cacophony. To be fair, buried underneath are the faintest traces of at least five halfway decent tunes. Unfortunately, there are 12 tracks on the album.

As well as being largely incoherent, Joe's lyrical vision is arguably at its most flawed since *Give 'Em Enough Rope*. Far too many tracks are nothing more than 'punk' rallying cries. However stylised it might have been, *The Clash* captured the flavour of life for disaffected youth in the inner city. *Cut The Crap*'s punks live somewhere else entirely. They stay cool on the street in 'Cool Under Heat', coolly bum cigarettes in 'Life Is Wild', coolly pick up chicks at the hop in 'Fingerpoppin', and coolly cruise cars in 'Dirty Punk': on the whole, more *American Graffiti* than British lowlife. What increases the wince-factor is knowing that the man singing these songs is 32 years old.

The lyrics which do genuinely attempt to address the state of Britain in 1984-85 are also undermined by inapposite romanticism. 'Three Card Trick', 'Movers And Shakers', 'North and South' and 'This Is England' are all rooted in the national turbulence and division caused by the recession as managed by Margaret Thatcher. One might have expected such events to be truly inspirational to Joe, but the results are at best mixed. At least the cornered, world-weary tone of 'This Is England' is appropriate to the times.

Overall, it would appear the 'political' material is aiming for a futurist vision not dissimilar to that of *The Clash*. Whereas the band's début album borrowed from urban models by Ballard, Orwell and Kubrick, though, *Cut The Crap*'s post-industrial wasteland is more suggestive of George Miller's *Mad Max 2*. Certainly, Joe himself had continued to sport his red-tinged mohican for much of the past two years, and a similarly-shorn leather-jacketed punk is pictured on the record's front cover. The film may even be the source of the album title. When a battered and broken Max volunteers to lead the escape by driving the tanker for the climactic chase sequence, doubts are expressed about his physical condition. 'Cut the crap!' retorts Our Hero. 'I'm the best chance you've got.' The fact that this cartoon vision was totally inappropriate to the Britain of 1984-85 merely serves to illustrate how far from reality Joe's filmic obsession had taken him. One is reminded instead of the Comic Strip's satirical film *Strike!*, in which the miners' conflict is given the full Hollywood treatment to 'unintentionally' ludicrous effect. Anticipation of a new Clash release allowed the album to climb to number 16 in the UK charts, although it faded away quickly thereafter. In the US, where *Combat Rock* had done so well, it reached no higher than number 88.

The 23 November 1985 issue of the *NME* carried a news report to the effect that Nick Sheppard, Vince White and Pete Howard had left the band. Whether they were being treated as scapegoats for the album's poor reviews, or whether the other two were making way for the mooted reunion of the former Clash line-up was not made clear...

No other statements were forthcoming...

As the following year progressed, it dawned that this was, in fact, the way the Clash were going to end: with a godawful racket followed by a defeated sigh.

It would be several more years before the full truth behind the last year of the new Clash's existence emerged; and it would take nearly as long for the machinations which had led to the departures of Mick Jones and Topper Headon to be revealed.

Last things first. Early in 1984, Joe's girlfriend Gaby gave birth to a baby girl, named Jazz Domino in honour of, respectively, Charlie Parker and the Van Morrison song as regularly performed by the 101ers. Joe had maintained his distance from his own parents for the last 14 years. His father, Ronald Mellor, died just before the March UK tour, leaving, as Joe himself told *NME* writer Stuart Bailie, 'a lot unsaid.' By the time Joe came home from the US visit in June that year, his mother, Anna, had started to sicken. 'She spent all year doing chemotherapy and radiation treatments because she had a form of cancer,' Joe revealed on BBC2's *Wired* in 1988. 'I spent most of the next year [1985] visiting her, and she died after the end of that year.'

The arrival of a first child usually reinforces the awareness of family, and facing the loss of his parents at a time when he was only just beginning to understand what it meant to be a parent himself was especially hard on Joe. As he later admitted, it required him to do a lot of thinking about all areas of his life: he had to reassess not only his personal relationships, but also how he felt about the Clash. For all his interview rhetoric, he had never been wholly sure that he was doing the right thing with the new band. His own doubts were reinforced by those of others. Johnny Green went to see one of the new Clash's March 1984 Brixton Academy gigs, and he told Joe that what he was doing was rubbish. 'I know,' came the forlorn reply. Stuart Bailie later described the Strummer of this era as 'a wounded, emotional mess'. More than the legal complications with Mick, this was the reason why there were very few gigs after the subsequent US tour, why preparations for the album were so desultory, and why Joe kept his distance from the new boys during this period.

The paradoxes, dichotomies and contradictions that had been the raw stuff of Joe's life for so long had finally spun out of control. With *Cut The Crap*, he was not making the album he wanted to make. Instead, Bernie was in residence behind the mixing desk and was making the album *he* wanted to make. At one point, during a brief absence by Bernie, Joe brought in the session guitarist who had played on Boney M's hits to add some slide guitar siren wails to 'This Is England'. Upon his return, Bernie wiped it. 'Like a "let me get control of my project again" vibe,' Joe – who had plenty of experience of such vibes from his days working with Mick Jones – told *Record Collector*'s Sean Egan in 2000. Joe finally came to realise that he had not really been in the driving seat for any part of the Clash's development over the past four years. Following a last blazing row with Bernie about the turkey they were basting in the name of the Clash, Joe washed his hands of the project before it was even completed. It was left to Bernie to oversee mixing in an unnamed Mayfair studio with engineer Simon Sullivan and his assistant Kevin Whyte.

Bearing in mind the comment Joe had made following Mick's sacking, that he would prefer to 'go back to busking and become a nobody' than carry on with a band that was not working out, the May 1985 busking tour can be seen in part as his acknowledgement that the Clash were on their last legs. Nick Sheppard saw the writing on the wall slightly later, en route to the Roskilde festival. 'That was when I realised how nasty things were between Joe and Bernie. He obviously hated his guts.'

After the Athens show, Joe faced up to the fact that the farce could not continue any longer. Knowing that the release of 'This Is England' was imminent, and that the contract Bernie had renegotiated with CBS meant he was powerless to stop it, he pulled a repeat of the disappearing trick that had presaged Topper's sacking three years earlier. This time Joe hid out in Spain 'sobbing under a palm tree'. 'He buggered off, and we were informed he'd buggered off,' says Nick. 'It became apparent that he might not come back, or if he did that he might not work with us.' Back in 1984, justifying firing Mick, Joe had told *Creem*'s Bill Holdship, 'I'd hope that if I started to act funny *I* would be fired, and the Clash would continue to roll on without me.' A year later, it looked as though Bernie and Kosmo might be prepared to take him at his word. 'Bernie was like, "Let's audition for another singer, and go out behind this record,"' says Nick. 'It was farcical. He and Kosmo were running around like headless chickens.' In 2000, Joe told Sean Egan that 'two or three' auditions to replace him did actually take place. Nick took his phone off the hook to avoid as much of it as possible, but says dates were indeed pencilled in for the following year.

Joe returned shortly after the single's release, but not to the bosoms of his manager and PR man. Instead, he conferred with Paul, then early in October invited the other three members of the new Clash round to Lancaster Road. 'He said, "I'm not going to work with Bernie any more, and I'm not going to carry on with the Clash anymore. I would ask you not to,"' says Nick. 'I had more respect for Joe than I did for Bernie. It was, "Right, that's it then!" We all went out and got really pissed, and the next day the rest of us got a grand each from Joe and Paul. Joe said, "Don't say anything, and you'll get paid for a while."'

'I think about those guys sometimes and hope it didn't fuck up their lives too much,' Joe told the *NME*'s Sean O'Hagan in 1988. 'Because they were good people in a no-win situation.' 'I was happy to be out of it. We'd all had enough,' Vince White told Ralph Heibutzki for the 1994 *DISCoveries* Clash retrospective. Although the end came as something of a relief for all concerned, the experience did leave its scars. 'It was great and it was very hard,' said Vince. 'It was both sides of the coin.' He and Pete Howard disappeared from the music business limelight thereafter. More resilient, and with ideas and contacts of his own, Nick used the money he was still receiving from the Clash to form Head with other leading lights of the Bristol music scene. Head recorded a couple of albums, but failed to make it big. By the late Nineties, Nick was living and playing in a new band in Australia. He feels no bitterness about his time with the Clash. 'I regret not being able to tour the world,' he says. 'And I would have liked to have got a better record out of it. But I made money, and I learned a lot.'

Had they been aware of what happened immediately after their dismissal, the trio might possibly have felt a little more aggrieved. Joe and Paul had suggested otherwise, but at that time both still hoped to persevere with the Clash. The rumours reported in the *NME* regarding a possible rapprochement with Mick Jones were not without foundation. Mick was in the Bahamas at the time, combining a vacation with some work in the studio for Talking Heads' Tina Weymouth. Taking Terry McQuade along for company, Joe followed him there. When they found Mick, Joe apologised profusely for his behaviour over the last two years, told him that his working relationship with Bernie was over for good, and asked Mick to come back and help reassemble the real Clash.

Mick accepted Joe's apology with reasonably good grace, and agreed to bury the hatchet, but he turned the offer down. He had spent two years conceiving his new music, building a new band, and recording their first album. He was now playing exactly what he wanted without having to fight anyone to get it recorded how he wanted. His private life was as rewarding as his professional one: in 1984, his girlfriend Daisy Lawrence had also given birth to a daughter, Lauren Estelle. Under the circumstances, he was reluctant to go back to the trouble and strife of life in the Clash. Joe listened to the rough mixes of the BAD album, and – according to the interview he gave Gavin Martin for the *NME* in 1986 – showed considerably less grace than his former partner when he informed him, 'It's the worst load of shit I've ever heard in my life. Don't put it out, man. Do yourself a favour.' Then he went home.

The 19 October 1985 statement purporting to be 'from the Clash', claiming they were temporarily off the road for legal reasons was, of course, a Rhodes-Vinyl attempt to obscure the real reason for the band's reclusiveness. Three weeks later, the Clash album came out and Joe was hardly surprised to find that *it* was now the biggest pile of shit he had ever heard in his life. He'd had no say in the trite title, the tasteless packaging – which was exactly what Mat Snow suggested it was – or the risible inner sleeve 'communiqué'. The photo of the band posing in Paul's basement flat, as used on both the back and inner cover, had been taken by Bernie's friend Mike Laye a whole year before the album's release.

Worse, Joe's songs – some of which he had last heard as half-finished demos – had been buried under a cacophony of synthesizer, sampled voices, overblown massed backing vocals, brass and electronic percussion. One or two had been varispeeded into different tempos. The songs selected for the album were not even necessarily the best of those stockpiled or even those recorded: played live on various occasions, but unreleased to this day are 'Glue Zombie', 'Ammunition' and the ballads 'In The Pouring, Pouring Rain' and 'Gallini'. Even worse still, although the composition of the single had been credited to Strummer & Co, Bernie had taken it upon himself to credit the tracks on the album to Strummer-Rhodes. 'He sort of served as a sounding board for me, but I thought it was a bit cheeky, all the same,' Joe told *Musician*'s Bill Flanagan in 1988. 'That's not to say he didn't write *anything*, but I wouldn't have said that it was half and half.' In 2000, he told *Record Collector* that Bernie's so-called songwriting contribution had been mostly structural: more a question of arrangement and production. 'He'd say to me, "Put half of that tune with the other half of that tune and you've got there."' 'Bernie had a lot of good ideas about sonic stuff like sampling,' says Nick Sheppard. 'But he had no understanding of melodics.' Worst of all, Bernie had attributed the production to 'Jose Unidos', a nod in the direction of the band's earlier imaginary Puerto Rican helper Pepe Unidos. Although this time a pseudonym for Bernie alone, the 'Jose' had been deliberately chosen to suggest Joe as a means of legitimising the project. 'It wouldn't have been so bad if Bernie had just got the blame, but that was unbearable,' Joe told Gavin Martin in 1986.

The reviews of the album appeared in the 9 November 1985 issues of the music press. The following week's papers carried reviews for BAD's *This Is Big Audio Dynamite*. The *NME*'s reaction was only marginally kinder than it had been to *Cut The Crap*, with John

McCready totally missing the point of BAD's hip hop-rock collision when he described it as 'an occasionally engaging mess which consists of eight dub-singed middle eights stretched, at times, to transparency'. Other critics were more receptive, and became increasingly more so as further singles were pulled from the album. It was no coincidence that the official announcement of Nick, Vince and Pete's departure from the Clash came the week following the BAD album's release. Lisa Robinson interpreted this apparent dissolution of the Clash at a time when BAD were in the ascendancy as a tacit acknowledgement on Joe's part that Mick had been in the right with regard to the tussle over musical direction. In a 1986 interview for *Hard Rock Video*, she asked Mick if he derived any satisfaction from that. 'No, I think it was a great shame,' he replied. 'It was a bloody great shame and it was too late. So I don't get any satisfaction whatsoever from that.'

Joe didn't really need his face rubbed in it any more, but in January 1986 it happened just the same: Topper's *Waking Up* was released to better reviews than either the BAD or Clash albums.

Despite this, Joe and Paul never officially called it quits, even between themselves. In Pat Gilbert's 1999 *Mojo* Clash retrospective, Paul recalled Joe telling him he had a new song, 'Shouting Street', and suggesting that the two of them get together and work on it soon. 'I said, "Fine," but I didn't get another call,' said Paul. 'I think Joe wanted to avoid any confrontation, which didn't bother me. I wasn't exactly looking at my watch.' Another retro rocker, 'Shouting Street' would eventually turn up in 1989 on Joe's first solo album, *Earthquake Weather*. Perhaps fittingly for the last song he wrote as – at least nominally – a member of the Clash, it is about the Portobello Road, just around the corner from his Lancaster Road home. Like his first major song for the Clash, 'London's Burning', its title is a close cousin of a MC5 song – this time 'Shakin' Street' – and its lyric finds both squalor and romance in the lee of the Westway. But the incisive anger of yore has given way to whimsy: its celebration of multi-cultural dodgy geezerdom is more *Only Fools And Horses* than *A Clockwork Orange*.

The beginning of 1986 saw a tacit understanding among the former members of its longest-lived and best-known line-up that the Clash were no more. This seemed to free them to talk about its demise with an unprecedented openness. Even the formerly close-mouthed Mick felt justified in speaking his mind by BAD's success, Joe's apology, and the dismissal of the new Clash boys.

The key to understanding what brought about the end of the Strummer/Jones/Simonon/Headon Clash is to be found in the discrepancy between what appeared to be going on, even to observers close to the band, and what was really going on. Early in 1981, Joe had brought back Bernie because the Clash had lost direction. The fact that Joe made this decision unilaterally made it all too easy to take at face value his subsequent domination of the Clash's media appearances and seeming dictation of musical direction and band policy. From 1981 onwards, nearly all music press reviews – for albums, singles and live shows – referred to the Clash as 'Strummer's band'.

Certainly, on the early 1982 New Zealand visit, journalists and tour managers alike were left in no doubt that Joe was calling the shots. When *Rolling Stone*'s Malcolm McSporran approached band roadie Jerry and asked him about Bernie's influence at that time, he received the following reply: 'The Clash have grown up. *Before*, he had four boys. *Now*, they're four world-weary hardened men. You can't tell them anything.' Returning to the Clash fold that May, Terry Chimes received much the same impression. 'There was a difference with Bernie,' he says. 'He was less powerful. He couldn't tell people what to do.'

In fact, Bernie had learned a salutary lesson from his first stint with the band. He was astute enough to realise that the now older and more experienced Clash would not stand for overtly authoritarian behaviour, but he had always been at his most effective when taking an indirect approach. The mask only slipped once in front of the music press. On the summer 1982 US tour, *Sounds'* Dave McCullough asked a drunken Bernie what his role with the Clash was second time around, and received the indignant answer, 'I OWN THIS GROUP!' Otherwise Bernie was content to remain in the background and play what amounted to a brothel-creepered and bespectacled Iago to Joe's increasingly wan Othello.

Returning as manager, Bernie's first priority was to make the Clash viable again, which meant getting the band out of debt. All other considerations were secondary, even artistic integrity. It was Bernie who started the grumbling about radio-unfriendly ragas. Although it was Joe who announced the band's intention to deliver a slick AOR full-price single album, then tour hard behind it in order to give it the hard sell, this was Bernie's agenda. It was certainly Bernie who brought in Glyn Johns to transform *Rat Patrol From Fort Bragg* into *Combat Rock*. As Joe told *Wired* in 1988, the original idea for his April 1982 disappearance scam came from Bernie, but the motive was not – as he claimed – solely to awaken interest in tour tickets or the forthcoming album. It was, as Topper suspected, also intended to reinforce the singer's dominance so that he could bring about Topper's dismissal. But it was Bernie, not Joe, who insisted this was necessary. He just got Joe to do the dirty work.

Although Joe took sole responsibility at the time for the decision to sack Topper, in 1986 he gave *Record Mirror*'s Jim Reid a somewhat different account: 'We were in Simonon's basement flat. It was dark and raining outside. We told Topper he was falling apart and he had to go. He split the flat, devastated. He walked around the block in the rain, and he came back.' Topper begged to be allowed to stay, and promised to clean up for good. 'That's when my heart went *ping*, y'know,' said Joe. 'It just rose up in me to say, "Look, he's come back. That's enough isn't it? What more do you want? Let's work with him. Let's help him!" Instead, I just shut my mouth, like everyone else in the room. Mick, me, Paul, Kosmo and Bernie.' Joe was trying to spread the blame around equally, but by casting himself in this more passive role, he was effectively pointing the finger at Bernie instead.

Up until the release of *Combat Rock*, the Clash were making money to pay off their debts, but from the 1982 dates with Terry Chimes onwards – especially the Who stadium supports, and the 1983 Us Festival – they were, as Mick claims, making it for the sake of making it. This was un-Clashlike behaviour, and – whatever his detractors might say to the contrary – it was not even particularly typical of Bernie. Back in 1980, the manager had attacked the Clash for selling out their original punk audience, but it is hard to imagine a more complete selling out of that audience than the events of 1982-83. Terry was certainly convinced that, whatever might have been said from the stage or in interviews, politics were no longer an issue behind the scenes. But then the sudden reversion to angry rebel rock and provocative political rhetoric following Mick's dismissal proved him wrong. In retrospect, the only explanation for the band's activities in the two years immediately prior to that upheaval is this: anticipating the showdown with Mick, Bernie was building a financial buffer to prepare for its impact, believing that, once Mick had gone, he would be able to get on and do what he *really* wanted to do with the Clash.

As early as December 1982, Joe and Paul gave Terry to understand that Mick was already heading for the sack. Again with the benefit of hindsight, Mick himself believes that part of the thinking behind Topper's dismissal in May of that year had been to make Mick's own subsequent expulsion easier for the remaining members of the band to countenance: the old McLaren-Rhodes principle of divide and rule in action. Talking to Lisa Robinson for *Hard Rock Video* magazine in 1986, Mick acknowledged that he had been difficult throughout the period following Bernie's return. 'I was right to be difficult,' he asserted. 'Because they were being run by the manager.' Lisa expressed amazement that anyone could take what Bernie said seriously. 'Well, I didn't listen that much, so that's why I stood out, right? But once he threw Topper out, and we all went along with that, he kind of knew that he had a free way. People were expendable. Basically, what happened was that Bernie wanted to sit where I was sitting in the group. The good seat, the comfy seat, the best seat in the house.' What about Joe? 'I think he sort of sat by and let it all happen.'

Mick's account of his own sacking differs somewhat from the 'go and write songs with your lawyer' version Joe trotted out to the music press in 1984. According to Mick, when Joe told him he didn't want to work with him anymore in August 1983, Mick responded by saying he believed Bernie was the destructive influence, and that they might be able to make the group work again if the manager left. 'I asked the band who they wanted, me or Bernie,' he told the *NME*'s Paolo Hewitt in 1986. 'The group said they wanted Bernie, and then just looked at the floor. I couldn't believe my ears. I stood there for about 10 seconds, stunned. Then I just picked up my guitar and walked out.' Reminiscing for the BBC2 programme *That Was Then, This Is Now* three years later, he added: 'I was set up, really. Bernie came running out after me with a cheque in his hand – you know, like a gold watch – which added insult to injury. But I took it anyway.'

'Sometimes I feel that I've only been a pawn in the game between Mick and Bernie,' Joe told *Record Mirror*'s Jim Reid in 1986. 'If you wanna look at the Clash story, the Titans in the struggle have been Mick and Bernie. They put it together, and then Mick said, "Let's get rid of Bernie," so we got rid of him. Three years later, I said, "Let's bring him back," so we brought him back. And then Bernie said, "Let's get rid of Mick," so we got rid of him.' Again, this overview casts Joe in a strangely passive role for someone with so much natural charisma. Lisa Robinson asked Mick how *anyone* could take Bernie seriously; which prompts the question, why did Joe?

'What you must realise is that a large percentage of people like me are idiots,' Joe explained to the *NME*'s Gavin Martin in 1986. 'I sit in a room and write ditties while others are selling stocks to Malaysia on the vodaphone. It's easy to manipulate people like me. What I do best is write doggerel, so part of me must be very childish. I gave Bernie a little too much. Bernie sort of coerced me into thinking that Mick was what was wrong with the scene. That wasn't hard because, as Mick will admit now, he was being pretty awkward.' Just in case that admittedly scathing self-criticism still suggested he was opting out of responsibility for his actions, he went on to acknowledge his own ruthless streak: 'Plus my ego – a bad thing an ego – was definitely telling me, "Go on! Get rid of the bastard!"'

Looking back, it is hard to believe that the five-piece new Clash's new direction could have been the brainchild of anyone *but* Bernie: the confrontational interviews, the retreaded punk polemic, the vitriolic denunciation of Mick, and the revisionist overhaul of the band's recent history all had a tell-tale Stalinist odour. 'Bernie's idea was to see if the original ideal of the Clash would still stand up in the Eighties,' Joe explained to Sean O'Hagan in 1988. 'I thought the idea was impressive, but it didn't work in practice. I didn't realise his full motives until it was too late and the whole thing had gone too far. It was too late to stop.'

Then, when it came time to record the album, Bernie's gameplan changed yet again. He did indeed end up sitting in Mick's seat, not only taking over his producer's chair, but – according to the album credits, at least – also usurping his role as Joe's principle co-songwriter. Keeping up with the Rhodes thought processes has never been a task for the faint-hearted, but it's worth noting that Bernie's experiments were not without precedent. Two years previously his rival Malcolm McLaren had released *Duck Rock*, a cross-pollination of other people's musical efforts, complete with samples, scratching and other hip hop adornments for which he took the creative credit: not a million miles from what Bernie attempted with *Cut The Crap*.

Joe was already disoriented by his family troubles, but Bernie exhibited no more respect for or interest in the finer feelings of his supposed henchman than he had with either Topper or Mick. 'I had a terrible time with Bernie Rhodes in the end,' Joe told Sean O'Hagan. 'In a nutshell, in order to control me, he destroyed my self-confidence.' All Joe felt able to do was make the gesture of the busking tour, and then run away.

Kosmo came to his senses in 1986, split from Bernie, and set up as a PR in New York. Bernie's own ambition did not come to a halt with the bad reviews for 'his' album and Joe's dismissal of the new Clash members. In spring 1987, Bernie took it upon himself to renegotiate the Clash's deal with CBS, claiming that Joe and Paul were still working together, and with him. Then he expressed surprise when the duo refused to play along. Eventually, a business meeting was called to agree a settlement. Bernie turned up in a black suit, 'for the funeral'. Tricia Ronane, Paul's girlfriend and manager-to-be, attended on the bassist's behalf. '[Bernie] couldn't deal with the fact that a woman was there arguing with him,' she told Chris Salewicz for *Q* in 1996. 'He wanted to take most of Paul's money away from him. I was telling him he couldn't.' Thereafter, Bernie also departed for New York, where he resumed his discussions about opening a club with Malcolm McLaren. Like all their previously mooted joint ventures, it came to nothing.

Bernie – the man for whom managing the Clash meant never having to say he was sorry – remains both estranged from his former charges and totally unrepentant to this day. In a 1990 *NME* retrospective interview with Stuart Bailie, he proclaimed, 'They're such squares, the Clash. They've gone back to how they really are.' He went on to call Mick a 'cry-baby' and Joe a 'coward'. In 1999, talking to *Mojo*'s Pat Gilbert, he rounded out his personal insults to cover the whole band, describing Paul as 'pussy-whipped' and Topper as a 'provincial tosser'. However, six years earlier, asked by *Q* magazine whether the band should reform, he initially said no, but then appeared to have second thoughts. As well as repeating the claim previously aired in the *NME* feature – that he had written the lyrics to the band's first album – he offered the following insight, in which the careful reader may well detect the faintest trace of unintentional irony: 'We had a great institution in punk rock English-style and we ruined it. But that's the music industry: see something good, sign it up, fuck it up. The kids end up feeling *molested*. If the Clash get involved with me again, then they can play for the right reasons.'

In their different ways, Topper, Mick, Joe and Paul did feel molested by the lead up to and immediate aftermath of their various departures from the Clash, and have all since admitted that they took a long time to get over it. 'I had to disassemble myself and put the pieces back together. I felt completely destroyed by that experience,' Joe said on the Channel 4 programme *Wired* in 1988. 'I'd lost my parents, my group. You want to think about things. You become a different person.' Topper's situation was complicated by denial related to his ongoing heroin problem: in the interviews he gave during 1985-86, he professed to feel no bitterness towards the other members of the band, but not everything he said supported this claim. He occasionally even refused to accept that his drug use had been a factor in his sacking. For their part, Mick and Joe now agree that things were never really the same after Topper left. In 1999's *Westway To The World*, Joe maintained that the group at its best had depended upon the chemical reaction between the four people involved. It had stopped working as soon as they messed with the formula. Talking to Gavin Martin for *Uncut* that same year, he went even further, saying he didn't think the Clash played a single good gig after Topper's departure...

Well, possibly one.

Although ultimately Bernie did end up with much of the blame for the Clash's demise, the former band members realised that making him the sole scapegoat would deny them the sturdy foundation necessary to rebuild their own relationship. Having already made his private apologies to Mick at the end of 1985, Joe began making his public ones in 1986. When talking to Gavin Martin for the *NME* that year, Joe expressed his amazement that Mick had accepted his overtures of friendship. 'I did him wrong. I really stabbed him in the back.' Topper finally took it on the chin in 1999, seizing the opportunity afforded by *Westway To The World* to apologise to the others for being out of control and acknowledge the part his addiction had played in creating the tensions that led to the end of the Clash. Having come to know his weaknesses all too well over the years, though, he also admitted that, given his time over, he would probably make all the same mistakes again.

Mick also had to let go of the belief that he was a wholly innocent victim. 'Consciously or unconsciously, Mick Jones always seems to be taking the piss,' wrote *Rip It Up*'s Duncan Campbell in 1982. 'His cockiness borders on arrogance, but it's an integral part of his personality.' Even in 1999's *Westway To The World*, when all the former band members were endeavouring to put the best possibly gloss on their working relationship, Joe felt bound to reiterate that, while with the Clash, Mick had not only habitually turned up late, but far too often 'like Elizabeth Taylor in a filthy mood'. Shortly after his late 1985 heart-to-heart with Joe, Mick began to face up to the fact that his arrogance and petulance had not only contributed to the creation of an impossible situation within the band, but had also robbed him of many potentially rewarding experiences. 'I missed a lot of the Clash because I was so self-involved,' he confessed to the *NME*'s Paolo Hewitt in 1986. 'Like when we toured, I'd get on the coach, and I wouldn't look out of the window. I was so far up my own arse. The change now is, I know what I'm doing. If I'm rude to someone, then I know why I'm being rude. And if I'm doing something fucked up, I know I'm doing something fucked up.' On *Westway To The World*, he – repeatedly – bemoaned his lack of self control as a younger man. Speaking to the *NME*'s James Brown in 1991, he said, 'It was a shame how communication broke down. It got too big. We couldn't take the pressure.' Two years earlier, on *That Was Then, This Is Now*, musing on the effects of success, he said, 'You become a different kind of arsehole.'

These were sentiments with which Joe heartily concurred, his most frequently-passed comment on the split remaining, 'we fell to ego'. As early as 1984, when the five-piece Clash were still trying to find their feet, he had already developed a fatalist attitude towards the previous incarnation of the band. In a radio interview he gave at that time, he admitted, 'We have fallen into each and every pitfall that you can possible fall into as a group starting from nothing and becoming something. We've probably invented a few new ones along the way. And there is no way around those pitfalls. You just do not get issued with a map. Every young group that starts is going to fall into them. I'm talking, specifically, about the success-goes-to-your-head pitfall, the ego-trip pitfall. You think you're musicians, you think you're artists, you think you're geniuses, you become drug addicts, you make over-indulgent records, you over-produce everything, you overdub the sound of ants biting through a wooden beam: all these things. We've gone through every damn one of them. We didn't even manage to shortcut one. I think it's inevitable. In fact, you can even say that one person cannot tell another person; it has to be learned by the actual pain of real experience. That's when you learn your lesson, living it. I remember reading advice like, "Don't sign anything," but you have to sign something sometime. There was no way of avoiding those things we fell into.'

As Mick suggested, better communication might have helped avoid some of them, but, thanks to Bernie, relationships within the band were established along confrontational lines right from the start. The Clash were mutually reliant creative people who were often capable of exhibiting true team spirit; but when that spirit flagged, they simply did not have the resources to rekindle it. Dressing up like an outlaw gang or an army platoon and playing football together was never going to be enough to see them through. During the early days of the Clash, they might have exaggerated or otherwise tweaked their personal histories for effect, but it remains undeniable that Mick, Joe and Paul were all from unsettled family backgrounds. The extent to which this left them emotionally damaged is arguable, but what it certainly did do was encourage determination, self-reliance and a strong survival instinct in each of them. These qualities gave them the drive they needed to persevere, but they also gave them a tendency to be selfish.

Interviewed by the *New Zealand Listener*'s Phil Gifford during the Clash's 1982 Australasian tour, Mick was asked why the Sex Pistols had burned out so quickly. 'I think the trouble was that the people in the band weren't caring enough towards each other. If you're not caring and supportive, it's impossible to keep going.' Maybe Topper ought to have helped himself, but maybe the others ought to have helped him too. Maybe Mick ought to have been less sulky, but maybe the others ought not to have pushed him into a corner. Maybe Joe ought not to have delivered ultimatums, but maybe the others ought to have taken more responsibility. Maybe Paul ought not to have taken sides so readily, but maybe he ought not to have been put in a position where he felt compelled to do so.

On *Westway To The World*, Joe pointed out that hindsight is all very well, but at the time 'things are moving so fast, you don't have time to step back and take a view'. All of the members were still in their early twenties when they first became involved with the band, and they were caught up in a whirlwind thereafter. It is difficult for experienced, well-balanced, mature adults in stable circumstances to maintain close relationships for seven years. To expect young men with no strong support network and next to no positive guidance to survive conditions of extreme stress for any longer than that was asking the impossible.

After thanking Mick for forgiving him in the July 1986 interview he gave to the *NME*'s Gavin Martin, Joe revealed that the two of them had agreed to work together again in the future. What circumstances forbade him to reveal at that time was that they had already begun to collaborate.

Before Christmas 1985, Joe had crashed the Portobello Basin end-of-shoot party for the Alex Cox film about the relationship between Sid Vicious and Nancy Spungen, at that time going under the title *Love Kills*. Alex had cornered Joe in the toilets and demanded a theme song as the price of admission. Given that Joe was feeling particularly down about everything at that time, and that the movie was set in the heyday of punk, concerned a deceased friend, and was already coming under regular attack in the music press from John Lydon, he was quite understandably reluctant to involve himself with the project. But when he later saw a rough cut, he decided it captured something of a musical and cultural movement that was far more exciting than anything else being offered to or created by 'the kids' of the day. Joe wrote 'Love Kills' as a dialogue between Sid and the policeman who arrested him for Nancy's murder. Joe also supplied the track 'Dum Dum Club'. Mick Jones accepted Joe's invitation to play guitar on both songs. He also produced the sessions, explaining the tell-tale beatbox adornments.

In some ways, the soundtrack turned out to be the equivalent of a high school reunion for the Class of '76 punk scene. Former Sex Pistol Steve Jones, now resident in LA, provided another track, and Glen Matlock played bass on the film's re-recordings of Sex Pistols songs. Shane MacGowan's band the Pogues also recorded material. But Alex ran out of both money and time before the soundtrack was complete. CBS had allowed Joe to donate the two songs already recorded on the understanding that the label retained the right to release them as a single. The soundtrack album was signed to MCA, though, and the terms of Joe's CBS contract forbade him to provide further material on an official basis. For the same reason that Mick's contributions to the first two songs remained completely anonymous, Joe wrote a further five pieces of incidental music under the assumed name Dan Wul and recorded them as Pray For Rain.

BAD began playing headlining gigs early in 1986. It was Joe who suggested the cover of Prince's '1999' which became their hardy perennial encore feature. Reviews of the shows remained more negative than positive. Mick had expected his new music to require some acclimatisation, but the general public proved more adaptable than the critics. The April UK tour was extended into May by popular demand once BAD's second single, 'E=MC2' charted. Celebrating their status as a multi-media band – and perhaps indicating that the Clash's boycott of the programme was one element of his previous band's policy with which Mick personally had not been in accord – BAD appeared on *Top Of The Pops* to promote it. It made number 11, equalling the Clash's best ever showing to date. Having been dismissive of that single, the *NME*'s Neil Taylor had the grace to eat his words and admit it was 'utterly brilliant' when also praising the album's third single 'Medicine Show', released in June. This peaked at number 29 in the charts. Although the album only made number 103 in the US, it reached number 27 in the UK on the back of the singles' successes. More importantly, it stayed on the charts for 27 weeks, going gold in the process.

In a public gesture of reconciliation with Mick, Paul and Joe made cameo appearances as policemen in the 'Medicine Show' video. Topper was too wrapped up in his own problems to appear. The encouraging reviews that greeted *Waking Up* had served to raise his expectations a little too high. In truth, there was little about the album that was new or challenging even at the time, and Topper's lyrics are frankly dire. Some of the songs do seem to be facing up to his heroin problem – 'When You're Down', 'Just Another Hit', 'Monkey On My Back' – and Topper claimed to have cleaned up in the interviews he gave. But he was quite clearly out of it for some of those same interviews. The album failed to chart or sell. Topper ruined his relationship with Phonogram by blaming the record company. Although his band continued to gig for the remainder of the year, they gradually lost all respect for him as his habit once more eroded his talents. By the end of 1986, he was reduced to selling off his Clash gold discs and collection of musical instruments to pay for drugs.

Joe became a father for the second time that year, the name Lola Maybelline suggesting tribute to the Kinks and Chuck Berry. That aside, his own life was going less than smoothly. He was arrested at 4 am on 25 April 1986 for driving his car erratically and at high speed along Kensington Park Road. Found to be over twice the legal alcohol limit, he was fined £200 and banned from driving for 18 months. The simultaneous release of the single 'Love Kills', the film, and the film soundtrack in late July should have boosted his spirits, but events conspired to undermine the impact of the début Strummer solo release.

Firstly, the title of the film and album had been changed at the last minute to *Sid And Nancy*, which meant there was no instant connection with the single. Secondly, the reception for both film and album was mixed. Thirdly, the video Alex Cox – returning a favour – had shot for Joe in Tabernas, near Almeria, where Sergio Leone had filmed most of his spaghetti westerns, received little exposure. Lastly, reviews of the single were not positive. In the *NME*, Steven Wells dismissed the memorable, if basic, rocker as 'weak and pitiful' and spitefully offered the following career advice to Joe: 'It's time

for the gold watch. P'raps you could get a job making tea at the BBC, or something.'
The single stalled at number 69 in the UK charts.

BAD were already back in the studio by this time, working on their second album at
the recently relocated Trident studios. The original site was where David Bowie had
recorded his albums from *Space Oddity* to *Aladdin Sane*. It was also where, in 1972, he
had produced Mott the Hoople's first CBS album, *All The Young Dudes*: Mick had now
pretty much collected the Mott the Hoople studio set... Joe was also present at Trident,
invited along after a casual street meeting with Don Letts. He stayed until the album was
complete, even sleeping under the piano. In the end, although Joe did not officially play
or sing on the album, he co-produced it with Mick. He also co-wrote two songs with
Mick alone and three more with Mick and various permutations of the other BAD
members. It was Joe's idea to mix the album in New York, a process that proved to be
so long drawn out and punitive to the BAD bank balance that it qualified as – admittedly
unintentional – revenge on his part for Mick's insistence on recording *Combat Rock*
there. Joe also suggested the album title, *No 10, Upping Street*, supposedly the home of
the alternative, *funky* Prime Minister.

Of the songs involving Joe, 'Ticket' identifies with the West Indian immigrant
experience on behalf of Don and Leo, while 'Beyond The Pale' does the same for Mick's
Russian roots. The former plays it for laughs, but both songs are highly contemptuous
of racism. 'Limbo The Law' and 'V Thirteen' take a more filmic approach. The former
is a cheery, upbeat Latino conflation of the themes of 'Bankrobber' and 'Death Is A
Star'. It assesses the impact of cinema on contemporary culture, making the valid point
that real life gangsters pick up all their best moves at the movies. 'V Thirteen' – its title
presumably a reference of the Second World War flying bomb known as the V2 – builds
a *1984*-like futurist vision on the deliberately banal foundations of the theme tune to TV
soap opera *EastEnders* and the opening snatch of dialogue from the London-set 1984
removals film *The Chain*. There is nothing remotely cosy about this post-'London
Calling' world. There is a crack epidemic, radioactive waste in the rainwater and food
chain, and news censorship. The only release to be found is in vague nostalgia for the
supposed good old days.

Last but not least is 'Sightsee MC!'. Reviewing the album for the *NME*, Danny Kelly
identified this pounding rock'n'rap guide to inner city London as the only track that
successfully realises BAD's 'Great Idea...' Sung in Mick's best yob Cockney, it takes the
listener on a guided tour of contemporary London, but *real* London, not tourist London:
from the Piccadilly Meat Rack to the Broadwater Farm riots. It also makes allusions to the
subject matter of the Clash's earliest material, a second, sub-textual tour which takes the
listener from 'Janie Jones' to '48 Hours' to 'London's Burning' to '1977' to 'White Riot'.

The second BAD album was released in late October 1986, and was generally deemed
to have failed to live up to the potential suggested by the band's début. Danny Kelly
believed most of the tracks to be 'doodles, sketches, blueprints, models or prototypes'.
It reached number 11, but faded quickly; the first two singles stalled around the 50 mark,
and 'Sightsee MC!' failed to show at all. The Strummer-Jones reunion did produce the
album's better songs, and understandably attracted a lot of attention from journalists. On
several occasions Mick found himself having to stress that Joe had no plans to join BAD.
He did admit that the duo planned to continue their writing partnership, this time with a
view to working up material for Joe's planned solo album.

It was not to be. After the BAD album sessions, Joe spent August 1986 back in
Almeria with Alex Cox, the Pogues and Elvis Costello, acting in a spoof spaghetti
western named – after the Clash song – *Straight To Hell*. Upon returning, he wrote and
recorded more music for the soundtrack, again under the respective aliases Dan Wul and
Pray For Rain. He spent the next year immersed in various film projects, while Mick

devoted himself to promoting and touring the BAD album. It would be late 1988 before Joe found time to record his first bona fide, non-soundtrack solo album. By this time Mick was gravely ill and in no position to contribute. Consultation on various Clash reissues excepted, Mick and Joe have never worked together since.

There was no new falling out, but it was not just conflicting schedules and assorted misfortunes that stood in the way of further collaborations. Promising though the joint compositions for *No 10, Upping Street* had been, they had required Joe to meet Mick on his home turf rather than halfway. It was not really the music that Joe loved, as was proved when his solo album was released in 1989. *Earthquake Weather* is the usual Strummer gumbo of punk, rockabilly, reggae and jazzy R&B stylings, recorded as close to live as possible in the studio using real drums and real guitars with – Simon Humphrey, the engineer on *The Clash*, would have been appalled to hear – no separation. In his happiness to have repaired his personal relationship with Mick, and his occasionally acknowledged hope that a Clash reunion might one day come about, Joe had initially overlooked one other significant factor in the break-up of the Clash: his and Mick's musical tastes had diverged dramatically.

He faced up to it in 1988 when speaking to Harold De Muir of the *East Coast Rocker*: 'You go on for 10 years, and it gets to a point where the other guy's taste is so far from yours that you think it stinks. People can start out as apprentices and sooner or later they want to become masters. People *grow*, y'know?' And some just change, while others become set in their ways. *No 10, Upping Street* is not a Clash album, but it does offer a glimpse of how the Clash might have progressed in the Eighties had Joe been prepared or able to put his own musical preferences second to Mick's. However much of a compromise 'Sightsee MC!' might be, its marriage of punk's baleful social commentary and cutting-edge rock'n'rap crossover stands as a more impressive last word from Strummer-Jones than *Cut The Crap* does from the Clash. After offering its lyrical précis of so many of the Clash's Greatest Themes, it even signs off appropriately, promoting the DIY ethic and passing on the baton to the next generation: 'Well, it's over to you, and bye from me…'

PART FOUR:
AFTER LIVES

18
FROM HERE TO ETERNITY

The Clash split occurred shortly before the 10th anniversary of the London punk movement. Since then, the 20th anniversary has also passed, and it is now possible to assess whether punk changed the world in any significant and lasting way.

Certain bands and individuals who came out of the punk movement could be said to have had a direct influence in the political arena, and several more to have had an indirect effect by influencing the thinking of their followers. Many were quick to align themselves with the anti-racist movement after the Clash and the Tom Robinson Band led the way with the massive April 1978 Anti-Nazi League gig in Victoria Park. Supporters of Artists Against Apartheid played no small part in effecting Nelson Mandela's release and establishing a democratic South Africa. Meanwhile, the Band Aid project created a climate where the playing of benefit gigs and espousal of causes came to be seen as a sort of moral dues-paying. CND, Greenpeace and Amnesty International have been among the organisations to benefit. One of the short term knock-on effects of punk was the raising of the standard of debate in the music press, and especially the *NME*. For much of the Eighties, it was no longer enough to talk about drugs, groupies and guitar solos. Musicians, whether representatives of new bands or established artists, were expected to have *opinions*. As a result, 'the kids' were given the strong impression that a degree of social and political awareness was a virtue.

A reaction seemed to set in at the end of the Eighties, when the loss of belief in a better tomorrow engendered by long-term unemployment and the general dampening effect of the recession encouraged an outbreak of the kind of apathy the Clash had warned about in 1976. The UK's rave culture was all about getting blissed out. Picking up on its influence, bands like the Stone Roses and Happy Mondays established the late Eighties Madchester scene and portrayed themselves as amoral, apolitical hedonists. In the US, grunge bands helped both create and reflect a depressed, self-obsessed environment. Their followers and contemporaries were characterised as slackers, or – thanks to the already overused title that Douglas Coupland borrowed for his 1991 novel – Generation X. The general picture was of a generation living a morbid, uninformed, insular existence, supposedly numbed to all positive thought and action by media overload and the meaninglessness and mendacity of modern society: life sucks, pass the drugs.

As already established, many of the first wave of punk bands and a fair proportion of the early punk fans had preferred to adopt a negative attitude to life, too; but it had been something of a pose, and there had invariably seemed to be at least some sense of anger or mischief behind it. Far more *knowing* in many respects than 'the kids' of the punk era, many of the kids of today – whether they live in the UK, US or elsewhere – seem to view existence as either a soap-standard self-indulgent confessional melodrama or a stylised action movie in which extreme violence has no lasting consequences. Responsibility is too often denied. Some have become so disengaged from life that they have become truly hopeless. Cynicism and negativity are fetishised. Morbid rock stars kill themselves, and laughing schoolboys mow down their classmates with automatic weapons.

This is about as far from the Clash's strain of punk influence – energy, creativity, protest – as it is possible to travel, but not all the signs have been bad. History has proved that the *NME* indulged in a little wishful thinking in trying to establish riot grrrls and the new wave of new wave as the Great Hopes of Rock just a few years before punk's 20th anniversary, but every so often an artist or album comes along to pick up the baton and pass it on. What the Eighties and Nineties have proved – if it was ever really in doubt – is that the bestower and recipient do not have to be skinny white boys (or girls) with electric guitars. Some of the best and most successful hip hop artists have been firmly intent on letting society know what time it is. In a 1990 interview with the *NME*'s Stuart Bailie, Bernie Rhodes claimed to have conceived the hugely influential hip hop label Def Jam with Russell Simmons. As ever with Bernie, it is tempting to laugh off the claim, but Chuck D has admitted that *The Clash* was one of the blueprints for Public Enemy's early albums. A few years later, one of the most erudite rap albums of all time, Disposable Heroes of Hiphoprisy's *Hypocrisy Is The Greatest Luxury*, was made by former members of US punk band the Beatnigs.

Did punk change its own, more immediate world, the music business? In some ways yes, in others – the most important – no. Some of the third wave punk bands went on to become the most commercially successful major rock'n'roll names of the late Eighties: the Cure, Simple Minds and U2. Punk took a more indirect route into the mainstream in the US, but it did eventually percolate through via first the localised hardcore scene, then the back-to-basics trad rock renaissance of the mid Eighties, and then the grunge movement of the late Eighties. Most of the big US bands of the early Nineties evidenced and acknowledged a strong punk influence, from Guns'N'Roses – who in 1994 released an album of punk covers entitled *The Spaghetti Incident?* – to R.E.M. to Nirvana and Pearl Jam. In 1993, when venerable New York noiseniks Sonic Youth released a video document of their European tour with Nirvana two years previously, the title they chose for it was not wholly ironic: *1991: The Year Punk Broke*. American pseudo-punks Rancid went on to sell millions of records.

Nevertheless, packing stadiums and shifting units by the trailer-load were not the goals to which punk originally professed to aspire. Although such successes are in one way a vindication of a musical genre, in another they help maintain the music business establishment in fine style. In so doing, they represent a betrayal of the original – admittedly poorly-articulated and confused – ideology that at least *seemed* to want to overthrow that establishment.

At first, it looked as though the glut of independent labels appearing on the market in the late Seventies might pose a threat to the status quo, capturing most of the vital new talent while the majors were left with their redundant long-haired, flared-trousered dinosaur bands. This was not to be. Independents usually operated on a hand-to-mouth basis, and even those with the most successful roster of artists were often only one bad record or distribution hitch away from bankruptcy. Plus, the majors quickly learned to turn predator. Why take on a chance on an untried artist when they could watch the indie charts, and move in to poach a dead cert? In these circumstances, few independent labels could compete with the kind of financial incentives, publicity and distribution guarantees offered by the majors. Those that did became like little majors themselves, often with all the disadvantages and few of the advantages.

There were other tactics. In the UK, Rough Trade set up its own distribution network, and in the Eighties various other independent labels and record shops got together to form a collective named the Cartel, but it was a losing battle. It was rare for even the most determinedly left-field bands to put the interests of an independent before their own. The Smiths stuck with Rough Trade for the duration of their career, though not always happily. New Order stayed with Factory until it went bust in 1992. But these bands were the exception rather than the rule, both in terms of loyalty and commercial success, and when their labels eventually ran into trouble, the rights to the bands' back catalogues were – inevitably – snapped up by majors.

Some of the independents that did survive compromised their status by arranging distribution deals through majors, or accepting financial investment from them. Also, because the independents' association with alternative music carried a considerable kudos, majors began inventing their own pseudo-independents: subsidiary labels with a specialised function – either set up for a particular sub-genre of music, or for the use of one particular band equally desperate for credibility by indie-association – but with all the power of the major behind them. When Bernie Rhodes returned to the UK in 1989 – following his brief association with Def Jam – he set up his own label, Sacred, through RCA. One of its first projects was a single with Bernie's original punk protégé, Glen Matlock. Glen says their relationship ended in some acrimony because he found Bernie was by now impossible to work with. The label duly folded.

In 1992, concern about the definition of 'indie' labels led to an attempt to reform the criteria allowing qualification for the indie charts. It was not easy. With the benefit of hindsight, the best answer to Mark Perry's criticism of the Clash for signing to CBS in preference to releasing independent records is: what's the difference, and how do you tell?

Since the mid Eighties, cheap sampling, programming and recording technology has been employed to make hip hop, acid house, techno and drum'n'bass music in garages and spare rooms. This amateur-hour approach has also extended to self-financed labels: true independents which, as they are offshoots of true street – or at least, club – level music cultures, can keep their fingers on the pulse of musical trends much more effectively than the less pliable majors, and thus make regular and successful forays into the mainstream charts. Such dance records have kept the indie sector alive.

They are also have-a-go DIY ventures. 'It's like punk, in a way,' Mick Jones told the *New Zealand Herald*'s Graham Reid in 1993. 'You don't need much, just a sampler and some records. It's that whole *Sniffin' Glue* thing. Get into the basement and form a band. But you still need an idea.' The addendum is an important one. In music, recording, writing, photography, design, film-making and any other creative endeavour, it may be true that anyone can do it, but it is not quite as true as punk sometimes seemed to suggest that anyone can do it in a way that is appreciated by others. The key point is that, without determination and application, talent and ideas are just unrealised potential. That lesson – there for anyone who wishes to learn it – is perhaps punk's greatest legacy.

Punk's new broom failed to change the major labels from within. The famous 'artistic freedom' clause demanded by the Clash and other punk and new wave bands was shown as worthless as soon as the issue of finance reared its head: he who controls the purse strings controls everything. The few skirmishes the majors were forced to fight in order to defend their position made them more contract-canny than ever before. If anything, the average artist's position is now considerably worse than it was immediately prior to punk. In the Nineties, both Prince and George Michael went on strike against contracts they viewed as 'professional slavery'. Like Clash members Joe Strummer and Mick Jones, George found himself trapped in a contract with Sony, who had inherited CBS's roster of artists when they bought out the label in 1988.

The Eighties recession caused a general slump in record sales, with singles being particularly hard-hit. Record shops began to narrow the range of their stock, sticking to safer bets. All of this hit the (non-dance-oriented) independent labels particularly hard. They were singles-led, had no real promotional budget with which to push their product into the public consciousness, and could not rely on large, steadily-selling back catalogues to keep their businesses ticking over.

The majors found it easier to adapt. As singles were no longer important in their own right, they were released as trailers or advertisements, with often four tracks – and occasionally more – being culled from an album for this purpose. Artists were increasingly required to help promote one album over three years and build it into a commercial monolith, rather than record an album every year or so and commence a new promotional campaign from scratch each time.

The cassette was already putting up a challenge to vinyl by the end of the Seventies, and the introduction of the CD in the early Eighties sounded the death knell for the traditional single and album medium of the vinyl disc. Some shrinkage in its share of the market was to be expected, but vinyl was certainly deliberately helped on its way to extinction by the majors. Any new format is initially expensive, but even by 1990, it was only marginally more costly to manufacture a CD than an LP – approximately 90 pence, as opposed to 70 pence – and yet the CD was still being retailed for anything up to two thirds as much again, making it much more profitable. Vinyl soon accounted for less than 10 per cent of the market. It was kicked while down by the mainstream record retailers, who deemed it to be a minority interest and stopped stocking it altogether. As well as hitting the consumer in the pocket, the switch from vinyl to CD again stuck the knife into the independent sector, which had always been vinyl-oriented.

Any sophisticated new technology has status symbol value, and CD was no exception. Between them, the gadget pioneers, hi-fi buffs and upwardly mobile poseurs got the format off to a good start, and word of mouth about its supposedly heightened sound quality soon spread. Before long, news reached former popular music fans now in their 30s and 40s, and with record collections long since banished to the attic and/or ruined by dust and scratches. Those with disposable income were tempted to investigate. As youth unemployment was running high, there followed a shift in the record-buying demographic away from youth cult-related artists and groundbreaking new acts towards fondly-remembered back catalogue classics and newer records by established name artists. Golden Oldie radio shows and even an adult version of MTV, entitled VH-1, ensued. It was the revenge of the Boring Old Farts, artists and consumers both.

The trend was a recession lifeline for the majors. The recording costs had already been met on the back catalogue product, years before, and here they were able to sell it again, often to the same customer, at a considerably inflated price. And not only in its original format: it became standard practice to release multi-disc CD boxed-set career retrospectives featuring several hours' worth of music. As the contracts with the back catalogue artists contained no clauses pertaining to the then-non-existent medium of CD, the record companies could also get away with paying them minuscule royalties.

Although the punk principle of VFM took a battering during the CD revolution, that revolution was not without its positive side-effects in other areas. Firstly, it dispensed with much of the knee-jerk ageism propagated by teen pop, hippy and punk cultures which said there was something wrong with you if you still liked rock'n'roll (or wrote about it) once past the age of 30. It created an environment where 40-plus artists like Neil Young, Paul Simon, Leonard Cohen and Lou Reed, instead of feeling they had to write for 'the kids', felt free to create something for people their own age without resorting to MOR platitudes.

It also – perhaps for the first time ever – encouraged the mass of consumers to think about popular music in historical, cultural and sociological terms that were not purely to do with nostalgia or kitsch. Previously, too much emphasis had been placed on the disposability of pop, with punk having been particularly guilty of dismissing the past out of hand rather than choosing more specifically deserving targets for its venom. Efforts were now made to contextualise rock's rich tapestry for a new market, not least with the publication – and success – of overview magazines like *Q*, *Vox* and *Mojo*, aimed at the older, less fad-oriented music buyer.

The inkies were predictably unimpressed. Having themselves suffered during the recession, they were unhappy to see the competition, and, especially in the case of the *NME*, annoyed by the climate that had engendered it. And they had a point. The CD boom not only further squeezed the independent sector, it threatened new music of any kind. With guaranteed revenue from back catalogues and name artists, the majors were under no pressure to find and develop new talent. A&R departments went hungry, even closed down. Fewer new bands got deals. Rather than being nurtured for several years, those that did were expected to deliver straight away. Those that couldn't deliver, or that failed to build on or maintain initial commercial success – whatever their artistic status – were simply let go. It was a case of hit, and keep hitting, or get off the pot.

Circulations continued to fall at the old school inkies, and their pop cultural influence waned. (*Sounds* would fold in 1991, and *Melody Maker* would be absorbed by the *NME* 10 years later.) *Q* was not without a sense of humour – occasionally biting – but compared to the iconoclastic savagery of the *NME*, it tended towards the deferential, especially for the first few years of its existence. And as far as the leading inky was concerned, a music scene that seemed to be hell-bent on returning to the smug, stagnant days immediately pre-punk was a music scene that needed its butt kicking on a regular basis. Thanks to the preservative powers of CD, many of the names reviled during the punk era were still dominating the charts with their risible tripe: Genesis and the solo Phil Collins, Yes (under that or any other name), the rump of Pink Floyd. By the beginning of the Nineties, some of the people who had initially set out to destroy them had instead joined them, both on the stadium circuit and in the extent of their pomp and pretension.

The summer of 1994 saw Boring Old Fart acts like the Rolling Stones, Pink Floyd and the Eagles charging up to $60, $75 and $125 respectively for tickets on their stadium tours of America. In an effort to uphold the standard of VFM, latter-day punks Pearl Jam – who had also done their bit to keep vinyl alive – attempted to set up a tour at a far more reasonable $18 a head. They found it impossible to book dates without the assistance of the Ticketmaster booking agency, who insisted on between $5 and $8 for themselves as a handling fee. As a consequence, the band were forced to cancel.

MP3 presents another challenge to the music business, permitting the free exchange of near-perfect quality recordings over the Internet. Where does DIY end and piracy begin? In 2000, the first of the copyright suits were filed...

These changes in the music business, its product and its target market in the few years preceding and the decades following the Clash split help explain much about the band's own posthumous reissue and compilation programme. Along with the more straightforward and predictable rose-tinting effect of nostalgia, awareness of the changes also contributes to an understanding of the post-split reversal of the music press and general public's attitude to the band. As a consequence, the Clash Myth quickly re-established itself, and then, if anything, grew in stature.

The well-deserved trashing handed out to *Cut The Crap* by the *NME*'s Mat Snow in November 1985 was offset by his acknowledgement that they were once worthy of far greater respect. Three weeks later, the paper proved his point when it ran a chart of its contributors' Top 100 all-time favourite albums, and *The Clash* came fourth. Both the generation of music writers who had been around since the late Seventies and the new generation, most of whom had reached adolescence during the heyday of punk, were more than a little disappointed that rock had failed to throw up anything to match it since. January and February 1986's 10th anniversary celebrations gave them the opportunity to hold forth about the good old days.

ZigZag devoted an entire issue to punk, with former editor Kris Needs providing a six-page overview-cum-update on the subsequent careers of the movement's leading lights.

The *NME* ran punk retrospectives over three issues, covering all aspects of the movement, its roots and its legacy. Danny Kelly – future editor of the paper, and subsequently of *Q* – volunteered his appraisal of the Clash: 'Later, it became pantomime parody, but… for nearly 18 months, the Clash were the greatest rock'n'roll band in the world.'

The London punk movement had not had quite the same direct impact in the US, but *Rolling Stone* journalists were given their opportunity to wax nostalgic in August 1987, when the magazine celebrated its own 20th anniversary with its contributors' Top 100 albums of the last 20 years. *London Calling* appeared at number 14, and *The Clash* (UK version) at number 27. Three months later, the *NME* responded with its readers' all time Top 100. *The Clash* made number 11 and *London Calling* number 28.

The next round of reappraisals accompanied the March 1988 release of *The Story Of The Clash, Volume 1*. CBS had been pressing for a 'best of' compilation since Mick's dismissal in 1983, and had been even keener to tap into the nostalgia market following the band's split. The dissolution of the Clash and the reconciliation of its previously warring former members cleared the path for the project. In 1987, the task of compiling the album was taken on by Mick Jones, assisted by Tricia Ronane, BAD's PR and Paul Simonon's girlfiend. Topper had other worries at the time, and both Paul and Joe were prepared to take a back seat as a gesture of apology to the guitarist.

The 28-track double CD or LP was originally put on the release schedule for the end of 1987. It was eventually held over until the following year, while Tricia helped sort out the Clash's business affairs with Bernie, and Sony bought out CBS. The bias of the album is towards singles – no fewer than 16 of the tracks previously having been released in that format – and towards the earlier part of the band's career: while even the original freebie version of 'Capital Radio' is included, *Sandinista!* supplies just two songs, *Combat Rock* just three, and *Cut The Crap* is not represented at all. Mick's track sequencing is not chronological. In fact, although it hops about all over the place, if any approximate trend is to be discerned, it is one that, perversely, moves *backwards* from 1982 to 1977. Thus, the 'story' the compilation tells is an elliptical one not too concerned with beginnings, middles or ends. Perhaps convenient when the end was so messy and, for Mick in particular, so distressing.

Joe was permitted some last minute tweaking. As well as the humorous memoir of 'band valet Albert Transom' included in the liner notes – almost as random in approach as the album itself – he is also responsible for the subtitle, *Volume 1*. The main title – a last minute switch from the proposed *Revolution Rock*, too much like *Combat Rock* – was meant to sound definitive. Joe's addition undermines it: he was still refusing to acknowledge that the Clash was over and done with. Dressed up in a Pennie Smith photograph and a sleeve by long-time Clash packaging designer Jules, the album was released in March 1988 – still on the CBS label in the UK, Epic in the US – preceded earlier in the month by the single 'I Fought The Law'.

Reviewing the album for the *NME*, Steven Wells concluded, 'The Clash were the catalyst that made (makes) punk such an intensely political "youth culture". They were the first break away from the pretentious hippyness of punk's London roots: putting anti-racism firmly on the top of the agenda, making 1977 the year of Rock Against Racism as opposed to 1976's Rock Against Being Bored In Art School. And this is a package put out by a subsidiary of a Japanese multinational. That's not ironic, it's just one of rebel rock's silly little contradictions.' At *Melody Maker*, Paul Mathur shared a similar perspective. 'It starts with the end. Ironically, but inevitably, the Clash's most commercially cherished moments came when they strapped on their funk fakery… empty music, drenched in the now familiar self-aggrandisement, but bereft of anything that even thinks of rhyming itself with irony… The second half of the double album is the Clash at the heart of your darkness... It's a great story.'

Rolling Stone's Elliot Murphy supplied the American angle. Although he awarded the album just three and a half stars, his impassioned tribute suggested that he had swallowed the Clash Myth more completely than his British counterparts: 'The Story of the Clash is a story that ended too soon... As this collection clearly shows, the Clash's political concerns remained in the forefront even as the band's musical influences moved beyond the Pistols to reggae and rap... the Clash's brand of rock, while commercially accessible, was truly revolutionary... We need this band more now than we did then.'

Aside from the last-minute comment Steven Wells made in his review, no-one seemed prepared to spoil the celebrations by raising the obvious issue: that the repackaging and reselling of the Clash's recorded history represented a capitulation to the record company's commercial motivations – especially as its main purpose was to tap into the growing CD reissue market – and was therefore the latest in a long line of sell-outs of the band's original principles. Back in 1979, talking to *Creem*'s Dave DiMartino, Joe had made sneering remarks about Americans' preference for repackaged nostalgia over contemporary music. And following his declaration 'THERE WILL BE NO SIX QUID CLASH LP EVER' – even allowing for inflation – a double CD initially retailing for £22.99 was straying just a little too far from the band's VFM policy. At least the *Night Network* TV programme asked Joe to defend himself. 'The LP is dead,' he said. 'Don't blame me that it's come out on CD. *I* don't have a player yet. It's just a retrospective: you can buy into it if you want, or just ignore it.' Quizzed about the amount of money he himself might expect to garner from the half million copies already sold, he grew evasive. 'No idea, but not as much as if it'd been on vinyl record. All groups are shafted on CD royalties.'

'I Fought The Law' climbed to number 29 in the UK charts, respectable enough to prompt a second single re-release in late April 1988, this time of 'London Calling'. It only reached number 46, but the album that spawned it climbed as high as number seven, and remained on the charts for 10 weeks.

The ground thus prepared, in late April 1989, Sony re-released the band's entire album back catalogue on mid-priced CD, still on the CBS label. As most of them retailed for approximately the same as a full-price LP, this hardly represented VFM, either. In the UK, the albums appeared as they had in their original vinyl versions, with one crafty anomaly: the version of *The Clash* that emerged was the US one. The excuse given was that 'technical delays' had held up the UK version, which would now not be available until later in the summer. In the event, it did not become available until October 1991. What this meant in real terms was that the record company had finally managed to side-step the band's 1979 objections to making the American version available in the UK.

That November, *Rolling Stone* magazine ran a feature celebrating the Top 100 albums of the Eighties, as selected by the magazine's editors. *London Calling* – released in the US in January 1980, and therefore qualifying for consideration by the skin of its teeth – was voted number one.

Aside from the numerous rebel rock bands that had followed in their footsteps over the years, the Clash also made a more direct and involuntary contribution to less likely areas of popular music. In February 1990, Beats International – a loose dance music collective formed by ex-Housemartin and future Fatboy Slim Norman Cook – released 'Dub Be Good To Me', which welded the SOS Band's 'Just Be Good To Me' to the bassline from 'Guns Of Brixton'. At the time of release, Norman openly admitted the source of the sample in interviews, telling the *NME* that it was an 'affectionate tribute to the Clash. It's like tipping my cap to them, because they were a huge influence on my growing up, both musically and politically'. The single reached number one, and remained there for several weeks during its 13-week residency on the charts.

When Paul Simonon approached Norman Cook for what he believed was his fair share of the royalties, however, Norman changed his tune (or, at least, the source of his tune), claiming he had lifted the bassline from an obscure ska track. The matter was eventually sorted out without recourse to legal action. In the meantime, Paul came up with another way to cash in, commissioning DJ and former Haysi Fantayzee member Jeremy Healy to remix the original 'Guns Of Brixton' for July 1990 single release as 'Return To Brixton'. By this time, though, 'Dub Be Good To Me' had used up most people's stock of affection for the bassline, and the Clash release stalled at number 57.

Mick's opportunity to exploit the Clash legacy came the following year. In an attempt to preserve their integrity, the band had always turned down approaches from advertising agencies wanting to use their music in commercials, from Dr Pepper to British Telecom. However, when Levi's jeans asked if they could use 'Should I Stay Or Should I Go' in a UK TV commercial, the response was different. The original approach was made to all the Clash members, but as it was Mick's song, the others left the decision up to him. He agreed. His excuse was that Levi's were one of the more enduring rock'n'roll accessories, and not a product to which anyone could object on moral grounds.

The real issue, as Mick well knew, was whether an anti-establishment band like the Clash – who had always made a stand for creativity and idealism over commercial exploitation – should involve themselves with any kind of advertising at all. Whether or not Levi's jeans were an acceptable product in themselves, there was no getting around the fact that the Clash were doing it for the money and the exposure: all previous Levi's ad songs had resulted in re-release hit singles. Mick's decision to put BAD II's 'Rush' on the B-side of the single when it was issued in February 1991 certainly smacked of opportunism. Paul – who had not been particularly keen on the idea of the ad in the first place – was not consulted about the use of the BAD II track. A 'spokesperson' told the *NME*, 'Paul felt Mick added insult to injury by putting "Rush" on. And that led to a few arguments.'

In the UK, the CBS label had now been supplanted by Columbia: the Clash had finally made it onto Big Red. That March, 'Should I Stay Or Should I Go' became the first and only Clash single to reach number one in the UK charts. Joe was fixing his 1955 vintage Morris Minor when it reached the top spot. 'I had my head under the bonnet, fucking with the fuel pump, and somebody came by and said, "Why don't you just go and get *another* one?"' he told the *NME*'s Stuart Bailie. 'It's kinda weird that you didn't have to lift a finger. It wasn't as if you were at the height of your touring and all that hard work, and you'd feel, "Ah, *we did it*!" It took a trouser advert to take it there, and it was very peculiar.' In the wake of the single's success, Sony re-released *The Story Of The Clash, Volume 1* on Columbia; this time, it climbed to number 13, and spent a further nine weeks on the chart.

There is no statute of limitations on integrity. As well as causing rifts between the former Clash members, the advertisement and single release tie-in was the last straw for many long term Clash fans who had always believed that – even if the band sometimes let themselves and others down – at least their heart was in the right place. It was a point of view eloquently stated by Billy Bragg when approached for comment by the *NME*: 'I came to terms with the fact that the Clash's pose was nothing but a sham years ago, but it still grieves me to see that advert. At least it's a song from their Parody Period. It could be worse. Imagine "White Levi's/ I want some Levi's/ White Levi's/ Some Levi's of my own." As Joe Strummer sang in "Death Or Glory", "He who fucks nuns will later join the church."'

The Clash's relaxation of principles reiterated what previous post-split commercial endeavours had already signalled: considerations like respect for the music and the fans no longer obtained. Sony had already begun to exploit the Clash's back catalogue, but from 1991 onwards, their exhaustive and repetitive re-issue and compilation programme evidenced their belief that they had a license to be as flagrant and shoddy as they liked.

'Should I Stay Or Should I Go' was followed by the late March 1991 re-issue of its fellow *Combat Rock* veteran 'Rock The Casbah'. It climbed to number 15 in the charts. To cater for this rekindled demand, May 1991 saw Sony re-release *Combat Rock* itself. On to a good thing, Sony then *re*-re-released the original two singles taken from *The Story Of The Clash, Volume 1*: 'London Calling', which reached number 64 in June, then 'I Fought The Law' which failed to show two months later. In late October, 'Train In Vain' followed, and also bombed.

The record releases were preceded by the similarly opportunist video compilation *This Is Video Clash*, released on CMV at the end of March 1991. An extremely lazy piece of work, its box cover recycles Caroline Coon's sleeve photo for the 1977 'White Riot' single, and it runs for just 30 minutes. It collects together only those promo videos directed by Don Letts, and includes no material at all from 1976-77: an unforgivable omission. Sony had CBS's April 1976 Dunstable promo film versions of 'White Riot', '1977' and 'London Calling' in the vault; alternatively – had they been determined to use exclusively Don Letts material – they could surely have included some of the footage he shot at the March 1977 Harlesden Colosseum gig. A more enterprising project might have included a few TV spots, or extracts from the extensive live footage available from all stages of the band's career. Rush-releases like *This Is Video Clash* are doubly annoying: they not only represent the squandering of an opportunity in themselves, but they also spoil the market for future, potentially more inspired projects.

In October 1991, Sony finally got around to issuing the original UK version of *The Clash* on mid price Columbia CD. To accompany it on the schedules, they also released *Black Market Clash* in the UK. As with the UK release of the US version of *The Clash* two years earlier, this was against the band's wishes as expressed at the time of the record's original release.

November 1991 saw the UK rush-release on Columbia of a CD compiling the band's singles A-sides. Although dressed in a cover featuring Pennie Smith photographs, it betrayed little in the way of thought or imagination, and evidenced no co-operation or collaboration from any member of the band. Witlessly entitled *The Singles*, it was yet another attempt to milk the success of 'Should I Stay Or Should I Go'. Once again, history was rewritten to exclude the last Clash hit, 'This Is England'. 'That's the one thing that really, really pissed me off,' says Nick Sheppard. 'They should have been able to admit, "Yeah, that's a great song. It doesn't matter that Mick's not on it."' The album climbed no higher than 68, and spent just two weeks on the charts.

The US had seen little Clash-related activity since the release of *The Story Of The Clash, Volume 1* and the reissue of the band's back catalogue on CD. While the success of 'Should I Stay Or Should I Go' precipitated a greedy smash-and-grab raid on the UK marketplace, the lack of activity in the US allowed an (on the whole) more considered and impressive project to get underway. Epic was just one of several major labels working through their backlists to feed the demand of the CD generation for the recording world's equivalent of coffee-table books: boxed set retrospectives.

Kosmo Vinyl, still resident in New York, had made peace with the former Clash members, and was now representing Joe's interests in a managerial capacity. He was given the job of overseeing a Clash boxed set. No one could question his dedication or enthusiasm. He unearthed all the documentation relating to the Clash's recording career, and tracked down masters for unreleased, obscure and – in some cases – forgotten tracks. He shortlisted the songs for inclusion and debated them with the band members. He collected together lyrics for nearly all the tracks, and had them printed up as a CD-sized booklet. He assembled another, larger 66-page booklet which included: a variety of photographs, mostly by Pennie Smith and Bob Gruen; a specially-commissioned essay by rock writer and former Patti Smith guitarist Lenny Kaye on the Clash and America; extracts from Lester Bangs's epic 1977 *NME* Clash feature as reprinted in *Psychotic Reactions And Carburetor Dung* (and probably suggested by Mick Jones); a discography; and – last but not least – a band history-cum-track-by-track breakdown consisting of excerpts from interviews recently conducted by Kosmo himself with the Clash, Bernie, former crew members and associates. The only thing he was not responsible for was producing the compilation, a task handled by Don De Vito and Richard Bauer.

Everything possible was done to make it feel like a bona fide Clash project. The title Kosmo gave it, *Clash On Broadway*, recycles that of the abandoned Don Letts film. The contentious 'Remote Control' is not included. An unlisted extra track, 'The Street Parade', has been snuck onto the end of the last disc, as 'Train In Vain' was onto *London Calling*. The boxed set matches *Sandinista!*'s supposed folly in including three discs, but instead of 36 tracks features a total of 64: adding up to over three and a half hours' worth of music, or the equivalent of approximately five standard albums. A possibly unintentional point made by the set: with their track skipping and random selection mechanisms, CD players had succeeded in changing the way people consumed music, something that the Clash had attempted but failed to do with *Sandinista!* 11 years previously; as a result, such a gigantic archive of material as *Clash On Broadway* was no longer considered as overbearing and unwieldy as the relatively petite triple album had seemed in 1980.

Not that the world was deemed ready for a wholesale re-evaluation of that album's delights. Other than its selling points for collectors – a few rare B-sides and alternative live versions; two of Guy Stevens's Polydor demos; the three previously unreleased tracks, 'One Emotion', 'Every Little Bit Hurts' and 'Midnight To Stevens' – *Clash On Broadway* takes a predictable-enough and near-chronological tour through the band's back catalogue. Although not necessarily in their original versions, it includes: 13 tracks from *The Clash* (that is, everything except 'Remote Control', making its exclusion even more of a statement), plus '1977'; all the singles, plus most of the key B-sides, 'Capital Radio', and the entire *Cost Of Living* EP except 'Capital Radio Two'; just five tracks (out of 10) from *Give 'Em Enough Rope*; 11 tracks (out of 19) from *London Calling*; just nine tracks (one of them unlisted, out of 36) from *Sandinista!*; only five tracks (out of 12) from *Combat Rock*; and nothing at all from *Cut The Crap*, which the discography also ignores. 'I think it was a pathetic attempt not to offend Mick,' Joe admitted to *Record Collector*'s Sean Egan in 2000.

Clash On Broadway is clearly a labour of love, but it is far from perfect. A true perspective on the Clash's career has been sacrificed for collectability; namely, the inclusion of the alternative versions, unreleased and rare tracks. A ploy to tempt people who already have the band's albums and/or *The Story Of The Clash, Volume 1* (the contents of which are repeated in their entirety), it throws the set's balance seriously out of whack. Whereas the early B-sides are worthy of inclusion on their own merit, later ones like 'Stop The World' are much less impressive than many of the omitted album tracks. Typically, the inclusion of these interesting but inconsequential oddities not only damaged the current project, but also compromised any future rarities compilation.

In addition to over-stressing the Guy Stevens connection, the boxed set's other failing is the overtly American bias of the packaging. Lenny Kaye and Lester Bangs's writings concentrate on the American perspective, as does the title *Clash On Broadway*. While the track selection trumpets the pre-eminence of the punk years, the packaging pretends that the American campaign was not only the most important thing to the band, but also the most significant thing *about* them. In fairness to Kosmo, the former Clash members were involved in the project, and could have said if they were unhappy with any aspect of it. They must have known that, although commissioned by their American record label primarily for the US market, *Clash On Broadway* would be their one and only chance to construct such a weighty memorial to their band; that, sooner or later, it would be released all over the world, and the American vision of the Clash it presents would become the general vision of the Clash.

The boxed set was released in the US in November 1991 as part of Epic's Legacy series, and helped along by a slick MTV *Rockumentary* which combined archive footage and contemporary talking head interviews with Mick, Paul and Joe. Despite being so openly courted by the project, and remarking that 'the power and ambition of the Clash went well beyond the time-capsule limitations of punk, with a go-for-the-throat urgency that rock has lost in the years since', *Rolling Stone*'s Don McLeese still found it ironic that 'the band that railed against "turning rebellion into money" now finds itself repackaged as pricy punk nostalgia'. He gave the project three and a half stars.

In February 1993, Columbia issued a five-track mid-priced CD in the UK entitled *Twelve Inch Mixes*, the sound of barrels being scraped. Evidence that it was not originated or approved by the band is provided by the inclusion of 'This Is England'. Reviewing it for *Q*, David Hepworth was surprisingly generous: 'Perhaps the Clash will ultimately be remembered not as a punk rock combo or even as rock'n'roll classicists but as a dance band.' He gave it four stars.

In November the same year, it was followed by yet another compilation. *Black Market Clash* had collected the Clash's oddities and B-sides up to August 1980, and it was now decided to update the project to cover their entire career; or rather, up to 1982, which was when the Clash now chose to pretend the Clash had ended. This time Kosmo Vinyl took the role of compilation producer, while project direction was taken care of by Gary Pacheco. Again, efforts were made to give it the feel of a bona fide Clash project: entitled *Super Black Market Clash*, it employs a colour-tinted version of the earlier album's Rocco Macauley cover photograph; 25 tracks are packed onto the single CD, but the compilation was also made available as a triple 10-inch vinyl album, a nod to both the original 10-inch release of *Black Market Clash* and the triple album *Sandinista!*; and a vintage Pennie Smith photograph appears on the inner sleeve. In addition, there are concise, but informative sleevenotes detailing each track's place and time of recording.

Once more, though, the album suffers from a number of shortcomings. Again, it was designed principally for the US market, where it was released on Epic. From an American point of view: although there are 10 obscure tracks – including several late-period B-sides, the instrumental 'Listen' from the *Capital Radio* EP, and the original *Black Market Clash*'s main attraction, 'Time Is Tight' – the other 15 all appear on *Clash On Broadway*. This time, the compilation was simultaneously released on Columbia in the UK, where *Clash On Broadway* had yet to appear. From a British point of view: it is irritating because it is so obviously oriented towards America, and includes the four tracks available on the UK version of *The Clash* but not on the US version. Nor was the CD update cheap. Reviewing it in *Q*, John Aizlewood took the now customary opportunity to state 'there's a reasonably strong case for arguing that the Clash were the greatest British rock band' before going on to find fault with this latest recorded testimonial: 'It's far from the treasure trove it could have been... There's little to recruit new converts and the whole exercise suggests a missed opportunity, but equally there's little that dispels the Clash's awesome aura.' He gave it three stars. It failed to chart.

Super Black Market Clash would become even more redundant in the UK when *Clash On Broadway* was finally released. As John Aizlewood suggested, the former could have been more of a treasure trove: if its larger, sister compilation had stuck to more conventional material, then *Super Black Market Clash* could have rounded up all the obscurities and oddities for those really interested in such things. It could certainly have made room for the still unreleased *Rat Patrol From Fort Bragg* outtakes. One possible reason for its failure to be more comprehensive was that there were further compilations in the pipeline. Talking to *Vox* in 1994, Kosmo denied this, insisting, 'There's nothing worth releasing.'

Clash On Broadway finally emerged in the UK – still on the Epic-Legacy label – in June 1994. It initially retailed for £33.49, hardly a give-away in itself, but by this time almost everyone keen enough on the band to buy it had given up on a UK release and paid closer to £50 for it on easily-available import. The flurry of re-releases over the previous three years had used up much of the UK music papers' patience. The *NME* ignored the boxed set altogether. *Q* contented themselves with a lukewarm review. In Vox, Mike Pattenden remarked: 'The deep irony of a jeans advert bringing them their only number one in 1991 was not lost on those who grew up with the Clash... They deserved better, but the suits could never swallow the real Clash. They were too jagged, too fucking unpalatable: like all great rock'n'roll. For that reason, a Clash boxed set can't but seem an incongruous monument.'

Mojo's forte was the multi-faceted career retrospective, and *Clash On Broadway* provided the magazine with an excuse to devote the bulk of its ninth – August 1994 – issue to the band. Slightly disappointingly, the magazine also took its cue from the boxed set when it came to focus and approach. Although the heading accompanying the cover photograph of the band announced 'The Clash: FROM WESTWAY TO BROADWAY', the Westway element consisted of a six page portfolio of Jonh Ingham's 1976 punk snapshots, only one of which was of the band. Equally tenuous – at least, more so than the boxed set would have the world believe – was the Guy Stevens feature tacked onto the end.

The rest of the epic feature was devoted to the Clash's American campaign. Ray Lowry supplied pen and ink drawings and a page of reminiscences from the second 1979 tour; Pennie Smith and Bob Gruen were chief among the photographic illustrators; Chris Salewicz provided a three-page account of the Clash's Bonds season, and interviewed Joe for a further page and a half of his recollections about America; and American correspondent Mark Coleman provided a two page essay on his country's reaction to the Clash. 'In America, the Clash didn't break down any barriers; gradually, they crept in through a side door labelled New Wave,' he wrote, noting that the band had already modified their punk sound into something softer and more musical by the time they reached the US. He concluded, 'The stridency and raw power of the Clash's pure punk roots certainly left a mark on America, but it's the controversial and "compromised" eclecticism of their New Wave phase that still rings in our ears.'

The problem with *Mojo*'s coverage was that it encouraged British people to think of the band in the same way; whereas, between 1986 and 1989, most UK commentators had held up *The Clash* as the band's shining moment and major contribution to the history of rock'n'roll, it now appeared that increasing historical distance from the impact of the punk movement was bringing them around to the American point of view: namely, that *London Calling* was the pinnacle of the band's achievements.

Will Birch attempted to redress the balance in his review of the boxed set, hidden away at the back of the same issue of *Mojo*. As the former drummer with pub rock band the Kursaal Flyers, who had headlined the Clash's fifth ever gig, and whom punk had quickly rendered obsolete, Will might have been expected to take the opportunity to settle an old score. Far from it. As far as he was concerned, it was the band's first two albums and handful of singles that provided the genuine foundation for the Myth. *London Calling*'s acceptance in America only served to launch 'the great trash-and-Vaudeville, coast-to-coast fancy dress party that culminated in Pennie Smith's epic photo album, *Before And After*'. Nevertheless, he concluded, 'The all-too brief career of the Clash is well represented and documented on this superb three-CD retrospective, and despite some dodgy moments their legend remains intact.'

The bias of the coverage towards the Clash's American years did indeed have its influence. In August 1995, a *Mojo* contributors' poll to establish the 100 Greatest Albums Ever Made put *London Calling* at number 23 and *The Clash* at number 59. The readers were asked to respond, and in January 1996, their poll placed *London Calling* at number 22 and *The Clash* at number 49.

In 1981, Joe had told the *NME*'s Paul Du Noyer that the Clash were resisting CBS's attempts to get them to record a live album. He would still be expressing his ambivalence about such projects 18 years later, being all too aware of the reasons that had prompted Buzzy Enterprises to re-record so much of the *Rude Boy* material in the studio: the Clash live were always more about impassioned communion than note-perfect reproduction or dazzling improvisation. In April 1998, though, Sony announced that Columbia would be releasing a Clash live compilation album the following year. Apparently, Joe had found a tape of the Clash's 13 October 1982 Shea Stadium concert when moving house. Recorded by Glyn Johns, it had revealed itself to be of surprisingly high quality. Thus inspired, the former band members were also considering other live tapes, including one of their 5 September 1976 Roundhouse show with Keith Levene.

That was the official version of events. In fact, the Clash live album had a much earlier genesis, something to which no-one involved with the project in 1998 wanted to draw attention. Tricia Ronane would probably not have been able to secure such a hefty advance for the project had the Clash camp reminded anyone at their record company that a live album drawn from the Shea Stadium concert had been proposed by CBS as early as 1982: that's why Glyn Johns had recorded the whole show. The split with Mick had put paid to that idea. Even the assembly of a live compilation album had first been planned as far back as 1990: Dave Mingay had been asked to provide his *Rude Boy* recordings, and Johnny Green his recollections for an accompanying booklet. This project had gradually evolved into *Clash On Broadway*, which ultimately had included just two live tracks. Upon completion of the boxed set, when Kosmo Vinyl told *Vox* there was nothing else in the vaults worth releasing, the largely overlooked live material was, in part, what he meant.

From mid 1998, Mick Jones spent the best part of a year working on the revived project with Bill Price. Joe and Paul did have some input when it came to song selection, but the source material was limited to shows that had been recorded to a high enough professional standard and could still be located in the vaults. Most of it came from the latter part of the band's career. The earlier, rougher material was rejected: nothing predating the 30 April 1978 Victoria Park show made it to the album. Keith Levene lost his chance to appear on the performance credit list; mysteriously, he also lost his co-songwriter's credit for the 27 July 1978 Music Machine version of 'What's My Name'. Most of the long-touted Shea Stadium material was supplanted by what the band believed to be superior versions of the songs recorded at the more intimate Boston Orpheum on the same tour. Terry Chimes played the drums at both gigs, contributing to a total of eight of the album's 17 tracks. When it came time to promote the album, Joe was still adamant that the Clash had hardly ever played a good gig after Topper Headon left.

Although 13 of the tracks were recorded in 1980 or afterwards – the Clash's America-oriented years – and 11 were actually recorded *in* the US, there is for once no real evidence of a bias towards the American market on the album. The Clash do play to their strengths, though, concentrating on their three most obvious career peaks: the critically acclaimed highpoints of the punk era and *London Calling*, and the commercially successful highpoint of *Combat Rock*. Of these, the first – when the Clash were consciously representing life in the UK, and even more specifically, London – is afforded the most attention. Although only three tracks are drawn from *The Clash*, a further five come from the 1977-78 inter-album singles. *London Calling* is represented by three tracks, with another two – 'I Fought The Law' and 'Armagideon Time' – drawn from singles also released in 1979. *Combat Rock* supplies three tracks, though the band's biggest US hit, 'Rock The Casbah' is not included. By contrast, *Sandinista!* provides just one track, and *Give 'Em Enough Rope*, like *Cut The Crap*, is not represented at all.

Paul Simonon prepared the cover artwork. He avoided one cliché in resisting the temptation to use a Pennie Smith live shot for the front cover – the Clash had already been there and done that for the covers of *London Calling* and *The Story Of The Clash, Volume 1* – but embraced another in choosing to feature photographs of the Westway at night. The title *From Here To Eternity* is lifted from a Fred Zinnemann film, starring Montgomery Clift – hence its namecheck in the 1979 Clash song 'The Right Profile' – of a James Jones novel about life in a Honolulu military barracks immediately prior to the Japanese attack on Pearl Harbour. Like the cover itself, the allusions it makes to Clash history and the Clash Myth are hardly subtle.

In addition to making a bold claim for the longevity of the band's music and legacy, the title also appears to be promising that there will be no further plundering of the archives. The album was released on 4 October 1999. For *Q*, Paul Do Noyer gave the album four stars: 'At last… we have a record of the Clash in their element.' Writing for *Mojo*, punk era *NME* contributor Neil Spencer was less convinced, opining that the Clash only really convince on the simpler songs. *From Here To Eternity* certainly failed to make the impression on the charts that its grandiose title warranted.

Released at the same time on Sony video, and broadcast on British terrestrial television – albeit late in the evening, and on BBC2 – was Don Letts's accompanying biographical documentary *Westway To The World*. This too had first been mooted at least five years earlier, before being resurrected to help stir up interest in the live album and the reissue programme that was due to follow. Drawing heavily upon Don's now decidedly well-worn archive footage, it also includes brief clips of some previously unseen Julien Temple footage from late 1976 and early 1977, and new interviews with all four principle band members conducted by Mal Peachey. Determined to preserve the legend, the Clash keep revelations to a minimum. Like the live album and all previous Clash-sanctioned posthumous material, the story ends with Mick's departure. The coverage again favours the punk era. Julien Temple's Sex Pistols documentary *The Filth And The Fury* was scheduled for higher profile cinema release the following year, and the Clash may well have decided that stressing their own association with the punk movement was their best bet for both immortality and short-term sales.

On 18 October 1999, to capitalise upon the band's return to the spotlight, Sony reissued the Clash's entire back catalogue on Columbia: all the studio albums, including both versions of the début and, almost unbelievably, *Cut The Crap*, plus the compilations *The Story Of The Clash*, *The Singles*, and *Super Black Market Clash*. Stickers attached to the CDs proclaim them to be restored, remastered and packaged in the original artwork.

The first of these boasts does not bear close inspection. (Restored from what, exactly?) Nor does the last. The UK version of *The Clash* now incorporates the artwork for the 'White Riot' single, though it does not include that single, and the cover's logo and typography are now a washed out orange rather than the original fiery red. *Give 'Em Enough Rope* includes the band portrait that was originally abandoned because it was printed back to front. It is still printed back to front. The map of international flashpoints that was meant to accompany it is not included. 'Train In Vain' has been added to the tracklist on the back cover of *London Calling*: 'secrecy' sacrificed for sales. The West Ham graffiti, formerly airbrushed out, is now evident on the front cover of *Sandinista!*, and 'The Sound Of The Sinners' is mislabelled on the back cover tracklist. *Combat Rock* incorporates the artwork for the 'Know Your Rights' single, but not that for the other two – far more successful – singles spawned by the album. With the exception of the artwork for the début album, none of this sloppy tinkering significantly diminishes the originals, but none of it significantly enhances them, either.

Mojo and *Uncut* – a new rival to *Q* – ran lengthy Clash retrospectives to coincide with the flurry of activity. The June 2000 edition of *Q* featured a poll in which magazine contributors voted for the best British albums ever made. One of the UK punk movement's shining moments again lost out to the Clash's take on Americana: *London Calling* came in at number four, *The Clash* at number 48. At the end of the year, *Mojo* published *The Mojo Collection: The Ultimate Music Companion*, listing albums the magazine's staff believed ought to be included in any comprehensive collection of popular music. Both Clash albums were listed.

In the years since the Clash split, parallel to the media re-examinations of their impact and legacy has run near-ceaseless speculation about the possibility of a reformation. The lack of an official statement about the band's demise left the door open, and rumours that Mick Jones was about to return to the fold – keeping BAD as a sideline – began to circulate in May 1986, when he and Joe Strummer were seen working together again. But for much of 1987, Mick toured hard with his new band, Joe busied himself with various acting roles and soundtrack work, and Paul Simonon rode with a motorbike gang in LA while assembling the personnel for his new band Havana 3 am. In November that year, Topper Headon was given a 15 month jail sentence – of which he eventually served 10 months – for supplying heroin to a friend who overdosed and died.

In March 1988, the release of *The Story Of The Clash, Volume 1* helped bring the band members back into the same orbit. Paul had been involved with BAD PR Tricia Ronane for some months, and had painted the cover for the band's third album, *Tighten Up Vol '88*. There was speculation that the Clash compilation album was a prelude to a reunion that might eventually provide volume two. During BAD's July-August 1988 UK tour, however, Mick contracted chicken pox from his four-year old daughter Lauren. The disease attacked his throat and lungs, and he contracted pneumonia, went into a coma and nearly died. The full process of recovery took nine months. Towards the end of that period, on 23 March 1989, Mick's Nan, Stella, died at 89.

Instead of persuading him to reform the Clash, Mick's travails inspired him to renew his commitment to BAD. As soon as he felt well again, he went straight back into the studio, bringing in Bill Price to help with production. The result, released in early September 1989, was *Megatop Phoenix*, an album which as its name – courtesy of Pete Wylie – suggests, represents a double, and doubly good, rebirth. It was inspired by the writings of Lester Bangs, De La Soul's 'daisy age' psychedelic rap album *Three Feet High And Rising*, Happy Mondays' acid house-influenced rock, and the acid house movement itself. 'It's just like punk was,' Mick enthused to *People Weekly*'s Steve Daugherty that November. The album came closer to capturing the mood of the times than anything else Mick or his former colleagues had released since *The Clash* 12 years earlier.

It is probably no coincidence that Joe Strummer chose this time to record *his* first solo album proper, *Earthquake Weather*. Released that October, it was musically unfocussed, lyrically clumsy and received mixed reviews. In the UK, the album went into the charts at number 58; the following week, it disappeared for good. It flopped everywhere else, too. Joe toured on the back of it, exhausting himself and losing £24,000 in the process.

Despite positive reviews for BAD's *Megatop Phoenix*, there were no hit singles, and the album failed to make up for lost ground. It climbed to 26, but remained on the charts for just three weeks. At least part of the reason it fell down the cracks was that yet another disaster was waiting to befall Mick: early in 1990, Don Letts, Greg Roberts and Leo Williams announced they were leaving BAD. They went on to form Screaming Target and then – minus Don – Dreadzone. Mick also split up with Lauren's mother, Daisy.

Announcing the 'not exactly amicable' defection of the original BAD members in January 1990, the *NME*'s newspages posed the question, 'CLASH FROM CHAOS?' By this time, though, Paul Simonon was rehearsing and playing with Havana 3 am. Mick Jones seemed to answer the NME's question by immediately forming BAD II to fulfil the original band's remaining live commitments. While his new outfit were writing and recording new material, Mick managed to remain in the public eye thanks to a collaboration with Aztec Camera's Roddy Frame. Roddy had written 'Good Morning Britain' in such a blatant plagiarism of BAD's style that he felt honour-bound to invite Mick to sing and play on it. Its release as a single in September 1990, and near-immediate climb to number 19 in the charts, could not have been better timed, coinciding as it did with the public emergence of BAD II.

BAD II's *Kool-Aid* was a limited edition release in October 1980, with a 'proper' album scheduled to follow the following year. It showed up in the charts for one week only, at number 55. The album was another lost classic: the lyrics were written by Mick at a period of emotional turmoil, and are consequently some of the most nakedly autobiographical he has ever recorded. They refer not only to the break-up of BAD, but also to that of the Clash. The opening lines of 'Change Of Atmosphere', later retitled 'Rush', revisit a sentiment already expressed in the previous album's 'Baby, Don't Apologise', but here stated far more defiantly in the first person (and, sadly, anticipating Topper's 1999 verdict on his heroin addiction): 'If I had my time again, I would do it all the same.'

Paul Simonon was let go by Sony. Havana 3 am signed a contract with Japanese label Portrait Records and recorded their eponymous album in Tokyo. Released in Japan in December 1990, it was accompanied by a short tour. In February the following year, the album was released in the UK by IRS. It failed to chart. The young woman reclining on the front cover is Tricia Ronane, now Havana 3 am's manager and Paul's wife. Paul had married the 26-year old Tricia in the Roman Catholic St Pius X Church, St Charles Square, Kensington on 28 July 1990.

Edited, remixed and revised by Mick and his cousin Andre Shapps, the previous year's BAD album was given a full release in July 1991 in a new cover and under the new title *The Globe*. In February, the lead single, 'Rush', had also been included on the B-side of the Clash single 'Should I Stay Or Should I Go'. In a deal arranged with the *NME* with the deliberate intention of recalling that for the Clash's *Capital Radio* EP, a sticker was enclosed with the first pressing of *The Globe*, a coupon was printed in the 10 August 1991 issue of the paper, and the first 2,000 people to return both together were sent a nine-track live album of BAD II's August 1990 show at the Alexandra Palace. Despite these promotional efforts, and an autumn tour, *The Globe* flopped in the UK, chalking up just one week in the charts at number 63.

Thereafter, BAD II moved straight onto a US tour supported by the Farm. It was a jaunt with more than its fair share of ups and downs. One night, the car in which Mick was a passenger crashed and rolled over four times. Although he emerged unhurt, he was badly shaken by yet another brush with death. The tour was successful enough to take the BAD II album to number one in the US college radio (alternative) charts, and although it only made number 73 on the mainstream charts, it went on to sell 250,000 copies. The single 'Rush' made number 32 in the mainstream charts, and was voted *Billboard*'s best modern rock song of 1991. In Australia, it made number one in the singles chart.

Meanwhile, the success of 'Should I Stay Or Should I Go' and the release of *This Is Video Clash* had prompted more rumours about a Clash reformation. BAD II's recent successes abroad encouraged Mick to restate his commitment to his new band, but he was evidently less happy with Columbia's work on his behalf in the UK. He told the *NME*'s James Brown, 'I think they want BAD II to fail so maybe I'll have to do the Clash again': as though reforming the Clash were his only other option. Paul Simonon was determined to stick with Havana 3 am, partly out of loyalty, and partly because he was still furious with Mick for putting a BAD II track on a Clash single. 'I want to retain my dignity,' he told the *NME*'s Mary Ann Hobbs. 'And I want to move on.'

The first public acknowledgement that substantial offers had actually been tabled came in April 1991. 'I don't think any of us would do it for the money,' Mick told *Vox*'s Mal Peachey. 'I don't think we'd do *anything* just for the money.' In early September, anticipating the November release of *The Singles* in the UK and *Clash On Broadway* in the US, the *NME*'s news pages carried the following story: 'Sources claim that Mick Jones has been approached by American promoters bidding £10 million for a one-off US Clash tour, and the offer has received serious consideration from Jones and Strummer.' By now, Mick seemed to be hedging his bets, telling *Rolling Stone* that he would not rule out a Clash reunion at some future date.

A few days later, Tricia Ronane told the *NME* the rumours were unfounded. 'The Clash haven't had any serious offers from promoters recently. But if there is an American promoter willing to put £10 million on the table, I'm sure the band would consider reforming. In fact, tell them to call me!' Joe, meanwhile, had accepted an offer to deputise for Shane MacGowan on a Pogues world tour. In early October 1991, he told the *NME*: 'There have been offers for sure, but really to answer the question, I have to get all the boys in one place at one time and we'd have to discuss it. I think we will. But Mick's on tour right now in America, Paul's just had a son and he might be going off with Havana 3 am, and I'm off around the world for the next six months with the Pogues, so it sounds a bit unlikely for the immediate future.'

In July 1993, Rick Sky's *Daily Mirror* pop column reported – in typically circumspect tabloid style – 'Punk kings the Clash are getting back together for a massive £50 million world tour after a 10 year break. The four-piece group have signed up with a top American manager and are currently lining up a string of dates: starting with a huge stadium tour of the US.' This, of course, did not happen, and the figure quoted was also wildly out. According to former Clash security man Ray Jordan, now working with BAD, the offer that had been put forward was for just $1.5 million. Ray also told *DISCoveries*' Ralph Heibutski that three members of the band were willing, but one refused.

On paper, all four members should have been keen. Joe had contemplated recording a second solo album in 1991, but Sony suddenly lost enthusiasm when they realised that for once the contract was weighted in Joe's favour: they would have to pay him an advance commensurate with his status as Clash frontman rather than someone who's last solo album had performed so miserably. They didn't want to pay the advance, but they didn't want to let him go, either. Stuck in a Catch 22, Joe resolved to sit back and wait until Sony lost interest. For most of 1991 he served out his time as an honorary Pogue.

That year, he and Gaby moved out of London to Basingstoke, partly for the sake of their two daughters' education. Two years later, Joe left Gaby, and moved back to the city alone.

Rather than follow up on what had been a promising 1991 – in the rest of the world, if not in the UK – BAD had gone back into hibernation. Like Joe Strummer, Ian Hunter had survived the mid Eighties doldrums of his solo career by contributing odd songs to movie projects, and Mick now followed suit. In 1993, he helped shape the music for the Rob Weiss film *Amongst Friends*, the soundtrack album for which was released on Atlantic. Credited as a solo artist for the first time, he contributed three instrumentals, as well as donating BAD II's Mott the Hoople-like 'Innocent Child' and suggesting Mott the Hoople's own 'All The Young Dudes'. Other soundtrack work followed, but Mick seemed to be marking time.

Paul Simonon's band, Havana 3 am, had split the previous year, so he was ostensibly free of other commitments. As long ago as 1983, though, Paul had revised his opinion of the relative merits of art and music. By 1993, he was devoting himself to painting full time. As well as on the front cover of *Tighten Up Vol '88*, examples of his work from the late Eighties – pop-cultural figures set against urban backgrounds, usually recognisably Notting Hill – can be seen on the back cover of the Clash's *Cut The Crap* and in Paul's interview sequence for 1991's MTV Clash *Rockumentary*. Entitled *The Last Supper*, this last painting is 'based on the Leonardo one, but I set it under the Westway with a bunch of characters on motorcycles, eating Colonel Sanders and drinking Special Brews'.

Topper Headon was no longer working as a musician. There were reports in the music press that he was driving a cab for a living, when able. The only obvious hindrance to a Clash reunion was Topper's continuing drug problem, and it was tempting to read more than generosity of spirit into Mick and Joe's joint funding at this time of yet another attempt at detox and rehab.

Q followed up Rick Sky's July 1993 *Daily Mirror* story, and were met with denials of an imminent reunion on behalf of Paul, Joe and Mick. Entering into the spirit of the debate, the December 1993 issue of *Q* included a two page feature under the title, 'The Big Question: Should The Clash Reform?' Twenty-three assorted former punks and Clash associates, record industry spokesmen, and current name performers were asked to pass their verdict. Predictability, the money men, thinking purely in terms of gain, said yes; as did the members of other reformed bands intent on justifying their own actions. Those with no agendas of their own to follow said no. Of course, Bernie Rhodes said yes, as long as he got to be manager...

Strangely, he was not the only person on the planet who thought this was a good idea. In 2000, Joe told *Record Collector*'s Sean Egan that the 1991 proposal for the Clash reunion had come from Mick Jones; or at least, from Mick's manager Gary Kurfirst. It had foundered when Joe – despite everything – insisted that Bernie Rhodes be offered his old job back. 'I'm terribly loyal in a stupid way, and I knew that the best combination was Strummer/Headon/Simonon/Jones on the floor and Bernie Rhodes managing it.' There was another reason. 'I didn't want Mick's manager to manage the Clash.'

Topper's musical inactivity continued, and with no incentive to stay clean, he began using again. So did Paul's, but he at least had found a satisfactory replacement. By the mid Nineties, the music-related sub-cultural figures had disappeared from his paintings, and the urban environment was losing ground to landscapes and river and seaside views. The themes might have changed, but the attitude had not: according to Joe Strummer, even in 1999, Paul was 'totally punk rock' about his art, painting for hours in all weathers. He wasn't entirely reliant on Clash royalties to fund his hobby, either. In 1995, a show at John Martin's private gallery in the West End of London offered his recent works for sale at prices ranging from £1,500 to £3,000 per canvas.

On 29 April 1994, BAD II appeared at the Hammersmith Apollo memorial concert for Mick Ronson, who had died from liver cancer exactly a year earlier. Ian Hunter was also on the bill. The following week, MTV carried news reports that Mick Jones had also died, of pneumonia. Perhaps taking the hint that he should get out more, Mick was often seen about London in the latter part of 1994, ligging and jamming with everyone from St Etienne to Primal Scream. In late 1994, BAD II, now trading as Big Audio, finally released *Higher Power*, the album they had recorded late the previous year. The CD sleeve mimics the speaker sleeve for the Clash's single 'Complete Control', and the inner sleeve revisits the Clash Manifesto circa 1976: 'anti fascist – pro creative'. Sadly, for the most part, the record within is twee, insipid and dull. It did not chart, and Sony finally agreed to let the band go.

In 1995, the first edition of this book predicted that the Clash would get back together again. Rumours were circulating that the Clash were to headline that year's Lollapalooza package tour of the US, and some of the support bands were even told this would be the case. 'That sort of went off without our knowledge,' commented Joe. Quoted on the *Music News Of The World* web page that September, Tricia Ronane confirmed that the band had been offered $5-7 million for the tour, but had turned it down. 'Basically, Mick's management thought it was a good idea, Joe was passionately against it, and Paul didn't give it the time of day.' Heidi Robinson, one of the tour's organisers, told a slightly different story. When phoned at home, Joe – apparently – had turned the offer down because Topper had only just completed yet another spell in rehab, the band hadn't played together in years and wouldn't have adequate time to rehearse, and they didn't have a new album to promote. Heidi claimed that Joe had told her the Clash were intending to record a new album in autumn 1995, and so might be available for the following year's Lollapalooza. Complementing Heidi's statement was another music industry rumour – reported by Chris Salewicz in a 1996 *Q* feature – that Dire Strait's manager Ed Bicknell was overseeing a multi-million dollar deal for a Clash tour and new studio album. 'I've never even met Ed Bicknell,' was Mick's response.

In 1995, BAD II signed to the independent label Radioactive, reverting to the name Big Audio Dynamite (BAD). A new album, *F-Punk*, was released that August. The project as a whole follows in the footsteps of lead single 'I Turned Out A Punk' as a semi-autobiographical exploration of Mick's punk roots. One track, 'Psycho Wing' is reminiscent of 'Clash City Rockers', and the album contains a DIY punk fanzine-style 'how to tune your guitar' guide. The front cover steals the green and pink typography of the *London Calling* cover, and, as with that album, there is an extra unlisted track: a cover version of David Bowie's proto-punk thrash 'Suffragette City', included as a tribute to Mick Ronson. *F-Punk* was sparsely and poorly reviewed. It was also poorly distributed, and failed to chart. When Nick Sheppard heard it, he was surprised by how much it reminded him of *Cut The Crap*. In September 1995, Sony swatted it aside with the compilation album *Planet BAD*.

In 2000, Joe would confess to laziness, telling *Q* that he had 'spent the last 11 years watching *Match Of The Day*'. This was not strictly true. Royalties from the Clash remained his chief source of income, but he continued to contribute to film soundtracks and take minor acting roles, guested on various projects – including a track with Rat Scabies for an Amnesty International album – did some DJ'ing on the dance scene, co-wrote some songs with and for former Stray Cat Brian Setzer, and helped out with Black Grape's unofficial Euro 1996 football anthem 'England's Irie'. It was with this last band and song that he finally abandoned another punk-era principle, and appeared on *Top Of The Pops*. That year, Joe again began to divide his time between London and the country, eventually setting up home in a Somerset farmhouse to raise his second family.

1996 was also the year that Sony finally let him go. He was the last member of the Clash to escape the 1977 CBS recording contract.

Joe began writing and recording some crossover dance tracks at Peter Gabriel's Real World studio with the Grid's Richard Norris. It was reported that these were due to be released as an album entitled *Strummerville*, but the duo were actually considering forming a group called Machine. Unfortunately, a spanner fell in the works. 'Because he was coming from acid house and I was coming from punk, we had to bridge a lot of ideological gaps,' Joe told *Record Collector*'s Sean Egan in 2000. 'We both fought our corners very hard, and eventually we fell out.'

In 1996, the surviving former members of the Sex Pistols – including Glen Matlock – were offered a reported one million pounds each for a reunion world tour. They accepted. It seemed that the last external factor preventing a Clash reunion – the opprobrium of their peers and mentors for selling out – had been removed. But the sight of 40-something men striking 20-year old poses and attitudes turned out to be not a little sad. The tour diminished the Pistols Myth in some way, and, more than anything else, it was probably fear of a similar fate befalling the Clash Myth that ultimately dissuaded the Clash from doing the obvious thing and following suit. No Clash reunion tour was scheduled. Nothing further was heard about a new studio album, either.

BAD lost two members after the failure of *F-Punk*, but Mick replaced them during 1996, and added former Beat and General Public toaster Rankin' Roger to the line-up. Delivering on one of the Clash's old promises, the BAD Soundsystem – featuring the DJs associated with the band, and Mick as occasional MC – began to present a peripatetic club night in London. In late 1986, work began on a new album, *Entering A New Ride*. 'It's all hooks,' Mick told Chris Salewicz for *Q*. 'I decided to miss out all the bits in between.' When Mick handed the album over to Radioactive the following year, the record label refused to release it. Given his long history of conflict with CBS, to have his creative freedom denied by the very independent label to which he had finally escaped must have been a crushing experience. In 1999, BAD set up a new website, and used it to release the rejected album track by track.

With BAD's position – and, presumably, finances – at an all time low, the chance to work on the live Clash compilation album came as a welcome relief to Mick during 1998-99. Inevitably, it begged the question whether the Clash would be reforming to promote it, and further cash in on both that project and the accompanying back catalogue reissue. Mick's obsessive recycling of Clash motifs with BAD would seem to suggest that he had not entirely laid the ghost of his previous band to rest, but during the course of an on-line interview he gave following the completion of the live album project, he insisted no reformation would be taking place.

More members of BAD jumped ship during 1999-2000. As if to rub it in, 2000 saw Sony release another BAD compilation album called *Super Hits*. Staying true to the Clash's amateur hour policy and BAD's multi-media ethic, Mick accepted an invitation to direct a video for the Shack song 'Oscar'. He also contributed guitar to Glen Matlock and the Philistines' album *Open Mind*. Mick has proved time and time again that it is unwise to write him off, but BAD would seem to have run its course as a commercially viable vehicle for his talents.

Topper also needed the money from the Clash live album. In 1998, he was involved in a car crash, and so badly hurt that he was pronounced dead on arrival at hospital. Although he lost his spleen, he made a full recovery, only to be diagnosed with hepatitis C. Far more serious than hepatitis B, the virus proves persistent in over 50 per cent of cases, and if untreated leads to progressive deterioration of the liver, cirrhosis and even cancer. This time, the choice Topper was given was quit heroin and all other drugs, or die sooner rather than later. The advance Tricia Ronane managed to secure for *From*

Here To Eternity enabled him to buy a house in Dover, where he joined a methadone programme. A Clash reunion would present him with an opportunity to salvage something from all the years lost to heroin addiction, but in *Westway To The World* he acknowledged that he might not be able to withstand the associated temptations.

Never a natural musician, Paul has not played bass with any regularity for the best part of a decade. The 1999 biographical documentary saw him restating his belief that the Clash were over and done: 'and that suits me fine'. For all his wild youth, Paul was always the most stable member of the Clash while the band were still together. It would appear that he has also adjusted best to life beyond the group. With an alternative creative outlet and a settled family life, he appears to be content with his lot...

August 1998 saw Joe begin a series of weekly desert island discs-type broadcasts on the BBC World Service under the inevitable banner *London Calling*: that radio station at last, however briefly. In the various interviews he gave to promote the Clash live album, Joe refused to say a band reunion would never happen, but appeared to have reconciled himself to the fact that it was unlikely. In 1999, he formed a new band, the Mescaleros, and recorded an album, *Rock, Art And The X-Ray Style*. Released at the same time as *From Here To Eternity*, on his own Casbah records through the Mercury label, it showcases Joe's eclectic tastes. Included are a couple of refugees from the aborted Machine project. *Top Of The Pops*'s spin-off show, *TOTP2*, played the video for one of them, the single 'Yalla Yalla'. The Mescaleros toured extensively, and in their live repertoire drew perhaps a little too heavily on the Clash's back catalogue. Joe, it seemed, had grown tired of waiting for the others, and had decided to have a Clash reunion of his own. It was especially hard to ignore such thoughts when the Mescaleros accepted the support slot on the Who's summer 2000 reunion arena tour...

Former leader of the Kilburns and the Blockheads, Ian Dury, succumbed to cancer on 27 March 2000. A memorial concert to benefit cancer charities was scheduled for 16 June that year. Among those pencilled in to take part were Mick Jones, Topper Headon and Joe Strummer. Fearing that the sentimental nature of the occasion might encourage those present to push for even a three-quarters reunion of the genuine Clash, though, Joe pulled out of the event at the last minute.

When the first edition of *Last Gang In Town* predicted that the Clash would reform, the somewhat glib reason offered was 'because they have made every other mistake in the book'. No other reformation has ever been 100 per cent successful, creatively and commercially. Admittedly, the reformed Buzzcocks and Sham 69 never had quite the same significance as the Clash, so their slide into relative obscurity second time around was hardly surprising. The Damned have reformed so many times it hardly signifies: splitting up is their equivalent of taking a break between albums or tours. The Velvet Underground reformation was eagerly awaited, but was something of an anti-climax and ended in bad feeling. The reformed Madness overstayed their welcome and began to feel like a rip-off. The Eagles' 1994 US tour was an even more obvious money-spinner. Ditto the Sex Pistols' 1996 outing.

The money and glory associated with a Clash reunion concert tour has tended to overshadow the prospect of the other possibility: a new studio-based creative collaboration. By far the most intriguing aspect of the 1995 wave of rumours was the possibility that a new studio album might be in the pipeline. It should be borne in mind, however, that previous projects of this ilk have also tended to disappoint. Bands that have reformed specifically for album projects, like the Small Faces, the original Animals, the Mark II incarnation of Deep Purple, and Television, have all succumbed to the same ego battles and musical differences that caused them to split in the first place. None has added anything of note to their musical legacy.

Relationships between the former Clash members are probably not solid enough to sustain the pressure. In particular, there was an edge to the way Joe talked about Mick in 1999-2000 that was missing for much of the Eighties and early Nineties. Perhaps ironically, Joe's recently demonstrated openness to dance grooves suggests that he and Mick might, in principle, find more common ground as songwriters in the Noughties than at any time since 1980. Somewhere between the styles of BAD and the Mescaleros might be located a 21st Century Clash sound that would please both. The result would probably sound not dissimilar to Black Grape, the Chemical Brothers or Fatboy Slim...

But why follow when once you led?

Also, in the *Record Collector* interview with Sean Egan, Joe revealed that *any* kind of collaboration between former Clash members was now unlikely to take place for contractual reasons. As ever with CBS/Sony, there was a price to be paid for Joe's solo escape and the substantial advance received by the former Clash members for *From Here To Eternity*. 'They've put into the contract that if I'm in the same studio with Paul, for example, then that thing is called the Clash and is owned by Epic [that is, Sony]. If I'm in the studio with Mick, it's a similar thing.'

Joe Strummer understands that – even if they seldom played the kind of arenas the likes of U2 play, and sold nowhere near the number of records U2 sell – the Clash still manage to hold at least equal status. 'The modern definition of "made it" is filling the 100,000-seat stadiums. U2 do five a week,' he told *Musician*'s Bill Flanagan back in 1988. 'But [when the Clash were together] there was still some vestige of true underground feeling. You saw us in arenas, but we were at our finest with 3,000 in an old theatre... if you look at our record sales, nothing sold until *Combat Rock* and "Rock The Casbah". I'd say we sold a *speck* overall to what U2 sell now. We made it, but in another way. We made it in the culture.'

In 1989, Panama's General Manuel Noriega rigged an election in order to hold onto power. Although previously they had been supportive, the US government now turned against him, accusing him of trafficking drugs to America. In December they responded in that most American of ways, by sending in the troops. Noriega went to ground in Panama City's Vatican embassy. The troops besieged the building, and rigged up loudspeakers to play high volume rock'n'roll music at him day and night in an effort to encourage his surrender. The most popular tune – with everyone, that is, except Noriega – was 'Should I Stay Or Should I Go'.

Following Sadam Hussein's order for Iraqi troops to invade Kuwait, the international community rallied behind the US's decision to reclaim the nation's oil for the free world. Allied troops began to gather in Saudi Arabia in October 1990, preparing for the following year's Gulf War. The first record played on the allied forces radio network was 'Rock The Casbah'. The Clash might be given pause to wince at such perversions of their original intention – the US's self-appointed role as the world's policeman being a long way from the sentiments expressed on *Sandinista!* or even *Combat Rock* – but in effect they were soundtracking significant historical events in much the same way the Doors and Jimi Hendrix had soundtracked the Vietnam war.

In 1992, after receiving a letter seeking guidance from former Transvision Vamp singer Wendy James, Elvis Costello replied by writing her an album's worth of songs he felt were suited to her persona. One of them, released as a single the following spring, was entitled 'London's Brilliant'. Including the line, 'Still digging up the bones of Strummer and Jones,' it is a celebration-cum-satire of the people who – like Wendy herself – have flocked to the Ladbroke Grove area over the years in pursuit of the Clash Myth. Its greater truth is that, when the generation who grew up with the Clash think of that area, they think of the band, just as the previous generation automatically associated Liverpool with the Beatles. In 1999, *From Here To Eternity* and *Westway To The World* acknowledged this connection and helped reinforce it.

Three Clash tribute albums were compiled and released between 1998 and 1999: *Burning London*, *City Rockers* and *Backlash*. The first of these had its tracks approved by Joe, features Topper drumming on the Afghan Whigs' version of 'Lost In The Supermarket', and includes versions of 'Cheat' by Rancid and 'Should I Stay Or Should I Go' by Ice Cube. The Clash's music also continues to be sampled regularly by new artists. You can hardly crack a novel by a thirty- or forty-something author without coming across a reference to a Clash song. An autumn 2000 magazine ad for Technics DVD Audio equipment projects a hologram of Pennie Smith's *London Calling* cover shot of Paul Simonon smashing his bass onto a suitably distressed-looking coffee table: it's an instantly recognisable icon for the generation(s) that might consider buying such equipment.

In August 1999, asked to vote for the 100 Greatest (musical) Stars Of The 20th Century, *Q*'s readers placed Joe Strummer – a man who at that time had been out of the public eye for the best part of a decade – at number 24, just two places behind Mick Jagger, 19 behind Elvis Presley, 22 behind Paul McCartney and 23 behind the winner, John Lennon. Elvis, Beatles and the Rolling Stones were still around in 1999… and so were the Clash. At *Q*'s annual awards ceremony in October 2000, Joe was presented with the Inspiration Award. Although never exactly a warm and cosy group, the former members of the Clash find themselves on the receiving end of handshakes, backslaps and hugs wherever they go.

For a while – thanks to the commercial success and resulting mass exposure they enjoyed during 1982, reinforced by the 1989 *Rolling Stone* poll and the signals given off by the 1991 *Clash On Broadway* package – it seemed as though the Clash were destined to be remembered as the US preferred to see them: as a conflation of *London Calling*, the black and white American outlaw chic as preserved in Pennie Smith's *Before And After*, the Bonds residency newscasts and Don Letts's videos for 'Rock The Casbah' and 'Should I Stay Or Should I Go'. Those were the days, after all, when anything seemed possible for the Clash. When they were soaking up influences from all the places they visited, both in real life and in their imaginations. When they were on the cusp of truly making it big, when stadium tours and multi-platinum discs seemed to be just around the corner.

There were other times – especially when punk's anniversaries rolled around – when it seemed as though the Clash would be remembered as the UK preferred to see them: in all their confused and contradictory glory as a conflation of *The Clash*, the Pollock/Pop Art/Lettrist-urban guerrilla looks as preserved on Sebastian Conran's Xeroxed gig flyers, their 1976-77 music press interviews, their 1977-78 singles and their early scenes in *Rude Boy*. Those were the days, after all, when they said and did everything they would subsequently fail to live up to and fail to live down. When they claimed they had come not only to shake up rock'n'roll but also to change the world. When it still seemed both reasonable and possible for representatives of a youth culture to do that.

A quarter of a century on from the band's formation, and 15 years on from their demise, those two views have mulched together. The Clash's painstaking efforts to create and nurture their own Myth have ultimately been eclipsed by the far more powerful myth-making capacity of the folk memory. Nothing contained in this book can hope to make a dent in it. Not even the Clash's well-oiled propaganda machine can hope to control it.

The way it appears to be working out for the band, though, they shouldn't mind too much…

When it comes to people we admire, it is in our nature to be selective with information, to load with personal associations, to elevate and make heroic. Mythopoeia is in our blood. When we think of the Clash now, we tend to forget or overlook the embarrassing moments, the mistakes, the musical filler, the petty squabbles, the squalid escapades, the unfulfilled promises. Instead, we take only selected highlights from the archive – the best songs, the most flatteringly-posed photographs, the most passionate live footage, the most stirring video clips, the sexiest slogans, the most memorable quotes, the warmest memories – and from them we construct a near-perfect rock'n'roll band, a Hollywood version of the Clash.

With the benefit of hindsight, it is clear this process had already begun even before the band went to America or consciously tried to make cinematic allusions with their music and clothes. As early as 1978, the *NME*'s Chris Salewicz described the band as being 'like Peckinpah's vision of the Western outlaws in *The Wild Bunch*, the loners whose high moral sense is one of the last relics of another time'. Chris knew about the individual band members' all-too-human frailties, but faced with the Clash's collective charisma, he could not prevent himself from falling under their spell. At this remove in both distance and time, how can we be expected to take any less romantic a view?

They have left us with the soundtrack to their own movie. And in any number of Pennie Smith's photos, taken at any point in their career, wearing whatever costume, the Clash do indeed resemble the central characters approaching the final confrontation in some elegiac sepia-tinted Western, noirish gangster flick, gritty Vietnam war film or grainy TV yob drama…

There they go, freeze-framed at the very moment they step out of history and into legend: the Last Gang In Town.

THE END

INDEX